A Soldiers' Chronicle of the Hundred Years War

A Soldiers' Chronicle of the Hundred Years War

College of Arms Manuscript M 9

Anne Curry and Rémy Ambühl

First published 2022

D. S. Brewer, Cambridge

ISBN 978-1-84384-619-2

D. S. Brewer is an imprint of Boydell & Brewer Ltd
PO Box 9, Woodbridge, Suffolk IP12 3DF, UK
and of Boydell & Brewer Inc.
668 Mt Hope Avenue, Rochester, NY 14620–2731, USA
website: www.boydellandbrewer.co.uk

A CIP catalogue record for this book is available
from the British Library

The publisher has no responsibility for the continued existence or accuracy of URLs for external
or third-party internet websites referred to in this book, and does not guarantee that any content
on such websites is, or will remain, accurate or appropriate

This publication is printed on acid-free paper

Printed and bound in Great Britain by
TJ Books Ltd, Padstow, Cornwall

Dedicated with love and thanks to our spouses
From Anne to John
From Rémy to Laura

CONTENTS

Illustrations

The authors and publisher are grateful to all the institutions and individuals listed for permission to reproduce the materials in which they hold copyright. Every effort has been made to trace the copyright holders; apologies are offered for any omission, and the publisher will be pleased to add any necessary acknowledgement in subsequent editions.

Contributors

Rémy Ambühl is a lecturer in Medieval History at the University of Southampton. His research interest has focused on the laws of war in the late Middle Ages. He was a Leverhulme Early Career Fellow in 2012–14 and a Fernand Braudel-IFER incoming fellow in 2015, and has published extensively on the issues of prisoners of war and the practice of surrender, including a research monograph, *Prisoners of War in the Hundred Years War* (Cambridge University Press, 2013).

Anne Curry is Emeritus Professor of Medieval History at the University of Southampton, where she was also Dean of the Faculty of Humanities from 2010 to 2018. She is the author of several books and articles on the Hundred Years War, especially the battle of Agincourt and English armies, and is co-director of www. medievalsoldier.org. She is currently preparing an online edition of the Norman rolls of Henry V (TNA C 64).

Richard Ingham is Visiting Professor at the University of Westminster (London) and was a Mercator Research Professor at the University of Mannheim. He was previously Professor of English Linguistics at Birmingham City University, having earlier taught at the University of Reading. His research areas have included first language acquisition of English syntax, and language contact between French and English in medieval England. His diachronic studies focus on bilingualism, sentence structure and negation.

Scott Lucas is a Professor of English and head of the department at The Citadel, the Military College of South Carolina. He is the author of *"A Mirror for Magistrates" and the Politics of the English Reformation* (University of Massachusetts Press) and *A Mirror for Magistrates: A Modernized and Annotated Edition* (Cambridge University Press), as well as a number of articles on early modern literature, history, and culture.

Deborah Thorpe is the Education and Outreach Manager at the Digital Repository of Ireland. She is also currently a Research Associate of the University of York, where she took her PhD, and was formerly a Marie Skłodowska-Curie COFUND Fellow of the Trinity College Dublin Long Room Hub (2017–18). Prior to that, she was an interdisciplinary postdoctoral researcher at the Centre for Chronic Diseases and Disorders and the English Department at the University of York and a researcher at the Ashmolean Museum, Oxford.

ACKNOWLEDGEMENTS

This project has been several years in the making and the authors have many people and institutions to thank. First, our thanks to the successive archivists of the College of Arms for their ongoing facilitation for our study of this and other manuscripts, and to the Chapter of the College for its permission to bring this chronicle to public knowledge. We are also grateful to the Neil Ker fund of the British Academy for funding to support research on the chronicle manuscript by Dr Deborah Thorpe, which underlies her contribution to Chapter 1. Thanks also to Richard Barber of The Boydell Press for his advice and support at all stages, and to Christy Beale for exceptional support in the final preparation for publication.

Professor Michael Brown has provided vital assistance on identification of the Scots, Dr Guilhem Pépin on the Gascons, Dr Pierre Courroux on the French, and Dr Hannes Kleineke and Dr Aleksandr Lobanov on the English. Professor Daniel Wakelin provided useful thoughts on William Worcester and his works. Dr Nigel Ramsay gave many valuable insights into the use of the chronicle by the heralds and on historical culture in London. In addition to his contribution to the volume on the 'Mirror for Magistrates', Professor Scott Lucas also kindly commented on our work on Edward Hall and the milieu in which he worked Alan Magary, currently producing an online edition of Hall, also gave useful advice here. Professor Richard Ingham advised on translation issues as well as providing an analysis of linguistics for the volume. The late Dr Jeremy Catto kindly shared his transcript of the manuscript many years ago. Our Southampton colleague, Professor Chris Woolgar, gave helpful advice on editing, as did Professor Michael Jones. Don Shewan produced valuable maps, so important for a work which includes mentions of so many places within its short length. Thanks also to the archivist of Magdalen College Oxford for facilitating consultation of the Fastolf Papers, and the many other archivists and librarians who have helped us over many years.

A special thanks to French colleagues, Professors Philippe Contamine, Bertrand Schnerb and Valérie Toureille, for their ongoing support and interest. Finally, we must thank our patient families who have lived with this project for too long.

All manuscript references are to materials in The National Archives (TNA) unless otherwise indicated. In the footnotes, * next to a personal name indicates there is a biographical entry in the *ODNB*.

AC	Archives Communales
ACO	Archives Départementales de la Côte d'Or
Actes	*Actes de la chancellerie d'Henri VI concernant la Normandie sous la domination anglaise (1422–1435)*, ed. P. Le Cacheux, Société de l'Histoire de Normandie, 2 vols (Rouen, 1907–08)
ADC	Archives Départementales du Calvados
Add. Ch.	Additional Charter
Add. MS.	Additional Manuscript
ADE	Archives Départementales de l'Eure
ADL	Archives Départementales du Loiret
ADN	Archives Départementales du Nord
ADO	Archives Départementales de l'Orne
ADS	Archives Départementales de la Sarthe
ADSM	Archives Départementales de la Seine Maritime
AM	Archives Municipales
AN	Archives Nationales
AND	*Anglo-Norman Dictionary* (2nd edn, London: Modern Humanities Research Association), http://www.anglo-norman.net
Anselme	Père Anselme de Sainte Marie, *Histoire généalogique et chronologique de la maison royale de France*, 9 vols (3rd edn, Paris, 1726–33)
arr.	arrondissement
Beaucourt	G. du Fresne de Beaucourt, *Histoire de Charles VII*, 6 vols (Paris, 1881–91)
BEC	*Bibliothèque de l'Ecole des Chartes*
Belleval	R. de Belleval, *Azincourt* (Paris, 1865)
Berry	Giles le Bouvier, dit Berry Herald, *Les chroniques du roi Charles VII*, ed. H. Couteault, L. Celier and M.-H. Jullien de Pommerol, Société de l'Histoire de France (Paris, 1979)
Bib. Mun.	Bibliothèque Municipale
BL	British Library
BNF	Bibliothèque Nationale de France
Bréquigny	'Rôles normands et français et autres pièces tirées des archives de Londres par Bréquigny en 1764, 1765 et 1766', *Mémoires de la Société des Antiquaires de Normandie*, 3e série, 23 (1858)

Cagny	Perceval de Cagny, *Chronique*, ed. H. Moranvillé (Paris, 1902)
cant.	canton
CCR	Calendar of Close Rolls
CFR	Calendar of Fine Rolls
Chartier	Jean Chartier, *Chronique de Charles VII, roi de France*, ed. A. Vallet de Viriville, 3 vols (Paris, 1858)
Chastelain	G. Chastelain, *Œuvres*, ed. J. Kervyn de Lettenhove 4 vols (Brussels, 1863–66)
Choix de pièces inédites	*Choix de pièces inédites relatives au règne de Charles VI*, ed. L. Douët-d'Arcq, 2 vols (Paris, 1863–64)
CIPM	Calendar of Inquisitions Post Mortem
Contamine, *GES*	P. Contamine, *Guerre, état et société à la fin du Moyen Age: études sur les armées des rois de France, 1337–1494* (Paris, 1972)
Cosneau	E. Cosneau, *Le Connétable de Richemont (Artur de Bretagne), 1393–1458* (Paris, 1886)
Cour amoureuse	*La cour amoureuse dite de Charles VI; étude et édition critique des sources manuscrites: armoiries et notices biographiques*, ed. C. Bozzolo and H. Loyau, 3 vols (Paris, 1982–92)
CPR	Calendar of Patent Rolls
Des Ursins	Jean Juvénal des Ursins, *Histoire de Charles VI*, ed. J. A. C. Buchon (Paris, 1836)
DKR 41	*Annual Report of the Deputy Keeper of the Public Records*, 41 (London, 1880)
DKR 42	*Annual Report of the Deputy Keeper of the Public Records*, 42 (London, 1881)
DKR 44	*Annual Report of the Deputy Keeper of the Public Records*, 44 (London, 1883)
DKR 48	*Annual Report of the Deputy Keeper of the Public Records*, 48 (London, 1887)
DMF	Dictionnaire du Moyen Français (1330–1500), http://www.atilf.fr/dmf
EETS	Early English Text Society
EHR	*English Historical Review*
English Suits	*English Suits before the Parlement of Paris, 1420–1436*, ed. C. T. Allmand and C. A. J. Armstrong, Camden Fourth Series, 26 (London, 1982)
ESTC	English Short Title Catalogue
Fauquembergue	*Journal de Clément de Fauquembergue, 1417–1435*, ed. A. Tuetey, 3 vols (Paris, 1903–15)
Fénin	Pierre de Fénin, *Mémoires*, ed. M. L. E. Dupont (Paris, 1837)
Foedera	*Foedera, conventiones, litterae et cuijuscunque generis acta publica*, ed. T. Rymer, 20 vols (1704–35)
FP	Fastolf Papers
Fr.	MS français

Gonzales	E. Gonzales, *Un prince en son hôtel: les serviteurs des ducs d'Orléans au XVe siècle* (Paris, 2004)
GR	G. Dupont-Ferrier, *Gallia Regia, ou état des officiers royaux des bailliages et des sénéchaussées, de 1328 à 1515*, 7 vols (Paris, 1942–46)
Gruel	Guillaume Gruel, *Chronique d'Arthur de Richemont, connétable de France, duc de Bretagne (1393–1458)*, ed. A. le Vavasseur (Paris, 1890)
Hall (1809)	*Hall's Chronicle*, ed. H. Ellis (London, 1809)
Hardy	*Rotuli Normanniae*, ed. T. D. Hardy (London, 1835)
HOCa	*The House of Commons 1386–1421*, ed. J. S. Roskell, L. Clark and C. Rawcliffe (Stroud, 1993)
HOCb	*The House of Commons 1422–61*, ed. L. Clark (Cambridge, 2020)
Itineraries	*William Worcestre, Itineraries*, ed. J. H. Harvey (Oxford, 1969)
Jarry	L. Jarry, *Compte de l'armée anglaise au siège d'Orléans, 1428–1429* (Orléans, 1892)
Jeanne. Dictionnaire	P. Contamine, O. Bouzy and X. Hélary, *Jeanne d'Arc. Histoire et dictionnaire* (Paris, 2012)
La Chesnaye	F.-A. Aubert de la Chesnaye-Desbois, *Dictionnaire de la noblesse, contenant les généalogies, l'histoire et la chronologie des familles nobles de la France*, 19 vols (Paris, 1863–76)
La France gouvernée	*La France gouvernée par Jean Sans Peur: les dépenses du receveur général du royaume*, ed. B. A. Poquet de Haut-Jussé (Paris, 1959)
L&P	*Letters and Papers Illustrative of the Wars of the English in France During the Reign of Henry the Sixth, King of England*, ed. J. Stevenson, 2 vols in three parts (London, 1861–64)
l.t.	*livre tournois*
Luce	*Chronique du Mont-Saint-Michel (1294–1376)*, ed. S. Luce, 2 vols (Paris, 1879–83)
MCA	Magdalen College Oxford, Archives
McFarlane	K. B. McFarlane, 'William of Worcester. A Preliminary Survey', in *Studies Presented to Sir Hilary Jenkinson*, ed. J. C. Davies (Oxford, 1957), pp. 196–221, reprinted in K. B. McFarlane, *England in the Fifteenth Century. Collected. Essays*, ed. G. L. Harriss (London, 1981), pp. 199–224
Monstrelet	Enguerran de Monstrelet, *Chronique*, ed. L. Douët-d'Arcq, 6 vols (Paris, 1857–62)
Morice	P. Morice, *Mémoires pour servir de preuves à l'histoire civile et ecclésiastique de Bretagne*, 3 vols (Paris, 1742–46)
NAF	nouvelles acquisitions françaises
NRS	National Records of Scotland
ODNB	*Oxford Dictionary of National Biography*
PL Davis	N. Davis, *Paston Letters and Papers of the Fifteenth Century Part II*, EETS (Oxford, 2014)

PL Gairdner	*The Paston Letters AD 1422–1509*, ed. J. Gairdner, 6 vols (London, 1872)
PO	pièces originales
Poli	O. de Poli, *Les défenseurs du Mont-Saint-Michel (1417–1450)* (Paris, 1895)
PPC	*Proceedings and Ordinances of the Privy Council of England*, ed. N. H. Nicolas, 7 vols (London, 1834–37)
PROME	*The Parliament Rolls of Medieval England, 1275–1504*, ed. C. Given-Wilson, P. Brand, S. Phillips, W. M. Ormrod, G. Martin, A. Curry and R. Horrox, 16 vols (Woodbridge and London, 2005)
Pucelle	Guillaume Cousinot, *Chronique dite de la Pucelle*, ed. A. Vallet de Viriville (Paris, 1859)
RDP	*Recueil des documents concernant le Poitou contenus dans les registres de la chancellerie de France*, ed. P Guérin, vol. VII: 1403–30; vol. VIII: 1430–47, vol. X: 1456–64 (Poitiers, 1888–1906)
Religieux	*Chronique du Religieux de Saint-Denis contenant le règne de Charles VI de 1380 à 1422*, ed. L. Bellaguet, 6 vols (Paris, 1829–52)
RMS	*Register of the Great Seal of Scotland (Registrum Magni Sigilli Regum Scotorum)*, ed. J. M. Thompson et al., 10 vols (Edinburgh, 1882–1914)
Rot. Scot.	*Rotuli Scotiae in turre Londensi et in domo capitulari Westmonasteriensi asservati*, ed. John Caley, 2 vols (London, 1814)
Rowe	B. J. H. Rowe, 'A Contemporary Account of the Hundred Years' War from 1415 to 1429', *English Historical Review* 41 (1926), pp. 504–13
Toison d'or	*Les Chevaliers de l'Ordre de la Toison d'or au XVe siècle. Notices bio-bibliographiques*, ed. R. de Smedt (Frankfurt, 2000)
Waurin	Jean de Waurin, *Recueil des croniques et anchiennes istories de la Grant Bretaigne a present nommé Engleterre, 1399–1422*, ed. W. Hardy, 5 vols (London, 1868)
Wylie	J. H. Wylie and W. T. Waugh, *The Reign of Henry the Fifth*, 3 vols (Cambridge, 1914–29)

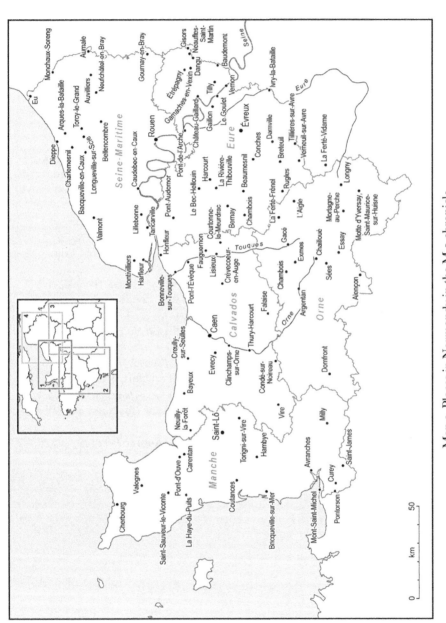

Map 1. Places in Normandy in the M 9 chronicle

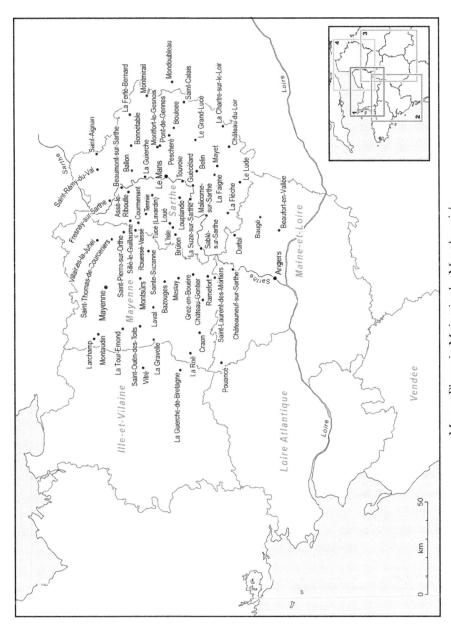

Map 2. Places in Maine in the M 9 chronicle

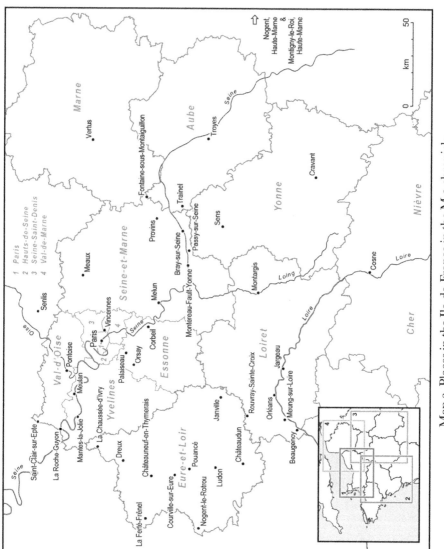

Map 3. Places in the Ile-de-France in the M 9 chronicle

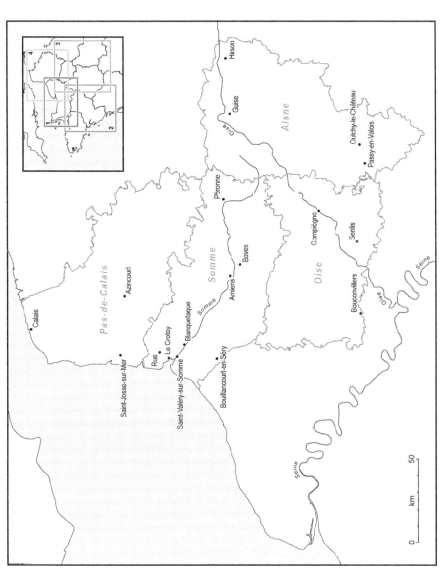

Map 4. Places in north-west France in the M 9 chronicle

Introduction

Between folios 31r and 66v of College of Arms MS M 9 there is a chronicle, in French and on paper, covering the Hundred Years War from Henry V's invasion of 1415 to the arrival of Joan of Arc at the siege of Orléans in May 1429.[1] The chronicle is only known to exist in this one copy. Its incipit at the top of the first folio, in the hand of William Worcester (1415–80/85), secretary of Sir John Fastolf (1380–1459), indicates that it was written for his master in the year of his death. At 18,217 words, the chronicle is relatively short, but it has several unique features. First, it is the only known English chronicle written in French in this period. Secondly, it is characterised by lengthy lists of people, French, English and Scottish, who participated in various battles and sieges, such names being presented in list format down the page, interspersed with narrative passages. Around 700 people are mentioned, along with around 230 places. Thirdly, the coverage of the English conquest of Maine from 1424 onwards, in which Fastolf was heavily involved, is much greater than that found in any contemporary chronicle, whether English or French.

The incipit offers an excellent starting point for the study of this fascinating chronicle but immediately raises questions since Worcester made several amendments to it. In his original version, he ascribed the work to only one author, Peter Basset, an English soldier, described as fighting under Henry V, Bedford and the later commanders in France in the reign of Henry VI. But in Worcester's revisions to the incipit, as indicated below by the italicised passages, a team of authors is indicated, which further marks out this chronicle as unusual. Those added are Christopher Hanson – who also appears twice in the narrative of the chronicle – who is described as a German who had previously served Thomas Beaufort, duke of Exeter (d. 1426), and Luket Nantron, a Parisian who was described as a clerk in the service of Fastolf. Worcester also ascribed to himself a supervisory role through the expression 'per diligenciam'.

> Iste liber de actibus armorum conquestus regni Francie, ducatus Normannie, ducatus Alenconie, ducatus Andegavie et Cenomannie cum aliis pluribus comitatibus compilatus fuit ad nobilem virum Iohannem Fastolf baronem de Cylleguillem [*added above*: *in anno Christi ml iiijc lix, 1459 anno quo dictus Iohannes Fastolf obiit*] per Petrum Basset armigerum Anglice nacionis exercentem arma in Francia sub [*added above*: *victoriose principe*] rege Henrico quinto [*added above*: *& Christoforum Hanson de patria almayn quondam cum Thoma Beaufort duce Excestrie et Luket*

---

[1]   The text of the chronicle ends abruptly at the top of folio 66r: the names of Joan of Arc and her companions were added by a later hand.

Nantron natum de Parys unum de clericis dicti Iohannis Fastolf et per diligenciam Willelmi Wircestre secretarii predicti Iohannis Fastolf] et sub Iohanne duce Bedfordie regente regni Francie necnon aliorum principum locumtenencium sub rege Henrico sexto, in toto per spacium xxxv annorum

This book concerning deeds of arms in the conquest of the kingdom of France, the duchy of Normandy, the duchy of Alençon, the duchy of Anjou and Maine and many other comtés was compiled for the noble man John Fastolf, baron of Sillé-le-Guillaume [*inserted above: in the year of Christ 1459, the year in which he died*] by Peter Basset esquire, of the English nation, who exercised arms in France under [*the victorious prince*] King Henry V [*and by Christopher Hanson of the country of Germany, at one time with Thomas Beaufort, duke of Exeter, and Luket Nantron, native of Paris, one of the clerks of John Fastolf, and by the diligence of William Worcester, secretary of the same John Fastolf*] and under John, duke of Bedford, Regent of the kingdom of France, and of other principal lieutenants under Henry VI, for thirty-five years in total.

It would appear that the chronicle was left incomplete at Fastolf's death but had been intended to cover the whole thirty-five years from 1415 to 1450.[2] The incipit also indicates the intended focus of the work on the 'deeds of arms of the English conquests'. Fastolf's own involvement in these wars was substantial.[3] After service in Ireland and marriage in 1409 to Millicent Tiptoft, widow of his commander Sir Stephen Scrope (d. 1408), Fastolf was active in France from 1412 onwards. Although invalided home from the siege of Harfleur he returned to serve in its garrison. Thereafter, he remained in service in France for twenty-two years, holding important garrison and field commands in both Normandy and Maine as well as enjoying a close association with John, duke of Bedford, Regent of France, as master of his household. He is known to have made much income from his French interests, especially the barony of Sillé-le-Guillaume near Le Mans granted to him in 1426.[4] Retiring from active service in 1438, he sought to sell his properties in Normandy but continued to hold Sillé and other lands in Maine. He received no compensation when Maine was surrendered and became highly critical of those deemed responsible for the final English defeat. In the mid-1450s he retired to Caister castle (Norfolk), dying there on 5 November 1459. In his constant service during his English retirement had been William Worcester, who was appointed one of his executors along with Sir John Paston.

This 'M 9 chronicle' (as we shall call it for ease of reference) has an independence of content, tone and flavour which marks it out as an important source for the Anglo-French wars. But its importance stretches beyond its medieval context. Even a brief glance at Edward Hall's *Union of the Two Noble and Illustre Famelies of Lancastre and Yorke*, published in 1548, indicates that the chronicle had been an important source, especially for the actions of the 1420s. Hall's text, printed by

---

[2]   Two fragments bound within College of Arms M 9 include information in William Worcester's hand which follows a similar format and type of content, giving credence to the assumption that the chronicle was intended to be continued after 1429. These are presented in the Appendix.

[3]   Harris, 'Sir John Fastolf', *ODNB*; Cooper, *The Real Falstaff*.

[4]   McFarlane, 'The Investment of Sir John Fastolf's Profits of War', pp. 91–116.

Richard Grafton after the author's death, even replicates the layout as well as the content of some of the lists. Study of the M 9 chronicle, therefore, necessarily involves two strands: its place as a chronicle of the fifteenth-century phase of the Hundred Years War, and its afterlife in the post-medieval period.

In 1619 we find the chronicle listed in a catalogue of books in the College of Arms made by Samson Lennard, Bluemantle Pursuivant.[5] By then, it had been bound with some early sixteenth-century texts to form what became College of Arms MS M 9. The catalogue description of 1619 reads: 'a boke in fol: concerning the warres of H.5. in France & also the ceremonies used at the creacion of the Prince, with other special notes'. In 1748 the chronicle was listed in Thomas Tanner's *Bibliotheca Britannico-Hibernica*, with a description notably close to the incipit.[6]

De actis armorum conquestus regni Francie, ducatus Normannie, ducatus Alenconie, ducatus Andegavie et Cenomannie cum aliis pluribus comitatibus compilatus fuit ad nobilem virum Iohannem Fastolf baronem de Cylleguillem per Petrum Basset manuscriptum in biblioteca Officii Armorum.

It was not until the early 1920s, however, that the chronicle's secrets began to be revealed. In carrying out an evaluation of English chronicles of the early fifteenth century as sources for French history, René Planchenault noted that Edward Hall's account of the wars in Normandy, Alençon, Anjou and Maine was particularly 'précieux'.[7] Planchenault was the first to suggest that Hall had drawn on an earlier text, his suspicions being boosted by the fact that Hall mentioned in his narrative a Peter Basset as a source of information for the disease which killed Henry V, as well as by Hall listing a 'John Basset' amongst the English sources he had used. Aware of the reference by Tanner to a work by Peter Basset in the College of Arms, Planchenault came to the initial conclusion that the chronicle used by Hall might be within Arundel MS 48. At this point, only the College's Arundel manuscripts had a printed catalogue and Planchenault was not able to visit to examine the chronicle.[8] In fact, he soon discovered, thanks to the work of Charles Kingsford, that the chronicle between folios 236 and 269 in Arundel 48 was a version of the *Croniques de Normandie*.[9] None the less, Planchenault was sure that within the vast

---

[5]   College of Arms, MS L 11 part 2, p. 15. The date given is 1 February 1618 which is in the dating system of the time 1619. We are grateful to Dr Lyndsey Darby, former archivist of the College of Arms, for this reference.

[6]   Tanner, *Bibliotheca Britannico-Hibernica*, p. 79. This was part of an effort by Thomas Tanner (1674–1735) to list every known pre-seventeenth-century writer, a project completed by David Wilkins in 1748.

[7]   'Au contraire, les détails que Hall nous fournit sur la lutte dans l'ouest de la France doivent lui être parvenus par cet intermédiaire. Les combats qui se sont déroulés dans les duchés de Normandie, d'Alençon et d'Anjou et dans le comté du Maine sont précisément ceux pour lesquels Hall nous est précieux. Ce Christophe Hanson, dont le nom est lié par Hearne à celui de Basset, ne nous est nullement inconnu et ses exploits ne nous sont justement rapportés que par le seul Edward Hall' (Planchenault, 'De l'utilité', pp. 123–4).

[8]   'Il n'est pas facile de faire la moindre recherché au College of Arms. J'ai pu, par grande faveur, consulter quelques manuscrits Arundel, mais non y travailler d'une façon suivie' (Planchenault, 'De l'utilité', p. 126).

[9]   Planchenault, 'De l'utilité', p. 125 n. 1; Kingsford, *English Historical Literature*, p. 69.

collections of the College the work of Peter Basset was 'sleeping', as he put it in his article of 1924.[10]

It was Benedicta Rowe who in 1925 identified the M 9 chronicle thanks to the assistance of Aubrey Toppin, Bluemantle Pursuivant.[11] Rowe was an Oxford postgraduate who produced in 1927 an excellent thesis on the duke of Bedford as Regent of France.[12] Her research was deeply based in the archives both in France and in England, and she was no doubt keen to seek out a potentially valuable chronicle relating to her period. In 1926 the results of her detective work were published in the *English Historical Review* under the title 'A Contemporary Account of the Hundred Years War from 1415 to 1429'.[13]

The significance of Rowe's article cannot be overstated. Her archival work had enabled her to trace Peter Basset and Christopher Hanson in the muster rolls and other records of the English administration of Normandy and Maine. As a result, their military careers were made apparent, prompting Rowe to the view that the chronicle

> is a plain soldierly account of the wars in which Fastolf had played so leading a part, intended to please the old man by awaking memories of his past adventures. It is rich in the names of those companions in arms and well-tried foes whom Fastolf would delight to recall.[14]

From a reading of Rowe's article, however, it is clear that she was able to spend only limited time reading the text in the College of Arms. All of her references about the content of the chronicle are actually to the corresponding section of Hall's *Union*. As a result – and also because of her disappointment that the chronicle ended before Joan of Arc's career took off – Rowe's opinion of the chronicle was rather negative: 'It must be admitted that, interesting as it is, it adds very little to our knowledge owing to the extensive use of it by Hall.'

It fell to Kenneth Bruce McFarlane (1903–66), Fellow of Magdalen College, Oxford, to probe more deeply. In 1957 he put forward some initial thoughts in his article, 'William Worcester: A Preliminary Survey',[15] but his premature death

---

[10] 'C'est, croyons-nous, dans un dossier de ses archives que doit dormir encore l'oeuvre de Pierre Basset' (Planchenault, 'De l'utilité', p. 126).
[11] Toppin (1881–1969) had joined the College as Bluemantle Pursuivant in 1923, becoming York Herald in 1932 and Norroy and Ulster King of Arms in 1957.
[12] Rowe went on to publish a number of seminal articles before pursuing a teaching career in India. Her staff file can be viewed in the Archives of the Friends of Women's Christian Colleges in Madras and of their predecessors, the British Boards of the Colleges: BL, MSS Eur F220/80 (1935–56). Her publications are listed in the bibliography.
[13] Her bringing the chronicle to light no doubt contributed to its selection for inclusion in the Heralds Commemorative Exhibition 1484–1934, held at the College of Arms. It features as item 95 in the exhibition catalogue which was published in 1936 and reprinted in 1970.
[14] Rowe, p. 513.
[15] Citations are taken from the reprinted article in *Collected Essays*, ed. Harris, where discussion of the chronicle is to be found on pp. 210–11. The microfilm purchased by McFarlane was subsequently used by Dr Jeremy Catto of Oriel College to produce a transcription. When he discovered that Anne Curry had also produced a transcription linked to her doctoral work on English military organisation in Lancastrian Normandy, he kindly shared his version with her.

prevented his making further use of the microfilm of the text of the chronicle which he had purchased. During Anne Curry's doctoral research in the early 1980s on military organisation in Lancastrian Normandy, she was able to visit the College of Arms and produce a transcript.[16]

Over the last forty years or so, research on the fifteenth-century phase of the Hundred Years War has expanded hugely. It is now possible, for instance, thanks to 'The Soldier in Later Medieval England' project co-directed by Curry, to discover more about military careers, not only those of Basset and Hanson but also others listed in the chronicle.[17] Curry's ongoing work on the Norman rolls of Henry V also provides relevant information on the conquest of Normandy, where names of both English captains and the French captains they supplanted at the point of surrender are given.[18] Rémy Ambühl's research on prisoners of war and on surrender has boosted understanding of martial culture and practice.[19] The collections of the College of Arms have also been extensively catalogued, which makes it possible to set the chronicle, and indeed the collected texts within MS M 9 as a whole, into context, as well as to explore the provenance of the text.[20] We also now know much more about Sir John Fastolf and his circle thanks to the work of Anthony Smith and Colin Richmond,[21] and to the new editions of the *Paston Letters and Papers* which show that Christopher Hanson, Luket Nantron and William Worcester were all key members of the knight's administration.[22] Worcester fell into dispute with the Pastons on the execution of Fastolf's will. It is therefore from that Paston archive, as well as from the papers of Fastolf and Worcester which came to Magdalen College Oxford, that we can gain many valuable insights into the context within which the chronicle was written.

But one name is strikingly missing from the *Paston Letters* and the Fastolf Papers – that of Peter Basset, whom, as we have seen, Worcester claims as the original author of the chronicle. Whilst, as Rowe first showed, Basset had certainly served as a soldier under Fastolf in France, no trace has been found of him after 1437, whether in France or in England after Fastolf's retirement. The waters are further muddied by Edward Hall's reference to a Peter Basset within his narrative as a chamberlain of Henry V,[23] as well as by his inclusion of a *John* Basset in the list of English authors used in the writing of his *Union*. The situation is further complicated by suggestion made in 1557 by the antiquarian John Bale that Peter

---

[16] In 2000 Curry included a translation of the chronicle's account of Agincourt in her collection of sources for the battle (*Sources*, pp. 85–8).

[17] www.medievalsoldier.org.

[18] Curry, 'The Norman Rolls of Henry V', pp. 265–82, along with a forthcoming online calendar.

[19] For instance, *Prisoners of War in the Hundred Years War*; 'Joan of Arc as Prisonnière de Guerre'; 'Henry V and the Administration of Justice: The Surrender of Meaux, 1422'; (with Dodd), 'The Politics of Surrender'.

[20] Campbell and Steer, *A Catalogue of Manuscripts in the College of Arms Collections*, vol. 1.

[21] Smith, 'Aspects of the Career of Sir John Fastolf'; Richmond's three volumes on *The Paston Family in the Fifteenth Century*, subtitled *The First Phase*, *Fastolf's Will*, and *Endings*.

[22] The first two volumes of the *Paston Letters and Papers of the Fifteenth Century* were edited by Norman Davis, and the third by Richard Beadle and Colin Richmond, and published by the Early English Text Society in 2004–05.

[23] Hall (1809), p. 113.

Basset was the author of a one-volume work on Henry V.[24] Such a work has never been discovered, but we need to explore the possibility that the M 9 chronicle had its origins in a work by Peter Basset which was then developed by Hanson and Nantron under the supervision of Worcester. To add further confusion, Worcester himself is credited with being the author of an *Acta* of Sir John Fastolf,[25] a work which, like Basset's book on Henry V, has never been discovered.

At the core of our book is the M 9 chronicle itself, which is presented in its original French, the linguistic aspects of which are explored by Professor Richard Ingham in Chapter 4. The scribe of the manuscript can be identified as Luket Nantron, as the contribution of Dr Deborah Thorpe in Chapter 1 confirms. The manuscript of the chronicle bears signs of use through annotations and additions. These begin with Worcester himself, whose distinctive hand is easily identified, but continue into the sixteenth century where they include heraldic symbols added against names of English soldiers. Through such annotations, and through the early sixteenth-century texts with which the chronicle was bound, we can explore what happened to the chronicle after the death of Fastolf. This shapes the content of Chapter 5. How did the chronicle find its way into the College of Arms? What use did heralds make of it? How might Hall have been able to access the text and to what use did he put it? A detailed comparison of the chronicle narrative against the relevant sections of his *Union* is vital to our understanding and is dealt with in Chapter 6. We know that Hall's narrative was drawn on in the creation of the Holinshed chronicles, sources used by Shakespeare (unless he drew on Hall directly). Can we see any possible influence of the mediated chronicle narrative on the plays which Shakespeare wrote about the period which the chronicle covers? This question is also addressed in Chapter 6. In Chapter 7, Professor Scott Lucas shows that the chronicle, as mediated by Hall, had a strong impact on the *Mirror for Magistrates*, another significant mid-Tudor work, through its story of the earl of Salisbury, a man prominent in the M 9 chronicle narrative. Taken together, therefore, the last three chapters of the book explore the 'afterlife' of the chronicle.

But what of its creation? Basset and Hanson were undoubtedly soldiers, and the chronicle was written for another soldier, Sir John Fastolf. Nantron and Worcester were in the employment of Fastolf. The authors are all intriguing and worthy of study as individuals, but it is also rare to find a chronicle written by a team. Chapter 1 reconstructs the careers of each man in turn before exploring how and when the work might have been compiled by the team in the last years of Sir John Fastolf. As noted earlier, the chronicle is unique in its format and content. Is there any sign that behind the surviving text there lies an earlier work by Basset which the rest of the team adapted and developed? Chapter 2 explores this problem as well as considering authorial choices of content and format.

---

[24] A one-volume work on Henry V by Peter Basset ('Edito in Anglico sermone libro cui titulum fecit Acta Regis Henrici Quinti. Lib. 1') is listed in the 1557 edition of Bale's *Scriptorum illustrium majoris Britanniae Catalogus*, p. 568.

[25] Bale's 1557 edition also lists a one-volume work by William Worcester on the deeds of Sir John Fastolf ('Acta Domini Ioannis Fastolfi. Lib. 1. Anno Christi 1421 et anno regni') (*Scriptorum illustrium majoris Britanniae Catalogus*, pp. 599–600). Worcester's preparation of such a work is also evidenced in a letter sent by John Davy to John Paston I which has been dated to 1460 (*PL Davis*, ii, Letter 602).

The incipit claims that the chronicle was written for Fastolf towards the end of his life. But to what purpose? Was it to help the ageing knight to reminisce? Or to comfort him with memories of past glories during the dark years after the loss of Normandy and of Maine. Might Sir John have played a personal role in stimulating the work and influencing its content? Why were the authors committed to the listing of the enemy as well as the English on such a large and unprecedented scale? On what sources might they have drawn? Following on from this, we explore in Chapter 3 how the chronicle portrays war. What image of war and of 'deeds of arms' was it intended to provide? Should we consider its approach 'chivalric', potentially reflecting the views and interests of the martial classes, and especially of Fastolf and the other serving soldiers associated with its production? The key question, perhaps, stimulated by Rowe's 'plain soldierly account', is whether we are indeed dealing with a 'soldiers' chronicle'.

The answers to such questions lie to a considerable degree within the text of the chronicle itself.[26] As a result, we have attempted to identify all of the people, places and actions which it mentions. This is no mean task given the quantity of individuals listed, a good number of whom are difficult to identify with certainty. But it is only through such research that we can understand the authorial choices of content and the intention of the chronicle. The text deserves to be brought to wider knowledge because of its unique form and perspective. To that end we have provided a full English translation which also includes identifications and commentary. We hope that the edition will provide an important addition to knowledge of Fastolf and his circle, a group already linked to a substantial amount of written output – complaints on the loss of France, efforts to revive interest in the war, translations of French works.[27] Undoubtedly, the M 9 chronicle stands as a complex and unique work whose study can provide valuable insights into the process of historical writing about the wars in France.

---

[26] For preliminary overviews of the chronicle and the issues it raises, see Curry, 'Representing War and Conquest, 1415–1429. The Evidence of College of Arms Manuscript M 9', and 'Une chronique écrite par des soldats'.

[27] Nall, *Reading and War*, pp. 41, 56–8, 149–50; Hughes, 'Stephen Scrope and the Circle of Sir John Fastolf', pp. 130–8. We are grateful to Professor Daniel Wakelin and Dr Cath Nall, currently preparing a new edition of Worcester's *Boke of Noblesse* of 1475, for discussion on this most famous of his works.

The M 9 chronicle and its authors

The incipit to the M 9 chronicle names four men as involved in its production, Peter Basset, Christopher Hanson, Luket Nantron and William Worcester. Each has a fascinating career which can be reconstructed to greater or lesser degree, but it is also relevant to discuss after each biographical study how they might have worked as a team in the creation of the chronicle. The manuscript of the chronicle itself is an important source in this study and therefore offers a useful starting point in discussion of the authors.

THE CHRONICLE MANUSCRIPT AND ITS SCRIBE, LUKET NANTRON
(DEBORAH ELLEN THORPE)

College of Arms MS M 9 is a compilation of fifteenth- and sixteenth-century texts which includes the chronicle which is the focus of this book.[1] The compilation was in its current form from at least the early seventeenth century; this is evidenced by the style of its binding as well as by its inclusion in the first catalogue of the collections of the College made by Samson Lennard in 1619.[2] The provenance and format of College of Arms MS M 9 as a whole will be explored in Chapter 5.[3] Here we shall concentrate only on the chronicle, which is only known to survive in this single manuscript.

The first folio is marked in a mid-fifteenth-century hand in small roman numerals as 'xxxj'. This style of numbering continues on all recto folios until the last folio of the chronicle 'lxvj'. Such original foliation indicates that the chronicle was previously part of another compilation, probably put together by William Worcester, but we cannot now know what else was originally bound with it. The first page of the chronicle is darkened, suggesting that it enjoyed a separate existence for some time before being grouped with later materials into College of Arms MS M 9. There is evidence of water damage to the head and fore-edge of the folios of the chronicle text, damage which is not seen elsewhere in MS M 9, which also confirms its separate existence for an extended period.

---

[1] This work is based on Thorpe, 'Writing and Reading', esp. pp. 47–8, 214–18, 293–301 and 315–30. Thanks also to Linne Mooney for palaeographical advice.

[2] The contents of the manuscript as a whole are set out in Campbell and Steer, *Catalogue*, vol. 1, pp. 129–31. There is further discussion in Chapter 5.

[3] We are grateful to the College of Arms conservator, Christopher Harvey, for his thoughts on the binding of MS M 9 as a whole and on the appearance of the chronicle section in particular.

In addition, it would seem that the chronicle has at some point been folded as a whole, rather like a newspaper might be. Other notebooks of William Worcester, such as his commonplace book, also show signs of folding, leading John Harvey to conclude that 'the original folded sheets of paper on which the books are composed must have been carried by Worcester on his journeys and used for immediate jottings. The narrow format of these books would make them easy to slip into a saddle-bag'.[4] These deep creases, though remedied by the later binding into the manuscript as a whole and by conservation techniques, are still evident in the chronicle folios. At some point, presumably in the sixteenth century, these medieval folios were disbound and sandwiched between later texts. Subsequently, the blank leaves and spaces following the chronicle text were used by sixteenth-century hands, with other writers making marginal annotations to the text of the chronicle itself. Such annotations have been noted in the edition provided later in this volume and are also discussed in Chapter 5.

The M 9 chronicle is the work of a single scribe who began writing midway down f. 31r, leaving the top half blank (Figure 1). William Worcester subsequently filled some of this empty space with the text's dedication or incipit, which begins 'de actibus armorum conquestus regni Francie'. Though Worcester wrote in this incipit that the chronicle was compiled under his supervision ('per dilgenciam'), he made relatively few corrections or additions to it, a contrast with other texts with which he is linked.

The relative lack of amendments by Worcester could suggest that there was a previous draft of the M 9 chronicle which has since been lost and which Worcester had amended substantially. This is supported by the neatness of the scribal hand of the chronicle and the text's large margins, which were scored but never filled. There are also thirty-one spaces left for enlarged initials. The scribe provided guide letters in every case but the decorative programme was never realised. Perhaps most striking are the large gaps left by the scribe within the text, which often rendered pages over half empty. If these gaps were intended for illuminations, then this programme of illumination was left unrealised. As a result, the text of the M 9 chronicle which survives today has a sparse, though neat, appearance. The text itself was left unfinished, ending abruptly near the top of f. 66r.

The elegant appearance of the M 9 chronicle, with its spaces for illumination, indicates that it was intended by William Worcester as a presentation piece for his master, Sir John Fastolf. Worcester's incipit states that it was written in 1459, 'anno quo dictus Iohannes Fastolf obijt' ('the year that the said Sir John Fastolf died'). It seems that the death of Fastolf put an end to Worcester's plans for a decorative, and expensive, celebratory chronicle, which would have covered a longer period. The text breaks off at the year 1429. Thus, the chronicle was abandoned, without a patron, incomplete and without its planned illuminations.

The first watermark of the M 9 chronicle is visible only on f. 31 and comprises two circles, with a vertical line in between and a triangle at the top of the line.[5] The second is a circle with two triangles inside, each divided into three. This is

---

[4]   *Itineraries*, p. xx. There are six surviving notebooks made by Worcester, 'four of them in an unusual elongated format, often called a holster book' (Wakelin, 'William Worcester Writes a History of His Reading', p. 56; Wakelin, *Humanism, Reading and English Literature*, p. 94).

[5]   For the use of paper in the circle of Fastolf, see Thorpe, 'Writing and Reading', pp. 214–18, which forms the basis of this section on the watermarks of the M 9 chronicle.

clearly visible on ff. 37 and 38 and again on ff. 49, 50, 51, 52 and 53. The third is another triangle, bisected from apex to base by a straight line (ff. 41, 42 and 45, 46). These marks are not amongst the repertoire that appears most commonly in material associated with Sir John Fastolf but four folios of the chronicle have a visible watermark that appears frequently in the corpus of writings associated with Fastolf: a bull's head, with a line topped with a star protruding from between its horns (ff. 59, 61, 63, 65). In addition, three of the folios – 119, 120 and 121 (the last being a half leaf bound after 120), bound within College of Arms MS M 9 – also show this watermark. Worcester's hand is apparent on ff. 120 and 121, the contents of which are provided in the Appendix to this volume.

This bull's head mark belongs to Charles Briquet's 'tête de boeuf' family of marks, an abundant group in the paper of the period, with the subgroup being either 'avec yeux et nez' or 'avec yeux et narines'.[6] A watermark from this group also appears in Magdalen College Oxford, Fastolf Paper (FP) 48. The mark is present also in another document at Magdalen College Oxford, Hickling 132, a document relating to Fastolf's dispute with the prior of Hickling. Both of these contain the hand of Fastolf's servant William Barker, with whom both Nantron and Worcester had a close working relationship. FP 48, as we shall see, contains writing by Luket Nantron. A similar bull's head watermark, though with longer horns and a thinner nose, appears on the folios of many texts in College of Arms, Arundel 48, a compilation made by William Worcester, reinforcing the connection between that manuscript and the M 9 chronicle.[7] Among the texts in Arundel 48 that feature this mark are the provisions of the Oxford Parliament spanning ff. 131r to 138r and the text on ff. 333 to 336 on reform of the coinage, which is in the hand of Luket Nantron.

The shared bull's head watermark in the M 9 chronicle, FP 48 and Arundel 48 combine with their shared scribal hands to create a picture of a closely-connected and collaborative community of scribes and compilers associated with Sir John Fastolf, including Luket Nantron, William Barker, and William Worcester. Worcester included Luket Nantron in his incipit to the M 9 chronicle, describing him as 'of Paris, one of the clerks of John Fastolf'. That Nantron is the only 'author' Worcester describes as a clerk suggests in itself that he was the scribe of the chronicle. That suggestion can be confirmed through a study of the hand, which does indeed identify it as that of Nantron.

Luket Nantron was in Fastolf's service by at least the mid-1450s, if not earlier.[8] In College of Arms, Arundel 48 there is a Latin text in his hand containing propositions for what could be done to save France. At the head of this document the date is given as August 1449. If this was written at that actual date, then it would suggest Nantron was already working for Fastolf and William Worcester at that

6   The *Thomas L. Gravell Watermark Archive* has one record from this group of watermarks, from 1469, on paper originating from Belgium (www.gravell.org [accessed May 2011], 'bull's head'). For the watermark in Briquet's compilation, see Briquet, *Filigranes*, 'tête de boeuf,' numbers 14096–15459, but especially numbers 14096–14442 and 14952–15207; and Thorpe, 'Writing and Reading', pp. 215–16.

7   Thorpe, 'Writing and Reading', p. 322. For the contents see *Catalogue of the Arundel Manuscripts in the College of Arms*, pp. 74–90.

8   For a short biography see https://www.englandsimmigrants.com/page/individual-studies/luket-nantron. See also Thorpe, 'Documents and Books', pp. 195–216.

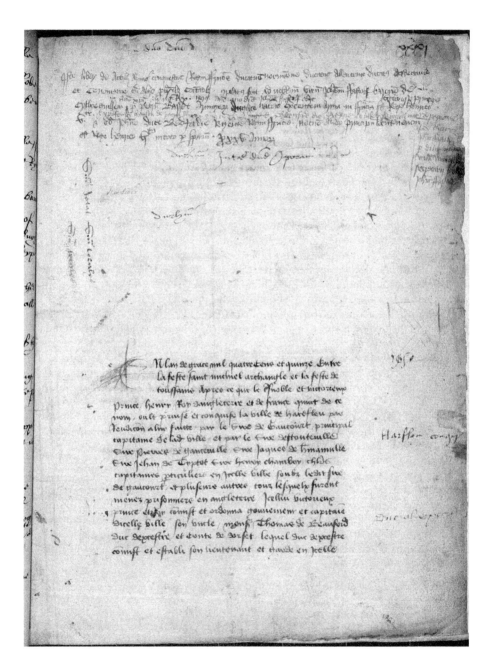

Figure 1. College of Arms, MS M 9 f. 31r. Reproduced by permission of the Kings, Heralds and Pursuivants of Arms

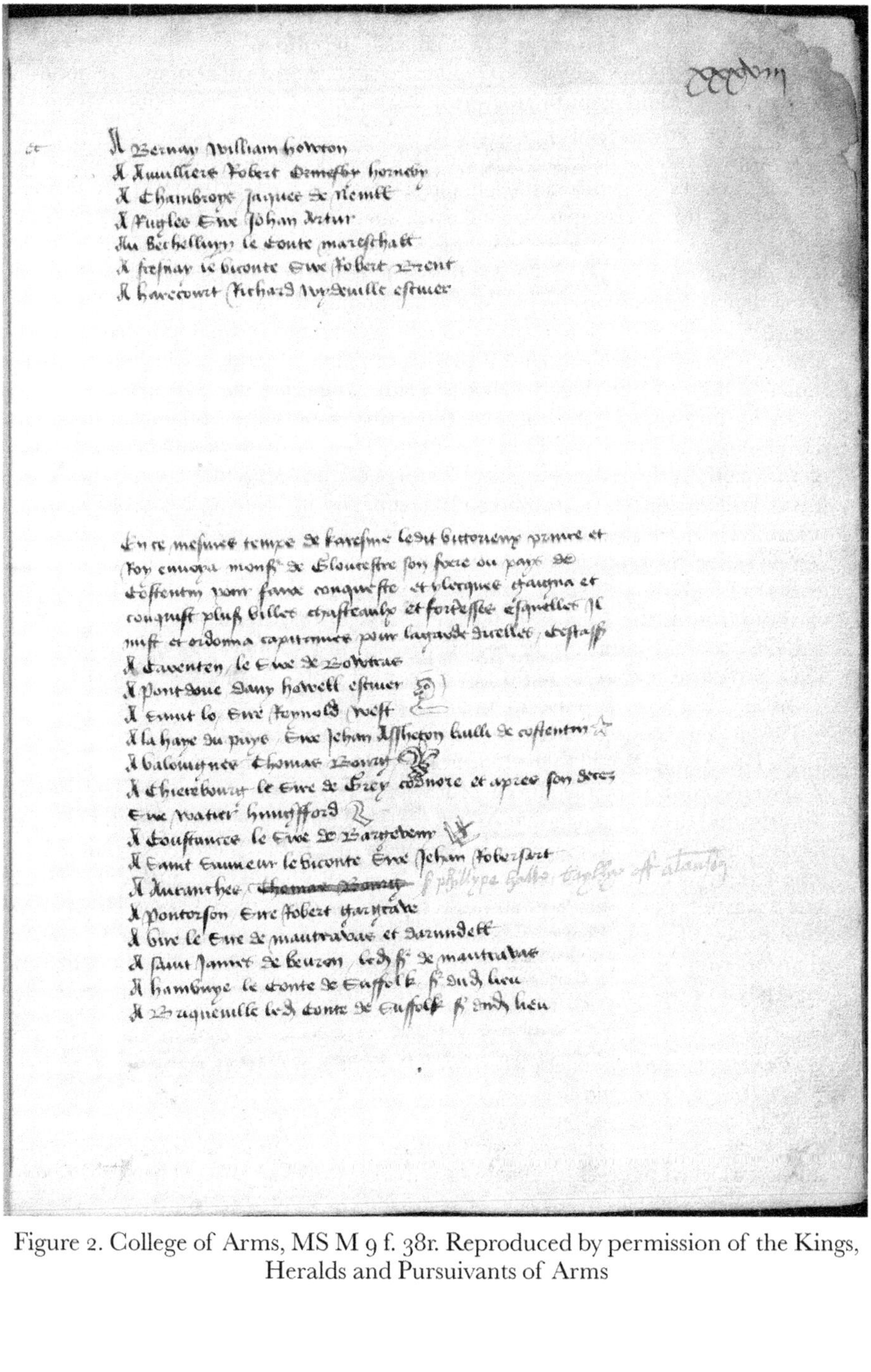

A Bernay William Howton
A Tuuilliers Robert Dmesby horneby
A Chambroys Jaquec de Nemll
A Fuglee Ewe Johan Artur
Ju Bethelluys le conte mareschall
A fresnay le biconte Ewe Robert Brent
A harcourt Richard Wyckuille esquier

En ce mesmes temps de karesme le dit bitonemy prinre et
Roy enuoia monsʳ de Gloucestre son frere ou pays de
Costentin pour faire conqueste et bloqune chascuna et
conquist plus villes chasteaulx et forteresse esquelles il
mist et ordonna capitannes pour lagarde duelles destaff
A sauenten le Ewe de Bouttue
A Pontdoue Dauy hotell esquier
A Cinut les Ewe fernold west
A la haye du puys Ewe Johan Assheton bailli de costentin
A baleuctmer thomas Bonay
A Chierebourg le Ewe de Grey ednore et apres son decez
Ewe wauer hunssford
A Couftances le Ewe de Bargedem
A Saint Enuueur le biconte Ewe Johan Robersort
A Auranchee thomas Bonay φ phillype Gatto tighne A atantog
A Pontorson Ewe Robert Harpcrake
A bire le Ewe de mautrauers et Arundell
A Saint Jamec de beuron les dʳ fᶦ de mautrauers
A hambuye le conte de Suffolk fᶦ dud lieu
A Baquienlle led conte de Suffolk fᶦ dud lieu

Figure 2. College of Arms, MS M 9 f. 38r. Reproduced by permission of the Kings,
Heralds and Pursuivants of Arms

point.[9] Nantron's name first appears in the Paston corpus in a letter dated tentatively by Norman Davis to November 1456 and numbered by him as Letter 569.[10] In this letter, Sir John Fastolf informed John Paston I, his legal advisor, that he had received correspondence from his servant William Barker, written in Nantron's hand, regarding his servants at Cotton manor in Suffolk.[11]

FP 48 presents further palaeographical evidence of a collaborative relationship between Barker and Nantron: the small, neat, hand of this draft petition written for Fastolf shares letter features with that of the M 9 chronicle.[12] These include minuscule *y* with a thin tail that curves to the right at its end and horned *g* with its straight back and a tail that bends to the left and then curves back to the right (see Figure 1, line 4 'Roy', line 4 'dangleterre'; Figure 3, line 1 'seyd', line 3 'Remaynyng'). The *s* and *f* lean forward towards the next graph in both samples and have slightly tapering tops and bottoms. Lower case *d* has the same shape in both petition and chronicle, being double lobed with the top lobe often tipping to the left (Figure 1, line 2 'de'; Figure 3, line 1 'seyd'). There is also an odd appearance of final rounded 'e' in M 9 (Figure 1, line 5, 'prinse') and in FP 48 (Figure 3, line 1, 'hadde'). The letter 'p' is also similar in the two texts (Figure 2, line 4, 'prince'; Figure 3, line 2 'apperith').

Such characteristics indicate that the scribe of both the M 9 chronicle and the draft petition in FP 48 was Luket Nantron. Though he evidently began the draft of the petition, the palaeographical features of the correcting hand indicate that it was William Barker who ultimately completed it.[13] The survival of Nantron's corrected hand in this document is rare evidence of the guidance and correction of one scribe by another within the context of gentry administration. Nantron's errors in FP 48 were those of a novice scribe rather than a French clerk struggling with drafting in the English language. Nantron had made some basic drafting mistakes, such as omitting the regnal year in the formula 'yere of the Regne of kyng herry the sext with ought any thyng yeldyng'. In this case, the correcting scribe inserted 'xxxi' superscript to indicate the missing year.

Paston Letter 569 was carried to Sir John Fastolf by a man named Henry Hanson. If this Henry was related to the Christopher Hanson listed in the M 9 incipit as one of the co-compilers of the chronicle, it would suggest a wider connection between Nantron and the Hanson family. As it is, we can easily trace links between Luket and Christopher Hanson. In a letter written after 1466, Fastolf's executors claimed that John Paston received certain items by the hands of several men, including Hanson and Nantron: 'Item, dictus Johannes recepit per manus dicti Thome Howys, Willelmi Paston, Thome Playter, Thome Plummer de London, scryvaner, Christofori Hanson armigeri, et Luce Nantron ad diversas vices tam Londonijs quam in Suthwerk ut patet per billam de parcellis' (Letter 906, lines 103–6). This indicates that

---

[9]   College of Arms, Arundel 48, ff. 329r–332r, printed in *L&P*, II, ii, pp. 723–9.

[10]   *PL Davis*, ii, Letter 569, lines 2–3. Further references to this edition are presented in the text as letter numbers, and line numbers if relevant, within parentheses.

[11]   'I receyvid by Henré Hannson on Thorsday last passid at iiij after none certeyn lettres, amonges whiche I receyvid on from William Barker writen of Lukettes hand' (Letter 569, lines 2–3). See Thorpe, 'Writing and Reading', pp. 47 and 297.

[12]   MCA, FP 48.

[13]   As indicated by a comparison with letters identified as being in the hand of William Barker by *PL Davis*, ii, such as Letter 578, an autograph letter from Barker to John Paston. See *PL Davis*, iii, Letter 1020 (image on p. 150).

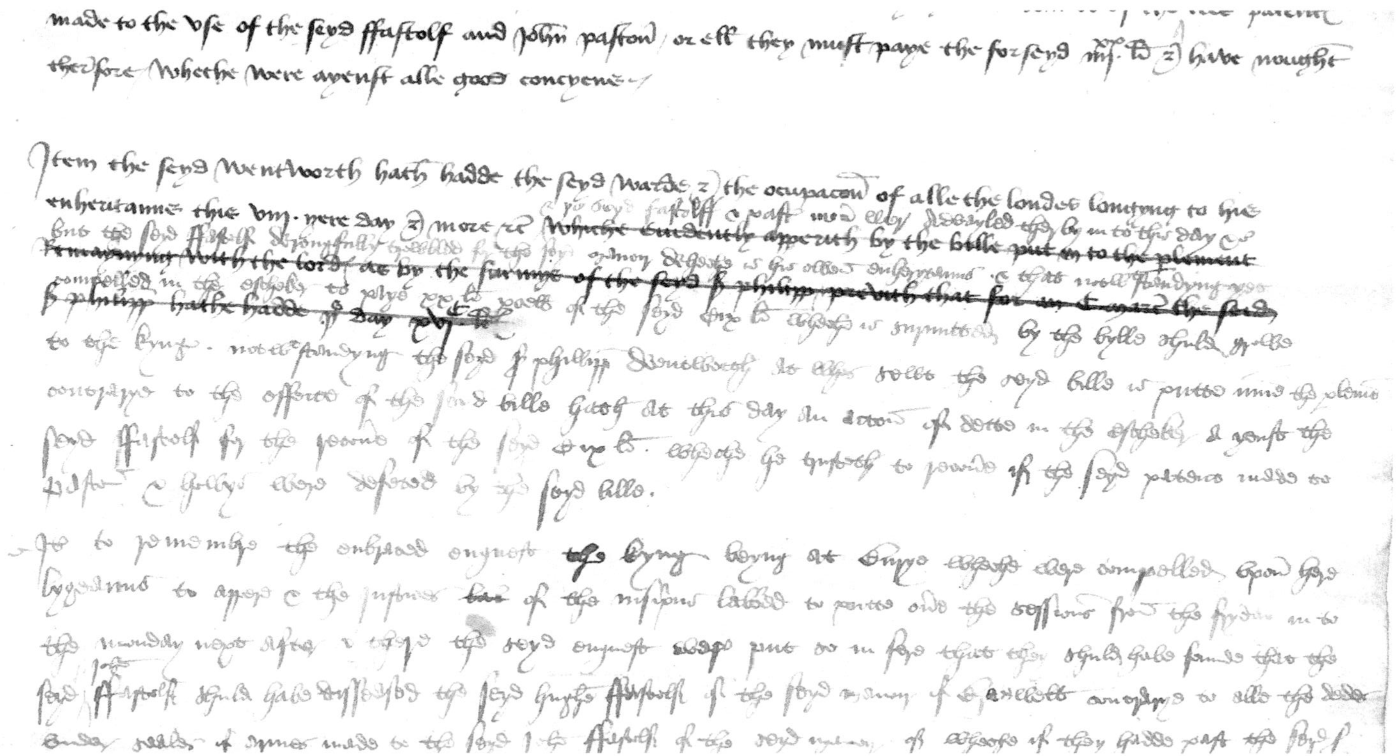

Figure 3. Oxford, Magdalen College FP 48. Reproduced by permission of the President and Fellows of Magdalen College Oxford

Nantron had been working as an assistant to Hanson whilst the latter was receiver of Fastolf's revenues in London.[14] However, there is no explicit record of Nantron ever working as a scribe for Hanson. For instance, FP 51 is an account roll of Christopher Hanson of rents due to Sir John Fastolf, but the hand is not that of the scribe of the M 9 chronicle. Regardless, the pair worked together during Fastolf's lifetime, in both an administrative and a literary capacity, and they later passed together into the service of John Paston.[15] Letters dating from after Fastolf's death demonstrate further the enduring nature of their close relationship when working together on behalf of the Paston family. In 1461 Clement Paston wrote to his father, John, promising him a delivery of money. Clement assured John that more money would be passed to Christopher Hanson and Nantron: 'þe remnawnte I trow I xall gett vp-on *Cristo*fire Hanswm *and* Lwket' (Letter 116, 25 August 1461).

We can see that Nantron had also worked with men from the wider circle of Sir John Fastolf. In around 1458, Henry Windsor, apparently a Chancery clerk, wrote to John Paston, excusing himself for using 'Luket' to copy documents for him which had been sent via William Worcester. Windsor had, he wrote, 'no leiser' to do so himself (Letter 574, lines 7–8).[16] That William Worcester also noted Nantron's death in London in his *Itineraries*, dating it to around 4 October 1471, also suggests a closeness from their common connections in the service of Fastolf.[17] It is possible that Nantron began to work for Fastolf whilst the latter was still in France: in that context he could also have known Hanson and even Basset. But to date, no evidence has been found of Nantron's links with Fastolf in France, nor have any Parisian origins for Luket been traced to substantiate Worcester's claim in the incipit of the M 9 chronicle.

It has been possible, however, thanks to the researches of Rémy Ambühl, to find a Parisian notary called Pierre de Nantron. Pierre was secretary of Jean II Le Maingre dit Boucicaut in Genoa in 1409–10.[18] Between 1413 and 1416 his name is found at the end of many acts of Charles VI,[19] and in mid-September 1415 we also find him executing royal orders to arm galleys against the English.[20] Pierre was dead by April 1424,[21] but given the relative rarity of the name, and the tendency for the area of activity to be hereditary, it would seem highly likely that Luket came from the same family and may even have been a close relative.

There is palaeographical evidence suggesting that Nantron copied texts in other collections connected with William Worcester and Sir John Fastolf. College of Arms, Arundel 48 was compiled and annotated by William Worcester, and includes texts which, as we shall see later, reflect Fastolf's concerns over the loss of Maine and of

---

[14]   See Hanson's biography in this chapter.

[15]   Thorpe, 'Writing and Reading', pp. 47–8.

[16]   Thorpe, 'Writing and Reading', pp. 47 and 252–3. Windsor married William Worcester's sister (Smith, 'Aspects of the Career of Sir John Fastolf', p. 66).

[17]   *Itineraries*, p. 255, although Thorpe suggests on the England's Immigrants website that, from the evidence of scribal work, this date may be too early for Nantron's demise.

[18]   Millet, 'Qui a écrit "Le Livre des fais du bon messire Jehan le Maingre dit Bouciquaut"?', pp. 136–47.

[19]   For example, AN, JJ 167/467, JJ 168/290; *Ordonnances des rois de France*, x, pp. 70, 150, 167, 181, 186, 201 (1413), 221, 226 (1414) 359, 382 (1416).

[20]   BL, Add. Ch., 259.

[21]   AN, X1a 64, f. 105v.

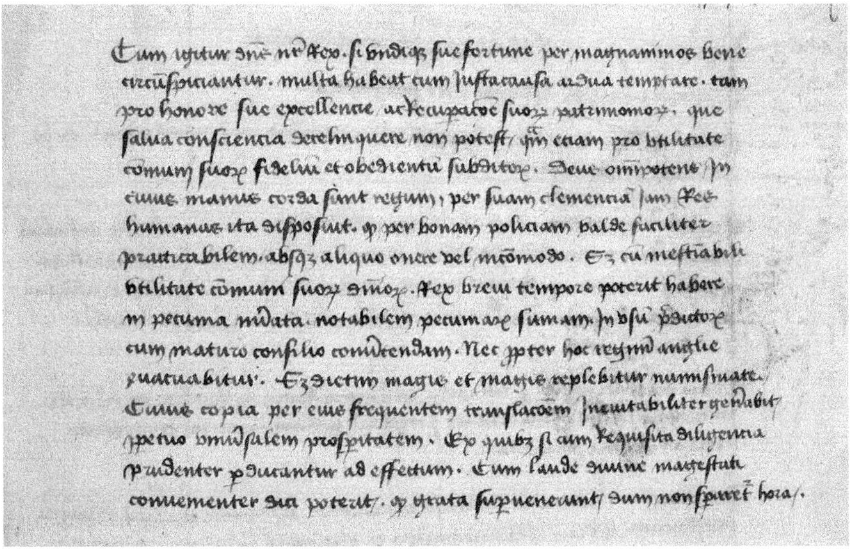

Figure 4. College of Arms, Arundel 48, f. 339. Reproduced by permission of the Kings, Heralds and Pursuivants of Arms

the war with France in general.[22] Arundel 48 contains the work of many scribes and includes paper with an array of watermarks.[23] However, certain texts within it share the aspect (the general appearance) and the ductus (the formation of individual letters) of the hand of the M 9 chronicle. The closest correspondence is in a collection of objections against certain ways and means for raising money to pay the king's debts on ff. 339r to 340r (Figure 4). There are numerous palaeographical similarities between the writing of this text and the hand of the M 9 chronicle. There is correspondence in the script's unconscious features, again with the forward-leaning aspect created by long *f* and *s* (Figure 1, line 2, 'feste'; Figure 4, line 1, 'sue fortune'); the minuscule *g* with horns and a tail which bends to the left, then sharply to the right at its tip (Figure 1, line 1, 'grace'; Figure 4, line 6, 'regum'); and minuscule *h* with an arch that extends below the bottom line, curving back towards the shaft (Figure 1, line 2, 'archangle'; Figure 4, line 6, 'humanas'). Final *s* is kidney-shaped and often spiky (Figure 2, line 3, 'Jaques'; Figure 4, line 1, 'domin*us*'). Majuscule letters, too, share features. For instance, the distinctive *R* has a loop that points towards the top line and a shaft that loops back on itself and horizontal cross bar (Figure 2, line 6, 'Robert'; Figure 4, line 2, 'Rex'). Majuscule *S* has a sigmoid shape, often with a spiky lobe, in both these texts in Arundel 48 and the M 9 chronicle (Figure 1, line 26, 'Suffolk'; Figure 4, line 8, 'Sz' [*sed*]).

It should be recognised that other scribes share some of the more common palaeographical features. In addition, shared features between hands influenced by the bâtârde style in this period introduce an element of doubt. However, the degree of correspondence in distinctive individual letters such as Nantron's 'g', the

---

22   Thorpe, 'Reading and Writing', pp. 316–17.
23   For more on the scribes and compilation of College of Arms, Arundel 48, see Thorpe, 'Reading and Writing', pp. 315–30.

general shared ductus, and the connection between Arundel 48 and the Fastolf circle, together suggest that this text in Arundel 48 ff. 339r–340r was written by Luket Nantron. There may be other texts in this compilation that are in the hand of Nantron.[24] However, though there are some palaeographical similarities between these texts (ff. 131r–138v; 141r–152v; 155v–157v; 329r–332r; and 333r–336v) and the hand of the M 9 chronicle, there are significant differences that make a certain attribution for these texts problematic. It may be that these three texts were copied by other French scribes with similar hands.

Overall, however, there is ample evidence of the interconnections of William Worcester, Christopher Hanson and Luket Nantron within the service of Sir John Fastolf in the 1450s. In this context, their collaboration on the M 9 chronicle is not surprising. McFarlane was inclined to ascribe a major role to Nantron, arguing that 'since the language chosen was Nantron's own and he was a clerk, it seems likely that he was responsible for the actual composition'.[25] As Professor Ingham shows in Chapter 4, the French of the chronicle is indeed the French of France – Nantron's language. Furthermore, it is significant that Fastolf chose to have in his service a French clerk. Would that we knew whether Nantron had already been associated with Fastolf in France. Without information of Nantron's earlier life and in particular whether he had direct experience of the Anglo-French war, it is difficult to assign him a greater role than that of the scribe of the chronicle.

PETER BASSET

The original incipit of the M 9 chronicle by William Worcester gives Peter Basset as the sole author, adding that he was English and served as a soldier in the wars in France. The soldiers of this period – whether in expeditionary armies dispatched from England or in garrisons maintained in France – received pay. As a result we have a considerable amount of archival information on them surviving in the records of the English Exchequer or of the *chambre des comptes* of Lancastrian France. On the face of it, therefore, it is simply a case of finding a Peter Basset in these records. Benedicta Rowe made a start in the 1920s, establishing a connection with Fastolf through service in his garrison of Alençon from at least 1429 to 1434,[26] although in her efforts to trace his earlier career, she misread as Peter a Philip Basset who was serving in April 1420 as an archer at Tombelaine.[27] With easier access to muster records through the 'Soldier in Later Medieval England' project, we can find further references to the service of a Peter Basset.

But how can we be certain that we are identifying the soldier who wrote the chronicle? At base we cannot. Worcester does not tell us that Peter Basset had served under Fastolf and, unlike Christopher Hanson, there is no mention of Peter in the chronicle text. We do have mentions within the text, however, of a John as well as a William Basset. William features on f. 39r in a list of appointments made

---

[24]   Thorpe, 'Writing and Reading', pp. 325–6.
[25]   McFarlane, p. 211.
[26]   Rowe, p. 506, citing BNF, Fr. 25768/239. However, this reference is to a muster of Fastolf's garrison of Alençon on 12 June 1427 and does not contain any Bassets. The muster of reinforcements in 1429 in which Peter appears is BNF, Fr. 25768/424. Rowe's reference, BL, Add. Ch. 11833, for Peter Basset's presence in the garrison of Alençon on 16 September 1434, is correct. See also Curry, 'Peter Basset', *ODNB*.
[27]   Rowe, p. 506, citing BNF, Fr. 25766/794.

by Henry V after the fall of Rouen where he is named as captain of Saint-Clair-sur-Epte, a location south of Gisors. Against his name is the additional description 'esquire, lord of the place', a wording which suggests that he had been given the place by the king in a land grant, but no such grant has been found in the surviving records nor is there any independent evidence of his holding this or any other captaincy. A John Basset is noted as one of those taken prisoner along with Sir John de la Pole during an action into Anjou in 1423 (f. 50r).

A number of William and John Bassets can be found within the muster rolls of Lancastrian Normandy but being certain they are the men of those names mentioned in the chronicle is not easy.[28] We face the same problem for Peter Basset. We can never be wholly certain that any Peter Basset we find in the records is definitely the man of that name who was the author of the chronicle.[29] But there are some interesting possibilities. The retinue which John Mowbray, Earl Marshal and earl of Nottingham, later duke of Norfolk (d. 1432), led on the 1417 expedition contained a Peter Basset, a William Basset and two John Bassets within the men-at-arms as well as a Richard Basset within the archers.[30] A Basset family can be shown to have earlier links with the Mowbrays. We find a William and a John Basset as men-at-arms and a Simon Basset as an archer in service under John's father, Earl Thomas (d. 1399), in 1389.[31] There has been a suggestion that John Fastolf started his career in the household of this earl who became first duke of Norfolk, which could mean he was acquainted even at this early stage with the Bassets but, without further evidence, this must remain a speculation.[32]

The account of the receiver-general of John Mowbray, Earl Marshal for 1414–15 (and hence covering the Agincourt campaign), notes under 'annuitates cum feodis hospicii' ('annuities and fees of the household') an annual payment of 5 marks to a John Basset 'armiger' ('esquire').[33] In the 'vadia guerrae' ('wages of war') section of the same account both this John and a Robert Basset were each paid for service on the campaign as a man-at-arms with three archers.[34] Since young soldiers often began their service as archers, it is not impossible that Peter was an archer within

---

[28]   A search on the names in www.medievalsoldier.org will reveal the problem of many men of these names appearing in muster rolls. One John Basset can be shown to have died by August 1427 since the land grant made to him by Henry V in July 1419 (C 64/11 m. 36, DKR 41, p. 788) was regranted then to Thomas Maistresson (AN, JJ 174/41). The Norman rolls also show there were Basset families within Normandy. A Jean Basset held a prebend at Mantes (C 64/15 m. 28, DKR 42, p. 396).

[29]   In the ensuing study, any possible spelling of Peter has been accepted: given that the muster rolls after 1422 were commonly written out by Frenchmen it is not surprising that variants of Pierre should be found alongside the customary English forms of Piers and Peter.

[30]   E 101/51/2 m. 27.

[31]   In a defensive force in the East March towards Scotland (E 101/41/17 m. 4).

[32]   In terms of geographical origins, there were a number of Basset families across England, including one in Cornwall (CPR 1422–29, pp. 217, 493), but so far it has not been possible to identify which is the family linked to the Earl Marshal.

[33]   Gloucester Record Office Microfilm 12. The original manuscript is held at Berkeley Castle, with the shelf mark D1/21/01/002/00/00.

[34]   A Robert Bassett (or Barsett) appears in the so-called Agincourt roll, a late sixteenth-century partial copy of a now lost original concerning the final stages of the campaign (BL, Harley 782 f. 75v).

one of these retinues on the 1415 campaign, from which the Earl was invalided home, as the M 9 chronicle notes on f. 31v.[35] It is also possible that Peter served within the company of 79 men-at-arms and 160 archers raised by the Earl in 1416 for the rescue of Harfleur, for which no muster roll survives.[36]

The first definitive evidence of Peter's service to the Mowbrays, as we have seen, is on the 1417 campaign. The presence of the Earl Marshal in the army which accompanied Henry to France at that point is mentioned on f. 34r of the M 9 chronicle. We find Peter again, as a man-at-arms alongside William Basset and John Basset, in the Earl Marshal's garrison of Pontoise between March and August 1422.[37] The M 9 chronicle mentions, on f. 41v, the Earl Marshal's appointment as captain of Pontoise when the king returned to England early in 1421. The Norman rolls confirm that the Earl was indeed appointed to this captaincy on 26 January 1421 and was still in post in the summer of 1422.[38] If Peter Basset had been in the Earl Marshal's company continuously, he would have been present with his master at the major events of the English conquest both before the sealing of the treaty of Troyes and subsequently, including the siege of Rouen, the advance towards Paris in the summer of 1419, the ceremonies at Troyes in May 1420, and the sieges of Sens and Melun which followed.[39] The Earl's presence at the siege of Melun is noted on f. 40v of the chronicle.

The Earl Marshal also led expeditionary troops from England to France in the summer of 1423.[40] Since there is no surviving muster roll for these troops we cannot be certain whether Peter Basset was in his company. But it is a strong possibility that he was the mounted man-at-arms of this name who mustered on 28 August 1423 in the garrison of Rouen.[41] Richard Beauchamp, earl of Warwick, was captain of Rouen at this point but the muster was headed by the lieutenant, Sir Thomas Gargrave. It is surely no coincidence that Gargrave is mentioned in

---

[35]   Sources for the Earl's company in 1415 include E 101/50/26 which appears to be a muster of part of the Earl's retinue before embarkation; E 101/44/30 no. 1, m. 10, a sick list following the siege of Harfleur; E 101/47/38 m. 1, which was a roll sent to the Exchequer some time after the campaign which lists the Earl's retinue. The Earl himself was invalided home after the surrender of Harfleur.

[36]   The size of the Earl's company is revealed in payments to him (E 101/48/10/144; E 403/624 m. 4).

[37]   E 101/50/19.

[38]   C 64/15 m. 21, DKR 42, p. 399 (appointment). See also an order of 2 June 1422 to muster his men in the garrison (C 64/17 m. 25d, DKR 42, p. 448).

[39]   From the Norman rolls we can trace the Earl's presence at the siege of Louviers, June 1418 (C 64/9 m. 32d, DKR 41, p. 711), Rouen, August 1418–January 1419 (C 64/9 m. 18d, 11d, 8d, 6d, C 64/10 m. 30d, DKR 41, pp. 715, 717, 718, 719, 753). The Earl was appointed in February 1419 to the captaincies of Neufchâtel and Gournay in anticipation of their capture (C 64/10 m. 32, DKR 41, pp. 730–1). In 1419 he mustered at Evreux in March (C 64/11 m. 78d, DKR 42, p. 313), Vernon in April (C 64/11 m. 48d, DKR 42, p. 318), Mantes in July (C 64/11 m. 35d, DKR 42, p. 322), Pontoise in August (C 64/11 m. 20d, DKR 42, p. 326), Gisors in September (C 64/11 m 20d, DKR 42, p. 326), Mantes in October C 64/11 m 15d, DKR 42, p. 328), Pontoise in early May 1420 (C 64/13 m 9d, DKR 42, p. 373), Sens (June 1421) (C 64/14 m 29d, DKR 42, p. 389), Melun (November) (C 64/14 m. 15, DKR 42, p. 391), and Paris (December) C 64/14 m 12d, DKR 42, p. 393).

[40]   E 403/658; E 404/39/165.

[41]   BNF, Fr. 25766/713.

the M 9 chronicle three times. On f. 51v, described as lieutenant for the earl of Warwick at Rouen, we find him at the English recovery of Compiègne (March 1424). The chronicle's account of this engagement is important since it provides the denouement of a story concerning Guillaume Remon dit Marjolaine, who had previously been taken prisoner by Sir John Fastolf at Passy in the summer of 1423, an event already recounted on f. 47v. If Basset had been with the Rouen detachment at the recovery of Compiègne, he would have known the fate of Remon, whose case is intimately linked with the interests of Sir John Fastolf.[42]

No other references have been found to a soldier called Peter Basset until 12 October 1429 when, as Rowe noted, a mounted man-at-arms of that name mustered in a company engaged for a month 'in addition to the ordinary retinue' at Alençon.[43] This is the earliest firm evidence of a link with Fastolf, who had taken up the captaincy of Alençon on 28 September 1423, holding command there until late 1429 or early 1430.[44] Whether Basset had served at Alençon earlier, or had been in Sir John's company during the invasion of Maine, is not known, but he continued to serve in the reinforcements at Alençon for at least another month into mid-November 1429.[45]

Further references to the service of a Peter Basset can be found in the 1430s. All are in the region of Alençon and therefore are likely to relate to the same person, who is consistently serving as a mounted man-at-arms. On 24 March 1431 a Peter Basset is found in the garrison of Essay under Sir Robert Harling.[46] Although temporarily absent on the day of muster, a Peter Basset, as well as an archer called William Basset, was listed in a muster of troops under Robert, lord Willoughby on 2 May 1432 for the siege of Saint-Céneri-le-Gérei.[47] This place, which lay 13 km from Alençon, had been used as a base by Amboise de Loré to launch attacks on the English.[48] The M 9 chronicle mentions de Loré several times as a highly proactive enemy. A counter-roll of January 1434 of the garrison of Alençon places a Peter Basset at a later siege of Saint-Céneri-le-Gérei, now serving in a detachment from the garrison to which Fastolf had returned as lieutenant to the duke of Bedford from at least September 1432.[49] This counter-roll notes that Basset had entered service on 18 January 1434 in place of a man who had been killed at the siege of Saint-Céneri three days earlier.[50] In March 1434 Peter Basset was still serving in the garrison of Alençon but was described as absent between 4 and 12 March in the company of the earl of Arundel 'a la journee de Sille le Guillaume',[51] a place intimately connected with Fastolf since he had been granted it during the conquest of Maine. William Worcester chose to refer to Fastolf by this title in the incipit of the chronicle. On 19 March, and again on 6 June 1434, Basset mustered

---

42   See below pp. 35 and 54.
43   BNF, Fr. 25768/424.
44   BNF, Fr. 4485 pp. 260–1. The last known reference so far discovered is November 1429 (BNF, Fr 25768/432).
45   BNF, Fr. 25768, no. 432.
46   BNF, Fr. 25769, no. 579
47   BNF, Clairambault 207, nos. 111–20.
48   Cooper, *The Real Falstaff*, p. 28.
49   BL, Add. Ch. 11838 (September 1432).
50   BNF, Fr. 25771/831.
51   BNF, Fr. 25771/843.

at Alençon within the garrison of Alençon.[52] Although he is not listed in the garrison musters taken on 16 November 1434 and on 18 August 1435,[53] we find him in the same garrison again on 31 October 1435 alongside a Thomas Basset who was also serving as a man-at-arms.[54] By this last date Fastolf had taken over full command of Alençon following the death of the duke of Bedford.

Basset mustered again at Alençon on 26 December 1437,[55] which is the last known reference to any service by a Peter Basset in France. Fastolf gave up the captaincy of Alençon in March 1438.[56] This marked the end of his service in France, although he spent the next year as governor of the Channel Islands before returning to England, where he remained until his death in 1459. So far no references have been found to Basset's service to Fastolf during the latter's retirement in England. Indeed, since references to Peter Basset dry up in France after December 1437 and none are found thereafter in English sources, it would seem likely that he died around this time.

As we have seen, there is a gap in the muster evidence between 1423 and 1429. Whilst we are at the mercy of the uneven survival of musters, we know that the garrison establishment in Normandy was decreased substantially after the English victory at Verneuil (17 August 1424).[57] This reduction released soldiers for the conquest of Maine in which Fastolf was heavily involved and to which the M 9 chronicle gives much space. That a Peter Basset participated in this conquest is borne out by a mention of him in 1426 in the *comptes de la fabrique* of the church of Pirmil, a village to the south-west of Le Mans which lay quite close to La Suze-sur-Sarthe, a lordship which Fastolf had been granted.[58]

After the surrender of Le Mans to the English in 1425, the inhabitants of its vicinity had little choice but to submit to the English. Each parish was to pay an annual *appatis* of 25 *l.t.* which could be part-paid in victuals. Towards the end of the year, the captain of La Suze, who is named in the Pirmil *comptes* as 'Grygryclere' (and in the M 9 chronicle f. 57r as John Suffolk), took four inhabitants of Pirmil prisoner. The *procureur* of Pirmil came to an agreement with the captain to redeem the prisoners by supplying more food, but in the following year Pirmil found itself at risk of a double render since the captain of Malicorne-sur-Sarthe, William Glasdale, claimed Pirmil lay within his jurisdiction. Glasdale's appointment to Malicorne after the surrender of Le Mans is noted on f. 57r of the chronicle. The *procureur* of Pirmil journeyed to Le Mans seeking a resolution; the village was formally placed under Malicorne with a render of victuals expected each month but it was not easy to find foodstuffs. In mid-March 1426 three barrels of wine were exchanged for oats with another village, Epineu-le-Chevreuil, but on the return home to Pirmil, the *procureur* and his companions were captured by soldiers from the English garrison in the castle of L'Isle-sur-Brûlon which lay to the north-west of Pirmil.

---

[52] BNF, Fr. 25771/826; BNF, Fr. 25771/864.
[53] BL, Add. Ch. 11838, ADO, A 411/A, respectively.
[54] BNF, Fr. 25772/1044.
[55] BNF, Fr. 25774/1279. A Thomas Basset served alongside him as a mounted man-at-arms, as did a Roger Basset as a foot man-at-arms.
[56] BNF, Clairambault 161/8. The captaincy was taken over by Edmund Beaufort.
[57] Curry, 'Military Organisation', i, pp. 218–23.
[58] Sarthe, arr. La Flèche, cant. Loué. Charles, 'L'invasion anglaise', p. 106, cited in Rowe, p. 507. See also, although with a very inaccurate narrative, Froger, 'La paroisse de Pirmil', pp. 281–95.

The soldiers of L'Isle-sur-Brûlon seized the wine, and Nicolas Molyneux (who, the *comptes* imply, was captain of the place) took the *procureur* prisoner. Molyneux claimed that Pirmil owed 6 *écus* for arrears of the *appatis*. The *procureur*'s companions went off to Sillé-le-Guillaume to borrow the money to pay his ransom. But whilst their return was awaited, an Englishman, Peter Basset, agreed to stand as surety for the *procureur* so that he could return to Pirmil, hoping that his fellow parishioners could find money and food to take back to L'Isle-sur-Brûlon to secure his release. The *procureur* duly went home to Pirmil, then returned with a gift for the captain's wife as well as a capon and a pheasant, and was eventually released from his bond. Basset's involvement in the matter is revealed in the *comptes de la fabrique* by a record of 15 *sous* which was due to be paid to him by the *procureur* ('Item à un Anglais nommé Pierres Basset qui avoit plegié envers le cappitaine quant je vins parler aux paroissens pour ce, en argent et en paisson xv *s*').[59]

No English captain is given for L'Isle-sur-Brûlon in the M 9 chronicle but a French captain is included on f. 36v within the list of captains at the time of the English invasion. The reference in the *comptes de la fabrique* of Pirmil does not make it explicit whether Peter Basset was a soldier in the garrison of L'Isle-sur-Brûlon or whether he had some other role. None the less, this reference places him firmly in Maine in the mid-1420s, and implies that he had participated in the conquest of the county. He seems to have remained in the area until the need for reinforcements in Normandy in the autumn of 1429 brought him to Alençon within the additional troops ordered there for the town's defence.

The reference to Molyneux in the case concerning Pirmil is highly significant. McFarlane's researches in the Fastolf Papers at Magdalen College Oxford brought Molyneux to notice through discovery of a risk-sharing agreement he entered into with John Winter at Harfleur in 1421, in the later implementation of which Fastolf became involved.[60] Both Winter and Molyneux are mentioned in the M 9 chronicle. On ff. 58r-v we find Winter appointed as captain of Mayet in Maine after its surrender to the earl of Warwick in 1426, with the additional comment that he was lord of the place because of a grant made to him by the Regent Bedford ('qui en estoit seigneur par don a luy fait par monditseigneur le Regent'). Molyneux is mentioned on f. 62r of the chronicle as a participant in the rescue of Le Mans by John, lord Talbot in the summer of 1427. Whilst no link with Fastolf is given in the chronicle, we know that from at least 1427 Molyneux was acting as Sir John's representative in the collection of garrison wages and that by 1433 he was his receiver-general in France, being rewarded with an annuity by Fastolf from one of his English manors in 1437.[61] He also became a master in the *chambre des comptes* at Rouen and bought up property in the Norman capital.[62] John Winter, who died in 1445, was described in Fastolf's will as 'late my servant',[63] being steward of Sir John's manor of Castle Combe from at least 1437, one of the knight's manors with which, as we shall see,

---

[59] Charles, 'L'invasion anglaise', p. 106.
[60] MCA, Southwark 213, discussed in McFarlane, 'A Business Partnership in War and Administration', pp. 151 74.
[61] McFarlane, 'A Business Partnership in War and Administration', p. 162. Molyneux continued in France, serving between 1445 and 1447 as receiver of the lands held in Normandy by Richard, duke of York (Johnson, *Duke Richard of York 1411–60*, p. 47).
[62] Massey, 'Lancastrian Rouen: Military Service and Property Holding', p. 275.
[63] *PL Gairdner*, iii, p. 156.

William Worcester was also associated. Whilst there is no surviving muster evidence to indicate their military service under Fastolf, both men clearly developed close and lasting links with Sir John. Winter also kept the counter-roll of Molyneux's account as receiver in Maine and Anjou for the duke of Bedford.[64]

There are a number of John Winters in muster rolls from 1415 onwards but it is not possible to identify with certainty which was the man who entered into the agreement with Molyneux in 1421. Molyneux, however, can be identified as a man-at-arms in the garrison of Rouen in 1422, serving alongside a Nicholas Basset.[65] As we saw, Peter Basset was in the Rouen garrison in the following year, and was also present at L'Isle-sur-Brûlon in Maine when Molyneux was captain there in 1426. There is no doubt, therefore, that they knew each other and that both developed links with Fastolf. Indeed, we can speculate that it was through Molyneux that Peter Basset came into the military service of Fastolf.

The career which we have elucidated for Peter Basset is typical of soldiers who chose to pursue their career in France after crossing with an expeditionary force, with periods of service under one captain but also movement between captains and places and theatres of war. Numerous military connections with Sir John Fastolf are evident for Basset from 1429. We have also been able to link Basset to other members of the Fastolf circle, such as Molyneux. There is no explicit evidence that Peter Basset knew Christopher Hanson but they were both active in Maine in the mid-1420s, and both were acquainted with Nicholas Molyneux, as we shall see when we consider the career of Hanson in the next section.

Assuming we have identified the same Peter Basset throughout, his personal experience of the conquest of Normandy and of Maine, and of others involved in it, was considerable. We have seen him in interactions with local inhabitants, and therefore presumably with a knowledge of French as well as some literacy. But there remains a leap of faith that he was the author of a chronicle. For this, we rely on William Worcester's incipit which suggests that Peter Basset was the original author of what became the M 9 chronicle. There is no evidence, however, that Basset was in Fastolf's service in the 1450s when the chronicle was compiled.

The waters are muddied by claims made by John Bale in the 1550s that a Peter Basset had written a one-volume life in English of Henry V ('edito in Anglico sermone libro cui titulum fecit Acta Regis Henrici Quinti Lib. 1)'.[66] This work, according to Bale, covered the king's life from its beginning and included the campaigns and victories in France as well as the peace settlement and regency. Basset, he wrote, was an esquire of good descent who had been in the personal service of Henry V, never leaving his side whether in war or peace, and so privy to things which were usually hidden. Bale added that whilst others had ascribed Henry V's death to certain causes, Basset had affirmed that the king died of pleurisy. Bale even gave a date for this information: 'claruit Petrus, anno domini 1430, Henrico sexti regnante'. If the soldier we have identified was also the author, we can show that he was in France in October 1429 and March 1431 but we have not been able to trace his whereabouts in 1430.

---

[64]   AN, KK 324 f. 1.

[65]   E 101/49/31. Nicholas Basset served in the 1417 army under Sir John Cornwall and under Sir John Radcliffe (E 101/51/2 m. 35, 40) and therefore a direct family link with the Bassets under the Earl Marshal is perhaps less likely. A Nicholas Basset was also granted forfeited lands in Normandy in April 1419 (C 64/11 m. 45, DKR 41, p. 782).

[66]   *Scriptorum illustrium majoris Brittaniae Catalogus*, p. 568. See Nichols, 'Peter Basset', p. 424.

The waters are further muddied by mention in Edward Hall's *Union* of 1548 that Peter Basset was a chamberlain of Henry V,[67] and yet further by Hall's inclusion of a John Basset in his list of English writers he had consulted. The Basset problem will be returned to in Chapter 6 since it more properly belongs to the sixteenth-century use of the M 9 chronicle. Suffice to say here that since Peter Basset does not seem to have been involved in the final compilation of the M 9 chronicle, it is possible that an English work on Henry V accredited to him by Bale was the source for Hanson, Worcester and Nantron in their creation of the version of the M 9 chronicle which is the subject of this current study.

To date, however, no English life of Henry V by Peter Basset has been discovered, nor has a Peter Basset been found in the service of Henry V, although a John Basset seems to have been in royal service.[68] All we can do in this study, therefore, is to examine the text of the M 9 chronicle to see whether it betrays any signs of the use of a pre-existing source. John Bale implies that such a source focused on Henry V alone. Yet Worcester's incipit to the M 9 chronicle implies that Peter Basset was the author of a work covering the whole of the English period in France – all thirty-five years of it from 1415 to 1450. Such an implication takes us back to the problem that Basset disappears from the historical record after 1437 and there is no evidence that he was in the service of Sir John Fastolf in England after the knight's retirement from France.

CHRISTOPHER HANSON

In the incipit of the M 9 chronicle the name of Christopher Hanson as an author was added by William Worcester, with the gloss that he was 'de patria almayn quondam cum Thoma Beaufort duce Excestrie' ('of the country of Germany, at one time with Thomas Beaufort, duke of Exeter'). Uniquely of all of those involved in the composition of the chronicle, Hanson also features within its narrative, being mentioned twice. During the siege of Pontorson in 1427 Hanson and other soldiers of the garrison of Sainte-Suzanne carried out an enterprise in the region of Anjou, advancing right up to Ramefort-de-Gennes (now Ramefort-sur-Seiche), where they took the castle by surprise attack (f. 59r). Shortly afterwards, Hanson along with Philip Goth, Martin Godefroy, the 'wall-scaler', and twenty or thirty Englishmen of the garrison of Sainte-Suzanne set off on another adventure of their own (f. 60 r), managing to enter the castle of Saint-Laurent-des-Mortiers whilst its captain, Jacques de Scépeaux, and his associates were at the nearby church hearing mass. As a result, Scépeaux became the prisoner of Christopher Hanson. These incidents are not found in any other contemporary narrative of the wars, whether English or French, and suggest the input of personal experience by a known contributor to the chronicle.

Sainte-Suzanne was a major fortress in Maine whose initial capture in September 1425 is noted in the chronicle on f. 57r. Turning to the muster roll evidence, we find a Christopher Hanson stationed there on 13 November 1426 under Sir John

---

[67]   Hall (1809), p. 113.

[68]   We are grateful to Dr Gwilym Dodd for discussion. John Basset acted as a musterer at Southampton of troops for naval service in March 1418 (*CPR 1416–22*, p. 148), and it is implied in June 1421 that he was a servant of the king employed in carrying messages between Normandy and England (*CPR 1416–22*, p. 400).

Popham, chancellor of Normandy, as part of a larger force ordered into the field under the earl of Warwick, lieutenant for war in Normandy, the Marches of Brittany, Anjou and Maine.[69] Popham had been appointed captain of Sainte-Suzanne on 29 November 1425.[70] His appointment to the captaincy after the capture of the place by the earl of Salisbury is noted in the chronicle on f. 57r. On the following folio we have mention of Warwick's appointment in May 1426 as lieutenant-general for war linked to his arrival with an expeditionary army from England (f. 58r). Hanson was undoubtedly involved, therefore, in the 1425–26 phase of the conquest of Maine, carrying out diversionary sorties from Sainte-Suzanne during the siege of Pontorson, a siege which the earl of Warwick commanded and at which Fastolf was present.

The earliest reference we have in the muster rolls to a Christopher Hanson in France is 10 January 1424 when a man of that name mustered as an archer in the garrison of Rue, the muster being taken by the lieutenant of the captain of Saint-Valéry, both locations being on the Somme estuary.[71] In this case the name is rare enough for us to assume it is the same man. The next reference is even more indicative given the already noted muster of November 1426 at Sainte-Suzanne. In September 1425 Christopher Hanson was serving as an archer in the retinue of Sir John Harpelay, *bailli* of Alençon. The location of the muster is given as 'before the fortress of Sainte-Suzanne', indicating that Hanson was involved in the initial capture of this place.[72] It is apparent, therefore, that he joined the garrison after the place was taken. A Christopher Hanson, military rank unknown, later appears in the personal retinue of John Beaufort, earl of Somerset (d. 1444), on 1 January 1440.[73] Whilst this is a long chronological gap from 1426–27, we know that John Beaufort had been captain of Sainte-Suzanne since at least 1439 if not 1438, when he was released from the French captivity which had begun with his capture at the battle of Baugé in March 1421.[74] Hanson's link with Sainte-Suzanne may therefore have persisted for some time.

Worcester notes in the incipit that Christopher Hanson was German ('de patria almayn'). No nationality is given for Hanson in any of the muster rolls in which he appears. That in itself is not problematic. The recording of nationality in muster rolls was unusual until rules were established in 1430 and even after that date it was recorded sporadically despite supposed requirements to note it.[75] A number of Hansons (given in various spellings) can be found in the Medieval Soldier database, but only once – a John Hanson serving as an archer in the garrison of Pont-de-l'Arche in November 1445 – is there annotation as 'German' ('allmand').[76] That term indicated an origin in High Germany as opposed to the Low Country areas within the empire, for which the term used was 'dutch'. Hanson is a common German name in this period but so far we have not been able to find a Christopher

---

[69]   BNF, Clairambault 186/45–8.

[70]   BNF, NAF 7626/461.

[71]   BNF, Fr. 25767/52.

[72]   AN, K 59/10. There is a post-medieval copy in BL, Add. MS 21,156/1, where the muster is misdated to 1415.

[73]   BNF, Clairambault 200/88.

[74]   BNF, PO 65 Angleterre 22.

[75]   Curry, 'The Nationality of Men-at-Arms', pp. 135–63.

[76]   BNF, Fr. 25777/1722.

Hanson in contemporary German sources.[77] We can see from the surname evidence, however, that several men of German origins served in English garrisons and field armies, most notably in the conquest of Maine in the mid-1420s.[78]

Worcester's incipit also claims that Hanson was formerly with Thomas Beaufort, duke of Exeter (d. 1426), but contemporary records have not so far substantiated this link. Christopher Hanson does not appear in any muster rolls for the duke nor is his name in the lists of the duke's household which William Worcester included in his *Itineraries*.[79] Nor does he appear in any of the duke's surviving archives although a Henry Haunson was bequeathed £10 in the duke's will.[80] A number of Hansons are found in muster rolls of the fifteenth-century phase of the war, some in retinues of other members of the Beaufort family.[81] The family relationships of these various Hansons are as yet unknown. We find, for instance, a Henry Hanson serving as a man-at-arms in the personal retinue of Edmund Beaufort, earl of Dorset, at the siege of Harfleur in October 1440.[82] This may be the same Henry Hanson who carried a letter to John Paston I which had been written by Luket Nantron for Sir John Fastolf and which has been dated to 1456.[83] By this date, Christopher Hanson was certainly also in Sir John's service in England.

The service in France of Thomas Beaufort, duke of Exeter, was extensive.[84] He is mentioned six times in the M 9 chronicle, emphasising key appointments as captain of Harfleur, Rouen and Paris as well as a very specific role in exposing to Henry V the wickedness of the Bastard of Vaurus at the siege of Meaux (f. 45v). No muster rolls survive for the duke's expeditionary companies but the timing of Christopher Hanson's first known appearance in the garrison of Rue in January 1424 would fit chronologically with the possibility that he had crossed in the duke's company in the previous year. Duke Thomas indented in March 1423 for six months' service with 800 men, his crossing being delayed to July because of illness.[85] It is likely that they

---

[77]   We are grateful to Dr Mark Whelan for his searches on our behalf in German sources.

[78]   Curry, 'Foreign Soldiers in English Pay', p. 309.

[79]   *Itineraries*, pp. 355–9.

[80]   *Testamenta Vetusta*, p. 209, cited in Elder, 'A Study of the Beauforts and Their Estates 1399–1540', p. 206. A Henry Hanson, archer, had served on the 1400 campaign to Scotland under Thomas Ratcliffe (TNA, E101/43/4).

[81]   For instance, John, an archer in Caen when it was captained by Cardinal Beaufort in 1429 (BNF, Fr. 22468/41–3); Richard, archer in Gisors in 1430 under the captaincy of Edmund Beaufort (BNF, Fr. 25769/517). A John Hanson and a Robert Hanson are listed as archers in a damaged undated muster roll which may relate to Thomas Beaufort or to another member of the Beaufort family. We are grateful to Ken Wise for his work on Beaufort family links based on the evidence of the names, which include Hansons, in an undated muster (E 101/45/17) for an expeditionary army where the captain's name is missing.

[82]   AN, K 66/1/47. A man-at-arms of this name was in the garrison of Alençon under Sir Richard Woodville in December 1442 (BNF, Fr. 25776/1602) and a Henry Hanson, archer, is found in the garrison in August 1436 under Richard Guethin (BNF, NAF 20522/67). These may all be the same person.

[83]   *PL Davis*, ii, Letter 569.

[84]   On all occasions he is called duke, even though at the time of his appointment to Harfleur he was earl of Dorset.

[85]   E 403/658 (4 March), E 402/661 (23 April and 17 July), E 404/39/163, cited in Ratcliffe, 'Military Expenditure', p. 6. Companies were also raised by the Earl Marshal, Robert, lord Willoughby and Sir Walter Hungerford.

were deployed at the siege of Le Crotoy, another location close to the mouth of the River Somme, which began on 24 June (an action which the M 9 chronicle does not include, however). Planned action at Le Crotoy would fit well with the chosen port of the duke's landing in France, which was Dieppe. If Christopher Hanson had served in Exeter's company, his entry to garrison service at Rue in January 1424 following a six-month contract (July to December) in the expeditionary army would make complete sense. Such was a common pattern for those who chose to stay in France after their expeditionary service rather than returning to England. Rue had fallen to the French in November 1422 but was recovered in May 1423 by Sir Ralph Butler. It was captained between Michaelmas 1423 and March 1424 by Hugh Warbreton with a garrison of twenty men-at-arms and sixty archers, as is confirmed by the muster of January 1424 in which Christopher Hanson appears.[86]

There is no surviving evidence that Christopher ever served within one of Sir John Fastolf's retinues or garrisons. Philip Goth, one of the men with whom, according to the M 9 chronicle, Hanson carried out a sortie from Sainte-Suzanne in 1426, was in Fastolf's personal retinue for the conquest of Maine which mustered at Alençon on 5 September 1424.[87] It is possible that Hanson's service with Fastolf eludes us because of the loss of many muster rolls, especially for the garrisons in Maine. Hanson's presence in Maine is confirmed, however, by Benedicta Rowe's discovery of his name in the 1433–34 account of Nicholas Molyneux as receiver for the duke of Bedford in Anjou and Maine.[88] In the section 'voyages' we find a payment of expenses to Christopher Hanson as the representative ('commis') of the receiver of Sainte-Suzanne, having been ordered by Molyneux to go from Sainte-Suzanne to Rouen. The purpose of the summons was for Hanson to present to Molyneux, then at Rouen (August 1434), a report on the state of Sainte-Suzanne ('pour monstrer et bailler son estat et besognes').[89] As we have seen when discussing Basset's career, Nicholas Molyneux had strong connections with Fastolf by this time. He had accompanied Fastolf and Bedford to England in 1433 and had only just returned to France when he summoned Hanson to Rouen in the summer of 1434.

Such connections place Hanson firmly in the circle of Fastolf and his associates in Maine even if we cannot establish a direct service link with Sir John before the latter's retirement. Hanson remained in France until the bitter end of the occupation. A list drawn up by William Worcester, and included in his compilation of documents which is now College of Arms, Arundel 48, of places lost by Edmund Beaufort as lieutenant-general, names Hanson as lieutenant at Bellême under Matthew Gough in 1449–50.[90] Another document in Arundel 48 mentions his presence in the cathedral of Le Mans in October 1447 during discussions on the instrument of surrender of Maine to Charles VII.[91] This last reference suggests a possible role in the landed interests of Fastolf. By his retirement Sir John had sold the majority of his Norman possessions to concentrate on his lands in Maine, espe-

---

[86]   Newhall, *English Conquest of Normandy 1416–1424*, p. 298.

[87]   BNF, Fr. 25767/93.

[88]   Rowe, p. 507.

[89]   AN, KK 324, f. 214.

[90]   'la ville et chastel de belesme dont estoit seigneur monseigneur de Boukyngham et capptaine et bailli mathiew goth et son lieutenant christofle hanson' (College of Arms, Arundel 48, f. 287, printed in *L&P*, II, ii, p. 627).

[91]   College of Arms, Arundel 48, f. 314.

cially the barony of Sillé-le-Guillaume. Henry VI's decision in 1446 to surrender Maine constituted a major threat to him unless compensation could be obtained.

After the loss of Normandy, we find Hanson in Fastolf's service in England holding the significant role of collector of the knight's rents, farms and other income ('collectoris reddituum, firmarum et denariorum forinsecorum Johannis Fastolf'). A roll of his accounts from Easter 1454 to 25 March 1457 survives within the Fastolf Papers at Magdalen College Oxford.[92] Hanson was undoubtedly part of the inner team in the last years of the knight's life at the very time the M 9 chronicle was being compiled. A letter of Sir John of 3 July 1459, where the intended recipient is in William Worcester's hand, mentions that Hanson had written to him about one of his tenements in London.[93] We also see that Worcester spent two weeks in Hanson's house in London during his visit to the capital immediately following Fastolf's death.[94] Significantly, too, it appears that Luket Nantron had been working as Hanson's assistant in London.[95] Given the complexity of dealing with Sir John's estates, Hanson's obligations as collector continued even after Fastolf's death, as several letters in the Paston archive reveal.[96] In October 1460 Margaret Paston reported that she was sending to her husband 'as many of Crystofr Hansonys acomptys as I and Jon Paston cane fynd'.[97] By this date Hanson was in the employ of John Paston I. We have a letter sent from London by Hanson to his new master on 12 October 1460 reporting on various political events of the time.[98]

In the summer of 1462 William Paston wrote to his elder brother John to tell him that Hanson had died in London at 2 a.m. on 17 July.[99] That this was newsworthy is indicated by the fact that Thomas Playter wrote to John Paston with the same news: 'please your maisterchip wete that Cristofer Hanson is ded and beryed and as for executor or testament he mad non'.[100] Playter went on, 'as for Christopher's papers that longeth to your tenants, I have goten of William Worcester, and as for all the remnaunt of Christopher good, William Worcester hath the rule as hym seemed most convenient'. In other words, Worcester had taken on the administration of Hanson's estate and archive after he died intestate. There can be no doubt, therefore, that Hanson, Nantron and Worcester were closely linked in their mutual service to Fastolf in the 1450s, including, it would seem, in the compilation of the M 9 chronicle.

---

[92]   MCA, FP 51. See also evidence of his work in *PL Davis*, ii, Letter 564 (October 1456). By 1458 he was also searcher of ships in the port of Great Yarmouth, the nearest port to Fastolf's seat at Caister (CFR 1452–61, p. 220).

[93]   *PL Davis*, ii, Letter 579.

[94]   MCA, FP 72 m. 8.

[95]   *PL Davis*, i, Letter 116 (25 August 1461), where they are mentioned together in a financial context. See also *PL Davis*, ii, p. 576, where claims made by Fastolf's executors after 1466 mention receipts by John Paston from Christopher Hanson, Luket Nantron and others both in London and Southwark.

[96]   For example, *PL Davis*, ii, Letter 888 (January 1460).

[97]   *PL Davis*, i, Letter 155 (29 October 1460).

[98]   *PL Davis*, ii, Letter 613. The letter is signed by Hanson but is not otherwise in his hand. See also *PL Davis*, i, Letter 231 (August 1461).

[99]   *PL Davis*, i, Letter 91.

[100]   *PL Davis*, ii, Letter 673 (July 1462). Playter noted Hanson's death again at the bottom of another letter (*PL Davis*, ii, Letter 674).

WILLIAM WORCESTER

Of all of the authors of the M 9 chronicle, the best known today is William Worcester.[101] His fame derives partly from his work for Fastolf during the knight's lifetime and as onooutor after his death in 1450, and partly from his subsequent writings. Worcester did not die until the 1480s, probably just before the death of Edward IV in 1483.[102] His most famous writings, *The Boke of Noblesse*, presented to Edward IV in June 1475 as the king set out for a campaign in France, and the *Itineraries*, notes of journeys made between 1478 and 1480, were products of the post-Fastolf period of his life.[103] A comprehensive study of Worcester's own writings and the collections he made of materials written by others would be valuable; both categories of texts are often difficult to date and to place in context because of Worcester's tendency to make additions and amendments, often over a number of years. Fortunately, his own handwriting is so distinctive that it is easy to recognise his involvement.

Much information about Sir John Fastolf, as well as about the end of the war with France, comes from what Worcester wrote as well as what he collected both during and after Fastolf's lifetime. We shall limit ourselves here largely to Worcester's activities up to the death of Fastolf in 1459, the year he gives for the compilation of the M 9 chronicle, but we shall return to him again in Chapter 5 when discussing the subsequent fate of the chronicle after Fastolf's demise.

Worcester was born in Bristol in 1415. His father was a whittawer, specialising in converting skins into white leather. His mother came from a more substantial local family which explains why he sometimes used her surname, Botoner. His intellectual capacity led him to Oxford around 1432 but he remained a layman. The exact date of his entry into Fastolf's service is uncertain – it may even have been whilst still at Oxford or shortly afterwards – but he is the only one of the knight's servants known to have attended university.[104] A first connection may have been as surveyor at Castle Combe as early as 1436 when Worcester was only 21. Fastolf had acquired this valuable Wiltshire manor through marriage in 1409 to Millicent Scrope née Tiptoft (1368–1446), co-heiress of Robert, Lord Tiptoft (d. 1372) and widow of Sir Stephen Scrope (d. 1408) by whom she had a son also named Stephen (1397–1472). Worcester's close personal service to Sir John began in 1438 at the point Fastolf left France and there is no evidence that he had been with him in France. Worcester was a pivotal figure within Sir John's household for the whole of the knight's life. In 1445 he married Margaret Howes, the niece of Thomas Howes, another member of Fastolf's household and rector of Castle Combe.

Although Worcester described himself as 'secretary' to Sir John only infrequently, that was essentially his role. In fact, he was rarely out of his master's company save when on the latter's official business elsewhere. Whilst totally committed to Fastolf and in awe of him, Worcester was on occasion intensely annoyed with his master and convinced, both before and after the latter's death,

---

[101]   Orme, 'Worcester [Botoner], William', *ODNB*.

[102]   This assumption is based on Lambeth Palace Library, MS 506, where the original dedication was to Edward IV, hastily changed by Worcester's son to Richard III, only to be changed back in due course.

[103]   *The Boke of Noblesse*, ed. Nichols, from BL, Royal MS 18 B xxii; *Itineraries*, ed. Harvey, from the unique MS Cambridge Corpus Christi 210.

[104]   Wakelin, 'William Worcester Writes a History of His Reading', p. 55; Smith, 'Aspects of the Career of Sir John Fastolf', p. 69.

that the rewards for his service were inadequate. Although Worcester had not served Fastolf overseas, the knowledge he developed of the knight's career and interests in France was substantial. Some of this derived from specific commissions by Sir John which involved visits to Normandy before the loss of the duchy. We only know about these visits, however, because of retrospective claims for expenses which Worcester put forward in the year following Fastolf's death.[105] The exact timing of his visits remains uncertain but Worcester mentioned three different areas of activity. All three have a bearing on the collection of materials and information which might have been relevant to the composition of the M 9 chronicle, both as we have it and in its intended extension to 1450.

First, Worcester was involved in collecting evidence in Normandy concerning the possessions of Sir Robert Harling, Fastolf's nephew, who died at the siege of Saint-Denis on 9 September 1435. Harling's military service had begun in the garrison of Harfleur in 1416 when Fastolf was lieutenant there. After his death, his body was excarnated to bring back to England,[106] where it was buried in East Harling church (Norfolk). According to McFarlane, Worcester's visit to France on the Harling matter 'cannot have occurred much later than 1440'. Worcester's interest in the matter continued even after Fastolf's death. In March 1460 we find him riding to East Harling with a Norwich marbler concerning the making of Sir Robert's tomb.[107] Even though Worcester presumably never knew Harling in person we can see how he came to know about his career. Harling is mentioned twice in the original text of the M 9 chronicle, the siege of Meaux in 1422 (f. 45r) and the battle of Verneuil in 1424 (f. 53v). William Worcester added in his own hand on f. 47r Harling's name as present at the siege of Meulan in 1423, adding that he was later lieutenant of the place. In fact this was being careless with the truth since Harling had been appointed captain of Meulan on 1 November 1422 and was therefore in charge of the town when it was retaken by the French in early January 1423,[108] necessitating a siege to be laid by the duke of Bedford.

Worcester's second major commission for Sir John in France was the collection of materials against an allegation of flight from the battle of Patay (1429).[109] This

---

[105] MCA, FP 72.

[106] *Parisian Journal, 1405–1449*, p. 297.

[107] MCA, FP 72 m. 9, cited in Richmond, *Paston Family: Will*, p. 74.

[108] There is evidence in the records of the *chambre des comptes* that Harling was appointed as captain on 1 November 1422, serving to at least Michaelmas 1425 (BNF, Fr. 25766/816; BNF, Fr. 4491 f. 72). Fastolf had entered into a five-year indenture on 19 May 1421 but only served to October 1422, passing on control to his nephew (E 364/749, BNF, Fr. 25766/816).

[109] MCA, FP 72 m. 8. Collins, 'Sir John Fastolf, John Lord Talbot and the Dispute over Patay', p. 129; and Taylor, 'John Talbot, John Fastolf and the Death of Chivalry', pp. 326–8. Fastolf had been described in a case brought before the Paris *Parlement* in the early 1430s by Thomas Overton as a 'chevalier fugitive qui est la plus [grant?] charge qu'on puist dire d'un chevalier'. This charge occurs in a testimony by Overton on 11 February 1435 but does not give specific clarification on the context of Fastolf's flight (*English Suits*, p. 264). Overton, who became Fastolf's receiver-general in the mid-1420s, made other charges against Fastolf in this testimony, including falsifying muster records, keeping back soldiers' wages and not keeping the right numbers in his retinues for which he had been paid. Overton added that as a result Fastolf's soldiers had deserted with disastrous military results ('et en a este tout perdu et a Laigny et a Patay et a Orliens et part tout'). We can expand on Overton's biography provided in *English Suits*, pp. 300–1. He had crossed as an archer in 1417 in the

charge had been put forward by John, lord Talbot, and had apparently led to Fastolf's suspension from the Order of the Garter, although the specially convoked meeting of Garter knights which heard the case and decided in Fastolf's favour is only known through Worcester's mention of it. In the expense claim put forward in 1460, Worcester asked for 100 shillings for collecting testimonials from various men concerning 'la journée de Patay'. He dated this activity to the twentieth year of Henry VI's reign (1441–42), adding that the dispute ('magnum litigium et guerra') between Fastolf and Talbot had lasted thirteen years. That length of time makes sense given that the matter arose out of Fastolf's flight from the battle of Patay on 18 June 1429 at which Talbot was captured, remaining a prisoner until 1433.[110] According to Monstrelet, Fastolf had initially been suspended from the Garter by the duke of Bedford, presumably close to the events of 1429, but was reinstated after investigation.[111] But it would appear from Worcester's expense claim that Talbot had reopened the matter in later years after Bedford's death. The M 9 chronicle ends before Patay but the information collected by Worcester in France could have touched on earlier actions in which Fastolf was involved.

The third commission related to Fastolf's responsibilities as an executor in France of the duke of Bedford and led to Worcester spending an extended period in Normandy, perhaps as much as nine months – his wording is 'per tres terminos anni'.[112] It was during this visit that he was captured by the French at Dieppe who had to be paid to secure his release. The exact date is not certain but McFarlane considered that it post-dated the other two commissions in France, and therefore is likely to have taken place in the mid-1440s, presumably after the English failed siege of Dieppe which ended in August 1443. Responsibilities as executor weighed heavily on Fastolf, who had been master of Bedford's household. He even tried to divest himself of his lands in Normandy for fear that they could be charged with liabilities arising out of the execution of the will.[113] As late as April 1449, Fastolf and the other surviving executor (Bedford's chamberlain, Sir Andrew Ogard, a fellow participant in the 1425 Maine campaign, as noted on f. 56v of the chronicle) were faced with claims from the bishop of Sées which triggered efforts to sequestrate Fastolf's remaining lands in Normandy.[114]

Given the focus on Bedford, it is likely that it was during this third commission that Worcester amassed copies of documents concerning Normandy and Maine

---

company of Sir William Bourchier (E 101/51/2 m. 23), moving in the next year to the company of Lord Fitzhugh as a man-at-arms (E 101/49/19 m. 1), being a man-at-arms in the garrison of Falaise in March 1421 under Fitzhugh and May 1423 under the earl of Salisbury (BL, Eg. Ch 146; Add. Ch. 89), and at Gamaches under Sir Ralph Butler in March 1423 (BNF, Fr. 25767/10). By 1428 he was in the garrison of Alençon (BNF, Fr. 25768/326). Not surprisingly given the later dispute with Sir John, Thomas is not mentioned in the M 9 chronicle (though he himself claimed in the case to have participated in the recovery of Le Mans in 1428), but his brother Clement is mentioned.

[110]   Pollard, *John Talbot*, pp. 16–18.

[111]   Monstrelet, iv, p. 332

[112]   MCA, FP 72, m. 7, printed in *The Bedford Inventories*, ed. Stratford, documentary appendix no. 19.

[113]   *The Bedford Inventories*, p. 34.

[114]   *L&P*, i, pp. 493–5, cited in *The Bedford Inventories*, ed. Stratford, pp. 34–5. Ogard was known to Worcester who noted his death on 14 October 1454 in his *Itineraries* and also claimed he had been dubbed knight at the battle of Verneuil (pp. 47, 335).

under the duke, especially for the financial year 1433–34. Towards the end of his life Worcester collated copies of these into a book for presentation to Edward IV, adding copies of other documents, such as Fastolf's advice of 1435 on how the war should be continued.[115] The book, now Lambeth MS 506, was intended to provide exemplars of good governance which Worcester hoped might inform and encourage renewed interest in France, as well as serving as a 'perpetuelle memorialle' of the duke of Bedford and those who had served in the earlier fifteenth-century campaigns.[116] The compilation included a list of garrison captaincies and sizes for 1433–34, indicating that Worcester had in his possession materials about the military administration of Normandy which could have been relevant to the making of the M 9 chronicle.[117] Also included was a list in Latin of the retinue of the duke of Bedford, as well as a list of the Frenchmen who served under him.[118] Such lists are reminiscent of the lists in the chronicle.

A much larger collection of copies of documents put together by Worcester is to be found in College of Arms, Arundel 48. These include a set of statutes of the Order of the Garter which have been dated to the reign of Henry V and which we might assume were acquired as part of the evidence gathering concerning Fastolf's suspension from the Order.[119] We also find further examples of good practice of the time of Bedford, such as a list of garrison captaincies and sizes following the Regent's military reforms of October 1434.[120] But a notable quantity of material in this volume concerns the end of the war with France, 1447–50.[121] There is much on the handover to the French of Maine, the area in which Fastolf's main landed interests lay by the 1440s and for whose loss he was keen to have compensation. One document bears the note 'copy made to show to Sir John

---

[115] Lambeth Palace Library, MS 506. This collection was being put together just before Worcester died, so that it fell to his son, also William, to complete the preface. The book was intended for presentation to Edward IV but did not reach him before his death. His name was scratched out and Richard III inserted, but the latter's subsequent fate led to another hasty reinsertion of the name Edward. There has been an argument that this book of evidences was intended to accompany the presentation of the *Boke of Noblesse* to Edward IV but there are timing issues here, since Worcester's annotation of the *Boke* indicates it was presented to that king in 1475.

[116] Wakelin, *Humanism, Reading and English Literature*, p. 108.

[117] That said, these do not appear to be simple copies of the originals which Worcester might have collected since all of the military administration of Normandy and Maine was conducted in French whereas the list of garrison sizes in Worcester's compilation is in Latin. See Curry, 'John, Duke of Bedford's Arrangements for the Defence of Normandy', pp. 235–51, and 'The Garrison Establishment in Lancastrian Normandy in 1436', pp. 237–69 at p. 239.

[118] Joseph Stevenson printed the list of the French (*L&P*, II, ii, pp. 529–32) but for the English chose instead to print an English translation of the late sixteenth century based on a collation of BL, Harley 782 and 6166. Another list in BL, Harley 782 appears to be derived from the M 9 chronicle, as is discussed in Chapter 5. See also Nall and Wakelin, 'Le déclin du multilingualisme dans The Boke of Noblesse', p. 76.

[119] College of Arms, Arundel 48, ff. 185–91; Jefferson, 'MS Arundel 48 and the Earliest Statutes of the Order of the Garter', pp. 356–85.

[120] Curry, 'John, Duke of Bedford's Arrangements for the Defence of Normandy', pp. 235–51.

[121] Black, *Catalogue of the Arundel Manuscripts in the College of Arms*; Thorpe, 'Writing and Reading', ch. 5.

Fastolf and others'.[122] Another mentions the presence of Christopher Hanson at Le Mans during negotiations in late 1447.[123] Worcester also collated in this volume a number of documents concerning failure in the war: suggestions on what might be done to keep hold of France, criticisms for the losses, and requests that questions be put to those who were to blame. We find here a text in Latin with the date August 1449, just after the French invaded Normandy, of nineteen propositions on how the situation might be reversed.[124] As we have already noted, this text is in the hand of Luket Nantron, whose hand is also seen elsewhere in Arundel 48.[125] The suggestion must be, therefore, that Fastolf or Worcester instructed Nantron to write, or else to copy, this text. The influence of Worcester himself on the content is suggested by classical allusions.[126] Unfortunately, we cannot be certain that the text which is bound in College of Arms, Arundel 48 itself dates to the summer of 1449 or whether it was a later copy, nor can we be wholly certain that the propositions in it were the ideas of Fastolf, who is mentioned within it in the third person concerning his successful administration of Maine under the duke of Bedford.

Whilst there is no material in this Arundel 48 collection which relates specifically to the period covered by the M 9 chronicle as we have it today, its compilation demonstrates Worcester's close involvement in his master's concerns about the French wars in the 1440s and early 1450s as well as his own continuing interest after Fastolf's death. In addition, several documents in the compilation demonstrate Worcester's keenness to make lists. One document is a list of places lost by Edmund Beaufort, duke of Somerset, at the end of the war with France, which gives the names of their captains.[127] It is here that we find mention of Christopher Hanson as lieutenant to Matthew Gough at Bellême. We can also see in the list evidence of Worcester's tendency to annotate and revise documents produced earlier. One of his additions to this particular list includes the date of 1462, indicating an ongoing interest in the French wars after 1459 which is also borne out in the notes Worcester made in his *Itineraries* in the late 1470s, where, for instance, he listed those involved in Henry V's taking of Caen and those who shared lodgings at the siege of Rouen.[128]

Worcester was undoubtedly fully aware of his master's distress at the loss of the war and the loss of his landed interests without compensation. In his writings and collections it is difficult to separate what was Fastolf's viewpoint and what was Worcester's. Worcester not only collected materials for Fastolf on the wars but also wrote papers to bring to book those deemed responsible for the defeat.[129] He served him throughout the difficult years of 1452–54 when Fastolf

[122] College of Arms, Arundel 48, f. 311.
[123] College of Arms, Arundel 48, f. 314.
[124] College of Arms, Arundel 48, ff. 329r–332r, printed in *L&P*, II, ii, pp. 723–9.
[125] For the other documents in Arundel 48 in Nantron's hand see Thorpe, 'Writing and Reading', pp. 325–6.
[126] Wakelin, *Humanism, Reading and English Literature*, p. 111.
[127] College of Arms, Arundel 48, ff. 286–90, printed in *L&P*, II, ii, pp. 619–34.
[128] *Itineraries*, pp. 353, 361. See also pp. 3–5, a list of captains at Verneuil 'according to what Ireland the herald told me on 1 Dec 1477' (i.e. Walter Bellengier), discussed in Chapter 5 below.
[129] Richard Beadle has shown that the duke of Norfolk's bill against the duke of Somerset in 1453 (BL, Add. MS 34888 f. 90, printed in *PL Gairdner*, ii, no. 230) was in Worcester's hand (Richmond, 'Sir John Fastolf, the Duke of Suffolk and the Pastons', p. 92 n. 63).

faced danger from those he criticised for recent war failures in France.[130] The madness of the king and the protectorship of the duke of York ended up saving Sir John from any planned action against him, and encouraged not only a final effort to bring Edmund Beaufort, duke of Somerset, to book for the loss of Maine and Normandy,[131] but also a request to the king for financial compensation for the loss of his lands in France. Several documents which listed Sir John's claims were produced to this end, no doubt with the involvement of Worcester and of John Paston I, Fastolf's legal counsel: these are headed 'the bill of debts owed by the king to Sir John Fastolf in the parts of France'.[132] The dating of these claims is problematic but we can be guided by the reference within them to the passage of fifteen years since service in France: since Fastolf left Normandy in 1438, the claims were produced in 1453–54.

The claims included adequate compensation for the loss of the barony of Sillé-le-Guillaume, occasioned by the handing over of Maine to the French king in the late 1440s. Money had apparently been allocated by the government for this but Fastolf had not been a beneficiary, whereas others, including the duke of Somerset, had been. We also find a request for arrears of wages for the keeping of fortresses in Normandy. There was in addition a claim for 4,000 marks for Fastolf's share in the capture of the duke of Alençon at the battle of Verneuil, and for the same amount due from the ransom of Guillaume Remon dit Marjolaine. As this last claim describes, Remon was a prisoner of Fastolf's own taking, for whom he had agreed a ransom of 20,000 *saluts d'or*. But without his knowledge, the prisoner had been taken from him by the duke of Bedford who used him to bring about the surrender of Compiègne. Fastolf had received some promise of compensation from Bedford through a prospective land grant in Normandy but only to the value of 1,600 *saluts d'or*. Now all lands in France were lost anyway and therefore Fastolf considered the full 4,000 marks due. No compensation was ever received. The M 9 chronicle does not mention Fastolf's role in the capture of the duke of Alençon at Verneuil, but it does refer to Remon as his prisoner. The latter's capture at Passy in 1423 is noted (f. 47v) as also is his use by Bedford later in that same year to persuade Compiègne to surrender by displaying him to its defenders with a noose around his neck (f. 51v).

From the summer of 1454 onwards Fastolf retired to Caister castle, remaining there permanently, it seems, until his death on 5 November 1459.[133] Worcester was one of three men (the others being Thomas Howes, Worcester's father-in-law, and

---

[130] Richmond, 'Sir John Fastolf, the Duke of Suffolk and the Pastons', pp. 73–103.

[131] In particular, an 'advertiriment' which can be dated to the attack on Somerset by the duke of Norfolk in 1453 (College of Arms, Arundel 48, ff. 324r–325v). Although this does not mention Fastolf by name it includes several clauses concerning the lack of compensation given to those who had lost lands in Maine and other allusions redolent of William Worcester's writings. It is also likely that a supposed petition in French from those who had lost their lands and livelihood by the surrender of Maine, which was added outside the collection of exemplars in Lambeth Palace Library, MS 506 (ff. 55r–56v, printed in *L&P*, II, ii, pp. 590–603), had its origins with Worcester and Fastolf. There is no evidence this petition was ever presented to the king.

[132] BL, Add. MS 34888; *PL Gairdner*, iii, pp. 55–64.

[133] Richmond, *Paston Family: First Phase*, p. 243

John Paston) upon whom the knight relied in the last years of his life.[134] Worcester was permanently in Sir John's company until his death (in fact, his post-mortem expense claim spoke of the last ten years involving continuous attendance day and night), and played a considerable role in organising his funeral.[135] As an executor, he spent much of the next twenty years in the troubled negotiations over Fastolf's will.

Worcester's devotion appears to have extended to writing a life of his master, intriguingly at around the same juncture as the dating he gave to the M 9 chronicle. His preparation of such a work is mentioned in a letter sent by John Davy to John Paston I reporting what John Bussard had told him:

> for he [i.e. Bussard] seyth the last tyme that he wrot on-to William Wusseter is was be-for mysommer [1460?], and thanne he wrot a cronekyl of Jerewsalem and the jornes that my mayster ded whyl he was in Fraunce, that God on his sowle have mercy. And he seyth that this drow more than xxᵗⁱ whazereys off paper, and this wrytyng delyverryd on-to William Wusseter and non other, ne knowyth not off non other, be is feyth.[136]

In other words, Bussard had been writing out Worcester's texts for him, and one of these was the *jornes that my mayster ded whyl he was in Fraunce*. This letter was dated by Norman Davis to 1460 but is considered by Colin Richmond potentially to date to 1459 and before Fastolf's death.[137] In the second edition of John Bale's listing of all known historical works, published in the late 1550s, we find within the writings of William Worcester (named there as Botoner) the *Acta Domini Ioannis Fastolfi Lib. 1. Anno Christi 1421 et anno regni*.[138] Although this work was not included in the 1548 edition, Bale made some relevant draft comments in his notebook which can be read as indicating that this *Acta* was in Magdalen College Oxford.[139]

No work with this title has been discovered in Magdalen College or elsewhere but, given the close alignment of the possible date of composition and the date on the incipit of the M 9 chronicle, we need to consider whether the M 9 chronicle is in fact the *Acta Ioannis Fastolfi* of William Worcester. There are several reasons why it cannot be. First, the opening line given by Bale (*Anno Christi 1421 et anno regni*) does not fit with the M 9 chronicle which commences in 1415. Bale's wording also implies that the *Acta* was written in Latin although it would not be impossible for a Latin title to be given to a work in another language. That is, after all, what Worcester did in the case of the M 9 chronicle by writing a Latin incipit to a French work. Secondly, Worcester names in that incipit the authors of the M 9 chronicle, giving himself a different role of 'diligence'. Thirdly, the scribe of the M 9 chronicle is Luket Nantron not John Bussard

---

[134] Richmond, *Paston Family: First Phase*, pp. 250–1, which also notes that eleven of the twenty-eight letters of Fastolf between November 1454 and July 1459 were written by Worcester.

[135] MCA, FP 72 m. 8. An inventory of Fastolf's goods speaks of the white draught chamber for William Worcester and Lewis, Fastolf's illegitimate son (*PL Gairdner*, iii, p. 185); Richmond, *Paston Family: Will*, pp. 71–2.

[136] *PL Davis*, ii, Letter 602.

[137] Richmond, *Paston Family: Will*, p. 74 n. 71

[138] *Scriptorum illustrium majoris Britanniae Catalogus*, pp. 599–600.

[139] *Index Britanniae scriptorium*, pp. 116–17.

who, as we have seen, is mentioned in the letter which John Davy sent to John Paston in 1459/60. Finally, the focus of the M 9 chronicle, as will be explored in Chapter 2, is not simply Fastolf, even though, of all those named in it, he is mentioned the most often.

It is possible, however, that information collected by Worcester for his proposed *Acta* was used in the compilation of the M 9 chronicle. There is evidence that Worcester was collecting information which would have been relevant to the continuation of the chronicle beyond 1429 (and, of course, equally of value in his own *Acta*). Two fragments in his hand have survived in archival association with the chronicle, being bound later into College of Arms MS M 9 and transcribed in an Appendix to this current edition.[140] A full page, mainly in French but with some Latin, lists those present at the siege of Lagny in June 1432; Sir John Fastolf is not included in this list. A following half page in Latin, but with occasional lapses into English as well as quite atrocious French, gives losses of places after the death of the duke of Bedford, as well as noting the rescue of Saint-Denis (at which siege, as mentioned earlier, Sir Robert Harling had died). Fastolf is mentioned here as 'lying safe in the castle of Gisors'.

We can also see that Worcester annotated Nantron's text of the M 9 chronicle on at least ten occasions. His purpose was largely to add other names. So, for instance, the names of Robert Harling and Richard Woodville are added as present at the siege of Meulan in 1423 (f. 47r). But he also added detail. On f. 31v he added that Sir Hugh Luttrell came from Somerset. In the list of English at the battle of Verneuil on f. 53v, he added against the name of Matthew Gough further information in Latin ('captus prisonarius in le chase ductus in ville de perche sed et redditur cum villa').

Worcester's tendency to annotate is seen in his other works. For instance, the last pages of the list of places lost in the fall of Normandy by Edmund Beaufort in College of Arms, Arundel 48 is covered with annotations. That concerning the fate of Thomas Gower, captain of Cherbourg, the last place to fall to the French, is dated by Worcester to 1457, again revealing Worcester's ongoing interest in the soldiers who served in France at the very time the M 9 chronicle may have been under preparation.[141] Substantial annotation by way of addition is also evidenced in Worcester's *Boke of Noblesse*.[142] The original text of the *Boke* does not mention Sir John Fastolf at all, but of the eleven additions in Worcester's hand, five explicitly concern Fastolf.[143] In one such addition there is explicit mention of a document.

[140] College of Arms, MS M 9, ff. 120–1.

[141] College of Arms, Arundel 48, f. 258.

[142] BL, MS Royal 18 B XXII, printed as *The Boke of Noblesse*, ed. Nichols. Its sole manuscript includes an *explicit* which dates its completion to 15 June 1475, indicating that it was consciously linked to the renewal of war with France by Edward IV in that year (f. 44r). There have been suggestions that the work was begun in the early 1450s (Allmand, 'France-Angleterre à la fin de la Guerre de Cent Ans: Le "Boke of Noblesse" de William Worcester', p. 104; Sutton and Visser-Fuchs, 'Richard III's Books: XII. William Worcester's *Boke of Noblesse*', pp. 154–65; Allmand and Keen, 'History and the Literature of War: The Boke of Noblesse of William Worcester', pp. 94–5). This is difficult to substantiate, but given Worcester's tendency to recycle it is hardly surprising that the *Boke* draws on ideas, such as the long-standing Plantagenet links of the English crown to Maine, which were also being put forward in the early 1450s when Fastolf was keen to gain compensation.

[143] Catherine Nall considers that the annotations were made by Worcester before the work was completed on 15 June and presented to Edward IV (pers. comm.).

Worcester tells us that he handed to Edward IV on the day of his departing out of London a copy of the ordinances of the duke of Bedford (1423), 'that remayned yn the kepyng of ser John Fastolfe'.[144]

Worcester was undoubtedly an 'active' reader, who generated a huge quantity of notes and annotations.[145] He claimed to have 'correctid and examined' as well as 'perrafed ... for more opyn and redye understanding' an English translation which Fastolf's stepson, Stephen Scrope, made of *The Dicts and Sayings of the Philosophers* sometime between 1450 and 1454.[146] Worcester dated his final revisions to this work to 1473. As with the *Boke of Noblesse*, many of his additions here were reflections on Sir John Fastolf.[147] Worcester's annotations on the M 9 chronicle are sparse in comparison with interventions in other works.[148] Presumably the death of Fastolf made the project a dead letter, not only curtailing the narrative at 1429 but limiting the need for revision and amendment of the text by Worcester.

TEAM WORK

Whilst in the medieval period the continuation of chronicles by an author different from the originator is not uncommon, it is unusual to find a work which had a 'team' of writers behind it. According to the incipit, four men were involved in the making of the M 9 chronicle. They fall neatly into two groups, with Christopher Hanson a member of both. The first group – Basset and Hanson – were soldiers who served in Normandy and Maine, although only for Basset do we have explicit evidence for military service under Fastolf. Whilst we cannot demonstrate unequivocally that Basset and Hanson knew each other, we can prove that they had mutual acquaintances within the circle of Fastolf, such as Nicholas Molyneux. The second group – Worcester, Nantron and Hanson – served Fastolf in his retirement in England, knew each other well and operated in the same spatial spheres in London and in Norfolk, linked to the business they carried out for Fastolf. What, then, might have been the respective roles of the four collaborators in the making of the chronicle?

Peter Basset and Christopher Hanson, as serving soldiers, were in a position to provide information from their own experiences. Only in the case of Hanson, however, do we see specific evidence of this in the chronicle. Twice we read of his personal involvement in military actions which were otherwise quite obscure. We can assume, therefore, that Hanson's input to the creation of the work involved oral testimony and comment. That Worcester chose to give so much detail in his incipit about Hanson's military background, as well as to note the longevity of Basset's service, suggests that he wished to emphasise the authenticity of their input to a work concerning 'de actis armorum'. But there remains the conundrum of whether Basset worked with the rest of the team at all in the final compilation

---

[144] BL, Royal MS 18 B xxii, f. 15r; *Boke of Noblesse*, ed. Nichols, p. 31. We know from other evidence that Edward left London en route to France on 30 May.

[145] For extended discussion see Wakelin, *Humanism, Reading and English Literature*, ch. 4.

[146] McFarlane, p. 211, the work being published as *The Dicts and Sayings of the Philosophers*. Worcester's corrected copy is Cambridge, Emmanuel College, MS I. 2.10. See also Bühler, 'Sir John Fastolf's Manuscripts of the *Epître d'Othéa* and Stephen Scrope's Translation', pp. 123–8.

[147] Richmond, *Paston Family: First Phase*, p. 259.

[148] Thanks to Deborah Thorpe for this observation.

of the chronicle since he does not appear to have been in Fastolf's service after the knight left France. Nantron was the scribe of the chronicle but it is impossible to know whether he composed as opposed to simply writing down what others dictated or else supplied to him in writing. Yet Worcester mentioned Nantron in the incipit in an explicit authorial role: as the scribe of the actual text Worcester considered him to have had a creative input. Nantron's service to Sir John was also emphasised in the incipit along with his French origins and professional capacity.

The team was undoubtedly multilingual but a decision had clearly been made to write the text in French. Basset was English but had an extended career in France which involved administration and contact with the local population in French. Hanson was German but lived and worked in France and subsequently in England. Worcester knew English, Latin and some French, and tried to learn a little Greek and Hebrew. As a clerk Nantron operated in Latin, French and English. Basset and Hanson had lived and worked in France but were not native speakers, nor were they educated in the way Nantron and Worcester would have been. Worcester had reading capacity in French. He had accumulated documents in French during his visits on behalf of Sir John. His notebooks mention two French works he read in 1450 and 1453,[149] but his written French was not strong. Indeed, it is notable that he preferred to keep his notes in Latin and to write his extended prose either in Latin or in English. None of his known writings include any extended work in French. The surviving fragments presented in the Appendix betray a rather shaky knowledge of French syntax. We know that in the late 1450s Worcester was concerned to improve his French.[150] We can be certain, therefore, that Worcester did not consider he could write the work in French himself. Whilst all four participants had a working knowledge of that language, only Nantron, therefore, was in a position to write to the high standard needed. The chronicle concerned the war *in* France – exclusively so – not Anglo-French relations. It included many French names. The military administration of Normandy and Maine was conducted entirely in the vernacular.[151] French was therefore the appropriate language for such a project.

---

[149] Wakelin, 'William Worcester Writes a History of His Reading', pp. 57, 64. In College of Arms, Arundel 48, ff. 236–69 we find a version of the *Croniques de Normandie* which Worcester had collected in France or ordered to be copied.

[150] A letter from Henry Windsor to John Paston, dated to August 1459, informed him that 'William hath goon to scole to a Lumbard called Karoll Giles to lern and to be red in poetre or els in Frensh, for he hath byn with the same Karoll every dey ij times or iij and hath bought diverse books of him'. Yet he was an enthusiastic learner. Windsor reported a further conversation in which William 'answered and said that he wold be as glad and as feyn of a good boke of Frensh or of poetre as my Maister Fastolf wold be to purchace a faire manoir' (*PL Davis*, ii, Letter 574). It has also been suggested that Worcester translated Cicero's *De Senectute* from French into English 'by ordenaunce dseyr of the noble knuyght Syr Johan Fastolf' (McFarlane, p. 218).

[151] In this context Worcester must have had translated into Latin the list of garrisons in 1433–34 in Lambeth Palace Library, MS 506 ff. 16v–20r, printed in *L&P*, II, ii, pp. 540–6, presumably because the exemplars for Edward IV were considered to be more appropriately in Latin or English. Only documents added later to the original text of this MS are in French, such as the supposed petition of those who had lost their lands and livelihood through the surrender of Maine. On the linguistic 'code switching' see Nall and Wakelin, 'Le déclin du multilingualisme dans The Boke of Noblesse', pp. 73–91.

There was another highly significant reason for French to be chosen for the chronicle. The work was intended for a patron whose own knowledge of French and appreciation of French book culture was strong. As master of Bedford's household Fastolf would have been fully aware of the duke's taste in French books, and of the library of the French crown which the duke had acquired in 1425 and which was housed at Rouen.[152] We cannot know whether any of these books came into Fastolf's possession after Bedford's death but we do have a list drawn up in 1448 of French books which Sir John owned.[153] In addition, we know that he commissioned a copy in French of Christine de Pisan's *Epître d'Othéa*,[154] as well as a no longer extant *Livre des Quatre Vertus*, both from Ricardus Franciscus in London in 1450, and both, we can assume, lavishly decorated by the 'Fastolf master'.[155] The French books known to be held by Fastolf were reflective, as Richard Beadle notes, of 'vernacular humanism prevalent in French courtly circles in the later fourteenth century … assembled with a view to emulating the choicest items in the princely and ducal collections that he would have known from his time in France'. Sir John was keen to demonstrate his taste for the best which money could buy since such possessions were a mark of high status. We can see within his copy of the *Epître d'Othéa* his motto on over twenty occasions, in one case entwined with the Garter.[156] Furthermore, we can point to a number of other participants in the war, including a number mentioned in the M 9 chronicle, known to have commissioned works in French or using French artists.[157] In other words, those who had served in France had been imbued with its noble culture, and the use of French in the chronicle served as a means of memorialisation of their experiences in the heady days of English success.

French was therefore the language to use for a work on deeds of arms of the English in France. It also emulated, although at a smaller scale, the *Grandes Chroniques de France* which could be found in Fastolf's collection of French books. This vernacular chronicle linked to the abbey of Saint-Denis was customarily elaborately illustrated. That there was an intention to add images to the M 9 chronicle is suggested by the spaces left, although we cannot know what form these might have taken. It was also intended to have a decorated first letter of each paragraph, a space being left for such a purpose with a small superscript letter to guide the rubricator.

---

[152] Beadle, 'Sir John Fastolf's French Books', p. 97. See also Barber, 'The Books and Patronage of Learning of a Fifteenth-Century Prince', pp. 308–18.

[153] MCA, FP 43, printed and commented on in Beadle, 'Sir John Fastolf's French Books', pp. 102–12.

[154] Oxford, Bodleian Library, MS Laud Misc. 570.

[155] Driver, '"Me fault faire": French Makers of Manuscripts for English Patrons', p. 420.

[156] Oxford, Bodleian Library, MS Laud Misc. 570, f. 93, illustrated in Driver, '"Me fault faire": French Manuscripts for English Patrons', p. 421.

[157] Sir William Porter commissioned a Sarum Hours which was illustrated by the Fastolf Master, and another collaboration between Franciscus and the Fastolf Master appears to have belonged to another member of the household of the duke of Bedford (Driver, '"Me fault faire": French Manuscripts for English Patrons', pp. 425, 433–4). See also Reynolds, 'English Patrons and French Artists in Fifteenth-Century Normandy', pp. 299–313, which mentions books produced in France linked to Thomas and John Burgh, Sir William Oldhall, Sir Robert Conyers, John, earl of Oxford, Thomas, Lord Hoo, and John, Lord Talbot.

As Daniel Wakelin puts it, 'during his life, Fastolf's household emerges as a cultivated place'.[158] Books in English and Latin were also held by Sir John, including a deluxe copy of John of Wales's *Breviloquium de virtutibus* also copied by Ricardus Franciscus. Within such an ambience, William Worcester was surely encouraged in his own scholarly endeavour and reading. He is known to have read widely; Wakelin has calculated that he 'took notes from, annotated or owned at least 23 particular works or volumes'.[159] Fastolf's household also saw translations from French into English by his stepson Stephen Scrope of the *Epître d'Othéa* as well as *The Dicts and Sayings of the Philosophers*,[160] works dedicated to Fastolf if not directly encouraged by him. Scrope had been involved in the wars, serving as a man-at-arms in Fastolf's garrison of Honfleur between at least 1427 and 1430, but he is not mentioned in the M 9 chronicle nor is there any evidence he played a role in its composition although he was resident in Caister castle from 1454 until he remarried in 1456.[161]

The incipit implies teamwork but under the supervision of William Worcester. His 'diligence' (*per diligenciam*) can be taken to extend to assembling information and directing the project as a whole. Indeed, we can argue that he was the driving force behind the chronicle. His notebooks confirm his liking for lists and facts, which abound in both the content and format of the M 9 chronicle. However, we need to bear in mind that Worcester's knowledge of the events covered by the chronicle was coloured by his service to Sir John and potentially over-dependent on what Fastolf had told him, as is suggested in the list of Fastolf's military appointments which Worcester wrote after his master's death.[162] This document reveals not so much errors of fact but carelessness with the truth, with the result that the knight's role is exaggerated. Worcester himself had little direct experience of the war with France other than through his missions for Sir John and what he heard from his master. Marginal additions Worcester made to the *Boke of Noblesse* reveal the impact of conversations with his master. For instance, he recalled what Fastolf had told him about the defence of Harfleur when threatened by the French in 1416, when the knight was lieutenant to the duke of Exeter in the town:[163]

I herd the seyd Ser Johan Fastolfe sey that every man kepyng the scout wache had a masty hound at a lyes to berke and warne yff ony adverse partye were commyng to the dykes or to aproche the towne for to scale yt.

Later he recalled another exchange – 'Hyt ys to remembre that I hafe herd myne autor Fastolfe sey, whan he had yong knyghtys and nobles at hys solasse' – concern-

---

[158] Wakelin, *Humanism, Reading and English Literature*, p. 103.

[159] Wakelin, 'William Worcester Writes a History of His Reading', p. 57.

[160] Respectively, Cambridge, St John's College, MS H.5; Cambridge, Emmanuel College, MS I.2.10, and CUL, MS Dd.9.18

[161] BNF, Fr. 25768/255, 284, 420; Fr. 26274/108. See also Hughes, 'Stephen Scrope', pp. 112, 114–15. Hanson tried after Sir John's death to assist Scrope in getting money from the knight's estate (p. 133).

[162] MCA, FP 69, where the list of commands (m. 6) is in the hand of Worcester himself; and he has heavily annotated the list of landholdings (m. 8). A list of Fastolf's military commands, written by Worcester in 1478, is also given in *Itineraries*, pp. 353–5.

[163] *The Boke of Noblesse*, p. 16, from BL, Royal MS 18 B xxii f. 8r.

ing the relative merits of the manly man and the hardy man.[164] This debate had classical origins, on which Worcester was particularly keen. His *Boke of Noblesse* reflects such interest in the classics but there is no sign of this in the M 9 chronicle.[165]

It is possible, if not likely, however, that the chronicle contains more of Fastolf's own reminiscences, especially in the section from 1424 onwards. The input of Sir John may also be revealed by the fifteen amendments and additions which Worcester made in his own hand. Take, for instance, extra names added to the lists of Englishmen present at specific engagements, as well as the deletion of Fastolf's name from those present at the betrothal of the duke of Bedford to Anne of Burgundy (f. 47v), presumably because the knight told Worcester that he had not been there. Such examples suggest that the work was read to Sir John and he responded with comments. It is not possible, however, to be sure of how much input Sir John had into the initial drafting of the chronicle, or whether the 'written for Sir John Fastolf' of the incipit should be taken as evidence of his request for the chronicle to be written in the first place.

The watermarks of the paper on which the chronicle was written suggest that it was written in England. Dating texts is always complex, since a work of this kind could have been in preparation for some time, not least if it had its origins in an earlier composition by Peter Basset which no longer survives. The incipit claims that the chronicle was compiled ('compilatus fuit') in the year Fastolf died – 1459. That it was certainly put together later than the events it narrates is confirmed by the use of anachronistic titles for some of its participants, as well as by errors which can be put down to the failings of memory. Yet such a work would also have taken time, not least in compilation of the lists. Worcester, Nantron and Hanson could have worked together on the chronicle at any time from the early to mid-1450s onwards. It is less likely that they cooperated before 1450 since Hanson was still in France at the loss of Normandy. A consideration of possible dating takes us back to Fastolf's response in the early 1450s to the defeat in France and his requests for compensation as well as for those responsible to be brought to book. As we have seen, Worcester was heavily involved in Fastolf's efforts in these areas. In this context the chronicle could have stood as a remembrance and celebration of happier days, a consolation and comfort for Sir John in his declining years.

That said, Fastolf generated mixed reactions from even those close to him. Whilst showing total dedication to him, Worcester frequently complained about his master, even in annotations to his reading and in his own works.[166] Whilst this is not seen in the M 9 chronicle, we can see perhaps a reason why there was little enthusiasm in the team to complete the work after Fastolf's death. Another long-serving servant, Henry Windsor, commented on how 'cruell and vengible he hath byn ever, and for the most part without pite and mercy'.[167] Stephen Scrope, Fastolf's stepson, frequently complained about Fastolf's manipulative and selfish actions towards him, and how he had reneged on promises about his inheritance, such promises being made, as Scrope recalled, 'in a garden in the parke

---

[164]   *The Boke of Noblesse*, pp. 64–5, from BL, Royal MS 18 B xxii f. 32v.

[165]   Worcester had looked at the *Gesta Henrici Quinti* (now BL, Cotton Julius E iv (4)) but after 1459 (Wakelin, 'William Worcester Writes a History of His Reading', p. 56).

[166]   Hughes, 'Stephen Scrope', p. 143.

[167]   *PL Davis*, ii, p. 145.

of Alaunson'.[168] Even whilst in France Fastolf had faced serious charges from his leading servant and administrator, Thomas Overton, which were made public in a case between them in the *Parlement* of Paris in the early 1430s.[169] Overton accused Fastolf of being corrupt, keeping to his own profit the wages of his soldiers and forcing them to live off the land. He also called him a 'chevalier futif', emphasising his flight from the battle of Patay which had brought thenceforth Talbot's wrath and even, it seems, briefly Bedford's displeasure. After Bedford's death and Fastolf's retirement from France, Talbot pushed again for this knight's removal from the Order of the Garter. Fastolf responded to Overton's charges with a tide of abuse, accusing him of being a bigamist who had made false claims about his competence as a clerk and who had defamed the men of the *Parlement* who were hearing the case. It is hardly surprising that neither Overton nor Scrope is mentioned in the M 9 chronicle!

We should also recall that Fastolf was in neither a strong nor safe position after the end of the French war. Whilst he sought to criticise others, it seems that at the time of Cade's rebellion in May 1450 Fastolf was himself amongst those that the rebels blamed, 'the which mynnyssshyed all the garrisons of Normaundy and Mauns and Mayn the which was the cause of the lesyng of all the Kynges tytyll and right of an herytaunce that he had by-yonde see'. In addition, the rebels claimed that he had assembled veterans at his London house 'to destroy the comens of Kent when that they come to Southewerk'.[170] Whilst his enemy the duke of Suffolk had been exiled and murdered in 1450, Fastolf's complaints against Edmund Beaufort, duke of Somerset, along with his support for Richard, duke of York in his attack on the duke, had placed Sir John in jeopardy in 1452–53, 'the worst years of Fastolf's life' according to Colin Richmond.[171] In August 1452 he felt threatened enough to convey his lands to feoffees. In the following year he was forced to enter into a bond for £1,000 and summoned to appear before the royal council.[172] Only the king's illness and the rise to ascendancy of the duke of York released him from suspicion in November 1453, the point at which Worcester was involved in helping the duke of Norfolk put together a case against the duke of Somerset.[173] Whilst Fastolf was in a safer position thereafter, there was still room for 'consolation' and for efforts to bring him solace as he retired completely to Caister.

---

[168] BL, Add. MS 28212 f. 22, discussed in Hughes, 'Stephen Scrope', pp. 118–19.

[169] *English Suits*, XX. Overton had crossed in 1417 as an archer under William Bourchier (E 101/51/2 m. 23) but in the following year was a man-at-arms under Henry, lord Fitzhugh (E 101/49/19 m. 1). He continued in Fitzhugh's service in the garrison of Falaise in 1421 (BL, Eg. Ch. 146), remaining there under the captaincy of the earl of Salisbury in 1423 (BL, Add. Ch. 89). In December 1428 we find him in the garrison of Alençon under Fastolf (BNF, Fr. 25768/326).

[170] *PL Davis*, ii, p. 314.

[171] Richmond, 'Sir John Fastolf, the Duke of Suffolk and the Pastons', p. 73. The enfeoffment, in MCA, FP 47, is transcribed there on pp. 74–6.

[172] CCR 1447–54, p. 398.

[173] BL, Add. MS 34,888, f. 90, printed in *PL Gairdner*, ii, pp. 290–2: Norfolk's bill against the duke, written by Worcester, as Richard Beadle has shown (see Richmond, 'Sir John Fastolf, the Duke of Suffolk and the Pastons', p. 92 n. 63); College of Arms, Arundel 48, ff. 324r–325v: a supporting text found in Worcester's collections and likely devised by him for Sir John and the duke of Norfolk.

If we take the incipit seriously then the chronicle as we have it is the product of the very last phase of Fastolf's life. This raises the possibility that Worcester wished to complete a work for Sir John before it was too late.[174] It cannot be a coincidence that Worcester was trying to complete his *Acta* at the same time as the M 9 chronicle. He gives every impression of a man who found it difficult to bring any project to completion, his constant returning to a text to annotate and add to it being a symptom of this. If Sir John was also feeding in reminiscences in a sporadic and unstructured manner, a 'final' version may have been hard to reach. A possible interpretation of the creation of the M 9 chronicle, therefore, is that, to speed up the process of producing a text for the consolation of the ageing Fastolf, a work by Peter Basset was used as a basis which was built upon by input from the three men in Fastolf's service in the mid-1450s, Worcester, Hanson and Nantron. This would pre-suppose that Basset's text was in the possession of any or all of Fastolf, Worcester or Hanson. This can only be an argument from silence given that we cannot trace Basset after 1437. Such a suggestion still leaves uncertain the nature and content of Basset's contribution to the final work. John Bale claimed in the mid-sixteenth century that a Peter Basset had written a one-volume work on Henry V in English. Although no such text has been traced, could this have been the work used by the rest of the team to compile the M 9 chronicle? But, if so, why did Worcester word the incipit to suggest that Basset, as original author, was intending to cover the whole period of the war and not only the reign of Henry V? Had there been earlier collaboration between the authors in France? A study of the careers of the authors can only take us so far in resolving these questions. We need to seek answers within the text of the chronicle itself.

---

[174] There has been some debate on Fastolf's state of health towards the end. Worcester tells us that he was ill from early June 1459 (BL, Sloane MS 4, f. 38v) and we know that he made his last will on the 14th of that month, but a letter of William Baker written on 24 June reports that he was 'as freshe as ever he was this ii yere thanked be God' (*PL Davis*, ii, Letter 578). According to his chaplain, Fastolf was unable to speak in the last three weeks of his life (Oxford, Bodleian Library, MS Top. Norf. c. 4, f. 10) but in general his lucidity to the end has been emphasised (Richmond, *Paston Family: First Phase*, p. 255).

2

The format and content of the M 9 chronicle

The format and content of the M 9 chronicle, as of any other text, are the result of authorial choices. As we have seen in Chapter 1, the authorship of the chronicle is complex. It is possible that the work as we have it was based on an earlier text by Peter Basset which may have focused exclusively on the wars of Henry V. In this chapter we shall look in detail at the format and content addressing key questions. To what extent does the chronicle show signs of being a 'work of two halves', divided by the change of king in 1422? William Worcester's incipit indicates that the chronicle was written for Sir John Fastolf. Does the content reflect that intention? What can we conclude on authorial choice in terms of the events covered and the people mentioned, both English and French? The chronicle provides a narrative of events but it is distinctive through its inclusion of many lists of participants, both in a range of military actions and as holders of captaincies. How might such lists have been drawn up and for what purpose?

A WORK OF TWO HALVES?

The M 9 chronicle provides a narrative of the Anglo-French war from Henry V's capture of Harfleur in September 1415 (f. 31r) to the arrival of the French 'in very great strength' at the siege of Orléans in early May 1429 (f. 66r). The last sentence of the original text indicates that there was an intention to name those involved in this French force but no names are given after the customary indicator 'Cestassavoir'. A later hand added seven names including that of 'La Pucell'. Such a curtailment indicates that the work was intended to continue beyond this point, presumably for the whole period of English rule from Henry V's conquest to the loss of Normandy in 1450 – the thirty-five years mentioned by Worcester in the incipit. Two stray sheets of notes in the hand of Worcester, later bound within College of Arms MS M 9, echo the format of the chronicle, being replete with names of participants in 1432 and 1434–35.[1] These suggest that Worcester had been collecting information about the military activity of later years for use in later sections of the chronicle. Furthermore, on f. 61r we find a reference to Matthew Gough holding office as captain of Laval up to 'the journée before Senlis, which will be mentioned later'. This is an explicit reference to the aborted battle of Montépilloy on 15 August 1429, and therefore serves as further evidence that it was intended to continue the chronicle beyond its current content and that there were plans for its later content.

---

[1]   These are transcribed in the Appendix.

The M 9 chronicle, as we have it, is 18,217 words long. The wars of Henry V, from 1415 to 1422, occupy 45 per cent of the wordage and those of Henry VI, from 1422 to 1429, 55 per cent. Within this second reign there is a distinctive concentration on the conquest of Maine which was begun after the battle of Verneuil (17 August 1424). This victory, won by the Regent, John, duke of Bedford, against a Franco-Scottish army, secured the English position in Normandy and made feasible expansion southwards into the county of Maine and duchy of Anjou, lands which Bedford had had granted to himself on 20 June 1424 in anticipation of their conquest.[2] By the summer of 1428 the English controlled most of Maine and had made some penetrations into Anjou. These southward campaigns of 1424 to 1428 occupy over half of the Henry VI section of the chronicle and 30.5 per cent of the text as a whole. Given Fastolf's prominence in the conquest of Maine, such statistics immediately provoke thoughts on his link to the chronicle, to which we shall return later in this chapter.

Another notable difference between the treatment of the reigns of Henry V and VI is revealed by analysis of the comparative proportions of narrative to lists. For the period 1415 to 1422, the chronicle contains twenty lists of varying lengths (see Table 4). Together, these contain 592 names covering presences, both English and French, on the major campaigns and at the major actions. This period contains the longest continuous list of names, occupying six folios (ff. 34v 37r) and with no intervening narrative, of French holders of garrison captaincies in Normandy, Maine and the Somme area at the time of the arrival of the English in 1417. Appointments to garrison commands made by Henry V in Normandy are subsequently presented between folios 37v and 39v but are interspersed with short sections of narrative summarising the various stages of the English conquest of the duchy. For Henry V's reign as a whole, narrative occupies 52.6 per cent of the wordage and lists occupy the remaining 47.4 per cent. There are few extended sections of narrative. Indeed, between the lists there are often only short summaries of events. The overall feel for Henry V's reign, therefore, is of a catalogue of names set within the barebones of a terse narrative.

A clear contrast can be drawn with 1422–29. Whilst there are twenty-one lists containing 455 names, narrative occupies 83.7 per cent of the wordage with lists taking up only 16.3 per cent. Furthermore, there are several long sections of narrative uninterrupted by any lists. This is particularly noticeable from the victory at Verneuil onwards. For the following nineteen folios until the battle of Rouvray in February 1429 (ff. 55v–64v) there is an extended narrative of the conquest of Maine and very few lists. As a result, the feel of the chronicle is quite different from its Henry V sections. The years 1424 to 1429, of course, marked Sir John Fastolf's greatest hour, from his elevation to knight banneret at the battle of Verneuil,[3] through his appointment to lead the first campaign of conquest of Maine in August 1424 and his subsequent governorship of Maine, to his battle victory against the French at Rouvray on 12 February 1429.

Contrasts between the two reigns can also be drawn in the level of accuracy and precision. It is notable how many errors there are in the first names of English lords in the 1415 campaign list, for instance, but the later sections of the work are more sure-footed in knowledge of names. A retrospective approach, reflective of

---

[2]   AN, JJ 172/518, JJ 173/315.
[3]   Fastolf's elevation to the Garter in 1426 is not mentioned in the chronicle.

the date of composition of the work, is revealed by the anachronistic use by the authors of titles which men were accorded in later years. For the reign of Henry V there is a distinct lack of precision in terms of dates. The opening mention of the capture of Harfleur, for instance, is given simply as 'between the feasts of St Michael and All Saints' (f. 31r). In reality, the surrender was made on 21 September, a week before Michaelmas. No more dates are given until the battle of Agincourt which the chronicle places on 'the vigil of the feast of St Crispin and St Crispinianus' (f. 33r). Such a date – 24 October – is strange since the battle date is well established as the 25th. Equally vague is the treatment of the English campaign of 1417 to 1419. For the initial landing the month of August is correctly given (f. 34v), but the many conquests of the first phase are given no specific dates nor do we find any indications of lengths of sieges. The siege of Louviers, which is known to have ended in June 1418, is the first for which a duration ('six weeks or so') is given (f. 38v). Thereafter, mention of the length of a siege is a common, and indeed distinctive, inclusion in the chronicle, with 'ou environ' invariably added.[4] Yet the political events of Henry V's reign are ubiquitously lacking in precise dating. On f. 39v, for instance, it is simply stated that 'at the beginning of the following year, 1419', negotiations began for a final peace. On the next folio, 1420 is given as the year when a settlement was reached but no specific dates are given for the actual treaty of Troyes. The murder of John the Fearless, which occurred on 10 September 1419, is mentioned only retrospectively within the narrative of the recovery in the late summer of 1420 by Henry V and his allies of Montereau, which enabled the duke's body to be recovered and given a fitting burial by his son (f. 40r). The date of the battle of Baugé is given obliquely through the description of the duke of Clarence lodging at Beaufort on 'Easter Eve', which was 22 March 1421.

To some degree, the same situation prevails in the narrative for the reign of Henry VI. The duke of Bedford is described as accepting appointment as Regent of France around 1 January 1422 (f. 46v). The year meant is, of course, 1423 since the chronicle consistently uses the French style of dating the year from Easter, a further indication of the fact that the text was written by the French clerk, Luket Nantron.[5] In fact the public proclamation of Bedford's appointment as Regent was made on 19 November 1422.[6] Later we read that 'In the year beginning at Easter in the year of grace 1423' negotiations began for Bedford's marriage to Anne of Burgundy (f. 47r), yet no date is given for any resulting marriage or for the treaty of Amiens. Thereafter, no further dates are given in the chronicle until mention of the Dauphinist attack on Compiègne 'the following winter of the year 1423' (f. 51r). There is a similar problem to that for Agincourt over the date given for the battle of Verneuil. The chronicle tells us that the assigned date for the English to meet the French in battle was 'the vigil of the feast of the Assumption of Our Lady in the month of August' (f. 54r). That would denote 14 August, the feast being on the following day. Such a chronology is out of line with the commonly accepted date

---

[4]   There is a fuller discussion of sieges in Chapter 3.

[5]   As a result, adjustment needs to be made in expressions such as the 'Lent tide' of 1417 (f. 37v), when Henry V's brothers were sent eastwards and westwards in Normandy to effect conquest, where the calendar year is actually 1418.

[6]   Fauquembergue, ii, pp. 72–5.

of 17 August.[7] Although we are told that the siege of Cravant was laid 'in the year 1423 around the month of July' (f. 48r) the date of the actual battle is not specified. Similarly, no date is given for Fastolf's action at Rouvray although we are told that a shortage of victuals at the siege came 'around the time of the following Lent', which began that year on 8 February.

Within such vagueness, we occasionally find striking detail. Take, for example, 'one Friday morning when it was extremely foggy the enemy took Compiègne'. And later, when the English managed to rescue Le Mans in 1428 after it had fallen briefly to the French, that troops entered the city at 5 o'clock in the morning (f. 62r). Notably, too, the various campaigns into Maine between 1424 and 1428 are demarcated by year as well as commander, with full detail being provided on the length of every siege. Although dating continues to be through phrases such as 'around the feast of Candlemas', 'when winter was nearly over, that is to say around the feast of the Purification', 'in the month of June', 'until just after Easter', there is notably more effort to provide a firmer chronology and a higher level of detail.[8] This is not limited to dates but also includes anecdotes on individual actions and situations in which the English invaders of Maine found themselves. Such details surely show the input of personal reminiscence and involvement, reflective of the input of Christopher Hanson in particular – including two mentions of his involvement in daring military actions – but also potentially of Peter Basset and Sir John Fastolf himself, all of whom participated in the conquest and garrisoning of Maine.

There are therefore perceptible differences in the chronicle between the two reigns yet there is also consistency across the whole work. The chosen format is always a mix of narrative and lists, differences being simply the relative proportions of each. In addition, an annalistic format is found throughout the chronicle. The narrative proceeds in chronological order with the beginning of each new year being indicated. The focus of the chronicle on military actions is also wholly consistent as is the tone and nature of the discussion. Non-military matters take up only 500 words, through extremely succinct mentions of the main political events directly related to the war: the treaty of Troyes (f. 40r); Henry V's proclamation as heir and Regent of France and the disabling of the Dauphin Charles from the succession (which must date to the *lit de justice* held in Paris in December 1420 but that event is not mentioned at all) (f. 41v); Henry's return to England in the spring of 1421 to have his wife crowned (f. 41v); the recovery of the body of John the Fearless after the siege of Montereau (f. 40r); Henry V's death (f. 46v); the acceptance by the duke of Bedford of the regency (f. 46v); and Bedford's marriage to Anne of Burgundy in April 1423 (f. 47v).

These appear as the only political events deemed important enough by the authors to disrupt the narrative on war. It is important to note that they are all chosen and constructed in such a way as to emphasise *English* success. By com-

---

[7]   August ('Geste des nobles', p. 198; Monstrelet, iv, p. 191; Waurin, iii, p. 109; Cagny, p. 132) or the 'Thursday (morning) after mid-August' (*Journal d'un Bourgeois*, ed. Beaune, p. 213; Chartier, i. 42; *Pucelle*, p. 224). Berry Herald gives no date and Fénin (p. 223) proposes the feast of Saint Rémy which is 1 October.

[8]   That said, the chronology becomes confused in 1427 when the French recapture of Le Mans and its recovery by Talbot, events of the early summer of 1428, are placed wrongly before the siege of Montargis. There is no obvious explanation for this error.

menting only on the recovery of Duke John's body as a result of Henry's siege of Montereau, the significance of the murder of the duke by the Dauphin's party in September 1419 as the explanation of subsequent Burgundian support of Henry's acceptance as heir to Charles VI is completely removed. This handling of the murder of Duke John helps to explain an extraordinary omission: the death of King Charles VI, which occurred on 21 October 1422. This authorial decision may have been simply because his death was deemed to have no real impact on the course of the war – as the French king's Regent as well as heir, Henry V had led all of the important sieges after the treaty of Troyes which are recounted in the chronicle. But the lack of mention of the death of King Charles also serves to emphasise that the English had enjoyed success by their own efforts and through their own rightful cause.

We must remember that the chronicle as we have it was written after the change of allegiance of the Burgundians in 1435. The presence of Burgundian allies is noted at the siege of Melun in 1420 (ff. 40r-v) and at the battle of Cravant in 1423 (f. 48v), as is also Henry V's appointment, when he became ill, of Duke Philip as his lieutenant for the Cosne campaign of 1422 (f. 46r). But it is notable with regard to this action that the chronicle adds explicitly that Bedford was appointed lieutenant 'for the English'. Similarly, in Bedford's appointment as Regent the emphasis is on the consent of the lords spiritual and temporal as well as the commons – in other words the English parliament (f. 46v). In addition, Burgundian-led military operations are omitted; there is nothing on the siege of Saint-Riquier or the battle of Mons-en-Vimeu (1421), or the relentless activity to subdue Picardy by Jean de Luxembourg, an ardent supporter of the Anglo-Burgundian alliance. In this context, the attention paid to Luxembourg's siege and capture of Guise in 1424 is puzzling (f. 55r). Whilst this was an important siege and its capture led to the surrender of several other fortresses in its neighbourhood, it was less significant to the English than the battle of Mons-en-Vimeu (30 August 1421), nearer to Normandy, which was not mentioned. The explanation is found in the fact that the chronicle highlights the presence of numerous Englishmen at the siege of Guise, and one person in particular, Sir Thomas Rempston, one of the most frequently mentioned individuals in the chronicle. The chronicle cannot be seen as overtly anti-Burgundian. The Burgundians are not removed from the narrative or indeed from the lists. That for the siege of Melun includes twenty-four names of Burgundians, just under a third of the total of those listed (ff. 40r–41r). Of note, the chronicle also mentions three Gascon lords serving the English, as well as the Navarrese ally, Charles de Beaumont.

What, then, does all this suggest in terms of the notion that the chronicle is a work of two halves? As we have seen, there are some possible indications that an existing work on the early campaigns had been taken up by Hanson, Worcester and Nantron in the 1450s and extended. The narrative for the military actions of the reign of Henry VI is much more extended than that of Henry V and includes a greater degree of detail, which surely reflects personal input by those intimately concerned with these particular campaigns. We cannot be certain, however, that any earlier work was presented in the 'list plus narrative' format. It is feasible that the later authors recast it into that form, and also that they had drawn from it only selectively. That said, if such an earlier work contained a mixture of narrative and lists, the later authors continued to follow this format, even if they changed the balance between them as they moved into the later chronological phases covered by the chronicle.

Whilst we can demonstrate that Christopher Hanson fed in his personal experiences, we cannot exclude the possibility that Fastolf also contributed to the content for the 1422–29 section. The input of Peter Basset to the final work remains problematic. We can show that he was active in Maine but not that he was in Fastolf's service in England in the 1440s and 1450s. None the less, it remains possible, even likely, that Hanson, Nantron and Worcester drew on Basset's earlier work. Based on the pattern of variations in format, it can even be speculated that Basset's work covered the reign of Henry V and perhaps also the first two years of the reign of Henry VI. It is after the battle of Verneuil that we see a real change in the format and content of the chronicle towards a more sustained and more detailed narrative.

THE ENGLISH IN THE M 9 CHRONICLE

The mention of individuals was clearly held by the creators of the chronicle to be a central element in their overall vision and purpose. By a simple count of occurrences of individuals in the chronicle some interesting findings emerge. The most frequently mentioned English participant is Sir John Fastolf, which would seem on the face of it to confirm that the chronicle was written for him as its incipit suggests. But of his twenty mentions only four fall within the reign of Henry V (Table 1).

Table 1. Mentions of Sir John Fastolf in the M 9 chronicle

---

f. 31r: appointed lieutenant of Harfleur by duke of Exeter

f. 39r: after the fall of Rouen, Sir Thomas Rempston is made captain of Meulan and later Sir John Fastolf

f. 40v: present at siege of Melun after treaty of Troyes

f. 45r: present at siege of Meaux

f. 47r: in army organised by Bedford as Regent for recovery of Meulan, described as master of the household of Bedford and seneschal of Normandy

f. 47v: present at betrothal of Bedford and Anne of Burgundy, but entry is deleted

f. 47v: commissioned by Regent to lay siege to castle of Passy, takes captain Guillaume Remon prisoner, also takes castle of Orsay, and appoints captains, then returns to Paris to Regent

f. 49v: appointed lieutenant for the king and Regent in Normandy in *bailliages* of Rouen, Evreux, Alençon, and pays de la Seine, and governor of the lands of Anjou and Maine

f. 53v: placed by Bedford in Ivry after its capture along with the whole of the Regent's host implying presence at battle of Verneuil

f. 54r: created a knight banneret before the battle of Verneuil

f. 55v: with Scales and Sir John Montgomery commissioned by Bedford after victory at Verneuil to take army into Maine

f. 56r: in 1425 in army of conquest into Maine and Anjou commanded by the earl of Salisbury, described as grand master of the household of the Regent and governor of Maine and Anjou

f. 56v: appointed captain of Le Mans following its surrender

f. 57v: at siege of La Ferté Bernard early in 1426, laid by Salisbury, is commissioned to a sortie against the enemy, along with Willoughby

f. 58v: in army of Warwick as lieutenant-general sent by Bedford when the enemy was threatening Pontorson, around Purification 1426

f. 60r: undertakes siege of Saint-Ouën, described as 'chevalier anglois' governor of Anjou and Maine, and leading the garrisons of the area and other men of his retinue in this action, then goes on to besiege castle of La Gravelle. A *journée* fixed for its surrender, to which Bedford leads an army which includes Fastolf and others

f. 60v: Fastolf is appointed by Bedford to take the surrender of La Gravelle but defenders refuse to keep agreement

f. 61r: around Michaelmas 1426 he is discharged from the governorship of Maine and Anjou and Talbot is appointed in his place

f. 64r: after death of Salisbury at Orléans is sent by Bedford to reinforce siege

f. 64v: with Rempston gets victuals from Paris for siege of Orléans and wins engagement near Rouvray

Fastolf's service in Harfleur can be substantiated from the records, including his lieutenancy to Thomas Beaufort in the spring and summer of 1417. (William Worcester added the size of his retinue into gaps left blank for the numbers suggesting that the knight himself had to be asked what figures to put.) Similarly, his succeeding Rempston in the captaincy of Meulan on 19 May 1421 is confirmed in the administrative records.[9] So far, no evidence has been found in the administrative records or in other chronicles of his presence at the sieges of Melun and Meaux but with such long engagements it is entirely feasible that he was present at some time.

These four mentions of Fastolf's service under Henry V do not show him to be a significant commander. Even more perplexing, given the chronicle was ostensibly written for him, are the omissions. In the *Boke of Noblesse* William Worcester added a note about his master's key role in the defence of Harfleur against the French when they besieged the port in 1416.[10] We also know that Fastolf had been granted the nearby manor of Frilense on 29 January 1416. By this date he was a knight, and as no dubbing is known during the Agincourt campaign from which he was invalided home, it would suggest some act of prowess in his Harfleur posting.[11] Yet no mention is made in the chronicle of his being made a knight, a contrast with

---

[9]   E 364/749. We also have surviving particulars of account for Fastolf's captaincy of Meulan (E 101/50/24 and 250).

[10]   *Boke of Noblesse*, p. 16 from BL, Royal MS 18 B xxii, f. 8r.

[11]   C 76/98 m. 4, DKR 44, p. 577. See also the claim put forward in Fastolf's case against Thomas Overton (*English Suits*, XX, p. 264) where he claimed to have been 'the first to disembark into the sea up to the sword belt and the king gave him the first house he saw in France'. This seems unlikely since the grant was not made until January 1416.

the mention of his elevation to knight banneret at the battle of Verneuil (f. 54r). Completely ignored in the chronicle is the valiant defence of Harfleur by Thomas Beaufort and his men under substantial French threat, and the expedition led by the duke of Bedford which gained victory in a naval battle in the Seine on 16 August 1416.[12] Similarly there is no mention in the chronicle of Fastolf's appointment as captain of the Bastille Saint-Antoine in Paris on 24 January 1421,[13] surely important as it placed him in a significant command position in the French capital during the king's absence in England.

Furthermore, if the chronicle had been intended as a eulogy for Fastolf's career in France we might have expected it to start in 1412 when he was a man-at-arms in the duke of Clarence's 4,000-strong army which was sent to support the Armagnac faction in France, and which marched from Saint-Vaast-la-Hougue to Bordeaux.[14] He stayed in service after Clarence's return to England, becoming lieutenant of the constable of Bordeaux,[15] under the overall command of Thomas Beaufort who was now lieutenant of Aquitaine. During this time Fastolf seems to have captured an important prisoner, the lord of Soubise,[16] and also to have been involved in the receipt of money which the duke of Orléans had promised to the duke of Clarence following a withdrawal deal sealed at Buzançais on 14 November 1412.[17]

A reading of the Henry V section of the chronicle reveals quite emphatically that the focus is the king himself. All of the actions and decisions are his and, until his absence in early 1421, his alone. Events in which he was not involved, such as the rescue of Harfleur in 1416, are ignored. A high proportion of paragraphs start with mention of the king. He captured Harfleur, he issued disciplinary ordinances, he won a great victory at Agincourt even though it was the enemy who delivered battle; he landed with a large army in 1417 and began his conquest; he sent his brothers and other lords out in different directions to effect more conquests; he succeeded in his negotiations with the French which led to his being made heir and Regent of France. His subsequent sieges all succeeded, and he acted with appropriate harshness towards all who opposed him, not hesitating to hang the Bastard of Vaurus who had behaved with such cruelty towards civilians before the siege of Meaux.[18]

We should also recall that, every time Henry is mentioned in the chronicle, the words 'victorious prince' are used to describe him, such a gloss also being inserted into the incipit by Worcester. The king's death is given extra emphasis on folio 46v by an invocation for all to weep at the loss of 'so very noble and

---

[12]   Curry, 'After Agincourt', pp. 30–41.
[13]   Nichols, 'Appointment of Sir John Fastolf'. See also the particulars of account of his period as captain in E 101/50/5.
[14]   As he prepared to cross to France, Fastolf had letters of protection issued on 10 July 1412 valid for six months (C 76/95 m. 12). Three white cloths were provided from his manor of Castle Combe 'for the livery of the lord beyond the sea' (cited in Cooper, *Real Falstaff*, p. 16).
[15]   E 101/185/6 no. 2, cited in Cooper, *Real Falstaff*, p. 180 n. 7; Vale, *English Gascony*, pp. 67–8.
[16]   CCR 1413–19, p. 173 (22 January 1415).
[17]   Milner, 'English Enterprise in France', p. 86.
[18]   Ambühl, 'Henry V and the Administration of Justice: The Surrender of Meaux, 1422', pp. 74–88.

victorious a prince, your protector and defender'. These lines stand out rather as
an intrusion into the customarily dry style of the chronicle. A similar intrusion
comes with the only use of direct speech in the whole chronicle where Henry
addresses Olivier de Mauny personally after his capture at *le park l'evesque* during
the siege of Meaux (f. 46r).[19] We are given a fascinating royal speech which told
Olivier that he would not be put to death for breaking his oath but would instead
be sent to England 'to learn English'. The king is the only person who speaks in
the entire chronicle.

Even if the king did not use these precise words, the conversation is so distinctive and unique that it surely reflects eye-witness testimony, perhaps by Fastolf
who, as we have seen, is noted as present at the siege. Or could it be that, as
Edward Hall and John Bale claimed in the mid-sixteenth century, Peter Basset had
some connection with the king as a chamberlain and was the source of the story?
To date, Basset has not been found within records of the king's household but, as
we have seen, there is no reason to doubt that he was in military service in France
in the conquest of Normandy and beyond, largely under the Earl Marshal.

Since the king was the focus, the chronicle started with his reopening of the
war in 1415 and not with the earlier campaign of 1412 which Clarence had led,
much to his brother's chagrin. The strategy of that earlier campaign – in support
of one faction in the French civil war and in the hope of obtaining a sovereign
Aquitaine – was not continued by Henry when he became king.[20] Henry's focus
was on Normandy. Hence the concentration of the M 9 chronicle is on the wars
in northern France which he conducted in person and which were continued by
Bedford after his death. The inclusion of the battle of Baugé in 1421 was a necessary exception, as it was fought by Henry's younger brother, the duke of Clarence,
during the king's absence in England. But his return to England is deliberately
prefaced in the chronicle by mention of the appointments he made to ensure good
governance in his absence (f. 41v): the duke of Clarence as his lieutenant-general
for France and Normandy with Salisbury as his deputy; the Earl Marshal as captain of Pontoise (which is significant given Basset's service under the Earl); and the
duke of Exeter as captain of Paris, a mention which, had the focus been on Fastolf,
would have allowed opportunity to mention Fastolf whose appointment as captain
of the Bastille was made at this same time in order to provide for defence during
the king's return to England.

Furthermore, Henry's return to France in the early summer of 1421 is noted in
the chronicle with the customary emphasis on the king, his actions and his success,
first at Dreux and in a *chevauchée* towards Orléans following news that the Dauphin
was assembling a large force. But the French, we are told, 'did not dare to await
him', withdrawing back across the River Loire in order to avoid battle (f. 44v). Even
though illness forced him to delegate military command to the dukes of Burgundy
and Bedford at Cosne, the chronicle tells us that it was Henry himself who made
preparations to raise a great army (f. 46v). The reader is thus left with the impression that the siege was lifted thanks to the king's foresight (and the cowardice of
the Dauphinists). Although the capture of Olivier de Mauny, who had gathered
French and Breton troops during the siege of Meaux in order to raid the Cotentin,
was the result of a successful action led by the earl of Suffolk (ff. 45v–46r), the last

[19]   The case of Olivier de Mauny is discussed further in Chapter 3.
[20]   Milner, 'English Enterprise in France', p. 96.

word is given to the king in his magnanimity to the prisoner, as we have seen. In these two examples, we can see how the chronicle keeps the attention on Henry V despite the fact that he took no part in these particular military endeavours. We can go one step further and argue that these episodes were included because they gave yet another opportunity for celebration of Henry, in the passages immediately before his death (f. 46v).

After the death of Henry V, however, Fastolf is the most frequently mentioned individual on the English side. His career really comes to life, fostered by his close service relationship with the duke of Bedford. His appointment as master of Bedford's household is correct but he was never seneschal of Normandy, although in early 1424 he was given some supervisory role over fortified places in the duchy.[21] A highly significant moment was Fastolf's capture, at the surrender of Passy in 1423, of Guillaume Remon, alias Marjolaine, whom Bedford subsequently used as leverage to obtain the surrender of the town of Compiègne in 1424 by parading him on a cart before the walls of the town, with a rope around his neck, ready to be hanged. Moved by the love of their captain, those inside negotiated the surrender of the town on condition that Remon was released. This account of the surrender is unique to the M 9 chronicle.[22] It is confirmed by a grant which Fastolf received from the king in January 1433 by way of compensation for several financial losses, including the ransom of Remon which was estimated at no less than 20,000 *saluts d'or*.[23] The wording of this grant confirms the circumstances in which Remon had fallen into the hands of Fastolf. Remon's release had indeed made possible the quicker surrender of Compiègne which was otherwise likely to hold out for much longer, but it had been made, as the grant explains, without the consent or even the knowledge of Fastolf, and without any compensation being made to him. Indeed, the matter continued to rumble on even after the end of the war, with Fastolf claiming he still had not received the full compensation for the loss of Remon's ransom.[24] The inclusion of this case within the chronicle therefore helps to confirm a special focus on Fastolf after the death of Henry V.

As we can see from Table 1, the chronicle dwells on military operations in which Fastolf had a significant command role. Such a situation followed the battle of Verneuil where he was elevated to knight banneret. There followed immediately an appointment alongside Lord Scales and Sir John Montgomery to begin the conquest of Maine. Although no date is given in the chronicle, the appointment was made on 25 August 1424, only a week after the battle victory.[25] The chronicle

---

[21] On 17 January 1424 he was appointed 'gouverneur et superveeur de toutes les villes, chasteaulx et forteresses' in Normandy and in the parts of Maine which were appatised (BNF, Fr. 26047/200), having powers similar to those held by Richard Woodville as seneschal of Normandy under Henry V. Woodville had been reappointed to that role on 11 March 1423 (BNF, Fr. 26046/47).

[22] Remon is not mentioned at all in the account of the surrender of Compiègne in Monstrelet (iv, pp. 176–7) and Fénin (pp. 210–12).

[23] AN, JJ 175/203, discussed at length in Armstrong, 'Sir John Fastolf and the Law of Arms', pp. 46–56.

[24] *PL Gairdner*, iii, p. 58. See above p. 35.

[25] BNF, Fr. 4485, pp. 319–20. The actual appointment exists in a sixteenth-century copy (BL, Arundel MS 26, f. 4, printed in Planchenault, 'La conquête' (1925), pp. 24–5, and in an earlier copy in College of Arms, Arundel 26, f. 56v).

subsequently goes into considerable detail on the successful sieges which Fastolf and his associates conducted. This campaign immediately after Verneuil was very much a pilot for the larger campaign of conquest of 1425 under the earl of Salisbury as lieutenant-general. In the list of participants which follows mention of the earl's commission by Bedford, Fastolf is the second name after Lord Scales, who was no doubt placed first because of his noble status, but, significantly, Sir John is also described as governor of Anjou and Maine, an office to which he had been appointed by Bedford on 11 March 1425.[26] In this capacity, we hear of his involvement in the capture of Le Mans which triggered the surrender of a number of other places.

The chronicle also emphasises Fastolf's prominence during Salisbury's siege of La Ferté-Bernard in the spring of 1426 when a Gascon of the English allegiance plotted to allow the French into Alençon. Fastolf, who was captain of Alençon, although strangely this is not noted in the chronicle,[27] and Lord Willoughby left the siege of La Ferté to engage with the French approaching the town. We hear later of Fastolf's success at other sieges as well as his victory at Rouvray in February 1429 when he successfully defeated French efforts to intercept the victuals he was bringing to the siege of Orléans. Whilst Sir Thomas Rempston is given as holding joint command at this time, the chronicle is explicit that it was Fastolf who gave the order for the archers to prepare stakes to break the cavalry charge, and also to place all the waggons as defence in the rear. In addition, the chronicle tells us that 'of Sir John Fastolf and all of his company none was killed or wounded'. On this occasion, as by Salisbury after the successful siege of La Ferté and the rescue of Alençon (f. 57v), Fastolf was received with great honour and joy by the earl of Suffolk and the other lords at the siege of Orléans. Here as elsewhere, the chronicle emphasises Fastolf's accepted place within the socio-military hierarchy.

Of course, by the time the M 9 chronicle was written, Fastolf's reputation was less strong than it had been in 1429. Only a few months after the 'battle of the Herrings', his flight from Patay (18 June 1429) challenged his reputation to a degree that it was still a live matter in the 1440s when his status as a Garter knight was at issue. It can be suggested, therefore, that the authorial team may have striven to create a wholly positive portrayal of Fastolf. Hence the extended treatment of his activities after 1424. It is relevant here that there is no explanation provided on why Bedford chose to remove him from his governorship of Maine and to appoint Talbot in his stead. Later historians suggested that Bedford had been disquieted by his failure to bring to satisfactory conclusion the surrender of La Gravelle.[28] Fastolf had come to a composition with the defenders that they would surrender at a set date and Bedford had sent him to receive the surrender, but, being well supplied with victuals, the defenders reneged on their promises and held out. The chronicle is elusive about what happened next but has to admit that the Regent had been forced to come in person with an army to force the surrender and to behead those who had gone against their agreement with

---

[26]   College of Arms, Arundel 26, ff. 59–63.

[27]   His indenture of June 1425 described him as 'capitaine et gouverneur des chateaux et ville d'Alencon et de Fresnay le Vicomte et la comte de Maine et de la marche environ' (BNF, Fr. 26048/432).

[28]   Hall (1809), p. 141; Holinshed (1577), iv, p. 1236, (1587), vi, p. 597.

Fastolf. The juxtaposition of 'once this was done, my lord the Regent went home with all his host without doing anything further' with the following sentence, 'after the departure of the Regent … Sir John Fastolf was discharged from the government of the areas of Anjou and Maine', is a skilful way of stating the facts without implying any failings on Fastolf's part.

Despite Talbot's later disputes with Fastolf arising from the latter's flight from Patay it is notable that the chronicle portrays Talbot in a wholly positive light. Indeed, it is important to note that the narrative for the reign of Henry VI, even after Verneuil, is never exclusively focused on Fastolf even though he is the individual mentioned the most often. That he shares the spotlight with leading commanders places him within the same high status group of this most successful period of the war – in other words, fame and reputation by association.

Table 2. Distribution of mentions of English participants

One mention	98 (49.4%)	
Two mentions	42 (21%)	
Three mentions	20 (10%)	
Four mentions	10 (5%)	
Five mentions	8 (4%)	
One to five mentions	178 (89.8%)	
More than five mentions	20 (10%)	
Six mentions	3	Exeter, Fitzhugh, Gloucester
Seven mentions	5	Oldhall, Popham, Roos, Talbot, Worcester
Nine mentions	2	Glasdale, Warwick
Ten mentions	4	Clarence, Gough, Rempston, Willoughby
Eleven mentions	1	Scales
Twelve mentions	1	Suffolk
Thirteen mentions	1	Bedford
Eighteen mentions	1	Salisbury
Twenty mentions	1	Fastolf
More than twenty mentions	1	Henry V
TOTAL	198	

As Table 2 shows, after Fastolf the Englishmen most frequently mentioned are indeed the commanders of noble birth. Given Fastolf's role as master of Bedford's household, which was his passport to fame and fortune from the mid-1420s, the attention given to Bedford is hardly surprising. After the death of Henry V, Salisbury was the leading commander in the field and was heavily involved in the conquest of Maine as well as providing an important link back to the late king.[29] His activities in Champagne, in which Fastolf was not involved, are also emphasised in the chronicle as is also his successful campaign along the Loire in 1428 which culminated in his tragic death. Fastolf had been associated with Scales in the initial conquest of Maine. The latter's prowess in defeating a group of French who tried to intercept his escort of victuals to the siege of Pontorson is also emphasised.[30] Fastolf also served under Warwick when the earl, recently arrived from England, was appointed as lieutenant-general in place of Salisbury (f. 58r). Subsequently, Warwick's successful sieges of Mayet, Le Lude and Montdoubleau are covered before the action moves to the siege which the earl was ordered to lay to Pontorson. This was a major engagement in its own right as well as crucial to securing the frontier with Brittany (ff. 58r–60r). Fastolf is again listed second after Scales in the list of commanders at Warwick's siege of Pontorson.

There are two men of lesser status who appear frequently – Sir Thomas Rempston and Matthew Gough. Rempston was almost an exact contemporary of Fastolf. He preceded Fastolf as captain of Meulan, and was closely connected through his role as Bedford's chamberlain as well as by a shared link with the duke of Exeter. Although Rempston's activities were largely in other theatres than those of Fastolf, he fought alongside Sir John at the battle of Rouvray in 1429. Rempston came from a well-established knightly family, being dubbed himself on the eve of the coronation of Henry V, and although he temporarily retired from military service in 1436, he was active in the Calais march, Gascony and Normandy again from the late 1430s to 1450.[31]

Although with Lancastrian connections and claims that his mother nursed John, lord Talbot, Matthew Gough's fame derived entirely from his personal initiative and boldness, as the often quite lengthy accounts of his exploits in the chronicle emphasise. Indeed, we are told the origins of his reputation for honour and courage in his formidable chase and capture of the Bastard of la Baume in 1423–24, braving the stones which were thrown at him by the garrison of Courcillon (f. 49v). The siege of Montaguillon, where this incident is meant to take place, is also related in other French chronicles, but Gough's chase is unique to M 9.[32] Interestingly, some elements of this story are evidenced in a legal suit before the *Parlement* of Paris between the earl of Salisbury and Pierre le Verrat, captain of Sens in 1426.[33] The dispute between the two men was over the escape of La Baume's hostages whose guard Salisbury had entrusted to Le Verrat. We learn in a plea delivered on behalf of Salisbury that Ymbert de la Baume 'fit une course sur lui ou sur ses gens'.[34] The English chased him so tenaciously that La Baume was caught up near to the fortress of Château-Renard,[35] which he held together with other fortresses in the area. Names and places differ between

---

[29]   In this context it is an unusual oversight that his presence on the 1415 campaign is not noted.

[30]   Fastolf's relationship with Scales soured when both were in England in the 1450s (Smith, 'Aspects of the Career of Sir John Fastolf ', p. 195).

[31]   *HOCa*, iv, pp. 192–4.

[32]   'Geste des nobles' (p. 195); Monstrelet (iv, pp. 154–5); Waurin (iii, pp. 31–3).

[33]   *English Suits*, pp. 148–53.

[34]   *English Suits*, p. 149.

[35]   Loire, arr. Montargis, cant. Courtenay.

the chronicle and the legal suit, but not the circumstances of the capture or the handing over of La Baume to Salisbury. Clearly, the chronicle shows here the benefit of inside knowledge. We know from surviving muster rolls that Gough served under Fastolf at the siege of Pontorson in 1427.[36] Whether there were earlier service links is uncertain.

Gough's distinctive qualities, this time as a spy, are featured again at Talbot's recovery of Le Mans in 1428, with the added circumstantial detail that having found out the information, he had a quick drink and a bit to eat before he went to tell Talbot and Scales, thereby facilitating their early morning raid on the city, taking the enemy so much by surprise that they had to flee in their nightshirts (f. 62r). Such circumstantial detail has all the signs of eye-witness testimony.

Gough is a unique character in the chronicle, although matched to a smaller degree by Hanson and his company in their surprise attacks on Ramefort (f. 59r) and Saint-Laurent-des-Mortiers (f. 60r). Gough's 'red carpet treatment' which is given by detailed anecdotes – of a type which even Fastolf did not enjoy – is a distinctive feature of the M 9 chronicle. He seems to have fascinated William Worcester, as is revealed by the annotations he made on him in the chronicle. On Worcester's list of places lost by Edmund Beaufort in 1449–50, in College of Arms, Arundel 48, he also glossed Gough's entry as captain of Bayeux with 'escuier vaillant'.[37]

Gough's presence at Cravant and Verneuil is only known through the chronicle, as are also the appointments to various captaincies in the conquest of Maine. It was not until 1431, it seems, that he was appointed to any captaincy in Normandy, that of Conches, and he never held any major command in the duchy.[38] Instead, he served a very useful purpose as a highly trusted rough diamond responsible for dealing with ex-soldiers living off the land, even being charged after the truce of Tours to take them off to Germany.[39] He was also involved in efforts to delay the surrender of Maine to the French, in which action he no doubt aligned with Fastolf's wishes. He remained active in the French wars to the bitter end. Indeed, there is a further link which explains his prominence in the chronicle: according to a list made by William Worcester, Christopher Hanson was lieutenant of Gough at Bellême at the end of the English occupation.[40]

By the time the chronicle was compiled, Gough had met an unchivalrous death at the hands of Cade's rebels. Fastolf's will included masses for his soul.[41] Were the plaudits of the chronicle an attempt to mitigate this, perhaps linked to Hanson's personal knowledge of him around that same time, and his opposition to the surrender of Maine to the French in 1448? Or was it simply that Gough had been a

---

[36]   BN, Fr. 25767/216, 25768/225.

[37]   College of Arms, Arundel 48, f. 287v, printed in *L&P*, II, ii, p. 625.

[38]   BN, Fr. 25769/590. He was appointed captain of Bayeux, one of the smallest garrisons in the duchy, in 1439 for life (ADC, F 1299). He was briefly lieutenant of Verneuil in 1442 (BL, Add. Ch. 12156). According to Worcester's list he was lieutenant at Carentan in 1449 (College of Arms, Arundel 48, f. 287v, printed in *L&P*, II, ii, p. 625).

[39]   On their return to Normandy in the spring of 1445 Gough was with his 'dirty dozen' in the vicinity of Lisieux but was bribed by the town council to keep his troops well away from the town (AC Lisieux, CC 17 f. 144).

[40]   College of Arms, Arundel 48, f. 287, *L&P*, II, ii, p. 627.

[41]   *PL Gairdner*, iii, p. 157.

larger than life figure in the wars, acting on his own initiative and in ways which did not fall easily into chivalric or command principle of the time? Not for Gough the prestige commands, land grants or a knighthood, but reward by the earl of Salisbury of a fine horse and a greater share in the ransom of the Bastard, as well as a reputation for daring and cunning which was also memorialised in Welsh praise poetry.[42]

Another commander mentioned frequently is William de la Pole, then earl of Suffolk. As is well known, in the late 1440s and early 1450s Fastolf did not hold de la Pole, by then duke, in high regard, blaming him for the surrender of Maine and the lack of compensation for those like Fastolf who had held lands there. Yet there is no sign in the M 9 chronicle of direct criticism of Suffolk, testimony perhaps to the fact that he had a distinguished war career before politics and royal intentions made him the scapegoat for defeat. Furthermore, Suffolk's career in France had begun in his father's company, alongside Fastolf, in 1415.

The chronicle's villain is William's younger brother, John. In 1423, as lieutenant for his brother in the Basses Marches of Normandy, he gathered troops for a raid into Anjou which ended in interception by the count of Aumale (f. 50r). In 1427 his lack of defence in one part of the English siege of Montargis eventually forced Warwick and Suffolk to abandon the siege (f. 62v). On both occasions, the French found the English in disarray, defeated them and forced them to flee, killing some and taking others prisoner. At Montargis the chronicle ascribes this failure directly to John de la Pole's poor maintenance of watch and his 'negligence and indolence'. Adding to the shame, the chronicle describes how he saved his own skin by fleeing to join his brother on another side of the siege. For the raid of 1423, the opprobrium is implicit in the description of de la Pole billeting himself and his troops in a nunnery for three days, taking prisoners, animals and 'all other kinds of booty he could find'. Five English prisoners were taken by the French on this occasion: John de la Pole himself, John Basset (an inclusion which could explain how inside knowledge of the event was gained), two John Affourds and – added in the hand of Worcester – John Clifton. This last addition is relevant since Clifton was also a Norfolk knight whom Worcester describes as sharing lodgings with Inglose and others at the siege of Rouen.[43] John de la Pole had probably served in the garrison of Harfleur under Fastolf in the early years of the conquest, so their hostility may have a longer history behind it. It is also possible that the attack on him was a veiled attack on his elder brother, since the chronicle makes clear that John was acting as William de la Pole's lieutenant.

John de la Pole is the only Englishman criticised in the whole chronicle. The defeat of Clarence at Baugé is skilfully handled to avoid any blame falling on the duke. Rather, the emphasis is on the treachery of André Lombart.[44] The duke and his nobles fought valiantly as much and for as long as they could (f. 43v). It cannot be a coincidence that a long and illustrious list of French and Scottish soldiers is given to emphasise what Clarence was up against, and also that after the engagement the enemy are portrayed as not daring to await the arrival of the English archers but departing as quickly as they could: 'They did not have time ("loisir") to carry off with them the body of my lord of Clarence, therefore it suited them

---

[42]   See Probert, 'Matthew Gough', and gutorglyn.net.
[43]   *Itineraries*, p. 361.
[44]   This matter is discussed further in Chapter 3.

to leave it behind' (f. 44r). The list of English prisoners and dead is comparatively extensive, not surprisingly when a number of those affected by Baugé, including Henry Inglose, had close connections with Fastolf,[45] through shared Norfolk origins and/or shared military experiences. Indeed, the M 9 chronicle may demonstrate Colin Richmond's suggestion that there may have been '"a Baugé generation" … sad and not triumphant, but committed to one another'.[46] Fastolf's first service had been under Thomas, duke of Clarence. A number of those active in France and featured in the chronicle were men with similar long-term links to the duke, as the biographies in the footnotes to the translation reveal.[47] Fastolf also requested prayers for Clarence in his will as also for the dukes of Bedford and Exeter.[48]

Several of those mentioned in the chronicle had military links with Fastolf, whether serving alongside him or under his command. Others had more personal links. Fastolf had sold the wardship of his stepson Stephen Scrope to the chief justice, William Gascoigne,[49] whose son, another William, is noted in the chronicle as dying at the siege of Meaux from an arrow, an unusual and unique point of detail (f. 45r). Fastolf's half-sister Margaret was married to Sir Philip Branche, who had served alongside Fastolf in Ireland. We find him as a man-at-arms in his brother-in-law's retinue as the conquest of Maine began in the late summer of 1424, alongside his own brother Henry.[50] Both are mentioned in the chronicle, as is Sir John Radcliffe, the second husband of Fastolf's other half-sister Cicely, who had served alongside Fastolf in Ireland and on the 1412 expedition. Also mentioned is the son of Cicely's first marriage, Robert Harling, a man towards whom Fastolf showed particular care both during his life and after his death at the siege of Saint-Denis in 1435.[51] Sir Henry Inglose, Sir William Oldhall, Sir Andrew Ogard, and Richard Waller were all feoffees of Sir John, and all feature in the chronicle. That said, another feoffee, Sir John Clifton, was not in the original text but added by William Worcester. Soldiers who served with Fastolf at Alençon, such as George Rigmaiden, Thomas Lound and Thomas Everingham, also receive mention. There is thus an evident bias of authorial selection especially when it comes to the more obscure men noted in the text, some of whom can be shown to have served alongside Basset and Hanson too.

Whilst some major campaigns in which Fastolf was not involved, such as the battle of Cravant, are not overlooked given their importance as English victories and a source of pride, it is instructive that the English sieges of Mont-Saint-Michel, laid from 1424 onwards, are completely omitted. These sieges were the concern of soldiers based in the south-west of the duchy, such as Nicholas Burdet. The latter was commissioned on 26 August 1424, the day after Fastolf, Scales and

---

[45]   Inglose was a councillor and feoffee of Fastolf and had a room kept for him at Caister (Richmond, *Paston Family: First Phase*, p. 208). His mother also had Fastolf blood.

[46]   Richmond, *Paston Family: First Phase*, p. 207.

[47]   Thanks also for discussion on this with Dr Mike Warner whose Southampton doctoral thesis on the company of Clarence in 1415 is published as *The Agincourt Campaign. The Retinues of the Dukes of Clarence and Gloucester.*

[48]   *PL Gairdner*, iii, p. 156.

[49]   Hughes, 'Stephen Scrope and the Circle of Sir John Fastolf', p. 111.

[50]   CPR 1408–13, p. 14; BNF, Fr. 25767/93; Smith, 'Aspects of the Career of Sir John Fastolf', p. 102.

[51]   E 101/50/4 where Fastolf acted on behalf of Robert after his death for the payment of wages.

Montgomery had been commissioned to begin the conquest of Maine, to lay siege to the Mont, the only place in Normandy which had not fallen to the English.[52] Successive sieges of Mont-Saint-Michel never involved the commanders featured in the chronicle, such as Bedford, Salisbury and Warwick, or Fastolf, and hence were not included. Not surprisingly, too, there is no mention at all of the armed clashes between Duke Philip and Humphrey, duke of Gloucester on behalf of the latter's wife, Jacqueline of Hainault, which much absorbed the Burgundian chroniclers of the period.

The M 9 chronicle's detailed treatment of the conquest of Maine is extremely important to historians.[53] It provides important insights into the service of English and French soldiers outside Normandy, all the more so as the administrative records for the English presence in that area have survived rather patchily. No other English chronicle treats of the war in Maine to any meaningful degree, nor do the *Croniques de Normandie* of which we know William Worcester had a copy.[54] Whilst a narrative of the conquest of Maine is found in some French chronicles, most notably that of Jean Chartier which also has overlap with the *Chronique de la Pucelle*, the chronology is often suspect and the events garbled.

Yet there are occasions when their information aligns with the M 9 chronicle. Notable here are the mentions in French chronicles of specific individuals such as Philip Branche at Saint-James-de Beuvron and William Blackburne at Le Lude, as in the chronicle.[55] A similar conclusion can be suggested for the mention in Monstrelet and Waurin of the failings of John de la Pole at Montargis.[56] Yet whilst Chartier mentions the capture of Henry Branche, describing him as Fastolf's nephew, at an action near Sainte-Suzanne against Ambroise de Loré, this incident is not found in the M 9 chronicle, nor is there any echo of the mention of Henry Biset at Montargis by Monstrelet and Waurin.[57] Direct links or influences between these French chronicles and the M 9 chronicle are unlikely. What we are seeing here is the impact of stories which were circulating, but also selectivity on the part of all chroniclers. Chartier was keen to mention the defeat of Henry Branche, his link to Fastolf being regarded as significant. The authors of the M 9 were not. Even so, whilst the M 9 chronicle puts forward a consistently patriotic English line, what it tells us about the activities of Fastolf and others involved in the conquest of Maine can be considered basically reliable precisely because it draws on the testimony of those directly engaged in this period of the war. In that context it is a 'soldiers' chronicle' interested in the actions of fellow soldiers.

---

52 BNF, Fr. 26047/309; Luce, i, p.j. xxiv.
53 Through Edward Hall's use of the chronicle it has already informed many works on the subject, both in French and English.
54 College of Arms, Arundel 48, ff. 236–69. It has also been speculated by Vallet de Viriville that there was a copy of the *Geste des nobles francois* in England sent to Jean, count of Angoulême (*Pucelle*, p. 25). The *Geste* gave a narrative to 1428 but does not show any notable similarities in the M 9 chronicle.
55 Chartier, i, pp. 49, 57.
56 Monstrelet, iv, p. 271; Waurin, iii, p. 216; Toureille, *Montargis*, p. 30.
57 Chartier, i, p. 56; Monstrelet, iv, p. 271; Waurin, iii, p. 216.

THE FRENCH IN THE M 9 CHRONICLE

The counting of Frenchmen mentioned in the chronicle is hardly an exact science.[58] Difficulties arise from the same individual appearing under different names, using both patronyms and toponyms, and from potential confusions between relatives, or even with unrelated homonyms whom we have not been able to identify. Our discussion comes with these caveats. The chronicle mentions around 421 separate French individuals, which is our best estimate. Of these, a large majority – 284 (67.5 per cent) – only appear once in the text. In an ideal world, we would need to compare the incidence of names in other chronicles of the period, but that is an ambitious task which would have been impossible to carry out for this edition.[59] We can, however, give some insights and detect trends by approaching the matter from the other direction – the small minority of individuals who have been cited five times or more.

Table 3. French name occurrences

1 mention	284 (67.5%)
2 mentions	78 (18.5%)
3 mentions	37 (9%)
4 mentions	15 (3.5 %)
5 mentions	4 (1%)
6 mentions	2
8 mentions	1
TOTAL	421

Baudouin de Champagne, lord of Tucé, is the most often cited Frenchman in the M 9 chronicle, who makes eight appearances, twice in the narrative and six times in the lists. His is not an obvious name. He was by no means a leading protagonist whose actions were widely reported in contemporary chronicles, unlike, for instance, Arthur, count of Richemont, mentioned six times. Richemont was of higher status, as a brother of the duke of Brittany, who was captured by the English at Agincourt (f. 33r), changed allegiance to the English cause (ff. 40v, 44v), but then reverted to the Valois cause (f. 47r) and became constable of the French army, and had a chronicle written about him by Guillaume Gruel. Baudouin de Champagne came from a family based in Maine.[60] The lordship of Tucé or Tussé

---

[58]   A similar conclusion applies to the Scottish, whose names are particularly garbled by the authors and sometimes difficult to identify. It can be hazarded that there are thirty-two individual Scotsmen named, of whom nineteen are mentioned only once, nine twice, three thrice, and one four times. Three Spanish are listed serving the French, as well as two Lombards. Gascons are found in both English and French service, as are Bretons, not least because of the double change of camp by the count of Richemont.

[59]   In fact, the naming practice and networks of individuals in chronicles could form an excellent research project assisted by existing computer software to extract and analyse relevant data on a large scale – this would be tremendously helpful to refine our understanding of chronicle writing.

[60]   La Roque, *Histoire généalogique de la maison de Harcourt*, ii, pp. 1884–9.

(today Lavardin), which he acquired from his marriage with Jeanne de Tucé, was only 13 km from the city of Le Mans.[61] Administrative records confirm that he was captain of Le Mans in 1424.[62] Chartier, who echoes the M 9 chronicle's comments here (f. 56v), places Tucé in command of Le Mans when the city was besieged and captured by the earl of Salisbury in August 1425.[63] This is of course the point at which Fastolf was, according to the M 9 chronicle, appointed to the captaincy of Le Mans, and therefore the two men may have met in negotiations for the treaty of surrender. Chartier's second (and last) mention of Tucé, which also aligns with the M 9 chronicle (f. 61v), is also related to Le Mans, the chronicler listing him amongst the French troops who briefly recaptured Le Mans in May 1428.[64] Tucé's participation in this operation is also evidenced by administrative record.[65]

But Tucé's scope of action in the chronicle looms much larger than simply Le Mans. He was present on virtually every battlefield and we can be certain there is no room for confusion over his identity in the text. 'Sire Baudouyn de Champaigne seigneur de Tucey' shared the captaincy of the town of Falaise with the lord of Longny in 1417 (f. 34v); 'Sire Baudouyn de Champaigne sire de Tusse' was at the battle of Baugé in 1421 (f. 42v); 'Sire Baudouyn de Champaigne seigneur de Tuce' was at the battle of La Gravelle in 1423 (f. 50v); 'Sire de Tusse' was among the French army which attempted to relieve Ivry and fought at Verneuil in 1424 (f. 52r); after the surrender of Le Mans in 1425, 'le Sire de Tusse, bailli de Tours' besieged the castle of Malicorne in 1426 (f. 59v);[66] and after the failed operation at Le Mans in 1428, 'le Sire de Tusse' fought at Rouvray (f. 64). This extraordinary activity of one single individual is unmatched in M 9. This portrayal of Tucé's activity also happens to be unique to this chronicle.

Tucé is not a major player in other chronicles. In fact, his existence is omitted in most chronicle accounts, even in *La Pucelle*, which is surprising given that chronicle's coverage of the war in Maine. Yet we find ample references to Tucé in Guillaume Tringant's commentary on *Le Jouvencel*. According to this source, Tucé was commissioned to the defence of the frontiers of Maine and Anjou in the aftermath of Verneuil in 1424, took part in the attempted recapture of Le Mans in 1428, was present at the aborted battle of Montépilloy in August 1429, and besieged Château-du-Loir in 1431.[67] Tucé's presence in this source can be explained by its high level of local interest in Maine and Anjou: de Bueil's family came from the Touraine on the borders of Maine. And Maine is indeed where the early action in *Le Jouvencel* is set. Tucé had also a personal connection with the de Bueil family since his daughter, Anne, married Louis de Bueil, Jean V's younger

---

[61]   *Le Jouvencel*, ii, p. 15 n. 5.
[62]   ADS, G 18, f. 104r, in Charles, 'L'invasion anglaise', pp. 198–9.
[63]   Chartier, i, p. 44.
[64]   Chartier, i, p. 58; see also Raoulet (ibid., iii, p. 194).
[65]   Baudouin de Tucé, knight, lord of Tucé and *bailli* of Touraine gave a *quittance* on 23 May 1428 for participation in the recovery of Le Mans (BNF, Clairambault 28/2055; Ledru, 'Tentative', p. 8).
[66]   Tucé was indeed *bailli* of Touraine but from 1431 to 1440. See *Le Jouvencel*, ii, p. 15 n. 5, which cites references from the Archives Municipales de Tours.
[67]   *Le Jouvencel*, ii, pp. 273, 275, 281, 284.

brother, in 1432.[68] In the light of this, we may have expected to see even more of Tucé in Tringant.

What can we infer from this 'French star' of the M 9 chronicle? Since there is no obvious connection between Fastolf or any of the authors of the chronicle and Tucé, apart from a possible link in the surrender of Le Mans in 1425, we are bound to see the chronicle's unparalleled showcase of Tucé and his military action in Maine as a direct result of its focus on war, and indeed on this particular theatre of war. Further supporting this point is the fact that Tucé shares the spotlight with his fellow countrymen – Ambroise de Loré (mentioned six times), from Le Mans, Jean du Bellay (five times), from Anjou, and Jean, lord of Fontaines-Guérin (five times), also from Anjou – all fighting actively against the English in Maine and Anjou in the 1420s. Such a situation could suggest that the chronicle displays an incomparable knowledge of the French military community of Maine and Anjou in the 1420s, provided of course that this information is correct: interest does not necessarily mean accuracy. For Tucé, we have managed to gather some evidence which supports *some* claims made in the chronicle's account, but a lack of surviving administrative records for Maine in this period makes this task difficult to apply across the board.[69]

In general, the information provided in the lists of Frenchmen can hardly be held as wholly accurate. The M 9 chronicle is the only chronicle to provide a detailed list of French combatants at Baugé. But what is the point if none of it is accurate? Out of the first ten dukes, counts and viscounts mentioned in the Baugé list (f. 42r), six individuals are highly unlikely to have been present on this battle-field, one count is invented, and only the presence of the count of Aumale can be established with any certainty.[70] The duke of Alençon is in the list as lieutenant-general of the Dauphin but he was aged only 12 in 1421. The *vicomte* of Thouars is listed as is the *vicomte* of Amboise but in fact they are the same person, as were the count of Aumale and the *vicomte* of Châtellerault. The lord of Albret was negotiating a treaty with Henry V at the time and most certainly not marshal of France; that is a confusion with his father.

Even so, we should not condemn or ignore the testimony of the chronicle completely. It appears to be better informed about the local community in Maine, including men of humble origins for whom we have been able to gather little information, or even none, from other sources. That said, we are fortunate here in the survival of the account of Bedford's receiver-general in Maine which gives many names of Frenchmen accorded safe-conducts.[71] This shows Baudouin 'soy disant sure de Tussé', knight, *bailli* of Touraine and captain of Tours and Saumur,

[68] *Le Jouvencel*, ii, p. 15 n. 5.

[69] On Tucé, we have already noted that the link with Le Mans in 1425 and 1428 is supported by administrative records, that Tucé indeed became *bailli* of Touraine albeit later. Note also that the participation at Baugé of Baudouin de Champagne, lord of Tucé, also seems to be evidenced in the *Journal de Jean du Bellay* (according to Planchenault, 'La conquête' (1925), p. 14 n. 1), but we have not managed to identify the source cited there.

[70] Jean de Harcourt, count of Aumale, was at Tours, 80 km from Baugé, on 1 April 1421, from whence he sent an order to his lieutenant, Olivier de Mauny, lord of Thiéville (Luce, i, pp. 107–8, no. 10). In light of this evidence, Aumale's presence at Baugé, which, curiously, is not mentioned in other chronicles, seems likely.

[71] AN, KK 324, discussed in Luce, 'La Maine sous la domination anglaise', pp. 226–41.

appears, for instance, as the recipient of a safe-conduct on 4 December 1433.[72] Many others named in the chronicle in relation to the campaigns in Maine, some of modest origins who appear nowhere else in the records that we have consulted, can be found mentioned in this administrative record, and thereby put flesh on some of the bones of the French of the chronicle. What our research has shown above all, as indicated in the footnotes to the English translation, is that the names, or at least the majority of them, are real names belonging to real people. The authors of the chronicle can be confused but do not normally make up names and individuals, although, as we shall see in the next section, there are oddities in the lists for the early battles, especially Agincourt.

THE LISTS

Names are central to 'chivalric' chronicles.[73] It is not uncommon for chronicle narratives of major battles to conclude with lists of dead, as is apparent in Monstrelet where we find lists of dead at Agincourt (273) and at Verneuil (60).[74] But the M 9 chronicle is unique in terms of its lists, bearing in mind its short length, the high number of names it gives and the range of contexts in which they appear, as well as in its systematic presentation of names in list form (Table 4).

Table 4. The lists in the M 9 chronicle

Key: E English; F French; B Burgundians; S Scottish

Event	Group	Number	Folio
Garrison put in Harfleur 1415	E	4	31r
Invalided home 1415	E	3	31r
With king to battle 1415	E	21	32r
Knighted at Somme 1415	E	11	32v
French at Agincourt 1415	F	43 (4 prisoners, 39 dead)	33r–v
Army of invasion 1417	E	24	34r–v
Garrison captains in Normandy 1417	F	111	34v–36r
Garrison captains in Maine 1417	F	67	36r–37r
Garrison captains elsewhere 1417	F	4	37r
Appointments of English garrison captains after siege of Caen 1417	E	14	37v
Appointments of English garrison captains under Clarence 1417–18	E	11	37v–38r
Appointments of English garrison captains under Gloucester 1417–18	E	15	38r

---

[72] AN, KK 324, f. 13r.
[73] Given-Wilson, *Chronicles*, pp. 100–1.
[74] Bouzy, 'Les morts d'Azincourt', pp. 221–55; Monstrelet, iv, pp. 195–6.

Appointments of English garrison captains after siege of Rouen 1419	E	34	39r-v
Siege of Melun 1420	E/B	77	40r–41r
Pre-Baugé knightings	F	3	42r
Battle of Baugé 1421	F/S	78 (62 French, 16 Scots)	42r–43r
Battle of Baugé 1421	E	30 (20 prisoners, 10 dead)	43v–44r
Siege of Meaux 1421–22	E	33	44v–45r
Action during siege of Meaux in Lower Normandy 1422	F	5	45v
Action during siege of Meaux in Lower Normandy 1422	E	4	45v
TOTAL NAMES 1415–22		592	
Siege of Meulan 1423	E	8	47r
Marriage of Bedford 1423	E	5	47v
Battle of Cravant 1423	E/B	32	48r-v
Battle of Cravant 1423	F/S	20 (5 French, all dead, 15 Scots, 13 dead, 2 prisoners)	49r
Action at Abbey of La Roe 1423	F	45	50r–51r
Action at Abbey of La Roe 1423	E	5 prisoners	51r
Action at Ivry 1424	E	5	51v
Action at Ivry 1424	F	111 (11 Bretons, rest French)	52r–53r
Battle of Verneuil 1424	E	43	53v–54r
Battle of Verneuil 1424	F/S	45 (10 Scots, 35 French)	54v–55r
Siege of Guise	E/B	4 (1 Burgundian, 3 English)	55r
Army under Salisbury in Maine 1425	E	21	56r-v
Appointments of English captains in Maine 1425	E	8	57r
Encounter with French during siege of Pontorson 1426	F	7	59r
Siege of La Gravelle 1426	E	12	60v
French recovery of Le Mans 1427	F	8	61r-v
English recovery of Le Mans 1427	E	10	61v
French action during siege of Montargis 1427	F	3	62v
Siege of Orléans after death of Salisbury 1428	E	9	64r

Battle of Rouvray 1429	F/S	48 including at least 2 Scots (4 dead)	64v–65r
(French arrivals at Orléans May 1429)	F	6	66r
TOTAL NAMES 1422–29		455	

The lists demonstrate considerable interest in those present at battles, not only those who died or were captured which were the groups which tended to interest other chroniclers. For instance, seventy-eight French and Scots are named in the list of those present in the army which met the duke of Clarence at Baugé. For the action at Ivry which preceded the battle of Verneuil, 111 French and Scots are named. What is distinctive about the M 9 chronicle, and consistent across its whole length, is the detailed attention given to appointments to garrison. Particularly noticeable are the long lists of French captains claimed to hold garrison commands in Normandy, Maine and the Somme area at the time of Henry V's invasion. With 182 names this is by far the longest continuous list in the chronicle. We also find sixty names of English appointed to commands between 1417 and 1419, distributed across three near contiguous lists interspersed with short sections of narrative outlining the progress of Henry V's conquest.

Another distinguishing feature is that the listing strategy includes the French, with due attention also paid to the Scots who supported them, as well as Burgundians and French who supported the English, and to the Bretons who are found in both camps. The contrast with other chronicles is again noticeable. Baugé illustrates this point well. The M 9 chronicle lists the names of some seventy-five combatants present in the Franco-Scottish army, a striking figure since we can gather only about a dozen names of combatants from the mainstream French and Burgundian chronicles reporting on the battle.[75] Even though Monstrelet gives sixty-seven names of dead and prisoners at Verneuil, which is a higher figure than the forty-four in the M 9 chronicle, the latter also names 114 Franco-Scottish combatants whilst Monstrelet does not name any.[76]

The lists in the M 9 chronicle raise several questions. The most obvious is why they were included at all. Were they a matter of record to give 'authenticity' to the narrative? This interpretation is not incompatible with the notion that inclusion of names was a means of honouring the 'chivalric class' of both sides. Such extensive naming might serve to promote fame and reputation: every single individual described as taking part in a successful encounter would thereby share the honour of the victory. Similarly, the focus on naming office-holders could be explained by the honour a person derived from holding an office of responsibility, be it a lieutenancy for the war of a given area or the captaincy of an important town. The lists contain solely 'men of name', an expression found twice in the chronicle relating to Cravant and Verneuil (ff. 49v, 55r). This is a chronicle of nobles, knights and gentry: there are no archers named.

It can be argued, however, that the inclusion of the lists was not in order to honour both sides, but only the English. The fame and renown of English warriors listed in the chronicle was enhanced by such comprehensive mention of those

---

[75]   The following chronicles have been used here: Berry, Cagny, Monstrelet, Waurin, Chartier, Fénin, *Pucelle*, Richemont, *Religieux*, and 'Geste des nobles'.

[76]   Monstrelet, iii, pp. 195–6.

against whom they had fought and won, hence the inclusion of lengthy lists of French nobles and gentry in the defeated armies. The names of the French were included simply to glorify the English victory. French men, or indeed those of other nationalities who resorted to guile or behaved treacherously, are named in order that they might be shamed.

A pressing question is where the lists came from. It has been a general assumption that lists of battle dead and prisoners were the product of heralds. The list of French casualties at Agincourt presented on f. 34r is followed by 'and several other knights to the number of 2,400, according to a declaration delivered by Montjoye, King of Arms of France'. Similarly, the list of French casualties at Verneuil is followed by 'and many others both French and Scots to the number of about 9,000 men, according to Montjoye, King of Arms for the enemy party. On the English side no man of name worthy of mention died' (f. 55r). These are, however, the only mentions of heralds in the M 9 chronicle and they relate to large-scale battles where heralds were present. Heralds would have had no dealings with, or interest in, appointments to captaincies, nor are they known to have dealt with presences at battles where this did not lead to death or capture. Therefore, whilst lists of dead and prisoners, or at least some of them, may have an origin in lists drawn up by heralds, there is no reason to believe that the heralds were behind the majority of lists in the chronicle.

Nor do the lists resemble the formal muster rolls of the period, whether for the French or English armies. The French are not known to have maintained lists of captaincies before the English invasion. For the English in Normandy there are some surviving lists. Those for 1436, however, do not name the captain but simply give the location and composition of the garrisons,[77] as is also the case for a list for the year following the truce of Tours in 1444.[78] This last mentioned list is found within a book of evidences (Lambeth Palace Library, MS 506) collected by William Worcester, although translated from its original French into Latin. Within this same book we find a list, again in Latin, of the garrisons in the year from Michaelmas 1433 to Michaelmas 1434 where the captains are named as well as sizes given.[79] Within another compilation made by William Worcester, College of Arms, Arundel 48, we also find a list of garrison sizes and captaincies in Normandy following reforms made by the duke of Bedford in October 1434.[80] This is in French and written in a French hand. None of these documents relates to the period covered in the M 9 chronicle but it is not impossible that Worcester had similar documents, now lost, for earlier years of the conquest of Normandy and Maine. There is a possibility that the administration in Normandy drew up an annual survey which gave names of captains as well as sizes of garrisons, as we see in the list for 1433–34 in Lambeth Palace Library, MS 506. However, that particular document cannot be a direct copying out of a government record since

[77]   Curry, 'The Garrison Establishment in Lancastrian Normandy in 1436', pp. 237–69.
[78]   Lambeth Palace Library, MS 506, ff. 28r–30r. There is another copy in a French archive: Dubosc, 'Manuscrit inédit tiré des archives de la maison de Matignon', pp. 33–51.
[79]   Lambeth Palace Library, MS 506, ff. 28r–31r (1444), and ff. 16v–20r (1433–34), printed in L&P, II, ii, pp. 540–6.
[80]   Curry, 'John, Duke of Bedford's Arrangements for the Defence of Normandy in October 1434', pp. 235–51.

it is in Latin; all of the documents of the administration of Lancastrian France were in French, as is seen in the lists of October 1434, 1436 and 1444.

We can see that William Worcester displayed an interest in the holders of English captaincies in Normandy at the loss of the duchy, creating such a list himself which he subsequently annotated and amended.[81] We also have in his own hand two lists giving information for 1432 and 1434–35 which were presumably drawn up in preparation for later sections of the chronicle.[82] In his *Itineraries* he also provides some lists, for instance for the rescue of Caen by Fastolf in 1434 from information provided by Thomas Fastolf.[83]

Given Worcester's interest in names it is tempting to consider that he lies behind the lists, which, in this scenario, were added in to the chronicle through his 'diligence'. But if there is substance in the argument that Peter Basset had been the original initiator of the M 9 chronicle, as Worcester himself suggests, we must assume that he had started the format of lists within an overall narrative which the rest of the team continued. As we have seen, there is more space given up to lists as opposed to narrative in the reign of Henry V. But if Basset was the controlling mind which the later authors copied, we still face the basic problem of where he might have acquired the information.

It is possible that the lists had no, or little, written material behind them, and that they were the result of oral recollection. As we have seen, Basset and Hanson were soldiers who had participated in some, but by no means all, of the events found in the chronicle. Fastolf similarly had been present on many occasions, and would have known personally English participants even at events where he was not engaged personally. His role as master of Bedford's household would have boosted his knowledge. He would have also known some French participants but it does not seem credible that he would have known all of the French listed in the chronicle. There are signs that reminiscence played a part in the writing of the chronicle: on occasion we see additional names inserted into a list as if, on hearing or reading it, someone thought of another person who should be mentioned.

On the face of it, however, the lists are so substantial and there are so many of them, as to imply that memory alone would not have been enough to create them, or at least not to create them accurately. To probe this further, we can carry out closer examination of the names within them.

The results of this examination are distinctly mixed. Thanks to the researches of Pierre Courroux, we can see that 28.6 per cent (12 out of 42) of the French dead

---

[81] College of Arms, Arundel 48, ff. 286–9.

[82] See Appendix.

[83] *Itineraries*, pp. 352–3 ('per relationem Thome Fastolf'). Given that Worcester made his note in 1478 this Thomas may be the man in whose wardship Sir John was keen to have an interest in the late 1440s and who was the son of John Fastolf of Oulton and grandson of Sir Hugh Fastolf, collateral lines of the same Norfolk family (Richmond, *Paston Family: First Phase*, p. 241). But Thomas Fastolfs are also found in the wars. A man-at-arms of this name is found in the company of the earl of Suffolk in 1415, but was invalided home like Fastolf himself (E 101/50/26, E 101/44/30 no. 1 m. 10). We also find men-at-arms of this name in Sir John's garrison of Honfleur in 1429–30 (BNF, Fr. 25768, no. 420, NAF 20522/23, Fr. 26274/108), and an archer of this name is found in the garrison of Caen under Ogard in 1439 and in a company for the field under Matthew Gough in 1440 (BNF, Fr. 25775/1435, 1450). Worcester's *Itineraries* contain other lists (for example, pp. 338–9, 358–61) but he does not report his source.

and prisoners at Agincourt are incorrect.[84] Amongst the dukes and counts the error rate is even higher (46.7 per cent, 7 out of 15 cases). Some names, such as the duke of Cleves, are simply invented: there was no such duchy at that time. The count of Namur was not at the battle and did not die until 1417, nor was the count of Hainault, who died in 1418. Oddly, too, a number of the famous Agincourt dead, such as the duke of Bar, the counts of Vaudémont, Roucy and Marle, are not found in the lists at all. Courroux's findings for the battle of Cravant are similar. Four French counts are listed as dead but in reality none of them died at this battle. Two of them are known to have died at Verneuil in the next year, another decade later.

Errors are not uncommon in English chronicles when it comes to foreign names. The chronicler Thomas Walsingham also made mistakes, naming, for instance, 'the count of Alençon, that is of Armagnac' as the opponent of the English at the battle of the Seine in 1416.[85] But the M 9 chronicle is guilty of some errors and confusions, listing men who did not fight at particular battles, creating two or three lords out of one, listing as dead men who were prisoners (as in the case of the count of Dammartin in 1415), or as prisoners men who were dead (as in the case of John of Bar, brother of the duke of Bar). Such errors make it unlikely that heralds' information lies behind the lists, and also suggest that the authors were keen to have the lists of French as long as possible in order to enhance the sense of English achievement even further. So arose additions, listing the same man more than once, and other devices.

Overall, our extensive identifications as given in the notes to the English translation suggest that the names of French given for the reign of Henry VI are generally much more reliable. Many revolve around actions in which we know that Fastolf and Hanson were involved. In addition, Fastolf held a command role in Maine which would also have increased his likely knowledge, especially of captaincies. The worst 'offences' concern the early period (1415–21), suggesting that their source of information – Basset? – was unreliable, or else that his lists were manipulated by the later authors to make them seem more impressive. In this context, it is particularly useful to examine the lists of French garrison captains in Normandy and Maine at the time of the landing of Henry V in 1417. These occupy six pages (ff. 34v–37r), with ninety-six places listed for Normandy, sixty-four for Maine and four in the Somme estuary. Overall we find 175 names of individuals since some captaincies were held jointly. This is the longest continuous list of names provided in the chronicle. Gaps left at the end of the Maine and Picardy list suggest there had been an intention to add more. Furthermore, it is unique: no other chronicle of the period ventured into giving even a small fraction of the information provided in this list. The insertion of an extensive list of French captains is puzzling, and the source of information from which it might have been drawn even more so, since there is no evidence the French kept lists as the English did later.

How accurate was this list? To check it, we can use information from the Norman rolls commissioned by Henry V for his acts issued in the duchy. These include treaties of surrender of places in the duchy where names of the French captains are usually given, as well as protections given to such captains. Out of the thirty-eight cases where we have such information, the name of the captain aligns with

---

[84]   We are very grateful to Dr Courroux for sharing his findings with us for this volume.

[85]   *St Albans Chronicle*, ii, pp. 686–7.

that in the M 9 chronicle on only nine occasions.[86] That said, despite the high rate of discrepancy, the names provided in the chronicle do not seem to be invented. On several occasions, the captain named in the chronicle appears in the Norman rolls in a different location or with a different role. What is clear, however, is that the chronicle cannot have been based on any official list compiled during the conquest, or that existed in France before the English arrived. However, it is not impossible that there had been a 'reshuffle' of French captains between the English landing and the actual surrender of each place.

Furthermore, it is difficult to see the logic of the order of the captaincies as given in the list. They do not follow the order in which places fell, which is revealed by comparison with the dates given in the treaties of surrender. Their ordering seems in part to be by geographical cluster, moving from Calvados into Manche, and then to Seine-Maritime and Eure, but locational clustering is less evident in the second half of the list. The list for Maine is doubly perplexing since the conquest of that area did not begin in earnest until 1424, although there was a limited amount of penetration in the reign of Henry V. Were the men listed French captains in place in 1417 or at the time of the actual conquest? This may be a question we can never answer since the surviving sources for the administration of Maine both by French and, after 1424, by English are very thin on the ground. This also makes it difficult to check the accuracy of the appointments of captains in Maine as given in the chronicle.

What of the lists of English captains appointed by Henry V in his conquest of Normandy?[87] As we have noted, sixty-eight are listed (ff. 37v–39v). Here the lists are more obviously chronological in nature since they follow brief narratives of the phases of conquest. The first fifteen relate to places taken in the first six months of the conquest by the king. Thereafter Henry sent his brothers, the dukes of Clarence and Gloucester, to the east and west respectively; we find lists given separately for the appointments each made. Subsequently we find a list of appointments made after the surrender of Rouen in January 1419. In all cases there is approximate, if not complete, alignment with the dates of surrender.

We can again compare with the evidence of the Norman rolls where many appointments of Englishmen to captaincies are enrolled. In sixteen of the forty-one cases (40 per cent) we find the same name as in the M 9 chronicle. So, for instance, Richard, lord Grey of Codnor is noted as captain of Argentan (f. 37v), and we have an enrolled appointment dated 13 October 1417. In other cases, it seems that the chronicle may be alerting us to the person put in command immediately after the capture of a place but who was soon replaced, allowing the initial appointee to continue with the field army to other sieges. So, for instance, the chronicle (f. 38r) notes Davy Howell as captain of Pont-d'Ouve, where a treaty of surrender is dated 17 March 1418 but where the Norman rolls indicate the appointment of William Rothelane as captain on 21 May 1418. For some places there is no early appointment of a captain found in the Norman rolls. Such is the case at Pont-de-l'Arche, where the first enrolled appointment of Sir Maurice Bruin dates to 3 April 1421, but

---

[86]   The notes to the English translation provide full details on the names of French and English captains for each place known from administrative sources.

[87]   For the sake of comparison, Walsingham (*St Alban's Chronicle*, p. 725) mentions sixteen appointments to captaincies made by Henry V in the first stage of the conquest, of which four align with the information in the M 9 chronicle.

where the chronicle gives the captain as the duke of Clarence (f. 39r). The Norman rolls indicate that the town surrendered to the duke in July 1418 and several entries confirm his subsequent captaincy, but there was no enrolled appointment.

We find problematic claims in the chronicle, however. At Cherbourg, we are told, Lord Grey of Codnor was captain until his death, being succeeded by Sir Walter Hungerford. Yet the latter's appointment as captain was enrolled on 11 August 1418 in anticipation of the formal treaty of surrender on 22 August. It is not feasible, therefore, that Grey had ever held the captaincy of Cherbourg, especially when he died on 1 August 1418. The Norman rolls record that Sir Walter Beauchamp was appointed *bailli* of Rouen on 19 January 1419 immediately after the surrender of the city, yet the chronicle claims that Sir John Kyghley held the post (f. 39r). Similarly, Thomas Burgh is given by the chronicle as captain of Avranches. This place surrendered on 14 July 1418 but was briefly recaptured in the spring of 1419 before being retaken in July 1419. On 27 August 1419 William de la Pole, earl of Suffolk, was appointed as captain. A later hand has crossed out Burgh and entered Philip Hall, *bailli* of Alençon, but no man of that name is known and the entry may be inspired by Edward Hall's later interest in the chronicle.

The strangest situation concerns the captaincy of Harfleur. According to the chronicle, Sir John Grey was appointed captain after the surrender of Rouen in January 1419 (f. 39r). In fact, Thomas Beaufort, duke of Exeter, who had been appointed at the surrender in 1415, remained captain until 21 January 1420. Grey was appointed at that date but died at the battle of Baugé, being replaced by Sir Ralph Cromwell and subsequently Sir William Phelip.[88] Given Fastolf's lieutenancy at Harfleur we might have expected greater accuracy in this case. But the example reflects a more general point about the lists of English captains, that they do not reflect a single particular point in time but rather give names of men who at one time or another held the post.

There can be no doubt that throughout the chronicle there is a great interest in who held a captaincy. In almost every case after a siege is mentioned, the man appointed to its captaincy is given. Indeed, the narrative is driven by this scenario of the capture of a place and the appointment of a captain, with the defeated French captain also being mentioned on occasion. This points to an important conclusion: that the authors of the chronicle interpreted deeds of arms to include the holding of military command, since it was proof of military standing and prowess. The narrative of the chronicle is very much driven by sieges and resulting appointments to garrison command, a reflection of the dominance of conquest in this phase of the Hundred Years War. This 'soldiers' chronicle' interpreted war as not simply battles and sieges. The authors' interest in garrison captaincies is consistent across the whole text. Therefore, if it had been a characteristic of an earlier work by Peter Basset then it was continued by Worcester, Hanson and Nantron. If not, then it was introduced or expanded by them retrospectively, which may explain the higher level of errors in the first half of the work.

The chronicle's constant emphasis on names draws attention to the 'naming practice' in chronicles and raises questions about record and memory in general. Our research has revealed inaccuracy but this is unlikely to be unique to the M 9 chronicle. The difference is that the extent of these lists and their high proportion in comparison with the narrative draws attention to the matter. The bias of the M

---

[88]   Curry, 'Henry V's Harfleur', p. 281.

9 chronicle is undoubted. It presents a deliberately selective view of a war which the English had lost by the time it was written. A sense of triumphalism and pride, even after this final defeat, was maintained by emphasising the contribution of so many brave Englishmen to the almost untrammelled success under Henry V and the Regent Bedford against the might of the French. In this respect, the naming strategy was a form of celebration and of consolation for Fastolf.

3

The portrayal of war in the M 9 chronicle

Despite offering a relatively short and truncated account of the war between 1415 and 1429, the M 9 chronicle stands out, as we have shown in the previous chapter, through its choice of content, thereby making an original contribution to the recording and memorialisation of this phase of the Anglo-French war. Clearly the M 9 chronicle belongs to the 'chivalric genre', but, at the same time, its tight focus on deeds of arms in war, its unmatched naming practice as well as its patriotic tone single it out. In this present chapter we will endeavour to situate it in the chronicling landscape of the period by looking closely at how it portrays war. We have attempted to keep this analysis as comprehensive as possible, addressing the chronicle's take on virtually all aspects of war, even those which it neglects.

THE JUSTIFICATION OF WAR

Just as the M 9 chronicle is disengaged with politics, it also shows no real interest in proving the justice of the English cause within the context of contemporary ideas of just war. The English claim to France is taken for granted.[1] Such a stance is hardly surprising since the chronicle was written for a veteran who had committed his life to the English cause. As Sir John Fastolf himself wrote in 1435, if Henry VI should renounce his title to the French crown, 'it might be said, noised and deemed in all Christian lands where it should be spoken of that not Harry the King nor his noble progenitors had, nor have, no right in the crown of France and that all their wars and conquest have been but usurpation and tyranny'.[2] The justification of the war in the chronicle is through the celebration of victory, as we see emphasised specifically in the case of Henry V who at every mention is called 'the victorious prince'. Victories proved that God was on the English side yet even this *a posteriori* justification through divine providence is not extensively exploited in the chronicle.[3] God is thanked on only two occasions: after the battle of Cravant we are told the lords gave thanks and praise to God and to His glorious mother (f. 49r); at Verneuil, which is described as an exceptionally cruel and amazing battle,

---

[1] Whilst the outline terms of the treaty of Troyes given on folio 41v are underlined, this is undoubtedly by a post-medieval hand.

[2] *L&P*, II, ii, p. 576, as modernised in Lewis, *Later Medieval France*, p. 37.

[3] For a similar 'martial bent' to divine intervention in the *Scalacronica*, a chivalric chronicle focused on battlefield victory, see King, 'War and Peace', pp. 148–62.

we read that 'at the end, as it pleased God our Creator and the Glorious Virgin, victory inclined towards and then remained with the English' (f. 54r).[4]

On occasion, we find implicit justifications that fit the doctrine of the just war as expressed in contemporary treatises.[5] For instance, the English fought in self-defence at Saint-James-de-Beuvron (f. 58r), resisting an enemy siege, and also at La Gueintre (f. 59r) and Rouvray (f. 64v) where the enemy tried to intercept their convoy of supplies. They fought to protect the population from the evils of the enemy at *le park l'evesque* (f. 45v), in the Ile-de-France (f. 47v) and at Ivry (f. 51v). Finally, they fought to recover possession of places which had been taken from them, as we find at Meulan (f. 47r), Compiègne (f. 51r) and Le Mans (f. 62r). Clarence's campaign in Anjou, which ended with his defeat at Baugé, is said to have happened after truces between Henry V and the duke of Anjou had been 'broken'. Reference to such a truce appears to be unique to the chronicle but there is no detail given on who had broken it or if it was simply a case of a period of truce coming to an end.[6] In general, however, the chronicle does not provide any explicit justification, even at the risk of making the English appear as outright aggressors, so convinced are the authors of the right of the English claim to France. In 1417, for instance, Henry V is described as raising a new army 'with the intention of making a conquest' (f. 34v). The same motive is repeated for the missions of conquest which the king entrusted to his lieutenants. Scales, Fastolf and Montgomery in 1424, and Salisbury in 1425, were appointed by Bedford 'to make conquest in the territories of Anjou and Maine' (f. 55v). But in this respect, the wording aligns with statements which we know to have been made by Henry V and, in the case of the appointments, with the wording of the actual commissions given to those appointed to lead the campaigns.[7]

STRATEGY AND TACTICS

Evidence for the discussion of strategy in chronicles is noticeably rare. Historians are thereby forced to engage with the perilous procedure of deducing strategic plans from the events described in such narratives.[8] The M 9 chronicle, being

---

[4]   All together the text makes only four references to God, the other two relating to the deaths, of the earl of Salisbury, who 'gave up his soul to God the Father and to Jesus Christ his son', having made the appropriate pre-death dispositions for his soul (f. 63v), and, earlier, of Henry V, with similar reference to the last rites and the giving up of his soul in full devotion (f. 46v). Indeed, in the case of the king, the post-mortem invocation is distinctly secular in nature, urging all people to lament the death of 'so very noble and victorious a prince, your protector and defender', and noting his burial in Westminster Abbey 'with his predecessors as kings'.

[5]   Contamine, *War in the Middle Ages*, pp. 260–302.

[6]   To what the chronicle is referring is not obvious. There is evidence of diplomatic activity between Henry V and Yolande of Aragon, queen of Sicily and Jerusalem, on behalf of her son, Louis of Anjou, in 1418 and 1419, including a truce agreement concluded on 7 March 1418, as well as subsequent evidence of an attempt by the English to redress infractions of these truces. Such diplomatic activity seems to end in July 1419, not long before the murder of Montereau (C 64/9 m. 9d, DKR 41, p. 689; *Foedera*, ix, p. 550, 692, 728, 773).

[7]   See for instance the appointment of Scales, Fastolf and Montgomery on 25 August 1424 for the conquest of Maine and Anjou (College of Arms, Arundel 26, f. 56v).

[8]   Prestwich, *Armies and Warfare*, p. 187.

tightly focused on the English perspective, can provide some insights, as, for instance, about how Henry V divided his army in the spring of 1418 to conduct conquests in specific areas (ff. 38r–39v), but in general there is a lack of engagement with strategic considerations. This is apparent in the prelude to the Orléans campaign. Salisbury, newly arrived in France with an army in the summer of 1428, is described as meeting and having discussions ('parle ensemble') with Bedford in Paris before he went on to besiege Janville-en-Beauce (f. 63r). It is known, however, that there was disagreement over the strategy to adopt against the French. Salisbury – and also the duke of Gloucester who headed the council in England – advocated a campaign to break through the Loire into the heartlands of the French king while Bedford wished to focus on the conquest of Anjou. Most significantly, Bedford, for the first time, had been denied full control of an English expeditionary force.[9]

Although it focuses on prominent individuals, the chronicle scarcely touches upon the strategic planning of commanders. That said, we find an important exception concerning the siege of Pontorson (f. 59r and v). The newly fortified town was besieged by the earl of Warwick in February or March 1427, surrendering to him by 8 May.[10] A failed attempt to intercept an English convoy of supplies near Mont-Saint-Michel on 17 April, according to the *Chronique du Mont-Saint-Michel*,[11] seems to have prompted Pontorson to negotiate a conditional respite, but surrender was necessary when no relief was received on the appointed day. These events, with typical chronological vagueness, are widely reported in French chronicles. The M 9 chronicle offers a relatively detailed account of this operation, but what is interesting and unique is the connection made with the contemporaneous operations in Maine of Gilles de Rais and Jacques de Dinan, lord of Beaumanoir. These, it claims, were intended to distract Warwick and force him to raise the siege of Pontorson, but they failed to do so. The only other sources which mention the operations of the two French lords – the besieging and capture of the fortresses of Ramefort, Malicorne and Le Lude – do not link them to efforts to distract the English from the siege of Pontorson and are particularly confused on their chronology.[12]

The chronicle proposes a more coherent account which can be substantiated from other evidence demonstrating the link between the siege of Pontorson and the French activity in the Maine. Fascinatingly, such evidence concerns none but John Fastolf himself. A surviving order of payment reveals that Fastolf, together with 100 men, was dispatched from Pontorson on 10 April 1427 for the relief of the fortress of Malicorne in Maine some 150 km distant which was under French siege.[13] According to the chronicle, Malicorne was forced to surrender to the French, with its captain, Olivier Kathersby, and all the English garrison being taken prisoner (f. 59v). Such a negative outcome may be the reason why the chronicle omitted to mention that Fastolf had been sent to Malicorne's rescue. On the other hand, Fastolf's direct involvement in these operations surely explains why the chronicle was better informed on the subject. We presumably owe this inside knowledge to Christopher

9   Curry, *The Hundred Years War*, pp. 110–11.
10   Beaucourt, ii, p. 26; Planchenault, 'La conquête du Maine' (1933), pp. 143–7.
11   Luce, i, p. 29.
12   *Pucelle*, pp. 242, 243, 250; Chartier, i, pp. 51–2, 53, 57 (between 1425 and 1428). The narrative of the siege of Pontorson follows after these events in Chartier, i, pp. 59–60, and *Pucelle*, pp. 253–4.
13   BNF, NAF 1482/47, printed in Planchenault, 'La conquête du Maine' (1933), pp. 151–2.

Hanson, one of its authors, who was able to contribute information on the contemporaneous sortie conducted by himself and twenty to thirty men of the garrison of Sainte-Suzanne, who included a man described as 'eschelleur' or 'wall-scaler', a rare and precious reference to this specialist role. Taking advantage at Saint-Laurent-des-Mortiers of the absence of Jacques de Scépeaux and his soldiers at church to take the castle, this action was a complete success (f. 60r).

Given its target audience, we might have expected to find a more sophisticated account of war in the chronicle. After all, Fastolf had written proposals for the overall strategy of war after 1435. His report, which is tainted by a sense of betrayal by the Burgundians, advocates 'sharp and cruel war'.[14] In Fastolf's view, the English should forget about sieges and focus their military efforts on raids of devastation and on attrition, burning and damaging the land. Such a vengeful policy belongs to the context of the Burgundian defection of 1435. The content of the chronicle was coloured by this event: relatively little place was given to the role of the Burgundians in the war, and, as we have seen, the murder of John the Fearless was downplayed as a cause for the triumph of Henry V in the treaty of Troyes. But mention of Fastolf's proposals in 1435 also draws attention to the fact that war in the chronicle is notably 'controlled'. Violence is markedly restrained, the war being conducted in a 'civilised' manner, based on shared practice promoting the control of violence. English expeditions, even those described as *courses* (ff. 56r, 58v), were aimed at conquering places or else confronting the enemy in a battle.

We find only two exceptions. In the first, the Bastard of Clarence's army on its return from Baugé is described as killing people and laying waste to the countryside of Maine (f. 44r). This description of deliberate devastation directly follows lamentations on the death of Clarence, as if emphasising that someone had to pay for his death. Since the French did not dare to face the Bastard's army, the English turned their anger against the 'people' to expiate the fault of the French knights. We see here a moral turn to the explanation of how the Anglo-French war was conducted. The second example offers a significant contrast, since here the English army had no moral grounds for its action. It indulged in a raid near La Gravelle which was aimed at capturing prisoners, cattle and 'all sorts of prey' (f. 50r). The fact that this pursuit for profits was carried out by John de la Pole, who comes under heavy criticism in the chronicle, implicitly tells of its disapproval for such behaviour. The scorched earth policy, advocated in such influential writings as Vegetius' *De re militari*, and scarcely hidden in chivalric chronicles such as Froissart's, does not fulfil the moral standard of the chronicle.[15] As we have seen, English action is driven on multiple occasions by the need to *protect* the population from the French. For instance, Henry V ensures the defence of the 'povres laboureurs' who have been the victims of the Bastard of Vaurus at Meaux (ff. 45r-v). Interestingly, the depiction of Vaurus's victims as (poor) ploughmen is more characteristic of accounts by clergy,[16] whereas lay authors such as Monstrelet, Le Fèvre de Saint-Rémy or Chastelain chose to portray them

---

[14]   *L&P*, II, ii, pp. 575–85; Vale, 'Sir John Fastolf's "Report" of 1435', pp. 78–84; Prestwich, *Armies and Warfare*, p. 185.

[15]   Allmand, *The De Re Militari of Vegetius*, pp. 314–21. Fastolf owned a copy of this work (p. 72).

[16]   *Religieux*, vi, pp. 450–1; Fénin, p. 354; *Vita et Gesta*, p. 315; Des Ursins, p. 566; 'Fragment', iii, p. 249.

as Englishmen and Burgundians, emphasising their political persuasion.[17] It could be argued that the chronicle promotes the view of Henry V as a paragon of justice, acting with a deep sense of equity.[18]

BATTLES

Whilst the chronicle is interested in military action, describing a number of engagements, it does not provide any sophisticated account of battlefield tactics. This situation is particularly noticeable in the account of Agincourt where other chronicle narratives, both English and French, are notably detailed. The chronicle blandly informs us that the 'opponents fought a battle' in which Henry V came out victorious, and then proceeds to mention the rallying by Guillaume de Thibouville of Frenchmen 'under a white banner to give a new battle' which triggered Henry's order that each man should kill his prisoner (f. 33r). Why does the chronicle dwell upon this episode whilst saying virtually nothing on the battle itself? As with other English chroniclers, the aim may simply have been to justify Henry's actions, but the mention of the 'pennon blanc', unique to this chronicle, points to another possible interpretation.[19] If the chronicle's 'pennon blanc' signifies a flag of surrender, the intention was surely to show a French manoeuvre of deception: they pretended they were going to surrender but instead launched an attack. The chronicle also makes a unique observation on the effects of the killing of the prisoners, explaining that was why so many French nobles met their end.

Clarence's choice at Baugé in leaving his archers behind, and his falling into an ambush set by the French, may seem a surprising inclusion. The chronicle's atypical interest in tactics on this occasion stems from its higher purpose to clear the duke's name (ff. 43r-44r). It gives no detail about the actual course of the fight. Ultimately, the disaster is presented as a result of Clarence's intention to win the honour of the victory for himself and his fellow nobles, but, as we will see, the chronicle also puts up the most vigorous defence of the duke's fateful decision. We can recall here, of course, that Fastolf had served under Clarence in Ireland. Some Burgundian accounts shift the blame to topographical features.[20] If Clarence rushed into the battle with only his best men, it was because his host had been slowed down by the difficult crossing of a river. According to Jean Le Fèvre, however, the river was not the problem. He records a rumour that Clarence had purposefully left his army behind because he was eager to achieve success and to prove himself in battle against the French in order to compensate for his missing Agincourt.[21] More elaborate French criticism comes from de Cagny who claims that the duke wanted to prove that the English could win a battle without archers.[22] English chroniclers tend either to minimise the significance of the battle, as in the case of Adam of Usk and the London chroniclers, or else to blame Clarence for his rashness, as with Walsingham and in the *Vita et Gesta*

---

[17] Monstrelet, iv, p. 96; Le Fèvre, *Chronique*, ii, p. 54; Chastelain, i, p. 303.
[18] Ambühl, 'Henry V and the Administration of Justice', pp. 74–5.
[19] For a detailed analysis of the chroniclers' account of this alleged massacre, see Curry, *Agincourt. A New History*, pp. 256–68.
[20] For instance, Monstrelet, iv, p. 38; Fénin, *Mémoires*, p. 153; Waurin, ii, p. 358.
[21] Le Fèvre, *Chronique*, ii, p. 36.
[22] Cagny, p. 120.

Henrici Quinti,[23] but there was also a popular view, as epitomised in the *Brut*, that the day was lost because Clarence had not taken the archers with him.[24]

The M 9 chronicle does not shy away from criticisms of Clarence. On the contrary, it brings them to the fore, but only to be in a better position to rebuke them. Clarence's fateful choice to leave his archers behind and to throw himself and the English nobility into the lions' den had been inspired by the Italian 'double traitor', André Lombart (f. 42v). He had misinformed Clarence about the size of the French army as well as warning the French of English intentions, thereby prompting them to set a deadly ambush. The chronicle makes it clear that Lombart worked for the French by including his name in the list of French combatants who fought at the battle of Baugé and adding 'traitre' next to it (f. 42v). Lombart's deception and responsibility for the English disaster are strongly emphasised. We are told that, as the English prepared to fight, Clarence thought that Lombart was telling the truth; subsequently, that the enemy were ready for battle because of the advice of Lombart, the traitor who had 'sold' the duke; and finally, after the list of casualties, that the duke had been 'falsely betrayed' (f. 44r). This is not the only chronicle of the period to shift the blame onto Lombart, suggesting this was rumour circulating at the time. John Streeche even suggests that Lombart had previously served the duke but had defected to the French after being disciplined by him for taking plunder at the capture of Pontoise in 1419.[25] But the chronicle's heavy-handed and repetitive method of dealing with Lombart suggests that its authors, who were no doubt aware of conflicting accounts which stained Clarence's reputation, were determined to convince, or even 'brainwash', its readers that Clarence was the victim of a most evil man in French pay.

A lack of interest in actual battle tactics is also evident in the chronicle's accounts of Cravant and Verneuil. Description is limited to an acknowledgement that the combat was fierce and cruel but eventually won by the English, the French being forced to run away. Bravery is emphasised at Cravant where the English and Burgundians, both foot and mounted, are described as throwing themselves into the hard fight with a loud shout and equal courage (f. 48v). At Verneuil the focus is on the elevation of Fastolf to the status of knight banneret and on divine will, as well as the two sides fighting bitterly. There is nothing on tactics or the bravery of the English as a whole.[26] A very similar description is made of the smaller-scale battles of *le park l'evesque* (ff. 45v, 46r) and La Gueintre (f. 59r). For the latter we are explicitly told that the English dismounted to fight, a mention which is puzzling since all battles previously mentioned had used the same tactic.[27] At La Gravelle (ff. 50r and v) and Montargis (ff. 52r and v) the French found the English 'in disarray' – in other words, not drawn up in battle formation – and defeated them.

---

[23]   See, on this, Milner, 'The Battle of Baugé', p. 500.

[24]   BL, Cotton MS Claudius A VIII, f. 10v (The *Brut Chronicle*), cited in Newhall, *English Conquest*, pp. 275–6.

[25]   Both John Streeche and John Hardyng place the blame on the same 'Andrew Lombard' (Milner, 'The Battle of Baugé', pp. 499–500). See below, p. 147, for the development of the story by Hall.

[26]   Courage, and especially that of a single Norman combatant, Jean de Saane (as described in the *Cronicques de Normendie*, p. 73), is elsewhere identified as a driving factor of the English victory at Verneuil (Jones, 'The Battle of Verneuil', esp. pp. 396–400).

[27]   On battle tactics and fighting on foot, see Prestwich, *Armies and Warfare*, pp. 316–23.

The only encounter for which the chronicle provides more details on tactics is the battle of Rouvray where the English were commanded by Fastolf himself (ff. 64v–65v). On seeing the French approaching the food convoy, Fastolf set his soldiers in battle array and ordered a sharpened stake to be planted in front of each archer in order to break the cavalry charge of the enemy. Such a tactic had been used at Agincourt and Verneuil, being commented on in several chronicles but not mentioned at all in the M 9 chronicle's account of these battles. In addition, at Rouvray Fastolf protected his rear with carts and horses tied together. The English thus defended themselves against the French within this enclosed area, and defeated them. Such a detailed account could be seen as opportunistic, since the information on Fastolf was readily available, but it was appropriate since it showed Fastolf himself, the dedicatee of the work, in favourable light as a skilful military commander. Rouvray stands as the greatest achievement of Fastolf recorded in the chronicle. We find it there described as a 'noble and glorious victory' and a 'victorious *destrousse*' (f. 65v), placing the engagement at the same level as another three 'glorious victories', namely Agincourt, Cravant and Verneuil (ff. 34r, 49r and 55r).

The high stakes and the great risks in pitched battle undoubtedly commanded admiration in the chronicle. This is by no means a unique standpoint – witness the comments of Geoffroy de Charny in the mid-fourteenth century[28] – but the chronicle also seeks to generate extra cultural capital by emphasising that the English seek this higher form of deeds of arms while the French shamefully avoid it. So, for instance, despite assembling a 'great power' in the region in the summer of 1421, the French withdrew when Henry V advanced towards Orléans because they 'did not dare to await him' (f. 44v). The desire to meet the French in battle, but which is disappointed by the latter who do not dare to face the English, is a recurrent theme in the chronicle. The situation reproduces itself at Baugé, where Clarence is described as expressing hopes that all might have the honour of this destruction (f. 43r), Ivry, where the French dare not come once they know the Regent is present in person (f. 53v), and Montargis, where Warwick offers battle but the French inside the town refuse it (f. 62v).

SIEGES

In large part, the military action described in the M 9 chronicle consists in captures, or attempted captures, of strongholds, whether towns or free-standing fortresses. This is hardly surprising because of the nature of a war which was firmly aimed at conquest. That said, Fastolf raised strong reservations against sieges in his 1435 memorandum where he described them as a waste of human and financial resources; if, none the less, a siege was to be laid, Fastolf highlighted the need for a force in the field ready to relieve and succour the besieging army.[29] His view could have been informed by siege warfare strategy between 1415 and 1429, in which he had participated but which finally failed. If this was the case, the chronicle does not show any sign of it. Should this be interpreted as evidence of the new sense of anger and rancour that warped Fastolf's judgement in 1435, or was it the case that the chronicle's portrayal of siege warfare was idealistic

---

28   *The Book of Chivalry of Geoffroi de Charny*, pp. 89–90.
29   *L&P*, II, ii, pp. 579 and 584.

and removed from the reality of war? We cannot offer a full answer here, but we can certainly contribute by examining the details of the sieges mentioned by the chronicle. We have identified sixty-four such operations in the text. These are listed in Table 5 together with the information which the chronicle provides about them: the type of place; whether a formal siege was laid; the length of the operation; and the outcome.

The list reveals a slight predominance of free-standing fortifications, mainly castles (28:64, 44 per cent), as opposed to towns (23:64, 36 per cent) or a combination of town and castle (12:64, 19 per cent). Whether this is an accurate portrayal or simply evidence of the selective bias of the chronicle would need further comparative study. The chronicle focuses on English operations to seize French-held strongholds: such incidents form the overwhelming majority of the corpus (52:64, 81 per cent). An interesting pattern can be seen here. Thirty-two operations out of sixty-four (50 per cent) involve explicit mention of a siege which ends in a surrender.[30] The fact that nearly all of these 'siege and surrender' situations (31:32, 97 per cent) are English-led operations indicates that this was not just a widespread practice, it was also an accepted norm – surrender predominated. Indeed, most English captures (44:52, 84.5 per cent) happened by way of surrender, whether or not they involved a siege. In the chronicle, therefore, with a single exception – Montargis in 1428 – the English are systematically successful in carrying out operations which avoid a violent storming and excessive bloodshed. Intriguingly, other methods by which a place might be taken – brute force (5:64, 8 per cent), surprise ('emblée') (5:64, 8 per cent), guile and trickery (2:64, 3 per cent) or treason (2:64, 3 per cent) – are only marginally represented and are associated with a French way of war. The French used either brute force or betrayal in five out of their eight successful operations. It is also worthy of note that three of the four unsuccessful sieges described in the chronicle are attributed to the French. In other words, the chronicle puts forward a 'proper way of war' which brings success. But that way of war, and the rewards which it brings, belong to the English.

Even so, trickery and guile were deemed worthy of praise on occasion. When a Gascon of the English party sold the town of Alençon to French partisans of Charles VII but then betrayed them by allowing Fastolf to carry out an ambush, the authors do not describe the Gascon action as treason and do not question the probity of the deed of arms. Similarly, they were not bothered – in fact the very opposite – by Christopher Hanson's use of trickery to seize the castle of Saint-Laurent-des-Mortiers during mass. The 'subtil moyen' used by Hanson is neither concealed nor criticised. Interestingly, such details on the way the English captured Saint-Laurent are unique to this chronicle, and are surely the result of input by Hanson himself. We can thus safely assume that this was a deed of arms that Hanson was proud of. What we detect here, therefore, is both pragmatism and political partisanship in the approach to questions of ethics in war.

---

[30] Siege and surrender was key to Henry V's strategy of conquest of Normandy (1417–19). The Norman rolls include some forty-nine treaties of surrender (Schnerb, 'Sauver les meubles', pp. 215–66).

Table 5. Siege operations in the M 9 chronicle

Key: T+C: town and castle

Place name	Place type	Date	Level of resistance (length, where given)	Outcome	Led by	Siege	Ref.
Harfleur	town	1415		surrender	English	yes	f. 31r
Touques	castle	1417		surrender	English	no	f. 37v
Caen	town	1417	'aucun espace de temps'	taken by force	English	yes	f. 37v
Falaise	castle	1418		surrender	English	no	f. 45v
Pont-de-l'Arche	T+C	1418	'aucun temps'	surrender	English	yes	f. 38v
Evreux	town	1418	'aucun temps'	surrender	English	yes	f. 38v
Louviers	town	1418	6 weeks	surrender	English	yes	f. 38v
Domfront	T+C	1418	'aucun temps'	surrender	English	yes	f. 38v
Rouen	T+C	1418–19	7 months	surrender	English	yes	f. 39r
Pontoise	town	1419		taken by 'emblée'	English	no	f. 39v
Sens	town	1420	15 days	surrender	English	yes	f. 40r
Montereau	T+C	1420	10 weeks	surrender	English	yes	f. 40r
Melun	T+C	1420	7 months	surrender	English	yes	f. 40r
Dreux	T+C	1421	6 weeks	surrender	English	yes	f. 44v
Meaux	T+C	1421–22	9 months	surrender	English	yes	f. 45r
Cosne	town	1422		siege lifted	French	yes	f. 46v
Passy	castle	1423	'brief temps'	surrender	English	yes	f. 47v
Orsay	castle	1423	'incontinent'	surrender	English	yes	f. 48r
Montaiguillon	castle	1423	half a year	surrender	English	yes	f. 49v
Meulan	T+C	1423		taken by 'emblée'	French	no	f. 47r
Meulan	T+C	1423	2 months	surrender	English	yes	f. 47r

Cravant	T+C	1423		siege lifted	French	yes	f. 49v
Saint-Pierre-sur-Orthe	castle	1424		surrender	English	no	f. 56r
Saint-Thomas-de-Courceriers	castle	1424		surrender	English	no	f. 56r
La Chartre-sur-le-Loir (1)	castle	1424		taken by force	English	no	f. 56r
La Chartre-sur-le-Loir (2)	castle	1424	'peu de jours'	surrender	English	no	f. 56r
Sillé-le-Guillaume	castle	1424	6 days	surrender	English	no	f. 55v
Touvoie	castle	1424	8 days	surrender	English	yes	f. 55v
Beaumont-le-Vicomte	castle	1424	15 days	surrender	English	yes	f. 55v
Ivry	castle	1424	6 weeks	surrender	English	yes	f. 51v
Compiègne	town	1424		surrender	English	yes	f. 51v
Verneuil	town	1424		surrender	English	no	ff. 55r-v
Compiègne (2)	town	1424		taken by 'emblée'	French	no	f. 51r
Verneuil	town	1424	'incontinent'	surrender	French	no	f. 53v
Guise	T+C	1424		surrender	English	yes	f. 55r
Sainte-Suzanne	T+C	1425	15 days	surrender	English	yes	f. 57r
Mayenne	castle	1425	6 weeks	surrender	English	yes	f. 57r
La Guierche	castle	1425	15 days	surrender	English	no	f. 56v
Le Mans	town	1425	6 weeks	surrender	English	yes	f. 56v
Lude	castle	1426		surrender	English	no	f. 58r
Malicorne	castle	1426		'conquered'	French	yes	f. 59v
Lude	castle	1426		taken by force	French	no	f. 59v
Mayet	castle	1426	2 days	surrender	English	no	f. 58r
Ramefort	castle	1426	none	taken by 'emblée'	English	no	f. 59r
Saint-Laurent-des-Mortiers	castle	1426		taken by 'subtil moyen'	English	no	f. 60r
Laval	castle	1426	4 days	surrender	English	no	f. 61r

Saint-Ouën-des-Toits	castle	1426	8 days	surrender	English	yes	f. 60r
La Gravelle	castle	1426	8 days	surrender	English	yes	f. 60r
Ramefort	castle	1426	10 days	surrender	French	yes	f. 59v
Montdoubleau	castle	1426	3 weeks	surrender	English	yes	f. 58v
Pontorson	town	1426		surrender	English	yes	f.58v–59v
Château-du-Loir	town	1426	8 days	surrender	English	yes	f. 58r
Saint-James-Beuvron	town	1426		siege lifted	French	yes	f. 58r
La Ferté Bernard	T+C	1426	Feb. to just after Easter (31 March)	surrender	English	yes	f. 57v
Laval	town	1428	none	taken by 'emblée'	English	no	f. 61r
Laval	castle	1428		treason	French	no	f. 61v
Le Mans	town	1427 (*recte* 1428)		treason	French	no	f. 62r
Le Mans	town	1427 (*recte* 1428)		scheme	English	no	f. 62r
Montargis	town	1428		siege lifted	English	yes	ff. 62r-v
Janville	town	1428	15 days	taken by force	English	yes	f. 63r
Janville	castle	1428	15 days	surrender	English	yes	f. 63r
Beaugency	town	1428	15 days	surrender	English	yes	f. 63r
Meung	town	1428	immediate	surrender	English	no	f. 63r
Jargeau	town	1428	immediate	surrender	English	no	f. 63r

The chronicle is noticeably vague with regard to the length of sieges during Henry V's conquest of Normandy: Caen, Domfront, Evreux, Pont-de-l'Arche are all described as conquered 'après aucun temps', suggesting that the authors were less well informed about this particular episode of the war. As a rule, operations leading to the capture of a place, according to the chronicle, were relatively short in duration. Out of the forty-two operations for which we are given a reasonably precise chronological marker, thirty (70 per cent) are described as being successfully concluded within fifteen days (given in the text as a *quinzaine*, equivalent to the modern fortnight), and thirty-six (86 per cent) within a month and a half.[31] The cases of Montaiguillon (six months), Rouen (six-and-a-half months, *recte* six months), Melun (seven months, *recte* five months), and Meaux (nine months, *recte* seven months) – are notable exceptions.

The chronicle provides interesting insights into the correlation between the length of siege operations and the terms of surrender. We might expect a greater length to result in harsher terms. This is true in the case of Meaux where, according to the chronicle, the town and fortified market offered the longest resistance to the English. The French garrison is described as surrendering at the will of Henry V, who ordered the execution of the Bastard of Vaurus and took prisoner the rest of the garrison (f. 45r). A treaty of surrender has survived.[32] Interestingly, and rather atypically, its preamble emphasises the 'will and pleasure of Henry V' but it is clear that the agreement was the product of negotiation between besiegers and besieged.

Yet the correlation between length and terms of surrender does not seem to apply further down the scale. The castle of Mayenne resisted six weeks, at the end of which the garrison secured the most liberal terms anyone could have hoped for: free departure with all personal belongings including horses and armour (f. 57 r). That said, the garrison of the castle of Saint-Ouën-des-Toits which surrendered after eight days only obtained terms that their lives be spared. One person accused of defamation and abusive language was excluded from the composition and executed, presumably at the behest of Fastolf himself who led the operations (f. 60r). (Unfortunately, the chronicle does not give any detail about the content or the target of this abusive language.) The garrison of the castle of Janville, which resisted around fifteen days, had to surrender at the will of Salisbury, who ordered the execution of some and the imprisonment of others (f. 63r), while those in the castle of Laval who surrendered after four days agreed to pay 20,000 *écus* for their safe departure (f. 61r). There are many more examples in Table 5 which undermine any correlation between length and terms, which suggests that other factors came into play, assuming, of course, that the chronicle is accurate.[33]

More fascinatingly perhaps, we can be struck by the wide variety of terms of surrender recorded in the chronicle; this underlines the significance of specific negotiations that led to a surrender as well as highlighting the contractual basis of such surrenders. Looking at the surrender of towns, we can be struck by the chronicle's focus on the fate of soldiers and on conditions for the departure of the garrison. Some additional elements can be noted. At Montaiguillon (1423), for instance, the two French captains had to swear that they would never make war against the king and Regent in the area north of the River Loire (f. 49v). The departing soldiers of Sainte-Suzanne (1425) had to perform a similar oath

---

[31]   We have included the places that surrendered 'in brief time' or 'at once' within the fifteen-day category for calculation purposes. The median of the length of the operations for which a precise number of days is provided is fifteen.

[32]   AN, J 646, no. 21 (2) (2 May 1422), discussed in Ambühl, 'Henry V and the Administration of Justice', esp. pp. 75–8.

[33]   Within the annotations to the English text, readers can find examples of the chronicle's errors in terms of the lengths it claims. For instance, the siege of Melun in 1420 lasted four rather than the seven months claimed by the chronicle. Worcester in his *Itineraries* (p. 359) claimed that the siege lasted thirty-one weeks and three days, which is close to seven months. The siege of Meaux in 1421–22 lasted for about seven months, not the nine claimed by the chronicle.

(f. 57r). The gunners were excluded from the terms of this surrender. Their fate is discussed below. By contrast, all those who departed from the town and castle of La Ferté-Bernard (1426) were allowed to do so without any specific condition, taking along with them goods, horses and equipment (f. 57v). Those who wished to stay under English rule are only rarely mentioned in the chronicle. The exceptions relate to the 1428 campaign of Salisbury in the Loire valley. Beaugency, Meung-sur-Loire and Jargeau are the only examples of surrender for which it is explicitly said that those in the towns who wished to live in the English obedience would be able to do so freely, while enjoying their lives and all their properties, a clause common in contemporary treaties of surrender but generally ignored by the chronicle in favour of military matters (f. 63r).

In some instances, we are given details about a special operation or events taking place during a siege. For example, the account of the siege of Meaux is focused on the denunciation of crimes committed by Vaurus and their just retribution (ff. 45r-v). Matthew Gough's heroic pursuit and capture of the Bastard of la Baume is given as taking place during the siege of Montaiguillon in 1423 and ends with Gough's presentation of his prisoner to the earl of Salisbury before the French town (ff. 49v–50r). The parading of Guillaume Remon, Fastolf's prisoner, before the walls of Compiègne in 1424, and the emotion this provoked amongst those within who decided to surrender the place in order to save the life of their captain, are both given detailed attention (f. 51r and v). Finally, the chronicle describes at length the secret operation led in 1428 by Matthew Gough into the city of Le Mans to effect its recovery and which facilitated its swift recapture (f. 62r).

The list of such anecdotes could easily be expanded. This form of information indicates what we might term 'insider knowledge', a special interest in individuals, and a distinct taste for the sensational. The 'nitty gritty' and daily routine of siege warfare, on the other hand, is conspicuously missing. When the chronicle alludes to such logistical issues as the need for the besiegers to be supplied with food, it is because this problem leads to further complications and more specifically to battle, at La Gueintre (f. 49r) and Rouvray (ff. 64v–65v). When the chronicle referred to a sally at Saint-James-de-Beuvron, it was because that action put an end to the siege laid by the French (f. 58r). Inhabitants of besieged towns are not well represented in the chronicle. They are seen as triggers which initiate an operation, whether begging the English authorities to protect them from the enemy (f. 47v), or betraying their English garrisons and causing the loss of the place, as at Laval (f. 61r) and Le Mans (f. 61v). In all instances, townspeople are simply accessories for either the celebration or the exculpation of the English. In situations of siege, civilians are denied any form of agency; they disappear altogether from the scene.

There is one important component of siege warfare which is underplayed in the chronicle, namely the use of gunpowder. It is handled in a similar way to the food supplies at the siege of Pontorson (1427) where a detachment of Anglo-Burgundian soldiers commissioned to bring back food supplies, ordnance and artillery was intercepted and defeated by a French army near Mont-Saint-Michel (f. 59r). At the siege of Montargis (1428), we can only infer that gunpowder artillery was in use from the mention that the English had to leave the ordnance behind them when they departed (f. 62v). Similarly, we hear that the French of Le Mans left the place in all haste (1428), leaving behind them horses, armour, ordnance and other war equipment (f. 62r). The actual *use* of gunpowder is much more fully reported in other chronicles than in the M 9 chronicle. Take the example of the chronicler

Guillaume de Cousinot's description of Salisbury's incursion into the province of Maine over the summer of 1425,[34] where the earl laid siege to Le Mans 'et y fit assortir grosses bombardes et autres engins pour abbatre les murs de ladicte cite; et de faict, il y en eut une grande partie d'abbatue du costé de la maison de l'évesque' (and ordered big bombards and other engines to be deployed there to bring down the walls of the said city; and indeed, a large segment of the wall was brought down on the side of the bishop's house). Salisbury then besieged Sainte-Suzanne 'et icellui comte y fit assortir et asseoir plusieurs grosses bombardes … et quand il eut esté quelques dix jours, il commença à faire tirer les dits canons et bombardes incessemment jour et nuit, tellement qu'ils abbatirent grand foison des murs de ladite ville' (and this earl ordered the deployment and positioning of several large bombards … and after around ten days, he began to make the said cannons and bombards fire relentlessly day and night so that they brought down a large part of the walls of the said town). Finally, Salisbury came before the castle of Mayenne 'et y fit mener plusieurs grosses bombardes, comme devant les autres places … lequel y fut fort merveilleusement batu de grosses bombardes' (and ordered several big bombards to be brought there, as he had done before the other places … the which [castle] was most amazingly battered by the large bombards). Salisbury's extensive use of cannons and gunpowder is also noted in Jean Chartier's chronicle. He describes the earl as having in his artillery train 'neuf grosses bombardes et plussieurs gros canons et vouglaires' (nine large bombards and several large cannons and fowlers) at the siege of Sainte-Suzanne.[35]

Most importantly, the testimony of these chronicles is supported by administrative records. A detailed receipt of the gunpowder Salisbury employed during the conquest of Maine in 1425 has survived, revealing that 1,000 *livres* of gunpowder were employed to subdue Beaumont, 200 *livres* for La Guierche, 3,000 *livres* for Le Mans, 2,800 *livres* for Sainte-Suzanne and, last but not least, 5,800 *livres* for Mayenne.[36] This reliance on gunpowder seems only to have increased when Salisbury returned to France in 1428. The artillery train which he brought with him, reconstructed from the records of the English Exchequer, included seventy-one cannons which were manned by ninety-six men.[37] Yet, most strikingly, there is not a single mention of English use of guns or gunpowder in the chronicle.

This peculiarity would surely classify the work as a conservative piece of literature on war, which emphasises individuals and deeds of arms while ignoring the growing presence and effect of artillery in the period.[38] We may even suggest reactionism, since it is not that guns and gunners are completely removed from the narrative. They appear at the siege of Sainte-Suzanne in a reference unique to this text. The French gunners, we are told, were excepted from the terms of surrender and were to be handed over to Salisbury to be disposed of at his pleasure. The earl proved to be merciless, ordering all of them to be hanged with a gun stone attached to their feet (f. 57r). Such detail is unique to this chronicle. The symbolism

34   *Pucelle*, p. 228.
35   Chartier, i, p. 45.
36   BL, Add. Ch. 17629 (2 May 1426), receipt for the artillery used by Salisbury during the sieges of the towns of Maine in 1425, printed by Planchenault, 'La conquête du Maine' (1925), pp. 29–31.
37   Spencer, 'The Provision of Artillery for the 1428 Expedition', pp. 179–92.
38   Worcester's *Boke of Noblesse* is also unforthcoming on gunpowder artillery.

of the punishment is compelling: the gunners were killed by their own weapon. The story is likely to have been communicated by Hanson who is known to have served in the garrison at Sainte-Suzanne after its capture and who was most probably present at the siege.[39] We are given no explanation as to why the gunners deserved such a cruel treatment. It cannot be imputed to strong resistance which they had provided, since the place had surrendered after fifteen days. We are given no judgement on this cruel execution: the authors appear to have considered it a fair retribution, possibly because the use of guns and gunpowder carried a sense of unfair play, where inanimate objects took the place of deeds of arms by living individuals. Guns gave men no chance of defending themselves through their customary feats of arms. This was an anonymous, faceless attack.

On the other hand, this cruel execution of gunners is specific to this event, which may suggest that something had happened during the siege which had displeased Salisbury, such as the killing of a friend, a servant or a fellow noble by a cannonball. We can imagine such a situation at the siege of Meaux in 1422 since in the surviving surrender agreement, gunners, along with perjurers and those complicit in the murder of John the Fearless, were excluded from the royal grace extended to other French defenders.[40] The gunners were held personally responsible by Henry V for the death of three English noblemen and were executed.[41] Yet none of this is noted in the M 9 chronicle.

It is striking that the only other mention of gunners in the chronicle relates to Salisbury's own death at Orléans. It is as if the Sainte-Suzanne incident was included by way of anticipation; Salisbury made gunners suffer and denigrated the tools of their trade, but in return he is made to suffer at their hands through a gun stone. In what is a particularly detailed passage for the M 9 chronicle, Salisbury, peering out of one of the upper windows of the tower of Les Tourelles which had been recently captured from the French, was struck on the face by a piece of the metal from the window frame or else by a piece of the gun stone, and died from his wounds eight days later (f. 63v). His death is widely reported in the narrative sources of the period. Many chroniclers highlighted that the identity of the individual who fired the gun remained unknown.[42] According to Perceval de Cagny, no one even knew from where the shot had come.[43] Le Fèvre specified that the person was not actually a gunner by profession but a man who happened to be by a gun and simply fired it.[44] The stress upon the anonymity of the shot in these chronicles may suggest that it was considered blameworthy and unchivalrous. In other words, that anyone would intentionally kill such a valorous and high-esteemed knight in such a manner – a shot from afar, leaving Salisbury defenceless and unable to protect himself – may have been difficult to accept, unless, of course, this was the

---

[39] See Hanson's biography in Chapter 1.

[40] AN, J 646, no. 21 (2). The anonymous chronicler of the Cordeliers (vi, p. 315) also mentions the 'cannoniers' among those excepted from the grace of the king. The English version of the agreement in *Foedera* (x, p. 212) mistook 'governers' for 'gunners' or 'cannoniers' in the original French text. See Ambühl, 'Henry V and the Administration of Justice', pp. 76 and 80.

[41] *Vita et Gesta*, p. 328.

[42] Monstrelet, iv, pp. 299–300; Chartier, i, pp. 63–4. There is nothing on the gunner in Waurin, iii, p. 246.

[43] Cagny, p. 145.

[44] Le Fèvre, *Chronique*, ii, p. 141.

(unquestionable) work of God. Cousinot claims that the earl was hit by the splinter of a cannonball 'by just judgement of God who is omniscient and who treats and rewards men according to their merits'.[45] The belief in divine intervention had spread precisely because the author of the shot could not be identified, according to the *Journal du siège d'Orléans*.[46]

By contrast, in the M 9 chronicle we are told exactly where the shot came from and who fired it. The gun had been targeted at the window of the upper chamber of the tower which was being used by the English to spy on the French. The author of the shot is not named but the chronicle provides ample details about him none the less. It was the son of a master gunner who fired the gun while his father was having dinner. The chronicle exculpates neither the son nor the father. The gun was set for the purpose of firing at the English looking through the window, and the son had acted on the command of his father. The chronicle therefore personalises this nefarious deed, making Salisbury the victim of an impersonal gun as well as the person who fired it.

The story was surely a way of criticising the French for their dishonourable behaviour, but it also suggests a certain moral discomfort about the use of guns. The chronicle therefore does not directly acknowledge any militarily effective use of gunpowder and cites it only to emphasise the culpability that it carries with it. We can see this in both of the examples cited above – the macabre and unique fate of French gunners at Sainte-Suzanne and the deplorable behaviour of the defenders of Orléans. The chronicle thereby shows itself as reactionary, harking back to the age of close-quarters, personal or group, combat and heroism. The use of guns ran contrary to such traditional 'deeds of arms'. Interestingly, the vengeful and pragmatic Fastolf of 1435, who was more in tune with the tactics and technology of his time, recommended that field armies 'shuld have with theme alle manere ordinaunces', including guns and cannons and the relevant staff to handle them.[47]

In this scenario, what, then, did the chronicle make of archers? Surely the arrows they dispatched were equally anonymous? The word 'archer' is only found six times in the chronicle, and only one person is noted as killed by an arrow, William Gascoigne at the siege of Meaux (f. 45r). It is significant that the prominent role that archers played at Agincourt is completely omitted even though a total number is given for men-at-arms (800) and archers (8,500) separately in the English army as it left Harfleur (f. 32v). A proposed figure (ten) for the archers killed at the battle is also given (f. 34r). There is no mention of archers at Cravant or at Verneuil. There are three mentions linked to the narrative of Baugé. The archers were left behind under the command of the Bastard of Clarence whilst the duke of Clarence advanced to meet the enemy since 'he wished that the other nobles and himself should have the honour of the destruction (of the French)' (f. 43r). Even so, archers are not depicted negatively in this narrative; in the Bastard of Clarence's attempt to rescue the duke, we are told that when the French heard that the archers were approaching, 'they did not dare risk a battle and in great haste retreated'. The potential importance of English archers at Fastolf's victory at Rouvray is mentioned but only by reference to Fastolf's skilfully protecting them behind stakes (f. 65v).

---

[45] 'ledit comte … fut, par juste jugement de Dieu qui tout connoist et qui traite et guerdonne les hommes selon leurs merites féry de l'esclat d'une pierre de canon' (*Pucelle*, p. 264).

[46] *Journal du siège*, pp. 9–10.

[47] *L&P*, II, ii, p. 581.

Intriguingly, the only mentions of the impact of ranged weapons are linked to French, not English, action. When the French recovered Le Mans by stealth in 1428, we hear that 'more than half the English were wounded or killed by the "trait" of the French' (f. 61r), this term being used in the period to describe cross-bow bolts as well as longbow arrows. Earlier, it is noted that Sir William Gascoigne was killed by 'un trait' at the siege of Meaux (f. 45r). Such references emphasised the danger and potency of bows of any kind. But there is also a sense of condemnation for causing the death – anonymously and at a distance – of a man worthy of honour in this celebration of 'deeds of arms'. In fact, Gascoigne is listed twice amongst the dead, the second time with mention of his cause of demise. The focus, then, is on the individual and his actions, but the authors were not interested in the hardware used. Further illustrating this point, 'horses and armour' appear on several occasions as items that departing French garrisons are authorised to take away with them (ff. 51v, 55v, 56v, 57r, 57v, 58v, 59v) or not (f. 59v). There is no mention in the chronicle of any other weapons. The direct reference to an 'eschelleur' (wall-scaler) (f. 60r) stands therefore as another example of a focus on the skill of an individual, not on his equipment.

NUMBERS AND ORGANISATION

Numbers are a perennial problem in chronicles especially when it comes to military matters. In theory, we might expect a chronicle written by soldiers to put forward more realistic numbers, but is this the case? The answer to this question is necessarily mixed, as is evident from Table 6 below.

Some ridiculously high figures for the French are put forward, most notably for the battles of Agincourt and Verneuil but also, quite strangely, for the French assault on Saint-James-de-Beuvron. Such numbers were for effect, to emphasise that the French were strong but the English defeated them none the less. For the reign of Henry V, numbers are only given for the 1415 campaign. Save for the size of the English army which marched from Harfleur – 800 lances and 8,500 archers, totals which are remarkably close to the numbers and composition deduced from the Exchequer records[48] – the other figures, all for the French, are exaggerated. This is not only noticeable in the 150,000 given for the French at Agincourt, a figure also found in Monstrelet's account,[49] but also in the 20,000 for the French who threatened to reopen the fight. No other chronicle advances such a high number for this action; indeed, most make no attempt to provide a number at all. It is possible that such a high number was chosen in order to justify Henry V's order to kill the prisoners, which, as the chronicle goes on to say, 'was the reason why so many nobles died'.

The contrast between the lack of figures put forward for the 1415–22 period and the frequent mention of numbers in the reign of Henry VI is striking. It provides yet another difference between how the two periods are handled, consonant with the idea that the narrative for Henry V's reign derived from an existing work, probably by Basset. The more granulated figures for the 1422–29 period are suggestive of personalised input, presumably by Hanson and even by Fastolf himself. Such potential involvement of actual participants does not remove the sense of exaggeration in

---

[48]   Curry, *Agincourt. A New History*, pp. 70–1.
[49]   'Cent cinquante mille de chevaucheurs' (Monstrelet, iii, p. 101).

French numbers. The example of the attack on Saint-James-de-Beuvron with an alleged 60–80,000 is the most extreme example, but we can note also the supposed 9,000 French and Scottish dead at the battle of Verneuil. The authors were wholly determined to emphasise English triumph against a powerful enemy.

Table 6. Numbers of troops given in the M 9 chronicle

March to Agincourt	English	800 + 8,500	f. 32r
French army at Somme 1415	French	50,000	f. 32v
French army at Agincourt	French	150,000	f. 32v
Dead and prisoners at Agincourt	French	2,400	f. 33v
French rallying at Agincourt	French	20,000	f. 34r
Cravant siege	French/Scottish	20,000	f. 48r
Cravant battle	English/Burgundian	15,000	f. 48v
John de la Pole action	English	2,000	f. 50r
French attack on John de la Pole	French	6,000	f. 50v
Verneuil	French	40,000	f. 53v
Verneuil	English	10,000	f. 54r
Verneuil dead	French/Scottish	9,000	f. 54v
First advance into Maine	English	2,000	f. 55v
Subsequent advance to Loire	English	1,500	f. 56r
Siege of Le Mans	English	10,000	f. 56v
Activity during siege of Fastolf and Willoughby	English	2,000	f. 57v
Garrison of Saint-James-de-Beuvron	English	500	f. 58r
Siege of Saint-James-de-Beuvron	French	60-80,000	f. 58r
Army from England under Warwick	English	6,000	f. 58r
Pontorson seized by Bretons	French	1,000	f. 58v
Siege of Pontorson	English	7,000	f. 58v
Victual search during siege of Pontorson	English/Normans	3,000	f. 59r
Encounter during siege; French dead	French	1,000	f. 59r
Siege of Malicorne	French	3,000	f. 59v
Attack by Hanson etc.	English	20–30	f. 60r
Siege of La Gravelle	English	20,000	f. 60r
French take Le Mans	French	6,000	f. 61r
English recovery of Le Mans	English	700	f. 61v
Prisoners at Le Mans	French	300–400	f. 61v
Siege of Montargis	English	6,000	f. 62v

Prisoners taken by French during siege	English	2,000	f. 62v
Army from England under Salisbury	English	7,000	f. 63r
Fastolf and Rempston force searching victuals (Rouvray)	English	1,500	f. 64v
French at Rouvray	French	9–10,000	f. 64v

As for English numbers, we also see exaggeration. The paid troops crossing in the expeditionary armies under Warwick in 1426 and Salisbury in 1428 can be calculated from Exchequer records as numbering 800 and 2,699 soldiers respectively as opposed to the 6,000 and 7,000 claimed in the chronicle.[50] The discrepancy is high, even if we allow for servants, grooms and others who crossed with such armies. Similarly, figures given by the chronicle for field operations in Normandy and Maine are too high, but not ridiculously so, in comparison with the level of exaggeration of French numbers. The siege of Pontorson can be shown from financial records to have involved over 2,400 troops,[51] boosted by some of the army from England under Warwick, but that still leaves the total lower than the 7,000 suggested by the chronicle.

Overall, however, it does not seem that our authors, despite their military experience and writing for a veteran, were consistently well informed on actual army sizes, or, if they were so informed, they chose to exaggerate. The chronicle's exaggerations of English numbers served to emphasise the consistently high level of commitment to the war. Where direct personal experience influenced the narrative, as in the case of Hanson's action at Saint-Laurent-des-Mortiers, the numbers (20–30) are realistic (f. 60r). Hanson's inside knowledge on the number of men from the garrison of Sainte-Suzanne involved in the action against Ramefort was clearly awaited when the chronicle was being written: we can see that a blank space was left to insert this information on f. 59r. Similarly, the first advance into Maine led by Sir John Fastolf, Sir John Montgomery and Thomas, lord Scales in 1424 involved at least 800 paid troops, the number doubling under Salisbury's command at the end of the year.[52] Such numbers are lower than the 2,000 mentioned in the chronicle (f. 55v) but that figure does not show the usual lack of realism to which chroniclers of the period were prone. Indeed, with additional troops recruited by the earl of Salisbury in Normandy through a *semonce des nobles*, the discrepancy may be even less marked.

The wording of the chronicle betrays other forms of inside knowledge. The creation of knights by Henry V at a proposed but then aborted crossing of the Somme (f. 32v) is unique to this chronicle, but wholly credible; dubbings before expected actions (and the crossing of rivers was a potentially dangerous affair) were relatively common.[53] The calling out of garrison detachments as a means of creating field armies, well evidenced in the financial records,[54] is also noted on several occasions. For his incursion into Anjou in 1421, for instance, Clarence is described as assembling troops from all the garrisons of Normandy at Bernay

---

50 Ratcliffe, 'Military Expenditure', pp. 21, 28.
51 BNF, Fr. 26049/698.
52 BNF, Fr. 4485 passim; BNF, Fr. 4491 f. 26v.
53 *Soldier in Later Medieval England*, pp. 70–1.
54 Curry, 'Organisation of Field Armies', pp. 207–33.

(f. 42r). Sir John de la Pole called out 'all the garrisons of the lower march' (of Normandy) in the same way two years later (f. 50r). Fastolf assembled men from the garrisons of the area as well as other men of his retinue for sieges in Maine in 1427 (f. 59v), and for the escort of victuals in 1429, which culminated in the battle of Rouvray. Here, the provost of Paris, Simon Morhier, led the *cinquantaine* of the city (a civilian crossbow company) and members of the household of the duke of Bedford to join with Fastolf and Rempston (f. 64v). A combination of English and Norman troops is also noted under Bedford in 1424 (f. 53v) and in the company sent out in search of victuals during the siege of Pontorson (f. 59r), with English, Burgundians and Picards being noted in troops for the siege of Guise (f. 55r). Other details reveal true military insights based on experience. The narrative on the siege of Ivry and battle of Verneuil indicates how major battles were pre-arranged by mutual consent (f. 54r). It is also in small coincidental remarks that we see evidence of practical understanding to be expected of military men, such as the time of day, the foggy conditions for the French recovery of Compiègne (f. 51v), which may have the additional value of offering excuses for English failure, and the icy conditions at Rouvray (f. 64v).

BRAVERY AND COWARDICE

M 9 is a chronicle about 'men of name' – nobles, knights, and armigerous gentry. War is shown through the prism of the ideals of this elite, which are commonly associated with 'chivalry'.[55] The chronicle places great emphasis on honour and moral values in the conduct of war. The English are exemplary in this respect, their impeccable behaviour being further emphasised by the moral failures of the French and the Scots.

The English are almost always brave as well as powerful. In a telling passage, the English garrison of Saint-James-de-Beuvron in 1426 faced a Breton army of (allegedly) 60–80,000 men which inflicted on the English 'many hard and cruel assaults', but the English defended themselves 'valiantly like lions' (f. 58r). Straight after this assault, the English sallied out and attacked the Breton camp. The Bretons were so frightened that, 'shamefully and in cowardly manner', they left the siege, leaving behind them food supplies and artillery. More than 4,000 Bretons on that occasion were either taken prisoner or killed, or so the chronicle claims.

The courage displayed by the English is heightened by the shame and coward-ice, as well as the fearfulness, of the French. On multiple occasions we read in the chronicle that the French did not dare to wait for the English and face them (f. 44r). For instance, they did not dare to challenge the Bastard of Clarence in the aftermath of Baugé. This helps to diminish the earlier French battle victory, alongside the claim that it had only been achieved through the treason of a foreign individual. The French were not brave enough to challenge Henry V near Orléans in the follow-ing summer (f. 44v), and they did not dare to face the joint forces of the dukes of Burgundy and Bedford at the siege of Cosne in 1422 (f. 46v). Similarly, they did not

---

[55]   For a discussion of the meaning and evolution of chivalry, see Kaeuper, *Medieval Chivalry*. In outlining the characteristics expected of knights, Craig Taylor (*Chivalry and the Ideals of Knighthood*, pp. 132–7) dedicated a long chapter to 'courage', a virtue brought to the fore in chivalric literature.

dare to engage Bedford at the siege of Ivry: on this occasion, they were intimidated by the presence of Bedford himself (f. 53v), as they had been by that of Henry V in 1421. Finally, the French who began raiding in Maine as a tactical manoeuvre to force Warwick to raise the siege of Pontorson are described as returning home because they could see that this manoeuvre did not work, and that the English were assembling an army to face them which they did not dare to wait for (f. 59v).

Such negative characterisation of the French is all the more striking because the English never lack daring. As we have seen, they seek danger by being battle-seeking. Through individual acts of bravery such as that of Matthew Gough at Montaiguillon, they face all challenges put their way (ff. 49v–50r). When the French do find the courage to fight the English, it is generally to their loss. The French are frequently portrayed as being overwhelmed by the power of the English and reduced to flight. The words 'flight', 'to flee' and 'fled' are used on at least fifteen occasions, with significant examples at *le park l'evesque* (f. 46r), Cravant (f. 49r), Courmenant (f. 55v), Saint-James-de-Beuvron (f. 58r), Avranches (f. 58v), La Gueintre (f. 59r), Le Mans (f. 62r), Les Tourelles at Orléans (f. 63v) and Rouvray (f. 65v). As if such mentions did not carry enough shame, both the flights at Saint-James-de-Beuvron and at Rouvray are morally condemned in the chronicle. We cannot help but be struck by how commonplace references to flights are. They are also ascribed to individuals such as Guillaume de la Baume (f. 49v), and even the Englishman John de la Pole (f. 51r). Such efforts at shaming gain further significance given the extent to which Fastolf's own reputation suffered from accusations of being a 'chevalier fuitif' on the field of Patay in 1429.[56]

The English are not infallible but when they fail there are always mitigating circumstances, except for John de la Pole, who, as we saw in the previous chapter and in the example just cited, is the subject of recurrent criticism. In a handful of other cases, the chronicle places the responsibility for failure on the perfidy of traitors, shifting the blame away from English captains. The most striking example is that of André Lombard at Baugé but we also read that the town of Laval (f. 61r) and the city of Le Mans (f. 61v) were lost because of the treason of, respectively, some citizens and a miller. The mention of this act of treason at Laval is rather awkwardly inserted in the narrative as if Matthew Gough, and the authors of the chronicle, had a pressing need for exculpation for any negligence.

When practised by the English, trickery and guile are deemed worthy of praise. Honorat Bovet, the author of the late fourteenth-century treatise *The Tree of Battles*, claimed that 'according to God and the scriptures, I may conquer my enemy by craft or fraud without sin, once the war has been ordained and declared and ordered between him and me, and I have given him defiance'.[57] As we have seen, the chronicle adopts a similar line, showing no concern about Christopher Hanson's use of trickery to seize the castle of Saint-Laurent-des-Mortiers during mass (f. 60r). This trickery is conceived as fair play and, furthermore, it is an act for which Hanson is credited. Our chronicle is ambiguous on the issue of guile,

---

[56]   The quote is taken from a lawsuit. These would have been the words used by Thomas Overton and which Fastolf claims in 1435 to see as 'la plus [?grant] charge qu'on puist dire d'un chevalier' (*English Suits*, p. 264).

[57]   Bovet, *The Tree of Battles*, p. 154 sq. Bovet's reflection on deceit is discussed in Whetham, *Just Wars and Moral Victories*, pp. 58–60.

trickery and treason. It unreservedly condemns as traitors those individuals who deceived the English, causing loss at Baugé, Laval or Le Mans. On the other hand, when a Gascon of the English party sold the town of Alençon to French partisans of Charles VII but then betrayed the latter by allowing Fastolf to carry out an ambush, the authors do not describe his action as treason nor do they question the fairness of the deed of arms (f. 57v). What we detect here, therefore, is pragmatism and political partisanship in the approach to ethics in war.

OATH TAKING AND OATH BREAKING

The M 9 chronicle puts distinctive stress upon individual oaths and specifically upon the failure of French prisoners to observe their parole. This point is epitomised by Olivier de Mauny's oath-breaking in 1422, information which is unique to the chronicle and which gives rise to its only utilisation of direct speech – words supposedly uttered by Henry V which were aimed at showing the king in a very good light (f. 46r):

> Old man, you had made an oath and promise to us that you would never make war against us and our subjects. You are a long-established knight and ought to have kept your promise. Because you have never before done anything like this in terms of falsehood and breaking your word, we do not crave your death but give you life and a trip to England to learn to speak English.

The promise not to re-arm against Henry V that Mauny is described as having given at the surrender of Falaise in 1418 was not common practice. Prisoners might be obliged not to re-arm against their masters or any of their masters' party, but once their ransom was paid, they were usually released from any form of obligation and could do as they pleased.[58] Terms of surrender of towns and castles occasionally included restrictions on the ability of the garrison to continue fighting but these are rare and do not seem to appear in any chronicle.[59]

Even if the meeting did not take place at Meaux between Henry V and Mauny as the chronicle describes and the king's words were simply invented, the explanation given for the fall of Mauny is supported by other evidence. All accounts agree that Olivier de Mauny was a leader of Franco-Breton troops and that he was captured on the battlefield at an engagement at *le park l'evesque* near Avranches. But there are divergences in dating. Chartier and Cousinot date the engagement to 1425 whilst in the M 9 chronicle it is made contemporaneous with the siege of Meaux in 1422 (f. 45v).[60] The person in question was Olivier de Mauny, lord of Lignières and Lesnen, who should not be confused with his two homonyms.[61] He was undoubtedly captain of the castle of Falaise at its surrender on 16 February 1418 and remained a prisoner of Henry V thereafter until he had satisfactorily repaired the walls of the castle, which task was completed by 28 June of the same

---

[58] Keen, *The Laws of War*, p. 169.
[59] Restrictions on re-armament may occasionally be included in terms of surrender during the French civil war. See, for instance, AN, JJ 166, no. 28 (12 February 1412); ACO, B 11879 (18 July 1417).
[60] Chartier, i, pp. 48–9; *Pucelle*, p. 213.
[61] See the English translation of the chronicle, note 199.

year.[62] One Olivier de Mauny – arguably the same person – appears in administrative records as a prisoner of Henry V on 1 May 1422 when the king rewarded one Robert Passage with a life grant for having captured him.[63] Henry was at this point at the siege of Meaux, the action during which the M 9 chronicle places Mauny's capture. There is also evidence that an Olivier de Mauny had crossed the Channel to England by the end of July 1422 together with other prisoners of Meaux.[64] These two pieces of evidence support the account in the chronicle of Mauny's capture and transfer to England. He died there, according to the chronicle.[65] This no doubt explains why we would find no trace of him in France later. Whilst this evidence cannot confirm Henry V's words, it suggests at least that we need to revise the chronology of the battle near Avranches, preferring the testimony of the M 9 chronicle over that of Chartier or Cousinot.

The M 9 chronicle mentions two similar oaths, not attested elsewhere, which were taken by French captains as part of terms of surrender. At the surrender of Sainte-Suzanne in 1425, Ambroise de Loré agreed not to wage war against the English for a whole year (f. 57r).[66] From the perspective of the chronicle, de Loré did not break his oath since he is mentioned as back in action only at the battle of Rouvray in 1429 (f. 65r).[67] At the surrender of Montaiguillon in 1423, Prégent de Coëtivy and Tugdual de Kermoysan dit 'le Bourgeois' promised never to fight again against the king and the Regent beyond the River Loire (f. 49v). Although the siege and capture of Montaiguillon is more fully recorded in other chronicles, this stricture remains specific to the M 9 chronicle.[68] Yet the chronicle records their presence on the battlefield of Rouvray in 1429 without comment (f. 65r), failing to recall the promise made earlier. Another mention of oaths is found in the wake of Henry V's conquests in the Ile-de-France in August 1422, where we are told that all the departing French garrisons crossed the Loire as they had promised (f. 46r). Such promises were common in surrender treaties; departing garrisons were often given safe-conducts which named a specified destination.[69] Rarely, however, do chroniclers interest themselves in such oaths. That the M 9 chronicle does so emphasises its concern with the honourable conduct of the military elite including the enemy.

In this context, it is not surprising that the chronicle is unforgiving about the duplicity of Guy Malet, lord of Graville, and of Arthur of Brittany, count of Richemont. Malet gave an oath of allegiance to the king and the Regent following the surrender of Meulan (f. 47r), an oath also noted by Monstrelet.[70] He was not the only person to give his oath of allegiance in these circumstances. A letter

---

[62] C 64/8 m. 2, 13; Hardy, pp. 308–12; C 64/9 m. 22, DKR 41, p. 692. He was still a prisoner of the king in April.

[63] CPR 1416–22, p. 437.

[64] Devon, *Issues of the Exchequer*, p. 375, under 29 July 1422, named as 'Olivier Mavne'.

[65] Hall (1809), p. 109, adds that he was buried in the White Friars in London.

[66] Cousinot, who gives a detailed account of this siege, makes no mention of this oath (*Pucelle*, p. 227).

[67] But earlier, in 1427, in Chartier, i, pp. 51–3, and *Pucelle*, pp. 242–3.

[68] *Pucelle* (p. 195) gives no details on the composition. According to Monstrelet (iv, p. 155), the defenders paid dearly to save their lives.

[69] See, for instance, the treaties for the surrender of Montagu, Braine and Soupir, La Ferté-Millon (May 1422) and Grancey (August 1434) in AN, JJ 172/61, J 1039/2; ACO, B 11880.

[70] Monstrelet, iv, p. 142.

of remission has survived which reveals that Geoffroy d'Alaines did so too and subsequently broke his word just like Malet.[71] What is unique to the M 9 chronicle is the explicit statement on the duplicity of Malet who fought on the French side at Verneuil and perished on the battlefield (f. 54r).[72]

Richemont's case is worth a detailed scrutiny not least as he is the second most frequently mentioned Frenchman in the whole chronicle. He is first mentioned as a prisoner taken at Agincourt (f. 33r). His subsequent captivity in England is well documented in financial records. He is next mentioned as succeeding the duke of Gloucester as captain of Ivry-la-Chaussée in Normandy (f. 39v). This handover, the chronicle claims, accompanied Henry V's grant to Richemont of the *comté* of Ivry in Normandy which can be dated through an entry in the Norman rolls to 10 January 1421.[73] The grant was made during the siege of Melun where Richemont's presence is recorded in the chronicle within the list of English and Burgundian lords who besieged the town (f. 40v). He is there called 'comte d'Ivry' even though the grant did not occur until after this service but, as we have seen, the chronicle commonly calls men by their later titles. He is similarly described as 'comte d'Ivry' at the siege of Meaux (f. 44v).

On 13 April 1423 a triple alliance was sealed at Amiens between the duke of Bedford, the duke of Burgundy and Richemont on behalf of his brother, the duke of Brittany, which also involved the marriage of Burgundy's sisters, Anne and Margaret, to Bedford and Richemont. Yet whilst the negotiations for the marriage of Bedford are mentioned in the chronicle, as also his wedding to Anne in Troyes (ff. 47r, 50r), there is no indication in its narrative that Richemont was involved or present at all in any of these negotiations or events. Rather, in the same section as the negotiations for Bedford's marriage are given, we read that Richemont, 'who had been given the county of Ivry, broke his faith and oath and went off secretly to Flanders and there joined with the enemy of the king and of the regent' (f. 47r).[74]

The chronicle is being careless with the truth. Richemont's rupture with the English and his change of allegiance did not occur until the middle of 1424 or even later in that year.[75] In 1423 he was a full and eager participant in the triple alliance and in the extra bond to Bedford and Duke Philip which marriage to Margaret of Burgundy had brought. As we can see, the chronicle is keen to anticipate Richemont's treachery. Mention of the grant to him of the county of Ivry at this same point is intended to heighten the outrage of his defection.[76] This change of allegiance, the chronicle continues, had an immediate effect on the garrison of the castle of Ivry. As soon as they heard of his volte-face they decided to hold the place against the king and the Regent. They introduced Gérard de la Pallière into the fortress together with

---

[71] AN, JJ 173/42 (12 December 1424).
[72] The death at Verneuil of the 'seigneur de Graville *ancien*', thereby avoiding potential confusion with his son, Jean Malet, is also noted by Monstrelet (iv, p. 195).
[73] The grant also included Aumale, Garentières and Berenguierville (C 64/14 m. 2 additional, DKR 42, p. 388).
[74] Monstrelet (iv, p. 175) and Waurin (ii, pp. 213–14) also describe this volte-face as a shock that was all the more brutal since the duke of Brittany had just renewed his oath and alliance with Burgundy and Bedford.
[75] Cosneau, pp. 79–80; Contamine, *Charles VII*, p. 118.
[76] Henry VI's grant of the *comté* of Ivry to John, earl of Huntingdon, on 12 July 1427 accused Richemont of 'rebellion, disobedience and lèse majesty' (Cosneau, pp. 529–30).

a great number of enemies who caused much trouble to the innocent subjects of the English king (f. 47v): Richemont's defection is therefore portrayed as causing damage to civilians as much as his previous companions-in-arms.

In addition to the deliberate omission of Richemont's involvement in the alliance of 1423, the chronicle's version of events at Ivry is undermined by other surviving sources. A letter of remission issued on 20 March 1424 to the captain of Ivry, an esquire called 'Pierre Glé', suggests that the castle had been seized 'par eschielle et faulte de guet' by La Pallière at some point in 1423,[77] well before Richemont's defection to the French. We can see, therefore, that the M 9 chronicle has constructed a narrative of Richemont's betrayal which revolves around Ivry and twists the facts in the process. The chronicle, writing retrospectively, antedates his defection with the intent of blaming it for the treasonable loss of Ivry to the French. This is directly linked in due course to the siege of Ivry (f. 51v) and ultimately to the need for the English to face the French in battle at Verneuil (ff. 54r-v). The causal chain which links these events together is well signposted even if implicit. This important example supports the idea that the chronicle interprets the course of the war through individual moral standards even, as here, to the point of rewriting it. We can also see how the narrative is brought to its inevitable culmination in victory at Verneuil as final retribution for Richemont's defection, creating again a particular emphasis on the importance of oaths and loyalties.

A moral perspective is also seen in two cases of failure to observe an oath to surrender a place on a fixed date: the castles of Saint-Pierre-sur-Orthe and Saint-Thomas-de-Courceriers (f. 56r) and La Gravelle (f. 60v). On both occasions, French misbehaviour resulted in their hostages being executed by the English. The beheading of the hostages of the first two fortresses is unique to this chronicle but the execution of hostages at La Gravelle is also noted by Chartier.[78] On both occasions, the M 9 chronicle places the blame on the French since they had no grounds for refusing to surrender and therefore were guilty of simply abandoning their hostages.[79]

CONCLUSION

Individual deeds of arms form an important dimension of the M 9 chronicle. Yet what is at least as distinctive and defining a trait of its portrayal of war is its principled and moralistic tone which is boosted by a very strong nationalistic flavour. In other words, we find both good and bad behaviour but the former is almost invariably English while the latter is inevitably French. In this context we can emphasise again that only the French are given guns!

The worth of individuals – and indeed groups of combatants – is measured by the yardstick of their courage and their capacity to expose themselves to danger, especially in battles, but it is also measured by their moral integrity and their capacity to keep their word. The chronicle also describes the 'normal' way to

---

[77]   AN, JJ 172/442.

[78]   Chartier, i, p. 56.

[79]   The practice of 'conditional respite' and hostage taking in such circumstances was widespread. Evidence shows that this system based on mutual trust worked well and smoothly. That said, failure to abide by the terms of the respite and the resulting execution of hostages were rare (Kosto, *Hostages in the Middle Ages*, pp. 99–110; Ambühl, 'Hostages and the Laws of War', pp. 188–205).

seize a stronghold which is through siege and surrender, acts which display both courage and mercy. It praises cunning and trickery when these are practised by the English but abhors acts of treason and subterfuge, as well as those men, such as Richemont, who have defected from the true cause.

The chronicle is not interested in the practical aspects of war. Strategy, tactics, logistics are systematically relegated to the background and emerge from it only when they explain the origins of a battle or when they feed a good story about an individual feat of arms. There is nothing on the reality of life on campaign. At one level, we might consider it disappointing that a chronicle by soldiers does not offer more practical insights and the 'nitty gritty' of warfare which would have given it a distinctive nature. After all, the combination of praise of individuals and vagueness around actual events is not at all unique to the M 9 chronicle but a commonplace of contemporary chronicles. There is one area, however, where the chronicle stands out from other writings of the period – its omission of the role of artillery and gunpowder. It is not simply that the chronicle overlooks the role of artillery: it despises it. It manifests its contempt in the impassioned account of the deliberate hanging of gunners as well as the denunciation of those who fired the gun which killed Salisbury at Orléans. These are unique inclusions. We can interpret this in two different ways. It may reflect the point of view of a soldier who fears cannons and dislikes the possibility of skilled 'chivalric' combatants becoming anonymous 'cannon fodder'. Or else, we can see here the reactionary nature of the chronicle, which praises the old ways of war and manifests a disdain for the new ways of gunpowder weapons. We should also note that archers are given little place in the chronicle despite the fact that they formed the largest part of the armies of the time, which those writing the chronicle knew well. The chronicle takes refuge in the old ideals of the aristocratic, chivalric, class. The distinct stress upon individual oaths further emphasises this tendency.

That said, the chronicle does not celebrate the whole of chivalry. Rowe suggested that the chronicle was 'marked by a genuine respect for the enemy'.[80] Our closer reading of the whole text indicates that this is not a valid judgement. Rowe placed emphasis on the willingness of the authors to criticise the English but in fact only Sir John de la Pole is ever really taken to task. The M 9 chronicle celebrates only the English. The French (and Scots) are named – often in some detail, and even erroneously, to raise the stakes which the English faced – and denigrated in order to show the English in the best possible light. They are simply an English foil. There is no chivalric honouring of the enemy at all. Interestingly, at Montargis where the French were able to raise the English siege, very few names of the victorious army are provided (f. 62v).

As the incipit tell us, the M 9 chronicle has the same professed aim of recording 'deeds of arms' that we find in Froissart's *Chroniques*. On the face of it, therefore, this apparently shared aim situates the chronicle within the chivalric genre, if such a genre exists. But, reading the incipit carefully, the work's purpose is to record the deeds of arms relating to the conquest of northern France *by the English*. It does not celebrate deeds of arms of all warriors. The chronicle was written for Sir John Fastolf and indeed, as we have seen in Chapter 2, some emphasis is placed on the deeds of the English knight. For instance, the engagement at Rouvray is portrayed

---

[80]   Rowe, p. 513.

as an individual deed of arms performed by Fastolf which was worth emphasising and elaborating by the inclusion of some rare tactical detail. It is indicative here that only Fastolf and Sir Thomas Rempston are mentioned by name, and the *prévôt* of Paris by his office, on the English side, whereas for the French and Scottish forty-five participants are named.

Yet, the chronicle is clearly not a chivalric biography like that of Marshal Bouci-caut, for instance. Fastolf has to share the spotlight with others, indeed a multitude of others. It is perhaps here that we come closest to the idea of a soldiers' chronicle, reflecting the composite nature and the multiple authorship of this work. Whilst individual prowess is noted, it is the collective effort of the English which predomi-nates, and which it portrays as being brought to its highest level of achievement by the good command of Henry V, Bedford, Salisbury, and others, including Fastolf himself. Furthermore, the English are well organised and well disciplined, and have a single united purpose which they fulfil. We might also see the influence of the undoubted English bureaucratic approach to military organisation through the chronicle's comprehensiveness when it comes to naming names. The conquest is narrated by means of mention of appointments to captaincies in places which were captured. No deeds in arms need to be attached to the appointment; the holding of the office is itself an expression of military success.

Such considerations explain the desire to include as many names as possible of participants. In this scenario, French names are also given in detail to emphasise the very level of achievement of the English soldiery in defeating this obvious French might of what is sometimes called – though not in the M 9 chronicle – the flower of 'chevalerie'. The naming of individuals on both sides who participated is therefore significant. The M 9 chronicle is orientated towards named individuals, both as victors and defeated, since the listing of high status French and Scottish individuals who were overcome added to the lustre of those who won. It also emphasises the dangers and challenges to which English soldiers had been exposed and yet over which they had triumphed by dint of their own personal bravery and involvement (and not through the 'distance' weapons, gunpowder or otherwise, which they had at their disposal). Where there had been setbacks, as in the case of Baugé – which was the result of a treacherous foreign individual – or the failings of John de la Pole, these were soon mitigated.

Above all, therefore, the chronicle is an expression of national pride, the pride of English soldiers (and on occasion a few loyal allies) who had participated in a remarkable period of English success. The chronicle was intended to cover the whole period of English presence in France from 1415 to 1450, as is indicated by the incipit and also by the evidence of Worcester's collection of similarly structured information covering later years. The years which it actually covers saw almost untrammelled English success, which makes possible the continuously positive stance of the text.

We can feel some regret, therefore, that the text ends just before the raising of the siege of Orléans and the reversals in English fortunes which that event initiated. Would that we could have known how a 'soldiers' chronicle' would have coped with the years of defeat, and indeed with Fastolf's apparent fall from grace after Patay. It is fair to say that whilst he continued in service in France until 1438, his glory days were over by 1429; Rouvray was the summit of his career. We must remember that the M 9 chronicle was not, as far as we can see, for public consump-tion but for a specific individual. We could even suspect that in Sir John Fastolf's last illness, the authors may have shrunk back from continuing the text, preferring to leave the knight with last memories of his success. We can only speculate that, had the chronicle been completed to cover the entire thirty-five years of English France, as Worcester's incipit suggests was the intention, we would have found within it the blame culture to which Sir John, ably aided by his secretary William Worcester, was prone in the early 1450s.

4

French in fifteenth-century England: what linguistic choices?

Richard Ingham

The M 9 chronicle is an intriguing text, not least because it was written in French for an English recipient at a time when the routine use of French among England's literate population was dying out. In this contribution to the present volume, I explore what options were available to someone wishing to write a French text in England in the fifteenth century, and examine the linguistic features of the M 9 chronicle against that background. It will be shown how the varieties of French existing in that period differed from each other, reviewing the main features of the late medieval French language as used on the continent,[1] and comparing them with those of the insular variety of French traditionally known as Anglo-Norman.

The later years of Anglo-Norman have benefited from greatly increased research attention since the millennium.[2] A rough consensus has emerged that it remained 'a perfectly serviceable variety of medieval French',[3] though a highly distinctive one in various linguistic respects, until its demise in the fifteenth century. In conventional textbook presentations, continental French, sometimes labelled 'Parisian', is taken as representing a prestige norm from which the French of England deviated in various ways.[4] As will be seen, continental French was far from being uniform, but in any event by the thirteenth century at the latest Anglo-Norman was clearly idiosyncratic in its spelling and grammar.[5] When it finally died out is debatable: records were still being kept in this form by some administrators in the 1420s and occasionally even beyond. However, it is safe to say that outside

---

[1]   Marchello-Nizia, *La langue française*; Buridant, *Grammaire nouvelle*.
[2]   See, for instance, Rothwell, 'English and French in England after 1362'; Trotter, 'Not as Eccentric as It Looks'; Ingham (ed.), *The Anglo-Norman Language and Its Contexts*; Wogan-Browne et al. (eds), *The French of England*; Ingham, 'The Transmission of Anglo-Norman'; Fenster and Collette (eds), *French in Medieval England*.
[3]   Trotter, 'Not as Eccentric as It Looks', p. 47.
[4]   See Price, 'Anglo-Norman'; and Kibbee, *For to Speke Frenche Trewely*.
[5]   Short, *Manual of Anglo-Norman*.

the law courts little use was still being made of insular French as a distinct variety by the 1450s, when the M 9 chronicle was composed.

The M 9 chronicle is in fact 'the only known example of a chronicle of the fifteenth-century phase of the [Hundred Years] war written in England in French'.[6] Its singularity in that respect was explained by McFarlane as due to the fact that the scribe responsible for composing the chronicle, Luket Nantron, was a Frenchman. In this current volume, an argument has been made for the various contributions of all those involved: Basset, Hanson and Worcester. Creating the work, including the provision of its content, would thus have been a team effort. On that basis, it is natural to wonder in what language the team members operated, and whether their linguistically mixed origin had any influence on the wording of the text. In this study, this issue is addressed first by presenting the distinctive characteristics of medieval varieties of continental and insular French, the latter to be referred to henceforth as A-N. The M 9 chronicle text will then be discussed in terms of how far it adheres to the features of the Central variety of continental French, the one used by scribes in the Île-de-France region around Paris. Orthographic and grammatical traits will mainly be discussed, as these have been most studied in the research literature, but the chapter concludes with some observations on lexis and phraseology, as further ways of judging how native-like the French in the M 9 chronicle should be considered.

INDICATIONS OF NON-NATIVE AUTHORSHIP?

Authorship of the earliest composed part of the text is attributed to Peter Basset, an English native speaker known to have spent twenty years in service in Normandy. Of the two other contributors mentioned, Luket Nantron is said to have been born in Paris, while Christopher Hanson can be assumed to have acquired some considerable knowledge of French during the twenty-five years he is attested as having been in military service in France. In one way or another, then, an authorial cluster of three non-native speakers and a native speaker had some input into the M 9 chronicle, leading to the possibility that the language of the text may have been influenced by non-native usage on the part of some of them. Some deviation from mainstream continental usage in the text would then not be surprising, depending on the proficiency of the respective non-native speakers, and the role they would have played in creating the text. That said, it is not impossible for highly proficient non-native speakers to create texts where the language employed is indistinguishable from native speaker use, especially if they take care over their work. This chronicle might be one such text, so that a study of its linguistic features would provide no clues as to authorial contributions.

We follow the reasonable assumption that the text was essentially scribed by Nantron. However, there are a certain number of French-language emendations to it in the hand of William Worcester. Worcester was an Oxford-educated scholar not known to have spent time in France, though he appears to have had a good reading knowledge of French.[7] In some half-dozen places, Worcester makes use of forms with clear insular associations (to be discussed in more detail below). These include unstable 'e', diphthong reduction, anomalous gender assignment, and an uncontracted preposition-plus-article combination:

---

[6]   Curry, 'Representing War and Conquest', p. 143.

[7]   He is said in the *Paston Letters* to have enjoyed reading French books (*PL Davis*, i. p. 131).

un lieue 55v; *bayllye* 31v (elsewhere: *bailli*); *jullet* 48r; *le chase* 53v; *de le counte de deven-shyre* 31v

In addition, Worcester uses the insular spelling *auxi* for the form *aussi* used in all other text instances of this word. These interventions by a known English native speaker stand out quite distinctly from the French used in the main body of the text.

The M 9 chronicle seems to present Central French uses almost all the time, along with a tiny scattering of insular uses, observable only in Worcester's emendations. This prompts the question of how the main text assumed the form it did, which in turn requires us to consider what options were available to someone wanting to write French in fifteenth-century England, and how late medieval insular and continental varieties differed. It therefore seemed worthwhile to pursue in this chapter an in-depth analysis of its linguistic character, measured against leading features of regular continental and insular usage.

CENTRAL FRENCH AND OTHER CONTINENTAL VARIETIES

There is a tradition of studying literary texts as typical examplars of Old and Middle French[8] which has restricted our appreciation of linguistic variation in those periods, according to Trotter:

> Investigation … of not only non-literary, but relatively 'lower-register' material representative of the attempts at writing of non-aristocratic and uneducated people, has led to a slowly growing awareness that the relative regularity (in grammatical matters) of the literary texts is by no means universally shared. Whilst we can never have access to a true range of sociolects of medieval or early modern French, it is possible to aspire to greater awareness of the diaphasic and diastratic range than has hitherto been achieved.[9]

The linguistic regularity of most mainstream literary texts in the medieval period tends to convey the notion of a standard 'Parisian' French, in which the written language would naturally have been couched, while other varieties had the status of no more than oral dialects. In fact, the Central or 'Parisian' French used in later medieval mainstream texts was a new variety, not some kind of original or 'pure' Old French: 'Parisian standard French was originally "a naturally occurring koiné" [sc. dialect contact variety – RI] which developed in the speech of the city through large scale in-migration and which was subsequently represented in the written language of Paris'.[10] Alternatively, it was a supra-regional variety adopted by thirteenth-century scribes that tended to avoid forms associated with regions outside the Central–East Central area.[11] Old and Middle French texts from before the fifteenth century nevertheless show considerable scribal variation, which has often been linked – for instance by Dees – with dialectal variation mediated through regional *scriptae*.[12] These were

---

8   Marchello-Nizia, *La langue française*; Buridant, *Grammaire nouvelle*.
9   Trotter, 'Une et indivisible', p. 369.
10 Lodge, 'The Sources of Standardisation in French', p. 41.
11 Grübl, 'La standardisation du français'.
12 Dees, *Atlas des formes et des constructions des chartes françaises*.

sets of graphemic conventions which need not have corresponded directly to speech in specific areas.[13] Whatever the precise circumstances in which it arose, a fairly consistent scripta was used from c. 1300 onwards by the French royal and law courts and by local administrators. It possessed in particular the following orthographic features, notated here in angled brackets and shown as they relate to the historical phonology of French:

(1) Latin tonic ō → <eu> e.g. *examinateur, leurs*

Latin C preceding I/E → /ts/ writtten <c> e.g. *icelle, ce*

Latin C preceding A → /tʃ/ written <ch> e.g. *chose, chauffer*

Latin 'closed' E → <oi> e.g. *soie, croire*

Latin tonic 'open' E preceding nasal → /je/ written <ie`> e.g. *vient, rien*

The following text, written in Paris towards the end of the fourteenth century, is typical of the orthographical norms operating in this area at the time. In addition to the above features, the plural agreement inflection is normally written <s>, e.g. *choses, bouches*, but <z> following /t/, as with /t/-final masculine past participles, e.g. *ausdiz, trovez*.

(2)

> Après lesqueles **choses** ainsi faites, demandé fu par ledit mons. le prevost ausdiz presens **conseilliers** leurs advis & oppinions comment il estoit bon de proceder contre lesdiz juifs. Tous lesquieulx, veu lestat d'iceulx, qui sont vacabons, les denegacions & confessions par eulx faites, & les accusacions dont ilz sont trouvez coulpables, par l'informacion faite sur lesdites accusacions par maistre Gieffroy Le Goibe, **examinateur** oudit Chastelet; attendu la quantité des larrecins & qualité dont ilz sont souspeçonnez; delibrerent & furent d'oppinion que, pour savoir par **leurs** bouches la verité desdites accusacions, ilz feussent mis a question … Et ledit Salemon de Barselone, juif, fu de **rechief** fait venir en jugement sur les quarreaux, et par le dit mons. le prevost lui fu dit que desdites accusacions il deist verité … Et pour **ce** que autre chose ne volt congnoistre que dit est, fu mis a question sur le petit tresteau, et incontinent requist que hors d'**icelle** l'en **le** meist, & il diroit verité. Si fu mis hors d'**icelle** question, mené **cho**ffer en la cuisine en la **maniere** acoustumee, & illec sans aucune force, cogneut et confessa qu'il estoit & est verité que lui present … print & embla en la mercerie du Palais … une bourse de soye & deux anneaux d'argent dorez. (*Registre criminel du Châtelet de Paris 1389–1392*, p. 45 (1391))

'These things having thus been done, the said Provost asked the said counsellors present for their advice and opinions how it was best to proceed against the said Jews. All the counsellors, taking account of those men's condition, who are vagabonds, the denials and confessions made by them, and the accusations of which they have been found guilty, by the information given on the said accusations by Master Geoffrey Le G., investigator at the said Chatelet; (and) given the quantity and nature of robberies, of which they are suspected; [the counsellors] deliberated and gave the opinion that, to know the truth from their own lips about

---

13 Grübl, 'La standardisation du français'.

the said accusations, they should be interrogated … And the said Solomon of Barcelona, Jew, was once again made to come to be judged in the paved area [sc. tribunal – RI], and was told by the Provost that he should tell the truth about the said accusations … And because he did not wish to acknowledge anything else than what was (already) said, he was interrogated on the little table, and immediately asked that he should be taken off it, and he would tell the truth. He was removed from this interrogation and taken to warm up in the kitchen in the usual manner, and there without force recognised and confessed who he was, and (that) it is true that he took and stole in the Palace cloth market a silk purse and two gilded silver rings.'

As time went on, the Central variety became increasingly prevalent in texts originating right across French-speaking regions, thanks to the political and cultural prestige of Paris. This would certainly have been the case at the time of writing of the M 9 chronicle. Regional scriptae outside the Central area were nevertheless common, as noted by Trotter, in documentary texts.[14] They used graphemic features indicating phonetic realisations that differed considerably from Central French, especially those corresponding to palatal phonemes such as /tʃ/ and /ts/, the initial sounds in Central French of the words *champ* and *ce*, respectively. Instead, they were given the values /k/ and /tʃ/, which appear in Picard texts in spelling forms such as *camp* and *che*. The following text is representative in displaying such features, as well as other distinctive Picard traits such as feminine definite article *le* and 1st conjugation past participles ending in <t>, e.g. *jugiet*:

(3)

Cest li ordonnance que messires li cuens de Flandres, messires de Guistiele et li **Eskievin** de Bruges commanderent a ordonner … en quel maniere li peseur doivent peser … Et choir pour la plainte que li estraigne marchant fisent de **chou** con ne lor pesa mie selon le fourme de **le** cartre, et pour le tort que il lor sembla con lor fist … Et quant li peseres ara miz son pois es **balanches**, si doit il ferir un cop au bauch encontre **le** langhe, **anchois** quil juge; et quant il ara **jugiet**, dont doit il dire a **lacateur** et au vendeur tant à chy: se vous volez, vous poez le pois conter, anchois que li peseres oste le pois des balanches; et li **markant** doivent dire et responde oil ou non. (*Ordinance of the Count of Flanders concerning weights and measures*, Bruges, 13 August 1282)

'This is the ordinance that My Lord the Count of Flanders, my lord G. and the eschevins of Bruges directed to be ordained … as to how weighers should weigh. As regards the complaint that foreign merchants made about the fact that they were not being given weights according to the charter and for the wrong that was being done to them … And when the weigher has placed his weight on the scales, he must strike the beam against the tongue, before he pronounces, and when he has judged, then he must say to the buyer and the seller words to this effect: If you wish, you can count the weight, before the weigher removes the weight from the scales: and the merchants must speak and reply yes or no.'

---

14   Trotter, 'Une et indivisible'.

The Picard *scripta* remained in common use in northern France until the fifteenth century.[15] Other late Old French *scriptae* presented their own distinct features. Those based in the North-East, Picardy and Burgundy used -*aige* for -*age* (Latin -*aticu*), e.g. <voyage> → <voyaige>, a trait which is frequently used in the M 9 chronicle. However, by the fifteenth century this spelling was common in Central French too, so no conclusions can be drawn about whether it reflected Nantron's own dialect. The same is not true of a Norman feature, the reduction of the /ie/ dipthong to /e/, e.g.:

(4)

> Le mois dauost, se ilz veullent ilz **vendront** a la fare et se eulx veullent ilz ni vendront mie.

> 'In August, if they wish, they shall come to the lighthouse and if they wish, they will not come.' (*Coustumes de l'eau de Saine*, Rouen (1380))

This can be found in the chronicle, but was not adopted in Central French, and seems to reflect a dialectal preference of one or more of the contributors to the M 9 chronicle.

Continental Old French displayed some grammatical variation, in morphology and to some extent in syntax.[16] Regional varieties diverged from Central French in pronoun forms. In the latter, weak form pronouns were used before tensed verbs, e.g.:

(5) a.

> Sire, fait Orians, je **m'acorde** a vous, mes se mez ceurs n'est mie bien a pais, ce n'est mie merveillez. (*Ysaye le Triste* p. 100)

> '"Sir," said O. "I agree with you, but if my heart is not entirely at peace, it's no surprise".'

(5) b.

> Et la dame **se tint** por fole / De la clamor qu'ele a fait. (*Fabliaux* MR VI 94; 188–9)

> 'And the lady thought herself mad, for the noise she had made.'

In Walloon and Poitevin, strong form personal pronouns could stand in such contexts, e.g.:

(6) a.

> Et à chest oppynion je **moy acorde**. (*Temporaliteit* §47 (c. 1330))

> 'And with this opinion I agree.'

(6) b.

> … dous quaus deners le dit vendeor **ssey tint** pleinerement por paiez. (*Poitou* I, 50 (1295))

---

[15] Lusignan, *Essai d'histoire sociolinguistique*.

[16] Buridant, *Grammaire nouvelle*; Ingham, 'L'anglo-normand et la variation syntaxique en français médiéval'.

' ... of which moneys the said vendor holds himself to be fully paid.'

This was also frequently the case in later Anglo-Norman, e.g.:

(7) a.

> Ne faut gueres qil **moi** ad mis a la mort. (AND: *Brut* 172 (c. 1300))

> 'He nearly put me to death.'

(7) b.

> Et si le bercher **sey** poet aquiter. (AND: *Seneschaussee* c.27 (c. 1280))

> 'And the shepherd can be discharged of responsibility.'

Use of ordinary personal pronoun (*eulx*) rather than reflexive (*se/soy*) was possible here in M. Fr.:

(8)

> Mes le premier cop fait et le second, firent semblant lesdiz Anglois de reculer arriere et de eulx en fuir. (DMF: Chastellain, *Chron.* IV D., 293 (c. 1461–72))

> 'When the first and second strikes were made, the aforesaid English pretended to retreat and run away.'

As was noted above, gender agreement marking on determiners and adjectives fluctuated in later Anglo-Norman, and this was also true of East Walloon:

(9)

> *Celle pain, blanke visaige, nulle bien, aigue benoit, bon confession, cest herbe, blancs dens.* (*Médecinaire Liégois* (thirteenth century))

> 'This bread' 'white face' 'no good' 'holy water' 'good confession' 'that herb' 'white teeth'

Verb conjugation was by no means uniform across the different varieties of medieval French. In Picard, the 1st person singular future often ended in -*a*.[17] In South-Western French, the present and preterite 3rd person plural ended in -*ont*, which was also found in A-N.

Having surveyed the characteristics of linguistic variation in French in the later medieval period, it is worth considering how much awareness insular writers had of such variation, and thus of the choices available to them when writing in French. As was pointed out by Lusignan, English Chancery scribes in the thirteenth and fourteenth centuries were capable of writing to continental correspondents using features of the recipient's dialect.[18] At least some English users were at this time aware of alternative versions of medieval French, in addition to their own. The small number of English clerics educated at the University of Paris would also have been conscious of them. Merchants in the wool trade having contacts with Flanders must have had some familiarity with Northern and North-Eastern French, and English administrators and soldiers who spent time in Normandy must have acquired some knowledge of the Norman dialect.

---

[17]   Buridant, *Grammaire nouvelle*.

[18]   Lusignan, *La langue des rois au Moyen Âge*.

It is known for sure that insular users were by the later fourteenth century aware of the superior prestige of Central French. Pedagogical texts written in England around 1400 extolled the virtues of 'Parisian' French and claimed to teach it, even though in fact they tended strongly to use insular forms.[19] So insofar as trade and cultural links with French-speaking northern Europe continued into the fifteenth century during the later stages of the Hundred Years War, insular users of French might also be expected to have retained some awareness of regional variation in the French spoken and written there. In the case of the contributors to the M 9 chronicle, Hanson and Basset are likely, from having spent many years in Normandy and Maine, to have been familiar with Western French: how far such influence is discernible in the chronicle text is a question to which I return in a later section.

THE FRENCH OF ENGLAND

The original Anglo-Norman[20] scripta established in the twelfth century had rather distinctive orthographic traits, which reflected Western Old French phonology in the use of <ei> and <u> rather than <oi> and <o>, e.g. in the forms highlighted below:

(10)

> Benëurez li **hue**m chi ne alat el conseil des fel**un**s … mais en la **lei** de nostre Seign**ur** la voluntét de lui, et en la sue lei purpenserat par **jur**n e par nuit. (AND: *Oxford Psalter*, Psalm 1: 1–2 (c. 1145))

> Original: *Beatus vir, qui non abiit in consilio impiorum … sed in lege Domini voluntas ejus, et in lege ejus meditabitur die ac nocte.*

Grammatically, little or no divergence is observable in the twelfth and early thirteenth centuries from continental Old French, except that the two-case system on nouns broke down sooner in England.[21] By the fourteenth century, A-N no longer made consistent use of the original scripta and typically displayed various grammatical features diverging from the Old/Middle French mainstream, e.g. the 1st conjugation *-er* infinitive ending was not uncommonly overgeneralised to other conjugations, as in *accompler, tener, metter, prender, saver, recever.*[22] As noted earlier,

---

[19] Kristol, 'L'enseignement du français en Angleterre'; Ingham, 'The Maintenance of French in Later Medieval England'.
[20] We will not explore here the question of whether different labels are needed for earlier and later insular French.
[21] As it did in Western varieties more generally, from which Anglo-Norman historically derived (Pope, *From Latin to Modern French*).
[22] This was probably a pronunciation feature, however, caused by the merging of /i/ and high /e/, metathesis of /re/ and /er/ (Short, *Manual of Anglo-Norman*), and the reduction of the diphthong /ei/ (Merrilees, 'La simplification du système vocalique de l'anglo-normand'). This explanation is supported by the almost total absence, even in later A-N, of 1st conjugation tensed forms overgeneralised to verbs of other conjugations, e.g. **accompla, *tena, *metta, *prenderent, *receverent,* i.e. where the above-mentioned vowel changes were not involved (Ingham, 'Later Anglo-Norman as a Contact Variety of French?').

apparent gender agreement errors were also common in later A-N, but this again appears to have been a pronunciation feature rather than a matter of grammar.[23]

The late fourteenth-century text below displays some of the regional (non-Central French) features discussed above, both insular idiosyncracies and those also found elsewhere. Gender agreement marking was erratic, verb conjugation divergent from Central French, and other distinctive traits are evident, such as *que* as subject relative pronoun, negation without *ne*, and strong forms of personal pronouns (e.g. *soy*) instead of clitic forms (e.g. *se*).

(11)

> Item, pur ceo que les soldeours que feurent ovek Moun Sieur de Surry, Lieutenant Dirlande, sont ore hors de soulde, et depart**ez** hors des gages, et ensi sont **nuls** souldeours demurantz sur la defens de la terre, ne **nulle monoie** entre **maines** pur paier ascunes souldeours, ne pur faire **relef** encontre les enemis en ascune manere, qar **le monoie que** estoit illeoqes en les maines del dit Lieutenant pur la defens de la terre est portez en Engleterre par Maudeleyn et les esquiers **que** feurent envoyez pur ycelle; et combien qils feurent sovent requis par le Conseil illoqes pur paier et deliverer parcelle **del dit monoye** pur trover souldeours en defens et salvacion **del dicte terre**, nientmains ils **soy** escuser**ont**, qils **avont** poair de rescevoir et **nul** poair de rien paier ne deliverer; et en **tiel** manere **la terre** est en peril de **final** destruccion. (AND: *A Roll of the Proceedings of the King's Council in Ireland*, 263 (1399))

> 'Next, because the soldiers that were with my Lord of Surrey, Lieutenant of Ireland, are now without payment, and have left without their money, so there are no soldiers remaining for the defence of the land, and no money at hand to pay any soldiers or to provide relief against the enemy in any way, for the money that was there in the hands of the said lieutenant for the defence of the land has been removed to England by M. and the squires who were sent for this purpose; and although they were often requested by the council there to pay and deliver some of the said money to find soldiers for the defence and preservation of the said land, nevertheless they refused to do so because (they said) they had power to receive and no power to pay or deliver; and in this way the land is in danger of ultimate destruction.'

The spelling in this text frequently deviates from mainstream continental usage, e.g.:

(12) Anglo-French: *ceo; feurent; soulde, pur; poair; rescevoir, esquiers; manere, tiel, relef; maines, deliverer*

Continental French: *ce; furent; solde, pour; povoir; recevoir, escuiers; maniere, tel, relief; mains, delivrer*

Some of these features are found systematically in later A-N texts, e.g. <e> for <ie> and vice versa, and <e> anomalously added or omitted.

Extracts from the following century, in which the same features remain present, will now be examined. In this petition, they include <-*e*> for Central French <-*ie*>, e.g. *chaunceller*, final -*e* omission, e.g. *layn*, <-*oun, -aun*> for <-*on, -an*>, e.g.

---

[23]   Ingham, 'Later Anglo-Norman as a Contact Variety of French?'; and Ingham, *The Transmission of Anglo-Norman.*

debruserount, graunter, anomalous gender marking, e.g. *son … discretion*, and lexical peculiarities such as *ascun* for *aucun* and *serche* for *cherche*.

(13)

> Please a vous, tressoveraigne seignur, par l'advys et assent dez seignurs espiritu-elx et temporelx en cest present parlement assemblez, d'ordeigner par auctorite de **mesme le parlement** qe le **chaunceller** d'Engleterre pur le temps este-ant eit poair par auctorite susdit de **graunter** severalx commissions, tantz come semblera a **son** tressage discretion … pur faire due serche parmy lour hundredes e **toutz maners** de draps de layn desore affairs deinz les ditz hundre-des … et si les ditz sercheours trovent **ascun** draps, per due serche et survieue, faux ou defectife, ou de male ou faux **faisour**, en partie ou en tout, q'adonqes lez ditz **sercheours** debruserount, emfrenderount et departerount les dit draps …
> (*PROME*, January 1431)

> 'May it please your most sovereign Lord, by the advice and assent of the most spiritual and temporal assembled in this present Parliament, to ordain by the authority of the same Parliament that the Chancellor of England at the time shall have power by the aforesaid authority to grant several commissions whenever it will seem suitable to his most wise discretion … in order to make due search throughout their hundreds of all kinds of woollen cloth to be made henceforth in the said hundreds … And if the said searches find any cloth fault or defective by due search and inspection, or badly or wrongly made, in part or completely, that then the said searches will break into, open and divide the said defective cloth.'

The following extract comes from a local government memorandum in very late A-N:

(14)

> … [various names] assembleez en la **counseil chaumbre** le x jour de Septem-bre, 34 Henr. vi. 1454, **ounte** ordine et **estable** que la somons **de lez** alder-manz et xxiiij du counseile de dite chaumbre de ceste jour en avaunt soit tenuz et ob-servez en la manere et fourme quensuite; ceste assavoir, que au **qile** joure q**ascun** dez ditz xij aldermanz et xxiiij **du dite counseile** ou de cez **succes-soures soite** summone destre devaunt le maire qore est, ou que pur le temps serra, et ne vient point al heoure assigne par le dite mair, paiera a **chescun foithe** iiij d., sil ne poet estre excuse par son **seremente faite** devaunt le dite mair, qil ne fuist mie a lostel de cele heure quaunt il fue summone. (AND: *York Memorandum Book* 2, 199)

> '… [various names] assembled in the council chamber on the 10th of September, 34th Henry VI, 1454, have ordained and set down that summonses of aldermen and 24 of the Council of the said Chamber should from this day forth be kept and observed in the shape and form following; that is to say, that on whatever day that any of the said 12 aldermen and 24 of the said councillors or of their successors should be summoned before the mayor who now is or who for the time being shall be, and does not come at the hour assigned by the said mayor, shall pay each time 4d, if he cannot be excused on oath performed before the said mayor, for not being at home at the time when he was summoned.'

Here, the vowel spellings <ou> and <au>, the 1st conjugation *-e* past participle ending overgeneralised to the 2nd conjugation verb *establir*, giving *estable* (treat as *establé*), rather than *establi*, and the uncontracted preposition + article form in *de lez aldermanz* are very distinctive insular features. Furthermore, the spelling forms *ounte, counseile, joure, soite, sermente* show the use of non-inherited *-e* to support a final consonant, as was then current in ME orthography. The graphemes <s> and <z> are both used for plural marking (*dez, aldermanz* versus *successoures*). Finally raising of /e/ to /i/[24] is indicated by *qile* for *quel* (as well as in *discharge* for *descharge* in the next extract).

Law French continued to display many of the same characteristics, as shown in the following extracts from reports of legal pleading in fifteenth-century King's Bench courts:

(15)

> *Paston*: A ce dioms nous qe nous mesmez fesoms vn fait testmoigne **mesme le resceit a mesme celui pleintif** et a R.H. par quels mayns le resceit est suppose, et demandoms iugement si saunz **mounstre** le fait **accioun** deuez **auer**.

> *Rolfe:* Ceo est al acompte par **quei** nous prioms laccompte qar **ieo** pose qil vst plede qe le pleintif vst done a luy lez deners, vncor le pleintif auera laccompte qar **ceo** plee va en **discharge** de laccompte et nemie en barre daccompte pur ceo qil ad **conuz** le resceit. (*Year Books 1 Henry VI*, pp. 114–15 (1422))

> '*Paston.* To this we say that we made a deed witnessing the same receipt to this same plaintiff and to RH, by this and the receipt is supposed. And we seek judgement whether without showing the deed you ought to have action.

> *Rolfe.* This is to the account, where for we pray the account, for suppose he had pleaded that the plaintiff had given the monies to him, still the plaintiff will have the account because this plea goes in discharge of the account, and not in bar of the account, because he has admitted the receipt.'

(16)

> *Danby.* Homme poet en diuers casez voider vn leez par especiell **mater**, comme si homme plede leez a terme danz dun maner, **ieo dirra** qe le lessour nauait riens en le maner al temps del leez, et ne sera chace a dire qil ne lessa pas. **Mesme le ley** si homme plede graunt de reuercion: ieo dirra qe le grauntour **nauera** rienz al temps del graunt.

> *Litilton.* Sir, il est voier en vestre case de leez a terme danz qar le leez est bon par parolle **saunz** liuere de seisin; mes si homme plede vn confirmacion ou feoffment il nest plee a dire qe le feoffour nauait rienz al temps, mes sera chace a dire qil nenfeoffe pas etc. qar al feoffment est **requisit** liuere de seisin.

> *Pigott*: A ce qe mon maistre Choke dit qil nest leez sil ne soit execute, sir, si ieo lesse terre a terme de vie et puis ieo graunt le reuercion a autre pur terme de vie et le tenaunt attourne, ore le defendaunt **poet barrer moy** en accion de wast par cell graunt. (*Year Books 10 Edward IV*, p. 77 (1470))

---

24 Short, *Manual of Anglo-Norman*.

'*Danby* C.J. A man can void a lease in diverse cases by especial matter, as when a man pleads a lease for term of years for a manor. I shall say that the lessor had nothing in the manor at the time of the lease and I shall not be driven to say that he did not lease. The same is the law if a man plead a grant of reversion, I shall say that the grantor had nothing in the reversion at the time of the grant.

Littleton J. The argument is good in your case of a lease for term of years, for a lease is good by parole without livery of seisin. But if a man plead a confirmation or feoffment, it is not a plea to say that the feoffor had nothing at that time, but he will be driven to say that he did not enfeoff etc. because for feoffment, livery of seisin is necessary.

Pygott: As for Master Choke J's remark that it is not a lease if it be not executed, sir, if I lease land for a term of life and then grant the reversion to another for the term of a life and the tenant attorns, then the defendant can bar me in action of waste by this grant.'

Anomalous gender marking and verb conjugation, as well as insular vowel realisations and spelling forms such as *jeo* and *ceo*, are strongly present in Law French. In addition, we see in both extracts an Anglo-Norman syntactic peculiarity, the order *mesme le* + noun, with the sense 'the same' + noun, rather than *le mesme* + noun.

What these administrative and legal texts show us is that from the late fourteenth century to roughly the time of the M 9 chronicle a variety of French was in existence in England which remained very distinct from the by now dominant mainstream form of French in use on the continent. Writing in this insular discourse tradition would have led a scribe to adopt a large number of grammatical and orthographic traits conferring a very different linguistic character on the text from what the M 9 chronicle actually presents, as will be shown in detail in the next section.

LINGUISTIC ANALYSIS OF THE M 9 CHRONICLE

i. Orthography and grammar

The main linguistic features highlighted in the examination carried out in preceding sections of Central French and other varieties, including A-N, will now be summarised. A Central French text of the fifteenth century would be expected to show the following orthographical features:

(17) <eu> e.g. *examinateur, leurs*

/ts/ writtten <c> e.g. *icelle, ce*

/ʃ/ written <ch> e.g. *chose, chauffer*

<oi> e.g. *soie, croire*

/je/ written <ie`> e.g. *rien, vient*

Final <s> would be expected for the plural inflection, but a <z> spelling after a noun stem or past participle ending in <t>. As regards grammar, regular gender agreement marking would be employed, as well as the verb forms normal in the Central variety such as the 3rd plural inflection *-ent*. Conjugation class differences would be maintained without overgeneralisation, and the use of clitic pronouns preceding tensed verbs would have been systematic.

In a text written in the later A-N linguistic tradition, however, the following features would be expected:

(18) unstable final <e>

<aun>, <oun> spellings

<ei> for <oi> spellings

<e> for <ie> spellings

The 3rd plural *-ont* inflection would not be unexpected, nor would overregularisation of 1st conjugation verb forms, and uncontracted preposition + article sequences such as *de les*. Various idiosyncractic forms such as *ceo* for *ce*, *jeo* for *je* and others noted in the previous section would also be likely.

Inspection of the chronicle text makes it immediately clear, however, that these A-N features are not followed, nor are those of Picard or of any other regional dialect variety. Virtually throughout, those of Central French are in regular use. No use is made, for example, of A-N <ou> for <eu>, of Picard <ch> and <c> for Central French <c> and <ch>, of Western French and A-N <ei> for <oi>. One A-N (but also Norman) feature does appear, however: <e> for <ie>, e.g. *chevaler* 45v, *bacheler* 54r, *vendroit* 54r. As regards final <s> or <z> spellings, the M 9 chronicle tends to treat reflexes of Old French /ts/ systematically. With a past participle, <z> is always used, e.g. *venuz, trahiz, retraiz*, etc. Where the pronounced form /ts/ arose from the addition of plural <s> to a stem ending in /t/, the grapheme <z> also features, e.g. *subgiez, touz*. But where the stem ends in /n/ or /r/, M 9 systematically uses <s> in plural contexts, e.g. *grans, gemissemens, embuschemens, contrains, fors* (= *forts*), *mors* (= *morts*).[25] Regular plurals normally also take the <s> spelling: *hommes, lieues, adversaires*, etc. Such consistently accurate distinctions would have been altogether alien to later insular French usage.

The clearly Central French character of the text is well exemplified in the following two extracts:

(19)

> [various names] … et pluseurs autres au nombre de sept cens hommes de fait, et de nuyt partirent dudit lieu dalencon et chevaucherent jusques a ung chastel a deux lieues pres ladicte[26] cite du mans nomme la guerche, et ylecques ledit Sire de Talbot commanda audit mathew goth [62r] quil chevauchast devant priveement, et espiast le gouverment desdiz adversaires, ['leq' cancelled] et Il yroit tout bellement apres lui, et que Ilz se Rencontrassent sur le chemyn pour

---

[25]   After /l/ there is some variation: the scribe mostly uses *ilz* but sometimes (and throughout the text) *ils*.

[26]   It should be noted that by the fifteenth century Latin-origin silent letters such as a <c> in *ledict* ('the said') were becoming common in Central French.

lui dire ce quil avoit trouver,[27] Lequel pour executer le commandement a lui fait comme dit est, chevaucha devant et saigement sans ce quil fust apperceu ne congneu par Iceulx adversaires, au plus matin tantost apres le point du jour, entra oudit chastel du mans, parla audit thomas gower qui lui dist le gouverment [sic] desdiz adversaires qui estoient dedens ladicte ville, et apres que Icellui matheu ot mengie un mors de pain et beu une foiz, Il sen party. (M 9 chronicle, ff. 61v–62r)

(20)

Ledit seigneur de Rustynam acompaignie de mil hommes de guerre et plus fist une course en normandie ou bas pays de costentin et jusques devant la ville et cite davranches, mais les anglois de la garnison dudit lieu yssirent hors contre lesdiz bretons et se combatirent contre eulx moult vaillamment … Le dit Sire de Scales en sa compaignie Sire Jehan herpelay chevaler bailli de costentin, Sire Guillaume Breton chevaler bailli de Caen, Sire Raoul Tesson, Sire Jehan Carbonnel, et pluseurs autres au nombre de trois mil hommes de fait tant anglois comme normans partirent dudit siege et alerent querir des vivres et des ordonnances et artilleries … le dit sire de Scales et les anglois descendirent a pie et se combatirent vaillamment contre lesdiz adversaires et y ot une bonne besoingne et forte bataille tant dun coste que dautre. (M 9 chronicle, ff. 58v–59r)

No anomalous uses of pronoun forms are observed here (or indeed elsewhere in the text). Gender marking, verb conjugation and pronoun use in these extracts are as in Central French. The masculine nouns *lieu chastel, gouverement, chemyn, commandement, point, jour, nombre, siege* and *coste*, and the feminine nouns *cite, ville, course, garnison, foiz, compagnie, besogne* and *bataille* all show gender-appropriate articles or adjectives. Verb conjugation distinctions are rigorously maintained, as with the *-ir* and *-re* verb forms *party, partirent, yssirent, combatirent, descendirent* and *querir*, along with *-er* verb forms *chevaucha, entra, parla, compta* and *alerent*. We also observe the citic pronoun *se* rather than *soi* used appropriately in *(ils) se recontrassent / se combatirent*.

Although these two passages are highly representative of the text as a whole, it does elsewhere contain a tiny number of exceptions. Occasional anomalous gender marking and verb forms occur:

(21) a. *la siege … le siege*, f. 38v; *un quartier du test*, f. 63v

(21) b. *lesdiz anglois les poursuirent* [preterite, for *poursuivirent*], f. 63v

These are so rare, however, as to be simple lapses, rather than showing insufficient knowledge of French.

ii. Lexis and phraseology

The M 9 chronicle makes recurrent use of items appropriate to describing familiar military events and offers very few opportunities for unusual lexis. Its very restricted vocabulary range would surely have been well within the competence of either a native speaker or a proficient second-language user of French

---

[27]   *Trouver* for *trouvé* is probably a slip of a kind not uncommon in contemporary French non-standard writing.

(especially one with a military background), and therefore does not allow us to investigate the main question at issue in this chapter. A rather different question might nevertheless be raised here, namely whether the two sections of the M 9 chronicle, the first running up to the death of Henry V in 1422, and the second from that point onwards, differ in lexical choices. This would be apparent if a given concept was lexicalised differently in the two parts of the text. Given the repetitive nature of the narrative, where similar military events are frequently described in both parts, opportunities for this question to be investigated are fortunately plentiful. The nouns *siege* and *bataille* show similar collocations in the two parts of the text: *tenir/lever un siege, mettre le siege,* and *livrer/donner bataille*. Other collocations used across both parts are the expressions *ordonna et commist [quelqu'un], gaigner une ville,* and *faire conqueste*. To these can be added the consistent preference for *adversaires*, rather than *ennemis*. In all these respects the M 9 chronicle is entirely in line with continental French practice, according to the relevant DMF entries consulted.

It is also worth mentioning that the two parts differ little in stylistic respects, e.g. the possible Latinate influence seen in initial participial clauses resembling a Latin ablative absolute clause:

(22)

Apres laquelle glorieuse victoire obtenue … (M 9 chronicle, f. 34r)

'After obtaining this glorious victory …'

(23)

Et tantost apres ledit traictee et mariaige faiz et acompliz … (M 9 chronicle, f. 40r)

'And as soon as the said treaty and marriage had been held and concluded.'

Thus the use by Nantron and his colleagues of Peter Basset's pre-existing life of Henry V when they compiled the text did not seem to affect the lexis in the narrative as a whole. This could of course be simply a matter of the authorial team having adopted a policy of continuing to use Basset's lexical preferences.

A possibly more revealing window on the native-like status of the text or otherwise can be obtained by considering its phraseology. A commonly noted hallmark of non-native language use is to use collocations between nouns and verbs, or nouns and adjectives, which do not sound natural to native speakers, e.g. **do a mistake, *have a concert, *make an end to, *high traffic, *hot regards, *large mistake*.[28]

Although much of M 9 phraseology is repetitive, limiting the scope for unusual collocations, a sample was taken of items that seemed to warrant further investigation, as they seemed to the present author suitable for validation as authentic in continental prose writing. Table 7 lists these selected collocational expressions, and shows whether they are recorded in dictionary sources (DMF and AND).

---

[28] Source: http://webdoc.sub.gwdg.de/edoc/ia/eese/artic25/marj2/8_2005.html

Table 7. Selected collocational expressions in the M 9 chronicle

Expression	Meaning	In DMF?	In AND?
tenir siege 39v	maintain a siege	✓	X (mettre s. ✓)
cheoir en maladie 31v	fall ill	✓	X (a-/enmaladir ✓)
*delivrer bataille 33r	give battle	X (livrer b. ✓)	livrer b. ✓; deliverer b. X
*purveoir pour son estat 41v	provide for her situation	X	X
*enfreindre son serment 45v	break his oath	X	X
*sa maladie lui engreiga 46v	(he) got worse	X (without pronoun ✓)	✓
passer hiver 38v	spend the winter	X (passer son h. ✓)	X
passa pays 47r	cross the country	✓	X
commander ... pour + infin 62v	ordered ... to do sthg	✓	X
coururent (le pays et) obeissance du Roy 47r	territory under jurisdiction of	✓	X
avoient necessite de vivres 58r	needed food	✓	X
estoient en aventure d'avoir este prins 61v	were at risk of being taken	✓	✓ but without complement
en entention de faire qqch 35v	intending to do sthg	✓	✓
*par emblee d'eschiele 39v	by the secret means of a ladder	X	X

Many of these collocations were attested in the DMF, and can thus be taken to accord with native-like continental French of the period. Indeed, the items investigated were mostly unrecorded in the AND, and none of the expressions not recorded in DMF could be found in AND either. There is almost no evidence here for insular French-influenced turns of phrase, except perhaps the malefactive dative construction *lui engreger*, cf.:

(24)

> ... se li mals **lui engregast**/Arere a li tost returnast. (*Prothesilaus* ANTS 2725 (c. 1180))

> (She told him) '... if the hurt should get worse, he should come back to her immediately.'

This construction is attested in AND, but not in DMF, although that may be merely an accidental gap.

The most interesting finding is that some collocations in M 9 are unattested in either DMF or AND: *par emblee de qqchose, purveoir pur son estat, delivrer bataille, enfreindre un serment*. The corresponding continental phrasing attested in DMF for these items is, respectively:

(25)

> Ou mois de mars dudit an mil CCCC quarante huit, fut **prinse d'eschielle et emblée** la ville et chastel de Fougières. (Escouchy, *Chronique* B., t.i, 14, 154 (c.1453))
>
> 'In March of the aforesaid year 1448 the town and castle of F. were taken by a concealed ladder.'

(26)

> Et pour **pourveoir à** la paix et transquilité des habitans de Paris et au gouvernement et bonne police de la Ville … (Fauquembergue, *Journal* I, 225 (1417–20))
>
> 'And to provide for the peace and quiet of the residents of P. and the good government of the city,'

(27)

> … qu'il ne voulloit point **ronpre son serment** qu'il m'a fait. (*Lettres Louis XI*, V, t.9, 71 (1481))
>
> '… that he did not want to break his vow which he made me.'

The unattested collocations in Table 7, if non-native-like, may betray a certain clumsiness a non-native speaker can sometimes display with phrasing in a second language. Conceivably, therefore, phraseology that is not attested in continental French might have arisen in contributions by Nantron's colleagues who were supplying him with the text content from their recollections, though this can be no more than speculative.

As a whole, there is no doubt that the text was written by a scribe thoroughly familiar with fifteenth-century Central French conventions. This leaves the puzzle of how to account for the presence in the text of a small number of discordant instances, some of which have an affinity with insular French (especially regarding gender marking and verb conjugation) or with Norman dialect. Should they be interpreted as indicating contributions to the text by regional/insular users? This is intriguing, as we know independently that the contributors to the M 9 narrative had connections with geographical areas outside the central French region. Hanson originated from an area described as Germany, as well as serving as a soldier in Normandy and Maine, while Worcester was an English second-language user of French. It is possible to suppose that the text owes the form it took to the generally expert competence of Nantron in deploying Central French, but also to input from the non-native French of other contributors, leaving traces in the shape of occasional conjugation and gender agreement errors.

On the other hand, one might suppose that Nantron, resident in England for some time and used to working with Englishmen who used their own second-language variety of French, may have experienced some influence from them on his own production of French. An individual's linguistic system is known to be to some extent porous and open to influence from those surrounding him or her. Many studies of bilingual speakers in contexts where their native language is not dominant show effects of their second-acquired language on the first,[29] and speakers of a second-acquired dialect may accommodate their speech to that dialect.[30] There is no reason to imagine that matters were different in the medieval period, assuming with the historical linguists Ringe and Eska that: 'The processes that we see operating around us in the present must be assumed to have operated in the same ways at any given time in the past, unless we can demonstrate a discontinuity in their causes between that past time and the present.'[31]

Finally, it must be borne in mind that the M 9 chronicle is an unfinished draft, which would have been given final revision. The occasional departures from Central French orthography, grammar and phrasing noted above are consistent with inattention on the part of a native speaker writer, rather than showing imperfect learning of French. The non-Central French features in the main text may therefore owe something to this factor, and would quite possibly have been removed in a corrected clean copy of the chronicle.

CONCLUSIONS

The main findings of this study may now be summarised. With respect to conjugation, gender marking and pronoun use, the M 9 chronicle is consistent with Central French of the fifteenth century. Its orthography shows no sign of typical insular French features. Its phraseology likewise lacks evidence of insular influence; the expressions selected for investigation were generally attested in continental texts cited in the DMF, and if they were not, did not appear in the AND either. In a text of 20,000 words, nothing of any consequence appears to conflict with the Central French character of the chronicle. Only an expert user of French would have been able to maintain such otherwise consistent adherence to the linguistic norms of continental spelling and grammar. There seems no reason to doubt, therefore, the assumption that Nantron, with his scribal training and experience, was responsible for the composition of the chronicle; Hanson, as a soldier, would not have possessed those qualities, and Worcester, though literate and a man of some scholarship, deviated noticeably from Central French in his rather few amendments to the text. While undoubtedly a 'team effort' in the compilation of information and the creation of the text, the chronicle contains almost no trace of any language variety that a member of the team other than Nantron himself would have used.

---

29   See review in Pavlenko, 'L2 Influence on L1 in Late Bilingualism'.
30   Chambers, 'Dialect Acquisition'; Nycz, 'Changing Words or Changing Rules?'
31   Ringe and Eska, *Historical Linguistics*, p. 3.

5

The post-medieval history of the chronicle and its use by the heralds

According to William Worcester's incipit, the M 9 chronicle was compiled in 1459, the year Sir John Fastolf died. The next firm date which we have for its existence is 1619 when the chronicle, bound together with a number of sixteenth-century texts, appears in Samson Lennard's handwritten catalogue of the College of Arms collections. The volume is described as 'a book in fol. concerning the warres of H. 5. in France & also the ceremonies used at the creacion of the prince, with other speciall notes'.[1] The inclusion in Lennard's catalogue indicates that it formed part of the foundation collection of the College. The L and M series are descendants of two pressmarks in the catalogue which represented 'the collection of the working manuscripts of the Tudor heralds'.[2]

In this chapter we shall consider when and how the chronicle might have come into the possession of the College of Arms. Helpful clues are provided by which later texts were chosen to be bound with it. Also relevant is evidence found in other texts of the sixteenth century of the use of the chronicle by heralds and others. First we shall turn to the immediate aftermath of Fastolf's death to consider the possible fate of the original chronicle manuscript.

THE IMMEDIATE FATE OF THE CHRONICLE

Sir John Fastolf died on 5 November 1459.[3] The knight had appointed William Worcester as one of ten executors of his will, but disputes soon arose with John Paston I, who claimed that he had been chosen by Fastolf as his main executor.[4] Worcester experienced repeated difficulties and high costs in not only trying to deal with Fastolf's affairs but also putting forward his own claims for money due to him for past and present services. Matters dragged on until 1470 when the

---

[1]   College of Arms, MS L 11 part 2, pp. 1–29, at p. 15. The date given for the catalogue is 1 February 1618 which is today's 1619. Lennard was Rose Rouge Pursuivant in 1613–16, and Bluemantle Pursuivant from 1616 to his death in 1633. Broadway, 'Lennard, Sampson (d. 1633)', *ODNB*.

[2]   Campbell and Steer, *Catalogue*, p. 1.

[3]   The chronicle is not amongst the books known to have been in Sir John's possession at his death (Beadle, 'Sir John Fastolf's French Books', pp. 96–112) nor to have been held by Sir John Paston I (Lester, 'Books of a Fifteenth-Century English Gentleman, Sir John Paston', pp. 200–17).

[4]   Richmond, *The Paston Family in the Fifteenth Century. Fastolf's Will*, especially chapter 2.

archbishop of Canterbury, Thomas Bourchier, transferred the administration of Fastolf's will to William Waynflete, bishop of Winchester (1398–1486), who had also been one of the initial executors. On 7 December 1472 Waynflete came to an agreement with Worcester, who was thereby paid for handing over to the bishop relevant Fastolf muniments.[5] Waynflete ended up in control of most of Fastolf's landed interests, which he put to the endowment of Magdalen College Oxford, the college he had founded in 1458. This explains why papers relating to Sir John produced or collected by William Worcester, including the papers drawn up in pursuit of his own claims, ended up in the muniments of Magdalen College as the Fastolf Papers, alongside various manorial records from Sir John's erstwhile estates which passed to the ownership of the College.

The settlement of the early 1470s left Worcester with more time to pursue other interests, but he never abandoned his interest in the wars with France. From 1477 to 1480 he undertook a number of journeys on which he made copious notes (Corpus Christi College Cambridge, 210), which were published in 1969 as his *Itineraries*. Whilst the majority concerned places he visited in England, he also included jottings on the French wars, including, for instance, lists of those involved in Henry V's taking of Caen and those who shared lodgings at the siege of Rouen.[6] Near the start of the notes on his first journey he included a list of captains at the battle of Verneuil 'according to what Ireland the herald told me on 1 December 1477'.[7] This note provides vital evidence to which we shall return shortly.

It is also important to remember that Worcester made broader reflections on the fifteenth-century phase of the Anglo-French war in his *Boke of Noblesse*, a text which bears an *explicit* dating its completion to 15 June 1475, indicating that it was consciously linked to the renewal of war with France by Edward IV in that year.[8] There can be no doubt that Worcester intended the *Boke* to guide and encourage the king in this endeavour.[9] The single manuscript, British Library MS Royal 18 B XXII, takes the form of a presentation copy. That it was within the royal collection suggests that it was indeed given to Edward IV. We can easily see, however, that it was heavily annotated by Worcester before he presented it to the king. On f. 15r, for instance, he notes that he had handed a copy of ordinances made by the duke of Bedford in 1423, which had been in the keeping of Sir John Fastolf, to Edward IV 'the day before youre departing out of London'. We can therefore date this action to 29 May 1475 before Edward set out on his campaign to France.[10]

Worcester's annotation indicates that at this point he still had in his personal possession copies and original manuscripts from the wars with France. This situation is further borne out by his preparation of a collection of copies of documents intended to serve as exemplars of good practice in encouraging Edward's renewal

5   MCA, Norfolk and Suffolk 75

6   *Itineraries*, pp. 353, 361.

7   *Itineraries*, pp. 3–5 (at p. 3).

8   BL, MS Royal 18 B XXII, f. 44 ('here endyth thys epistle under correction the xv day of June the yeere of crist m^l iiij^c and of the noble regne of kyng Edward the iiii^{the} the xv^{ne}').

9   There have been suggestions by McFarlane and Allmand that the work was begun in the 1450s (Allmand, 'France-Angleterre à la fin de la Guerre de Cent Ans: Le "Boke of Noblesse" de William Worcester', pp. 104–11), but the version which exists certainly dates to the mid-1470s.

10   Nall, *Reading and War*, p. 55.

of war. The collection, now Lambeth Palace Library MS 506, was not completed by the time of Worcester's death. It therefore fell to his son, another William, to change the dedication to Richard III and then after that king's demise, back to Edward IV,[11] although it is not certain that the book was ever actually given to either king. A further collection of texts on the war with France and on other matters which Worcester assembled, and which is now College of Arms, MS Arundel 48, certainly remained in Worcester's own possession. This collection contains a number of texts in the hand of Luket Nantron, who died in October 1471.

In this context, therefore, it is feasible, if not likely, that the manuscript of the M 9 chronicle also remained in Worcester's hands until his death. Its original foliation starts at 'xxxj' indicating it had been bound with other materials, although we cannot be certain that this was whilst it was in the possession of Worcester. The folding of the pages of the chronicle follows a pattern seen in other manuscripts linked to Worcester.[12] We have also noted that Worcester had made fifteen annotations to the text of the chronicle.

Worcester's date of death is uncertain but is deemed to have occurred between 1480 and 1485; 1482 is a popular choice since Lambeth Palace Library MS 506 contains a preface dedicated to Edward IV which Worcester's son William amended to dedicate the work to Richard III, who came to the throne in July 1483. From the late 1470s Worcester's base was Pockthorpe, just outside Norwich. Norwich city records mention a payment of rent by his widow at Michaelmas 1485, this reference giving a *terminus ante quem* for her husband's death.[13]

The fact that William junior was able to amend the dedication of his father's text in Lambeth Palace Library MS 506 indicates that the volume was still in William senior's hands at his death. But the fate of the latter's manuscripts as a whole – totalling twenty-nine or thirty works – would repay further research.[14] Given the pattern of their later archival homes it would seem that they had been dispersed at least by the middle of the sixteenth century, if not earlier, but the exact situation of each work remains elusive.[15] For example, the notes which formed the 'Itineraries' were acquired by Corpus Christi College Cambridge in the last decade of the sixteenth century, having been previously in the collection either of Matthew Parker, archbishop of Canterbury (d. 1575), or of Henry Aldrich, a fellow of the College from 1569 to 1579.[16] Edward VI wrote out some pages from what

---

[11] Sutton and Visser-Fuchs, *Richard III's Books*, p. 87.

[12] See the discussion of the manuscript in Chapter 1.

[13] Norwich City Archive, Chamberlain's account book 1479–88, folio 82v, cited in *Itineraries*, p. ix.

[14] In addition to six or seven notebooks, there are twenty-three manuscripts which can be linked to him through marginalia or an *ex libris* in his hand (Wakelin, *Humanism, Reading and English Literature*, p. 94; Wakelin, 'William Worcester Writes a History of His Reading', p. 56).

[15] Worcester (*Itineraries*, p. 253) noted that he had presented his English translation of Cicero's 'De Senectute' to William Waynflete, bishop of Winchester, on 10 August 1473. Could more of his works have passed into the possession of Waynflete? Paston papers also include a list of places taken by Henry V in his second campaign which has some similarities with the narrative of the chronicle, making Paston possession of the chronicle another possibility (*PL Gairdner*, ii, pp. 5–8).

[16] *Itineraries*, pp. xviii–xx.

became Lambeth Palace Library 506,[17] suggesting that it could have been in the royal library in the 1540s. We know that subsequently the manuscript was in the possession of George Carew, earl of Totnes (1555–1629), before it came into the collection of Gilbert Sheldon, who was archbishop of Canterbury from 1663 to his death in 1677.[18]

College of Arms, MS Arundel 48 came into the College of Arms in 1678 from Henry, duke of Norfolk, grandson of the collector, Thomas, earl of Arundel (d. 1646). British Library Royal MS 13 C I, a compilation of chronicles and other historical and religious notes probably made by Worcester, was in the royal library by 1666.[19] Worcester's commonplace book, now British Library Cotton Julius F VII, was owned by Thomas Allen of Oxford, a mathematician and antiquary (d. 1632), but came into the Cotton library which was donated to the nation in 1702. Medical jottings which Worcester had made between 1464 and 1478 were combined with texts authored by others in a volume within the collection of Sir Hans Sloane (d. 1753) which was purchased for the nation at his death and is now British Library Sloane MS 4. Astronomical tables made by Worcester, in one case explicitly for Sir John Fastolf in 1440, and other miscellaneous materials, including a medical text copied by Worcester at Pockthorpe near Norwich in 1463, came into the collection of William Laud (1573–1645) and thence into the Bodleian Library at Oxford (MS Laud. Misc. 674). In almost all cases, therefore, the immediate fate of Worcester's papers at his death is not known. The M 9 chronicle is no exception to this.

In the mid-sixteenth century, John Bale (1495–1563) attempted to list all known historical works, publishing his *Illustrium majoris Britanniae scriptorum, hoc est, Angliae, Cambriae, ac Scotiae summarium* in Ipswich in 1548–49. An extended version, *Scriptorum illustrium majoris Britanniae Catalogus*, was published in Basel between 1557 and 1559. Six works of 'Guilhelmus Botoner' (in other words, William Worcester) are noted by Bale in this later edition, with the additional note that there were undoubtedly others of which Bale was as yet not fully apprised.[20] One of the six works is listed as '*Acta Domini Ioannis Fastolfi Lib. 1. Anno Christi 1421 et anno regni* [sic]',[21] although as we have already argued in Chapter 1, it does not seem that this is the M 9 chronicle.

There is no reference to Botoner in Bale's 1548 edition but there are some relevant draft notes in Bale's notebook which is believed to date to the same year.[22]

---

[17] Jordan, *The Chronicle and Political Papers of Edward VI*, pp. xxi–xxxiii, 185–90.

[18] For full details of provenance see the online catalogue of Lambeth Palace Library and also James, *A Descriptive Catalogue of the Manuscripts in the Library of Lambeth Palace: The Medieval Manuscripts*, p. 711. A seventeenth-century transcript of part of MS 506 is to be found in the Society of Antiquaries, MS 41 (Willetts, *Catalogue of Manuscripts in the Society of Antiquaries*, p. 20).

[19] In this manuscript Worcester's hand is evidenced in annotations. There is also a reference on f. 141b to his making extracts in 1453 from a book on Roman history acquired by Fastolf when the latter lived in Paris.

[20] 'Pluraque alia congessit, quae an adhuc extent plano ignore'. For the entry see *Scriptorum illustrium majoris Britanniae Catalogus*, pp. 599–600.

[21] The other five are *Antiquitates Anglicas. Lib. 3. Eximiae probitatis et prudentiae; Epistolarum aceruum Lib. 1. Oratori necessaria est sapientia; Collectiones Medicinales Lib. 1 Recipe in nomine individuae trinitate; Abbreviationes doctorum Lib. 1. Post locorum descriptionem debet sequi; De astrologiae valore Lib. 1. Post locorum descriptionem debet sequi.* Thomas Tanner (*Bibliotheca Britannico-Hibernica* (1748), p. 115) repeats the entry of Bale, adding further works noted by John Pitts in *De Illustribus Angliae Scriptoribus* (Paris, 1619), pp. 648, 861.

[22] *Index Britanniae scriptorum*, ed. Poole and Bateson, pp. 116–17.

Only three works are listed for Botoner in this notebook: the *Anglorum antiquitates*; a description of Bristol; and the *Acta domini Ioannis Fastolf*, noted as in 1557 as being in one volume with the opening line 'Anno Christi 1421 et anno regni'. The location is given by Bale as follows: *Ex collegio Magdalene Oxonii*. Since Bale claimed to write from personal visits to libraries and actual sight of the texts he listed, there is a possibility that at least some of Worcester's works had passed into the hands of Magdalen College, presumably with other manuscripts in his possession linked to Sir John Fastolf. Yet there is today no known evidence of such works in the possession of the College. If they had been there in the late fifteenth/early sixteenth century it would seem they had been dispersed or destroyed. If a Latin life of Fastolf had existed (as Bale suggests) then either it no longer exists or has continued to elude detection. There is no suggestion, however, that the M 9 chronicle was ever at Magdalen College.

HERALDS AND THE M 9 CHRONICLE

a. Walter Bellengier

Worcester's mention, in the notes concerning his first journey begun in 1477, of Walter Bellengier (sometimes anglicised to Bellingham) as a source of information on presences at the battle of Verneuil is a potentially significant *point de départ*.[23] Bellengier was the last holder of the office of Ireland King of Arms, a post which he held from 1467 to around 1484.[24] He had accompanied Edward IV to France in 1475 and was most likely the herald who took the English king's letter of defiance to Louis XI of France.[25] One of the grants of arms for which he was responsible was issued on 13 July 1475 at Fauquembergues, significantly close to the battlefield of Agincourt where we know the king spent two nights.[26]

That Worcester knew Bellengier is confirmed by the reference to him as a source of information on those present at the battle of Verneuil. The Latin wording used here by Worcester – 'secundum relacionem Irland le herolde mihi factum anno Christi 1477 primo Decembris' – suggests personal contact between the two men on a matter of mutual interest. The M 9 chronicle includes a list of those present with the duke of Bedford at the siege of Ivry who then, implicitly, accompanied him to meet the French in battle at Verneuil (ff. 53v–54r). Bellengier's list as supplied to Worcester in 1477, however, included five names not in the original M 9 list: Sir John Salvain; the earl of Suffolk; Sir Andrew Ogard; Davy Howell; and [Walter] Charlton, where we find further information ('who married the duke of York's

---

[23]   *Itineraries*, p. 3.

[24]   London, 'Walter Bellengier', pp. 232–6. In 1455 he was in the service of the earls of Northumberland as their Esperance Pursuivant (CP 40/776 m. 278 dorse, cited in Mead, 'Walter Belyngham, Esperance Pursuivant', p. 103).

[25]   Hall (1809), p. 309. As Hall notes, he was confused by French writers with Garter. See also London, *Life of William Bruges*, p. 33.

[26]   For the king's presence at Azincourt see *Appendix to the Second Report of the Royal Commission on Historical Manuscripts*, p. 94; Scofield, *The Life and Reign of Edward IV*, ii, p. 133. For mention of the presence of Ireland King of Arms on the campaign in France see *Calendar of State Papers: Milan, 1385–1618*, pp. 189–200. The arms granted were a differenced version of his own arms but the reason for this is not clear. Thanks to Dr Adrian Ailes for this observation.

mistress'). In three further cases Bellengier provided further information of the county of origin of participants (Gilbert Halsall of Lancashire; Lancelot de Lisle of Hampshire; Glazedale (i.e. William Glasdale) of Blackmoor beyond York). This information can be seen to have had an impact on William Worcester. On M 9 he added in his own hand Salvain's name to the original chronicle list of those present with Bedford. He also amended the original spelling of Thomas Burgh. Alongside that same name Worcester added 'armiger valens in armis', and with a longer addition after the name of Matthew Gough, that he had been taken prisoner during the rout but later released.

We cannot be sure when Worcester made these specific amendments, but such changes, alongside his record of information gleaned from Bellengier, indicate that he remained keen to discuss and compare information on the wars. It was surely in the mid- to late 1470s that Worcester was himself drawing up a list of the retinue of the duke of Bedford for inclusion in the book of exemplars of which his son changed the dedication and which is now Lambeth Palace Library MS 506.[27] Around the same time, Bellengier was commissioning copies of materials concerning the wars in France. On f. 56v of British Library Add. MS 4101 (sometimes referred to as Birch 4101) we find the following:

> Lan mil cccclxxvii et le xiij jour du moys de decembre fut fait et escript ces livres en la cite de Londres a la Request de honnorable et saige homme Water Bellengier natif de Dyeppe Roy darmes dirlande De tres victorieux tres hault et trespuissant prince Le Roy edowart dangleterre quart de ce nom Lequel livre a este escript par Jean Pelhisser escollier de luniversite de paris et serviteur dudit Roy darmes direlande Lequel Roydarmes dirland a este officier darmes par lespace de cinquante cinq ans et plus a content de la date dessus mise. Explicit.

British Library Add. MS 4101 includes a number of texts relating to the war in France under Henry V and Henry VI including, on the folio following the comment given above, ordinances made at a meeting of heralds in Rouen in January 1421.[28] Hugh Stanford London assumed that the comment related to the ordinances.[29] But its position on the dorse of the preceding folio and the use of the word 'Explicit' makes it much more likely that the comment is placed at the end of the material which precedes it. This material, occupying folios 37 to 56, is copies of extracts from the *chambre des comptes* of Normandy during English rule. Most concern the English garrison of Avranches in the 1440s, and refer to the actions of Edmund Beaufort, duke of Somerset.[30] It is tempting to think that their copying

---

[27]   Lambeth Palace Library, MS 506, ff. 8r–11r.

[28]   For the full contents see *Catalogue of Additions to the Manuscripts 1756–1782: Additional Manuscripts 4101–5017*, pp. 15–16. BL, Add. MS 4101 was bequeathed to the British Museum by Thomas Birch (1705–66) and formed the first addition to the initial collection of manuscripts bequeathed by Hans Sloane (d. 1753). We are grateful to Dr Adrian Ailes for discussion of this manuscript.

[29]   London, *The Life of William Bruges*, p. 98, although he cited the manuscript reference incorrectly as Harley 4101 and gave the date as mil cccclxvii rather than the correct mil cccclxxvii.

[30]   BL, Add. MS 4101, ff. 37–56. The copies also include a safe-conduct given by Charles VII in favour of Robert Don, master of a ship of 300 tuns, on 28 January 1452 (f. 52r). This

may have been linked in some way to the interests of Worcester in attacking the duke. We also find between folios 65r and 69v copies of the ordinances which the duke of Bedford issued in Normandy in December 1423. Worcester referred to these same ordinances in an annotation to his *Boke of Noblesse*, noting that he had presented them to Edward IV just before his departure from London for France in late May 1475, and which had been preserved in the keeping of John Fastolf.[31]

We can conclude, therefore, that Worcester's continuing interest in the Anglo-French wars of the early part of the century was matched by that of the herald Bellengier. Edward IV's invasion of northern France in 1475 had, it seems, stimulated that interest further. It is credible that Bellengier was shown or even given the M 9 chronicle by Worcester. A study of the text of the chronicle indicates that it contains annotations in hands other than that of William Worcester. Whilst it is extremely difficult to identify or date such hands, there is indication by the style of writing that one or more Frenchmen were involved. For instance, the names of La Pucelle and her companions which were added at the very end of the chronicle (f. 66r) are in a French-style hand which has a late fifteenth-century appearance.[32] We also find several marginal headings in French in a late fifteenth-century French-style hand. Walter Bellengier, as a herald of French origins domiciled in England for an extended period, is certainly a candidate to have been this annotator even if we cannot be certain he ever owned the chronicle.[33]

b. Christopher Barker

There is very strong evidence, however, that the chronicle was in the possession of a later herald, Christopher Barker (d. 1550). This is revealed by what is written on the dorse of the last page of the original chronicle (f. 66v). Here in an early sixteenth-century hand we find the text of an oath taken by Francis I of France in 1515 to uphold the treaty of Montargis with the English. The oath is followed by an annotation in the hand of Christopher Barker which reads as follows:

> at the taking of the othe was west then mayd[e] bishop Elette of Ey[ly] and w[t] hym xpofer' barker alias Lysely pourcevant to the Duek of Suff' after Suffolk harould after Richemond harould after that Norray Kyng of armes after that gartier principall king of arms.

Christopher Barker was Lisle Pursuivant from 1513 and subsequently Suffolk herald from 1517 to Charles Brandon, duke of Suffolk (c. 1484–1545), and was

---

seems a random inclusion. We can speculate that it could be linked to a visit of William Worcester to Normandy to collect information for Fastolf.

[31]   BL, Add. MS 4101, ff. 65r–69v, with Worcester's annotation in his *Boke of Noblesse* in BL, MS Royal 18 B XXII, f. 15r. Worcester also referred to Bedford's ordinances in the Advertiriment, probably prepared for the attack on Somerset by the duke of Norfolk in 1453 (College of Arms, MS Arundel 48, ff. 324r–325v). See also Nall, *Reading and War*, pp. 52–3.

[32]   The chronicle text in Nantron's hand ends close to the top of f. 66r with 'autres chevaliers, escuiers et nobles dont de partie diceulx les noms sensuivent. Cestassavoir'. But no names follow in Nantron's hand. Rather, seven names have been added in a later French-style hand: 'le bastard dorleans, la pucell, le Hyre, le sire de Rays, le sire de lorese, messyre Robrt Bodrycourt capytayne vawcolour'.

[33]   We are grateful to Dr Nigel Ramsay for discussion on this and other points.

present with his master in France in 1514–15.[34] He transferred into royal service in 1522, becoming Richmond herald. In June 1536 he was appointed Norroy King of Arms and on 15 July of the same year finally Garter at the death of Thomas Wall (Garter 1534–36). The annotation on folio 66v must therefore post-date his appointment as Garter in 1536 but precede his death in 1550. The M 9 chronicle can therefore be shown to be in Barker's possession at some point between these dates. He was involved in overseas negotiations linked to Henry VIII's proposed invasion of France in the early 1540s, and accompanied the king on the expedition of 1544. Within London he had a house in Paternoster Row, where chapter meetings of the heralds were sometimes held.

By 1619 our chronicle was bound with sixteenth-century materials to form MS M 9.[35] This composite volume contains 100 folios in total but there are several blank pages. As we have seen, Barker used the dorse of the last page of the chronicle (f. 66v) for a note of the oath paid by the French king in 1515. But another link to Barker is indicated through the first seven folios of the composite volume, numbered in pencil from f. 1 to f. 7, which contain the proclamation of a tourney. There is a high degree of certainty that this relates to the Field of the Cloth of Gold (7–24 June 1520) at which Charles Brandon was present, with Suffolk herald Barker no doubt in his company. The hand is contemporary or close to the date of the event.

On the dorse of the last page of this tourney proclamation (i.e. f. 7v) we see written 'The ordre of the states of the blode Ryalle' in a mid-sixteenth-century hand. The chronicle follows immediately afterwards. Since the chronicle already had its own contemporary foliation from xxxj to lxvj, folio 7r was at some point also numbered as 30 in order to suggest a direct sequence. There are therefore no folios 8 to 29 in the volume, nor is there evidence of any effort to introduce a new foliation to the chronicle section when the various elements were put together. The folio following the chronicle is numbered as 119 in the same hand as the first seven folios of the volume. If there had been intervening folios from 67 to 118, they were not included in the final binding. Folio 119r contains notes 'of the vyolatynge or breakynge of a Sepulchre or monument' in the same mid-sixteenth-century hand as 'The ordre of the states of the blode Ryalle' on f. 7v. On its dorse there are two lines of Latin verse to St George in a sixteenth-century hand.

The following folio, marked 120, is paper of fifteenth-century date and contains a list in Latin of those present at the siege of Leysaye (*recte* Lagny) in the hand of William Worcester.[36] The page also bears two later additions. At the top is written in a sixteenth- or early seventeenth-century hand 'Ihus Maria Amen dico vobis Amen Thome Chorum Angelorum'. Immediately below Worcester's list we find 'Thomas Hudson merchant tailor of London', in a sixteenth-century hand.[37] On the back of the sheet (f. 120v) we find in a mid- to late sixteenth-century hand 'Memorandum delyvyrd unto master palgrave iiij pec[es] of gren say for the anging of ys chambare Item a bedsted Item to aloue for the glass iij^s iiij^d'. The rest of

---

[34]   Yorke, 'Barker, Sir Christopher (d. 1550)', *ODNB*.

[35]   For the full description see Campbell and Steer, *Catalogue*, pp. 129–31.

[36]   See Appendix.

[37]   No one of this name seems to be mentioned in N. V. Sleigh-Johnson's unpublished doctoral thesis (UCL 1989), 'The Merchant Taylors Company of London 1580–1645'. A Thomas Hudson, son of Richard Hudson, merchant taylor, was admitted to the Merchant Taylors' school in 1593 (Robinson, *Register of Scholars*, p. 34).

the volume is made up of fifty folios of sixteenth-century paper but only the first seven of these have been used.[38] They contain an account of jousts held in Paris in November 1514, written in the same hand as the proclamation of a tourney written on the opening folios of the volume, and therefore probably arising out of the direct interest, if not involvement, of Christopher Barker. The remaining forty-three folios are blank.

It would appear, therefore, that Barker's specific interest in Anglo-French relations arising out of his personal experiences, as well as his enthusiasm as a herald for deeds of arms past and present, had encouraged him to collect materials on the war with France in the fifteenth century as well as of his own period. It is easy to see how such cognate materials, perhaps already held together as a distinct group, would subsequently be bound together by the time of the 1619 catalogue. The binding is typical of an early seventeenth-century format used in the College, mirroring that of heraldic visitations of this time. The volume as a whole measures 270 x 210 mm and is bound using reversed calf boards. On the front and back is an indented stamp in gold of the seal with the arms of what was then commonly called the Office of Arms. It bears the legend 'sigillum commune corporationis officii armorum'. There is evidence of later re-stitching and improvements to the binding using inner paste boards, carried out most likely in the late nineteenth or early twentieth century.[39] We also find bound into the volume after folio 120 another sheet in Worcester's hand which contains information which would have been relevant to the continuation of the chronicle beyond 1429,[40] This could suggest that Barker had collected such stray pieces but the fact that it is not foliated makes it more likely that the sheet was added during later refurbishments when some herald spotted it was in the same hand as folio 120.

Whilst ownership by Christopher Barker of the chronicle is very likely indeed, it is impossible to know precisely when the chronicle came formally into the custody of the College of Arms (or Office of Arms as it was known then). Since Barker died in 1550 before a permanent home for the Office was acquired, we would expect his collections to have been held within his own house in Paternoster Row during his lifetime. Individual heralds were active in creating their own collections of materials, both historical and relating to their duties. Ordinances ascribed to Richard, duke of Gloucester as constable of England and Earl Marshal between 1469 and 1483 urged the heralds to 'apply them selfes in redyng bokes of dyvers langages as cronycles and storyes for the better inducement of understanding in gestes (of) honour and feates of Armes'.[41] It was common for royal heralds to pass on their collections to their successors but in a rather haphazard manner. The small quantity of materials held collectively in the house in Coldharbour on Upper Thames Street, which had been granted to the heralds at the time of Richard III's charter of incorporation in 1484, were taken by John Writhe (Garter 1478–1504) to his own house when the charter was rescinded by

---

[38] The first five are numbered in pencil 1–5, the next is unnumbered, and the following two are numbered as 6 and 7.

[39] We are very grateful to the College of Arms conservator Christopher Harvey for his thoughts on the binding of the manuscript and on the chronicle section.

[40] See Appendix.

[41] BL, Cotton Tiberius E VIII, ff. 159r-v, printed in Ramsay, 'Richard III and the Office of Arms', p. 158.

Henry VII. These materials, along with Writhe's own, subsequently passed to his son and successor as Garter, Thomas Wriothesley.[42] In the 1540s the heralds petitioned for new premises for themselves and their libraries, without success in the short term although it seems that some books may have been stored in the interim in the dissolved Augustinian friary in the city of London.[43]

A new charter was given to the College in 1555 along with a new site in Derby Place, the site of the present building facing Queen Victoria Street, where a building was constructed by 1564. It remains uncertain, however, how much 'historic', or even current, material was brought to these new premises by the then heralds. When an official inquiry was carried out in 1595 it was alleged that many ancient books and records had been 'robbed'. The resulting reforms of 1597 urged the College to preserve the old books and records in their keeping as well as to purchase the records of two recent Clarenceux Kings of Arms, Robert Cooke (d. 1593) and Richard Lee (d. 1597).[44] Samson Lennard's catalogue of 1619 therefore reveals the state of play following these reforms, showing also the origins of an alphabetical press system although some subsequent reorganisations took place. The College building of 1564 was destroyed in the Great Fire of London in 1666 but the library was saved and returned to the new building erected between 1670 and 1690, which has survived to this day.

Christopher Barker's papers, along with those of his predecessors as Garter, Thomas Wriothesley and Thomas Wall, are known to have formed a significant part of what became the foundation collections L and M of the Heralds' Library in the early seventeenth century: indeed, it has been noted that their manuscripts 'typically … include accounts of events in which the writers themselves played a role'.[45] That situation is particularly noticeable in the case of the M 9 chronicle where an event concerning Barker has been noted on the dorse of the last folio of the original chronicle, to which he has added his own observation.

We can trace another item relating to Anglo-French relations in the foundation collections which is known to have come from Barker. This compilation, MS M 16 bis, with documents in the hands of a scribe known to be linked to Barker, includes an early sixteenth-century copy of the commission of 25 August 1424 to Sir John Fastolf, Thomas, lord Scales and Sir John Montgomery for the initial invasion of Maine as well as the treaty for the surrender of Sillé-le-Guillaume which the same men made on 1 October 1424.[46] Within the same volume is a copy of a

---

[42]   Wagner, *Records*, p. 9.

[43]   'In 1545 there was a Council enquiry into the fate of a great number of books of the Office of Arms which were said to have been there' (Ramsay, 'London. Clarenceux King of Arms and the Office of Arms', p. 171).

[44]   Wagner, *Records*, pp. 12–13.

[45]   Campbell and Steer, *Catalogue*, pp. 10–11.

[46]   College of Arms, MS M 16 bis, ff. 121–3; Campbell and Steer, *Catalogue*, pp. 141–54. Copies of these two documents along with further materials concerning Sir John Fastolf are also found in College of Arms, MS Arundel 26, which seems to have been compiled in the late fifteenth century and later to have been owned by John Writhe, Garter (1478–1504). Further copies of documents concerning Henry V's wars in France, including the arrangements for the laying of siege to Rouen in 1418–19, are found in MS Arundel 29, which also seems to date to the late fifteenth century but whose provenance is not known (*Catalogue of the Arundel Manuscripts in the College of Arms*, pp. 38–9, 43).

document of 1371 concerning Charles V's decisions on which fortresses should be demolished.[47] Barker's interest in French history and heraldry is also revealed by the contents of MS M 4 in which his own hand appears.[48]

OTHER HERALDS AND THE ANNOTATIONS WITHIN THE M 9 CHRONICLE

That there was genuine interest by other early sixteenth-century heralds in the late medieval Anglo-French wars is also evidenced by the bequest of Thomas Benolt (Clarenceux 1511–34), to his deputy and eventual successor, Thomas Hawley, of 'all my four volumes of Froissart … with all other my books of chronicles, gestes and honour', along with rolls of arms, visitation records and other materials linked to his office of arms.[49] This quotation might suggest Benolt as a candidate for possession of the M 9 chronicle but an inventory of his books at his death does not contain anything which quite resembles it.[50] That said, Benolt did own 'cronicles in French of popes emperours and kings of England with the armes of divers gentilmen painted', described as the work of William Whiting, Huntingdon herald and later Chester herald.[51] Whiting appears to have been Chester herald between 1447 and c. 1455 but, as yet, nothing has been discovered about his writing activity nor has his chronicle come to light. The description of his work is not consonant with that of the M 9 chronicle nor has evidence been discovered of links between him and the known authors of the chronicle. But mention of the work suggests that the taste for chronicles in French in the middle of the fifteenth century was not restricted to the M 9 chronicle.

Thomas Wriothesley (Garter 1505–34) came into possession of Sir John Paston's 'Grete Booke' of 1468–69, a miscellany which included the 'Mantes' military ordinances of Henry V. The volume subsequently passed through a number of heralds until it came into the hands of the first marquess of Lansdowne whose papers were sold to the British Museum in 1807.[52] Wriothesley also owned what is now British Library Additional MS 4101 in which the copy commissioned by Walter Bellengier of the heralds chapter at Rouen in 1420–21 is to be found.[53]

There is a possibility that some of the annotations in the M 9 chronicle are in the hand of Wriothesley who had been present on the 1513 expedition to France and at the Field of the Cloth of Gold in 1520, and who resided in London at Garter House in Barbican Street.[54] Passages in English added immediately below the end of the chronicle on its last page (f. 66r) − on the taking of Cherbourg in 1450, a

---

[47]   College of Arms, MS M 16 bis, ff. 123–4. See Caumont, 'Relation de la visite des forteresses'.

[48]   Campbell and Steer, *Catalogue*, p. 4. The 'French' folios linked to Barker include ff. 24–25v, a computation of the annual military expenditure for the kingdom of France, and f. 136, the lands held by Richard, duke of York in Normandy.

[49]   Wagner, *Records*, p. 10.

[50]   College of Arms, MS Heralds I, ff. 189r–191r, summarised in Wagner, *Heralds and Heraldry in the Middle Ages*, appendix, and printed in full in Ramsay, 'London. Clarenceux King of Arms and the Office of Arms', pp. 176–202.

[51]   Ramsay, 'London. Clarenceaux King of Arms and the Office of Arms', p. 178.

[52]   See the detailed record for BL, Lansdowne 285 on the bl.uk site.

[53]   London, *Life of William Bruges*, p. 98.

[54]   Yorke, 'Wriothesley [formerly Writhe], Sir Thomas (d. 1534)', *ODNB*.

short description of Normandy and a note of the ransom and release of the duke of Orléans in 1440 – are very close to other proven examples of his handwriting.[55]

A number of different hands can be seen in the annotations. A desire to add supplementary details was a common motivation for early modern owners and readers of texts. In the case of the heralds their annotations were stimulated by the visitations they undertook since the presence of ancestors at the great military events of the past was taken as a mark of armigerous status. This may explain the sixteenth-century additions of John Mortimer, Philip Hall, William Hall and James Ormond to the list of those knighted by Henry V at the Somme (f. 32v). Philip Hall was also named as *bailli* of Alençon, replacing the original name in Nantron's hand, Thomas Burgh, which was deleted (f. 38r); Sir Ferry Mortimer was similarly added as *bailli* of Honfleur (f. 39v) – a spurious addition since this office never existed in the period covered by the chronicle; Richard Merbury was added as captain of Conches (f. 39v); Philip Hall, Sir John Aubemond and Sir John Radcliffe were added to the list of those present at the siege of La Gravelle (f. 60v); and Sir Henry Mortimer was added to the list of those at the siege of Orléans (f. 64r). It should be noted that two family names feature more than once – Hall and Mortimer – suggesting some specific interest on the part of the annotator.

Significantly, in the context of possible ownership of the chronicle by heralds and its eventual deposit within the collections of the College of Arms, heraldic annotations have been added against the names of certain Englishmen. By their style they look to be of an early to mid-sixteenth-century date. From f. 37r to f. 39v, where we find lists of appointments made by Henry V to various captaincies in his initial conquest, a garter symbol has been drawn against the names of certain men (Figure 5). There are eighteen such garter marks overall. The intention was surely to indicate that the man concerned had been a Knight of the Garter. For eight individuals the assumption was correct. Humphrey, duke of Gloucester has the Garter mark against his name in two places, and Thomas, duke of Clarence thrice, the last being alongside a further marginal note 'obijt' (f. 43v), in the narrative of his death at the battle of Baugé. In five cases, however, the mark was placed against the name of a man for whom there is no evidence of his being a Garter knight. Furthermore, the approach does not appear to have been systematic, since there are several other men named in the chronicle who were KG yet did not have the Garter mark placed against their name, including Sir John Fastolf himself.[56] Such errors and omissions do not, however, detract from the probability of the involvement of heralds since in the sixteenth century knowledge of who had been KG in the past was flawed. It is also possible that the annotator did not complete the task he had begun.

A similar conclusion can be drawn for other heraldic annotations. In ten cases on folios 37v and 38r, the first lists of appointments made by Henry V in Normandy, and in one case each on folio 39r and folio 45r, we see small drawings to the left or right of names in the form of heraldic symbols which were intended to reflect the coat of arms or crest of the individual concerned (Figure 5). A good example here is the hunting dog of the Talbot crest. In all, there are twelve symbols given, but in

---

[55]   For instance, in BL, Add. MS 45131, f. 68r, printed as fig. 10a of Walker, 'The Westminster Tournament Challenge', p. 13. We are grateful to Dr Nigel Ramsay for this reference.

[56]   These are Thomas Beaufort, earl of Dorset and duke of Exeter; John Cornwall; John Fastolf; John Grey of Ruthin; William Harrington; Walter Hungerford; William Phelip; Thomas Rempston. Data has been taken from Collins, *The Order of the Garter*, appendix 1.

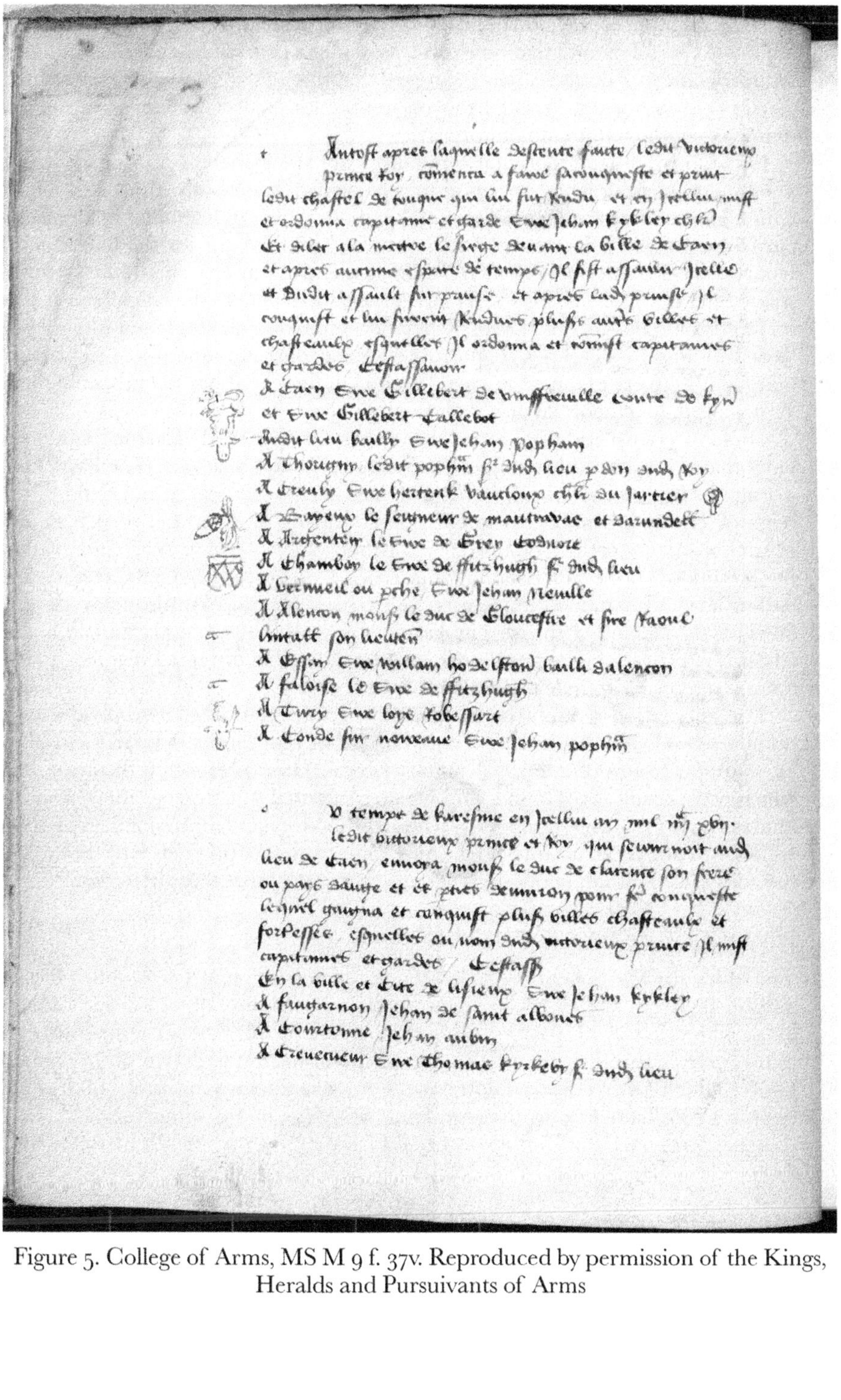
Tantost apres laquelle descente faicte ledit victorieux
prince Roy commenca a faire sa conqueste et print
ledit chastel de touque qui lui fut rendu et en icellui mist
et ordonna capitaine et garde Sire Jehan kykeley chlr
Et dela ala mettre le siege devant la ville de Caen
et apres aucune espace de temps il fist assaillir icelle
et dudit assault fut prinse et apres ladite prinse il
conquist et lui furent rendues plus autres villes et
chasteaulx esquelles il ordonna et commist capitaines
et gardes cestassavoir
A Caen Sire Gillebert de umfreuille conte de kyme
et Sire Gillebert tallebot
Audit lieu bailly Sire Jehan popham
A thoucque ledit popham sr dudit lieu par don dudit Roy
A creuly Sire hertenk vanclous chlr du Jartier
A bayeux le seigneur de mautravas et darundell
A Argenten le Sire de grey codnore
A chambray le Sire de ffitzhugh sr dudit lieu
A vernueil ou perche Sire Jehan Nevill
A Alencon mons le duc de Gloucestre et sire Raoul
lentall son lieuten
A Essay Sire William hodelston bailli dalencon
A faloise le Sire de ffitzhugh
A Tury Sire loys robessart
A Conde sur noireau Sire Jehan pophm

Au temps de karesme en icellui an mil iiij c xvij
ledit victorieux prince et Roy qui sejournoit audit
lieu de Caen envoia mons le duc de clarence son frere
ou pays dauge et es pties denviron pour faire conqueste
lequel gaigna et conquist plus villes chasteaulx et
forteresses esquelles ou nom dudit victorieux prince il mist
capitaines et gardes cestass
En la ville et cite de lisieux Sire Jehan kykeley
A ffaugarnon Jehan de saint albones
A Courtonne Jehan aubin
A Crevecueur Sire Thomas kykeley sr dudit lieu

Figure 5. College of Arms, MS M 9 f. 37v. Reproduced by permission of the Kings, Heralds and Pursuivants of Arms two cases (Sir John Popham and Sir William Porter) the same drawing is repeated at a later mention of the individual concerned. The fact that these annotations are limited to two folios, and that no effort was made to provide a heraldic annotation for every one even on those folios, suggests that this was a process which was initiated but not completed. Perhaps, too, the annotations reflect individuals of interest to the sixteenth-century annotators.

Other forms of later marginal annotations are also evident. For instance, we see a pointing finger, drawing attention to a particular point but without any explanation given. Others take the form of headings which indicate the content at a particular point, for instance, 'mariage du roy' on folio 40r for the marriage of Henry V and Catherine. All such headings are given in French and in a French style of hand, which, as discussed earlier, appears to date to the late fifteenth century and could possibly be that of Bellengier. There is a much greater intensity of these headings in the post-1422 narrative. 'Azingcourt' is found in the right-hand margin of folio 31v in the same French hand but there is also a second annotation, 'Agingcourt', in a different, distinctly English, hand.

On folio 34v we find what looks like 'Tongne' rather than 'Tougue' in the left-hand margin against the taking of the castle of Touques in 1417. The hand here is English. Intriguingly, there was a Thomas Tonge who was York herald in the reign of Henry VII and subsequently Norroy King of Arms between 1522 and 1534. This may therefore be further indication of the reading of the text within the community of heralds, where Tonge wished to note his personal fascination in finding a place mentioned which was close to his own name. We also see from 1420 onwards the placing of the date in Arabic numerals in the margin, and additionally, from the death of Henry V onwards, the indication of regnal year (e.g. 1 H6), but it is impossible to date these annotations securely.

The annotations within the M 9 chronicle were undoubtedly the work of a number of individuals over an extended period of time, and are not in themselves an unusual feature of medieval manuscripts.[57] Their presence indicates a text which was consulted and used, and which generated some engagement from its readers. Save for Worcester himself, whose distinctive hand makes for firm identification, we cannot be certain who the annotators were nor precisely why they made the additions they did, but there is enough to suggest links to the heralds.

THE USE OF THE CHRONICLE BY ROBERT GLOVER

The M 9 chronicle appears to have been in the possession of Christopher Barker (Garter 1536–50) and to have come into the possession of the College of Arms along with other of his papers, although the date of this transfer remains uncertain. There is strong evidence that the M 9 chronicle was drawn on by Robert Glover after Barker's death. Glover was Portcullis Pursuivant from 1568 to 1571, deputy to William Flower, Norroy King of Arms in 1570 (marrying Flower's daughter by 1572), and Somerset herald from 1570 to his death in 1588.[58] He

---

[57]   There are also miscellaneous scribbles in sixteenth-century hands on the first page of the chronicle. On the inserted half leaf after folio 120 we see 'a 16th C signature (?) Ricardii Jaakys, and other jottings, including the name Robt. Dowland", also "fischer"' (Campbell and Steer, *Catalogue*, p. 131).

[58]   Ramsay, 'Glover, Robert (1543/4–1588)', *ODNB*.

was an avid collector and copyist, perhaps most famous for his multiple copying of the 'Agincourt roll'.[59] Of the three copies he made, the copy in British Library MS Harley 782 has engaged the most historical attention. This volume also contains several other lists in Glover's hand concerning the Hundred Years War. That of direct interest in the context of the M 9 chronicle is a list of appointments to captaincies made by Henry V,[60] which begins 'In the yere 1417 anno Domini, King Henry the v[te] conquered theis townes in Normandey and in France and made the noblemen capetaynes of the same tounes and castelles'. The list which follows is very close to the appointments to captaincies found between f. 37v and f. 57r of the M 9 chronicle. The suggestion is, therefore, that Glover derived his list from the chronicle.

Glover's list is not, however, a simple copy of the chronicle where the lists are in French. Glover provided a heading in English and throughout his list he uses 'At' to begin each entry. Until the entry for Cherbourg he writes the entries in English. He there begins 'At Cheerebourg Sir Grey de Codnor', but then continues in French 'et apres son deces sir Walter Hungerford'. Thereafter he commonly uses French in each entry until he reaches the entry for Sir John Fastolf's appointment at Le Mans. This suggests that Glover was making his list directly from the chronicle, rather than from any pre-existing translation into English made by a third party. The result is a strange mixture of English and French.

In the chronicle, the appointments to captaincies are not presented in a continuous form. Rather, they are given in separate blocks, following the chronology of the conquest, with intervening narrative. By contrast, Glover places all the appointments within a single continuous list. In order to do this, he would have had to read the chronicle to choose the information for extraction. We can see his mediation in the case of Montaiguillon where he notes the appointment of Matthew Gough ('Et Mathe Goghe esquire capytayne de at Montaiguillon en Brie') and also adds 'dont estoient capitaines Pregent de Coëtivy et Guillem bourgeois Bretons firent sarment au comte de Sallisbury qui james ilz ne feront guerre contre le Roy deca la revere de Loyre'. Glover's wording is essentially a paraphrase of the chronicle account on folio 49v, where in fact we are told of the French captains, the military action and the oath within the text before we are told of the appointment of Gough. Glover would therefore have had to read the surrounding narrative in order to paraphrase it. Indeed, since he included appointments mentioned over forty pages of the chronicle text, and also made some rearrangement in the order in which they were presented in the chronicle, we can assume he read all, or at least most, of the text.

His interest, however, was primarily heraldic rather than historical. His purpose in creating the list was linked to his duties as a herald. Campaign and battle presences of ancestors were useful for the gentry of Tudor England who wished in the heraldic visitations to prove their status. The heralds collected such lists in order to

---

[59] Wylie, 'Notes on the Agincourt Roll', pp. 105–40; Curry, *Sources*, pp. 407–8. The earliest copy of the roll is deemed to be in Bodleian Library, Ashmole MS 825, ff. 15–35. There is another in College of Arms, MS 1 bis, ff. 17–34, which lies within a collection made by Robert Cooke, Clarenceux herald (d. 1593). The BL Harley 782 copy was published by Nicolas, *History of the Battle of Agincourt* (1827), pp. 331–64, and collated with the other two copies in the second and third editions of this work.

[60] BL MS Harley 782, ff. 49v–50v.

act as checks on claims. Appointments to captaincies were indications of suitable status. In the case of the Agincourt roll, Glover chose only to list the men-at-arms by name and to count up the number of archers. After all, an archer ancestor was not deemed likely in the sixteenth century to be evidence of gentle status.

Glover mentions all of the appointments to captaincies noted in the chronicle save for one: Breteuil. This is potentially interesting since in the original chronicle (f. 39v) Breteuil had been listed without any captain's name being given. The name of a captain (Ferry Mortimer) had been added later, probably in the sixteenth century. This could indicate that Glover consulted the chronicle before the addition had been made. But this argument is potentially undermined by the fact that he does include another addition which seems to be in the same hand: Sir Richard Merbury as captain of Conches. Glover's omission of Breteuil may be a simple copying error or else a deliberate omission for a reason which we can only guess. Could it be that he did not consider 'Ferry Mortimer' an English name and therefore relevant to his heraldic visitations?

British Library MS Harley 782 contains other lists which show signs of being drawn by Glover from the chronicle. On folios 49r-v, for instance, we find lists of the English dead and prisoners at the battle of Baugé. Glover gives the dead first, and the prisoners second, a reversal of the ordering in the chronicle (ff. 43v–44r). That Glover shows some confusion is illustrated by the fact that he starts the list of dead with the duke of Bedford, although he has subsequently added '& Clerens'. Thirteen names follow. Ten of these are in the chronicle list and are given in the same order, but Glover has added three more (Sir John Lumley, Lord Roos and the earl of Tancarville, Lord John Grey). The chronicle placed the latter erroneously in the list of prisoners, an error which Glover has corrected. Otherwise both provide the same list of prisoners in the same order although we can spot small variations. For instance, the chronicle names Thomas Burgh, correctly, as esquire; Glover calls him Sir Thomas Burgh. But as with the list of appointments to captaincies, we can conclude that Glover read the surrounding narrative in the chronicle when drawing up his list since his heading refers to the treachery of André Lombart.[61]

Without labouring the point, similar conclusions can be reached about Glover's lists in British Library MS Harley 782 of English lords in Henry V's army of 1415 (f. 49r), at the siege of Meaux (f. 50r), and at the battles of Cravant and Verneuil (ff. 51r–52r), where there is a closeness, especially in order of names, if not always an exact replication of the chronicle lists. But the list he includes of those serving in the household and retinue of the duke of Bedford as Regent of France (ff. 52v–53v) and in Gascony (ff. 53v–54) cannot have been derived from the chronicle, or at least not exclusively, and may reflect use of other lists drawn up by William Worcester, as in Lambeth Palace Library MS 506.

Glover was an inveterate copier. In the case of the Agincourt roll he seems to have produced three copies, perhaps in order that various heralds conducting visitations might have the material simultaneously. In College of Arms L 15 folios 24r and 27v we find a list in Glover's hand with the following heading, 'The names and arms of dyvers noblemen and gentlemen that had the gouvernement

---

[61] 'The battaill of Bauge in the yere of christe Mccccxxi in France in the tyme of Kinge Henry the vte where was slayne and taken prisoners their noblemen who wer be trayed by on Andreu Lambert a doubell traiter'.

of certeyn cities, townes, castelles and forteresses conquered in France by the most victorious prince King Henry the fifte'. This is essentially the same list as in British Library Harley MS 782, with the chronicle list therefore also its source. Note here too Glover's reference to Henry V as 'victorious prince', an epithet used in the chronicle every time the king is mentioned.

College of Arms L 15 also includes another copy of the list of men serving under Bedford (ff. 144r–145v). In this version we find some coats of arms drawn next to names, much as we saw in the annotations to certain entries in the M 9 chronicle. These coats of arms are not in Glover's hand but that of Robert Cooke (d. 1593), who was Rose Blanche Pursuivant from 1561–62 before becoming Chester herald in 1562 and then Clarenceux King of Arms in 1567.[62] In 1584 Glover and Cooke, then acting in the place of Garter King of Arms, travelled together to France to invest King Henri III with the Garter. We can be certain that College of Arms L 15 was put together by Cooke, using, editing and adding to Glover's work.[63] Cooke dedicated the resulting book to the Queen to whom it was given as a New Year's gift. Its opening folios had been drawn up by Glover to remind the queen 'How your Maiestie is heir to the dukedom of Normandy and the kingedom of England', but Cooke had altered this to 'How the queenes maijestye is heire [etc.] by William Conqueror'. The volume also included, probably also in Glover's hand, a copy of the Battle Roll, the names of those who were believed to have accompanied William the Conqueror to England in 1066.[64]

Where and when did Glover read the chronicle and draw up lists from it? Given what we know about his career, it was most likely whilst he was Somerset herald. He had begun to carry out visitations shortly before his appointment to this role in 1570. By 1584 he had compiled an Ordinary of 15,000 arms, reflecting something of a culmination in his research activity. Drilling down further, it can be suggested from a note on Glover's list of appointments in L 15 that the New Year's gift to the queen was made in 1572.[65] Undoubtedly, our chronicle had been accessible to him. This in turn suggests that after Barker's death in 1550 it had either been handed on to individual heralds and kings of arms, such as Glover's father-in-law William Flower, or his associate Robert Cooke, or else was placed in the collection of the College of Arms, which had its own building from 1564.

Glover's manuscripts were widely dispersed at his death. The owner in the early seventeenth century of British Library MS Harley 782 was another herald

---

[62]   Day, 'Cooke, Robert (d. 1593)', *ODNB*.

[63]   We are grateful to Dr Nigel Ramsay for this information and for discussion on this text. The College of Arms purchased Cooke's papers at the end of the sixteenth century at the impulse of William Camden, who was Clarenceux from 1597.

[64]   A link with the manuscripts associated with William Worcester can be hazarded here too, since he is credited by the antiquarian Henry Spelman (1562–1641) with making a copy of the Battle Roll in May 1449 (Norfolk Record Office, Norwich Public Library Manuscript Collection MS 7197, f. 299v).

[65]   College of Arms L 15, f. 24r. The note reads 'Dr W 1572 to the queen for a neweresgyfte' and is not in the hand of either Glover or Cooke. Identification of Dr W is problematic. Dr Nicholas Wotton, who became dean of Canterbury after the dissolution, has been suggested, but he died in 1567.

who signed on the first folio 'Ralf Broke, Yorke Herald, 1604'.[66] By 1630 the volume was in the hands of Thomas Cole, a lawyer of the Inner Temple, and was amongst many of his manuscripts which came to Edward Stillingfleet (d. 1699) before being purchased by Robert Harley (1661–1724). The Harleian Library was purchased for the nation in 1753 as one of the foundation collections of the British Museum. It was there that it was seen by Bréquigny (1714–95), a Norman historian, who had been sent to England in 1764–66 to search for materials concerning the history of France.[67] He transcribed the list of Henry V's appointments but it remained unpublished until 1847 when Champollion-Figéac included Bréquigny's transcript in *Lettres des rois et reines de France et d'Angleterre*.[68] The list was published again in 1858 within a selection of Bréquigny's transcripts published by the Société des Antiquaires de Normandie.[69] The list, as mediated by Bréquigny, has been much drawn on by English historians but without appreciation of its provenance. Although it is two stages removed from the M 9 chronicle, there can be no doubt that this chronicle is its original source.

---

[66] Brooke was York herald from 1593 to 1625. We are grateful to Dr Nigel Ramsay for details of its later history. The volume was rebound in 1786.

[67] Bémont, 'Bréquigny, Louis Georges Oudard Feudrix de'.

[68] Champollion-Figéac, *Lettres*, vol. 2, pp. 339–43. This work was published under the auspices of the Comité des Travaux Historiques.

[69] 'Rôles normands et français', no. 1359, pp. 249–50.

6

The M 9 chronicle and the histories of the mid-Tudor period

Benedicta Rowe was the first to identify the M 9 chronicle as a major source for Edward Hall's *Union of the Two Noble and Illustre Famelies of Lancastre and Yorke*, which was published in 1548.[1] In this section we shall look closely at the use which Hall made of the chronicle, whilst also considering how he might have had access to it and how his work (and hence his use of the chronicle) influenced other Tudor writers of the later sixteenth century. However, there is a conundrum facing us here. At the beginning of Hall's work we find a list of his sources: 'The names of the aucthors aswell Latin as other out of the whiche this work was first gathered and after compiled and conioyned'.[2] Under the heading 'Englishe writers' is the name 'Ihon (i.e. John) Basset'. Yet the M 9 chronicle is, according to the incipit written by William Worcester, the work of Peter Basset, and it is in French. Could it be that Hall did not draw directly on the chronicle but on a now lost English text by a Basset which was linked in some way to the chronicle? We shall return to this question at the end of the section, but first let us consider Edward Hall and his *Union*.

EDWARD HALL

Hall's *Union*, which covered events from the last years of the reign of Richard II to the author's own lifetime in the reign of Henry VIII, marks a distinctive turning point in the writing of history in England and in English. The significance of Hall's approach is neatly summed up by his biographer in the *Oxford Dictionary of National Biography*: 'Hall's text represents an important confluence of humanist and vernacular historical writing. He did not produce a raw chronology of events; rather, he absorbed the lessons of humanist historiography both in giving his history a narrative shape and in concerning himself with political rather than divine

---

[1] Even in its own time it was better known as Hall's Chronicle (Lucas, 'Hall's Chronicle and the Mirror for Magistrates', p. 357). An edition was produced in London in 1809 by Henry Ellis with the title *Hall's Chronicle containing the History of England during the reign of Henry the Fourth and succeeding monarchs to the end of the reign of Henry the Eighth*. A link between Basset and Hall had already been speculated by Sydney Lee in his biography of Peter Basset for the first edition of the *DNB* (vol. 24, pp. 63–4), and Planchenault also believed that there was a Basset text behind Hall's work.

[2] Hall (1809), p. viii.

causes.'[3] Hall's overarching aim was to explain how the political problems in the last years of Richard II's reign, which led to his deposition and the coming of the house of Lancaster, were worked out over the course of the fifteenth century until resolved by the coming of the Tudors. This aim is explained at the very beginning of Hall's work and also explains the title which he gave it, as he outlined in his preface. Hall's inclusion of a list of authors at the beginning of the *Union* is further evidence of a new approach to English historical writing, where sources and evidence took on a significance they had not held hitherto. In this current discussion, it is not simply that Hall listed a work by a so called (mistakenly?) John Basset but that within his text he also credited a Peter Basset, a chamberlain of Henry V at the time of the latter's death, as a source of information for the king's last illness.[4] The Basset problem is returned to at the end of this chapter.

The dominant form of non-Latin chronicle writing in England before Hall was that of the London Chronicle, which was closely linked to the tradition of the vernacular Brut. Here the division of time was by the mayoralty of the City: the names of the mayor and sheriffs were followed by a narrative of 'their' year. The Chronicles of London formed a source listed by Hall under 'Englishe writers'. The same list includes 'Fabian', a reference to *The Newe Cronycles of England and Fraunce* written by the London draper Robert Fabyan (d. 1513) but printed three years after his death, which were also organised by mayoral year. Fabyan served as sheriff of the City in 1493–94 and came close to election as mayor.[5]

Fabyan's second son was apprenticed to Edward Hall's father, who was a member of a well-established London family which for many generations had been leading members of the Grocers' Company. Edward was born in 1496 or 1497 in the parish of St Mildred Poultry. After an education at Eton and King's College Cambridge he entered Gray's Inn around 1521. He may have entered parliament as early as 1523 but was most certainly a member in the parliaments of 1529 and 1539 for Much Wenlock (and perhaps 1536 too) and then for Bridgnorth in the parliaments of 1542 and 1545. It has been speculated that there was a Shropshire connection in his family, but London was undoubtedly Hall's home and his place of business. He held the office of common serjeant in London from 1533 to 1535, when he became under-sheriff of the City, an office he held to his death on 15 April 1547.

Hall's historical writing was a side-line to his professional activity in the law.[6] He admitted that he was not an original writer of history, seeing himself as a compiler.[7] This is well expressed in the dedicatory preface for the *Union* which he penned just before his death for Edward VI: 'I have compiled and gathered (and not made) out of diverse writers as well forayn as Englishe this simple treatise …'.[8] Hall's exposure

---

[3]   Herman, 'Hall, Edward (1497–1547)', *ODNB*. See also www.historyofparliamentonline.org/volume/1509-1558/member/hall-edward-i-149697-1547.

[4]   Hall (1809), p. 113.

[5]   McLaren, M.-R., 'Fabyan, Robert (d. 1513)', *ODNB*. Fabyan's chronicle had been printed in 1516 by Richard Pynson as *The New Chronicles of England and France* without attribution, but the 1533 edition printed by John Rastell bore the author's own name. For a later edition of 1811 see *The New Chronicles of England and France*, ed. H. Ellis. 'The one without name' is presumably the anonymous author of a Chronicle of London.

[6]   For his activities as a lawyer see Baker, *The Men of Court*, i, pp. 804–5.

[7]   Smith, 'Date and Authorship of Hall's Chronicle', p. 254.

[8]   Hall (1809), p. vii.

to humanist education coloured his thoughts on the need to record what had happened in the past 'so that evidently it appereth that Fame is the triumphe of glory, and memory by literature is the verie dilator and setter furth of Fame'.[9] Historical writing was, as Hall saw it, a way of keeping memories alive, both positive and negative. 'Thus memorie maketh men ded many a thousand yere still to live as though thei wer present. Thus Fame triumpeth upon death and renoune upon Oblivion, and all by reason of writing and historie.'[10] As Scott Lucas has summed up neatly, Hall's intention in the *Union* was also 'the preservation for future generations of the glorious and inspiring deeds of prominent figures of England's past'.[11] In this context the wars in France no doubt proved attractive as a subject.

London had a strong tradition of its citizens being involved in historical writing. Given the link between the two families, we can speculate that Hall was inspired by Fabyan's example. Indeed, he paid his respects in his preface with the comment that, since Froissart, no man in the English tongue 'hath either set furth their honours accordyng to their desertes, nor yet declared many notable actes worthy of memorie dooen in the tyme of seven kyngs which after kyng Richarde succeeded, except Robert Fabian and one without name which wrote the common English chronicle'.[12] In 1534 the court of aldermen of the city of London ordered that a copy of Fabyan's chronicle should be kept in the court, presumably as a source of reference. This was, as we have seen, very shortly after Hall took up office as common sergeant.

Scott Lucas has argued that Hall's historical writing began around 1529 and was initially aimed at producing an account of Henry VIII's reign.[13] But this plan was abandoned in 1533. In the early 1540s he turned to the fifteenth century. By then he was able to draw extensively on Polydore Vergil's *Anglica Historia* (listed in his Latin authors as 'Polidorus') which had been published in 1534.[14] The inspiration of Polydore is wholly evident in the *Union* not only in content but also in style.[15] Especially apparent is the influence of classical-style rhetoric on Hall's composition of imagined speeches. For his account of the battle of Agincourt he provided a pre-battle speech for the French constable as well as for Henry V. Whilst the latter draws largely on historical sources, the speech for the Constable of France is pure invention, fanned by xenophobic views of the French in the mid-sixteenth century.[16] Polydore Vergil organised his history by reign, an approach reminiscent of the Lives of the Twelve Caesars of Suetonius (d. 122). Hall adopted the same format, with organisation by reign intended to contribute towards his

---

[9]   Hall (1809), p. v.
[10] Hall (1809), p. vi.
[11] Lucas, 'Hall's Chronicle and the Mirror for Magistrates', p. 360.
[12] Hall (1809), p. vi. Froissart was not in Hall's list of French writers but this is unsurprising given that his *Chroniques* ended in 1400. John Bourchier, Lord Berners (c. 1467–1533), had translated one of the versions of Froissart's *Chroniques* into English, the work being printed by Richard Pynson in 1523 and 1525.
[13] Lucas, 'The Consent of the Body of the Whole Realm', pp. 60–1.
[14] Smith ('Date and Authorship of Hall's Chronicle', p. 255) considers therefore that Hall could not have begun this project until after 1534. John Stowe claimed that Hall began to write when he became under-sheriff and was 'stired up by men of Authoritie' to do so (Lucas, 'Holinshed and Hall', p. 205).
[15] Kelly, *Divine Providence in the England of Shakespeare's Histories*, pp. 109–37.
[16] Curry, 'The Battle Speeches of Henry V', pp. 91–2.

overall aim of considering the political divisions in fifteenth-century England and their resolution by the Tudors. Each reign-based chapter was given an indicative title. For the two reigns covered by the M 9 chronicle we find 'The victorious acts of King Henry the v', and 'The troubleous season of king Henry the vi'. Tudor success was epitomised by 'The politicke governaunce of king Henry the vii', and 'The triumphant reigne of king Henry the viii'. Within each reign Hall organised his narrative by regnal year.

By 1546 Hall appears to have completed his narrative of the period from 1398 to 1509 but not to have continued his initial work on Henry VIII. This situation is suggested by the wording of his will made in 1546 and proved on 25 May 1547, 'Item I give to Richard Grafton prynter my Cronycle late made trusting that he will sett it forward'.[17] Grafton carried out Hall's wishes. When he printed the work in 1548,[18] he added his own preface to that already written by Hall making clear that Hall had reached only the 24th year of Henry VIII in his writing (1532–33). Grafton claimed that the subsequent content to the 38th year of Henry VIII (1546–47) was put together by him based on notes and papers which Hall had assembled, 'but utterly without any addition of myne', but there is some suggestion that his intervention was greater.[19] In 1550 Grafton reissued the *Union* with a new address to the reader, and a third edition was printed in 1560.[20]

HALL AND THE M 9 CHRONICLE

The most obvious indication of Hall's use of the M 9 chronicle is his inclusion of most of the lists found within the latter. It is notable too that the printed text has a distinctive layout with names being presented in list form, deliberately echoing their appearance in the chronicle itself. This layout suggests that Grafton himself saw the chronicle and that he wished to echo its appearance when typesetting Hall's chronicle, a desire which may have been expressed to him by the author. Significantly, Grafton's own composition, *A Chronicle at Large*, published in 1568–69,[21] included some of the lists from M 9 which had been included in Hall, and again replicated their special layout in the printing process. Even in this small example we gain an insight into the community of writers and printers in the highly productive and inventive environment of mid-Tudor London.

That the M 9 chronicle was not the only source which Hall drew on for his chapters on Henry V and VI is wholly apparent. His intention was to provide a rounded account of domestic as well as French events, and to that end he needed to consult other sources. The prefatory list of authors indicates that in addition

---

[17]   TNA, PROB 11/31/518. The will was made in 1546 but no specific date is given in it. Pollard, 'Edward Hall's Will and Chronicle', pp. 171–7.

[18]   ESTC 12721 and 12722. The claim by Tanner in his *Bibliotheca Britannico-Hibernica* of 1748 (p. 372) that there was a 1542 printing by Berthelet is not substantiated. See Pollard, 'The Bibliographical History of Hall's Chronicle', pp. 12–17.

[19]   Hall (1809), p. vii. For discussion on Grafton's level of intervention see Devereux, 'Empty Tuns and Unfruitful Grafts: Richard Grafton's Historical Publications', pp. 40–1. It is possible therefore that the list of authors and other preliminary material was the creation of Grafton since it follows immediately after his preface, but this should not detract from the evidence in the text of his *Union* that it was Hall who used the works of the authors cited.

[20]   ESTC 12723 and 12723a.

[21]   ESTC 12147.

to Polydore and Fabyan he also made use of the Chronicles of London, John
Hardyng (which Grafton had printed in 1543–44), and the first English printer,
William Caxton (drawn from the Polychronicon and the Brut). Hall also listed
twelve French authors, amongst whom we find one of the leading chroniclers of
the fifteenth-century phase of the Hundred Years War, Enguerran de Monstrelet.
Dozens of fifteenth- and sixteenth-century manuscripts of Monstrelet's work are
extant but his chronicle was also printed by Antoine Vérard around 1500 and 1508.
Other printed editions followed in 1512 and 1518.[22] Hall can be shown to have used
Monstrelet through a printed version since he replicated an error introduced by
Vérard.[23] That would also have been the case for the *Anglica Historia* of Polydore
Vergil. Also in Hall's list of French authors was *Le Rosarie*, better known as *Le
rosier des guerres*, which was written by Pierre Choisnet at Louis XI's request, for
the education of his son.[24] This work was printed in 1489–90 in Lyon and three
times in the 1520s in Paris. *Les Croniques de Normandie* is also listed. Several versions
are known. One, probably authored by Gilles le Bouvier, Berry Herald (1386–c.
1455), was printed in 1487 by Guillaume Le Tailleur.[25] Another was composed by
Georges Chastellain (1404–74) in the 1460s. A copy of that particular text is found
in College of Arms, MS Arundel 48, made for William Worcester.[26]

Hall's City connections made it possible to gain easy access to materials for
the writing of the *Union*. Erler has pointed out how important an entrée to the
administration of London was in this respect, especially given the ever-developing
library kept at the Guildhall.[27] We have already noted that a copy of Fabyan's
history was placed there in 1534. A copy of the *Croniques de France*, which dealt with
the fourteenth century, was included in a list of books in the custody of the corpo-
ration in 1470, but it was certainly back in the city's possession by 1516, having been
'borrowed' by Fabyan.[28] The books and archives were kept in a room between the
mayor's court and the inner council chamber used by the aldermen.[29] It is also
known that Hall used a copy of the Chronicle of London which Fabyan had been
continuing in his own hand.[30] In addition, Hall had his own collection of books
for which he made provision in his will, bequeathing one work to the Guildhall,

---

[22]   Wijsmann, 'History in Transition', p. 224.
[23]   This was the attribution on p. 156 of the capture of Aumale in July 1430 to William de
la Pole, earl of Suffolk, rather than to Humphrey, earl of Stafford, whose name was in the
original manuscript versions. We are grateful to Dr Scott Lucas for this information. See
also W. C. Hardy's note in his edition of Waurin, iii (1422–31), p. 351. The error was copied
by Monstrelet.
[24]   We are grateful to Dr Lydwine Scordia of the University of Rouen for information on
Le Rosier.
[25]   Reprinted by Hellot as *Les chroniques de Normandie 1223–1453*.
[26]   College of Arms, MS Arundel 48, item 66.
[27]   Erler, 'The Guildhall Library, Robert Bale and the Writing of London History', p. 185.
[28]   'At this Court Water Smyth which hath mayred the Wyff of M. Fabyan late alderman
of this Citie brought in a grete boke of the Croniques de ffraunce wreton in ffrench and
belongyng to this Citie which long lyme (sic) in the Kepyng of the seyd M. ffabyan' (Repertory
3 of the Court of Aldermen, f. 93v) (Ramsay and Willoughby, 'London Guildhall', pp.
148, 156, SH47 no. 13). The volume of chronicles is now London Metropolitan Archives,
CLC/270/MS00244.
[29]   Barron, *London in the Later Middle Ages*, p. 153.
[30]   Boffey, *Manuscript and Print in London*, p. 199.

a Latin text which we find within the list of authors in his *Union*: 'all my Frenshe bookes and Englysshe bookes I will to my brother and all other my books not being of the lawe I will shalbe given to my freends or sold according to the discretion of my executours saving that I will that my Cronica Cronicorum shalbe given to the chamber of London to lye in the council chamber'.[31]

It was common in this period for books and manuscripts to be lent and borrowed, a further reflection of the active intellectual community in the city. Given the extent of Hall's use of the M 9 chronicle and in particular his inclusion of many of the lists of names, it would have been necessary for him to have extended access to the actual text. It is likely, therefore, that Hall was able to borrow the chronicle, which is believed in the 1530s and 1540s to have been in the possession of Christopher Barker, who had become Garter King of Arms in 1536. Barker lived in Paternoster Row at a house identified by the sign of the Tyger's head. This street lay close to St Paul's churchyard, which was the area in which a number of printers were based at this time.[32]

We know that Hall was acquainted with heralds, and most particularly Charles Wriothesley, the only surviving son of Thomas Wriothesley, Garter King of Arms from 1505 to 1534. Charles (1508–62) was appointed Rouge Croix Pursuivant at the age of 16 but was from 1529 a member of Gray's Inn, with which Hall was associated. In 1534 he became Windsor herald, a post he still held in 1554 when the College received its charter. He was himself the author of a chronicle covering the reigns of the first Tudor kings.[33] Since he inherited his father's important library it is wholly feasible that Hall had access to it.

COMPARISON OF THE M 9 CHRONICLE AND HALL'S *UNION*

The level of use which Hall made of the M 9 chronicle varies across the period from 1415 to 1429, the years which the chronicle covers, both in terms of the influence of the lists and of the narrative.[34] But that he did use the text is directly indicated by the fact that, once the coverage of the chronicle ceases, we find no further lists in Hall relating to the war in France. Hall was, of course, writing in English, but we can see on some occasions that his prose is a direct translation of the chronicle. We know that Hall knew French well: he used Monstrelet and other French works in their original language. Therefore, he could easily have translated the lists and narrative passages from a French text into English. This is not to exclude the possibility that he drew on an English version of the chronicle, but given that no such work is known to exist and

---

[31]   TNA, PROB 11/31/518; Ramsay and Willoughby, 'London Guildhall', p. 149.

[32]   Raven, *The Business of Books*, pp. 26–7.

[33]   *A Chronicle of England during the Reigns of the Tudors from AD 1485 to 1559*, ed. Douglas. Christopher's mother was Thomas Wriothesley's first wife Joan, daughter of a William Hall of Salisbury, but as yet no family link with Edward Hall's ancestors has been discovered. We are grateful to Dr Alan Magary of San Francisco for the information on the link between Hall and Charles Wriothesley.

[34]   Hall (1809), pp. 62–148. See Rowe, pp. 508–13, for her perceptive remarks on the use which Hall made of the M 9 chronicle. This section of our edition is not intended as a full analysis of all of the sources which Hall drew on in his treatment of this period but only as a study of his use of the M 9 chronicle. We are grateful to Dr Alan Magary for sharing his current work on an online edition of Hall's chronicle.

that the M 9 chronicle is extant, we shall assume for the purposes of comparison that Hall did use the chronicle which is the subject of this current study.

In general, Hall's use of M 9 was less intensive in his account of the reign of Henry V than that of Henry VI. For both reigns, however, he both selected which information from the chronicle to use whilst at the same time adding information which he had gleaned from elsewhere or expanding the text with his own words. So, for instance, he noted verbatim from the chronicle the appointment of Thomas Beaufort as captain of Harfleur 'which established his leuetenaunt there Ihon Fastolffe with .xv. C men and .xxxv. knightes, whereof the baron of Carew and Sir Hugh Lutterell were two counsaillers' (f. 31v; p. 63). But he chose to ignore the two further names given in the chronicle (John Standish and Thomas Lord) as well as to omit mention of the geographical areas (Devon and Somerset) from which Carew and Luttrell hailed. Such information was presumably discounted because it was of lesser contemporary interest to Hall and his readers. Hall also used vocabulary of his own time, as in the addition of the word 'counsaillers'. But his close following, on occasion, of the chronicle meant that he also replicated its errors, such as the incorrect first names for the earl of Arundel and the Earl Marshal when their invaliding home was mentioned.

Hall included the names of those knighted by Henry V at the Somme (f. 32v; p. 64), information only found in the M 9 chronicle, but added the explanatory gloss that those so dubbed were 'hardy and valeant gentlemen'. The original list in Nantron's hand, with seven names, was repeated, although the chronicle's 'Raoul de Graystoke' was erroneously accorded the first name 'Reginald' by Hall.[35] Hall also included the four names which had been added to the chronicle in a later sixteenth-century hand. Two of these were Philip Hall and William Hall, so a personal interest was no doubt in play here. We see this again where Hall follows the later insertion of Sir Philip Hall in preference for Thomas Burgh as captain of Avranches (f. 38r). Indeed, had Hall discussed the chronicle with Christopher Barker or others then it is possible that some additions to and annotations of the chronicle text were influenced by Hall himself. We should not dismiss the possibility of a more complex relationship between Hall, the M 9 chronicle, and the additions made to it in the sixteenth century. That said, Hall's text is sometimes at odds with the later changes. So, for instance, he puts 'Henry Mortimer' as knighted at the Somme where the amended chronicle text speaks of a John Mortimer.

For the battle of Agincourt, Hall had much fuller material to draw on, especially the *Chroniques* of Enguerran de Monstrelet. It is apparent that he did not use M 9's list of French dead and prisoners, even though he presented the material in a similar list format (pp. 71–2). Almost none of the names in the chronicle list are found in Hall's list. For the king's order to kill the prisoners Hall took his account from Monstrelet and not the chronicle. The latter (f. 34r) ascribed the king's decision to the attack on the English camp by a group of local lords, whilst Monstrelet (and Hall) portrayed it as the response to the rallying of 20,000 French to give a new fight. We may perhaps detect some slight influence from the distinctive concluding sentence of the account in the M 9 chronicle: 'and that was the reason why so many nobles died', although Hall reshapes a positive into

---

[35]　Such confusion is not surprising since there was no member of the family of barons Greystoke called Ralph who could have been knighted in 1415.

a negative form: 'so that in effecte havyng respecte to the greate nombre, few prisoners or none were saved'.

For the army with which Henry invaded in 1417 Hall had replicated the names provided in the chronicle but placed them within the text. He also amended the chronicle's entry of 'the two lords of Ferrers Groby' to 'Ferreys of Groby and Ferreys of Chartley', which he presumably saw as a factual improvement (ff. 34r–v; p. 77). He chose to omit completely the long list of French garrison captains given in the chronicle but his comment suggests that he was fully aware of it:

> so were al the walled tounes and castles in Normandy and Mayne wel furnished with men and vitaile. The names of the Frenche capitaines were to tedious to reherse and therefore I overpass them. (p. 77)

Such a conscious omission suggests that Hall had read the chronicle and chosen what to include and what to ignore. A further indication of selection is seen in the way he treats the appointments to captaincies made by Henry V and his brothers. In the chronicle they are presented as three separate lists with short narratives in between (ff. 37v–38r). Hall preferred to present them in one block, whilst distinguishing between the appointments made by the king and those made by each of his brothers (pp. 80–1). We find some slight alterations in order, and also some omissions. For instance, no mention is made of the membership of the Order of the Garter by Van Clux: such information on a Silesian knight was presumably not seen of interest at the time of Hall's writing. The appointments made by Henry after the fall of Rouen were also presented in list form by Hall but it is significant in terms of his selectivity that he omitted some of the more obscure places noted in the chronicle (f. 39r; pp. 89–90). His conclusion gives insights into his rationale, but also confirms that he had seen the full evidence as provided in the chronicle:

> if I should here rehearse what tounes wer conquered, what fortresses were yelded, and who wer made capitaines of the same, this Pamphlet would turne to a volume more tedious then pleasaunt, and therefore I over passyng small names and muche doing, will returne again to the principall thynges touching the sequel of this historye. And who so desireth to know all the circumstances of the delivery, lette hym overloke the Frenche writers, which to advoyde shame confesse and write the verite.

The M 9 chronicle gave very little space to the siege of Rouen. Hall's account is much more substantial, including as it does the whole text of the treaty of surrender. The detail given by Hall on the positioning of the various English contingents at the siege is also distinctive, and is most likely derived from an early sixteenth-century text in College of Arms, Arundel 29, ff. 57r–v,[36] whose hand has similarities with that of some of the amendments to the M 9 chronicle. This is another potentially important link with Christopher Barker and other heralds of the 1530s and 1540s, suggesting that Hall's consultation of manuscripts associated with them went beyond the M 9 chronicle.

For the last years of Henry V's reign, Hall included, in list form, those present at the siege of Melun, thereby repeating the error in the M 9 chronicle that all three of

---

[36] *Catalogue of the Arundel Manuscripts in the College of Arms*, pp. 40–1.

the king's brothers were in France at this point (ff. 40r–41r; pp. 104–5). We can see here that Hall had some problem in understanding the names: 'Artur de bretaigne conte dyvry', for instance, is given as 'the archbishop of Britayne earle of Yvry'. Hall also added other names ('Syr Guy Moyle, Syr John Stanley, Syr Lewes Mohun and xv maister soldiers'). Similar conclusions can be advanced for Hall's list of the French and Scots who fought against the duke of Clarence at Baugé, which is also presented in list form as in the chronicle (ff. 42r–v; pp. 103–4). Hall here cites most, although not all, of the names provided in the chronicle's list but there is more variance between the lists of Scots. Whilst there are fifteen names in common between the chronicle and Hall, six other names are found uniquely in the chronicle and seven only in Hall. Here we can see that Hall was able to draw on other information.

Hall also drew on the chronicle for the knighting by Clarence of three of his own soldiers at the entry into Anjou. As with Henry V's dubbings at the Somme, Hall chose to add a fourth: 'Sir Thomas Beaufforde called the bastard of Clarence', an addition which shows his confusion over branches within the royal family of the time. Hall also followed the narrative of the chronicle in the story of a Lombard who misled the duke into thinking that the enemy were small in number. Whilst the chronicle simply calls the traitor André Lombart, Hall, uniquely it seems, names him more precisely as 'A Lombard … called Andrewe Forgusa', and whilst the chronicle provides a list of thirty-one English dead and captured, presented in list form, Hall chooses to name, within the text, only sixteen, erroneously adding the earl of Suffolk to the prisoners.

Hall included a cut-down version of the list of men in Henry V's army at the siege of Meaux but presented it in list form emulating the layout of the chronicle (ff. 44v–45r; p. 108). A Sir William Hall finds his way additionally into Hall's list. Hall omitted the story of the Bastard of Vaurus but included in full the anecdote of the king's treatment of Olivier de Mauny. Hall's text here is a direct translation of the king's supposed words. But we can also see important additions which Hall made to the story. To Henry V's comment in the chronicle that he could indeed have put Mauny to death, Hall added 'although by the lawe of armes we might lawfully so dooe'. Hall also emphasised Mauny's demise in England by adding not only that he died 'for very shame and mere melancholy', but also that he was buried in the White Friars, a reflection of Hall's intimate knowledge of London. The location specified by Hall was the former Carmelite priory, dissolved in 1540, which lay between Fleet Street and the Thames.[37]

The overall conclusion for the reign of Henry V, therefore, is that Hall drew on the M 9 chronicle for its names and for occasional stories whilst building up his often extensive narrative from other sources, especially Monstrelet, and from his own skills as an imaginative writer. Furthermore, whilst Hall puts forward a positive portrayal of Henry V, there is no sign that he sought to emulate the use of the chronicle's constant description of the king as 'victorious prince'.

For the reign of Henry VI, Hall used some of the lists of names provided in the chronicle but we also find him using more of its narrative. His reason for doing so was surely because other accounts of English actions in the period from 1422 to 1429 were scarce. This was particularly the case for the English invasion of Maine, a campaign which, as we argued in Chapter 2, was a notable focus of the M 9 chronicle.

---

[37]   Holder, *The Friaries of Medieval London*, pp. 97–118. A vaulted cellar, probably of the prior's mansion, remains under 65 Fleet Street.

On the siege of Meulan in 1423 Hall used the chronicle's comment that the lord of Granville swore an oath to Bedford but later broke it (ff. 47r-v; p. 166). But he embellished the information provided by the chronicle. For instance, he added a gloss to his mention of the earl of Salisbury: 'a manne bothe for his greate pollicie and haute corage more to be compared to the old valiant Romans than to men of his daies' Whilst the chronicle left blank the name of the captain whom Bedford appointed after Meulan was taken, Hall put that the earl of Salisbury appointed Sir Henry Mortimer and Sir Richard Vernon to the captaincy. But he chose to omit two names which had been added later to the chronicle as men present at the siege (Richard Woodville and Sir Robert Harling, who is described as at that time lieutenant of Meulan).

With regard to Fastolf's successes at Passy and Orsay, Hall (calling the places Pacy and Cursay/Coursay) followed the chronicle quite closely, as also in the narrative of the arrival of Scottish troops and the formation of an army under the earl of Salisbury which proved victorious at the battle of Cravant (ff. 47v–49r; pp. 117–18). Here we find Hall copying, in list format, the list of English participants with very little variation, save for the omission of Sir John Crafford and the replacement of the chronicle's Jenkin Banaster by Davy Lloyd. The list of Burgundians provided in the chronicle was of lesser interest to Hall, with the result that he copied only twelve of the sixteen names given. Hall's account of the battle of Cravant is notably close to that of the chronicle, the first time we find such a close liaison in the narrative of the chronicle as opposed to the lists, although Hall omits the chronicle's mention that the Franco-Scottish army numbered 20,000. And whilst the chronicle tallies the dead and prisoners as 800, Hall's figure is 8,000. We could consider this simply a transcription lapse, or else a deliberate heightening, or an effort to correct what Hall perceived to be an error. Hall then proceeded to a list of French and Scottish dead and prisoners (ff. 49r-v; p. 118). Whilst Hall drew fully on the list in the chronicle, he added other names, of both French and Scots. He also estimated the totals of dead and prisoners for each nationality and added four names of English dead (one of whom is Sir William Hall, and another Sir Gilbert Halsall whom Hall has as still alive a few years later when appointed to a captaincy) 'and xxi C other slaine'. Hall's figures here are exceptionally high, even taking into account the rise in army sizes by the 1540s. Newer military organisation is revealed by his use of the word 'billmen' in his narrative of the battle. Given his desired elevation of English glory, Hall rejigged the chronicle text which had spoken of the advance across the river of English and Burgundians, 'at the same time and with equal courage', both on foot and on horse. In his version the English led the way and the Burgundians merely followed: 'both horsemen and fote men of the Englishe part coragiously put themselves into the river and with fine force recovered the bank, who the Burgonions incontinent folowed'. The impact of the new religious sensibilities is revealed in the sentence which follows after Hall's list of dead and prisoners. Whereas the chronicle has the lords giving thanks and praise for the victory 'to God and his glorious mother', Hall was careful to avoid any whiff of mariolatry and mentioned God alone.

In the narrative of the events of the third year of Henry VI's reign (1424–25), Hall's use of the M 9 chronicle is more complex, but that again indicates that he read it and decided to omit some events whilst rearranging the order of others. So, for instance, he reverses the order of Gough's bravery at Courcillon with the activities on the southern frontier involving John de la Pole and also the siege of Compiègne. But in points of detail it is clear that the chronicle was his main source of information on military actions in France at this point. That said, his own interests affected his choice of content. Hall included the siege of Le Crotoy, an action which the chronicle omitted completely, since he had clearly found information elsewhere that the Regent Bedford sent Sir Philip Hall with 800 men to besiege the town (p. 120). Hall chose to omit the chronicle's long list of French who attacked John de la Pole (ff. 50r-v), instead mentioning only two French peers by name 'and vi thousand Frenchmen', the same figure as given in the chronicle. But he included the same English prisoners as listed in the chronicle, rationally deleting the duplicate entry for John Afford (whom the chronicle listed twice, first as lieutenant at Falaise and secondly as marshal of Argentan), and adding a new name – Henry Mortimer. He also noted the total number of English dead and prisoners as 600 rather than following the chronicle's claim of 1,000.

Hall's lack of interest in the French also led to his omission of the long list in the chronicle of the Frenchmen who lay siege to Ivry (ff. 51v–53r), picking out only a handful of names to mention and adding in names of the Scottish leaders with the French who are not mentioned at this point in the chronicle (pp. 121–2). Hall also chose to reduce the numbers in the Franco-Scottish army from the chronicle's total of 40,000 to 15,000 French and 5,000 Scots. Oddly, perhaps, he did not replicate the list of English involved in the battle of Verneuil (ff. 53v–54r), although he selected a few names to mention within the text, adding to them Sir Philip Hall whose name did not appear in the chronicle's list for the victory. Hall's date for the battle (27 August 1425) is distinctly odd, but he was at pains to avoid the chronicle's dating as the vigil of the Assumption of the Virgin May (14 August). Needless to say, he also omitted, after a hard fight, the gaining of the victory by the English, 'as it pleased God our creator and the Glorious Virgin'. He felt on less contentious ground in copying, in list form, most of the chronicle's list of French and Scottish dead and prisoners (f. 54v–55r; p. 125), although advancing a more precise total for French and Scottish dead (9,700 as opposed to 'about 9,000' in the chronicle) whilst retaining the chronicle's comment that the tally derived from Mountjoye, King-of-Arms of the French. Hall also added that 2,100 Englishmen had been killed at Verneuil where the chronicle had given no figure for casualties and, whilst he copied the chronicle's comment that 'no man of name' had died on the English side, he added 'savyng five young esquires'. In dealing with the aftermath of the battle, such as in noting the appointment of Sir Philip Hall as captain of Verneuil, and Bedford's reception in Rouen with great honour and joy before he returned to Paris, Hall followed the wording of the chronicle almost verbatim, save for the linguistic shift.

The same situation prevails in Hall's narrative of the beginning of the campaign into Maine for which Montgomery, Scales and Fastolf were commissioned. But he chose to cut the detail of the chronicle in terms of the places that surrendered to them (ff. 55v–56r),

> which for prolixity of tyme, I thynke necessary to be omitted. For surely the Englishe puissance was so tried, proved, assaied and spred abroad throughout all France that the Frenche men thought that in conclusion the English men would have or should have all thynges which they either wished or enterprised. (p. 126)

Hall's narrative therefore moved swiftly to the subsequent army sent into Maine and Anjou under the earl of Salisbury (f. 56r). The chronicle here provided a list of participants but Hall again curtailed the information rather dismissively, simply mentioning

'Lorde Scales and other approuved capitaines whose names you have heard before'. 'These lusty captains', Hall tells us –an excuse for not giving their names, we might think – entered Maine and besieged Le Mans. His subsequent narrative followed the chronicle very closely, even to the point of giving the same French captains' names and the summary of the terms of surrender which he had read in the chronicle.

After mention of Fastolf's appointment as captain of Le Mans, however, Hall chose to overlook at this point the details of the other captains appointed in other places (f. 57r), moving instead straight to Salisbury's siege at Sainte-Suzanne. His narrative here is much longer than that of the chronicle, but whether this is from another source or simply his own imagination remains uncertain. Whilst Hall emphasised the use of gunpowder artillery, he omitted the chronicle's story of the earl allowing all the defenders to depart save for the cannoneers, whom he hanged, a cannonball tied to their leg. This omission is intriguing given Hall's general liking for such anecdotes. Perhaps we are seeing the effect of gunpowder weapons being so commonplace that the story was less interesting. Or perhaps it did not fit easily with the special accolade which Hall chose to accord to Salisbury at his death (p. 146). The appointment of Sir John Popham as captain of Sainte-Suzanne was noted as in the chronicle, but with Hall's gloss that he was 'a valiaunt and circumspect knight'. Hall's narratives of the sieges of Mayenne and La Ferté-Bernard follow the chronicle quite closely, as does the plot by a Gascon to betray the English garrison of Alençon. Here Hall adds as a piece of circumstantial evidence the actual sum of the French bribe to the Gascon of 400 crowns. He then noted the appointments to the other captaincies which he had ignored earlier, thereby rearranging the information which the chronicle presented. 'Improving' on the chronicle, he added a summation of the progress the English had made in Maine, in which 'all men rejoysed and wer very glad, not only for the conquest of so many towns but also that God had sente theim victory in pitched felde and in a mortall battle', before concluding that 'it is not convenient that I should talke so muche of Fraunce and omit all thynges done in England'. By such a signpost, Hall left the chronicle's narrative and moved to the campaigns of the duke of Gloucester in Hainault.

At the beginning of the section headed the fourth year, Hall returned to the chronicle for an account of the activities of Thomas Rempston and others in fortifying Saint-James-de-Beuvron, and the failure of Arthur de Richemont to effect a siege there (f. 58r; p. 129). Here Hall followed the chronicle almost verbatim until its account of the rout of the force under Richemont, save that Hall emphasised the latter's office as Constable of France, a title completely ignored by the chronicle. Thereafter Hall's account seems to draw on Monstrelet's *Chroniques*, although Lucas has pointed out that there are enough differences to suggest that Hall may have drawn on another unknown source:

> in particular, whereas the M 9 chronicle and Monstrelet note in general that the French army left behind much in the way of supplies and munitions, Hall quantifies the number of abandoned materials, mentioning among other things 500 barrels of herring and 300 pipes of wine. He also claimed that the Constable went to Anjou to attack villages after the loss at Saint-James, whereas Monstrelet claims he returned to Brittany.[38]

---

[38] Personal communication. We are grateful to Dr Lucas for his observations and his further comment that although Hall owned a copy of Alain Bouchart's *Grandes Croniques de*

After this episode, Hall turned to an extensive discussion of English affairs in the summer of 1426, most notably the attempted resolution by Bedford of the quarrel between Henry Beaufort and Humphrey, duke of Gloucester. He returned to the chronicle with the arrival of the earl of Warwick in France with an expeditionary army and his ensuing conquests in Maine, where his text is again very close to his source (ff. 58r; p. 138). After a brief excursion into the departure of Bedford from England at the beginning of the section on the fifth year of the reign, Hall followed the chronicle narrative on the activities of the lord of Rostrenen,[39] marshal of Brittany, in fortifying Pontorson and the commissioning of Warwick to lay siege, continuing his close use of the chronicle throughout the whole of this campaign and beyond to the sieges laid by Sir John Fastolf at Saint-Ouën and La Gravelle (ff. 58v–61r; pp. 139–41). In two places, however, Hall chose to bring into his text names which the chronicle had presented in list form: the French defeated by Lord Scales during the siege of Pontorson (f. 58v; pp. 139–40), and the English designated by Bedford for the siege of La Gravelle (f. 60v; p. 141), where we see some selectivity on the part of Hall about who should be mentioned.

When the appointment of Talbot to the governorship of Anjou and Maine is mentioned by Hall we are given an insight into his method, since he used the opportunity to emphasise the bravery and success of Talbot and the fear which the French had towards him, comments not found within the chronicle. But the chronicle was clearly the source for the appointment of Sir Gilbert Halsall as captain of Laval after its capture by Talbot, since its retrospective comment that Halsall remained captain until his death at the siege of Orléans is reflected in Hall's wording 'which after was slain at the siege of Orleance'. After this, the chronicle went first to the French seizure and subsequent English recovery of Le Mans (May 1428), misdating it to 1427, and then to the siege of Montargis, which began in June 1427. Hall corrected the error by following the correct chronological order, placing the siege first. Hall gave a longer account of this action although the wording of the chronicle is revealed on a number of occasions (ff. 62r-v; pp. 141–2). The same is true for the recovery of Le Mans where the special role of both Thomas Gower and Matthew Gough is replicated, as also the surprise 5 a.m. (an hour later in Hall) entry of the English to the town, catching the French in disarray, and forcing them to flee in their night clothes or even naked (ff. 61r–62r; pp. 142–3).

Hall's powers of imagination as a story teller are evident in his development of this key action at Le Mans. To the bare narrative of the chronicle Hall added explanatory glosses with an emotive and nationalistic purpose. Thus, in the prelude to the French capture of the city, he added a long section on how the release from his English captivity of the duke of Alençon 'revived again the dul spirits of the Dolphyn and the fainte hertes of his captaines, promisying to theim grete victory with little travail and much gain with small labour wherefore in hope of good lucke, he determined to do some notable feate against thenglishmen'. An unexpected chance for the French, in his words, arose from the inhabitants of Le Mans who 'began sore to lament that they were subiectes and vassals to the yoke and power of the Englishmen'. By setting up French hopes of success, the bravery and skill of Talbot, Gower and Gough in recovering Le Mans are made to seem all the more glorious and enabled Hall to heap opprobrium on the 'ungracious coniu-

---

Bretagne, that work was not the source of this information.
[39]   Given as Rustynan in M 9 and Rustinan in Hall.

racion' within the city which had allowed the French to enter. Whilst the chronicle concentrates on the military outcome, claiming that 300–400 French were taken prisoner or killed in the recovery and victorious rout of the city, Hall ends with an inquiry into the civilian plot, with thirty citizens, twenty priests and fifteen friars 'which accordyng to their desertes were put in execution'. As in earlier sections, post-reformation political correctness has an impact.[40] Where the chronicle has the English at their entry to Le Mans crying 'Our Lady, St George, Lord Talbot', Hall's cry is simply 'St George and Talbot'.

The final part of the M 9 chronicle concerns the campaign of the earl of Salisbury along the Loire, leading to the siege of Orléans and concluding with the imminent arrival of Joan of Arc, although her name, and those of her leading companions, were added later to what was Nantron's original text (ff. 63r–65v). Whilst there is much similarity for Salisbury's campaign between the chronicle and Hall's narrative (pp. 143–7), there are differences in the route taken by the earl and in the size of the army he brought from England (7,000 in the chronicle, 5,000 in Hall). Hall also inserted several lines about the count of Dunois, the Bastard of Orléans, who is only mentioned in passing in the chronicle. After the narrative of Fastolf's victory at Rouvray, Hall's use of the chronicle came to an inevitable end. But his account of that battle (where he added the name 'battle of the herrings', a name not in the original text of the M 9 chronicle but given in a marginal annotation of the sixteenth century) was taken from the chronicle although Hall chose to omit most of the names of English participants and French victims, both of which the chronicle had presented in list form, and to alter the numbers of English troops from 1,500 to his own 500 – making it an even greater English victory! Hall's account of the specific circumstances of the death of Salisbury at the hands of the son of the gunner follows the chronicle but was expanded by his consummate narrative and rhetorical skill, as is apparent in the eulogy at the death of the earl; this, Hall noted, was the real turning point of English fortunes in France, and, for the duke of Bedford, 'as if he had loste his right hand or lacked his weapon' (p. 147).

In conclusion, there is ample evidence that Hall drew extensively on the M 9 chronicle narrative and on the names it provided. We can see that he *used* the chronicle in the full sense of that word, necessarily reading the whole text, making choices and selections from it, manipulating and expanding on it to suit his purpose and his style. On eight occasions chronicle lists were reproduced in Hall's *Union* in list form, although sometimes lightly edited. The last of these lists in Hall concerned the French and Scottish dead at Verneuil. After that point, Hall chose to include only a handful of names within his narrative from the chronicle's subsequent lists. The preponderance of his use of lists in list form – five out of the eight – occurs, therefore, in his chapter on Henry V. That said, the layout of the chronicle with its names in list form influenced Hall (and his printer) more broadly beyond the war in France. In his account of the reign of Henry VI, Hall also presented in list form the lords who took an oath in the 1426 parliament and those who were dubbed by the duke of Bedford at the same parliament alongside the king (pp. 135, 138).

---

[40]   Lucas, 'The Consent of the Body of the Whole Realm', pp. 69–72, points out how Hall used his narrative of parliamentary activity in the fifteenth century, such as efforts towards disendowment in the 1410s, as a retrospective justification of the controversial acts of the Reformation parliament.

On a few occasions Hall reordered the events as given by the chronicle but generally he followed its chronology precisely. His text is closest to the M 9 chronicle
in the narrative of campaigns in Maine between 1424 and 1427, where he had
no other major source to draw on. Otherwise, we see the influence of his use of
Monstrelet's chronicles but also the power of his own imagination and ability as a
writer. Hall's *Union* was by its nature longer and more discursive than the chronicle,
and was imbued with contemporary preferences, not least the avoidance of pre-
reformation invocations. For both reigns covered by the chronicle, Hall aimed to
provide a much fuller, more rounded and interconnected account of English history, which included the activities of the English crown in France. His anticipated
audience was much larger than that ever envisaged by the chronicle, since his work
was intended to be printed. In that respect, Hall aimed to tell a good story for his
readers. Towards his stated objectives the M 9 chronicle offered useful material
but was hardly enough by itself. We should not forget, however, that the use of the
chronicle by Hall did not end with the publication of his *Union*, since his work, as
we shall see, was taken up by other Tudor writers, through whom the chronicle's
content was perpetuated. Here we shall look at the work of Richard Grafton and
Raphael Holinshed. In the following chapter, Scott Lucas will consider the impact
of the chronicle, through Hall, on the 1554 poem concerning the earl of Salisbury
that was published in the first edition of *A Mirror for Magistrates* (1559).

THE INFLUENCE OF HALL'S *UNION*

The first use of Hall was by Richard Grafton (1506/7–1573), who, as we have
seen, was instrumental in bringing Hall's *Union* into print. Like Hall, Grafton was
a prominent Londoner, being MP for the city in the parliament of 1553–34 and a
governor of the city's hospitals as well as a member of the Grocers' Company, of
which he was twice master.[41] His City and company links facilitated easy access to
materials just as it had for Hall. Grafton oversaw the printing of the Great Bible in
English (1539), of which Miles Coverdale was editor. Based in a house in what had
previously been Greyfriars, the Franciscan friary near Newgate which had been
dissolved in 1538 (and in whose re-opened church Hall had expressed his wish to
be buried),[42] Grafton became printer to Edward VI and was responsible for many
key texts of the period, including the Prayer Book of 1549. His career courted
controversy, initially on religious grounds but later through scholarly disputes with
John Stow and questions about his financial probity.

Grafton's own interest in historical works is revealed as early as 1543–44 when
he printed John Hardyng's metrical chronicle, adding a prose continuation and a
dedication to the duke of Norfolk which had been prompted by the latter's successful Scottish campaign of 1542. In the early 1560s Grafton turned to composing and
printing his own historical works.[43] The first, *The Abridgement of the Chronicles of Eng-*

---

[41] Ferguson, 'Grafton, Richard (1506/7–1573)', *ODNB*.
[42] TNA, PROB 11/31/518: 'and my body I will to be buried honestly in the church of Christ
lately called the Greyfriars'. The church was reopened on 30 January 1547 but Hall's family
had him buried at St Benet Sherehog. We are grateful to Dr Alan Magary for this observation.
[43] Devereux, 'Empty Tuns and Unfruitful Grafts: Richard Grafton's Historical
Publications', pp. 33–56.

land (1563),[44] followed the form and content of the London chronicles organised by mayoral year. The second, *A Chronicle at Large* (1568–69), shows direct evidence of the use of Hall's chronicle.[45] Hall is listed by Grafton at the outset of his work among 'The Names of the Authors that are Alleged in this History'. There is no mention of any work by Basset but 'Clarenseaux King of Arms' is listed.[46] This link with the heralds demonstrates their inclusion within the scholarly community of London. Exactly which Clarenceux was meant is unclear, but the office had been held by two men, Thomas Benolt and Thomas Tonge, both of whom may have had connections with the M 9 chronicle. The inventory of Benolt's books at his death in 1534 included early printed editions of Froissart's chronicles and the *Croniques de France* printed in Paris in 1476–77.[47]

In *A Chronicle at Large*, Grafton included some of the lists which Hall had taken from the M 9 chronicle, choosing again to replicate the layout inspired by the chronicle. We find, for instance, identical lists of those dubbed by Henry V at the Somme as well as those present at the siege of Melun in 1420.[48] There are also close similarities of text between Hall and Grafton, as, for instance, in the account of the battle of Verneuil.[49] A list of the French and Scots slain is printed by Grafton in list form down the page following exactly the list provided in Hall, which was, as we have seen, only moderately amended from the list provided in the M 9 chronicle. Grafton's *Chronicle at Large* therefore perpetuated the material of the chronicle. As already noted, it is likely that he had himself seen the chronicle. That said, Grafton did not simply copy Hall's text but edited out some of the information and some of the lists which Hall had derived from the chronicle.[50]

Grafton's works were much less influential, however, than the major historical compilation of the second half of the sixteenth century which is commonly known as Holinshed's *Chronicles*. Raphael Holinshed (1525–80) was employed in the printing house of the evangelical Reyner Wolfe, who had a plan to produce a comprehensive history and geography of the world.[51] In the event the work was limited to England, Scotland and Ireland. A first edition in two volumes was produced in 1577,[52] and was an immediate commercial success, its attractiveness being boosted by its wood-cuts as well as its comprehensiveness. After Holinshed's death the work was further expanded to three volumes in 1586–87.[53] Of all histories written in the Tudor period, this second edition of Holinshed's chronicles was exceptionally influential, both at the time (Shakespeare used it extensively in his plays) and over the centuries to come.

---

[44]   ESTC 12148.

[45]   ESTC 12147. For a later edition, *Grafton's Chronicle or History of England*, ed. H. Ellis, 2 vols (London, 1809).

[46]   Thomas Tonge held this office between 1534 and 1536. His predecessor Thomas Benolt (1511–34) had a number of books, as noted earlier. Thomas Hawley was Clarenceux from 1536 to 1557, being followed by William Harvey (1557–67) and then Robert Cooke (1567–94).

[47]   Ramsay, 'London. Clarenceux King of Arms and the Office of Arms', pp. 185, 190.

[48]   *Chronicle at Large*, pp. 483, 485–6.

[49]   *Chronicle at Large*, p. 506.

[50]   To cite but one example (*Chronicle at Large*, p. 468), he omitted the names of the appointees to places taken by the duke of Gloucester in 1418 which Hall had derived from the chronicle.

[51]   Clegg, 'Holinshed [Hollingshead], Raphael (c. 1525–1580)', *ODNB*.

[52]   Amongst other copies, ESTC 13568.

[53]   For the relevant volume on England, ESTC 13569.5.

Holinshed directly acknowledged use of Hall's *Union*,[54] but he also drew on other relevant works for the early fifteenth century, such as Tito Livio's *Vita Henrici Quinti*, which Hall had not used. In the context of this present study, the question is the extent to which Hall's use of the M 9 chronicle was continued by Holinshed. Even though there is no evidence of any direct consultation of the chronicle in the preparation of either of Holinshed's editions, given their high level of popularity, any adoption of lists or narrative from Hall would undoubtedly have had the effect of perpetuating the transmission of the content of the M 9 chronicle which Hall had begun.

Holinshed's narrative of the French wars replicates very closely that of Hall.[55] Take, for instance, Holinshed's narrative on the launching of the conquest of Maine under Scales, Fastolf and Montgomery. This followed Hall's wording almost exactly, with the same list of conquered places being given, followed by 'and twentye other, whyche I doe heere passe ouer', which is reminiscent of Hall's comment on the same subject 'which for prolixity of tyme, I thynke necessary to be omitted'.[56] The story of Matthew Gough's bravery at Courcillon was copied verbatim from Hall, who himself had taken it from the M 9 chronicle (f. 37v).[57] But there are differences between Hall and Holinshed which reflect authorial intervention and 'improvement', no doubt based on Holinshed's consultation of other sources of information. So, for instance, Holinshed provides a date for Henry V's arrival at Argentan (4 October 1417) for which no precise date was given in Hall or in the M 9 chronicle.

We can see that Holinshed's chronicles replicate the names of participants which Hall had derived from the M 9 chronicle. On almost every occasion, however, they integrate such names within the prose of the narrative rather than presenting them separately in list form, as can be seen in the case of the dead and prisoners at Verneuil.[58] There are only two exceptions where Holinshed replicates in list form the lists which Hall had taken from the M 9 chronicle. The first is the list of appointments to captaincies made by the dukes of Clarence and Gloucester in 1418, although here Holinshed made some changes to Hall's spellings.[59] The second is the list of garrison captains appointed by Henry V after the fall of Rouen. The source is here directly acknowledged since Holinshed adds the comment 'as we find them in the Chronicles of Maister Hall'.[60]

SHAKESPEARE

Shakespeare's use of Holinshed's *Chronicles* is well known. Reflecting upon his plays 'Henry V' (1599) and 'Henry VI Part 1' (1592) – the latter believed to be the first of his history plays – we can see a very interesting example of the mediated influence

---

[54]   See Lucas, 'Holinshed and Hall', pp. 204–16.

[55]   The account of Agincourt is close to that of Hall although Holinshed includes only a very short list of French dead, choosing not to copy Hall's longer list (Curry, *Sources*, pp. 249–59). There is no significant difference in the two editions of Holinshed's chronicles in the sections concerning the wars in France.

[56]   Holinshed (1577), iv, p. 1225; Hall (1809), p. 126.

[57]   Holinshed (1577), iv, p. 1223; Hall (1809), p. 90.

[58]   Holinshed (1577), iv, p. 1225; Hall (1809), p. 125.

[59]   Holinshed (1577), iv, p. 1192; Hall (1809), p. 90.

[60]   Holinshed (1577), iv, p. 1202; Hall (1809), pp. 89–90.

of the M 9 chronicle. This concerns 'Henry VI Part 1' Act I, scene 4, where the earl of Salisbury is injured at the siege of Orléans by gunshot. Shakespeare has the son of the gunner at Orléans responsible for the earl of Salisbury's death, a story which has its origins in the M 9 chronicle.

Shakespeare's scene begins with the stage instruction: 'Enter on the walls a master gunner and his boy'. It is soon clarified that the boy is in fact the son of the gunner. He tells his father that he has often shot at the English but always missed his aim. His father reassures him that 'now thou shalt not. Be thou ruled be me', adding that he has seen the English come to 'a secret grate of iron bars in yonder tower to overpeer the city' and has therefore set a piece of ordnance against it. This echoes the text of the M 9 chronicle which had been taken up by Hall and thence Holinshed.[61]

> Quite soon, and within a short time after the taking and capture of the tower – in which there was a room, amongst other chambers, which had a window barred with iron bars through which you could see all along the bridge and into the city – several lords and other Englishmen frequently went to this window to observe and look out into the city. Those inside the city were annoyed by this. As a result, they had one of the master cannoneers aim a cannon straight against the window to shoot when necessary. (f. 63v)

Shakespeare's scene continues. Since the master gunner himself 'can stay no longer' he asks his son to keep watch but if he sees any English at the window to run to bring him word. We can anticipate what is going to happen in the boy's reply: 'Father I warrant you, take no care. I'll never trouble you if I may spy them.'

The scene continues with the stage instruction: 'Enter on the turrets the lords Salisbury and Talbot, Sir William Glasdale, Sir Thomas Gargrave and others'. The M 9 chronicle has Salisbury, Glasdale and Gargrave and others entering the tower at dinner time and going into the chamber. The earl went straight to the window and began to look out towards and across the town. This is followed in Hall and Holinshed although both authors have all of the three men going to the window and looking out. Shakespeare has made a significant change, therefore, by adding Talbot at his own volition.

Then comes a third stage instruction: 'Enter the boy with a linstock'. Salisbury tells the company that it is supper time in Orléans. 'Here through the grate I count each one and view the French how they fortify. Let us look in: the sight will much delight thee. Sir Thomas Gargrave and Sir William Glasdale, let me have your express opinions where is the best place to make our battery next.' After

---

61   Hall (1809), p. 145: 'In that toure that was taken at the bridge ende, as you before have heard, there was a high chambre hauyng a grate full of barres of yron by which a man might loke all the length of the bridge into the citie, at which grate many of the chief capitaines stode diverse times, vieuying the cite & devising in what place it was best assailable. They within the cite perceived well this toting hole and laied a pece of ordynanace directly against the wyndowe'; Holinshed (1577), iv, p. 1240, and (1587), vi, p. 599: 'In the Tower that was taken at the bridge ende (as before you haue hearde) there was an high chamber, hauing a grate full of barres of yron, by the which, a man myghte looke all the length of the bridge into the Citie, at whiche grate, many of the chiefe Captaynes ſtoode many times, viewing the Citie, and deuiſing in what place it was beſt to giue the aſſault. They within the Citie well perceyued thys tooting hole, & layde a peece of ordinance directly againſt the windowe.'

giving their advice, another stage instruction reads: 'Here they shoot'. Salisbury and Gargrave fall. Both cry out 'O lord have mercy', but it is left to Talbot to make a eulogistic speech on Salisbury which begins 'What chance is this that suddenly hath crossed us', making it clear that the earl has been seriously injured ('One of thy eyes and thy cheek's side struck off. Accursèd tower! accursèd fatal hand that hath contrived this woful tragedy').

The original inspiration undoubtedly derived from the M 9 chronicle which Hall, and Holinshed repeating Hall, followed closely.[62]

> Immediately the son of the master cannoneer noticed that there were people at the window. So he took the fuse and did just what his father, when going off for his dinner, had shown and instructed him. He fired the cannon and let fly a ball directly against the window, which broke the iron bars. The earl was hit on the head by one of the bars, or else by the shattering of the ball, to such an extent that it took out one of his eyes and smashed up a quarter of his head right through to his brain.

The personalisation of the person who brought about the death of Salisbury suits Shakespeare's dramatic purpose, emphasising also the role of fate in this 'woful tragedy'. Furthermore, as Michael Hattaway argues in his edition of the play, the emphasis on Salisbury, a 'surviving titanic hero from the reign of Henry V', being 'sniped down by a cannon fired by a boy' is intended to expose significant changes between the past and present in terms of both warfare and politics.[63] As it also supposed that Henry VI was played by a boy actor, there is also the intriguing possibility – indeed likelihood – that the son of the gunner was also cast as the king.

Shakespeare's addition of Talbot to the scene also serves a specific and important purpose. Talbot is throughout the play a significant protagonist, as witnessed in his exchanges in later scenes with La Pucelle. But the scene also takes us back to the beginning of the play. The funeral of Henry V immediately triggers a sense of doom and gloom and is followed by news of failures in France. Amongst these is the defeat at Patay and the capture of Talbot. Whilst the content and chronology are suspect here since Orléans has not yet been besieged – Shakespeare subsequently has Joan besieging Rouen – it emphasises the significance which Talbot is going to have in the play, with some critics claiming that he is in fact the hero of it,[64] as well as providing the first mention of Sir John Fastolf. The messenger bringing news of Patay stresses Talbot's bravery but continues 'Here had the conquest fully been

---

[62] Hall: 'with in a short space the sonne of the master gonner, perceived men lokyng out at the wyndowe, toke his matche as his father had taught hym, which was gone doune to dinner, and fired the gonne whiche brake and shevered the yron barres of the grate, whereof one strake therle so strongly one the hed that it stroke away one of his iyes and the side of his cheke'; Holinshed, 1577 and 1587: 'within a short space, the sonne of the master gunner, perceiuing men looking out at the window, tooke his match, as his father had taught him, who was gone downe to dinner, and fired the gunne, the shot whereof brake, and sheeuered the iron barres of the grate, The Earle of Salisbury slain so that one of the same barres strake the Earle so violently on the head, that it stroke awaye one of hys eyes, and the fye of hys cheeke.'

[63] *The First Part of King Henry VI*, ed. Hattaway, p. 18.

[64] *The First Part of King Henry VI*, ed. Hattaway, p. 17.

sealed up, if Sir John Fastolf had not played the coward. He, being in the vaward, placed behind, with purpose to relieve and follow them, cowardly fled, not having struck one stroke.'[65]

This early reference allows a second mention of Fastolf when Talbot goes into the tower at Orléans with Salisbury, Gargrave and Glasdale. Explaining that he has been exchanged as a prisoner he expresses his anger at Fastolf's behaviour which had led to his capture 'But O, the treacherous Fastolf wounds my heart, whom with my bare fists I would execute, if I now had him brought into my power.'[66] Treachery therefore sets the scene for the death at the hands of an inexperienced boy of a valiant earl ('In thirteen battles Salisbury overcame; Henry V he first trained to the wars').[67] Fastolf appears in person in Act 4, which is set during the king's visit to France, and is immediately challenged by Talbot. 'I vowed, base knight, when I did meet thee next to tear the Garter from thy craven's leg.' Having done this, he speaks again of Fastolf's cowardice in battle, and that such behaviour does not make him worthy of membership of the Order. Fastolf is given no chance to reply but is banished by the king forthwith ('Be packing therefore, thou that wast a knight, henceforth we banish thee on pain of death').[68] Such a failing of chivalry is emphasised by the letter from the duke of Burgundy with which Fastolf had arrived to give to the king, for it announced the duke's decision to change his allegiance from Henry VI to Charles VII.

Shakespeare was influenced in his portrayal of Fastolf by his reading of Holinshed's account of Patay which followed very closely that of Hall, telling of Fastolf's departure from the battle without fighting at all. Bedford, we are told, had initially taken the Garter from him but it was quickly restored 'by meane of frendes and apparent causes of good excuse by hym alledged ... against the mynd of the lorde Talbot', such information being taken from Monstrelet by Hall, who makes clear that the dispute between Talbot and Fastolf, begun by the latter's flight from Patay, was further exacerbated by the return of the Garter.[69] Of course, none of this is found in the M 9 chronicle which ends before the raising of the siege of Orléans. Nor does the chronicle make any explicit link between the outwitting of Fastolf by the defenders of La Gravelle (f. 60v) and his replacement by Talbot as governor of Maine and Anjou, but Hall and Holinshed do make the connection, linking Fastolf's discharge from this office with the appointment of Talbot and using the opportunity to comment positively on the latter's military prowess.[70]

---

[65] Act I, scene 1, lines 130–4.
[66] Act I, scene 4, lines 34–7.
[67] Act I, scene 4, lines 77–8.
[68] Act IV, scene 1, lines 15–16, 46–7. It would not be correct, however, to identify this Fastolf with the Falstaff of the later plays 'Henry IV parts 1 and 2' and 'Henry V'. That character was not initially intended to be called 'Falstaff' but by the name of Oldcastle, being changed by Shakespeare because of the reverence to the latter as a precursor of Protestant martyrs (*The First Part of King Henry IV*, ed. Weil and Weil, p. 5; Cooper, *The Real Falstaff*, p. 6).
[69] Hall (1809), p. 150; Holinshed (1577), iv, p. 1242, (1587), vi, p. 601; Monstrelet, iv, p. 332.
[70] Hall (1809), p. 141; Holinshed (1577), iv, p. 1236, (1587), vi, p. 597.

It is possible that Shakespeare used Hall directly. It has been suggested that he possessed a copy of the *Union* and even annotated it.[71] Whatever the case, it can be argued that the general content and tone of the M 9 chronicle, as well as the tragedy at Orléans through the son of the master gunner, reached him through the mediation of Hall and Holinshed. By such means was transmitted to Shakespeare the martial and chivalric traditions of the wars of Henry V and VI, as well as the names and actions of at least some of those involved. Also communicated was the sense of the honour and national pride which participation in these wars embodied – or at least the successful parts of these wars, since the M 9 chronicle only covered the years of English ascendancy from 1415 to the reversals of 1429. Such a jingoistic spirit is particularly apparent in Shakespeare's 'Henry V'. Failure in France is pivotal in 'Henry VI Part 1', with feuds such as that between Talbot and Fastolf presaging the dynastic disputes which followed in the Wars of the Roses.[72]

THE BASSET PROBLEM

At the beginning of his *Union* Hall listed a 'Ihon Basset' amongst the English authors he had used. So far no historical work by a John Basset has been discovered. As we have seen, Peter Basset was noted by William Worcester to be the principal author of the M 9 chronicle, a work in French. We could dismiss the different first name in Hall's list of authors as a transcription or typographical error, not least as Hall mentions a Peter Basset within his *Union* as a source of information on the death of Henry V. But the issue of the difference of language – English/French – remains problematic. Might it be that Hall included Basset in his English authors on the grounds that the writer was English by nationality and not necessarily that he wrote in English? That interpretation does not seem credible since all the other writers in Hall's list of English authors wrote in English. Why should Basset be an exception? If there is any truth in the suggestion that Hall used an English work by someone called Basset, it would seem more likely that there was once such a work which is now lost.

In exploring this hypothesis, we can point to another mid-sixteenth-century mention, made by John Bale, of an English work by a Peter Basset. Bale (1495–1563) was an English Protestant cleric who was briefly bishop of Ossory in 1552–53 before being forced out of his see by the accession of Queen Mary.[73] For many years he worked to produce a list of all works written by past English, Welsh and Scottish writers. Much of his research had been carried out in the libraries of recently dissolved monastic houses, his project being motivated by regret at the loss

---

[71]   Zeeveld, 'The Influence of Hall on Shakespeare's English Historical Plays', pp. 317–53. The argument that Shakespeare had a copy of Hall which still survives is put forward by the bookseller Alan Keen, 'A Short Account of the Recently Discovered Copy of Edward Hall's Chronicle', pp. 255–62, and developed in Keen and Lubbock, *The Annotator*. For comment see the online paper of George, 'A Lost Annotated Text and an Unrecognized Folio Corrector'.

[72]   In the scene immediately following Fastolf's dismissal by the king, Shakespeare has a 'Basset of the Red Rose or Lancastrian faction' in dispute with Vernon of the White Rose or Yorkist faction, leading to the first scene explicitly presaging the subsequent civil wars. Shakespeare would have read in Holinshed (taken from Hall) of a Peter Basset, chamberlain of Henry V, but it can only be speculation that this led him to the use of the surname.

[73]   King, 'Bale, John (1495–1563)', *ODNB*.

of so much past intellectual achievement. As Bale put it, 'to destroye all without consyderacyon, is and wyll be unto Englande for ever, a moste horryble infamy amonge the grave senyours of other nacyons'.[74] The initial fruits of his labour were published in 1549 in *Illustrium majoris Britanniae scriptorum*.[75] In this edition, however, there is no mention of any work by a Peter or a John Basset. Nor do we find any mention of such a work in the surviving notebook kept by Bale in which he made draft lists of authors and works as well as their locations.[76]

After his expulsion from Ossory, Bale sought exile in Basel. In 1557–59 he produced there an expanded version of his list, *Scriptorum illustrium majoris Britanniae Catalogus*.[77] It is here that we find mention of a one-volume work in English by Peter Basset concerning Henry V ('Edito in Anglico sermone libro cui titulum fecit Acta Regis Henrici Quinti Lib. 1'). The full entry reads as follows:[78]

> Petrus Basset, clari generis armiger, et Henrico Quinto Anglorum regi a cubiculis, eorum omnium testis oculatissimus fuit, quae idem rex magnificus tam apud Anglos quam etiam in Galliis olim fecit. Nam aderat illi ad latus semper hic Petrus, seu domi seu foris quicquam ageret, sive vel in pace vel in bello fuisset occupatus, et omnibus in locis notabat eius tum dicta tum facta precipua. Descripsit illius ab ipsis incunabulis vitam varias in Franciam expeditiones, gloriosas de Gallis victorias ac triomphos: cum Carolo sexto francorum rege pacifactionem & affinatatem post bella, atque tandem eius regni administrationem plenissimam, Henrico filio regi ipsius diademate Parisis tum demum insignito. Et hec omnia in eius regis laudem plenissime congessit, edito in Anglico sermone libro, cui titulum fecit *Acta regis Henrici quinti Lib. 1*
>
> Praeter hoc, nihil opusculorum eius extare novi. Et ubi scriptorium aliqui, predictum regem ex venenata potione, alii ex fiacrii male aut igne Antonii interisse fingunt, iste ex pluresi obiisse illum affirmat. Claruit Petrus anno Domini 1430, Henrico sexto regnante.[79]

Bale even gave a date (1430) for the clarification that Peter Basset had made about the cause of Henry V's death.[80] For Bale, Basset was an esquire of rank and cham-

---

[74]   Much of Bale's research had been carried out in the libraries of recently dissolved monastic houses, motivated by regret at the loss of so much past intellectual achievement: 'To destroye all without consyderacyon, is and wyll be unto Englande for ever, a moste horryble infamy amonge the grave senyours of other nacyons', cited in Aston, *Lollards and Reformers*, p. 327.

[75]   The full title is *Illustrium majoris Britanniae scriptorum, hoc est Angliae, Cambriae ac Scotiae summarium, in quasdam centurias divisum a Japheto sanctissimi Noah filio ad annum domini 1548*. This edition was published in Wesel in 1549.

[76]   Oxford, Bodleian Library MS Selden supra 64, printed as *Index Britanniae scriptorum quos ex variis bibliothecis non parvo labore collegit Ioannes Baleus, cum aliis*.

[77]   See also Warner, *John Bale's Catalogue of Tudor Authors*.

[78]   *Scriptorum illustrium majoris Britanniae Catalogus*, p. 568.

[79]   *Scriptorum illustrium majoris Britanniae Catalogus*, p. 568; and Nichols, 'Peter Basset. A Lost Historian of the Reign of Henry V', p. 424.

[80]   Monstrelet claimed Henry's death was due to 'St Anthony's fire' (now better known as ergotism). The Religieux of Saint-Denis had ascribed it to 'St Fiacre's sickness', which is an otherwise undocumented illness which seems to have been intended to make a political

berlain to Henry V. As a result of this role he knew things about the king which were otherwise secret and not known to others; he never left the king's side and so was able to note all that Henry did, both in war and in peace. Bale also added that Basset's account went right from the beginning of the king's life, through all his military activity and triumph and the peace with France, adding that Henry was invested with insignia in Paris as the king's son.

There is no firm evidence, however, that Bale had actually seen or read this *Acta regis Henrici quinti* in English by Basset. He gave no location for it, whilst his usual practice was to indicate the current whereabouts of the works he listed. Indeed, his description implies that the work was no longer extant. The possible implication, therefore, is that Bale heard of it because of the mentions in Edward Hall's *Union*, printed in 1548, of an English author called (John) Basset, and of a Peter Basset as a source of information on the death of Henry V and a chamberlain of the king. That would explain first why Basset's *Acta regis Henrici quinti* had not been included by Bale in the first edition of his list which was published around the same time as Hall's *Union* was being printed, and secondly, why it *was* included by Bale in his edition of 1557–59, by which time the *Union* had gone through two printings. Furthermore, in 1555 Queen Mary had ordered all copies of the *Union* to be destroyed, because of the 'reformation' sections on Henry VIII and Edward VI,[81] thereby making it a work of interest to as rabid a Protestant as Bale.

In Hall's narrative of the death of Henry V, copied by Holinshed, we find the following: 'For Peter Basset esquire which at the time of his death was his chamberlain affirmeth that he [Henry V] died of a Plurisis'.[82] What Bale tells us in his entry both repeats and develops this further. The entry in Bale's second edition suggests that Basset's work covered the whole of the king's life. Bale could simply have invented all of this based on the apparent closeness of Peter Basset to Henry V and also perhaps the inclusion of a Basset in Hall's list of English authors. There remains no proof that Bale had actually seen Basset's work himself. It is equally possible that he was told about the work by Edward Hall, or by Richard Grafton, who, as we have seen, was a well-known Protestant printer.

It seems likely, as we have argued in Chapters 1 and 2, that the M 9 chronicle has its origins in a work by Peter Basset. We saw that a soldier by that name existed but there is no proof of anyone of that name as chamberlain to Henry V. Hall claims that (John) Basset wrote in English. Bale follows this line, but, as we have suggested, is unlikely to be an independent source on this point. But if we take both Hall and Bale at face value, then it would seem that a Peter (or John) Basset did write a life of Henry V in English. On the face of it, there is no reason why the Peter Basset named by William Worcester did not write in English since he was English by birth, nor why Nantron, Hanson and Worcester could not have drawn on his work in English, nor why such a work was a one-volume life of Henry V. All we can say is that if such a work existed, it no longer appears to do so. All we have is the M 9 chronicle in French, with an involvement in its creation of a Peter Basset.

---

point since St Fiacre was of Scottish origin: Henry had allegedly allowed his troops to ravage the lands of St Fiacre, plundering the church which held his relics (Wylie and Waugh, *Henry the Fifth*, iii, p. 418 n. 11).

[81]   *Tudor Royal Proclamations*, ii, pp. 58–60. The *Union* was printed again in 1565.

[82]   Hall (1809), p. 113; Holinshed (1577), iv, p. 1218; (1587), vi, p. 584.

In the early eighteenth century a solution was proposed by Thomas Tanner (1674–1735) – namely that there were *two* works by Basset.[83] By the time his *Bibliotheca Britannico-Hibernica*, a listing of pre-seventeenth-century authors in England, Wales and Ireland, was published in 1748, the existence of the M 9 chronicle in the College of Arms was known. It had been mentioned by Thomas Hearne (1679–1735) in the preface to his edition of the *Vita et Gesta Henrici Quinti* (often called the Pseudo Elmham) which was published in 1727. Hearne notes 'Petri Basset et Christophori Hansoni inprimis adversaria potius quam historiam imperfecta'.[84] Hearne knew that this text was in French and that it was in the library of the College of Arms ('In bibliotheca collegii fecialium'[85]), having been informed of the work by John Anstis who had become Garter King of Arms in 1718. He also knew that the work had a link to Sir John Fastolf, suggesting that Anstis had told him of the whole incipit on its first page.

In Tanner's entry for Peter Basset in the *Bibliotheca Britannico-Hibernica* we find the following work accredited to this author, the description being extremely close to the incipit by William Worcester, suggesting therefore that Tanner may also have seen the work, or else been told of it by Hearne, although no mention was made by Tanner of its language:[86]

> De actis armorum conquestus regni Francie ducatus Normannie ducatus Alenconie, ducatus Andegavie et Cenomannie cum aliis pluribus comitatibus compilatus fuit ad nobiliem virum Iohannem Fastolf baronem de Cylleguillem per Petrum Basset manuscriptum in biblioteca Officii Armorum London.

Tanner had also been influenced, however, by a reading of Bale's entry concerning Peter Basset in *Scriptorum illustrium majoris Britanniae Catalogus*. As a result, Tanner also listed for the same Basset a one-volume *Acta regis Henrici quinti* in English, adding further information taken from Bale: 'Bassetus [Petrus] clari generis armiger, et Henrico Quinto Anglorum regi a cubiculis, eorum omnium testis oculatissimus fuit, quae idem rex magnificus tam apud Anglos quam etiam in Galliis olim fecit'.

Tanner also knew that Edward Hall had listed a John Basset amongst his English sources. He therefore added an entry in his *Bibliotheca Britannico-Hibernica* for 'Bassetus [Johannes]', describing him as a 'historicus Anglus teste Edw. Hallo, inter alia scripsit Anglice Chronicorum lib. 1'. Tanner added that no other work of John Basset was known, but that a man of this name had been vicar of Gedney (Lincs.) in the reign of Richard II, information Tanner had found in Rymer's *Foed-*

---

[83]   Sharpe, 'Tanner, Thomas (1674–1735)', *ODNB*.

[84]   Hearne, *Vita et Gesta*, pp. xxxi–xxxii, cited in Rowe, p. 505 n. 3.

[85]   *Fecialis* (or more commonly *fetialis*) was a classical Latin word signifying a college of priests responsible for formally making peace or declaring war and was commonly used from the sixteenth century as the Latin for herald. Our thanks to Nigel Ramsay for this clarification.

[86]   Tanner, *Bibliotheca Britannico-Hibernica*, p. 79. (This work had been completed after Tanner's death by David Wilkins.) Tanner also noted that the work had been listed on p. 615 of Pitts, *De Illustribus Angliae Scriptoribus*, published in Paris in 1619. Pitts (1560–1616) studied at Oxford but was ordained a Catholic priest in Rome and had a distinguished career in France.

era printed earlier in the eighteenth century.[87] To date, no work on English history of any period by a John Basset has been discovered.

Thanks to Tanner, John Basset was deemed to be the author of one work and Peter Basset the author of two works, even if only one was extant. When Peter Basset's biography was written for the first edition of the *Dictionary of National Biography* in 1885, its author, Sydney Lee, replicated the idea that there were two works by Basset. Lee knew that there was a chronicle in French in the College of Arms. His source for this was presumably Hearne's preface to the *Vita et Gesta Henrici Quinti*, since Tanner had not noted the language of the work. But Lee did not know the reference number for the text in the College of Arms. He simply noted the thought of William Macray that it was possibly College of Arms, Arundel 48, item 66, which was an incomplete history of Henry V's wars in France written in French.[88] Yet, as Lee reminded his readers, 'Both Bale and Tanner distinctly state … that Basset's history of Henry V was written in English'. Dodging the problem of a John Basset as listed in Hall's English authors, Lee concluded that 'It is probable that Hall, who was obviously acquainted with Basset's work, made liberal use of it in his well-known chronicle.'

To date, no English text(s) by Peter or John Basset have been discovered. But Hall's reference to an English work by a Basset has an implication for the study of the M 9 chronicle. Could it be that Hall did not use the extant chronicle in French as his source, but rather a lost work in English which contained the same, or mostly the same, narrative and lists of participants? As we have seen, there is a very strong suggestion that the M 9 chronicle was based on an earlier work by Basset, and, in reality, we have no evidence what language that work was in.

Hall wrote his lists using English forms of names, which might suggest that he was taking the information from an English chronicle by Basset, yet his French was also good enough to allow him to translate the lists and narrative passages from French into English. As we saw in Chapter 5, the lists which Robert Glover copied into British Library Harley 782 were partly in French and followed the wording of the M 9 chronicle, and partly in English but following the order presented in French in the same chronicle. This would suggest that Glover used the chronicle which is extant today, and translated some parts of it, leaving the rest in the original language.

In conclusion, therefore, unless we discover an English work on Henry V by Peter Basset – in other words, Bale's 'in Anglico sermone libro, cui titulum fecit *Acta regis Henrici quinti Lib. 1*' – or an English historical work by a John Basset, as listed amongst Edward Hall's 'English Auctors', the only known authorial product involving a Basset – in this case, with the first name Peter – is the M 9 chronicle.

---

[87] *Foedera*, vii, p. 199, an entry taken from the French rolls, where John Basset was nominated by Sir Philip Despenser in letters of attorney of June 1378 as the latter prepared to cross to France in the company of John of Gaunt, duke of Lancaster

[88] Citing *Notes and Queries*, 2nd ser. ix, p. 512. William Dunn Macray (1826–1916) was librarian at the Bodleian Library from 1845 to 1905. A guide to the Arundel manuscripts was already in the public domain, printed in 1829, but there was no printed catalogue of the foundation collections of the College until 1988. In 1913 Macray's idea was demolished by Charles Kingsford, who showed that the chronicle in College of Arms, Arundel 48 was a *Cronique de Normandie*.

7

'In the Mids of his Glory': the M 9 Chronicle, 'A Mirror for Magistrates', and the tragedy of English imperialism

Scott Lucas

The military narrative preserved in College of Arms MS M 9 may have begun its life as a chronicle designed for a single fifteenth-century reader, but its unique status as a detailed account, offered from the English perspective, of martial activity in France between 1415 and 1429 helped to win for it a wide audience in the succeeding century and beyond. Two early modern authors in particular became inspired by this narrative's material, and they employed it to enrich their own written works. As we have seen in Chapter 6, the first was the chronicler Edward Hall, who introduced sixteenth-century readers to the M 9 chronicle's narrative by incorporating nearly all of it (with his own additions and emendations) into his massive history of English affairs c. 1398–1547, *The Union of the Two Noble and Illustre Families of Lancaster and York* (1548). The second was the anonymous author of the tragic verse monologue 'How Thomas Montagu the Earl of Salisbury, in the Mids of his Glory, was Chanceably Slain with a Piece of Ordnance' (composed 1554, first published 1559).

In the conceit of this 280-line, rhyme-royal work, a ghostly Thomas Montague, fourth earl of Salisbury, rises from the grave to recall his many military triumphs and his shocking, untimely death (3 November 1428). After a brief lament for the tarnished memory of his father, a man executed for his participation in the Epiphany Rising against King Henry IV (December 1399–January 1400), Salisbury's ghost embarks on a stirring account of his own glorious career in the second and third decades of the fifteenth century. As a young man, Salisbury quickly rose to prominence under Henry V, winning numerous military victories abroad and participating in the negotiation of all English treaties. After Henry V's death, Salisbury found favour with Humphrey, duke of Gloucester, and John, duke of Bedford, the two great noblemen who ruled as protector of England and Regent of France respectively during the infancy of King Henry VI. Both men held great confidence in him, Salisbury's ghost recalls in the poem, trusting him to 'rule at home as often as they willed' and sending him several times to campaign in France 'when they it needful deemed'. A man in both 'peace and war well skilled', Salisbury won many forts and towns simply by assuring their defenders that they would be 'friendly used' if they surrendered; whenever a stronghold resisted him or an army offered him combat in the field, however, Salisbury's fierce courage and the overwhelming 'force and furies' he deployed in battle assured that victory was always his. Salisbury's long string of triumphs in the 1420s only came to an end by a tragic accident, when, while besieging the powerful city of Orléans, he was wounded by a piece of iron grating dislodged by a cannonball that struck a tower wall near to him. He died from this injury several days later, seemingly on the cusp, his ghost suggests, of yet another great victory and still in 'the Mids of his Glory'.[1]

For his information about Salisbury's French campaigns, the poet relies heavily on the M 9 chronicle narrative as it was presented in Hall's *Union*. The poet employs this material to accomplish two goals in his poem. Most immediately, he seeks to extol the fifteenth-century warrior Salisbury and to lament the unfortunate circumstances that led to Salisbury's demise. Beyond that, he artfully shapes the matter to awaken in his intended audience fond memories of mid-Tudor England's own glory days of bellicose imperialist expansionism. He does so to celebrate this sort of aggressive English foreign policy and to offer a modicum of consolation to those currently suffering from its shocking reversal and collapse in the early 1550s.

The collection of historical verse tragedies for which 'Salisbury' was composed, *A Mirror for Magistrates*, began as the brainchild of the printer John Wayland. In early 1554, in the initial year of Mary I's reign, Wayland sought to release a new edition of John Lydgate's venerable *de casibus*-tragedy collection *The Fall of Princes* (c. 1431–37), which recounted in poetic form the downfalls of famous figures who lived from the time of Adam and Eve to the year 1364. To make his edition more marketable, Wayland planned to supplement Lydgate's text with a collection of new tragic poems relating the unfortunate lives and deaths of chiefly English notables who had met their ends in the years after those covered by Lydgate's work.[2]

To oversee this project, Wayland selected the well-known mid-Tudor poet William Baldwin (d. 1563). Recruiting seven other men to contribute to the collection, Baldwin oversaw the creation of twenty historical verse tragedies stretching from the last years of Richard II's reign to the end of Edward IV's. Following Lydgate's own conceit, each of these new tragedies would be related by the ghost of the person who had experienced its misfortunes. The authors broke, however, with Lydgate's method of paraphrasing what the ghosts supposedly uttered, in order to employ a much more emotionally powerful and dramatic form in which the ghosts themselves told their tales in their own voices.

Late in 1554, the collection was printed under the title *A Memorial of such princes, as since the time of Richard II were unfortunate in the Realm of England*. Mary I's lord chancellor Stephen Gardiner ordered the work suppressed before publication, however, almost certainly because of the topically allusive, controversial content some of the *Memorial* authors added to their poems. Only after Mary's death and the accession of Elizabeth I could this collection finally appear, in lightly edited

---

[1]		Lucas, ed., *A Mirror for Magistrates: A Modernized and Annotated Edition*, pp. 58–67. All further references to *A Mirror for Magistrates* will be to this edition.
[2]		Of the twenty ghostly speakers intended for this work, eighteen were English, one Scottish (King James I), and one Welsh (Owain Glyn Dŵr).

form, under the new title *A Mirror for Magistrates* (1559). From the moment of its publication, the *Mirror* enjoyed great success, eventually appearing between 1559 and 1621 in seven often-expanded editions and numerous reissues of earlier printings. By the time of its last edition, the *Mirror* had grown to three times its original size and had inspired a host of Tudor and Stuart authors to emulate its style and to draw on its poems' contents for their own literary creations.[3]

In choosing to present notable English political and military events stretching from the Merciless Parliament of 1388 to King Edward IV's death in 1483, the 'Salisbury' poet and his fellow authors by necessity confronted one of the most traumatic occurrences of England's fifteenth century, the loss of nearly all English-held lands in France in the late 1440s and early 1450s. The failure of England to maintain its control of French lands, despite the inspiring victories of Henry V and subsequent decades of hard-fought struggle, would have resonated particularly strongly with many living in 1554, for Englishmen and women of this time too had recently witnessed – and a great number had suffered from – a similar reversal of a proud period of martial success and imperial expansion, one hauntingly reminiscent of the stunning territorial losses experienced by England in the mid-fifteenth century.

From the beginning of his reign (1509–47), King Henry VIII sought to present himself to the world as a proud, bellicose monarch, one eager to make England a major force in European affairs.[4] Vigorously promoting the English monarch's claim to the title 'King of France', Henry VIII yearned to restore English sovereignty over French lands lost under Henry VI. To this end, the king led an expedition into France in 1513, and he and numerous of his subjects soon celebrated the resultant capture of the French towns of Thérouanne and Tournai as proof positive of English might and military skill.[5]

Although subsequent noble-led enterprises against France were not as successful as the king's own invasion in 1513, Henry VIII never abandoned his dream of extending his authority over neighbouring lands. In the early 1540s, Henry adopted an aggressively imperialistic foreign policy. In 1542, the king had Wales joined to England and Ireland made a kingdom, with the English monarch as its sovereign. In the same year, Henry ordered a devastatingly successful attack on Scotland; in its wake, he dictated a compact (the treaty of Greenwich, 1543) that promised to wed the infant Mary, Queen of Scots, to his own son Prince Edward, in a bid to unite the Scottish and English crowns under English dominance. When the Scottish parliament rejected this agreement, Henry ordered the powerful soldier Edward Seymour, first earl of Hertford, to lay waste to the country as punishment (1544). Seymour put to fire Leith and Edinburgh, acts that earned for him (in the words of Edward Hall's chronicle) 'great honour [and] the great reioysyng aswel of the kynges maiestie as of all his faithful and louyng subiectes'.[6]

---

[3]   For the creation of *A Mirror for Magistrates* and the topically allusive, controversial material several of its contributors added to their tragedies, see Lucas, *'A Mirror for Magistrates' and the Politics of the English Reformation*.

[4]   For the bellicose, chivalric culture at Henry VIII's court and the king's eagerness to rival the chief princes of Europe, see, among other works, Kipling, *The Triumph of Honour*; and Richardson, *Renaissance Monarchy*.

[5]   Scarisbrick, *Henry VIII*, pp. 31–8; Murphy, 'Henry VIII's French Crown'.

[6]   Hall (1809), p. 861. On the attempts in the 1540s to bring the Scots under English hegemony, see Merriman, *The Rough Wooings*.

In 1544, Henry himself travelled to France to witness his forces besiege Boulogne.[7] Greeting news of that city's surrender as one of the highest achievements of his reign, he joyously entered the newly defeated town with 'the sworde borne naked before him ... like a noble and valyaunt conqueror'. In the wake of Boulogne's capture, Henry was reluctant ever to give up this highly visible symbol of English might; he ultimately agreed (in the treaty of Campe, 1546) to return it only in the year 1554 and for great monetary compensation.[8]

Shortly after Henry VIII's death (28 January 1547), the celebrated military commander Edward Seymour, now duke of Somerset, assumed chief power as protector during Edward VI's minority, and he continued Henry VIII's policy of imperialist expansionism. In September 1547, Seymour led an expedition into Scotland designed to compel the Scots to honour the provisions of the treaty of Greenwich, winning a crushing victory over Scottish forces at the battle of Pinkie Cleugh. Once again pride ran high in response to another English vanquishing of foreign foes. So fervent were the celebrations of Somerset and his Scottish conquests that London magistrates even offered the returning protector a triumphal entry into the city, in the manner usually reserved only for monarchs.[9]

After Pinkie, the bellicose expansionism that had so strongly guided English foreign policy in the 1540s quickly stagnated, declined, and, within a few years, ended in ruin. Somerset had followed his victory at Pinkie by establishing numerous English garrisons in the Scottish lowlands. France, however, sent 10,000 troops to bolster Scottish resistance to England, and the expense of protecting the border and maintaining Seymour's garrisons quickly became enormous. In response, Somerset once again turned his thoughts to invasion; he was in the process of building up a new expeditionary force when his fellow privy councillors, stirred both by his domineering treatment of them and his mishandling of the ferocious popular risings of summer 1549, deposed Somerset from office in October. To the sorrow of those who had once championed the protector and his foreign and domestic policies, Seymour's rivals blamed nearly every trouble England experienced between the years 1547 and 1549 on him.[10] Although later pardoned by the king and restored to the privy council, Seymour was never able to regain control of English affairs. He lost his life in February 1552, executed on a charge of plotting against those councillors who had supplanted him in authority.

In the wake of Somerset's deposition, England withdrew all of its Scottish garrisons. English-held Boulogne fared no better. Troubled by financial pressures and numerous French assaults on Boulogne and its environs, the new government led by John Dudley, earl of Warwick, came to the conclusion that Boulogne was not worth keeping for the full term of the Campe treaty. Dudley sought to end hostilities with France by offering Boulogne's return long before the negotiated date. The result was an inauspicious peace (1550) that saw Boulogne yielded four years

---

[7]   Murphy, *Tudor Occupation of Boulogne*, pp. 21, 83.
[8]   Hall (1809), p. 862; Scarisbrick, *Henry VIII*, pp. 450, 464.
[9]   Jordan, *Edward VI*, pp. 252–63; *Grafton's Chronicle*, ii, p. 504.
[10] Bush, *The Government Policy of Protector Somerset*, pp. 2, 7–40, 160–1; Jordan, *Edward VI*, pp. 268–91; for the charges made against Seymour by his enemies before and after his deposition, including his alleged diversion of military funds for his personal use and his unwillingness properly to defend England's foreign holdings, see *Troubles Connected with the Prayer Book of 1549*, ed. Pocock, pp. 96, 115–16; Stow, *Annales*, pp. 1008, 1011, 1015–17.

before it was due and for only half the compensation that the treaty of Campe had specified. Under Dudley, the grand expansionist policies of the previous years were completely abandoned, and, to the dismay of many, England simply surrendered all the foreign possessions its forces had fought so hard to win and keep over the preceding decade.[11]

By the time the poems of *A Memorial of such Princes* were being composed (1554), English foreign policy could not have been more distant from the ethos of proud imperialist expansionism that had guided it in the 1540s. Not only did the current monarch, Queen Mary, decline to challenge Scotland or France, but, to the horror of many, she announced that she intended to wed the powerful Habsburg prince Philip of Spain. In contemplating Mary's Spanish match, many feared that England would be reduced to permanent status as a second-rate power: the 'common humour' of Englishmen and women at the time, according to one contemporary, was dread that England would become nothing more than an inglorious, submissive client of the mighty Habsburg empire. To the pain and bewilderment of many, the nation's proud pursuit of martial glory and imperialist expansionism seemed to have ended in complete and apparently lasting failure.[12]

Through his account of his ghostly speaker's great victories, the 'Salisbury' poet seeks to valorise once more the abandoned policy of bellicose English expansionism, presenting readers with a narrative, based heavily on that of the M 9 chronicle, designed to convince them of the ease that England once enjoyed in extending its influence abroad and defeating foreign foes. To revive such memories – and the concomitant sense of pride they once engendered – the poet sharply pared down the information in the M 9 chronicle as it was conveyed to him in Hall's chronicle. He included nothing from the text not directly related to Salisbury himself, dispensing with the long lists of captains and knights who served with Salisbury, the detailed declarations of the named foes who opposed this great commander in the field, and in most cases the accounts of actions leading up to or following the great victories the M 9 chronicle relates. The result is a remarkably brisk and exhilarating display of English martial prowess, as expressed in the career of a single great Englishman.

Thus, in having Salisbury's ghost recall the battle of Cravant (31 July 1423), the poet mentions neither the other English leaders present nor their Burgundian allies. Instead, he has his Salisbury emphasise solely his own role in fighting against England's enemies, making it seem almost as if a single English warrior alone had been sufficient to defeat the besieging army of Frenchmen and Scots. 'Force and furies fit be for the field', Salisbury's spirit observes to his auditor, *Mirror* editor William Baldwin,

---

[11]   Elton, *Reform and Reformation*, pp. 359–60; Jordan, *Edward VI*, pp. 299–300.

[12]   Ham, 'The Autobiography of Sir James Croft', 53. Two of the four known contributors to the 1554 *Memorial of such Princes* and the 1559 *Mirror for Magistrates* served in the campaigns of the 1540s. Poet and courtier George Ferrers travelled with Henry VIII under arms to Boulogne, and he took part in two of Edward Seymour's incursions into Scotland (1545 and 1547). Author and clerk of the privy council Sir Thomas Chaloner accompanied Seymour on his 1544 Scottish invasion, and he served as Seymour's chief secretary during the September 1547 expedition, for which Somerset knighted him on the field (Lucas, *'A Mirror for Magistrates' and the Politics of the English Reformation*, pp. 41–9; Leland, 'Ad Georgium Ferrarium', p. 99; Millar, *Tudor Mercenaries*, p. 148).

> For when Lord Stewart and Earl Vantadore
> Had cruelly besieged Cravant town,
> Which we had wan and kept long time before,
> Which lieth in Auxerre on the river Yonne,
> To raise the siege the regent sent me down,
> Where, as I used all rigour that I might,
> I killed all that were not saved by flight.[13]

The poet implies a sense of Salisbury's vigour and alacrity by the swift flow of these lines. The reader's eye quickly glides over the passage, as the poem moves quickly from news of cruel foes besieging Cravant, to Regent Bedford's command for Salisbury to break the siege, to Salisbury's sudden appearance on the field, and then to his seeming sole personal dominance over his French and Scottish foes.

The poem keeps up its rapid pace in the next several stanzas, compressing several years of military action described in the M 9 chronicle into a few brief references. Just five lines after his victory at Cravant, Salisbury appears at Montaiguillon, whose twenty-week siege the poet condenses into two lines of poetry. Thereafter, Salisbury is immediately off to Ivry and, a few lines after that, to Verneuil, which similarly receives only two lines of verse before Salisbury places himself at the siege of Le Mans. Only here does his narrative slow, in order to emphasise the glory of his victory over a particularly proud, 'warlike' town and a particularly worthy, stubborn foe.[14] The poet packs two full years of sieges and fighting into a brief, compact space, to make it appear as if this representative of English martial prowess had not only been a skilled general but also a man relentless and untiring in his zeal to place foreign lands under English royal authority.

After Le Mans, the poet brings Salisbury's tale of conquest and capture to something of a crescendo, when he combines Salisbury's taking of Sainte-Suzanne, Mayenne and La Ferté-Bernard, whose captures are recounted with some detail in the M 9 chronicle narrative, with the bare list of other forts and towns seized in the wake of the fall of Le Mans.[15] The poet discards the careful record of the captains to whom these holdings were entrusted, leaving solely the names of the conquests themselves listed one after the other. The result is a breathless, even disorienting rush of victory upon victory, as nothing seems to be able to stop Salisbury's headlong drive to bring all of Maine under English control:

> But to return, in Maine wan I at length,
> Such towns and forts as might either help or hurt;
> I manned Mayenne and Suzannes, towns of strength,
> Fort Barnarde, Thanceaux, and S. Cales the curt,
> With Lile sues Bolton, standing in the dirt;
> Eke Gwerland, Susze, Louplande and Mountsure,
> With Malicorne, these wan I and kept full sure.[16]

---

[13]   *A Mirror for Magistrates*, p. 62.

[14]   *A Mirror for Magistrates*, pp. 63–4.

[15]   College of Arms, MS M 9, f. 57r.

[16]   *A Mirror for Magistrates*, p. 64. 'Thanceaux' derives from Hall's mistaken reading of the first word of the M 9 chronicle's 'Chasteaulx lermitage', the fortified priory Château-

Stripped of their details, the M 9 chronicle's record of Salisbury's actions in Maine becomes a splendid roll call of quick, decisive English conquests. The poem's readers are invited to revel in this impressive assertion of the fullness of English warriors' mastery over their foreign enemies and their seemingly easy seizure of even the strongest foreign holdings.

The poet's swift and confident account of Salisbury's actions between 1423 and 1425 is meant to reawaken in Tudor readers all the pride and good memories associated with past English conquests, whether England's victories in France in the 1420s or its forces' capture of Boulogne and their several successful invasions of Scotland in the 1540s. If the English crown had lost almost all of its holdings in France by the 1450s (and again in the 1550s), it was not – the poet's long list of historically verified triumphs seems to assert – because of English commanders' inability to defeat foreign foes or to seize foreign possessions. To the contrary, the poem insists on the ease with which English troops under a competent English leader can devastate all who come before them. Thus, the poem's Salisbury boasts of how his 8,000 Englishmen at Verneuil were all that were needed to slaughter 10,000 members of a much larger ('two thousand score') foreign army. At Saint-James-de-Beuvron, Salisbury later recalls, 500 English soldiers shouting Salisbury's name were enough to cause the retreat of 40,000 frightened foes. Salisbury even uses the term 'Frenchly' to describe the way England's enemies fled at Saint-James-de-Beuvron, to suggest that cowardly flight is natural to French fighters when faced with the threat of having to meet determined English troops.[17] English prowess has won mighty victories in the past, readers are to consider, whether in the 1420s or the 1540s; why should anyone expect it not to do the same in the 1550s, if only England's governors had the will to pursue the expansionist aims so many had celebrated under Henry VIII and Protector Somerset?

Unfortunately, England's glorious period of expansion and conquest in foreign lands did, in fact, fail, and Protector Somerset's enemies were quick to blame him for its collapse. Beyond his general celebration of aggressive English imperialism, the poet shapes his poem as a means indirectly to contest the painful claims that Edward Seymour's own failings were the cause both of his downfall and that of the proud imperialist policy that had so long guided English foreign affairs. He does so by inviting readers, through his highly suggestive description of Salisbury and his methods, to recall Seymour in the same manner as they view the Salisbury of his poem, as a victorious man who was brought low not by his own weakness or incompetence but solely through undeserved misfortune.

To guide readers to thoughts of Edward Seymour, the poet adds details to his description of Salisbury not found in his three sources – the rendering of the M 9 narrative in Hall's *Union*, Hall's own words about Salisbury in his chronicle, and Robert Fabyan's brief references to Montague in his *New Chronicles of England and France* (1516). The M 9 chronicle, Hall and Fabyan all present Salisbury solely as a fierce and devoted campaigner. The poet, by contrast, has his Salisbury claim an important domestic career for himself, declaring that under Henry VI he often 'bare rule at home' in place of Protector Humphrey, duke of Gloucester. The people loved him in his role as England's governor, Salisbury asserts, since his rule

---

l'Hermitage (Sarthe, arr. la Flèche, cant. Le Lude). See College of Arms, MS M 9, fol. 57r; Hall (1809), p. 127.

[17]   *A Mirror for Magistrates*, pp. 63–5.

ever expressed his 'virtuous life, free heart, and lowly mind'. His unusually kind, loving governance led grateful English subjects to call him 'the good earl'.[18]

It was precisely his characteristically mild disposition, Salisbury's ghost then surprisingly declares, that helped him to win many of his conquests in France. Salisbury explains that his native kindness always led him to try to negotiate in a friendly manner with French-held towns before besieging them,

> For in assaults due mildness passeth far
> All rigour, force, and sturdy violence,
> For men will stoutly stick to their defence
> When cruel captains covet them to spoil
> And, so enforced, oft give their foes the foil.
> But when they know they shall be friendly used,
> They hazard not their heads but rather yield;
> For this, my offers never were refused
> Of any town, or surely very seld.

While such assertions sharply contradict the poem's accounts of Salisbury's long siege of Montaiguillon (which Hall mistakenly describes as a town) and his battering of Le Mans, the poet has Salisbury adduce as proof Beaugency, whose assault, Salisbury claims, 'began' with a successful offer to show its townspeople favour if they submitted to Henry VI. To make this claim, the poet ignores the fact that Hall states that Salisbury 'tooke' Beaugency and suggests he offered clemency only after seizing it. The poet then exaggerates the reaction of the towns of Meung and Jargeau, claiming without ground in any of his sources that the towns' leaders were so taken with Salisbury's offer of friendly treatment to Beaugency's citizens that they brought him the keys to their cities before he was within two days of their gates.[19]

The author adds such unprecedented claims to stir thoughts not of the fifteenth-century military general Salisbury but of the sixteenth-century political and military leader Edward Seymour, duke of Somerset. The poet's assertion that his protagonist ruled England in place of the lord protector recalls to mid-Tudor readers Edward Seymour's own tenure in that office, and his identification of Salisbury as the 'good earl' stirs thoughts of Edward Seymour's own well-known title of 'the good duke', bestowed upon him by his popular supporters. More pointedly, the poet's description of Salisbury's 'virtuous life, free heart, and lowly mind', as well as his reputation for mild domestic governance, conjures up memories of the idealised public image of a benign, loving ruler that Edward Seymour had enjoyed in the days of his protectorate.[20]

---

[18] *A Mirror for Magistrates*, pp. 61–2. The chronicler Fabyan notes that 'dyuers writers' termed Salisbury 'the good erle'; the poet supplies his own reason for this epithet (Fabyan, *New Chronicles*, p. 598).

[19] *A Mirror for Magistrates*, pp. 62, 65–6; cf. Hall (1809), p. 144; College of Arms, MS M 9, f. 63r.

[20] See, for instance, John Foxe's description of Edward VI's late protector: 'there was alwayes in hym great humanitie, and such meekness and gentlenes, as is rare to be founde in so highe estate. He was prone and readye to geue eare vnto the complaints and supplications of the poor, and no lesse attentiue to the affayres of the co[m]mon wealthe. Which, if he had lyued together with king Edward, was like to do much good in reformyng many misorders within this realme' (*Actes and Monuments*, p. 1323).

Likewise, Salisbury's insistence that 'in assaults due mildness passeth far/ All rigour, force, and sturdy violence', and his claim that he always sought to offer recalcitrant French towns friendly use rather than initially threatening them, echoes the rhetoric of kindness and amity that Seymour publicly adopted in his attempts to bring Scotland under English hegemonic control. Seymour most famously employed such language in a proclamation widely disseminated in England and Scotland shortly before his 1547 Scottish invasion, in which he insisted that he and his English forces 'come into this realme not as an enemie … but as a frend', and in which he promised that the English would do 'the least hurte or domage that we can' to Scottish lands, since he sought only to help the Scots join the English in 'a frendly kynde of liuyng' as members of a single kingdom. It is this image of Seymour as the loving, reluctant, yet, when need be, ferociously powerful English military leader that the poet urges readers to recall through the Salisbury of his poem.[21]

By connecting Seymour to his poem's Salisbury, the poet seeks to offer his intended audience an exemplary guide for coming to terms with the sudden downfall of the late lord protector and the painful, unlooked-for collapse of his 'glorious' imperialist designs.[22] They are to interpret Seymour's failure to join Scotland to England in the last years of his life in the same way they interpret Salisbury's failure to take Orléans, not as a consequence of weakness or incompetence but of unmerited misfortune. No foreign opponent could ever match Salisbury in battle, the poem asserts; only a lucky shot against a tower window grate ended Salisbury's career of magnificent conquest. In endowing his unvanquished Salisbury with attributes of Edward Seymour, the poet urges readers to revive memories of Seymour's own remarkably successful military career and to entertain the notion that the fallen lord protector could have achieved equal success in the future, had he only been allowed to remain in power long enough to pursue his expansionist designs to ultimate victory.[23] Seymour's career in the furtherance of English imperialism, the poet subtly guides readers to believe, ended as Salisbury's did, not in military defeat but in glorious promise unfulfilled.

In a similar manner, the poet invites readers to understand Seymour's troubling fall from power in terms of Salisbury's sudden loss of life, as itself the result of malign misfortune. In confronting Salisbury's sudden downfall, the poet – almost alone among the contributors to the 1559 *Mirror* – seeks no failing in his protagonist himself to explain his loss. Rather, Salisbury's spirit execrates 'froward Fortune' for its sudden, hostile turn against him, blaming it rather than himself for his presence in the 'cursed' tower whose splintered window grate gave him his death wound. Thus,

---

[21] *A Mirror for Magistrates*, p. 62; Edward Seymour, duke of Somerset, *Edward, Duke of Somerset…: To all…of the Realme of Scotlande*, printed by Richard Grafton (London, 1547). For a more detailed analysis of the poet's evocation of Seymour in the figure of Salisbury, see Lucas, *'A Mirror for Magistrates' and the Politics of the English Reformation*, pp. 142–8.

[22] Several of the poems in *A Mirror for Magistrates* are shaped to offer exemplary models by which to come to terms with the shocking, dismaying fall of Protector Somerset, the failure of his expansionist aims, and his public vilification by his rivals in the wake first of his deposition and then of his execution. For these poems, see Lucas, *'A Mirror for Magistrates' and the Politics of the English Reformation*, pp. 67–157.

[23] Until the end of his rule, Seymour's rhetoric was that of complete confidence that Scotland would be his (whether by peaceful overtures or war) after a planned final invasion of the nation. See, for instance, *Troubles Connected with the Prayer Book*, pp. ix, 148–9; Pollard, *England under Protector Somerset*, p. 139.

the sole lesson Salisbury draws from his untimely death is that even the greatest of men can never know the outcome of their plans. Recalling how he had renewed his campaigns in France in 1428 and seemed poised to take Orléans, Salisbury exclaims,

> See Baldwin, see the uncertainty of glory,
> How sudden mischief dasheth all to dust!
> And warn all princes by my broken story
> The happiest fortune chiefly to mistrust.
> Was never man that alway had his lust.
> Then such be fools, in fancy more than mad,
> Which hope to have that never any had.

That Salisbury did not win Orléans and that Seymour did not win Scotland should be seen as the consequences of bad luck and not as failings either of English imperialism itself or of the abilities of the men who had championed it. Seymour, readers may believe, lived at a time in which his plans for a new invasion of Scotland were thwarted by a sudden, malign turn of domestic fortune: the unlooked-for popular rebellions of 1549 that diverted troops from England's foreign aspirations and set the conditions for Seymour's removal from principal authority. Both Seymour and Salisbury had experienced only success in the past and could have been expected to enjoy more such success in the future, if fortune had only remained in their favour. No matter what the ultimate outcome of the two men's dreams of conquest, the poem prompts readers to conclude, Salisbury and Seymour alike should ever be remembered as men who ended their lives on the cusp of new victory and who were lost while still 'in the Mids of [their] Glory'. Such thoughts could not hope to offer great consolation to the two men's admirers, but they could at least offer some.[24]

The narrative of the M 9 chronicle sparked both admiration and inspiration in the anonymous author of the *Mirror for Magistrates* poem 'How Thomas Montagu, the Earl of Salisbury, in the Mids of his Glory, was Chanceably Slain with a Piece of Ordnance'. The poet seized on the chronicle's detailed record of Thomas of Salisbury's many victories in the 1420s (as it was presented in Hall's *Union*) as proof positive of the long-standing prowess of English soldiery and the ease with which a determined English commander could vanquish foreign enemies and extend English royal authority. For readers demoralised by what many feared was the permanent and humiliating loss of English power in Mary I's reign, the poem this author created could revive feelings of pride in native might and martial skill, even if England's current governors chose to pull away from the stirring, if costly, course of aggressive expansionism that had so recently won for England famous victories in France and Scotland. It could also offer its readers a means to a comforting understanding of the failure of this proud period of imperialist conquest, one that blamed mere bad luck rather than the incompetency of revered military and political leaders for its collapse. Through his exciting, inspiring, and yet also consolatory verse narrative, the author of the 'Salisbury' poem ensured that the matter of the M 9 chronicle would continue to speak movingly to generations of early modern Englishmen and women even a century and more after it was composed.

---

[24]   *A Mirror for Magistrates*, pp. 58, 66–7.

The Edition of College of Arms MS M 9
folios 31r–66r

Editorial practices

In the text and the translation, square brackets are used to indicate authorial interventions and post-medieval annotations, and round brackets are used for editorial interventions.

In the chapters, quotations are given in English unless the original wording is relevant to the discussion.

FRENCH TEXT

Punctuation has been modernised, as also capitalisation of nations and their subjects, and of proper names, with apostrophes being used in relevant cases (as in, for example, d'O). The chronicle's spelling of first names has been retained: in some cases, therefore, we find 'Guillaume' and 'William' applied to both English and French. The spelling 'Willam' is used for some English and Scots.

All abbreviations have been extended. Contextual assumptions have been made on the extension of 'sire' and 'seigneur'. The word for knight is commonly given in the text in abbreviated form: extension has deployed the common French spelling of the period, 'chevalier'. Where the chronicle's use of 'u' rather than 'v' would lead to confusion, 'v' has been used, for instance in the name 'Olivier'.

The scribe has sometimes left sizeable gaps between the sections of text. The dimensions of these gaps have not been noted in the transcription. Otherwise, however, there has been an effort to replicate the layout of the chronicle text, in order to emphasise the distinctive list layout.

TRANSLATION

Spellings have been modernised to the most common current usage. Where there is a widely accepted equivalent, French titles are given in English (i.e. 'sire' as lord; 'comte' as count; 'duc' as duke). Other French titles and offices such as *vicomte*, *vidame* and *bailli* have been left in French. The appellation 'Sire' given immediately before the first name has been given as 'knight' after the person's name.

Identification of places follows the French administrative arrangements at the date of publication of this edition.

Unidentified people and places are indicated in italics.

Translation is an art rather than a science. We have endeavoured to produce a translation which is close to the original but which is comprehensible and readable in a modern setting. Where no equivalent modern term has been found, and where there would be a risk in imposing one, we have left the expression in the original language.

IDENTIFICATIONS

Many people are mentioned in the M 9 chronicle. Identification has been a considerable undertaking but has been deemed essential to the production of an edition of the chronicle, given its focus on the listing of individuals. That said, given the constraints of space and time, it has not been feasible to provide full biographies. The principal aim of the editors has been to identify the person named and, where possible, to add information relevant to the context in which they are listed. In this, the use of administrative records has been privileged over that of chronicles.

For the English, we are fortunate to have a considerable quantity of administrative records on which we can draw. Particularly valuable for the reign of Henry V are the Norman rolls (TNA, C 64) which were started at the landing of 1 August 1417 and continued to the king's death on 31 August 1422. They provide a firm record for the English of office holding and presences at various military engagements (as well as giving names of French garrison captains and landholders). We can also draw on English Exchequer records which concern the payment of armies. Such a source continues to be relevant for expeditionary armies sent to France in the reign of Henry VI. For garrisons and field actions in France under Henry VI, we can draw on the surviving records of the *chambre des comptes* although these have suffered loss and dispersion over later centuries and are now found in archives world-wide,[1] which both editors have used in their researches. The muster rolls from the English Exchequer and the *chambres des comptes* formed the basis of the database prepared by Anne Curry and Adrian Bell (medievalsoldier. org), which has also proved hugely helpful.

In identifying Englishmen we have been hugely assisted by another two major projects. The new *Oxford Dictionary of National Biography* (oxforddnb.com) includes biographies of some of those named in the chronicle. Such cases are indicated in the notes by an asterisk after the person's name in the first note concerning them: readers are urged to consult the full biography in that work. In the case of the English nobility the *ODNB* also corrects where relevant *The Complete Peerage*, although that remains an important source of reference.

The History of Parliament Trust has produced biographies of all MPs from 1376 to 1461, some of whom also served as soldiers in France during the period of the M 9 chronicle. The first set of volumes, published in 1993, cover the period from 1376 to 1421 and are available online (histparl.ac.uk). Where there is a relevant biography which readers can consult, this is indicated by 'HOCa'. The volumes for 1422 to 1460 were published in 2019 and are not yet online. Where there is a relevant biography this is indicated in the footnotes by 'HOCb'.

For the French, the task of identification has been considerably more challenging. In many circumstances, as is commonly the case with chronicles, the individual is named in the M 9 chronicle by lordship in his possession or his function as a royal official. Whilst it is often possible to identify lordships through modern maps, the spelling of place names and surnames is inconsistent in the chronicle and does not always match their modern form. It can therefore be difficult to identify the individual with certainty. A number of approaches have been deployed.

There is no equivalent in France to the *ODNB* but there are a number of older genealogical and biographical dictionaries of the nobility, such as those compiled by Père Anselme and La Chesnaye des Bois, along with Magny's *Nobiliaire Universel*. All three are available online. These works have proved useful, and not only for the most obvious higher status individuals, but the information these old studies include must sometimes be handled carefully. Anselme's work is particularly

---

[1]   Curry, 'English Armies in the Fifteenth Century', pp. 49–50.

important as he consulted material which has now disappeared, but he is not always wholly accurate. We have drawn on more recent prosopographical studies, such as the members of the 'Cour Amoureuse', researched by Carla Bozzolo and Hélène Loyau; the members of the household of the dukes of Orléans, researched by Elizabeth Gonzalez; participants at Agincourt, as researched by René Belleval and Anne Curry (medievalsoldier.org/agincourt600); the clients of Pierre de Brézé, as researched by Gareth Prosser; the defenders of the Mont-Saint-Michel, as researched by Siméon Luce and Oscar de Poli. Also valuable are biographies of the leading protagonists (such as Gaston du Fresne de Beaucourt's biography of Charles VII; André Bossuat's study of Perrinet Gressart; Eugène Cosneau's of Richemont; Pierre Champion's of Guillaume Flavy) and studies of major families such as the Lavals, Trémoilles, Anthenaises, Harcourts, etc. The fact that so many older books, articles and editions have been placed online on archive.org and Gallica.fr has proved extremely helpful in the pursuit of identifications, since it opens up access to studies of individuals, families and places carried out within the context of French local scholarship over the last one hundred and fifty years or so. Such older works often include a wealth of printed primary sources in their 'pièces justificatives'.

In France, we have also carried out archival research in the Archives Nationales and Bibliothèque Nationale de France as well as various Archives Départementales and Archives Municipales. Particularly valuable has proved AN, KK 324, the account of the duke of Bedford's receiver-general in Anjou and Maine from 1 October 1433 to 30 September 1434.[2] The conquest and defence of Maine is a particular topic of interest in the M 9 chronicle but is not a topic well covered in other chronicles or printed sources. Although it deals with a slightly later period, the names of individuals found in KK 324 (who include one of the chronicle authors, Christopher Hanson) are important to this study, as are also local studies by Robert Charles, Louis Froger and René Planchenault. That said, whilst there are surviving *chambre des comptes* records for garrisons and military activity in Normandy and the Ile-de-France, such materials concerning Maine have not generally survived. Therefore, it has proved more difficult to identify captains of garrisons in Maine, and also to confirm through administrative records the appointments of English captains in Maine which are given in the chronicle.

---

[2] Luce, 'La Maine sous la domination anglaise en 1433 et 1434', pp. 226–40.

Edition of the original text and
its annotations

[31r]¹ Incipit added in hand of William Worcester, with insertions also in his hand:
Iste liber de actibus armorum conquestus regni Francie ducatus Normannie,
ducatus Allenconie ducatus Andegavie et Cenomannie cum aliis pluribus comitatibus, compilatus fuit ad nobilem virum Johannem Fastolf baronem de Cylly-
eguillem [inserted above with caret mark: in anno Christi mˡ iiijᶜ lix .1459. anno
quo dictus Johannes Fastolf obiit] per Petrum Basset armigerum Anglice nacionis
exercentem arma in Francia sub [inserted above: victoriose principe] Rege Henrico vᵗᵒ et [inserted without caret mark, above 'et', continuing above line and
down right-hand margin: & Christoforum Hanson de patria almayn quondam
cum Thoma [deleted: duce] Beauford duce Excestrie et Luket Nantron natum de
Parys unum de clericis dicti Johannis Fastolf et per diligenciam Willelmi Worcestre secretarii predicti Johannis Fastolf] sub Johanne duce Bedfordie regente regni
Francie necnon aliorum principum locumtenencium sub rege Henrico vjᵗᵒ, in toto
per spacium .xxxv. annorum

[E²] n lan de grace mil quatre cens et quinze³ entre la feste Saint Michiel archangle
et la feste de Toussains, apres ce que le tresnoble et victorieux prince, Henry, roy
d'Angleterre et de France quint de ce nom, oult prinse et conquise la ville de
Harefleu par rendicion a lui faitte par le sire de Gaucourt, principal capitaine de
ladicte ville,⁴ et par le sire d'Estouteville, Sire Pierres de Gauceville, Sire Jaques de
Hermanville, Sire Jehan de Typtot, Sire Henry Chamboy, chevaliers, capitaines
particuliers en icelle ville soubz ledit sire de Gaucourt, et pluseurs autres, touz
lequelx furent menez prisonniers en Angleterre, icellui victorieux prince et roy
commist et ordonna gouverneur et capitaine dicelle ville son uncle, monseigneur
Thomas de Beauford duc d'Excestre et conte de Dorset,⁵ lequel duc d'Excestre
commist et establi son lieutenant et garde en icelle [31v] Sire Johan Fastolf chevalier a notable retenue [inserted above in hand of William Worcester: de .xvᶜ.] de
chevaliers [inserted above in hand of William Worcester: et .xxxv. auxi de] escuiers

---

¹   There are a number of post-medieval doodles on this page. At the very top of the page,
'domino domino d'; after the incipit, randomly before the start of the main chronicle text:
'duchm'; 'int' dme' comperam'; 'duchm'. Written down the page at left side below the
incipit. Summa total' Sum totally'.
²   An 'e' in the top left of the space for the initial. Three lines are allowed for this initial.
A series of squiggles to some degree representing an E have been placed in the location.
³   In right-hand margin in a later hand '1451' [sic], an error for 1415.
⁴   In right-hand margin in later hand 'harfleur conqu'.
⁵   In right-hand margin in later hand 'duc of exeter'.

et autres gens de guerre pour la garde seurete et defense de ladicte ville dont partie
diceulx les noms ensuivent. Cestassavoir
[added in hand of William Worcester: le baron de Carrow de le counte Devenshyre]
Sire Hue Loutrell chevalier [added in hand of William Worcester: de counte de
Somersett]
Johan Stanndysh escuier
Thomes (sic) Lord escuier et pluseurs autres
Et pour ce que durant le temps que ledit victorieux prince et roy avoit tenu siege
devant ladicte ville de Harefleu, pluseurs seigneurs cheyrent en grandes maladies,
icellui roy leur donna licence de retourner en Angleterre, cestassavoir a
Monseigneur Thomas duc de Clarence frere dudit roy
Monseigneur Johan Conte Mareschal et de Nothingham
Monseigneur[6] Johan conte d'Arrundell et de Waryn tresorier d'Angleterre

[32r]
[L[7]] es choses dessusdictes et autres notables statutz et ordonnances faictes et
establies, ledit victorieux prince roy, acompaignie des princes et seigneurs dont les
noms ensuivent, cestassavoir
Monseigneur Umfroy duc de Gloucestre frere dicellui roy
Monseigneur ['Johan' deleted; added in hand of William Worcester: Edouart] duc
de York
Johan conte de Huntyngton[8]
Johan conte de la Marche[9]
Thomas conte de Oxenford
Richart conte de Devenshire
William conte de Suffolk
Gilbert de Umfreville conte de Kyn'
Johan sire de Roos
Thomas sire de Wyllugby
Johan sire de Clyfford
Le sire de Fitzhugh
Le sire de Clynton[10]
Le sire de Ferieres Groby
Le sire de Ferieres de Shartley
Le sire de Cameys
Le sire de Bowser
Johan de Beauchamp Sire Despencer et de Bargevenny
et depuis conte de Worcestre
Le sire de Haryngton
Le baron de Karue du pays de Cornewaille
[added in the hand of William Worcester: Le baron de duddeley]
et pluseurs autres jusques au nombre de huit cens lances et huit mil cinq cens arch-
iers ou environ, party dudit lieu de Harefleu et chevaucha par terre jusques a la

---

6   In left margin in later hand '[..]ke'.
7   A letter 'l' at left side of the space left for the capital letter.
8   In left-hand margin against his name a paragraph mark.
9   In left margin in a later hand 'Edmond'.
10   In left-hand margin against his name a paragraph mark.

Blanque Take, pres Saint Wallery pour ylec passer oultre la riviere de Somme, mais il trouva que [32v] les adversaires jusques au nombre de cinquante mil hommes de guerre estoient de lautre coste de la dicte riviere pour lui defendre le passaige. Parquoy et aussi pour le dangier du flot de la mer, icellui victorieux prince party dudit lieu de la Blanque Take, et chevaucha a tout son host contremont la dicte riviere de Somme jusques au Pont Saint Maxence, pour ylec passer oultre icelle riviere, et ylecques trouva de rechief lesdiz adversaires en grant nombre qui gardoient ledit passaige. Et pour ce que icellui victorieux prince pensa ylec avoir bataille il fist chevaliers pluseurs dont partie diceulx les noms ensuivent. Cestassavoir
Jehan seigneur de Ferieres Growby
Raoul de Greystok
Pierre Tempest
Christofle Morysby
Thomas Pykkeryng
William Hodelston
Jehan Hosbalton
[added in a later hand: John Mortymer
Phillipe Halle   }
Guillaume Halle   } freres
Jaques de ormond]
[11]et pluseurs autres. Mais lesdiz adversaires ne luy donncrent ne livrerent aucune bataille audit lieu. Aincois icellui victorieux prince party dicellui lieu avecques tout son host et chevaucha sanz avoir aucune bataille jusques a une lieue pres la cite d'Amiens en une ville pres ung chastel nomme Boves ou il loga par deux jours. Et apres passa icelle riviere de Somme a deux lieues pres la ville de Peronne, et chevaucha par devant icelle ville vers la riviere de Sourdon jusques a ung chastel nomme Agincourt.[12] Auquel lieu il ot nouvelles certaines que les adversaires jusques [33r] au nombre de cent et cinquante mil hommes de guerre venoient pour luy delivrer bataille. Pourquoy icellui victorieux prince fist ses ordonnances et se appareilla pour recevoir ladicte bataille. Et en la vigile de la feste Saint Crespyn et Saint Crispinian oudit an mil iiii[c] et quinze iceulx adversaires delivrent bataille, de laquelle icelluy victorieux prince et roy ot lonneur et victoire. Et desdiz adversaires furent en icelle mors et prins les princes et seigneurs dont les noms ensuivent, premierement
Monseigneur [Johan deleted] Charles duc d'Orleans nepveu du roy Charles de France sixiesme de ce nom prisonnier[13]
Le conte Jehan d'Alencon nouvellement fait duc d'Alencon mort
Le duc de Bourbon prisonnier[14]
Le duc de Brabant mort
Le duc de Cleves mort
Le duc de Baviere mort
Le conte de Nevers et de Rethel mort
Le conte de Namur mort

---

[11]   Just before this paragraph in the left-hand margin in a later hand is 'Azingcort'.
[12]   In left-hand margin in a later hand (not the same hand as in the previous marginal note) 'Agingcourt'.
[13]   There is an indecipherable erasure following the word 'prisonnier'.
[14]   A small squiggle in a later hand to the right-hand side of his name.

Le conte de Haynau mort
Le conte de Foix mort
Le conte de L'Estrak mort
Le conte de Eu prisonnier
Le conte de Vendosme prisonnier
Artur de Bretaigne conte de Richemond prisonnier
Le conte de Tancarville mort

Le sire de Rambures	}
Le sire de Gamaches	}
Le sire de Torcy	}
Le sire de la Heuze	}
Le Sire d'Aurrichier	} mors
Le sire de Maugny	}
Le sire de Heugueuille	}
Le sire de Preaulx	}
Le sire de Fontaines	}
Le sire de Ferieres et de Chambroys	}
Le sire de Beaumesnil	}
Le sire de Hambye	}

[33v]

Le sire de Rouvrou	}
Le sire de Crecy	}
Le conte de Vertuz	}
Le sire de Creuly	}
Le sire de Tylly	}
Le sire de Chamboy	}
Le sire de Gacey	}mors
Le sire de Vypont et de Chaillouay	}
Le sire de Sillie le Guillaume	}
Le sire de Tucey	}
Le sire d'Asse le Riboule	}
Le sire de Nouens	}
Le sire de la Suze	}
Le sire de Sable	}
Le sire de la Bret	}
Le sire de Partenay	}

et pluseurs autres chevaliers jusques au nombre de deux mil quatre cens chevaliers, bailliez par declaracion par Mont Joye roy darmes de France. Et pour ce que Sire Guillaume de Tybouville chevalier, seigneur de la Riviere de Tybouville [34r] ralia lesdiz adversaires jusques au nombre de vingt mil hommes de guerre et plus soubz ung pennon blanc, pour donner et livrer nouvelle bataille, icellui victorieux prince roy fist crier par son host que tout homme occist son prisonnier. Et ce fut la cause parquoy tant de nobles furent occis. Et en icelle bataille de la partie dudit victorieux prince furent mors les seigneurs qui ensuivent. Cestassavoir

Monseigneur le duc de York	}
Le conte de Suffolk	} mors
Sire Richart Kykley	}
Davy Gam escuier galoys	} et environ dix archiers

Apres laquelle glorieuse victoire obtenue ainsi que dit est, icellui victorieux prince ordonna pour la sepulture des seigneurs et autres mors en icelle bataille tant de son party comme du party de sesdiz adversaires. Et puis chevaucha atout son host paisiblement jusques en sa ville de Calais, en laquelle il sejourna par aucuns jours pour soy rafreschir, et puis passa la mer en son royaume d'Angleterre a grant honneur et victoire.

[E[15]] n lan mil quatrecens dixsept le dit tresnoble et victorieux prince et roy Henry quint fist nouvelle armee pour passer oultre la mer en entencion de faire conqueste. En laquelle armee furent les seigneurs dont les noms ensuivent. Cestassavoir

Monseigneur Thomas duc de Clarence	}
Monseigneur Umffroy duc de Gloucestre	} freres dudit roy

Le conte de Huntyngton[16]
Le Conte Mareschal
Le conte de Warrewyk
Le jeune conte de Devenshire
Le conte de Salysbury
Le conte de Suffolk
Le conte de Somerset
[34v] Sire Jehan de Nevile
Le sire de Roos
Le sire de Wylugby
Le sire de Fitz Hugh
Le sire de Clynton[17]
Le sire de Bowtras
Le sire de Scrope
Le sire de Mautravers
Le sire de Bowser
Les deux seigneurs de Ferieres Growby
Sir Jehan Cornewaille
Le sire de Grey Codnore
Sire Gylbert de Umfreville
Sire Gylbert seigneur de Talbot
et pluseurs autres

Et ou mois daoust endit an mil iiij[c] xvij, icellui victorieux prince entra en mer et descendi ou dit pays de Normandie pres ung chastel nomme Touque[18] pour commencier sadicte conqueste. Et en ce temps oudit pays de Normandie pour la partie des adversaires estoient les capitaines dont les noms ensuivent. Cestassavoir
Oudit chastel de Touque Sire Guillaume de Pombray chevalier
A Caen le sire de Montenay et le sire de Fontaines
Marmyon son cousin germain
A Nully l'Evesque Robert de Pierrepont escuier
A Bayeux Sire Jehan Ffortescu
En la ville de Faloise le seigneur de Longny et Sire Baudouyn de Champaigne seigneur de Tucey

---

15   A letter 'e' at left side of the space left for the capital letter.
16   In left-hand margin against his name a paragraph mark.
17   In left-hand margin against his name a paragraph mark.
18   In left-hand margin in a later hand 'Touque'.

Ou chastel dudit lieu Sire Olivier de Maugny et Charles de Maugny son frere bailly de Caen

A Argenten Sire Jehan de Carrouges et Sire Guillaume Martel

[35r] A Saint Sauveur le Viconte Sire Guillaume de Hermanville et Sire Ambroys de la Gresille

A Sees Sire Loys de Clamorgan

A Tury Sire Hemery de Clinchamp

A Essay Sire Loys Tremorgan

A Alencon le Galoys d'Achey chevalier

A Danfront le baron de Blosset seigneur de Saint Pierre

A Vire Sire Jehan Carbonnel

Au Mont Saint Michiel Sire Jaques et Sire Nicole Paynel freres

A Conde sur Noireaue le sire d'Annebek

A Saint Lo le sire de Briqueville

A Creuly le sire d'Argouges

A Carenten Sire Guillaume Mortysmer seigneur de la Haye du Puys

A la Haye du Puys le dit Sire Guillaume seigneur du dit lieu

A Valoignes le baron de Byars

A Chierebourg Sire Jehan Picquet et Sire Guillaume de la Luyserne

A Avranches Sire Richart de Rocheford

A Pontorson Sire Hue Tesson

A Saint Jame de Beuron Sire Guillaume Pigas

A Hambuye le seigneur dudit lieu

A Honnefleu Sire Loys de Braquemont et Sire Jehan d'Onnebault

Au Bechelluyn Jehan d'Ellebeuf et Huguelin du Quesnay

A Harecourt Guillaume de Mellemont escuier

A Loviers le Sire du Grippon

A Evreux Guillaume de Craon escuier

A Dreux Raymonnet de Laguerre escuier

Au Pont de l'Arche le sire de Graville

Ou chastel et ville de Rouen Sire Guy le Bouteillier

Au pont de Rouen Henry de Chauffour escuier

A la Porte Cauchoise dudit lieu Jehan de Gyngy

A la Porte Beauvoisine le sire de Pesmes

A la Porte Saint Hyllaire le Bastart de Tyan

A la Porte Martaynville le Grant Jaques

A Bellencombre le roy d'Yvetot

A Caudebec le sire de Vilequier

[35v] A Tancarville Sire Ector de Dompierre

A Dieppe Sire Guillaume Martel

A Torchy le seigneur dudit lieu

A Charlemesnil le seigneur dudit lieu

A Arques le sire de la Heuze

A Lillebonne le seigneur de Caleville

A Aubmarle Sire Coquart de Cambron

A Longueville Guillaume Hartbouel

A Valemont Sire Pierre de Gauceville

A Gamaches Sire Loys de Tyennebronne

A Neufchastel Sire Morelet de Bethencourt

A Gournay Sire Davyot de Poix chevalier bourgoingnon
A Gisors Sire Rigault de Fontaines
A Bouconvillier Sire Jaques de Bouconvillier seigneur du dit lieu
A Pontoise le sire de Lisleadam et le sire de Motry
Au Pont de Meulent le seigneur d'Aunoy
A Mante Sire Jehan Dartye
A Vernon Sire Jehan Courcelles et le Bastart de la Bausme de Savoye
A la Roche Guyon Olivier de Dampont
A Monceaux Robert de Pierrecourt
A Eu le baron de la Heuze
A Boillancourt Sire Gilles de Gamaches
A Gaillart le sire de Baqueville et le sire de Mauny
A Yvry le seigneur du dit lieu
A Estrepaigny Guillaume d'Anesy escuier seigneur de Roucheroles
A Courtonne Jehan de Famysson escuier
A la Riviere de Tybouville Guillaume de Tybouville escuier
A Chambroys la dame du dit lieu
A Beaumesnil la dame du dit lieu
A Lisieux nul capitaine fors les bourgois de la cite
Au Ponteaudemer nul capitaine
A Faugarnon Robert de Maillot
A Crevecueur en Auge
A Chamboy la dame du dit lieu
A Chaillouay Jehan le Beauvoisien
A Conches Guillaume Tournebeuf
Au Pont l'evesque Jehan de Vypont
[36r] A Tylly Jehan de Chantepie
A Torigny Sire Thomas du Boys
A Exmes Sire Pierre le Beauvoisien
A Exmes Sire Jehan de Tournebeuf
A Mortaigne ou Perche Sire Jehan de Mongoubert
A Belesme le bastart d'Alencon
A Vernueil Sire Robert de Milant
A Longny Sire Robert d'O seigneur de Maillebois
A la Mote d'Yvercey Sire Johan Rafeton
A Tillieres Jehan de Bellegarde escuier seigneur de Bellegarde
A la Ferte Ernault le vidame de Chartres
A Chasteauneuf en Tymeroys le dit vidame
A Gacey Jehan seigneur de Clery
A Rugles Jaques de Nevyll
A Gaillon Sire Pierre du Couldray
Aux Goulletz Loys d'Abecourt
A Neaufle Sire Jehan de Saint Cler seigneur du dit lieu
A Baudemont le dit Sire Jehan de Saint Cler
A Dangu Pierre de Saint Cler
A la Ferte Fresnel le seigneur de Gripont
A Courville le sire de Vypont
A L'Esgle

La conte du Maine
A Fresnay le Viconte Sire Jehan de Combres
A Beaumont le Viconte Huet de Fontenay escuier
A Tonnoye Sire Jehan Canu
Au Mans le sire de Fontaines principal, le sire de Bellay et le Roncin particuliers capitaines
A Saint Aignen Sire Guillaume de Mauny chevalier seigneur du dit lieu
A la Guierche Robert d'Asse et les espaignolz
A Asse le Riboule Guillaume de Saint Denis
A Sillie le Guillaume Pierre le Forestier et Olivier le Forestier bretons
A Antony Gawayn de Montigny
A Tuce Sire Pierre Boterel
A Loue Guyon du Coing escuier
A Tennye Sire Jehan de Tournemyne
A Courmenant le dit sire Jehan de Tourmemyne
A Orte Jehan Vachereau
[36v] A Courceuers Michiel Taillebert
A Sainte Suzanne Sire Ambroys de Lore
A Sable Sire Guy de Laval
A Laval Sire Guy Turpin[19]
A Mayenne la Juhez Sire Jehan d'Avaugour
A la Ferte Bernard Jehan d'Avaugour escuier
A Clinchamp Jehan Pesaz
A Saint Kalez Jehan Tybergeau
A Peschere Patry le Voyer seigneur du dit lieu
A Boulouere Astergon
A Montfort l'Aillier Michiel de Ferieres
A Chasteaux l'Ermitaige nul capitaine
A Bonnestable Jehan Courtvalain
A Balon Huet de Channoy
A la Faigne le sire de Periers
A Luce Guillaume Papillon
A Chasteauduloir le sire de Mailly
A la Suze Foulquet de Mauley
A Lisle soubz Brulon Sire Jehan de Matefelon seigneur du dit lieu
A Malicorne le seigneur du dit lieu
A la Flesche Jehan le Beauvoisien
A Saint Ouen d'Estaiz Sire Guillaume d'Orenge
A Vilaine la Juhez Pierre d'Anthenaize
A Montaudain le Bastart de la Fueillie
A la Tour Edmond Sire Jehan de Vaulx
A Mellay Sire Guillaume Voyer
A Ramefort Jehan de Saint Aulbin
A la Chartre sur le Loir Dyago de Sales
A Saint Laurent des Mortiers Sire Jaques de Sepeaulx
A Montmirail Huet de Prez bailli de Chartres
A Nogent le Rotrou Sire Fleurent d'Ylliers

---

[19]   In left-hand margin against his name a paragraph mark.

A Montdoubleau Sire Jehan des Croix
A Saint Romy du Plain le seigneur de Vauhuet
A Torigny et Basogiers le sire des Escotays
A Montseur Sire Pierre d'Arqueney
A Chasteauneuf Jaques de Corches
A Lisle Ronde Guillaume de Breuedent
A Louppelande Loys de Valoges
[37r] A Ludon Pierre Morel
A Lude Henry de Moyen
A Gerlande Jehan Derien
A Bauge Sire Jehan Cueurdommes
A Durestal Sire Jehan d'Averton
A Belin le dit d'Averton seigneur du dit lieu
A Grez sur Mayne Emery d'Antenaise
A Chasteaugontier Sire Hardouyn de Mymber
A Craon Sevestre de Sepeaulx
A Vitrey le sire de MontJehan
A la Guierche en Bretaigne Sire Jehan de Champaigne
A Pouence Guillaume Boves
Au Crotoy Sire Jaques de Harecourt
A Saint Wallery Sire Guillaume de Semembron
A Saint Baussay ledit Sire Guillaume seigneur du dit lieu
A Saint Esperit de Rue Loys de Ellecourt

[37v] [T²⁰] antost apres laquelle descente faicte, ledit victorieux prince roy commenca de faire sa conqueste et print ledit chastel de Touque qui lui fut rendu, et en icellui mist et ordonna capitaine et garde Sire Jehan de Kykley chevalier. Et dilec ala mectre le siege devant la ville de Caen, et apres aucune espace de temps il fist assaillir au icelle et dudit assault fut prinse, et apres ladicte prinse il conquist et lui furent rendues pluseurs autres villes et chasteaux esquelles il ordonna et commist capitaines et gardes. Cestassavoir
A Caen Sire Gillebert de Umffreville conte de Kyn' et Sire Gillebert Tallebot[21]
Au dit lieu bailly Sire Jehan Popham[22]
A Thorigny ledit Popham seigneur du dit lieu par don dudit roy
A Creuly Sire Hertenk Vanclouz chevalier du Jartier[23]
A Bayeux le seigneur de Mautravas et d'Arundell[24]

---

[20] A letter 't' at left side of the space left for the capital letter.
[21] In the left-hand margin against this entry a drawing in a later hand of a dog with collar, presumably a Talbot, a hunting hound. That it was a badge of the Talbots can be seen in the image of John Talbot, first earl of Shrewsbury, presenting the Shrewsbury book to Queen Margaret in 1445 (BL, Royal MS 15 E VI f. 2v).
[22] In the left-hand margin against his name a drawing in a later hand of the head of a deer with antlers, as found on the Popham coat of arms and badge (Siddons, *Heraldic Badges*, ii part 2, p. 235).
[23] To the right of his name a garter mark. Van Clux became KG in 1421.
[24] In the left-hand margin against his name a drawing in a later hand of an oak leaf and acorn, emblems associated with the Fitzalan earls of Arundel (Siddons, *Heraldic Badges*, ii part 2, pp. 117–18).

A Argenten le sire de Grey Codnore
A Chamboy le sire de Fitzhugh seigneur du dit lieu[25]
A Vernueil ou Perche Sire Jehan Neville
A Alencon monseigneur le duc de Gloucestre et Sire Raoul
Lintall son lieutenant[26]
A Essay Sire Willam Hodelston bailli d'Alencon
A Faloise le sire de Fitzhugh[27]
A Tury Sire Loys Robessart
A Conde sur Noireau Sire Jehan Popham[28]

[E[29]] n temps de karesme en icellui an mil iiij^c xvii ledit victorieux prince et roy, qui seiournoit audit lieu de Caen, envoya monseigneur le duc de Clarence son frere ou pays d'Auge et es parties denviron pour faire conqueste, lequel gaigna et conquist pluseurs villes, chasteaulx et forteresses, esquelles ou nom dudit victorieux prince il mist capitaines et gardes. Cestassavoir
En la ville et cite de Lisieux Sire Jehan Kykley
A Faugarnon Jehan de Saint Albones
A Courtonne Jehan Aubin
A Crevecueur Sire Thomas Kirkeby seigneur dudit lieu
[38r] A Bernay William Howton[30]
A Auvilliers Robert ['Ormesby' cancelled] Horneby
A Chambroys Jaques de Nevill
A Rugles Sire Johan Artur
A Bechelluyn le Conte Mareschall
A Fresnay le Viconte Sire Robert Brent
A Harecourt Richard Wydeville escuier
En ce mesmes temps de Karesme ledit victorieux prince et roy envoya monseigneur de Gloucestre son frere ou pays de Costentin pour faire conqueste, et ylecques gaigna et conquist pluseurs villes chasteaulx et forteresses esquelles il mist et ordonna capitaines pour la garde dicelles. Cestassavoir
A Carenten le sire de Bowtras
A Pont d'Ove Davy Howell escuier
A Saint Lo Sire Reynold West[31]
A la Haye du Puys Sire Jehan Assheton bailli de costentin[32]

---

[25]   In the left-hand margin against his name a drawing in a later hand of a cross-hatched shield, as in the Fitzhugh coat of arms.
[26]   In left-hand margin against his name a paragraph mark.
[27]   In left-hand margin against his name a paragraph mark.
[28]   In the left-hand margin against his name a drawing in a later hand of a deer with horns, as in the Popham coat of arms.
[29]   Small letter 'e' at top left-hand corner of the space left for the initial.
[30]   In left-hand margin against his name a paragraph mark.
[31]   To the right of his name a small drawing in a later hand of a coiffed head. This does not appear among the emblems of the Wests, lords de la Warr (Siddons, *Heraldic Badges*, ii part 2, pp. 311–12).
[32]   To the right of his name a drawing in a later hand of a five-point star, as found in the Ashton coat of arms, although it does not feature as badge for the Assheton family of Lancashire (Siddons, *Heraldic Badges*, ii part 2, p. 16).

A Valoingnes Thomas Bourg[33]

A Chierebourg le sire de Grey Codnore et apres son decez Sire Watier Hungerfford[34]

A Coustances le sire de Bargeveny[35]

A Saint Sauveur le Viconte Sire Jehan Robersart

A Avranches [Thomas Bourg cancelled; added by a later hand: Sire Phillype Halle baylly off Alanson][36]

A Pontorson Sire Robert Gargrave

A Vire le sire de Mautravas et d'Arundell

A Saint James de Beuron ledit seigneur de Mautravas

A Hambuye le conte de Suffolk seigneur dudit lieu

A Briqueville ledit conte de Suffolk seigneur dudit lieu

[38v] En icellui mesme temps icellui victorieux prince envoya monseigneur le conte de Warewyk pour faire conqueste, lequel mist le siege devant les ville et chastel de Dampfront en Passais, lesquelx apres aucun temps lui furent renduz et delivrez, et y mist capitaine Sire Hue Staffort seigneur de Bowser, et si conquist pluseurs autres places et forteresces ou il mist divers capitaines.

[A[37]] pres ce que icellui roy [deleted: d] et victorieux prince oult tenu son Karesme et fait ses Pasques et passe hyver au dit lieu de Caen, en leste suivant en lan de grace mil cccc et xviij et que par son mandement furent venuz devers lui dudit royaume d'Angleterre monseigneur le conte de la Marche et le sire de Clyffort avecques notable armee, icellui victorieux prince mist la siege devant la ville de Loviers ou il fut par lespace de six sepmaines ou environ, et lui fut rendue et delivree, et dicelle fist capitaine monseigneur le duc de Clarence son frere, lequel fist son lieutenant Sir Jehan Godart chevalier. Et en ce temps icellui victorieux prince envoya monseigneur le duc d'Excestre pour faire conqueste lequel mist le siege devant la cite et ville de Evreux, laquelle apres aucun temps lui fut rendue et delivree, et y mist capitaine Sire Gylbert de Halsalle chevalier, qui fut fait bailli dudit lieu. Et icellui victorieux prince ala mectre le siege devant la ville ['et ch' cancelled] pont et chastel du Pont de l'Arche lesquelz apres aucun temps lui furent renduz et delivrez et diceulx

[39r] fist capitaine monseigneur le duc de Clarence son frere.

[E[38]] n icellui an mil iiij[c] xviij ledit victorieux prince environ le commencement du moys daoust mist le siege devant la cite ville chastel et pont de Rouen, ou il fut par lespace et temps de sept moys ou environ que ilz lui furent renduz et delivrez par composicion. Et diceulx fist capitaine monseigneur le duc d'Excestre, et son lieutenant monseigneur de Wyllugby et Sire Jehan Kykley fut fait bailli dudit lieu. Et tantost apres que ladicte ville de Rouen fut rendue come dit est se rendirent

---

[33] To the right of his name a drawing in a later hand of a fleur de lys as found in the coat of arms of the Burgh family of Lincolnshire (Siddons, *Heraldic Badges*, ii part 2, p. 56).

[34] To the right of his name a drawing in a later hand of a sickle, used as a badge by the Hungerford family (Siddons, *Heraldic Badges*, ii part 2, p. 164).

[35] To the right of his name a drawing in a later hand of interlaced staples, to represent the coat of arms of the Neville lords of Abergavenny (Siddons, *Heraldic Badges*, ii part 2, p. 205).

[36] Possibly the same hand as in the addition on folio 39v.

[37] A letter 'a' at left side of the space left for the capital letter.

[38] A letter 'e' at left side of the space left for the capital letter.

et conquist icellui roy pluseurs autres villes chasteaulx et forteresses, esquelles il ordonna et commist capitaines, cestassavoir

A Caudebec Sire Loys de Robessart[39]

A Tancarville Sire Jehan Grey conte dudit lieu[40] [added by a later hand: par don]

A Harefleu ledit Sire Jehan Grey

A Moustriervillier Clement Overton escuier[41]

A Belencombre Sire Thomas Rameston seigneur dudit lieu

A Dieppe monseigneur Guillaume Bowser conte de Eu par don[42]

A Eu ledit monseigneur Guillaume conte dudit lieu

A Longueville le Captal de Buch conte dudit lieu[43]

A Arques Sire James Ffynnes bailli de Caux[44]

A Aubmarle monseigneur de Warrewyk qui fist son lieutenant audit lieu Sire Willam Montfort[45]

A Neufchastel Sire Phelipe Leesche[46]

A Monceaux ledit Sire Phelipe[47]

A Gournay Sire Gilbert d'Umfreville conte de Kyn'[48]

A Baqueville le sire de Roos seigneur dudit lieu par don

A Gaillart ledit sire de Roos[49]

A Estrepaigny Richart Abraham escuier[50]

A Dangu Richart Wydeville escuier[51]

A Saint Cler sur Oecte Guillaume Basset escuier seigneur dudit lieu

A Neaufle le conte de Worcestre[52]

A Gisors ledit conte de Worcestre

A Bouconvilliers Jehan Abourgh escuier bailli de Gisors[53]

A Mante le conte de la Marche[54]

---

[39] In left-hand margin against his name a garter mark. Robessart became KG in May 1421.

[40] In left-hand margin against his name a garter mark. Grey became KG in October 1419.

[41] In left-hand margin against his name a paragraph mark. In right-hand margin in a later hand 'not for the lord guerton'.

[42] In left-hand margin against his name a garter mark. There is no evidence Bourchier was ever KG.

[43] In left-hand margin against his name a garter mark. The captal became KG in c. 1439.

[44] In left-hand margin against his name a paragraph mark.

[45] In left-hand margin against his name a garter mark. Warwick became KG in July 1403.

[46] In left-hand margin against his name a paragraph mark.

[47] In left-hand margin against his name a paragraph mark.

[48] In left-hand margin against his name a garter mark. There is no evidence Umfraville was ever KG.

[49] In left-hand margin against his name a paragraph mark.

[50] In left-hand margin against his name a paragraph mark.

[51] In left-hand margin against his name a garter mark. There is no evidence Woodville was ever KG.

[52] In left-hand margin against his name a garter mark. There is no evidence the earl of Worcester was ever KG.

[53] In left-hand margin against his name a paragraph mark.

[54] In left-hand margin against his name a garter mark. There is no evidence the earl of March was ever KG.

A Vernon Sire Guillaume Porter chevalier[55]

[39v] A la Roche Guyon Sire Guy le Boutillier seigneur dudit lieu

A Meulent Sire Thomas Rameston et depuis Sire John Fastolf

A Yvry la Chaucee[56] monseigneur de Gloucestre.[57] Et apres Artur de Bretaigne conte et seigneur dudit lieu par don

A Danville Sire Christofle Corwen

A Honnefleu monseigneur le conte de Salisbury. Et apres monseigneur de Clarence[58] seigneur par don, lequel y commist son lieutenant Robert Inkebarow escuier

A Conches [added in later hand: Sire Richard Merbury]

A Breteuil [added in later hand: Sire Ferry Mortymer bayly off Honeflew][59]

[E[60]] n lannee ensuivant mil iiii^c xix au commencement fut commencie par ambaxadeurs a parler de traictie de paix final entre les deux royaumes de France et d'Angleterre, et durant ledit temps par emblee deschiele fut prinse et conquise la ville de Pontoise. En laquelle monseigneur le duc de Clarence fut commis capitaine. Et dicelle fist son lieutenant Sire Raoul seigneur de Cromwelle.

[40r][61] [E[62]] n lannee commencant lan de grace mil iiii^c et vingt[63] le traictie de la paix final entre les deux roys et royaumes de France et d'Angleterre dont parle a este cy devant fut accorde conclut et conferme par le moyen de ce que ledit victorieux prince et roy espousa en la ville de Troyes en Champaigne Madame Katerine fille dudit roy de France Charles de ce nom sixiesme, et fut fait heritier et regent de France par adopcion. Et tantost apres ledit traictie et mariaige faiz[64] et acompliz, ouquel furent le roy de France dessus nomme la royne Ysabel sa femme, le duc de Bourgoingne et pluseurs autres seigneurs, ledit victorieux prince et roy a tout son host mist le siege devant la ville et cite de Sens en Bourgoingne, ou il fut par lespace de quinze jours ou environ, et mena avecques lui ledit roy Charles. Ausquelx deux roys icelle ville et cite fut rendue et delivree et y fut mis capitaine et garde le sire de Jonvalle. Et dilecques iceulx deux roys partirent, et ala ledit victorieux prince mectre le siege devant la ville et chastel de Montereau ou Foulq d'Yonne, ouquel lieu le duc Jehan de Bourgoingne avoit este occis. Et apres quil ot este et tenu siege par lespace de six sepmaines ou environ, iceulx ville et chastel lui furent renduz et delivrez. Et ylecques fut trouve le corps dudit duc Jehan moins que honnourablement mis en sepulture. Pourquoy le duc Phelipe de Bourgoingne son filz le fist tout de nouvel en sepulturer honnourablement. Et apres ces choses faictes et acomplies, ledit victorieux prince fist capitaine et garde diceulx ville et

---

[55] In left-hand margin against his name a bell, as on the coat of arms of the Porter family.

[56] A word has been written in a later hand above 'charite' but is not decipherable.

[57] In left-hand margin against his name a garter mark. Gloucester became KG in September 1399.

[58] In left-hand margin against his name a garter mark. Clarence became KG in September 1399.

[59] Possibly the same hand as in the additions on folio 38r.

[60] A letter 'e' at left side of the space left for the capital letter.

[61] The page number is actually given as x rather than xl.

[62] A letter 'e' at left side of the space left for the capital letter.

[63] In right-hand margin in a later hand '1520' [sic].

[64] In right-hand margin in a later hand 'Mariage du roy'.

chastel monseigneur le conte de Warrewyk. Et party icellui prince et roy et mist le siege avant la ville et chastel de a (sic) Meleum, ou il sist par lespace de sept moys ou environ. Et oudit siege avecques ledit victorieux prince estoient ledit roy Charles de France son beau pere,[65] et le roy d'Escoce et pluseurs autres princes et seigneurs, cestassavoir

Monseigneur le duc de Clarence[66]　}

Monseigneur le duc de Bedford[67]　} touz freres dudit victorieux prince et roy

Monseigneur le duc de Gloucestre[68]　}

Monseigneur le duc de Bourgoingne

Monseigneur le duc de Bar

[40v] Le prince d'Orenge

Le conte de la Marche

Le conte de Huntynghton[69]

Le conte de Stafford

Le conte de Somerset

Le Conte Mareschal

Le conte de Warrewyk

Le conte de Worcestre

Le conte de Suffolk

Artur de Bretaigne conte d'Yvry

Sire Charles de Navarre

Le conte de Perche

Le conte de Mortayng

Le conte d'Ormont

Le conte d'Essemont

Le conte de Eu

Le conte de Tancarville

Le conte de Longueville captal de Buch

Le conte de Saint Pol

Le conte de Brayne

Le conte de Ligny

Le conte de Vaudemont

Le conte de Joingny

Le sire de Roos

Le sire de Mautravers

Le sire de Grey Codnore

Le sire de Bowser

Le sire de Audeley

Le sire de Wyllugby

---

[65]　In right-hand margin in a later hand 'Le roy de France arme avecque le roy d'Angleterre'.

[66]　In left-hand margin against his name a garter mark. Clarence became KG in September 1399.

[67]　In left-hand margin against his name a garter mark. Bedford became KG in September 1399.

[68]　In left-hand margin against his name a garter mark. Gloucester became KG in September 1399.

[69]　In left-hand margin against his name a paragraph mark.

Le sire de Clynton[70]
Le sire de d'Aucourt
Le sire de Clyffort
Le sire de Ferieres de Groby
Le sire de Ferieres Chartley
Le sire de Fitzwater
Le sire de Talbot
Le sire de Fournywall
Le sire de Fitz hugh
[41r] Sire Jehan de Cornewaile sire de Fennop
Le sire de Scrope de Bocton
Le sire de Scrop
Le sire de Haryngton
Sire William Phelip sire de Bardolf
Le sire de Scales
Le sire de Karu
Le sire de Duras
Le sire de la Lande
Le sire de Montferrant
Le sire de Louvel
Le sire de Boutras et de Bourg
Le sire de Chasteluz   }
Le sire de Lille Adam   } mareschaulx de France
Le sire de Vergier
Le sire de Chastillon
Le sire de Crouy
Le sire de Saint George[71]
Le sire de Pesmes
Le sire d'Anguyan
Le sire de la Tremoille
Le sire de Jonvale
Sire Hue de Launoy
Sire Jehan de Courcelles garde du corps dudit roy Charles
Le sire de Varembon
Le sire de Jalons
Sire Guy de Bar
Sire Jehan Ffastolf
Sire Phelip Leessh
Sire[72] Rodevall
Sire Jehan Heron
Sire Morice Brown
Sire Guillaume seigneur de Bonneville
Sire Pierre Tempest
Sire Robert Tempest

---

[70] In left-hand margin against his name a paragraph mark.
[71] In the left-hand margin in a later hand a pointing finger against his name.
[72] Inserted above in a later hand 'John'.

[41v] et pluseurs autres. Et apres ce que lesdiz roys et seigneurs ourent ylecques tenu siege par le temps de sept moys ou environ, la dicte ville et chastel de Meleum (sic) furent renduz et delivrez ausdiz roys, car lesdiz adversaires qui dedens estoient plus aucuns vivres pour la sustentacion de leurs vies.[73] Et fut le dit Barbazon capitaine principal comme dit est prisonnier. Et apres icellui victorieux prince commist et establi capitaine et garde diceulx ville et chastel monseigneur le conte de Huntyngton.[74] Et tous iceulx trois roys et autres princes et seigneurs dessusdiz alerent en la cite de Paris. Et ylecques fut ledit noble et victorieux prince proclame heritier et regent le royaume de France. Et Charles de Valoys filz dudiz roy Charles et soy nommant Daulphin de Viennoys fut proclame inhabile a succeder a la couronne de France et prive dicelle succession.[75] Et ces choses et autres ordonnances faictes et establies pour la gouvernement dudit royaume de France icellui [struck through: Ro] victorieux prince print licence dicellui roy Charles son beau pere et de la royne pour aler en Angleterre et mener avecques lui la royne sa femme pour la faire couronner. Et ordonna monseigneur le duc d'Excestre capitaine de Paris, et monseigneur le Conte Mareschal capitaine de Pontoise. Et pour la garde de France et Normandie ordonna et commist monseigneur le duc de Clarence son frere, son lieutenant general, et monseigneur le conte de Salisbury son lieutenant particulier en Normandie dela la riviere de Seine. Et sen ala en Angleterre et mena avecques luy ladicte royne Katherine sa femme,[76] laquelle il fist couronner a Westm' pres Londres en royne d'Angleterre, et luy fist pourveoir pour son estat et assigner son douaire.

[42r] [E[77]] n lanne (sic) dessusdite mil iiij[c] et vingt ou temps de karesme,[78] ouquel temps ledit victorieux prince estoit oudit royaume d'Angleterre, monditseigneur de Clarence son frere et lieutenant general de France et Normandie, pour ce que les treves et abstinence de guerre qui prinses avoient este entre ledit victorieux prince dunepart, et le duc d'Anjou dautrepart pour les pays d'Anjou et de Maine estoient rompues, assembla toutes les garnisons de Normandie en la ville de Bernay. Et dilecques parti et entra oudit pays du Maine et passa oultre la riviere de Yengne a Pont de Genne et dilec passa tout oultre le pays jusques a Lucy, ou il passa oultre la riviere du Loir et entra en pays d'Anjou, et chevaucha jusques devant la cite d'Angiers ou il fist pluseurs chevaliers, cestassavoir
Sire Guillaume Roos[79]
Sire Henry Godart
Sire Rawland Ryde

---

73 This is an accurate reading but seems to lack grammatical sense. 'Estoient' is presumably an error for 'navoient'.
74 In left-hand margin against his name a garter mark and a paragraph mark. Huntingdon became KG in October 1415.
75 This section is underlined in a later hand and to the left in the margin there is a note also in a later hand 'Henry the vth proclamed of France heir and regent' as well as a finger emerging from a cloud.
76 In the left-hand margin in a later hand 'royne corone'.
77 A letter 'e' at left side of the space left for the capital letter.
78 In right-hand margin in a later hand '1420'.
79 In left-hand margin against his name a paragraph mark.

et pluseurs autres.[80] Et ce fait, il sen retourna prenant prisonniers et proyes jusques
a Beauford[81] en Valee auquel lieu il se logea et y seiourna jusques a la vigille de
Pasques commencans lan mil cccc xxi. Pendant lequel temps il ouyt nouvelles que
les adversaires, cestassavoir le duc d'Alencon soy nommant lieutenant general du
roy

Le conte de la Marche francois
Le comte de Commynges
Le conte de L'Estrak
Le conte d'Aubmarle
Le conte de Peyteure
Le viconte de Rohan
Le viconte de Thouars
Le viconte de Chasteauleraut
Le viconte d'Amboise
Le sire de L'Esgle
Le bastart d'Alencon
Le bastart de la Marche
Le bastart de Vendosme
[42v] Le sire de Champaigne
Sire Baudouyn de Champaigne sire de Tusse
Sire Antoyne de Champaigne
Le sire de Fontaines
Le sire de Bellay
Le sire d'Averton et de Belin
Caignart capitaine
Le sire de Rambures
Sire Tanneguy du Chastel
Sire Jehan Tournemyne
Le sire d'Asse le Riboule
Le sire de Bueil
Le sire de Gaules
Le sire de Graville
Le sire de labret   }
Le sire de la Fayecte   } mareschaulx de France
Le baron de Coulonces
Le sire d'Auzebosc
Le sire de Vypont
Alain Gyron capitaine
Guillaume Remon dit Marjolayne capitaine
Le Roncin capitaine
Oudin Chynart capitaine
Sire Fleurent d'Ylliers
Sire Jehan d'Avaugour
Sire Jehan de Vaulx
Jehan d'Avaugour capitaine de la Ferte Bernard

---

[80]   In right-hand margin in a later hand '1421'.
[81]   This word is underlined in a later hand and a note added in the right-hand margin 'the
na.. beauford'.

Sire Jehan des Croix
Roberton des Croix
Girart de Lawe capitaine
Sire Jehan de Montgoubert
Le sire de Goussall espaignol
Dyago de Sales espaignol
Andre Lombart traitre
Le sire du Grippon
Poton sire de Sentrailles
Sire Jehan de Raveton
Sire Jehan de Beauveau
[43r] Le sire de Precigny
Sire Pierre Chapperon
Sire Pierre de Beauvau
Sire Guy de Fromentieres
Sire Jehan de Champaigny seigneur de la Montagne
Le sire de Montboursier
Le sire de Chastelgiron
Sire Jehan de Mathefelon
Sire Guy Turpin
Sire Guillaume de Maugny
Sire Guillaume de la Mote
    Et des Escossoys
Le conte de Boukham
Le conte de Wyghton
Sire Willam Steward
Sire Willam Douglas
Sire Jehan Tourneboule
Sire Robert Lille
Sire Willam Conyngham
Sire Alissandre Meldryn
Sire Alyssaundre de Homme
Sire Jehan Balglavy
Sire Willam Lille
Sire Jehan Halyberton
Sire Jehan Crawfforth
Sire Willum Candey
Sire Jehan Grey
Le sire de Coughersawte

et pluseurs autres tant Francoys comme Escossoys estoient assemblez[82] a grant puissance en une ville pres ung chastel nomme Baugey pour venir rencontrer monditseigneur de Clarence. Pourquoy icellui seigneur parla audit Andre Lombart qui estoit traitre double[83] et enquist quele puissance lesdiz adversaires avoient et quel nombre ilz estoient, lequel lui dist que lesdiz adversaires nestoient que en petit nombre et navoient pas puissance de resister contre la moictie du povoir

---

[82]   In right-hand margin in a later hand 'Battaile de Baugy'.
[83]   In left-hand margin in a later hand a stem with three dots drawing attention to this matter of Lombart's treason.

de monditseigneur de Clarence, et quil se avancast et il auroit une tresbelle et
honnourable victoire. Lequel monseigneur de Clarence, pensant [43v] que icellui
Andre lui eust dit la verite, ordonna pour gouverner les archiers de sa compaignie,
cestassavoir Sire [blank] Sire [blank] chevaliers freres du pays de Portingal capitaines de Fresnay le Viconte, et avecques eulx le bastart de Clarence, et leur commanda que ilz le actendeissent audit lieu de Beauffort jusques a son retour, et quil
vouloit que luy et les autres nobles [deleted: eu lonneur] eussent lonneur de celle
destrousse. Mais il advint tout autrement dont tresgrant fut la douleur et perte. Car
aussi tost comme icellui monseigneur de Clarence et les nobles de sa compaignie
furent passez oultre aucuns passaiges et destroiz rencontrerent lesdiz adversaires
tous prestz en bataille par ladmonicion dudit Lombart traitre[84] qui avoit vendu
icellui seigneur, et si avoient fait grans embuschemens de leurs gens pour defendre
que icellui seigneur et ceulx de sa compaignie ne peussent eschaper sans estre
mors ou prisonniers, lesquelz adversaires incontinent luy coururent sus de toutes
pars, et luy et ses nobles se defendirent moult vaillamment tant comme ilz peurent,
mais en la fin ilz ne porent endurer le faiz desdiz adversaires, et fut monditseigneur
de Clarence[85] piteusement occis, et pluseurs autres seigneurs [deleted: fur] furent
prisonniers et occis dont en partie les noms ensuivent, cestassavoir

Le conte de Somerset	}
Le conte de Huntyngton[86]	}
Le conte du Perche	}
Le sire de Fitzwatier	}
Sire Jehan Grey conte de Tancarville	}
Sire Jehan Barker	} prisonniers
Sire Raoul de Neville	}
Sire Henry Ingloux	}
Sire Willam Bowys	}
Sire Willam Longton	}
Thomas Abourg escuier	}
Sire Willam ['Heron' cancelled] Wolf	}
Sire Edmund Heron	}
Sire Richart Benet[87]	}
Sire Willam Crafford	}
Sire Willam Roos[88]	}
[44r]	
Sire William Roos[89] (sic)	}
Richard Waller escuier	}
Sire Guillotin de Lansac	} prisonniers
Sire Richard Stother[90]	}

---

[84]   In right-hand margin in a later hand a small squiggle drawing attention to this matter
of Lombart's treason.
[85]   In left-hand margin against his name a garter mark and to the left of it 'obiit'. Clarence
became KG in September 1399.
[86]   In left-hand margin against his name a pointing finger.
[87]   In left-hand margin against his name a paragraph mark.
[88]   In left-hand margin against his name a paragraph mark.
[89]   In left-hand margin against his name a paragraph mark.
[90]   We have inserted a line here to separate prisoners from dead.

Sire Gilbert de Umfreville[91]   }
Sire Robert Ver frere au conte d'Oxenforde }
Sire William Roos[92]   } mors
Sire Henry Godart   }
Sire Robert Brend   }
Sire Jehan Knyvet   }
Sire Robert Boutevillain   }
Sire James a Ryde   }
Sire Jehan Pondessay   }
Sire Thomas de Marny   }

et pluseurs autres. Et incontinent que lesdiz deux chevaliers de Portyngall et le
dit bastart de Clarence oyrent nouvelles comme monditseigneur de Clarence et
sa compaignie estoient faulsement trahiz ilz partirent hastivement avecques touz
les archiers esperans venir assez a temps pour secourir icellui seigneur et donner bataille ausdiz adversaires. Mais iceulx adversaires qui oyrent nouvelles de la
venue desdiz archiers noserent actendrent la bataille et hastivement se retrayrent
et sen alerent avecques leurs prisonniers, et noient pas loisir demporter le corps
de monditseigneur de Clarence aincois leur convint le laissier derriere eulx.[93] Et
quant lesdiz chevaliers et bastart virent que lesdiz adversaires sen estoient ainsi alez
et retraiz, ilz prindrent a grans pleurs souspirs et douleurs les corps de monditseigneur de Clarence et daucuns des autres seigneurs qui ylecques avoient este occis,
et lez emporterent avecques eulx et le demourant firent ensepulturer le mieulx que
ilz peurent. Et puis sen retournerent par la conte du Mayne et passerent pardevant
la cite du Mans occians le peuple et gastans le pays par ou ilz passoient, et vindrent
jusques en la ville d'Alencon, auquel lieu ilz se departirent et alerent chacun en la
garnison dont il estoit party.

[44v] [E[94]] n lannee mil cccc xxi ou moys de may ledit tresnoble et victorieux
prince a notable armee passa la mer et descendi a Calais et vint en Normandie,
et mist le siege devant les ville et chastel de Dreux, auquel siege il fist et commist
chief capitaine et gouverneur le roy d'Escosse. Et apres que ledit siege oult dure
lespace de six sepmaines ou environ iceulx ville et chastel furent renduz et delivrez
audit victorieux prince, desquelx il fist et commist capitaine et garde monseigneur
le conte de Worcestre.
[T[95]] antost apres le prinse desquelx ville et chastel de Dreux ledit tresnoble et
victorieux prince qui avoit ouy nouvelles que les adversaires estoient assemblez a
grant povoir vers les parties d'Orleans, chevaucha et ala a tout son host vers ladicte
cite d'Orleans, et jusques devant icelle, mais iceulx adversaires qui noserent actendre sen estoient desia departiz et passez oultre le riviere de Loire. Et pour ce ledit
victorieux prince sen retourna sans autre chose faire et passa pardevant Baugency,
et dillecques ala tout droit mectre le siege devant les cite ville et marchie de Meaulx

---

91 In left-hand margin against his name a small garter symbol. There is no evidence
Gilbert Umfraville was ever KG but his uncle Sir Robert was elected in 1408.
92 In left-hand margin against his name a paragraph mark.
93 In left-hand margin in a later hand 'corps recovere'.
94 A small letter 'e' placed at left-hand side of the space left for the capital letter.
95 A small letter 't' placed at left-hand side of the space left for the capital letter.

en Brie, lequel siege dura par le temps et espace de neuf moys ou environ, et en sa compaignie estoit oudit siege les seigneurs dont les noms ensuivent, cestassavoir

Monseigneur de duc d'Excestre

Le conte de la Marche
Le conte de Warrewyk
Le conte de Stafford
Le conte de Worcestre
Artur de Bretaigne conte d'Yvry
Le conte de Brayne
Le sire de Clyfford
Le sire de Fournyvall
Le sire de Louvel
Le sire de Audeley
Le sire de Seyntmer qui y mourut
Le Sire d'Aucourt qui y mourut
[45r] Le sire de la Swych
Le sire de Morley
Sire Jehan Cornewayle sire de Fannop et son filz lesquelx moururent durant ledit siege
Le sire de Ferieres Chartley
Le sire de Bowtraz
Le sire de Clynton[96]
Le sire de Haryngton
Le sire de Wyllugby
Le sire de Fitzhugh chamberleyn du roy
Sire Jehan Germeyn mareschal
Sire Jehan Fastolf
Sire Lowys de Robessart
Sire Willam Gascoing qui y mourut
Sire Jehan Radclyf
Sire Robert Harlyng
Sire Willam Philip
Sire Willam Porter[97]
Sire Thomas Rampston
Sire Willam Gascoing qui mourut oudit siege dun trait

et pluseurs autres. Et apres que ledit siege avoit este continuelment tenu devant lesdit ville et marchie de Meaulx par lespace desdit neuf moys ou environ, cestassavoir environ le moys daoust en lan mil iiij^c et xxii, icelles ville et marchie de Meaulx furent renduz et delivrez audit victorieux prince, et tous les gentilz hommes et autres gens de guerre qui estoient dedens se rendirent a la voulente dicellui victorieux prince. Et pour ce que ledit bastart de Vaulru, audevant dudit siege mis avoit fait prendre et cruellement mourir tresgrant nombre de povres laboureurs, qui avoient este prins prisonniers en faisant [45v] leurs labours, et lequelx estoient encores pendans a ung hault arbre nomme Ourme, quant ledit victorieux prince vint pour mectre ledit siege auquel ilz furent monstrez par monditseigneur le duc

---

[96]   In left-hand margin against his name a paragraph mark.
[97]   In left-hand margin against his name a small bell, as on the Porter family coat of arms.

d'Excestre, dont il ot tresgrant pitie, et les fist despendre et ensepulturer, et jura que sil povoit avoir ledit bastart que il le feroit mourir de pareille mort quil avoit fait mourir ledit (sic) povres laboureurs, et sur larbre mesmes ce qui fut fait, car incontinent que ledit bastart de Vaurru fut venu et se fut rendu a la voulente dudit victorieux prince, icellui victorieux prince incontinent le fist mener audit arbre,[98] ou il fut pendu et mort. Et Peron de Lupee et touz les autres adversaires furent prisonniers, et une partie diceulx furent envoyez en Angleterre, et une autre partie furent menez en diverses villes et chasteaulx et mis en diverses prisons.

[D[99]] urant lequel siege de Meaulx, Sire Olivier de Mauny qui avoit este capitaine du chastel de Faloise et par la composicion et reddicion dicellui avoit fait serement que jamais ne feroit guerre contre ledit victorieux prince, en enfraignant sondit serement et venant contre sa foy et promesse, assembla grant puissance de gens de guerre tant Francoys comme Bretons, cestassavoir
Le sire de Montboursier
Le sire de Coynon
Le sire de Chastelgiron
Le sire de Tyntignac
Le sire de la Houssaye et pluseurs autres, et entra ou pays du Costentin ou ilz firent pluseurs maulx et eussent encores plus fait, mais monseigneur le conte de Suffolk qui estoit gouverneur de la basse marche incontinent quil ot ouy nouvelles de ladicte entreprinse, assembla, cestassavoir
Monseigneur de Scales
Sire Jehan Assheton bailli de Costentin
Jehan Banaster escuier
Rix Amadok escuier et pluseurs autres gens de guerre des garnisons dudit pays, et chevaucha contre lesdiz adversaires et les vint rencontrer pres ung chastel qui est nomme le park l'evesque, ouquel lieu ilz assemblerent [46r] les ung (sic) contre les autres et firent pluseurs beaulx faiz darmes dunepart et dautre. Et en la fin lesdiz Francois et Bretons qui ne povoient plus endurer le faitz desdiz Anglois sen tournerent en fuite et a desconfiture, et ylecques moururent desdiz Francois,[100] cestassavoir, ledit sire de Coynon et le ledit (sic) sire de Chastelgiron et pluseurs autres, et le sire de la Houssaye et ledit Sire Olivier de Mauny furent prins prisonniers et pluseurs autres. Et tantost apres ce, nouvelles furent apportees audit victorieux prince de la prinse dudit Sire Olivier, pourquoy icellui victorieux prince manda et fist venir devers lui icellui Sire Olivier, et lui dist teles paroles en substance, Beau pere, vous nous aviez jure et promis que jamais ne feriez guerre contre nous et nos subgiez, vous estes ancien chevalier et deussiez tenir vostre promesse. Et pour ce que ne lavez pas ainsi fait aincois lavez faulsee et enfraincte toutesfoiz, nous ne voulons votre mort, mais vous donnons la vie et yrez faire ung voyaige en Angleterre pour aprendre a parler anglois. Et apres ce fut mene oudit royaume d'Angleterre ouquel il est depuis ale de vie a trespassement.

---

[98]   In left-hand margin in a later hand 'Capitayne pendeu'.
[99]   A letter 'd' placed at left-hand side of the space left for the capital letter.
[100] In right-hand margin in a later hand 'Francoys desconfit'.

[E[101]] n cellui mesmes an environ ledit moys daoust tantost apres que icellui mar-chie de Meaulx avoit este rendu et conquis, icellui victorieux prince sen vint en la cite de Paris, et tantost se rendirent et lui furent delivrees toutes les places et forteresses que les Francois tenoient et occupoient en lisle de France, en Lannoys et en Brie et Champaigne, et sen alere (sic) touz iceulx adversaires oultre la riviere de Loyre ainsi promis et jure lavoient.

Et tantost apres, cestassavoir environ la feste de l'Assumpcion Nostre Dame furent apportees nouvelles audit victorieux prince qui desdiz adversaires en grant puissance avoient mis le siege devant la ville de Cosne en Bourgogne. Pour laquelle ville secourir icellui victorieux prince assembla et fist grant armee et party de la dicte ville de Paris et ala jusques a la ville de Corbueil a sept lieues dudit Paris, auquel lieu il commenca a estre malade, pourquoy ordonna son lieutenant general pour ledit voyaige, monseigneur le [46v] duc de Bourgoingne. Et aussi ordonna son lieutenant pour les Anglois, monseigneur le duc de Bedford son frere, lesquelx firent le dit voyaige et alerent jusques audit lieu de Cosne, mais les adversaires aussi tost comme ilz ouyrent nouvelles de la venue desdiz seigneurs pour la rescousse dicelle ville, ilz noserent actendre aincois leverent leur siege et sen alerent, telle-ment que a la venue diceulx seigneurs ils ne trouverent point lesdiz adversaires et par ainsi fut icelle ville rescousse. Et icellui victorieux prince retourna dudit lieu de Corbueil a ung chastel pres la ville de Paris nomme le Bois de Vincennes, auquel lieu sa maladie lui ['agrava' cancelled] engreiga de plus en plus et apres ses ['do' cancelled] ordonnances envers dieu notre createur faictes et acomplies, il rendi devotement son esperit. Alas quele pitie,[102] quelz douleurs, quelz gemissemens, quels pertes, quelz damaiges, et fut le derrenier jour du moys daoust en lan de grace mil iiij[c] xxij et depuis son corps fut porte en Angleterre et ensepulture en labbaye de Westmonstr' pres la cite de Londres, avecques ses predecesseurs roys. Pleurez touz princes seigneurs nobles bourgois populaires et touz bons vraiz et loyaulx subgiez la mort et perte de si tresnoble et victorieux prince votre protecteur et defendeur.

[T[103]] antost apres le trespassement duquel victorieux prince, et pour ce que son filz et heritier estoit encores de petit et tendre aaige, cestassavoir de laaige de neuf moys ou environ et pour pourveoir a la garde gouvernement tuicion et defense dudit royaume de France, fut ordonne commis et establi du consentement de touz les seigneurs et nobles tant espirituelz comme temporelz et par les communes du pays que monseigneur Jehan duc de Bedford, ainsne frere dudit defunct victorieux prince, seroit regent le royaume de France, lequel tantost apres quil ot accepte ladicte charge, cestassavoir environ le premier jour de janvier oudit an mil iiij[c] xxij, ouy certaines [47r] nouvelles que la ville et pont de Meulenc sur la riviere estoient prins par emblee, par le sire de Graville et autres adversaires, pourquoy il fist armee et assembla cestassavoir
[added in the hand of William Worcester: Richard Wydeville armiger, Robert Harlyng de Norfolk chevalier pour lors lieutenant dudit lieu]
Monseigneur le conte de Salisbury

---

101 A small letter 'e' placed at left-hand side of the space left for the capital letter.
102 In the right-hand margin in a later hand 'Le roy Henry morrust 1422'.
103 A small letter 't' placed at left-hand side of the space left for the capital letter. In the left-hand margin in a later hand '1422/1/H/6'.

Monseigneur le conte de Suffolk
Le sire de Scales
Le jeune sire de Ponyngges
Sire Jehan Ffastolf grant maistre dostel dudit monseigneur le regent et seneschal
de Normandie, et pluseurs autres, et mist le siege devant lesdiz ville et pont de
Meulenc, lequel siege dura deux moys ou environ, et finablement ledit sire de
Graville rendi et delivra a monditseigneur le regent iceulx ville et chastel, et fist le
serement destre vray et loyal subgiet et obeissant du roy notre souverain seigneur et
monditseigneur le regent, mais tantost apres il se rendi adversaire en alant contre
sondit serement. Et diceulx ville et pont fist monditseigneur le regent capitaine [no
name given]

[E[104]] n lannee commencant a Pasques lan de grace mil iiij^{c}xxiij ledit monseigneur
de Bedford commenca a faire[105] parler et traictier pour le mariaige dentre luy et
Dame Anne, seur de Phelipe duc de Bourgoingne. Pendant lequel temps Artur de
Bretaigne conte de Richemond et de Montfort, lequel auoit fait serement a tresvic-
torieux prince le roy Henry cinquieme, dont cy devant est fait mencion, et qui lui
avoit donne la conte d'Yvry, en faussant sa foy et serement sen party secretement et
ala en Flandres et dylecques passa pays et sen ala rendre avecques les adversaires
du roy et de monditseigneur le regent, pourquoy les gens quil avoit commis a la
garde du chastel dudit lieu d'Yvry, quant ilz ouyrent nouvelles de la reddicion dudit
conte, tindrent ledit chastel contre le roy et monditseigneur le regent et mistrent
dedens avecques eulx pour estre plus fors Girault de Pailliere et grant nombre de
adversaires lesquelx coururent le pays et obeissance du roy, robans et pillans les
povres subgiez et faisans tout le mal [47v] qui a eulx estoit possible. Et non obstant
ce icellui monseigneur le regent continua sadicte poursuite, et fut ledit mariaige
fait accorde et furent ensemble a Troyes en Champaigne, ausquelles espousailles
furent en la compaignie de monditseigneur le regent, cestassavoir
Monseigneur le conte de Salisbury
Monseigneur le conte de Suffolk
Le sire de Scalles
Le sire de Ferieres et de Chambroys
['Sire Jehan Fastolf' cancelled]
et pluseurs autres. Et icellui mariaige consumme, ledit prince party dudit lieu de
Troyes pour aler a Paris, et en son chemin prist et conquist pluseurs chasteaulx et
forteresses, cestassavoir
Traynel
Bray sur Seine et pluseurs autres, et apres sen ala a Paris ou il fut bien notable-
ment receu honnourablement et a grant joye. Et pour ce que lesdiz adversaires
occupoient deux chasteaulx et forteresces qui faisoient infiniz maulx et dommaiges
aux citoiens dudit Paris et au povre peuple denviron, les bourgois dudit lieu prier-
ent et requirent monditseigneur le regent quil lui pleust sur ce pourveoir telement
que lesdiz adversaires feussent mis hors desdictes places, cestassavoir de Pacy et de
Oursay. Pourquoy icellui monseigneur le regent a leur priere et requeste ordonna
et commist pour conquerir lesdiz deux chasteaulx Sire Jehan Fastolf, son grant
maistre dostel, avecques certaine notable armee, lequel incontinent mist le siege

---

[104] A small letter 'e' in the left-hand side of the space left for the capital letter.

[105] In right-hand margin in a later hand 'mariage du duc de Bedford'.

devant ledit chastel de Pacy qui dedens brief temps lui fut rendu, et le capitaine dudit lieu nomme Guillaume Remon dit Marjolayne escuier fut pour ladicte rendicion prisonnier dudit Fastolf. Et apres mist le siege devant ['le dit' cancelled] [48r] ledit chastel de Oursay, mais incontinent les adversaires qui dedens estoient firent appoinctement et le rendirent. Et en iceulx chasteaulx ledit Fastolf commist capitaines et gardes et puis sen retourna audit lieu de Paris devers monditseigneur le regent.

[E¹⁰⁶] n icellui an mil iiijc xxiii ['environ' cancelled; added in hand of William Worcester: moys de jullet]¹⁰⁷ le conte de Ventadour, le conte de Comminges, Sire Willam Styward connestable d'Escoce et pluseurs autres, jusques au nombre de xx mille hommes de guerre du party des adversaires, mistrent le siege devant la ville et chastel de Cravant en la conte d'Auxerre ou pays de Bourgoingne, mais incontinent monditseigneur le regent et monseigneur le duc de Bourgoingne assemblerent grant povoir dont les noms des principaulx seigneurs ['et' cancelled] chevaliers et escuiers qui y furent ensuivent, cestassavoir
Monseigneur le conte de Salisbury lieutenant general de monditseigneur le regent
Le sire de Wylugby
Le jeune sire de Ponyngges
Le sire de Molyns
Sire Thomas Rameston
Sire Willam Oldhall
Sire Jehan Passhelay
Sire Thomas Flemmyng
Sire Edmund Heron
Sire John Grey
Sire Reynault Grey
Sire Jehan Artur
Sire Henry Byset
Sire Willam Peyto
Sire Richard Lewyk
Sire John Crafford
Sire Guilbert Halsalle
Sire Lancelot de Lisle
Thomas Abourg
Willam Glasdalle
[48v] Matheu Goth, Digon Amore
Rix Apmadok
Jennekyn Banaster
et pluseurs autres Et des Bourgoingnons
Le sire de Saint George lieutenant general pour le duc de Bourgoingne¹⁰⁸
Le conte de Joingny
Le conte de Brayne
Le sire de Chasteluz marcschal de Bourgoingne

---

¹⁰⁶ A strange-shaped medium-sized 'e' placed at left-hand side of the space left for the capital letter.
¹⁰⁷ In right-hand margin in a later hand '2 H6'.
¹⁰⁸ In left-hand margin a pointing hand next to his name.

Le sire de Vergyer
Le bastart de Vergyer
Le sire de Chastillon
Le sire de Crouy
Le sire de Lisleadam
Le sire de Pesmes
Le bastart de Thyan
Pierres Gressart
Francois l'Arragonoys
Jehan de Gyngy
Davyed du Clou
Henry Chauffour

et pluseurs autres au nombre tant Anglois comme Bourgoingnons quinze mil hommes de guerre ou environ.[109] Et vindrent devant ladicte ville de Cravant pour a icelle donner secours et livrer bataille ausdiz adversaires. Et pour ce que la riviere de Yonne qui passe devant icelle ville de Cravant estoit entre lesdiz adversaires tenant ledit siege, et les Anglois et Bourgoingnons venuz pour ledit secours, pourquoy ilz ne povoient bonnement assembler pour batailler car lesdiz adversaires gardoient tresfort la rive et passaige de ladicte riviere. Et non obstant, tout a une voix et dun mesme couraige, lesdiz Anglois et Bourgoingnons tant a pie comme a cheval se ferirent dedens icelle riviere et a force la passerent oultre et vindrent joindre a bataille contre lesdiz adversaires, et ylecques [49r] eurent tresforte et dure bataille et en la fin lesdiz adversaires ne peurent endurer les grans cops desdiz Anglois et Bourgoingnons et tournerent a desconfiture, et en fuite, et en icelle bataille furent mors et prins prisonniers desdiz adversaires jusques au nombre de viij^m hommes de guerre ou environ, dont des principaulx seigneurs et autres nobles qui y furent mors et prins les noms ensuivent, cestassavoir

Le conte de Ventadour	}
Le conte de Lestrak	}
Le conte de Commynges	} mors
Le conte de Tonnere	}
Sire Conquart de Cameron	}

Escossoy

Le sire de Saint Johnsson	}
Johan de Balglavy	}
Sire Johan Tourneboule	}
Sire Johan Halybourton	}
Sire Robert Lysle	}
Sire Willam Conyngham	}
Guillaume Douglaz escuier	} mors
Sire Alixandre Homme	}
Sire Willam Lisle	}
Sire Johan Rotherfford	}
Sire Willam Crafford	}
Le sire de Coggessale	}
Sire Georges Lysle[110]	}

---

109 In left-hand margin in a later hand 'bataille de Cravant 2 H6'.
110 We have inserted a line here to separate dead and prisoners.

Sire Alixaundre Meldryn   } prisonniers
Sire Lowys de Serigny   }

Apres laquelle bataille et glorieuse victoire faicte et obtenue, dont lesdiz seigneurs rendirent graces et louenges a dieu et a sa glorieuse mere, iceulx seigneurs anglois et bourgoingnons departirent densemble, et sen alerent les Bourgoingnons en leur pays, et monditseigneur de Salisbury et les autres seigneurs anglois retournerent a Paris devers monditseigneur le regent qui les receut a grant joye et honneur. Et diceulx a ladicte bataille ne mourut aucun homme de nom et peu dautres dont il nest mestier de en faire apresent aucune mencion.

[49v] En ce temps tost apres ladicte ville de Cravant recouvree comme dit est, monditseigneur le regent commist et ordonna monseigneur le conte de Salisbury, lieutenant general pour le roy et pour luy es pays de France, Brye et Champaigne, Sire Jehan Ffastolf fut commis lieutenant pour le roy et monditseigneur le regent en Normandie es bailliages de Rouen, Evreux, Alencon et du pays denviron dela la riviere de Seyne, et avec ce gouverneur des pays d'Anjou et du Maine. Guillaume Glasdalle escuier fut commis bailli et capitaine de Mascon, Sire Thomas Gargrave et Sire Thomas Flemmyng furent commis capitaines de Montigny le Roy, Sire Edmund Heron et Digon Avoine (recte, Amore) furent commis capitaines de Vertus en Champaigne, et Matheu Goth escuier fut fait capitaine de [blank].

Et ces choses ainsi faictes, monditseigneur de Salisbury mist le siege devant les tour et chastel de Montaguillon en Brie,[111] dont estoient capitaines Pregent de Coëtivy et Guillaume Bourgois, bretons. Et apres que ledit siege ot dure par le temps et espace de demy an ou environ, lesdiz tour et chastel furent renduz et delivrez es mains dudit conte de Salisbury, et lesdiz Pregent de Coëtivy et Guillaume Bourgois firent serement que jamais ilz ne feroient guerre contre le roy et monditseigneur le regent deca la riviere de Loyre, et par ceste condicion sen alerent. Durant lequel siege advint que le bastart de la Baume et ung nomme Caignart, capitaines de Courcillon, firent une course en Masconnoys, et daventure Matheu Goth escuier et autres de sa compaignie qui estoient sur les champs a leur adventure rencontrerent lesdiz bastart de la Baulme[112] et Caignart, et ylecques de plaine venue sentrerencontrerent bien asprement et y oult une bonne petite besoingne et bien aspre, et en la fin ledit bastart sen fuy, et ce voyant icellui Matheu laissa toute sa compaignie et le suyuy jusques audit lieu de Courcillon tout seul, et quant ledit bastart vist quil ne povait soy sauver dedens ladicte place, habandonna son cheval et entra es fossez pour soy sauver, mais ledit Matheu Goth descendi de son cheval et suyuy tout seul icellui bastart, et non obstant que ceulx qui estoient dedens la dicte place de Courcillon gettoyent pierres et autres choses [50r] pour vouloir sauver leur capitaine, icellui Matheu Goth print icellui bastart son prisonnier, le admena avecques luy, et depuis le presenta a monditseigneur le conte de Salisbury, estant audit siege devant Montaguillon, lequel pour la vaillance que ledit Matheu Goth avoit faicte, et en recompensacion dicelle lui donna ung bon coursier avecques tout le droit de tierces qui lui pouoit appartenir en icellui prisonnier, et touz les heritaiges dicellui bastart. Et ce fut le premier commencement pourquoy ledit Matheu acquist le nom de honneur et de vaillance.[113]

---

[111] In right-hand margin in later hand 'Montaguillon prise par le [...]'.

[112] In right-hand margin in a later hand 'par vaillance de Matheu Goth'.

[113] In left-hand margin a paragraph mark. In right-hand margin in later hand 'not[a] Math'Gothe'.

[V¹¹⁴] ous avez ouy cy devant comment monditseigneur de Bedford regent faisoit traictier du mariaige dentre luy et Dame Anne de Bourgoingne, et comment il ala en la cite de Troyes pour icellui mariaige parfaire acomplir et confermer, durant lequel temps et voyaige Sire Jehan de la Pole, frere du conte de Suffolk,¹¹⁵ lieutenant dudit conte en la basse marche de Normandie et capitaine d'Avranches, assembla toutes les garnisons de ladicte basse marche au nombre de deux mil hommes de guerre ou environ, et chevaucha ou pays d'Anjou devant la cite d'Angiers, et dilecques a labbaye de la Roe, et jusques a une religion de nonnaynes en laquelle il seiourna par trois jours, et puis retourna jusques a une ville plate pres le chastel de la Gravelle, tousiours prenans prisonniers bestaulx et toutes autres proyes que ilz povoient recouvrer. Et eulx ylecques estans survindrent les adversaires, cestassavoir

Le conte d'Aubemarle
Le visconte de Nerbonne
Le sire de Laval
Le sire de Loheac
Le sire de Champaigne
Sire Jehan d'Avaugour
Sire Jehan de Vaulx
Le sire de Park
Sire Guy de Champchevrier
[50v] Sire Ambroys de Lore
Sire Pierres le Porc
Sire Guillaume de Pont briant
Sire Pierre d'Arkeney
Le sire des Escotays
Sire Baudouyn de Champaigne seigneur de Tuce
Sire Anthoyne de Champaigne son frere
Sire Hardouyn de Mynedere
Sire Pierre Herysson
Sire Loys de Tremorgan
Sire Guy Turpyn
Sire Jehan de Lore
Sire Jehan de *Champigny*
Sire Robert de Chauvigny
Le sire de la Feullie
Sire Guy d'Orenge
Sire Jehan de la Rochiere
Le sire de Juigny
Le sire de Juvigny
Le sire de Bellay
Le sire de Fontaynes
Le sire de Malicorne
Le sire de la Suze
Le sire de Champaigne
Sire Loys le Gros

---

¹¹⁴ A small letter 'i' at top left-hand corner of space left for the initial.
¹¹⁵ In left-hand margin in hand of William Worcester 'nota malum viagium predictum et ex fortuna'. In right-hand margin in later hand 'langloys prise'.

Sire Hue le Gros son frere
Sire Guy de Laval
Le sire d'Asse le Riboule
Le sire d'Averton et de Belin
Le sire de la Saugiere
Sire Jehan le Voyer
Sire Jehan le Bervier
Sire Pierres de Berouille
Sire Jehan de Beaurepaire
Jehan le Beauvoisien
Jehan d'Avaugour
et pluseurs autres au nombre de vi m hommes de guerre ou environ, et trouverent les Anglois en desarroy [51r] et frapperent soubdaynement sur eulx, parquoy ilz furent desconfiz et tournerent en fuyte, et en icelle desconfiture furent prins prisonniers et mors les seigneurs chevaliers et escuiers dont en partie les noms ensuivent, cestassavoir
Le dit Sir Jehan de la Pole   }
Jean Basset   } prisonniers
Jean Affourd lieutenant de Faloise }
Jean Affourd mareschal d'Argenten }
[added in hand of William Worcester: Jehan Clyffon chevalier]
et pluseurs autres jusques au nombre de mil Anglois ou environ.

[E[116]] n hyver ensuivant oudit an mil iiijc xxiij, Yon du Puys, Girart de Lawe et Gaultier de Brusac escuiers du party des adversaires assemblerent avecques leurs gens et passerent deca la riviere de Loire et chevaucherent le plus coyement et secretement que ilz peurent, tant quilz vindrent jusques au pres de la ville de Compiengne, sans ce que aucunes nouvelles en feussent sceues audit lieu de Compiengne, ne es parties denviron, et telement que par ung vendredi matin quil faisoit tresgrant broillaz prindrent et par emblee icelle ville de Compiengne. Pour laquelle recouvrer, incontinent que monditseigneur le regent ouyt nouvelles de la dicte prinse,[117] il fist une armee et fist mectre le siege devant ladicte ville, et dun des costez de la riviere estoient, cestassavoir le conte de Suffolk, le conte de Ligny et pluseurs autres, et de lautre coste estoient le sire de Lisleadam, le prevost de Paris, Sire Thomas Gargrave, lieutenant a Rouen pour monseigneur le conte de Warrewyk, capitaine dudit lieu, et pluseurs autres. Et pour ce que lesdiz adversaires estoient fors dedens ladicte ville et avoient assez vitailles, parquoy ledite siege estoit en voye destre longuement ylec, aussi que len doubtoit quilz neussent secours de leur party, monditseigneur le regent fist prendre ung nomme Guillaume Remon [51v] dit Marjolayne escuier, lequel avoit este prins prisonnier a Pacy par Sire Jehan Fastolf chevalier, car il estoit maistre et capitaine des adversaires qui estoient dedens ladicte ville de Compiengne. Et ledit Remon monditseigneur le regent fist mectre et lyer sur une charrecte, la corde ['dedens' cancelled] entour le col prest pour estre pendu. Et en cest estat fist mener icellui Marjolayne devant ladicte ville et a la veue desdiz adversaires, en leur affirmant que se ilz ne rendoient icelle ville en lobeissance du roy et dudit regent icellui Marjolayne seroit pendu et estrangle.

---

116   A small letter 'e' in top right-hand corner of the space left for the initial.
117   In left-hand margin in hand of William Worcester 'compiegne predict […]'.

Lesquelx adversaires, voyans leur dit capitaine en tel peril de mort et pour lamour quilz avoient a luy, pensans quilz nauroient aucun secours, composerent et rendirent icelle ville moyennant que ledit Marjolayne fut delivre, et quilz sen alerent franchement atout leur biens chevaulx et harnoys.

[A[118]] pres laquelle ville de Compiengne ainsi recouvree et conquise comme dit est,[119] ledit regent qui avoit de jour en jour complaintes des horribles et infiniz maulx et dommaiges que les adversaires occupans le chastel de Yvry faisoient chacun jour sur les povres subgiez du roy, fist nouvelle armee et envoya pour mectre le siege devant ledit lieu d'Yvry, cestassavoir
Le conte de Salisbury
Le conte de Suffolk
Le sire de Willugby
Le sire de Scales
Le sire de Ponyngges, et pluseurs avec notable armee, lesquelz mistrent le siege devant ledit chastel de Yvry, ou ilz tindrent siege par lespace de six sepmaines ou environ. Pendant lequel temps les adversaires firent une grosse armee ['en laque' cancelled] pour donner secour audit lieu d'Yvry. En laquelle armee estoient les princes et seigneurs dont les noms ensuivent, cestassavoir
Le duc d'Alencon chief et lieutenant general
Le bastard d'Alencon son uncle
[52r] Le conte d'Aubemarle
Le conte de Ventadour
Le conte de Tonnerre
Le conte de Maulevrier
Le conte de Forestz
Le viconte de Nerbonne
Le viconte de Touars
Le sire de Graville
Le sire de Gaules
Le sire de Malicorne
Le sire de Mauny
Le sire de Bellay
Le sire de Fontaines
Le sire de Montfort Lailler
Sire Loys de Harecourt seigneur de Bonnestable
Le sire de Tusse
Le sire de Champaigney
Le sire de Mont Jehan et de Sillie le Guillaume
Le sire de la Suze
Le sire d'Amboys
Le sire de Beaumesnil
Le sire d'Ausebosc
Le sire de Moyon
Le baron de Coulonces

---

[118] A small letter 'a' in top right-hand corner of the space left for the initial.
[119] In right-hand margin in a later hand '2 H6 Compiegne de francoys gayne et recouvr' par langloys'.

Le baron des Byars
Sire Jehan de Tollevast
Sire Jehan de Villiers
Sire Nicole Paynel
Sire Jaques Paynel son frere
Sire Jehan Donnebault
Sire Henry de Tylly
Sire Loys de Braquemont
Sire Jehan Tournebeuf
Sire Gauvain de la Haye
Sire Jehan Pigache
Sire Florent Dylliers
Sire Rigault de Fontaines
Sire Robert de Dreux
[52v] Sire Olivier de Milanc seigneur de Saint Celerin
Sire Coquart de Cambron
Sire Pierres le Beauvoisien
Sire Pierre de Bereville
Sire Jehan de Bourgneuf
Sire Groingnet de Vasse
Le sire des Escotaye
Sire Pierres d'Arkeney
Sire Robert de Feschal
Sire Olivier de Feschal
Sire Guy d'Orenge
Sire Guillaume d'Orenge
Sire Ambroys de Lore
Sire Guy de Champchevrier
Sire Antoyne de Champaigne
Sire Sanson de Sens
Sire Robert d'Aungne
Le sire da la Roche Bowet
Sire Guillaume de Mauny
Sire de Pontberengier
Sire Guillaume de la Mote
Sire Jehan de Tyval
Sire Ambroys de Gaigny
Sire Guillaume de Verdell
Sire Hue le Gros
Sire Guillaume de Montahier
Sire Jehan de Vaulx
Sire Jehan Oudart
Sire Jehan de la Rochiere
Sire Pierre de Beauvau
Sire Jehan Quatrebarbes
Sire Jehan le Verrier
Sire Robert de Boiscornu
Sire Jaques de Mathefelon
Sire Pierres le Voyer seigneur de Ballay

Sire Hardouyn de Myndiere
Le sire d'Averton
Le sire d'Asse le Riboulle
[53r] Le sire de Peschere
Sire Jehan de Ville Prouvee
Sire Jaques de Sepeaulx
Le Galoys d'Asche
Sire Jehan de Beaurepaire
Sire Guillaume Bellengier
Sire Robert de Freulay
Sire Guillaume de Chauvigny
Sire Pierres le Porc
Sire Robert de Montchauvel
Le sire de la Marvaille
Sire Lancelot Giron baron en Bretaigne   }
Jehan de Chauvigny seigneur de la Montaigne }
Sire Jehan Tournemyne   }
Sire Jehan de Pontbryant   }
Sire Jehan Giffart   }
Sire Jehan Gerart   }
Sire Henry de Puskalet   } bretons
Sire Pierres Boterel   }
Sire Jehan Testenowe   }
Le bastart de Beaumanoir   }
Olivier de la Forest   }
Pierres de la Forest   }
Le sire de Grippon
Ambroys d'Anthenaize
Pierre d'Anthenaize
Ffoulquet Pesaz
Guyon du Coing
Jennekyn Kent
Huet de Fontenay
Michiel Tailleuer
Hue de Channay
Charles de Villiers
La Manne
Ffoulquet de Coulonges
Guillaume de Landereposte

[53v] et pluseurs autres chevaliers de escuiers et autres gens de guerre jusques au nombre de quarante mil hommes ou environ. Et aussi tost comme nouvelles vindrent devers monditseigneur le regent, il assembla tout quil pot bonnement, tant Anglois comme Normans, et sen ala audit siege pour le renforcier. Pour quoy lesdiz adversaires, quant ilz oyrent nouvelles que icellui regent estoit en personne oudit siege, noserent ylecques venir et sen alerent a Verneuil ou Perche,[120] laquelle ville leur fut incontinent rendue. Et ce pendant les adversaires qui estoient dedens ledit chastel d'Yvry voyans que le socour leur estoit failly et quilz navoient plus de

---

[120]　In left-hand margin in a later hand 'Verneuil en Perche'.

quoy vivre, composerent et rendirent icellui chastel au roy et a monditseigneur le regent et sen alerent. Duquel chastel icellui monseigneur le regent mist gardes, et avecques tout son host, ouquel estoient, cestassavoir

Monditseigneur le conte de Salysbury
Le sire de Willugby
Le sire de Scales
Le sire de Ponyngges qui estoit malade
Sire Jehan Grey
Sire Reynault Grey de Ruthin freres
Sire Jehan Fastolf
[added in hand of William Worcester: Sire Jehan ['Salvyan' cancelled] Salveyn bayllye de Rouen]
Sire Lancelot de Lisle
Sire Jehan Passhelay
Sire Gilbert de Halsalle
Sire Jehan Grey de Northumberland
Sire Thomas Blount
Sire Robert Harlyng
Sire William Oldhall
Sire Jehan Harpelay
Sire Alayn Bukessell
Sire Jehan Artur
Sire Richart Merbury[121]
Sire Thomas Gargrave
Thomas Abourgh [added in hand of William Worcester: h [at end of his name] armiger valens in armis]
Willam Glasdalle
Matheu Goth [added in hand of William Worcester: captus prisonarius in [inserted above: Le chase] ductus in ville de Perche sed et redditur cum villa]
Johan Banaster
[54r] Rix Apmadoc
Richart Waller
Johan Abourg
Sire Phelippe Braunche
Sire Jehan de Montgomery
Sire Jehan Kyrkley
Sire William Crafford
Sire Raoul Boutellier
Sire Willam Torbok
Richart Gethyn[122]
Sire Henry Byset
Sire Rauland Staundyssh[123]
Sire Johan Robersart
Sire Nicole Burdet
Thomas Lounde

---

[121]   Against his name in left-hand margin a memorandum sign.
[122]   In left-hand margin against his name a paragraph mark.
[123]   In left-hand margin against his name a paragraph mark.

Willam Minoz[124]
Georges Rygmayden
Willam Kyrkeby
Thomas Everingham
et autres, tant Anglois comme Normans, jusques au nombre[125] de dix mil hommes
de guerre ou environ. Tantost quil ot nouvelles certaines que lesdiz adversaires
avoient prinse ladicte ville de Vernueil party et chevaucha droit vers lesdiz adversaires et manda audit d'Alencon et au Duc Douglaz et du conte de Boukam connestable d'Escoce que se ilz le vouloient actendre ylecques il les vendroit veoir. Et
ilz lui remanderent que il venist hardiement, et que ilz le actendroient et estoient
prestz pour le recepvoir. Et ainsi en la vigile de la feste de l'Assumpcion Nostre
Dame ou moys daoust, monditseigneur le regent arriva devant ladicte ville de
Vernueil, ou il trouva lesdiz adversaires prestz et en bataille, Et ylecques avant que
il donnast bataille ausdiz adversaires fist baneret Sire Jehan Fastolf[126] qui audevant nestoit que bacheler. Et ce fait les deux parties assemblerent aigrement a
bataille moult forte cruele et espoventable, mais en la fin, comme il plaisoit adieu
nostre createur et a la glorieuse vierge, la victoire tourna et demoura aux Anglois
et ['lesdiz' cancelled] la desconfiture [54v] tourna sur lesdiz adversaires et en icelle
bataille furent prins prisonniers et mors tant Francois comme Escossoys les princes
seigneurs et autres chevaliers et escuiers dont les noms ensuivent, cestassavoir

Ledit duc d'Alencon	}
Le bastart d'Alencon	}
Sire Loys de Tremorgan	} prisonniers
Sire Pierre Herysson	}
Sire Jehan Tournebeuf seigneur de Courronne	}
Le conte d'Aumarle[127]	}
Le conte de Ventadour	}
Le viconte de Nerbonne	}
Le sire de la Forest[128]	}
Le sire de Graville	}
Le sire de Galles	}
Le sire de Fontaines	}
Le sire d'Amboys	} mors
Le viconte de Touars	}
Le sire de Bellay	}
Le sire d'Averton	}
Le sire d'Asse le Riboulle	}
Le Rousin	}
Oudin Chynart	}
Yvor du Puys	}
Sire Pierre de Champaigne	}

---

[124]   In left-hand margin against his name a paragraph mark and to the left of that, a small cross.
[125]   In right-hand margin in a later hand '1423 battayle de Vernoyl lan du roy Henry le vi ijd'.
[126]   Immediately to right of line a paragraph mark.
[127]   From this point, the following are 'mors'. We have inserted a blank line for the sake of clarity.
[128]   In left-hand margin against his name a paragraph sign.

Sire Pierre Boterel Breton }
Sire Robert de Dreux }
Sire Jehan de Montgoubert }
Le bailly de Touraine }
Sire Pierre Chapperon }
Le sire de Malicorne }
Le sire de Bourg Nouvel }
Sire Jehan de Tournebeuf Seigneur de Beaumesnil }
['Sire Jehan de Tournebeuf' cancelled]
Sire Loys de Harecourt seigneur de Bonnestable }
Michel de Ferieres }
Sire Jehan Pigache }
Sire Jehan Quatre Barbes }
[55r] Et des Escossays
Le duc de Touraine conte Douglas }
James Douglaz son filz }
Le conte de Boukam connestable de France }
Le conte de Wyghton } mors
Sire Alixaundre Meldryn }
Sire Henry Balglavy }
Sire Johan Sterlyng }
Sire Willam de Homelesdon }
Sire James Grey }
Sire Robert Kandey }

et pluseurs autres, tant Francois comme Escossoys, jusques au nombre de neuf
mil hommes ou environ par compte fait par Mont Joye roy darmes pour la partie
desdiz adversaires. Et pour la partie des Anglois ny mourut aucun homme de nom
dont il soit a faire mencion.

[E[129]] n ce mesme temps Sire Jehan de Luxembourg conte de Ligny,[130] en sa compaignie certain nombre d'Anglois, cestassavoir
Sire Thomas Rampston
Nicolas Warberton
Willam Lynoz et pluseurs autres tant Anglois comme Bourgouignons et Picquars,
avoit mis et tenoit le siege devant la ville et chastel de Guyse en Therache, laquelle
par composicion lui fut rendue avecques le chastel de Herisson et autres pluseurs
chasteaux et forteresses environ icelle ville de Guyse.

[A[131]] pres laquelle bataille et glorieuse victoire obtenue par ledit monseigneur le
regent comme dit est, incontinent les adversaires qui estoient et sestoient retraiz
dedens la dicte ville de Vernueil ou Perche firent composicion que [55v] en rendant
et delivrant la dicte ville et chastel de Vernueil ilz sen yroient franchement avecques
leurs biens chevaulx et harnoys. Et ainsi le firent. Et en icelle monditseigneur le
regent commist capitaine et garde [added in later hand: Messire Phillippe Halle]
et party et sen retourna en la cite de Rouen a grant honneur, joye et victoire,

---

[129]   A small letter 'e' in top left-hand corner of the space left for the initial.
[130]   In the right-hand margin in a later hand '3 H6'.
[131]   A small letter 'a' in top left-hand corner of the space left for the initial.

et dylecques ala a Paris. Auquel lieu tantost apres il commist et ordonna le sire de Scalles, Sire Jehan Fastolf et Sire Jehan Montgommery, avecques deux mil hommes ou environ en leur compaignie, pour aler faire conqueste es pays d'Anjou et du Maine. Lesquelx seigneurs, ou moys de septembre oudit an mil iiij^c ['xxiiij' cancelled; added by William Worcester: xxv], entrerent oudit pays et conte du Maine et mistrent le siege devant le chastel de Beaumont le Viconte, dont estoit capitaine Huet ['deprez es' cancelled] de Fontenay escuier, qui dedens quinze jours apres rendi le chastel par telle composicion que une partie de ceulx qui estoient dedens demourerent et furent prisonniers et lautre partie sen alerent leurs vies sauves. Et dylecques mistrent le siege devant le chastel de ['Thouvioye' cancelled; added in later hand: 'Tennye'] a un lieue pres la cite du Mans, dont estoit capitaine Sire Jehan Tournemyne breton, lequel au bout de huit jours rendi ledit chastel par ainsi quils sen alerent ung baston en le main.

Et dilecques alerent devant le chastel de Sillie le Guillaume, dont estoient capitaines Pierre le Forestier, et Olivier le Forestier bretons, qui dedens six jours apres se rendirent et delivrerent ledit chastel par composicion que ilz sen yroient leurs vies sauves, et payeroient certaine somme dargent dont lesdiz capitaines demourerent pleiges et hostaiges. Et ce fait, alerent devant les chasteaulx de Orte et de Courceriers, dont estoient capitaines Michiel Tailleuer et Guillaume Vachereau, lesquelz firent composicion de rendre lesdiz places ou de combatre dedens ung moys prochain ensuivant. Et de ce faire, baillerent hostaiges. Pendant lequel temps lesdiz seigneurs conquirent autres places, cestassavoir Roussy, Vasse, Courtmenant et pluseurs [inserted above hand B: autres] qui leur furent abandonnes par les capitaines et gens desdiz lieux, qui sen estoient fuyz et nosoient actendre la venue desdiz seigneurs. Et dedens la [56r] fin dudit moys iceulx seigneurs retournerent devant lesdiz chasteaulx de Orte et Courceriers, pour iceulx recevoir en lobeissance du roy et de monditseigneur le regent ou pour combatre. Et non obstant que les adversaires ne comparurent point, lesdiz capitaines, en alant contre leurs foy et promesses, ne voulurent delivrer icelles forteresses et abandonnerent leursdiz hostaiges, lequelx hostaiges ce voyans incontinent firent devant lesdiz places decoler iceulx hostaiges, et apres sen retournerent vers leurs places. Assez tost apres ces choses faictes, cestassavoir environ la feste de Chandeleur, les seigneurs devant nommes accompaigniez de mil et cinq cens hommes de guerre firent une course vers la riviere du Loyr, et prindrent dassault la premiere garde du chastel et forteresse de la Chartre sur le Loir, mais le donjon se tint et en peu de jours se rendirent, et ledit donjon, et diceulx fut fait capitaine Richard Gethyn escuier.[132] Et durant le dit temps firent fortiffier Montfort L'Aillier, dont ilz firent capitaine Thomas Lound escuier, et apres sen retournerent en leurs places et garnisons avecques leurs proyes et prisonniers.

[L[133]] annee ensuivant mil iiij^c vingtcinq,[134] monditseigneur le regent ordonna et commist pour et ou nom du roy et de luy lieutenant general monseigneur le conte de Salysbury, et lenvoya avec notable armee esdiz pays d'Anjou et du Maine pour ylec faire conqueste, lequel compaignie des seigneurs dont les noms ensuivent, cestassavoir

---

[132] In left-hand margin in a later hand 'r getyn'.
[133] A small letter 'l' at top left-hand corner of space left for the capital.
[134] In right-hand margin in a later hand '1425'.

Le sire de Scalles
Sire Jehan Fastolf grant maistre dostel dudit monseigneur le regent et gouverneur
desdiz pays d'Anjou et du Mayne
Sire Jehan Grey filz du seigneur de Grey Ruthin
Sir Reynault Grey son frere
Sire Alan Bukessell
Sire Thomas Blowet
Sire Willam Oldhall
Sire Lancelot de Lisle
[56v] Sire Andreu Ogard
Sire Jehan Montgomery
[added by William Worcester: Thomas Popham chevalier]
Le sire de Ferieres et de Chambroys
Guillaume Glasdalle
Matheu Goth
Richart Whetherton
Thomas Gower
Robert Stafford
Thomas Abourg
Thomas Everyngham
Willam Kyrkeby

et pluseurs autres au nombre de dix mil hommes de guerre ou environ entra oudit
pays du Maine ou moys de juing et mist le siege devant la cite du Mans, dont
estoit principal capitaine Sire Baudouyn de Champaigne seigneur de Tusse, Sire
Guillaume de Maugny, Sire Hue le Gros, Sire Guillaume de la Mote et Huet de
Fontenay petiz capitaines.[135] Et apres que ledit siege oult dure par lespace de six
sepmaines ou environ, et que ceulx de dedens virent que ils ne seroient point secouruz, firent traictie et composicion, cestassavoir que ilz rendirent et delivrerent en
lobeissance du roy et de monditseigneur le regent icelle cite, et touz les bourgois,
gens deglise, gens de guerre et autres qui vouldroient demourer auroient leurs
vies sauves et touz leur biens, et leurs heritaiges non denuez, et qui ne vouldroit
demourer, il sen pourroit aler avecques touz ses biens, chevaulx et harnoys. Et
dicelle cite fut et demoura capitaine ledit Sire Johan Fastolf, gouverneur desdiz
pays. Et en venant mectre le siege devant ladicte cite du Mans, ledit conte passa
par devant le chastel de la Guierche a deux lieues pres dicelle cite, et y logea par xv
jours ou environ que les adversaires qui dedens estoient lui rendirent ladicte place.
Apres laquelle cite ainsi rendue et conquise comme dit est dessus, furent rendues
et mises en obeissance du roy et de monditseigneur le regent diverses places et
forteresses, esquelles furent mis et ordonnez capitaines, dont en partie les noms
dicelles ensuivent, cestassavoir
[57r] Saint Kalez, ouquel fut mis capitaine Richart Gethyn escuier
Chasteaulx l'Ermitaige et la saigne, dont fut ordonne capitaine Matheu Goth
escuier Guerlande dont fut fait capitaine Jehan Banaster escuier
Malicorne dont fut capitaine Guillaume Glasdalle escuier
Lisle soubz Brullon dont fut capitaine Sire Lancelot de Lisle chevalier Louppelande
dont fut ordonne capitaine Henry Braunche
Montseur dont fut fait capitaine Sire Willam Oldhall chevalier

---

[135] In left-hand margin in a later hand 'Mauns pris'.

Le Suze dont fut fait capitaine Jehan Suffolk escuier
et pluseurs autres furent abatues et desemparees.

[E[136]] t en celle mesmes annee environ le moys de septembre, monditseigneur
le conte de Salisbury et les autres seigneurs dessous nommez en sa compaignie
mist le siege devant les ville et chastel de Saincte Suzanne, dont estoit capitaine
Sire Ambroys de Lore chevalier, lequel dedens quinze jours apres ou environ fist
composicion et rendi audit conte lesdiz ville et chastel, moyennant ce que ilz firent
tous serement que jusques a ung an ensuivant ilz ne feroient point guerre et ne se
armeroient point contre les Anglois, et par ce moyen ilz sen alerent avecques leurs
biens, excepte les canonniers lequelz furent reservez et delivrez a monditseigneur
le conte pour en faire a sa voulente, qui touz les fist pendre une pierre a canon a
chacun pendue au pie. Et dudit lieu de Saincte Suzanne, dont il fist capitaine et
garde Sire Jehan Popham chevalier, incontinent party et ala mectre siege devant
le chastel de Mayenne la Juhez dont estoit capitaine le sire des Escotaiz, et dura
ledit siege environ six sepmaines que ilz firent composicion tele, cestassavoir que
ilz rendirent icellui chastel et sen alerent touz leurs vies biens chevaulx et harnoys
saufs, et dicellui chastel fut fait et ordonne capitaine et garde Sire Jehan Montgommery chevalier. Et apres ce que le temps dyver fut en partie passe, cestassavoir
environ la feste de la purificacion nostre dame, icellui conte de Salisbury mist le
siege devant les ville et chastel de la Ferte Bernard, dont estoit capitaine Jehan
d'Avaugour dit chieure, qui dura jusques apres Pasques. Pendant le temps duquel
siege durant [57v] une vendicion fut machinee et faicte par ung Gascoing du party
des Anglois,[137] avecques Charles de Villiers, Pierre le Beuf, Pierre d'Anthenaize
et Emery d'Anthenaize et Guillaume de Landereposte, touz tenans le party des
adversaires, cestassavoir que le dit Gascon devoit mectre dedens le chastel dudit
lieu d'Alencon les dessus nommez, moyennant que lesdiz adversaires lui devoient
faire certain don. Laquelle vendicion ainsi faicte comme dit est, icellui Gascon fist
savoir audit conte de Salysbury, lequel ordonna le sire de Willugby et Sire Johan
Fastolf pour aler rencontrer lesdiz adversaires. Et au jour qui mis avoit este entre
le dit Gascon et lesdiz adversaires pour faire delivrance dicellui chastel, iceulx
adversaires dessusnommes et autres en leur compaignie jusques au nombre de ij[c]
hommes de fait, vindrent en ung matin jusques pres ledit lieu d'Alencon pensans
de verite et sans nulle faulte entrer dedens, mais il fut tout le revers. Car lesdiz sire
de Wyllugby et Sire Johan Fastolf, qui sestoient departiz dudit siege de la ferte
accompaigniez de ij[m] Anglois, vindrent raencontrer et encloure lesdiz adversaires
au pres dudit lieu d'Alencon, et ylecques furent touz iceulx adversaires mors et
prins prisonniers, excepte ledit Pierre d'Anthenaize qui sen fuy et eschappa. Et ce
fait lesdiz sire de Wyllugby et Sire Jehan Fastolf retournerent audit siege devant la
Ferte devers ledit conte de Salisbury qui les receut a grant joye pour la destrousse
quilz avoient faicte. Et assez tost apres que la feste de Pasques fut passee, les adversaires qui estoient dedens ledit lieu de la Ferte Bernard, voyans que aucun secour
ne aide ne leur venoit, et que leurs vivres amenuysoient fort et que bonnement ilz
ne pouvoient plus garder lesdiz ville et chastel contre lesdiz Anglois qui chacun
jour et nuyt leur livroient fors assaulx et escarmuches en diverses manieres, traicterent et composerent avecques ledit conte et lui rendirent et delivrerent iceulx

---

[136] Small letter 'e' at top left-hand corner of the space left for the initial.
[137] In left-hand margin in a later hand 'jorne de alaunson'.

chastel et ville moyennans que ilz sen alerent avecques leurs biens chevaulx et harnoys. Et diceulx ledit conte de Salisbury fut fait seigneur par don qui lui en fut fait par monditseigneur le regent.

[E[138]] n ce temps mesmes et durant icellui siege, cestassavoir [58r] ou temps de karesme, Sire Thomas Rampston, Sire Phelip Braunche, Sire Nicole Bourdet et autres Anglois en leur compaignie jusques au nombre de cinq cens hommes ou environ fortiffierent et emparerent la ville de Saint James de Beuron sur la marche de Bretaigne, mais incontinent que Artur de Bretaigne conte de Richemond ouyt nouvelles de la dicte fortifficacion, il manda et assembla les barons de Bretaigne et autres du party des Francois, avecques le peuple dudit pays de Bretaigne ['jusques' cancelled] et estoient bien nombrez tant ungs comme autres au nombre de soixante a quatre vings mil personnes, lesquelz vindrent et mistrent siege devant ladicte ville de Saint James, et donnerent aux Anglois tresgrans cruelz et fors assaulx,[139] mais lesdiz Anglois qui dedens estoient se deffendirent vaillamment comme lyons et tellement que apres ung tresfort assault que lesdiz Bretons avoient fait aladicte ville dont ilz estoient travailliez, lesdiz Anglois saillirent hors de leur dicte ville et fraperent sur iceulx Bretons en leurs logeis, et tellement furent lesdiz Bretons effrayez que honteusement et couardement ilz sen fuirent et leverent leurdit siege, et laisserent leurs biens vivres et artilleries, et en celle destrousse furent mors et prins prisonniers desdiz Bretons quatre mil hommes et plus.

[E[140]] n lannee mil cccc vingt six environ le moys de may[141] monditseigneur le regent duc de Bedford commist et ordonna lieutenant general du roy et de luy le conte de Warwyk qui nouvellement estoit venu d'Angleterre acompaignie de six mil hommes de fait, et en descharga ledit conte de Salysbury, lequel conte de Warrewyk entra ou conte du Mayne, et mist le siege devant la ville de Chasteauduloir, la quelle dedens huit jours apres lui fut rendue par [space for name left blank] qui en estoit capitaine, et dicelle fist capitaine et garde Matheu Goth escuier. Et apres ala devant le chastel de Mayet, qui le second jour lui fut rendu et delivre et y mist capitaine Jehan Wynter escuier qui en estoit seigneur [58v] par don a luy fait par monditseigneur le regent. Et dylecques ala devant le chastel du Lude qui lui fut rendu et y mist capitaine Guillaume Glasdalle. Et pour ce que ledit conte avoit nouvelles que les adversaires faisoient une assemblee ou pays de Beausse, icellui conte fist une course oudit pays esperant trouver et rencontrer lesdiz adversaires lesquelz il ne trouva point et sen retourna sans autre chose faire. Et a son retour mist siege devant le chastel de Montdoubleau dont estoit capitaine Roberton des Croix escuier, et y fut par lespace de trois sepmaines que ledit Roberton rendi ladicte place moyennant que lesdiz adversaires sen alerent leurs biens chevaulx et harnoys avecques eulx. Et dicelle fist et ordonna capitaine et garde le sire de Wyllugby. Et ce fait, ledit conte sen retourna devers ledit duc de Bedford regent qui pour lors estoit en la ville.[142]

---

138 Small letter 'e' at top left-hand corner of the space left for the initial.
139 In right-hand margin in a later hand 'les Bretons discomfit'.
140 Small letter 'e' at top left-hand corner of the space left for the initial.
141 In right-hand margin in a later hand '1426'.
142 There is no name given for the town although a space appears to have been left for it at the end of the line.

Et[143] en icelle mesme annee environ la feste de la purificacion nostre dame, le sire de Rustynam mareschal de Bretaigne ['a g' cancelled] assembla grant compaignie de Bretons et ala fortiffier la ville de Pontorson, et durant le temps de ladicte fortifficacion ledit seigneur de Rustynam acompaignie de mil hommes de guerre et plus hst une course en Normandie ou bas pays de Costentin et jusques devant la ville et cite d'Avranches, mais les Anglois de la garnison dudit lieu yssirent hors contre lesdiz Bretons et se combatirent contre eulx moult vaillamment et telement que ilz obtindrent la victoire et furent lesdiz Bretons desconfiz et mis en fuyte, et ledit seigneur de Rustynam prins prisonnier, et grant partie de ses gens mors et prins. Et tantost apres nouvelles vindrent audit duc de Bedford de ladicte fortifficacion, pourquoy incontinent il envoya mectre le siege devant icelle ville par le conte de Warrewyk son lieutenant general, en sa compaignie le sire de Scales, Sire Jehan Fastolf, Sire Jehan Popham, Sire Thomas Rampston, Sire Nicole Burdet, Matheu Goth et pluseurs autres a notable armee de sept mil hommes de fait ou environ, durant lequel siege, pour ce que ilz auoient necessite de vivres, le dit sire de Scales en sa compaignie Sire Jehan Herpelay chevalier bailli de Costentin, Sire Guillaume Breton chevalier [59r] bailli de Caen, Sire Raoul Tesson, Sire Jehan Carbonnel, et pluseurs autres au nombre de trois mil hommes de fait, tant Anglois comme Normans, partirent dudit siege et alerent querir des vivres et des ordonnances et artilleries, et ainsi comme ilz retournoient audit siege, sur les greves de la mer environ le Mont Saint Michiel rencontrerent les adversaires a grant puissance, ou estoient, cestassavoir

Le baron de Coulonces

Le sire d'Ausebosc capitaine du Mont Saint Michiel

Le sire de Montboursier

Le sire de Chasteaugiron

Le sire de Tyntignac

Le sire de Montauban

Le sire de Chasteaubruyant

et pluseurs autres nombrez a plus de six mil hommes de fait, et y lecques le dit sire de Scales et les Anglois descendirent a pie et se combatirent vaillamment contre lesdiz adversaires et y ot une bonne besoingne et forte bataille tant dun coste que dautre, mais en la fin les adversaires qui ne poient plus endurer les grans cops des Angloys se desconfirent et tournerent en fuyte, et ylecques fut occis ledit baron de Coulonces et plus de mil Francois mors et prins.[144] Apres laquelle belle et notable destrousse, ledit sire de Scales et autres de sa compaignie sen alerent audit siege avecques leurs vivres artilleries et prisonniers a grant joye honneur et victoire, et ou ilz furent tresjoyeusement receuz par ledit conte de Warrewyk. Ou temps mesmes dudit siege Christofle Hansson et autres souldoyers de la garnison de Saincte Suzanne au nombre de [blank] hommes de fait firent une entreprinse ou pays d'Anjou et alerent jusques a ung chastel nomme Rameford, lequel chastel par eschielle et emblee fut prins, laquelle prinse venue a la congnoissance des adversaires qui estoient assemblez pour aler secourer ladicte ville de Pontorson au nombre de vingt mil personnes ou environ, rompirent leur voyaige et sen alerent mectre de siege devant ledit chastel de Ramefort [59v] ou Ils furent par lespace de dix jours entiers, que les Anglois qui dedens estoient, voyans le grant nombre des

---

[143] A letter (possibly R) in left-hand margin in later hand.

[144] In right-hand margin in a later hand 'mil francois mors'.

adversaires estant devant eulx, le petit nombre quilz estoient dedens et aussi que vivres leur failloient, furent contrains de appoinctier avecques lesdiz adversaires et delivrerent icellui chastel moyennant que ilz sen alerent, leurs vies sauves et perdirent touz leurs biens chevaulx et harnoys. Et ce fait, lesdiz adversaires se departirent et nalerent point audit lieu de Pontorson pour lui donner socour. Mais tantost apres, le sire de Rays, soy disant lieutenant du roy es pays d'Anjou et du maine, en sa compaignie le sire de Mont Jehan, le sire de Beaumanoir, le sire de Tusse bailli de Tours et pluseurs autres jusques au nombre de trois mil hommes de guerre, entrerent oudit conte du Maine et mistrent siege devant le chastel de Malicorne dont estoit lieutenant et garde Olivier of Batyrsby escuier, lequel chastel ilz conquirent et fut ledit Olivier et touz les autres qui estoient dedens prisonniers. Et dilecques alerent devant le chastel du Lude, dont Willam Blakborne estoit lieutenant et garde soubz Guillaume Glasdalle escuier, lequel chastel ilz assaillirent et le prindrent dassault, et touz ceulx dedens furent mors et prins prisonniers, et apres firent une course ou pays et puis sen retournerent, pour ce que ilz aperceurent bien que le dit conte de Warrewyk ne leveroit point le siege quil avoit mis et tenoit devant ladicte ville de Pontorson, aincois avoient ouy nouvelles que les Anglois se assemblerent pour les combatre, ce que lesdiz adversaires ne oserent actendre. Et pour ce que ceulx que estoient dedens ladicte ville de Pontorson virent et congnurent bien que ilz nauroient aucun socour, considerans aussi que vivres leur commencoient a faillir et que lesdiz Anglois leur livrerent chacun jour divers assaulx, traicticrent et composerent avec ledit conte de Warrewyk, cestassavoir que ilz rendirent et delivrerent icelle ville de Pontorson es mains dicellui conte de Warrewyk moyennant quilz sen alerent franchement avecques leurs biens chevaulx et harnoys. Et apres ledit comist commist (sic) gardes et capitaines dicelle ville le sire de Roos et le sire de Talbot et sen retourna devers ledit regent. Et depuis par certain appoinctement qui fut fait de treves et abstinences [6or] de guerre entre ledit regent et le duc de Bretaigne, icelles deux villes et forteresses de Pontorson et Saint James de Beuron furent desemparees. Tantost apres que ledit sire de Rays et autres adversaires qui estoient entrez a puissance oudit conte du Maine, comme vouz avez ouy cy devant, se furent departiz, Christofle Hansson,[145] Phelipe Goth, Martin Godeffroy eschelleur, et pluseurs autres de la garnison de Saincte Suzanne jusques au nombre de vingt a trente Anglois, alerent a leur adventure, et par ung matin ainsi comme Sire Jaques de Sepeaulx chevalier qui estoit capitaine et garde du chastel de Saint Laurens des Mortiers estoit yssu hors dudit chastel avecques pluseurs Francois et alez en leglise dicellui lieu, estant devant la porte dudit chastel pour ylecques ouyr la messe, et durant le temps que len chantoit icelle messe, les Anglois dessus nommez par subtil moyen entrerent par ladicte porte et prindrent ledit chastel et fut ledit sire Jaques de Sepeaulx capitaine dessus nomme prisonnier dudit Hansson. Et depuis garderent ledit chastel et en fut ordonne garde et capitaine Sire Willam Oldhalle chevalier.

[E[146]] n icellui mesme an cestassavoir environ le moys de [blank][147] Sire Jehan Fastolf chevalier anglois gouverneur desdiz pays d'Anjou et du Maine assembla les gens des garnisons dudit pays et autres gens de guerre de sa Retenue et mist le

_____

145   A paragraph mark in left-hand margin.
146   Small letter 'e' at top left-hand corner of the space left for the initial.
147   In right-hand margin note in later hand '4 H6'.

siege devant le chastel et forteresse de Saint Ouen d'Estais pres la ville de Laval, dont estoit capitaine pour les Francois Sire Guillaume d'Orenge chevalier, lequel au bout de huit jours rendi (sic) audit Fastolf ladicte forteresse par composicion tele que [deleted: il] lui et tous ceulx qui estoient dedens, excepte qui estoit diffamateur et avoit dit pluseurs iniurieuses parolles dont il fut execute auroient leurs vies sauves, et fut ledit capitaine prisonnier.

Et dilecques icellui Fastolf party et ala mectre le siege devant le chastel de la Gravelle. Et au bout de huit jours ceulx qui estoient dedens firent composicion de rendre ladicte forteresse dedens certain jour, ou cas que ilz ne seroient secouruz et que lesdiz adversaires ne se trouveroient les plus devant ladicte place audit jour. Et de ce tenir et acomplir iceulx [60v] adversaires baillerent et delivrerent pleiges et hostaiges, cestassavoir Guillaume de Cordouen et Jehan de la Maisiere escuiers, lesquelx prins et receuz par ledit Fastolf, il se party de devant ladicte place et ala devers ledit monseigneur le regent et lui fist savoir ledit appoinctement et composicion. Pour quoy icellui monseigneur le regent fist armee pour aler audit jour mis et assigne pour combatre ou rendre ladicte place et en sa compaignie estoient, cestassavoir Le conte de Mortaing

Le sire de Roos

Le sire de Talbot

Sire Jehan Fastolf

Sire Jehan Montgommery

Sire Jehan Popham

Sire Willam Oldhall

Sire Thomas Blunt

Sire Nicole Bourdet

[added by later hand: Sire Phillippe Halle

Sire Jehan de Aubemond

Sire Jehan Radclyff]

et pluseurs autres jusques au nombre de vingt mil hommes de guerre ou environ. Et chevaucha jusques a labbaye de [space for name left blank] en esperance de combatre lesdiz adversaires, lesquelx comme len disoit estoient assemblez a grant puissance, mais ce non obstant, iceulx adversaires ne comparurent point audit jour. Et pour ce monditseigneur le regent envoya ledit Fastolf pour recevoir ladicte forteresse comme appoinctie et promis avoit este. Mais lesdiz adversaires qui dedens estoient, sestoient tresfort pouveuz de vivres, parquoy en alant contre leurs appoinctements et promesses et en abandonnant leursdiz pleiges et hostaiges, furent du tout reffusans dicelle deliverer, et pour ce par lordonnance dicellui monseigneur le regent, lesdiz hostaiges furent decapitez devant et voyans ceulx de ladicte place. Et ce fait monditseigneur le regent a tout son host retourna sans autre chose faire.

[61r] [A[148]] pres lequel retour dicellui monseigneur le regent, cestassavoir environ la feste saint michiel ou dit an mil cccc xxvi, ledit Sire Jehan Fastolf fut deschargie du gouvernement quil avoit desdiz pays d'Anjou et du Maine et en son lieu y fut commis le sire de Talbot, lequel ou temps de karesme ensuivant fist une entreprinse secrete, et dicelle entreprinse print et gaigna par emblee deschielle la ville de Laval, mais le sire de Loheac et pluseurs nobles et bourgois de ladicte ville se

---

[148] A small 'a' is noted in the top left of the space left for the initial letter.

retrayrent dedens le chastel et icellui tindrent par quatre jours ou environ, durant lequel temps ils traictierent et appoincterent avecques ledit sire de Talbot, cestassavoir que ledit sire de Loheac et touz les autres nobles gens de guerre, bourgois et autres qui estoient retraiz dedens icellui chastel sen yroient franchement en payant la somme de vingt mil escuz pour toutes choses, et icellui chastel delivre comme dit est icellui sire de Talbot commist et ordonna garde et capitaine dicellui et de ladicte ville Sire Guillebert de Halsall chevalier, lequel en fut capitaine et garde jusques au temps que le siege estoit devant la cite d'Orleans, ouquel il fut occis ['au' cancelled]. Et apres en fut ordonne capitaine et garde Matheu Goth escuier qui en ot la garde jusques au temps de la journee devant Senlis dont mencion sera faicte cy apres. Ouquel temps ledit Matheu goth estant aladicte journee par le moyen et trayson de ung traitre monnyer qui gardoit ung moulin joingnant les murs dudit lieu de Laval, lesdiz adversaires entrerent dedens ladicte ville et icelle gaignerent et mistrent en leur obeissance.

[E[149]] n lannee mil cccc vingt sept environ la feste[150] de penthecouste, les adversaires firent une grosse entreprise secrete et se assemblerent au nombre de six mil hommes de guerre ou estoient les seigneurs qui ['en' cancelled] ensuivent, cestassavoir
Le sire de Labret   } mareschaulx de France
Le sire de la Fayete   }
[61v] Le sire de Mont Jehan
Le sire de Bueil
Le sire d'Orval
Le sire de Tusse
Le sire de Beaumanoir
La Hyre
Regnault Guillaume son frere
et pluseurs autres, et par laide et trayson daucuns des gens deglise et bourgois de la cite du Mans, iceulx adversaires entrerent et gaignerent icelle cite par ung [blank]. Mais les Anglois qui estoient dedens icelle cite se retrayrent dedens le chastel que nouvellement len ediffioit, et dont estoit lieutenant et garde Thomas Gower, et se deffendirent moult puissamment et vaillamment contre lesdiz adversaires qui toute la journee du [blank] prochain ensuivant leur avoient divers fors et merveilleux assaulx et telement que plus des deux pars diceulx Anglois estoient bleciez et navrez du trait desdiz Francois et estoient en adventure davoir este prins le lendemain neust este que nouvelles vindrent audit sire de Talbot de ladicte prinse lequel hastivement assembla les souldoyers de la garnison dont estoit capitaine et autres denviron, ou estoient, cestassavoir
Le sire de Scales
Sire Thomas Blount
Sire Thomas Rampston
Sire William Oldhalle
Mathew Goth
Willam Glasdalle
Olivier of Batyrsby
Osberne Mundeford

Nicolas Molyneux

Thomas Lound

et pluseurs autres au nombre de sept cens hommes de fait, et de nuyt partirent dudit lieu d'Alencon et chevaucherent jusques a ung chastel a deux lieues pres ladicte cite du Mans nomme la Guierche, et ylecques ledit sire de Talbot commanda audit Mathew Goth [62r] quil chevauchast devant priveement, et espiast le gouverment desdiz adversaires, ['leq' cancelled] et il yroit tout bellement apres lui, et que ilz se rencontrassent sur le chemyn pour lui dire ce quil auroit trouve, lequel pour executer le commandement a lui fait comme dit est, chevaucha devant et saigement sans ce quil fust apperceu ne congneu par iceulx adversaires, au plus matin tantost apres le point du jour, entra oudit chastel du Mans, parla audit Thomas Gower qui lui dist le gouverment (sic) desdiz adversaires qui estoient dedens ladicte ville, et apres que icellui Matheu ot mengie un mors de pain et beu une foiz, il sen party et vint rencontrer ledit sire de Talbot et ledit sire de Scales environ a ung mille pres la dicte [blot: ville?], et lui dist et compta tout ce quil avoit trouve. Et incontinent lesdiz seigneurs et leur compaignie descendirent a pie et vindrent et entrerent dedens icellui chastel, et par icellui entrerent environ leure de cinq heures du matin dedens ladicte cite du Mans, et commencerent acrier a haulte voix Notre Dame Saint George A monseigneur de Talbot. Laquelle chose oyans lesdiz Francois qui estoient encores couchiez dedens leurs lits, furent touz espoventez et se leverent hastivement, et commencerent a eulx en fuyr, les ungs touz nuz en leurs chemyses, sailloient oultre les murs, les autres sen fuyoient parmy les portes,[151] et sauvoient leurs vies au mieulx que ils povoient et habandonnerent leurs vestemens chevaulx harnoys ordonnances et artilleries, et diceulx Francois en celluy recouvrement et victorieuse destrousse furent desdiz Francois mors et prins prisonniers environ trois a quatre cens.

[T[152]] antost apres, cestassavoir environ la feste de la Nativite Saint Jehan Baptiste, ledit monseigneur le regent fist mectre le siege devant la ville de Montargis dung coste et dautre de la riviere qui passe par ylecques qui est nommee [blank]. Et dicellui bailla la charge et gouvernement au conte de Suffolk, et a Sire Jehan de la [62v] de la (sic) Pole son frere au nombre de six mil hommes de guerre ou environ. Et oultre monditseigneur le regent commanda audit conte de Warewyk qui estoit son lieutenant general pour estre a certain nombre de gens a Saint Mathelin de Larchamp, a fin de renforcier ledit siege si mestier en estoit, et les Francois deussent venir pour donner secour a ceulx qui estoient dedens. Et apres ce que ledit siege ot dure par lespace de deux moys ou environ les Francois, cestassavoir

Le sire de Boussac mareschal de France

La Hyre

Ponton de Sentrailles

et pluseurs autres au nombre de trois mil hommes de fait ou environ chevaucherent le plus secretement que ilz peurent vers ledit siege. Et de la partie dont ledit Sire Jehan de la Pole avoit le gouvernement, trouverent les Anglois en desarroy par faulte de bon guet et par ['la' cancelled] negligence et paresce dudit Sire Jehan de la Poole,[153] frapperent sur eulx et les mistrent en fuyte, et en tuerent et prindrent

---

[151]   In right-hand margin in a later hand 'La citie de mans recouvre par angloys'.

[152]   Small letter 't' at top left-hand corner of the space left for the initial.

[153]   In left-hand margin in a later hand 'pereient par neglience deux mil anglois'.

prisonniers jusques au nombre de deux mil Anglois ou environ, et ledit sire Jehan
de la Poole passa la riviere sur ung cheval vers lautre partie dudit siege ou estoit
ledit conte de Suffolk son frere, et par ce moyen fut a grant peine sauva. Et ledit
conte de Warrewyk, tantost quil ouyt nouvelles de la venue desdiz Francois, party
dudit lieu de Saint Mathelin de Larchamp, et hastivement se vint joyndre audit
siege, et a grant peine ralya lesdiz Anglois et offry donner bataille ausdiz Francois lesquelx estoient desia retraiz dedens ladicte ville de Montargis, mais iceulx
Francois reffuserent ladicte bataille. Et ce voyans lesdiz seigneurs anglois, et que
autre chose ilz ne povoient faire pour ledit temps leverent et rompirent ledit siege,
sen partyrent et retrayrent et laisserent et perdirent toutes les ordonnances quilz
avoient menees en icellui siege et sen retournerent devers icellui monseigneur le
regent.

[63r] [L¹⁵⁴] an de grace mil quatrecens vingt huit¹⁵⁵ environ la feste de Penthecouste, le conte de Salysbury, comme lieutenant du roy d'Angleterre et de France
a notable armee de sept mil hommes ou environ, passa la mer et descendi a Calais.
Et dillecques passa par le pays de Picardie tendant son chemyn vers la cite de Paris
en laquelle ledit monseigneur le regent estoit pour le temps. Et apres quilz eurent
parle ensemble, ledit conte avecques son armee party de Paris et ala mectre le siege
devant les ville et chastel de Yainville¹⁵⁶ en Beausse, et au bout de quinze jours
apres fist assaillir ladicte ville, et par force et dudit assault la prist et conquist. Mais
les Francois se retrayrent dedens ledit chastel et le plus que ilz porent se defendirent. Et au bout de autres quinze jours lesdiz Francois qui estoient dedens ledit
chastel rendirent et delivrerent eulx et ledit chastel a la voulente dicellui conte,
lequel pour certaines causes en fist une partie diceulx mourir et lautre partie furent
touz prisonniers. Apres incontinent ledit conte ala mectre le siege devant la ville
de Baugency et dura ledit siege pour quinze jours ou environ, durant lequel temps
ceulx dedens ladicte ville traicterent et composerent avecques icellui conte, cestassavoir que ilz rendirent icelle ville moyennant que touz ceulx demourerent en
lobeissance de Anglois ourent leurs vies et touz leurs biens et heritaiges sauves. Et
dillecques ala devant Meun sur Loire mais ceulx dedens se rendirent incontinent
par sembable composicion comme ceulx dudit lieu de Baugency. Et pareillement
se rendirent ceulx de la ville de Jargueau. Et quant ledit conte avoit mis capitaines
et gardes es villes et places dessusdictes,¹⁵⁷ cestassavoir ou moys de Septembre
oudit an mil iiijᶜ xxviij, icellui conte mist le siege devant la cite d'Orleans de lun des
costez dicelle seulement, dedens laquelle estoient capitaines et gouverneurs principaulx le bastart d'Orleans, et l'evesque dudit lieu, qui avoient soubz eulx grant
nombre de gens de guerre tant Francois comme Escossoys. Et apres que ledit siege
ot este devant ladicte cite par lespace de [blank] ou environ, ceulx dedens firent
une saillye par le pont dicelle et vindrent escarmucher contre les Anglois [63v]
lesquelx les receuvent moult bien et vaillament se combatirent ensemble dune
part et dautre. Mais en la fin lesdiz Francois ne pouvoient plus porter le faitz et
charge desdiz Anglois et commencerent a eulx desconfire et tourner en fuyte vers
ledit pont pour eulx sauver, mais lesdiz Anglois les poursuirent de si pres occians

---

¹⁵⁴ A small 'I' at top left-hand corner of space left for the initial.
¹⁵⁵ In right-hand margin in a later hand '1428'.
¹⁵⁶ In right-hand margin in a later hand 'yanvile prise'.
¹⁵⁷ In right-hand margin in a later hand 'sege d'orlians'.

que ilz entrent ensemble dedens le boulouerk dudit pont, lequel avecques latour qui estoit au bout dicellui pont fut gaignee par lesdiz Anglois, et pluseurs desdiz Francois occis et prins prisonniers, et ce fait ledit conte comist et ordonna capitaine et garde diceulx tour et boulouerk, Willam Glasdall escuier. Assez tost et dedens peu de temps apres le prinse et conqueste faicte dicelle tour, en laquelle entre autres chambres avoit une chambre qui avoit une fenestre barree de barreaulx de fer, par laquelle len povoit veoir tout au long dudit pont et dedens ladicte cite, et pour pluseurs seigneurs et autres Anglois souventeffoiz aloient en icelle fenestre pour regarder et veoir dedens ladicte ville, parquoy ceulx de dedens qui en estoient desplaisans firent par ung des maistres canonniers dicelle assorter ung canon tout droit contre ladicte fenestre et pour tirer contre icelle quant mestier leur seroit. Advint ung jour a heure de disner ou environ que ledit conte de Salysbury, Sire Thomas Gargrave,[158] ledit Glasdalle et pluseurs autres vindrent en ladicte tour et entrerent en ladicte chambre, et ledit conte ala droit a ladicte fenestre et commença a regarder vers et dedens ladicte ville. Et incontinent le filz dudit maistre canonnier apperceut quil y avoit gens en icelle fenestre si print le feu, et ainsi comme son pere lui avoit monstre et commande quant il estoit ale a son disner, mist le feu oudit canon et tira une pierre tout droit contre icelle fenestre et rompy les barreaulx de fer, et de ung diceulx ou de ung esclat de ladicte pierre fut icellui conte frappe par la teste tellement et si piteusement que il emporta ung de ses yeulx et rompy un quartier du test jusques ['a la' cancelled] au cervel, et pareillement ledit sire Thomas Gargrave fut pareillement atteynt dun autre esclat tellement que dedens deux jours apres il trespassa. Et ledit conte [64r] fut emporte a Meun sur Loire, auquel lieu il fut malade par lespace de huit jours ou environ, pendant lequel temps il ordonna et disposa pour le salut de son ame comme ung bon vray crestien, receut touz les sacremens de saincte eglise et le vray corps nostre seigneur, et apres rendi son esperit a dieu le pere et a Ihesucrist son filz.

[C[159]] es nouvelles tresdouloureuses venues devers ledit monseigneur le regent de la mort de si tresnoble victorieux et vaillant seigneur, dont ne fait pas a merveillier se il en avoit grant douleur et desplaisance a son cuer, icellui monseigneur le regent commist et ordonna leutenant general pour le roy et pour luy le conte de Suffolk, lequel estoit audit siege et dicellui siege et de toute larmee le fist chief capitaine et lui en bailla la charge et gouvernement et conduite. Et pour reconforter et renforcer icellui siege envoya cestassavoir
Le sire de Talbot
Le sire de Scalles
Sire Jehan Fastolf
Sire Thomas Rampston
Sire Raoul de Neville
Sire Guylbert de Halsalle
Sire Lancelot de Lisle
Sire Henry Byset
[added by later hand: Sire Henry Mortymer]

---

[158]   In left-hand margin in a later hand 'cont de Sallysbure sire Thomas Gargrave tues de ung cannon'.
[159]   A small letter 'c' at top left-hand corner of space left for the initial.

et pluseurs autres a notable armee, lesquelz continuerent ledit siege et oultre firent faire et asseoir pluseurs bastilles tout autour devant les portes dicelle cite, pour destreindre ceulx dedens. Et environ le temps de Karesme ensuivant,[160] pour ce que vivres et artilleries commencoient a faillir oudit siege, fut appoinctie et ordonne que Sire Jehan Fastolf et Sire Thomas Rampston avec leurs gens yroient devers ledit regent a Paris pour querir et leur admener oudit siege des vivres et artilleries, lesquelz [64v] venuz et arrivez audit lieu de Paris, par lordonnance dudit monseigneur le regent firent chargier grant nombre de vivres tant blez farines harencs et autres comme artilleries, sur chariotz, charrectes et chevaulx. Et pour iceulx mener et conduire plus seurement audit siege, ordonna Sire Simon Morhier[161] chevalier prevost de Paris, avec lui les arbalestriers de la cinquantaine de Paris, et une partie des gens du propre hostel dicellui monseigneur le regent por aler avecques lesdiz Fastolf et Rampston conduire iceulx vivres jusques audit siege, lesquelz partirent touz ensemble jusques au nombre de quinze cens hommes de guerre ou environ, et alerent avecques leursdiz vivres jusques a Yaynville en Beausse. Et ung matin quil avoit tresfort gele et faisoit grant froit, partirent dudit lieu de Yainville tendans leur chemin vers ledit siege. Et comme ilz furent alez jusques environ ung village nomme Rouvroy, en unes grans landes, apperceurent les Francois adversaires ['venir' cancelled] de loings venir alencontre de eulx, et estoient bien en nombre tant Francois comme Escossoys de [written in gap but probably in the main hand: neuf a dix] mille ou environ, ou estoient les seigneurs et autres nobles dont les noms en partie sensuivent, cestassavoir

Sire Charles de Bourbon filz ainsne du duc de Bourbon
Sire Willam Styward connestable d'Escoce
Le conte de Perdriac
Le bastard d'Orleans
Sire Jehan de Vendosme vidame de Chartres
Le sire de Touars
Le sire Loheac
L'evesque d'Orleans
Le sire de L'Esgle
Le sire de Beauvau
Le sire de Tusse
Le sire de Maylly
Le sire d'Orval
Le bastart de la Tremoille
Jehan de la Roche
La Hyre et ses freres
Poton de Sentrailles
[65r] Ferrebourg capitaine
Le bourg de Bar
Pierres Jaillet
Blanchefort
Henry de Villeblanche
Le bastart de Vendosme
Pevot capitaine

---

[160] Doodle in left-hand margin at end of line.
[161] In left-hand margin in a later hand 'nota Morhier'.

Stevenot de Talloche
Sire Jehan Fourquault
Sire Guillaume de Lyons
Sire Robert de Savoye
Gaultier de Brysac
Sire Pierre Brysac
Sire Pierre de Beauvau
Sire Ambroys de Lore
Le sire de Bourg Guerart
Le sire de Bueil
Pierre de Champaigne
Sire Pierre de Berouille
Kannedey escossoyes
Le bourg de Maskernam
Le bourg de Cornylliam
Sire Thuault de Valperungue lombart
Sire Giles de Saint Simon
Le sire de Chabannes
Roberton de Croix
Pregent de Coityvy
Guillaume Bourgois

[65v] et pluseurs autres.[162] Pourquoy ledit Fastolf ordonna et mist tous les Anglois et autres de sa compaignie en bataille, et fist planter devant chacun archier ung pal agu pour rompre la force des chevaulx a larriver des adversaires et derriere fist mectre enclaver et lyer touz les chevaulx et charroiz quilz avoient admenez avecques eulx, et ylecques actendirent la venue desdiz adversaires qui vindrent et assaillirent lesdiz Anglois dedens ledit cloz quilz avoient ainsi fait comme dit est, mais iceulx Anglois se deffendirent moult viguereusement et vaillamment, et tellement que lesdiz Francois se desconfirent et retrayrent et honteusement perdirent le champ et sen fuyrent. Et acelle noble victoire et destrousse furent occis, cestassavoir

Ledit Sire Willam Styward connestable d'Escoce [added in later hand: et son frere
Le sire d'Orvall
Le sire de Chateauberry
Messire Jehan Lesgott]

et pluseurs autres tant Francois comme Escossoys jusques au nombre de [added in later hand: xxv^c] ou environ. Apres laquelle noble et glorieuse victoire icellui Sire Jehan Fastolf et touz ceulx de sa compaignie, dont aucun ne fut occis ne navre dont il doyt estre fait mencion, partirent avecques leurs vivres et autres artilleries, et sen alerent audit siege, ouquel par ledit conte de suffolk et autres seigneurs ilz furent receuz notablement a grant joye et honneur. Apres laquelle victorieuse destrousse, ledit siege fut tenu et continue jusques apres la feste de Pasques commencans lan de grace mil iiij^c xxix, tousiours faisans grans et merveilleuses escarmuches ['aussi' cancelled] assaulx et autres faiz de guerre les ungs contre les autres. Et jusques ou moys de may oudit ouquel temps lesdiz adversaires a tresgrant puissance et ou estoient les seigneurs et [66r] autres chevaliers escuiers et nobles dont de partie diceulx les noms sensuivent, cestassavoir
[added in later hand: le duc d'Alanson

---

162   In left-hand margin in a later hand, 'Le Bataille de Harenk'.

Le bastard d'Orleans
La Pucell
Le Hyre
Le sire de Rays
Le sire de Lorese
messyre ['Rob' cancelled] Robert Bodrycort capytayne ['ess' cancelled] Vawcolour]

[Added in a later hand, not same hand as previous entries: Memorandum in the yere of our lord god m^l iiij^c l the laste day of July was Cherbourg the laste toune in Normandy delivered to Thomas Gonell in the tyme of kinge Henry the vjth

The contree of Normandy conteniethe in lengthe vj journayes and iiij in bredethe and there ys in yt a hundreth tounes and stronge castelles, there be vij cittees and v bishoprekes and tharchbishoprecke of Rouen. In the last conquest reigned in Fraunce kinge Charles the viith.

Anno domini m^l iiij^c xl Charles duke of Orliannce was delivered oute of pryson in englond, who was presonner xxv yeres, and he payde for his rauncon iiij^c m^l crounes.]

English translation, identifications and commentary

(31r) This book concerning deeds of arms in the conquest of the kingdom of France, the duchy of Normandy, the duchy of Alençon, the duchy of Anjou and Maine and many other counties was compiled for the noble man John Fastolf, baron of Sillé-le-Guillaume [in the year of Christ 1459, the year in which he died] by Peter Basset esquire, of the English nation, who followed the pursuit of arms in France under [the victorious prince] King Henry V [and by Christopher Hanson of the country of Germany, at one time with Thomas Beaufort, duke of Exeter, and Luket Nantron, native of Paris, one of the clerks of John Fastolf, and by the diligence of William Worcester, secretary of the same John Fastolf] and under John, duke of Bedford, Regent of the kingdom of France, and of other principal lieutenants under King Henry VI, for thirty-five years in total.

In the year of grace 1415, between the feasts of Michaelmas (29 September) and All Saints (11 November), the most noble and victorious prince, Henry, king of England and of France, fifth of that name, took and conquered the town of Harfleur.[1] Surrender was made to him by the principal captain of the place the lord of Gaucourt,[2] and by the lord of Estouteville,[3] Pierre de Gausseville knight,[4] *Jacques de Hermanville knight, Jean de Typtot knight, Henri Chamboy knight,*[5] knights,

---

[1]   Seine-Maritime, arr. Le Havre, cant. Le Havre 2. A treaty was agreed on 18 September 1415 for surrender on the 22nd. The text is no longer extant but its terms are noted in several chronicles and in a letter which the king sent to London on 22 September (Curry, *Agincourt. A New History*, pp. 90–2).

[2]   Raoul de Gaucourt (c. 1371–1462), lord of Gaucourt, Hargicourt and Maisons-sur-Seine, chamberlain of the dukes of Orléans and first chamberlain of Charles VII between 1437 and 1453, was prominent in the defence of Harfleur. He, together with sixteen others from the garrison, including Jean d'Estouteville, were taken to England as prisoners by the end of the year (E 404/34/260 A, B). Gaucourt and Estouteville regained their freedom in 1425 through a complex operation involving the payment of a ransom and the liberation of the earl of Huntingdon (SC 8/85/4229; *PROME*, x, pp. 172–3; BL, Add. Ch. 3594; Gonzales, pp. 253–6; Ambühl, *Prisoners*, pp. 72–5, 155–6).

[3]   Jean II, lord of Estouteville (d. 1435), 'écuyer échançon' of Charles VI, was, according to Burgundian chroniclers, captain of Harfleur in 1415 (Curry, *Agincourt. A New History*, pp. 84–5). He shared the fate of Gaucourt (see preceding note). See also Morandière, *Histoire de la Maison d'Estouteville*, pp. 200–2, 207, 226, 238, 244, 288, 300–1, 330–1.

[4]   Pierre de Gausseville appears as an esquire in the Tabellionage of Rouen in 1409 (Beaurepaire, 'Notes et documents', p. 511). A knight by 1415, he was taken to England in November and remained in captivity in the Tower of London until mid-1417 (E 404/34/260 A, B).

[5]   Surviving sources record the names of twenty-nine men who were taken prisoner at the surrender and sent to England, some in 1415 and others in 1417 after captivity in the castle

sub-captains in the said town under the lord of Gaucourt, and several others, all of whom were taken as prisoners to England. The victorious prince and king ordered and appointed as governor of the town his uncle Thomas Beaufort, duke of Exeter and earl of Dorset,[6] the which duke of Exeter commissioned and established as his lieutenant and keeper therein (31v) Sir John Fastolf with a notable retinue [of fifteen] knights and [thirty-five] esquires and other men of war for the guard, safekeeping and defence of the said town,[7] some of whose names follow, to wit, [the 'baro' of Carew of the county of Devon][8]
Sir Hugh Luttrell[9] [of the county of Somerset]
John Standish esquire[10]
Thomas Lord esquire[11] and several others.

---

of Hammes, but there is no 'Jaques de Hermanville', 'Henry Chamboy' or 'Jean de Typtot' amongst them. The chronicle may have mistaken the latter for Thomassin de Tybutot who was taken to England in 1415 (E 101/47/35; E 404/34/260 A, B; *PPC*, ii, p. 205). Monstrelet (iii, p. 83) mentions a lord of Hermanville among the defenders of Harfleur.

[6] Thomas Beaufort (1377–1426)* was the third son of John of Gaunt by Katherine Swynford. Created earl of Dorset in 1412, he indented for the service of 400 in 1415 (E 101/45/5 m. 1) and was appointed captain of Harfleur at its surrender with a garrison of 1,200 men (*PPC*, ii, pp. 147–8). As a reward for his defence of the town, he was created duke of Exeter in November 1416. He remained captain of Harfleur until February 1420 but was often absent in England or elsewhere in Normandy.

[7] Fastolf*, then an esquire, served on the 1415 campaign with a retinue of forty men within the company of Michael de la Pole senior, earl of Suffolk, but was invalided home after Harfleur fell (E 101/45/5 m. 8d; E 101/50/26; E 101/46/24 m. 3; E 101/44/30 no. 2). Exactly when he returned to the town is uncertain but he appears as a man-at-arms in a muster of the Harfleur garrison covering the period from 31 December 1415 to 1 April 1416 (E 101/47/39) and received a grant of the nearby lordship of Frilense on 29 January 1416, by which time he was a knight (C 76/98 m. 4, DKR 44, p. 577). The accounts of the treasurer of Harfleur show that he held command between 2 March and 30 August 1417 in the absence of the duke of Exeter, holding under his command between March and June 2 knights, 61 mounted and 145 foot men-at-arms and 608 archers, and between June and August 3 knights, 52 mounted and 52 foot men-at-arms and 596 archers (E 101/48/7, ff. 12–12v).

[8] Although domiciled in south Devon, Sir Thomas Carew* (1368–1431) bore the courtesy title 'Baro de Carew' based on his tenure of the castle of Carew in Pembrokeshire, but he was never summoned as a peer to parliament. He was commissioned in February 1415 to patrol the sea in anticipation of the invasion of France but subsequently indented for the land campaign with thirty-six men (E 404/31/385; E 101/45/5 m. 8; E 101/45/21 m. 27; E 101/47/15). Financial records suggest that his whole company was put into the garrison of Harfleur. Thomas was still serving there as a man-at-arms between December 1415 and April 1416 (E 101/47/39; C 76/99 m. 24, DKR 44, p. 581). It is unlikely, but not impossible, that he was present at Agincourt.

[9] Sir Hugh Luttrell (c. 1364–1428) of Dunster (Somerset) does not appear in the surviving records for the 1415 expedition but served in the campaign to save Harfleur in the following year (E 101/48/10/104; E 403/624 m. 4). He was formally appointed lieutenant of Harfleur from 2 August 1417, holding office until February 1420 (E 101/48/7, ff. 13–13v) (HOCa).

[10] A John Standish appears as a man-at-arms on the muster roll of the Harfleur garrison for the period 31 December 1415 to 1 April 1416 (E 101/47/39).

[11] A man of this name can be found serving as a man-at-arms in the garrison of Harfleur from 31 December 1415 to at least the autumn of 1419 (E 101/47/39; E 101/48/6; E 101/48/19). He was involved in the capture of Vittefleur, Blacqueville and Saint-Valery-en-Caux in 1418–19 (E 101/48/7, ff. 8v; C 64/11 m. 17, DKR 41, p. 800).

Since during the time that the victorious prince and king had laid siege before the said town of Harfleur several lords had fallen into great sickness, the king gave them licence to return to England, to wit,

Thomas, duke of Clarence,[12] brother of the king

John, earl Marshal and earl of Nottingham[13]

John (recte, Thomas), earl of Arundel and of Warenne, treasurer of England.[14]

(32r) Once this had been done and other notable statutes and ordinances established and made,[15] the said victorious prince the king, accompanied by princes and lords whose names follow, to wit,

Humphrey, duke of Gloucester,[16] brother of the king,

John (erased: Edward entered by a later hand), duke of York[17]

John, earl of Huntingdon[18]

John (recte, Edmund), earl of March[19]

---

[12]   Thomas, duke of Clarence* (1387–1421), the king's eldest brother, had indented for the service of 960 men in 1415 but, falling ill at the siege, he returned to England in early October with forty-seven of his men (E 404/31/155; E 101/45/5 m. 3; E 101/45/4; E 101/45/1; E 101/44/30 no. 1, m. 1; E 358/6 m. 1).

[13]   John Mowbray, Earl Marshal, earl of Nottingham and Norfolk* (1392–1432), who became duke of Norfolk in 1425, crossed in 1415 with 200 men but was invalided home after Harfleur surrendered (E 404/31/170; E 101/45/5 m. 4d; E 101/45/1; E 101/44/30 no. 1, m. 6; E 101/47/37 and 38).

[14]   Thomas Fitzalan, earl of Arundel* (1381–1415), crossed with 400 men but was invalided home on 28 September and died at Arundel castle on 13 October 1415 (E 404/31/149; E 101/45/5 m. 3d; E 101/44/30 no. 1, m. 8; E 101/45/1; E 101/47/1; E 358/6 m. 2). He had been appointed treasurer when Henry V came to the throne. The Warenne title came from the inheritance by the Fitzalans in 1347 of the earldom of Surrey previously held by the de Warennes, which was therefore often called the earldom of Surrey and Warenne. The error in the first name is presumably explained by confusion with Thomas's cousin and heir, John, lord Maltravers (1385–1421).

[15]   On the ordinances issued by Henry V in 1415 see Curry, 'The Military Ordinances of Henry V', pp. 226–8.

[16]   Humphrey, duke of Gloucester* (1390–1447), the king's youngest brother, had indented for 800 men and was present at Agincourt with at least 507 (E 404/31/250; E 101/45/5 m. 5; E 101/45/13; E 101/44/30 no. 1, mm. 2–5; E 358/6 m. 4).

[17]   Edward, duke of York* (c. 1373–1415) was the son of Edmund (d. 1402), fourth son of Edward III and first duke of York. Indenting for the service of 400 men in 1415, he was killed at Agincourt (E 101/69/4/389; E 404/31/184; E 101/45/5 m. 3; E 101/45/22 m. 3; E 101/45/2; E 101/45/19; E 101/47/40; E358/6 m. 3d). It is unclear why there was authorial confusion over the first name since there was never a Duke John of York.

[18]   John Holland* (1395–1447) was restored in 1416 to the earldom of Huntingdon, which had been lost by his father's rebellion in 1400, and was made KG probably in 1415. He indented in 1415 for eighty men and was present at Agincourt (E 404/31/89; E 101/45/5 m. 1, m. 2d; E 101/45/22 m. 3v; E 101/45/18 m. 2; E 101/44/30 no. 1, m. 9; E 101/45/7; E 358/6 m. 9d).

[19]   Edmund Mortimer, earl of March* (1391–1425), was the great grandson of Lionel, second son of Edward III, making him the focus of plots against the first Lancastrian kings. He was given livery of his lands by Henry V in June 1413 and served on the 1415 expedition with 200 men, being present at Agincourt (E 404/31/169; E 101/45/5 m. 4; E 101/45/20 m. 40; E 101/45/1; E 101/44/30 no. 1, m. 6).

Thomas (recte, Richard), earl of Oxford[20]
Richard (recte, Edward), earl of Devon[21]
William, earl of Suffolk[22]
Gilbert Umfraville, earl of Kyme[23]
John, Lord Roos[24]
Thomas (recte, Robert), Lord Willoughby[25]
John, Lord Clifford[26]
Lord Fitzhugh[27]
Lord Ferrers of Groby[28]
Lord Ferrers of Chartley[29]
Lord Camoys[30]

---

[20]   Richard de Vere, earl of Oxford* (1385–1417), led a retinue in the 1415 army but there is conflicting evidence on its size, between 100 and 140 men (E 404/31/254; E 101/45/5 m. 4; E 101/45/21 m. 13; E 101/44/30 no. 1, m. 7; E 101/46/36; E358/6 m. 8d). There was never an Earl Thomas.

[21]   Edward Courtenay, earl of Devon (1357–1419), was blind and did not participate in the 1415 campaign. There was never an Earl Richard of Devon.

[22]   William de la Pole* (1396–1450), second son of Michael de la Pole senior, earl of Suffolk, served on the 1415 campaign as a man-at-arms in the company of his father but was invalided home after the surrender of Harfleur (E 101/50/26; E 101/46/24, m. 3; E 101/47/33 no. 4, m. 2; E 101/44/30 no. 1, m. 10). He became earl of Suffolk at the death of his elder brother, Michael junior, at Agincourt, and was elevated to marquess in 1444 and duke in 1448.

[23]   Sir Gilbert Umfraville* (1390–1421) was a Northumberland knight who had a putative claim to the Scottish earldom of Kyme in Scotland through descent from the Umfraville earls of Angus and was thereby known by this courtesy title. For the 1415 campaign he indented for the service of 120 and was present at Agincourt (E 101/69/6/480; E 404/31/233; E 101/45/5 m. 5).

[24]   John, lord Roos (or Ros) (c. 1397–1421) of Helmsley (Yorks. NR), crossed with sixty men and was present at Agincourt (E 404/31/32; E 101/45/5 m. 6; E 101/45/21 m. 40).

[25]   Robert, lord Willoughby* (c. 1385–1452) of Eresby (Lincs.), crossed with ninety men and was present at Agincourt (E 404/31/183; E 101/45/5 m. 3; E 358/6 m. 10d; E 101/46/33). The confusion on his first name presumably arises from the service in Normandy of Thomas Willoughby, probably his nephew.

[26]   John, lord Clifford (c. 1389–1422) was a northern lord whose estates included the honour of Skipton (Yorks. WR). He crossed with 120 men and was at Agincourt (E 404/31/358; E 101/45/5 m. 7; E 101/45/1; E 101/44/30 no. 1, m. 12).

[27]   Henry, lord Fitzhugh* (c. 1363–1425) was a northern lord whose base was at Ravensworth castle (Yorks. NR). He crossed with 120 men and was at Agincourt (E 404/31/279; E 101/45/5 m. 2; E 101/45/1; E 101/44/30 no. 1, m. 11).

[28]   William, lord Ferrers of Groby* (Leics.) (1372–1445) is not known to have served on the 1415 campaign.

[29]   Edmund, lord Ferrers of Chartley (Staffs.) (1386–1435) crossed in 1415 with forty-eight men and was present at Agincourt (E 404/31/249; E 101/45/5 m. 2d).

[30]   Thomas, lord Camoys* (c. 1351–1421), whose estates focused on Trotton in West Sussex, was related to the king through his marriage to Elizabeth Mortimer, granddaughter of Lionel, the second son of Edward III. He crossed with ninety men and was present at Agincourt, being assigned, according to the *Gesta Henrici Quinti* (p. 83), command of the rearguard (E 404/31/357; E 101/45/5 m. 5d; E 101/45/21 m. 30; E 101/45/1; E 101/44/30 no. 1, m. 15; E 101/47/13; E 358/6 m. 3).

Lord Bourchier[31]
John (recte, Richard) de Beauchamp, Lord Despenser and Bergavenny and later earl of Worcester[32]
Lord Harington[33]
Baron Carew of Cornwall[34]
[added: the baron of Duddeley][35]
and several others to the number of around 800 lances and 8,500 archers.[36] He left Harfleur and rode overland to Blanquetaque[37] near Saint-Valery-sur-Somme[38] in order to cross over the River Somme, but he found that (32v) the enemy, to the number of 50,000 men of war, were on the other side of the river to prevent his passage. For this reason and also because of the danger of the tides, the victorious prince left Blanquetaque and rode with all his host downstream of the River Somme to *Pont Saint Maxence*[39] in order to cross the river there. There he found the enemy again in large numbers guarding the crossing. As the victorious prince

---

[31] Hugh Stafford, lord Bourchier (d. 1420) was a younger son of Hugh, second earl of Stafford (d. 1386). He was summoned to parliament from 1411 as Lord Bourchier as a result of his marriage to Elizabeth Bourchier (d. 1433), daughter of Bartholomew, lord Bourchier of Halstead (Essex) (d. 1409). In 1415 Hugh crossed with sixty men but both he and his company were placed in garrison at Harfleur and were not present at the battle (E 404/31/152; E 101/45/5 m. 2d; E 101/47/6). His widow later married Lewis Robessart.

[32] This must be Richard Beauchamp, lord Bergavenny (1397–1422), who was created earl of Worcester in February 1421. He was a grandson of Thomas Beauchamp, earl of Warwick (d. 1369), and so half cousin of Richard Beauchamp, earl of Warwick (d. 1439). He had been knighted on the eve of Henry V's coronation and was close to the king. Although no evidence has been found of his presence on the 1415 campaign – it is more likely he was defending the Welsh marches – he was active in military actions against the French from 1416 onwards.

[33] John, lord Harington* (c. 1384–1418), whose lands were mainly in Lancashire but who had come into possession of Porlock (Somerset) by marriage, indented for a company of 120 in 1415 but he was not at Agincourt, being invalided home after Harfleur surrendered (E 404/31/161; E 101/45/5 m. 3; E 101/45/21 m. 12; E 101/44/30 no. 1, m. 13; E 101/46/1; E 101/47/33; E 358/6 m. 5).

[34] Carew's interests lay in Devon but he held a grant from the duchy of Cornwall.

[35] There was no man of this title in 1415. John Sutton* of Dudley (Staffs.) (c. 1401–87) was created Lord Dudley in 1440. Men-at-arms called John Sutton are found in the companies of the dukes of Clarence (E 101/45/4 m. 3) and of Gloucester (E 101/45/13 m. 2) but it is not certain whether either was the later peer, whose service in France can be traced only from 1418.

[36] This is intriguingly close to the figures derived from the financial records of the campaign. See Curry, *Agincourt. A New History*, pp. 113–31.

[37] A crossing point of the River Somme used by Edward III in 1346 at Port-le-Grant (Somme, arr. Abbeville, cant. Abbeville 1).

[38] Somme, arr. Abbeville, ch. l. cant.

[39] This cannot be the modern Pont-Sainte-Maxence which is close to Beauvais (Oise). There is a place called Saint-Maxent (Somme, arr. Abbeville, cant. Gamaches) which lies 16 km south-west of Abbeville but which is not on the Somme, nor is Pont-de-Metz (Somme, arr. Amiens, cant. Amiens 7) which lies south of Amiens. The most likely location intended is Pont-Rémy (Somme, arr. Abbeville, cant. Rue) which was an ancient crossing point of the river 11 km to the south-east of Abbeville.

thought that he might have battle there he made several knights, some of whose names follow, to wit,
John (recte, William), Lord Ferrers of Groby[40]
Ralph Greystoke[41]
Peter Tempest[42]
Christopher Moresby[43]
Thomas Pickering[44]
William Hoddleston[45]
John Osbaldeston[46]
[John Mortimer[47]

---

[40]   William, lord Ferrers of Groby (1372–1445) is not known to have served on the 1415 campaign, nor is a John Ferrers of Groby known; William's sons were Henry and Thomas.

[41]   A Sir Ralph Greystoke served as a knight in the army of 1417 in the retinue of Richard Beauchamp, earl of Warwick (E 101/51/2 m. 12), but there is no other evidence of service in 1415. Ralph, third baron Greystoke (1353–1418), with estates in Yorkshire and Cumberland, is rather too old to have been knighted in 1415 and cannot be found on the campaign, nor can his heir John (d. 1436).

[42]   A presence on the 1415 campaign is not otherwise evidenced but on the 1417 expedition a Sir Peter Tempest served under John, lord Clifford (E 101/51/2 m. 21). His identity remains unknown.

[43]   No man of this name has been found in the surviving records of the 1415 campaign but this is presumably Sir Christopher Moresby who served as a knight in the retinue of John, lord Clifford in the 1417 expedition (E 101/51/2 m. 21). An earlier link with Lord Clifford is indicated by his serving as feoffee for lands in Westmorland and Yorkshire, including the honour of Skipton in May 1415 (CPR 1413–16, p. 320). Sir Christopher is found active in Westmorland in the late 1420s and early 1430s, as well as being sheriff of Cumberland in 1429 (CPR 1422–29, p. 405; CPR 1429–36, pp. 40, 71, 361), but no service in France after 1417 is known.

[44]   We find two archers called Thomas Pykeryng in the company of the duke of Gloucester in 1415 (E 101/45/13 m. 2, 3d). A Thomas Pykering is found as a man-at-arms in the company of John, lord Roos in the 1417 expedition (E 101/51/2 m. 44). But no knight of this name has been identified.

[45]   William Hoddleston (or Hodilston) (1365–1422) of Copeland (Cumb.) served on the 1415 campaign in the royal household (E 101/69/6/471; E 404/31/292; E 101/407/10 m. 1; E 101/45/18 m. 7). That he was knighted is confirmed by his status in the 1416 campaign for the rescue of Harfleur (E 101/48/10/133; E 403/624 m. 4).

[46]   John Osbaldeston esquire indented for the 1415 campaign with four other esquires, probably within the royal household, each providing two archers (E 101/45/5 m. 1d). He is given as a knight on the late sixteenth-century Agincourt Roll, suggesting that he had indeed been knighted during the campaign (BL, Harley 782, f. 83). He led a retinue on the 1417 expedition (C 76/100, m. 21, DKR 44, p. 593). He was a younger son of the family which took its name from Osbaldeston (Lancs.) but established himself in Chadlington (Oxon) (Longford, 'Some Notes on the Family of Osbaldeston', p. 75).

[47]   A John Mortimer took out letters of protection in 1415 in the company of Sir John Baskerville (C 76/98, m. 17, 19, DKR 44, p. 566). A Sir John Mortimer appears in the post-campaign retinue roll of the earl of Arundel (E 101/47/1 m. 1). Presumably the knight of this name (b. c. 1378) who was executed for treason in 1424 is intended here, although this identification is uncertain.

Philip Hall[48]   }
William Hall[49]   } brothers
James Ormond[50]]
and several others, but the enemy did not give or deliver battle at the said place. So the victorious prince left that place with all his host and rode on without having any battle until he came within a league of the city of Amiens[51] to a town near a castle called Boves,[52] where he lodged for two days. Afterwards he crossed the River Somme two leagues from the town of Péronne,[53] and rode on past that town towards the River Soudon[54] as far as a castle called Azincourt,[55] at which place he heard definite news that the enemy (33r) to the number of 150,000 men of war had come to give battle against him. So the victorious prince made his deployments and prepared to give battle. On the vigil of the feast of Saints Crispin and Crispinian in the year 1415 the enemy gave battle, in which the victorious prince and king had honour and victory. Of the enemy were killed or taken prisoner in the battle the princes and lords whose names follow:
First, [Johan cancelled] Charles, duke of Orléans, nephew of King Charles VI, prisoner[56]
John, count of Alençon, newly made duke of Alençon, dead[57]
the duke of Bourbon, prisoner[58]
the duke of Brabant, dead[59]
the duke of Cleves, dead[60]

---

[48]   Other than a Philip Hall serving as an archer in the 1440s no man-at-arms or knight of this name has been found in the surviving military records.
[49]   There are a number of William Halls serving in the fifteenth century, including a man who took out in June 1415 letters of protection to cross in the retinue of the earl of March (C 76/98, m. 16, DKR 44, p. 567) and another who served as a man-at-arms in the company of Lord Maltravers in the 1417 expedition (E 101/51/2 m. 36), but no knight of this name has been found.
[50]   The identity here is uncertain. James Butler* (1390–1452), who inherited the earldom of Ormond in 1405, is not known to have served in 1415 although he is found in France from 1418.
[51]   Somme, ch. l. d'arr.
[52]   Somme, arr. Amiens, cant. Amiens 5.
[53]   Somme, ch. l. d'arr.
[54]   There is no river of this name. The village of Sourdon (Somme, arr. Montdidier, cant. Ailly-sur-Noye) lies 16 km south of Amiens. The river intended is presumably the River Ternoise, which the author of the *Gesta Henrici Quinti* (pp. 76–7) calls 'fluvium gladiorum', translated by the editors as the 'River of Swords'.
[55]   Pas-de-Calais, arr. Montreuil, cant. Auxi-le Château.
[56]   Charles, duke of Orléans (1391–1466), nephew of Charles VI, spent the next twenty-five years of his life in captivity in England, being released in 1440 in return for the payment of a ransom of 240,000 écus (Champion, *Vie de Charles d'Orléans*, esp. pp. 133–313).
[57]   Jean I's (1385–1415) *comté* of Alençon had been elevated to a *duché-pairie* in 1414.
[58]   Jean I, duke of Bourbon (1381–1434) died in captivity in England in 1434 (Leguai, 'Le problème des rançons', pp. 41–58).
[59]   Anthony, duke of Brabant (1384–1415), eldest brother of John the Fearless, duke of Burgundy, arrived late at the battle and was killed (Boffa, 'Antoine de Bourgogne', pp. 255–85).
[60]   Adolph, count of Cleves (1373–1448) was a German prince within the alliance network of the dukes of Burgundy (Schnerb, *État bourguignon*, pp. 144 and 279), but Cleves was not a duchy until 1417 and there is no evidence he was present at Agincourt.

the duke of Bavaria, dead[61]
the count of Nevers and Rethel, dead[62]
the count of Namur, dead[63]
the count of Hainault, dead[64]
the count of Foix, dead[65]
the count of Astarac, dead[66]
the count of Eu, prisoner[67]
the count of Vendôme, prisoner[68]
Arthur of Brittany, count of Richemont, prisoner[69]
the count of Tancarville, dead[70]
the lord of Rambures[71]   }
the lord of Gamaches[72]   }

[61]   Presumably Louis VII (c. 1368–1447), duke of Bavaria (1413) and brother of the French queen Isabeau of Bavaria, is intended, but he was not at Agincourt.
[62]   Philip (1389–1415), count of Nevers and Rethel, youngest brother of John the Fearless, duke of Burgundy, was knighted by Boucicaut not long before the battle in which he died (Belleval, p. 236).
[63]   Guillaume II of Flanders (1355–1418), count of Namur, was not present at Agincourt (Uyttebrouck, *Le gouvernement du duché de Brabant*, ii, p. 714, no. 175; and see Balon, *La Maison de Namur*).
[64]   Guillaume IV of Bavaria (1365–1417), count of Hainaut, Holland and Zeeland, was a German prince within the alliance network of the dukes of Burgundy (*Cour amoureuse*, i, p. 49), but was not present at Agincourt.
[65]   Jean I (1382–1436), son of Archambaud de Grailly, became count of Foix at the death of his father in 1412 or 1413 (Flourac, *Jean Ier, comte de Foix*). His allegiance was wavering between the French and English at the time of Agincourt. He did not take part in the battle.
[66]   Jean II, count of Astarac (d. 1458), a Gascon lord, served the king of France from the mid-1420s, being councillor and chamberlain of Charles VII in 1426, but his presence at Agincourt is unlikely (Anselme, ii, p. 619; Gaussin, 'Les conseillers de Charles VII', p. 106).
[67]   Charles d'Artois, count of Eu (1394–1472), was captured and taken to England. He regained his freedom in 1438 through a complex operation involving the liberation of John Beaufort, earl of Somerset, who was captured at Baugé in 1421 (Ambühl, *Prisoners*, pp. 66–70).
[68]   Louis de Bourbon (1376–1446), count of Vendôme, was taken as prisoner to England. He agreed to pay a ransom of 100,000 écus in 1417 (*Foedera*, ix, p. 442), but being unable to meet the costs, he was eventually released in 1426 through an exchange with John Holland, earl of Huntingdon, who was captured at Baugé.
[69]   Arthur (1393–1458), count of Richemont, was a younger brother of Jean V, duke of Brittany and son of Joan of Navarre, who had become queen of England by her second marriage to Henry IV in 1403. He was released on parole in 1420 and subsequently served the English as part of a deal which involved the two brothers swearing obedience to the treaty of Troyes (Cosneau, pp. 57–69).
[70]   The Norman, Guillaume IV, count of Tancarville (d. 1415), vicomte of Melun, had had a long military and diplomatic career in French royal service before Agincourt where he lost his life (Anselme, viii, p. 553; *Cour amoureuse*, no. 17).
[71]   David de Rambures (d. 1415), a knight from Picardy, was initially attached to the duke of Burgundy but later became a faithful servant of Charles VI and the Dauphin Louis, duke of Guyenne, who made him grand master of the crossbowmen in 1412. He was sent, together with the lord of Longroy, to defend the borders of the Calaisis in 1415 because it was believed that Henry V would land at Calais. Rambures and his three sons died at Agincourt (Belleval, pp. 244–5).
[72]   Guillaume II, lord of Gamaches (d. 1441), knight, councillor and chamberlain of Charles VI and Louis, duke of Guyenne, was made 'maître veneur et de gouverneur de la vènerie' in 1410. In reward for his past services, the king helped him to pay his Agincourt

the lord of Torcy[73] }
the lord of La Heuze[74] }
the lord of Avrichier[75] } dead
the lord of Mauny[76] }
the lord of Heugueville[77] }
the lord of Préaulx[78] }
the lord of Fontaines[79] }
the lord of Ferrières and Chambrais[80] }

---

ransom in April 1417 and appointed him *bailli* of Rouen four months later. He was captain of Compiègne in July 1418 but surrendered the town to the English in 1422. The chronicle makes no mention of the first English capture of Compiègne (but does emphasise the second English capture which involved a prisoner of Fastolf), nor does it allude to Gamaches's capture at Cravant, which is noted in other texts (Anselme, viii, p. 690; *Cour amoureuse*, i, p. 163; Carolus-Barré, 'Compiègne', p. 391 n. 14).

[73] Colart d'Estouteville (d. 1415), lord of Torcy, a member of Charles VI's household, already had a very long career by the time of Agincourt, where he died (Morandière, *Histoire de la Maison d'Estouteville*, pp. 155, 190, 208, 215; *GR*, ii, pp. 269; *Cour amoureuse*, i, p. 101).

[74] The identity of this lord of la Heuze (Heuse), who also appears in Monstrelet (iii, p. 115), is uncertain. Robert de la Heuze, dit le Borgne, lord of la Heuze, a Norman knight, had been involved in the defence of Normandy against the English in 1413 and was present at the great council of Charles VI in November 1414, but died shortly afterwards. It is possible that the member of the family who died at Agincourt was his younger brother Jean de la Heuze, dit le Baudrain, lord of Quévilly, a chamberlain of Charles VI (Demurger, 'Guerre civile', p. 265; Bouzy, 'Les morts d'Azincourt', p. 244).

[75] This may be Jean d'Avrichier, knight, lord of Avrichier and Plasnes, who was dead by 14 March 1419 (C 64/10 m. 14, DKR 41, p. 744), although he seems unlikely to have been killed at the battle. The lordship was later acquired by Sir John Fastolf who obtained on 28 December 1433 a licence to sell it (*Actes*, ii, p. 385 no. 700–1).

[76] Bouzy ('Les morts d'Azincourt', p. 240) suggests that 'le seigneur de Maunes' who appears in Monstrelet's list of battle dead (iii, p. 114) might be Guillaume IX Crespin, lord of Mauny, whose lands were redistributed to John Fastolf. On 15 January 1419 Fastolf was granted the lordship of Bec-Crespin held by Guillaume de Maugny known as Crespin (C 64/10 m. 13, DKR 41, p. 745).

[77] This may be Jean de Hangest, lord of Hangest and Avesnecourt, knight, a chamberlain of Charles VI in 1383 and 1400, and grand master of the crossbowmen (1407–11), who is believed to have died at Agincourt (Anselme, VI, p. 640; *Cour amoureuse*, i, no. 95). He would have inherited the lordship of Heugueville (Manche) or Heuqueville (Eure), from another Jean de Hangest (d. 1407), who held the office of grand master of the crossbowmen from 1403 to 1407 (*Cour amoureuse*, i, no. 96). We cannot exclude the possibility that the chronicle, as Anselme, confused the two men.

[78] The chronicle's lord of Préaulx, presumably the man designated as 'le filz au seigneur de Préaulx' in Monstrelet's list of dead (iii, p. 113), seems to refer to Louis de Bourbon, the eldest son of Jacques I de Bourbon (d. 1417), lord of Argies, Préaux, Dangu and Thury, who, according to Anselme (i, p. 364), bore the title of lord of Préaux while his father was still alive.

[79] Jean de Fontaines, lord of Fontaines, served Louis, duke of Orléans and joined the Orleanist party after the murder of his master in 1407, defending the rights of the duke's son and heir, Charles. Gonzales (pp. 228–31) lost track of him after 1413–14. His presence and death at Agincourt is possible but the chronicle may intend his son, Enguerrand de Fontaines, who had followed in his father's footsteps, siding with the Orleanist party in the early 1410s (Gonzales, pp. 226–7). The death of Enguerrand de Fontaines at Agincourt is also noted by Monstrelet (iii, p. 115).

[80] A 'Raoul de Ferrières' appears in Monstrelet's list of dead (iii, p. 117). A lord of Ferrières was alive when the town and castle of Chambois (Orne, arr. Argentan, cant. Argentan 2, co.

the lord of Beaumesnil[81]   }
the lord of Hambye[82]   }
[33v]
the lord of Rouvroy[83]   }
the lord of Créquy[84]   }
the count of Vertus[85]   }
the lord of Creully[86]   }
the lord of Tilly[87]   }
the lord of Chambois[88]   }

Gouffern-en-Auge) surrendered to the English in March 1418, and remained in possession of his estates in return for submission to the English (C 64/8 m. 5, Hardy, pp. 294–6). A letter of protection was accorded to the lord of Ferrières and Chambrais in April 1419 (C 64/11 m. 78, DKR 41, p. 763).

[81]   In January 1416, Charles VI authorised Louise de Hangest, wife of Guillaume de Tournebu, lord of Beaumesnil, to manage the latter's estates in his absence, given that he was missing after the battle ('comme son dit mari ait esté a la battaille qui nagueres a esté en Picardie contre nos ennemis et adversaires d'Angleterre, et ne scet ne ne puet encore savoir la certaineté s'il y est mort ou prins') (AN, Dom Lenoir, vol. 21, p. 173; Lenoir, *Preuves généalogiques*, pp. 149–50, no. 184). In June 1416, Louise appears as a widow in an inquiry regarding the ward of her under-age children (AN, Dom Lenoir, vol. 5, pp. 165–170; Lenoir, *Preuves généalogiques et historiques de la maison d'Harcourt*, p. 151, no. 186). We are grateful to Adrien Dubois for these references.

[82]   The lordship of Hambye was disputed. It would appear to have passed from Jeanne Paynel of Moyon and her husband to Louis d'Estouteville, lord of Auzebosc, yet Estouteville does not seem to have titled himself lord of Hambye before 1432. It is not known, therefore, whom this entry describes.

[83]   This is possibly Mathieu du Rouvroy, dit le Borgne, lord of Saint-Simon, who mustered as knight banneret at Arras in August 1414. Rouvroy and his brother, Jean, dit Gallois, fought at Agincourt where both died, according to Monstrelet, iii, p. 114 n. 10 (Anselme, iv, p. 397; *Cour amoureuse*, no. 161; Bouzy, 'Les morts d'Azincourt', p. 252).

[84]   This may be Raoul de Créquy, dit 'l'Etendard', lord of Créquy. According to Douët-d'Arcq in his edition of Monstrelet (iii, p. 113), where death at Agincourt is also noted, he was called 'l'Etendard' because he had conquered many a banner over the English (Anselme, vi, p. 782; Belleval, p. 181; *Cour amoureuse*, no. 208; Bouzy, 'Les morts d'Azincourt', p. 240).

[85]   Philippe d'Orléans (1396–1420), count of Vertus, a younger brother of Charles, duke of Orléans, served in the armies of Charles VI in Picardy and Artois in 1414 but there is no evidence of his presence at Agincourt. He was made lieutenant-general for the king and the Regent in Guyenne and Poitou beyond Dordogne in March 1418 (Anselme, i, p. 462; *GR*, iii, p. 421).

[86]   This may be Jean, lord of Croÿ, councillor and chamberlain of the king, and the dukes of Burgundy, governor of Artois (1405), captain of Le Crotoy (1411), and *grand bouteiller* of France (1412), who, according to Monstrelet (iii, p. 113), died at Agincourt (Anselme, v, p. 636; *Cour amoureuse*, no. 184).

[87]   This 'lord of Tilly' and the 'lord of Chambois' who follows are almost certainly the same person: Jean de Tilly, lord of Chambois. This may be a scribal oversight or else a desire to expand the list.

[88]   Jean de Tilly (d. 1415), knight, lord of Chambois, councillor and chamberlain of the king, mustered as knight bachelor along with six other knights and four esquires on 22 September 1415 in Rouen (BNF, Clairambault, 106/74). His death at Agincourt is also mentioned in Monstrelet (iii, p. 115). See Belleval, p. 167.

the lord of Gacé[89]   }
the lord of Vieuxpont and Chailloué[90]   }
the lord of Sillé-le-Guillaume[91]   }
the lord of Tucé[92]   }
the lord of Assé-le-Riboul[93]   }
the lord of Nouens   }
the lord of la Suze[94]   }
the lord of Sablé[95]   }
the lord of Albret[96]   }

---

[89]   There was seemingly no lord of Gacé in 1415. In August 1421 Henry V granted to William Glasdale the lands of Gacé in the *vicomté* of Orbec late belonging of the lady of Moyon, a rebel (in other words, Jeanne Paynel of Moyon) (C 64/16 m. 31, DKR 42, p. 414). She had inherited the barony of Gacé from her mother Jeanne de Champagne, and retreated to Mont-Saint-Michel with her husband, Louis d'Estouteville, lord of Auzebosc, after the English invasion.

[90]   Yves de Vieuxpont (c. 1360–1415), baron of Neubourg, was also lord of Vieuxpont, Courville and Chailloué before he inherited the barony of Neubourg from his uncle. He was a chamberlain of Louis, duke of Orléans (1389–1403) and Charles VI (1400–15). Those who drew up an inventory of his movable goods in April 1416 thought that he might have survived the battle and was either a prisoner or else had died in England. It may be that his body had not been found after the battle (Plaisse, *La baronnie du Neubourg*, p. 304 n. 2). Royal letters issued on 22 May 1416 were more certain that he had died at the battle (Belleval, p. 263). See also Gonzales, pp. 560–2.

[91]   Anne de Sillé, who inherited the barony of Sillé-le-Guillaume from her father Guillaume VII, first married Jean de Montjean, lord of Montjean. There is a 'seigneur de Montegen' in Monstrelet's list of dead (iii, p. 115) but he has been identified as Renaud de Montjean, lord of Guillebourg (Anselme, vii, p. 175; Bouzy, 'Les morts d'Azincourt', p. 248). Favre and Lecestre found evidence in the *Registre des comptes de Tours* showing that 'Regnault' de Montjean acted as governor of Touraine in 1416 and 1417 (*Jouvencel*, i, p. lxvii n. 1). They also claim that Jean de Montjean died at Agincourt but fail to engage with Anselme's claim that this Montjean, Renaud's nephew, died in 1418.

[92]   We know that a Jeanne inherited the lordship of Tucé at the death of her father, Guillaume II, and married in turn Guillaume de Sources, and after his death in 1423, Baudouin de Champagne (ADS, G18), but it is unclear who is meant here.

[93]   The lord of Assé-le-Riboul is also in Monstrelet's list (iii, p. 115). Belleval (p. 133) identified him as Foulques Riboul, knight, lord of Assé-le-Riboul and Lavardin, chamberlain of Charles VI, but this Foulques died in 1412 (Piolin, *Histoire de l'église du Mans*, pp. 197–8). The person intended might be his son Jean of whom we know nothing save that he died soon after his father without an heir (Roquet, 'Mansigné', pp. 185–7).

[94]   Jean de Craon (1363–1432) was lord of la Suze in 1415 but did not die until 1432 (Anselme, viii, pp. 573–4; Berry, p. 122 n. 4).

[95]   The lordship of Sablé changed hands several times between 1390 and 1415. Louis II, duke of Anjou, was lord but was not present at Agincourt and died in 1417 (Menage, *Histoire de Sablé*). There is possible confusion with Antoine de Craon, lord of Beauverger-en-Vermandois, chamberlain of Charles VI and 'grand panétier' of France (1411–13), whose father Pierre de Craon was between 1390 and 1392 lord of Sablé and whose death at Agincourt is mentioned in Monstrelet (iii, p. 115) (Anselme, viii, p. 623; *Cour amoureuse*, no. 98; Bouzy, 'Les morts d'Azincourt', p. 23).

[96]   Charles I d'Albret (1368–1415), count of Dreux and vicomte of Tartas, was constable of France from 1403 but temporarily lost this office between 1411 and 1413 because of the civil war, in which he was actively involved on the Orleanist side. Albret and Boucicaut

the lord of Parthenay[97]   } dead

and several other knights to the number of 2,400, according to a declaration delivered by Montjoye, King of Arms of France. Because Guillaume de Thibouville, knight, lord of La Rivière-Thibouville[98] (34r) rallied the enemy to the number of 20,000 men of war and more under a white banner to give a new battle, the victorious prince the king had it cried throughout his host that every man should kill his prisoner. That was the reason that so many nobles were killed. In the said battle on the side of the victorious prince there died the lords whose names follow, to wit,

the duke of York   }
the earl of Suffolk[99]   } dead
Sir Richard Kyghley[100]   }
Davy Gam esquire,[101] Welshman } and about ten archers.

After this glorious victory had been thus obtained, the victorious prince ordered the burial of the lords and others killed in the battle, both those of his own side and

---

were made 'chefs principaux de notre dite guerre' by Charles VI in July 1415, and shared command of the French army at Agincourt, where Albret died (Anselme, vi, pp. 205–6; Belleval, pp. 127–8). See also Courroux, *Charles d'Albret*.

[97]   Jean II Larchevêque (d. 1427) inherited the lordship of Parthenay (in Deux-Sèvres) in 1401. Treated as a Burgundian partisan and a rebel in 1414, his lordship and other estates were confiscated by the king and passed to the count of Richemont, who was therefore lord of Parthenay at the time of Agincourt. Jean II obtained the restitution of his estates in September 1416 (AN, JJ 169/258), and sold them to the king and the Dauphin in November 1419 (AN, J 183, no. 135). Richemont re-entered into possession of the lordship of Parthenay in 1425 (Cosneau, pp. 485–93).

[98]   The M 9 chronicle is the only one to blame Guillaume de Thibouville, lord of la Rivière-Thibouville, for a last ditch attempt at reversing the outcome of the battle which resulted in the slaughter of the French prisoners (Curry, *Agincourt. A New History*, pp. 158–60). The 'seigneur de la Riviere de Tybouville' appears in Monstrelet's list of casualties (iii, p. 115 n. 3) and has been identified as Bureau de la Rivière, lord of Perchin and Tybauville (or Thibouville) (Bouzy, 'Les morts d'Azincourt', p. 254), or else Jean de Fricamps, lord of La Rivière-Thibouville (Belleval, p. 216). The Norman rolls on which Belleval based his assumption show unequivocally that the lordship of La Rivière-Thibouville was a possession of the Thibouville family. Guillaume de Thibouville acted as captain of the castle of La Rivière-Thibouville when it surrendered to the English on 11 March 1418 (C 64/8 m. 5, Hardy, pp. 292–4). Henry V's grant of the lordship to the earl of Salisbury on 1 June 1418 indicated that these lands belonged to Louis de Thibouville who had died recently (C 64/ 9 m. 13, DKR 41, p. 698) but presumably this death post-dates Agincourt.

[99]   Michael de la Pole held the comital title for barely over a month following the death of his father at Harfleur on 18 September 1415. Michael junior had crossed to France in his father's retinue (E 101/46/24 m. 4). His body was brought back to England for burial in Wingfield (Suffolk).

[100]   With his seat at Inskip (Lancs.), Sir Richard Kyghley (1370–1415) indented to serve with five men-at-arms and eighteen archers in 1415 and was also in charge of fifty archers from Lancashire (E 404/31/252; E 101/69/4/386; E 101/45/5 m. 4d; E 101/46/5; E 101/47/30; E 101/44/29; E 358/6 m. 4d).

[101]   Dafydd Gam (c. 1380–1415) hailed from Brecon and had indented for the 1415 campaign to serve as a man-at-arms with three archers (E 101/69/4/404; E 404/31/362; E 101/45/5 m. 5). His death at the battle is mentioned in a number of chronicles (Chapman, 'Posthumous Knighting').

those of the enemy. Then he rode peacefully with all his host to Calais[102] where he stayed for several days to refresh himself, then he crossed the sea to his kingdom of England with great honour and victory.

In the year 1417 the said most noble and victorious prince and king Henry the fifth made a new army to cross overseas with the intention of effecting a conquest. In this army were the lords whose names follow, to wit,

my lord Thomas, duke of Clarence[103]   }
my lord Humphrey, duke of Gloucester[104]   } brothers of the king
the earl of Huntingdon[105]
the Earl Marshal[106]
the earl of Warwick[107]
the young earl of Devon[108]
the earl of Salisbury[109]
the earl of Suffolk[110]
the earl of Somerset[111]

---

[102] Pas-de-Calais, ch. l. d'arr.

[103] According to the *Vita Henrici Quinti*, p. 31, Clarence had a company of 960 for the 1417 campaign, but it seems that he had an additional 240 men under his command (E 404/33/219). On the day of the landing, 1 August 1417, he was appointed constable of the army (C 64/8 m. 2, Hardy, pp. 316–17).

[104] According to the *Vita Henrici Quinti*, p. 31, Gloucester had a company of 400 for the 1417 campaign. The names of 321 men in his company are found on the muster roll (E 101/51/2 m. 1).

[105] The earl of Huntingdon indented for 160 men (E 101/70/1/583; *Vita Henrici Quinti*, p. 32) but 176 names are found on the surviving muster roll (E 101/51/2 m. 26).

[106] The Earl Marshal indented for 400 men (E 101/70/1/576; *Vita Henrici Quinti*, p. 32) but 415 names are found on the surviving muster roll (E 101/51/2 m. 28).

[107] According to the *Vita Henrici Quinti*, p. 32, Richard Beauchamp*, earl of Warwick (1382–1439), had a company of 400 for the 1417 campaign. The names of 402 men are found on the muster roll (E 101/51/2 m. 12). Warwick had not participated in the 1415 campaign because he held the captaincy of Calais.

[108] At the time of the expedition the earl of Devon was the blind Edward Courtenay (1357–1419), who did not participate, nor, it seems, did his second son and eventual comital successor, Hugh (1389–1422). The person intended is presumably his eldest son, Sir Edward Courtenay (c. 1385–1418), who indented to serve with a company of 120 men (E 101/70/1/582). The surviving muster roll lists 121 men in his company (E 101/51/2 m. 20).

[109] Thomas Montague*, earl of Salisbury (1388–1428), indented for the service of 376 men in 1417 (E 101/70/2/618 and 619), although the *Vita Henrici Quinti*, p. 32, notes a retinue of 400, and 423 names are found on the surviving muster roll (E 101/51/2 m. 9). Surprisingly, the M 9 chronicle does not note his presence on the 1415 campaign when he had a retinue of 120 and was present at Agincourt (E 404/31/174; E 101/45/5 m. 5d; E 101/45/21 m. 40).

[110] William de la Pole, earl of Suffolk, indented for the service of 120 men in 1417 (E 101/70/1/575). That number is found in his company on the muster roll (E 101/51/2 m. 13).

[111] The earl of Somerset in 1417 was Henry Beaufort (1401–18), son of Earl John (c. 1371–1410) who was the eldest son of John of Gaunt and Katherine Swynford. In 1415, although under age, Earl Henry had served within the company of his stepfather, Thomas, duke of Clarence, but had been invalided home from Harfleur (E 101/45/4; E 101/45/1; E 101/44/30 no. 1, m. 1). It is likely that Earl Henry was in the company of the duke of Clarence on the 1417 campaign since the latter's warrant for payment notes the service of an earl (E 404/33/219), but no muster roll survives for Clarence's company.

(34v) Sir John Neville[112]
Lord Roos[113]
Lord Willoughby[114]
Lord Fitzhugh[115]
Lord Clinton[116]
Lord Botreaux[117]
Lord Scrope[118]
Lord Maltravers[119]
Lord Bourchier[120]
the two lords of Ferrers Groby[121]

---

[112] Sir John Neville (c. 1387–1420) was the eldest son of Ralph Neville, earl of Westmorland (c. 1364–1425). On the 1417 campaign he led a company of 166 (E 101/51/2 m. 22).

[113] John, lord Roos indented for a company of forty (E 101/70/1/585). Forty-five names are found on the surviving muster roll.

[114] According to the *Vita Henrici Quinti*, p. 32, Willoughby indented for a company of 160 men in 1417. On the surviving muster roll 161 names are found (E 101/51/2 m. 15).

[115] Henry, lord Fitzhugh indented for a company of 240 in 1417 (E 101/70/1/577; E 404/33/217). On the surviving muster roll 275 names are found (E 101/51/2 m. 3).

[116] There is no evidence that William, lord Clinton (1378–1431), whose seat was at Maxstoke (Warks.), served in 1417. He had been present on the 1415 campaign and was at Agincourt (E 404/31/346; E 101/45/5 m. 5; E 101/44/30 no. 1, m. 13; E 101/45/1). He was serving in Harfleur in the first months of 1416 (E 101/47/39).

[117] William, lord Botreaux (1389–1462), whose seat was in North Cadbury (Somerset), does not appear in the surviving sources for the 1417 campaign. In 1415 he had crossed with a retinue of sixty but was invalided home after Harfleur surrendered (E 404/31/151; E 101/45/5 m. 5; E 101/45/22 m. 23; E 101/45/18 m. 3; E 101/47/7).

[118] There is no evidence that Richard, lord Scrope of Bolton (1394–1420) served on the 1417 campaign. This is therefore most likely Sir John Scrope (c. 1388–1455) who was restored in 1425 to the title of Lord Scrope of Masham which had been forfeited by the involvement of his elder brother Henry in the Southampton plot of 1415. Although Sir John does not appear in the surviving sources for the 1417 expeditionary army, he can be shown through entries in the Norman rolls to have been active in Normandy thereafter.

[119] John FitzAlan, lord Maltravers (1385–1421) was the cousin and male heir of Thomas, earl of Arundel who died on 13 October 1415 but he never formally came into possession of the earldom because of opposition from the Earl Marshal, the late earl's heir general. John bore the courtesy title of Maltravers by inheritance from his grandmother. He served in 1415 with sixty-five men and was at Agincourt (E 404/31/375; E 101/45/5 m. 3d; E 101/45/1; E 101/44/30 no. 1, m. 15). He indented for a company of 160 for the 1417 campaign (E 101/70/2/604), and appears on the surviving muster roll with 159 men (E 101/51/2 m. 36).

[120] According to the *Vita Henrici Quinti*, p. 32, Hugh Stafford, lord Bourchier had a company of 120 for the 1417 campaign. The surviving muster records 119 names (E 101/51/2 m. 22). He was created KG in 1418.

[121] Identification is uncertain here. William, lord Ferrers of Groby* (1372–1445) is not known to have served on the 1417 campaign nor is he mentioned in the Norman rolls. Sir Henry Ferrers, his son, was present in 1417 in the retinue of the Earl Marshal (E 101/51/2 m. 27), whose daughter he had married in 1416. Henry died before his father. Although his presence is not noted in the M 9 chronicle, Edmund, lord Ferrers of Chartley served on the 1417 campaign with eighty men (E 101/70/1/580; *Vita Henrici Quinti*, p. 32).

Sir John Cornwall[122]
Lord Grey of Codnor[123]
Sir Gilbert Umfraville[124]
Sir Gilbert, Lord Talbot[125]
and many others.

In the month of August of this year 1417 this victorious prince put to sea and landed in Normandy near to a castle named Touques[126] in order to begin the conquest. At this time within Normandy on the enemy side were the captains whose names follow:

at the castle of Touques *Guillaume de Pombray knight*[127]
at Caen the lord of Montenay and the lord of Fontenay-le-Marmion, his first cousin[128]
at Neuilly-la-Forêt *Robert de Pierrepont esquire*[129]
at Bayeux Jean Fortescu knight[130]

---

[122] Sir John Cornwall* (1364–1443), created Lord Fanhope in 1432, appears in the surviving muster for the 1417 campaign with a company of 174 men (E 101/51/2 m. 35). He had served on the 1415 campaign and was at Agincourt (E 404/31/263; E 101/45/5 m. 4d; E 101/45/21 m. 2).

[123] Richard Grey*, fourth baron Grey of Codnor (Derbys.) (c. 1371–1418), appears in the surviving muster for the 1417 campaign with 224 men (E 10/51/2 m. 18). He had not served in 1415 as he was Warden of the East March towards Scotland.

[124] Umfraville indented for the service of 240 men for the 1417 expedition (E 404/33/220). The surviving muster roll lists only 179 names (E 101/51/2 m. 33) but it is possible that the remainder had crossed in an advance force.

[125] According to the *Vita Henrici Quinti*, p. 32, Gilbert, lord Talbot (1383–1418), with his seat at Goodrich (Herefs.) had a company of 400 for the 1417 campaign. He had extensive military experience, having led a company of 120 in 1415 (E 101/45/5 m. 2). He was the elder brother of John, lord Talbot (1384–1453).

[126] Calvados, arr. Lisieux, cant. Pont-l'Évêque (Bonneville-sur-Touques). The landing was deliberately arranged to occur on 1 August 1417, the date subsequently being used by Henry V in his dealings with the Norman population as well as a definition of legal memory.

[127] The treaty of surrender of the castle was negotiated by Guillaume le Comte and Jean Bonenfant, two lieutenants of Jean d'Augère, knight, and captain of the place, on 3 August 1417 (C 64/8 m. 6, Hardy, pp. 284–5).

[128] Calvados, ch. l. d'arr. The chronicle is mistaken since the lords of Montenay and Fontenay-le-Marmion were the same person. Guillaume IV de Montenay, a Norman knight, councillor and chamberlain of Charles VI and Charles VII, was captain of Carentan and defended Honfleur and Caen during the English invasion in 1415 (*GR*, ii, p. 266). He appears in the treaty of surrender of the castle of Caen on 19 September 1417 as its sole captain (C 64/8 m. 6, Hardy, pp. 287–8). Henry V granted Montenay's confiscated lordships of Faugernon, Fontenay-le-Marmion and le Hommet to Edward Holland, earl of Mortain, on 29 March 1418 (C 64/9 m. 24, DKR 41, p. 690). Montenay was present with the Dauphin at the fateful meeting of Montereau in 1419. He met his end at Verneuil in 1424. See also Poli, p. cxxxix and preuves nos. 771, 798, 891; Gaussin, 'Les conseillers', p. 110; Schnerb, 'Sauver', p. 254 n. 219).

[129] Calvados, arr. Bayeux, cant. Trévières, known in this period as Neuilly-l'Évêque as a residence of the bishops of Bayeux. Thomas de Creully, esquire, negotiated the surrender of the castle as its captain on 15 May 1418 (C 64/9 m. 32, DKR 41, p. 686).

[130] Calvados, ch. l. d'arr. As captain of Pont-d'Ouve, Jean Fortescu, esquire, agreed the treaty for the surrender of Bayeux on 17 March 1418 (C 64/10 m. 9, DKR 41, p. 746). He

in the town of Falaise the lord of Longny[131] and Baudouin de Champagne knight, lord of Tucé[132]

in the castle of Falaise Olivier de Mauny knight[133] and Charles de Mauny his brother, *bailli* of Caen[134]

at Argentan Jean de Carrouges knight[135] and Guillaume Martel knight[136]

(35r) at Saint-Sauveur-le-Vicomte Guillaume de Hermanville knight[137] and *Ambroise de la Grésille knight*[138]

---

seems to have accepted English rule and participated in ongoing administration (C 64/10 m. 24; /11 m. 39d; /15 m. 29d, DKR 41, p. 756, DKR 42, pp. 321, 406).

[131] Calvados, ch. l. d'arr. The treaties of surrender for the town (20 December 1417) and castle of Caen (1 February 1418) suggest that Olivier de Mauny assumed the role of captain for both (C 64/8 m. 2, Hardy, pp. 308–15). This 'seigneur de Longny' seems to be Louis de Longny whose barony of Longny was confiscated by Henry V and granted to Thomas de Montague, earl of Salisbury, on 16 October 1419 (C 64/11 m. 11, DKR 41, p. 803).

[132] Baudouin de Champagne, knight, lord of Tucé, a councillor and chamberlain of Charles VII, was captain of Le Mans in 1424 (ADS, G 18, fol. 104r; published in Charles, 'L'invasion anglaise', pp. 198–9). He is the most cited Frenchman in the chronicle, reflecting his sustained activity in Maine and Anjou between 1425 and 1428 as a lieutenant of the Valois king, including the recovery of the fortresses of Le Lude and Malicorne and a failed attempt to recapture Le Mans in 1428. (See also Planchenault, 'La conquête' (1925), p. 14 n. 1.)

[133] Olivier de Mauny, lord of Lignières and Lesnen, issued from an old Breton family, and was a chamberlain of Charles VI, in the service of the French crown from the late 1380s. In October 1415, he was in Normandy under the command of the duke of Alençon in an effort to halt the English (BNF, Clairambault, 72/18; *Songe véritable*, p. 188). He was captain of the castle of Falaise at its surrender in February 1418 (C 64/8 m. 2, Hardy, pp. 302–8) and remained a prisoner of Henry V until he satisfactorily repaired the walls of the castle, which task was completed by 28 June (C 64/9 m. 22, DKR 41, p. 692). By virtue of the surrender, he would have sworn not to re-arm against the English. But he broke his word according to M 9 (f. 45v), with fateful consequences.

[134] Charles de Mauny, knight, lord of Lingèvres and La Haye-Pesnel, was councillor and chamberlain of Charles VII in 1416 and *bailli* of Caen from November 1415 until the town was captured by the English in 1417 (*GR*, i, pp. 453–4; Demurger, 'Guerre civile', p. 216). He received a safe-conduct on 2 February 1418 which anticipated his return to the castle within fourteen days (C 64/8 m. 14, Hardy, p. 240).

[135] Orne, ch. l. d'arr. Jean de Carrouges and his wife Amisia accepted English rule. On 30 January 1420 Henry V confirmed them in the lands they had held on 1 August 1417 (C 64/12 m. 43d, DKR 42, p. 337). For Robert de Carrouges who first embraced the English cause and then rebelled against it, see Lefèvre-Pontalis, 'Épisodes de l'invasion', pp. 497–500.

[136] The name 'Guillaume Martel' appears on two occasions in this list of captains, first as co-captain of Argentan and secondly as captain of Dieppe. Note also that the chronicle's 'lord of Bacqueville', who was co-captain of Château-Gaillard, was Guillaume IX Martel. There is evidence of at least one homonym who was lord of Longueil and Languetot and 'panetier' of Charles VI in the 1400s (BNF, PO 1868, Martel, no. 63 and 65; *Songe véritable*, p. 186) and who was still active in 1420 (BNF, Clairambault 71/24; *Songe véritable*, p. 186).

[137] Manche, arr. Cherbourg, cant. Bricquebec. The treaty of surrender of Saint-Sauveur-le-Vicomte was negotiated on 25 March 1419 by Robert de Fréville as captain (C 64/10 m. 6, DKR 41, p. 746). The Norman Guillaume de Hermanville was an 'écuyer d'écurie' in 1380, 1400 and 1405 (*Cour amoureuse*, ii, 93, no. 476).

[138] This may be Aimery de la Grésille, knight, who according to Monstrelet (iv, p. 196) was killed at Verneuil in 1424.

at Sées *Louis de Clamorgan knight*[139]
at Thury-Harcourt *Hemery* de Clinchamp[140]
at Essay Louis de Trémagon knight[141]
at Alençon Jean dit le Galois d'Achy, knight[142]
at Domfront Guillaume Blosset, dit le Borgne, lord of Saint-Pierre-en-Caux[143]
at Vire Jean Carbonnel knight[144]

---

[139] Orne, arr. Alençon, ch. l. cant. The identity of Louis is uncertain but Thomas, Colin and Jacques de Clamorgan accepted English rule and participated in the ongoing administration of the duchy (C 64/10 m. 24; /16 m. 25, 40; /17 m. 16, DKR 41, pp. 738; 42, pp. 425, 432, 450).

[140] Calvados, arr. Caen, ch. l. cant. The castle of Thury had surrendered by 28 September 1417 when a safe-conduct was issued to all in the castle to leave (C 64/8 m. 26, Hardy, p. 158). Vigor de Clinchamp, knight, lord of Clinchamp, de Mezerets and la Chapelle, was captain of Saint-James-de-Beuvron on 1 May 1418 (Gerville, 'Recherches sur les anciens châteaux', p. 149). The brothers Colin and Richard de Clinchamp mustered in the garrison of Mont-Saint-Michel in May 1421 (Luce, i, no. xii), but there is no trace of an Aimery.

[141] Orne, arr. Alençon, cant. Radon. Louis de Trémagon (Tromagon, Trémaugon), knight, received a safe-conduct to leave Alençon on 24 October 1417 (C 64/8 m. 21, Hardy, pp. 187–8). He is presented as an 'Armagnac' captain who was lord of La Chapelle-près-Sées in a letter of remission of 1427 which detailed the circumstances of his capture of the town of Sées some six years earlier (*Actes*, ii, p. 22, no. 163). He fought in the army which raised the siège of Orléans in May 1429 (Raguier's accounts in *Journal du siège*, pp. 195–8) and, with his wife Catherine du Bellay, received safe-conducts in Maine in 1434 (AN, KK 324, ff. 63r, 96r). This Louis de Trémagon, seemingly of Breton origin, is not to be confused with a Gascon, named simply 'Tromagon', who was militarily active at that time.

[142] Orne, ch. l. d'arr. From Picardy, Jean dit le Galois d'Achy, knight, captain of the castle and town of Alençon, received a safe-conduct to leave there on 24 October 1417 (C 64/8 m. 21, Hardy, pp. 187–8). Henry V granted lands which had been confiscated from le Galois d'Achy, knight, a rebel, to Thomas Walton in tail male, in April 1419 (C 64/11 m. 50, DKR 41, p. 778).

[143] Orne, arr. Alençon, ch. l. cant. Clément le Bigot, lieutenant of the captain of the castle of Domfront, negotiated its surrender with the English in July 1418 (C 64/10 m. 8, DKR 41, p. 746). Guillaume Blosset, dit le Borgne, lord of Saint-Pierre-en-Caux, described himself, in a receipt of 18 January 1418 for payment of wages, as an esquire, captain of the men-at-arms and archers in the castle and town of Neufchâtel-d'Ellecourt rather than Domfront (BNF, Clairambault 140/2725). He had been knighted and had become a chamberlain of Charles VII by 1430 (BNF, Clairambault 140/2727). There is evidence of his military activity in Maine in the early 1430s (*RDP*, viii, p. 336 n. 1).

[144] Calvados, ch. l. d'arr. The captain of the town, castle and tower of Vire upon its surrender on 21 February 1418 was the 'compagnon de Gaule' (that is to say Pierre de Mornay, dit Gauluet, lord of Gaules) (C 64/8 m. 6, Hardy, pp. 289–92). The Carbonnel were a Cotentin family, seemingly Orléanist during the civil wars (Prosser, 'Affinity', pp. 42–3). There were at least four of them who accepted English rule: Jean, Guillaume, Henri and Caryot. Evidence suggests that there must have been more than one 'Jean Carbonnel' in Lancastrian Normandy. A Jean Carbonnel, knight, gave his oath of fealty to Henry V on 3 March 1419 (C 64/10 m. 16, DKR 41, p. 759). This was probably the same 'Jean Carbonnel' whose lands held before 1 August 1417 were confirmed on 4 March 1419 (C 64/10 m. 25, DKR 42, p. 736). This cannot be the same 'Jean Carbonnel' who appears as a negotiator on the English side for the surrender of Evreux on 20 May 1418 (C 64/10 m. 8, DKR 41, p. 746). This other 'Jean Carbonnel' might well be the same person who was robbed while riding with goods and chattels from Henry V's army to Harfleur sometime before 22 October 1418 (C 64/ 9 m. 10, DKR 41, p. 518).

at Mont-Saint-Michel Jacques Paynel knight[145] and Nicole Paynel knight, brothers[146]

at Condé-sur-Noireau *the lord of Annebecq*[147]

at Saint-Lô the lord of Bricqueville[148]

at Creully-sur-Seulles Jean d'Argouges[149]

at Carentan *Guillaume Mortysmer knight, lord of La Haye-du-Puits*[150]

at La Haye-du-Puits *the said Guillaume, lord of the place*[151]

at Valognes Guillaume le Soterel, baron des Biards[152]

---

[145] Manche, arr. Avranches, cant. Pontorson. Jacques Paynel, esquire, mustered in the garrison of Mont-Saint-Michel on 7 June 1424 (Morice, ii, pp. 1144–5). He is not to be confused with Jacques Paynel, lord of Orlonde, who accepted English rule in November 1421 (AN, JJ 172/358; Luce, i, p. 100 n. 1). Robert Jolivet, the abbot of Mont-Saint-Michel, was also acting as captain of this place (Fiasson, 'Un chien couché', pp. 47–8).

[146] Nicole Paynel, lord of Bricqueville, mustered as a knight banneret in the garrison of Mont Saint-Michel on 1 May 1421 (Luce, i, no. xii) and became lieutenant and *de facto* captain there in March 1425 (Luce, i, p. 195, no. 56) but was forced to hand over the captaincy to Louis d'Estouteville, lord of Auzebosc, on 26 October 1425 (Luce, i, p. 210, no. 64).

[147] Calvados, arr. Vire, ch. l. cant. On 28 December 1417 Nicholas Whitfield was given power to take into royal hands the castle of Condé-sur-Noireau and to implement agreements between the king and the (unnamed) captains of the castle (C 64/8 m. 16, Hardy, p. 225).

[148] Manche, ch. l. d'arr. Jean Tesson and Guillaume Carbonnel, knights, are mentioned as the two captains of Saint-Lô in the treaty of surrender on 12 March 1418 (C 64/8 m. 4, Hardy, pp. 298–300). In 1418 the lord of Bricqueville-sur-Mer was apparently another Nicole Paynel (d. 1419), father of the defender of Mont-Saint-Michel. Either he or his son acted as 'gardein de la dite ville et cité' of Coutances at its surrender on 16 March 1418 (C 64/8 m. 5, Hardy, pp. 296–8). His castle and lordship of Bricqueville were confiscated by Henry V and granted to the earl of Huntingdon on 5 April 1418 (C 64/9 m. 40, DKR 41, p. 680). He was dead by May 1420 (Luce, i, pp. 96–7, no. 5).

[149] Calvados, arr. Caen, cant. Bretteville-l'Orgueilleuse. Jean d'Argouges, knight, rebel, had his lordship of Argouges confiscated in 1418 (AN, JJ 173/640; *Actes*, ii, p. 349, no. 487). He was elected to the chivalric order of the Camail in 1439 (Poli, p. xcxvi, and no. 1227).

[150] Manche, arr. Saint-Lô, ch. l. cant. Jean de Villiers was captain of the town and castle of Carentan in the treaty of surrender negotiated on 16 March 1418 (C 64/8 m. 4, Hardy, pp. 300–3). The castle and barony of la Haye-du-Puits, which was held by the house of Mortemer in the fourteenth century, were confiscated by Henry V from the late Henri de Colombières and his widow Jeanne Campion on 1 April 1418 (C 64/9 m. 33, DKR 41, p. 685).

[151] Manche, arr. Coutances, cant. Créances. A Guillaume des Hayes received a safe-conduct on 1 January 1419 to travel from Rouen into France and back (C 64/ 9 m. 3, DKR 41, p. 706).

[152] Manche, arr. Cherbourg, ch. l. cant. Guillaume le Soterel, baron des Biards, appears as a knight bachelor defending Rouen in 1415. He defended his castle of Les Biards against the English towards the end of 1418, but eventually yielded and retreated to Mont-Saint-Michel. Henry V granted all his lands in the Cotentin, estimated to be worth 800 *écus* per annum, to Thomas Bowet on 19 April 1419 (C 64/11 m. 67, DKR 41, p. 771). See Luce, *La France*, p. 221; Poli, p. ciii and preuves nos. 810, 893, 983, 1027–8, 1036, 692.

at Cherbourg Jean de la Haye, dit Piquet knight[153] and Guillaume de la Luzerne knight[154]
at Avranches *Richart de Rocheford knight*[155]
at Pontorson *Hue Tesson* knight[156]
at Saint-James (de-Beuvron) *Guillaume Pigas* knight[157]
at Hambye the lord of the place[158]
at Honfleur Louis de Braquemont knight[159] and Jean d'Onnebaut knight[160]

---

[153] Manche, ch. l. d'arr. Jean de la Haye, dit Piquet, lord of la Luthumière, esquire, councillor of Charles VI from 1413 to 1418, was captain of Valognes from 1401 to 1412 (*GR*, ii, p. 291). In September 1415 he was appointed by the king to raise troops against the English (BNF, PO 573, Callar-Calmart 42; PO 2289, Piquet 49). He appears as the sole captain of the town and castle of Cherbourg in the treaty of surrender which he negotiated with the English on 22 August 1418 (C 64/10 m. 8, DKR 41, p. 746). He was a member of the *Cour amoureuse* (ii, p. 93, no. 478). See also *Songe véritable*, pp. 153–6; and Gonzales, Fiches.
[154] Guillaume de la Luzerne, esquire, appears as one of the negotiators in the treaty of surrender of Honfleur, negotiated on 25 February 1419 (C 64/10 m. 4, DKR 41, p. 746). He subsequently served in the defence of Mont-Saint-Michel (Luce, i, pp. 113–16, no. 13, 114 n. 6).
[155] Manche, ch. l. d'arr. The town of Avranches was taken by the English sometime in April 1418, recovered by the French on 18 June 1419, and taken again by the English on 14 July 1419. The last capture occasioned a treaty of surrender which makes no reference to a Richart de Rocheford (C 64/10 m. 1, DKR 41, p. 746). See also Newhall, *English Conquest*, pp. 94, 113, 137–8.
[156] Manche, arr. Avranches, ch. l. cant. No information has been found on this captaincy. The Tesson were a well-established Norman family but no Hue has so far come to light.
[157] Manche, arr. Avranches, cant. Saint-Hillaire-du-Harcouët. No information has been found on this captaincy.
[158] Manche, arr. Coutances, cant. Quetteville-sur-Sienne. Philippe de la Haye, knight, was captain of the castle of Hambye at its surrender on 10 March 1418 (C 64/10 m. 10, DKR 41, p. 746). Foulques Paynel, knight, lord of Hambye and Bricquebec, died in 1413. His brother, Nicole Paynel, lord of Moynon, seems to have acted as guardian for his niece, Jeanne Paynel, until his death, possibly at Agincourt in 1415. According to Fauquembergue (i, p. 14) in August 1417 the lordships of Hambye and Bricquebec were in the hands of the king following the death of the lord of Hambye. This lord may have been Louis d'Estouteville, lord of Auzebosc, who had a claim through his wife, another Jeanne Paynel, Nicole's daughter. On 13 March 1418 Henry V granted the castles and lordships of Hambye and Bricquebec to William, earl of Suffolk (C 64/8 m. 2, Hardy, p. 319; C 64/11 m. 55, DKR 41, p. 775). See also Luce, i, pp. 95–110.
[159] Calvados, arr. Lisieux, cant. Honfleur-Deauville. Thomas de Carouges, Guillaume d'Anfernet, knights, and Guillaume de la Luzerne, esquire, acting on behalf of 'Jean Bethas' (perhaps the captain), negotiated the surrender of the town of Honfleur on 25 February 1419 (C 64/10 m. 4, DKR 41, p. 746). The Braquemont were a Cauchois noble lineage. Louis de Braquemont (1391–1424), 'échanson' of Louis de Guyenne (1413–15), was defending Harfleur in 1415. He is described as an esquire banneret in a receipt for wages for his service in arms in 1420. He was a pensioner of the Dauphin in 1421, and seems to have met his end at Verneuil in 1424 (Gonzales, pp. 75–87).
[160] Jean d'Onnebaut, knight, received a safe-conduct to leave the fortress of La Roche-Guyon following its surrender on 28 April 1419 (C 64/11 m. 65, DKR 41, p. 771). He was a member of the garrison of Mont-Saint-Michel in the early 1420s. He died at Verneuil in 1424 (Luce, i, p. 99 n. 2; Poli, p. xcvi and nos. 1010 and 1039).

at Le Bec-Hellouin *Jean d'Elbeuf and Huguelin du Quesnay*[161]
at Harcourt Guillaume de Mellemont esquire[162]
at Louviers the lord of Grippon[163]
at Evreux Guillaume de Crannes esquire[164]
at Dreux Raymonnet de la Guerre esquire[165]
at Pont-de-l'Arche the lord of Graville[166]
in the castle and town of Rouen Guy le Bouteillier knight[167]

---

[161] Eure, arr. Bernay, cant. Brionne. The treaty of surrender of the abbey and fortress of Bec-Hellouin was negotiated by the prior of the abbey and Jean Du Fay, esquire, lieutenant, on 4 May 1418 (C 64/ 9 m. 26, DKR 41, p. 688).

[162] Eure, arr. Bernay, cant. Brionne. Férand de Fréville, captain of the castle of Harcourt, together with Guillaume de la Lande, *bailli* of the lordship of Harcourt, negotiated the surrender on 9 March 1418 (C 64/9 m. 29, DKR 41, p. 688). Guillaume de Mellemont, esquire, mustered at Honfleur on 6 October 1415 (BNF, Clairambault 73/21).

[163] Eure, arr. Les Andeleys, ch. l. cant. Jean Tesson, knight, who was then lord of Grippon, shared the captaincy of Saint-Lô with Guillaume Carbonnel at its surrender on 12 March 1418 (C 64/8 m. 4, Hardy, pp. 298–300). As he refused English rule, his estates were confiscated by Henry V and granted to Thomas Bersyngham. We hear of this transaction from a later grant by the English king on 9 April 1422. By that time, both Jean Tesson and Bersyngham had died, and Henry granted Jean's estates to Raoul Tesson who, unlike his elder brother, had accepted English rule (C 64/17 m. 24, DKR 42, p. 441). On 11 September 1430, Raoul Tesson paid homage to Henry VI in Rouen for his lordship of Grippon (AN, P 267(2), no. 459). The Norman knight remained in possession of his estates when he rallied the French cause two years later (AN, JJ 175/284). See also Luce, i, p. 289 n. 1; Sauvage, *Les capitaines*, pp. 26–30.

[164] Eure, ch. l. d'arr. Guillaume de Crannes was captured by the Orleanists at the siege of Soissons in 1414 and narrowly escaped death. He was 'écuyer d'écurie' of the duke of Burgundy from 1415. He defended Evreux during the English invasion and, acting in his capacity as *bailli* of the city, negotiated the treaty of surrender on 20 May 1418 (C 64/10 m. 3, DKR 41, p. 756). He was dead by 30 July 1419 (C 64/11 m. 30, DKR 41, p. 791). See also Demurger, 'Guerre civile', p. 247; Schnerb, *Enguerrand*, pp. 133–4; Schnerb, "'A l'encontre des Anglois'", pp. 200–2.

[165] Eure-et-Loir, ch. l. d'arr. Raymonnet de (la) Guerre, a Gascon captain, was actively campaigning against the English and the Burgundians in northern France between 1415 and 1418. He was in the county of Étampes at the head of 1,000 men in October 1415 (AN, JJ 169/5). A few months later, he was in garrison in Saint-Denis, subsequently campaigning in the *pays de Santers* in January 1416. A letter of remission confirms that he was captain of Dreux for Charles VI in March 1417 (*Choix de pièces inédites*, ii, p. 31). He was killed in the massacres in Paris in June 1418. See also *Journal d'un Bourgeois*, ed. Tuetey, p. 67 n. 2.

[166] Eure, arr. Les Andelys, ch. l. cant. Guy Malet (d. 1424), lord of Graville, mustered as a knight banneret in Rouen on 22 September 1415 (BNF, Clairambault 69/89). Either he or his son was in command of Pont-de-l'Arche during the English invasion. The son, Jean de Graville, received safe-conducts to go to Henry V at Pont-de-l'Arche between 5 and 19 July 1418 (C 64/ 9 m. 17, 19, DKR 41, pp. 694, 695). The lordship of Graville 'lately held by Guido Malet knight, lord of Graville', together with a house in Rouen belonging to Jean de Graville, were confiscated by Henry V and granted to Lewis Robessart on 19 January 1419 (C 64/10 m. 28, DKR 41, p. 733). On Jean Malet, lord of Graville, master of the crossbowmen of France, see also Contamine, *GES*, p. 238 n. 26.

[167] Seine-Maritime, ch. l. d'arr. Guy le Bouteillier, lord of la Bouteillerie, was a Norman knight from the *pays de Caux*. Burgundian supporters in Rouen overthrew the Armagnac regime and handed over the control of the city to him in January 1418. Le Bouteillier, acting

at Rouen bridge Henri de Chauffour esquire[168]
at the Porte Cauchoise of Rouen Jean de Gingins[169]
at the Porte Beauvoisine (of Rouen) the lord of Pesmes[170]
at the Porte Saint-Hillaire (of Rouen) the Bastard of Thian[171]
at the Porte Martinville (of Rouen) Le Grand-Jacques[172]
at Bellencombre the 'king of Yvetot'[173]

---

as captain during Henry V's siege, led the negotiations for surrender on 4 January 1419 (C 64/10 m. 6, DKR 41, p. 746), but he does not appear in the treaty of surrender of 13 January in the list of signatories (C 64/10 m. 5, DKR 41, p. 746). He changed allegiance shortly afterwards and served the English thereafter.

[168] The bridge at Rouen over the River Seine. Henri de Chauffour or Chaufour, 'écuyer d'écurie' of the king and the duke of Burgundy, was sent to the Norman capital in 1418. He acted as one of the captains of Rouen during the siege, defending the 'Grand-Pont and the Barbacane' (Puisieux, *Siège et prise de Rouen*, pp. 54 and 91). He received a safe-conduct on 2 January 1419 as part of the negotiations, and another on 21 January after the surrender to go to Gisors (C 64/9 m. 1, DKR 41, pp. 705, 7). He received 1,280 *francs* as compensation for his losses at the siege of Rouen (Schnerb, '"A l'encontre des Anglois"', p. 209). He was among the ambassadors who negotiated with Henry V in late 1419, receiving instructions from Philip the Good and the queen. Henri de Chauffour, described by Chastellain as a 'bien vaillant escuier et tres adroit homme' (i, pp. 122–3), was fatally wounded in 1420 (Bonenfant, *Philippe le Bon*, pp. 17–18, 301, 317 and 321).

[169] The north-western entrance to the city of Rouen, on the road leading to Dieppe. The chronicle has confused Jean de Gingins, a nobleman from Savoy, with 'Laghen, bastard d'Arly' who guarded la Porte Cauchoise and was the most trusted captain 'en qui la communauté avoit la plus grant fiance' and who died during the siege (Monstrelet, iv, pp. 116, 129).

[170] The north-eastern entrance to the city of Rouen, on the road towards Beauvais. Guillaume de Grandson, lord of Pesmes (d. 1429), a knight from Franche-Comté and a vassal of the dukes of Burgundy, served his lord during the civil war, witnessed the murder of John the Fearless at Montereau, and later supported the dual monarchy (Perchet, *Recherches sur Pesmes*, pp. 257–77). His presence at the siege of Rouen is attested by a safe-conduct to leave the city with his retinue on 21 January 1419 (C 64/9 m. 1, DKR 41, p. 707).

[171] The eastern entrance to the city of Rouen, on the road leading to Darnétal. The Picard knight Jean, Bastard of Thian or Thien was a zealous supporter of the dukes of Burgundy. John the Fearless rewarded the courage he had shown during the siege of Senlis in 1418 with a grant of the lordship of Mouchy-le-Vieux (AN, JJ 172/62; *Journal d'un Bourgeois*, ed. Tuetey, p. 85 n. 4). He was in Rouen during the siege guarding the 'porte de Martainville' (Puisieux, *Siège et prise de Rouen*, p. 91). He was one of the signatories of the treaty of surrender on 13 January 1419 (C 64/10 m. 5, DKR 41, p. 746), and received a safe-conduct to leave on 21 January (C 64/9 m. 1, DKR 41, p. 707). The Bastard of Thian held the office of *bailli* of Senlis (1418–19, 1424–8) and of Meaux (1430, 1439?) (*GR*, iv, p. 97; v, p. 388). References to his deeds of arms in the 1420s and 1430s populate the pages of Monstrelet. He was eventually captured at the siege of Meaux in 1439 and beheaded shortly afterwards (Monstrelet, iii, pp. 150, 181, 239, 255, 281, 386; iv, pp. 44, 92, 124, 136, 172, 174, 176, 325, 329; v, pp. 2, 68, 126, 184, 388).

[172] Another entrance on the eastern side of Rouen on the road leading to Paris. The Lombard, Le Grand-Jacques, a 'chef' of condottieri, was among the captains of the garrison of Rouen in 1418 (Puisieux, *Siège et prise de Rouen*, p. 54).

[173] Seine-Maritime, arr. Dieppe, cant. Neufchâtel-en-Bray. The lord or 'king' of Yvetot was then Pierre de Villaines. He is described as a rebel in the Norman rolls and his lands were confiscated by Henry V and granted to John Holland, earl of Huntingdon, on 20 February 1419 (C 64/10 m. 29, DKR 41, p. 732). See also Beaucousin, *Histoire de la Principauté d'Yvetot*.

at Caudebec-en-Caux the lord of Villequier[174]
(35v) at Tancarville Hector de Dampierre knight[175]
at Dieppe Guillaume Martel knight[176]
at Torcy-le-Grand the lord of the place[177]
at Charlesmesnil the lord of the place[178]
at Arques the lord of La Heuze[179]
at Lillebonne *the lord of Calleville*[180]
at Aumale Coquart de Cambron knight[181]

---

[174] Seine-Maritime, arr. Rouen, cant. Notre-Dame-de-Gravenchon. Robert le Conte appears as captain of Caudebec in the treaty of surrender negotiated on 7 September 1418 (C 64/10 m. 7, DKR 41, p. 746). The lordship of Villequier confiscated from Robert de Villequier was granted to John Boutiller on 21 April 1419 and to Walter Hungerford on 19 May 1421 (C 64/11 m. 65, C 64/16 m. 31, DKR 41, p. 771, DKR 42, p. 413).

[175] Seine-Maritime, arr. Le Havre, cant. Bolbec. Guillaume, lord of Crasmenil, captain of the castle of Tancarville, reached a surrender agreement on 31 January 1419 (BNF, Fr. 26043/5435). The terms of surrender of the castle of Saint-Germain-sous-Cailly, returning to the obedience of Charles VII, on 10 April 1436, anticipated that Hector de Dampierre would be entrusted with the guard of the keep (BNF, PO 1882, Masquerel 4).

[176] Seine-Maritime, ch. l. d'arr. The surrender of Dieppe on 8 February 1419 was negotiated by townsmen (C 64/10 m. 1, DKR 41, p. 746).

[177] Seine-Maritime, arr. Dieppe, cant. Luneray. Guillaume d'Estouteville (d. 1449), knight, lord of Torcy and Blainville, became a prisoner of Henry V when Harfleur surrendered in 1415 (C 64/14 m. 26, DKR 42, p. 375). He was taken to England in November and remained in captivity in the Tower of London until mid-1417 (E 404/34/260 A, B). We find him in his castle of Torcy during Henry V's invasion, as suggested by the chronicle, negotiating its surrender in March 1419 (C 64/10 m. 17, DKR 41, p. 742), following which he swore fealty to Henry V (C 64/11 m. 77, DKR 41, p. 764). He left the English obedience in 1424 (AN, JJ 172/600) and made an attempt to capture Rouen in 1432 (*Actes*, ii, pp. 178–80, no. 206).

[178] Seine-Maritime, arr. Dieppe, cant. Luneray, co. Anneville-sur-Scie. Jean d'Estouteville, lord of Charlesmesnil, had established his nephew, Guillaume d'Estouteville, lord of Torcy as his heir in November 1416 and died shortly afterwards. The lord of Torcy was thus also lord of Charlesmesnil in 1417 (Anselme, viii, pp. 96, 878; Morandière, *Histoire de la Maison d'Estouteville*, pp. 221, 232, 256).

[179] Seine-Maritime, arr. Dieppe, cant. Dieppe 2, today known as Arques-la-Bataille after the battle victory of Henri IV in 1589. On the 'baron de la Heuze' see note 197.

[180] Seine-Maritime, arr. Le Havre, cant. Bolbec. The chronicle may be confusing Calleville and Malleville. Guillaume de Malleville appears as captain of the castle of Lillebonne in its treaty of surrender negotiated on 31 January 1419 (C 64/10 m. 1, DKR 41, p. 746). There is evidence of three Callevilles in the Norman rolls, all dead by the end of April 1419, when Henry V redistributed their estates. Colard de Calleville, knight, had died by 12 April 1419, when his lands of Auberville-le-Manuel, Manneville and *Chipouville* (Gerponville?) were granted to William Fitzharry (C 64/11 m. 68, DKR 41, p. 769). Guillaume de Calleville, knight, was dead by 26 April 1419 when his lands in Caux were granted to John Harpelay (C 64/11 m. 50, DKR 41, p. 779). Jean de Calleville, knight, lord of Donville, had died by 28 April 1419 when his lands of 'Tremouville' and 'Vinemesville' in Caux were granted to Hugh Spencer (C 64/11, m. 62, DKR 41, p. 773).

[181] Seine-Maritime, arr. Dieppe, cant. Gournay-en-Bray. Henry V granted the lands in Caux of the rebel Jean, alias Coquart, de Cambron, knight, to Adam Frost on 18 May 1419 (C 64/12 m. 31d, DKR 42, p. 341). Coquart or Choquart de Cambron, a gentleman from Artois, was joint captain of the castle of Airaines in 1421 with Jean Sarpe, lord of Saint-Maulvis, when the place was captured by Jean de Luxembourg. The two men took refuge in Le Crotoy,

at Longueville-sur-Scie Guillaume d'Harbouville[182]
at Valmont Pierre de Gausseville knight[183]
at Gamaches-en-Vexin Louis de Thiembronne knight[184]
at Neufchâtel-en-Bray Morelet de Béthencourt knight[185]
at Gournay-en-Bray Daviot de Poix, a Burgundian knight[186]
at Gisors Rigault de Fontaines knight[187]
at Bouconvillers Jacques de Bouconvillers knight, lord of the place[188]

---

then commanded by Jacques de Harcourt. It was Cambron who surrendered the keys of Le Crotoy to the duke of Bedford on 3 March 1424. Cambron was in the company of the duke of Alençon when the latter was taken prisoner at Verneuil (Huguet, *Aspects*, pp. 146–51).

[182] Seine-Maritime, arr. Dieppe, cant. Luneray. On 7 January 1419 Robert de Grosmesnil, captain of the castle of Longueville, was provided by Henry V with a protection (C 64/9 m. 2, DKR 41, p. 707). The chronicle's captain of Longueville could be Guillaume d'Harbouville, knighted by 1405, chamberlain of Charles VI in 1405 and 1408 (*Cour amoureuse*, i, no. 243).

[183] Seine-Maritime, arr. Le Havre, cant. Fécamp. Pierre de Gausseville was taken prisoner at the surrender of Harfleur in 1415 and brought to England in November. He remained in captivity in the Tower of London until at least mid-1417 (E 404/34/260 A, B).

[184] Eure, arr. Les Andelys, cant. Gisors. Louis de Bournel, knight, lord of Thiembronne, was taken prisoner at Mons-en-Vimeu in 1421 and handed over to the duke of Burgundy (Monstrelet, iv, p. 63). He later appears as captain of the town and castle of Gamaches in the treaty for its surrender which he negotiated on 11 June 1422 in the wake of the fall of Meaux (AN, J 646/20, AN, JJ 172/360). It is likely that his release had been conditional upon the surrender of Gamaches.

[185] Seine-Maritime, arr. Dieppe, cant. Neufchâtel-en-Bray, commonly called 'de Lincourt' in the Middle Ages. Renaud VI, alias Morelet, de Béthencourt (c. 1364–c. 1440) issued from a noble family of the *pays de Caux*. Morelet was a chamberlain of Charles VI from 1397 to 1412, and a member of the household of John the Fearless, whom he served in arms during the civil war. He was found guilty of fraud and murder and spent five years in prison between 1414 and 1419, when Duke Philip released him. Béthencourt, who embraced the double monarchy, assumed high responsibilities in the government of Paris in the 1420s (Schnerb, 'Morelet de Béthencourt', pp. 449–72).

[186] Seine-Maritime, arr. Dieppe, ch. l. cant. Daviot de Poix was a staunch supporter of the duke of Burgundy. His sustained military activity earned him many a chronicle mention (Monstrelet, iv, pp. 59, 67, 136, 205, 230). We find him at the battle of Mons-en-Vimeu (in 1421), at the siege of the Pont-de-Meulan (in 1423) and the siege of Guise (in 1424). According to Fénin (p. 105), the castle of Gournay was under the command of Philippe de Saveuses in 1418.

[187] Eure, arr. Les Andelys, ch. l. cant. Rigault (or Regnault) de Fontaines, lord of Fontaines, was attached to the duke of Orléans. He defended the castle of Coucy on his behalf in 1412 (AN, JJ 166/28). He was an 'écuyer échanson' of Philippe de Vertus in 1413, governor and *bailli* of Valois in 1436 and chamberlain of the duke in 1441 (Gonzales, p. 232). It was Lionel de Bournonville who was captain of the town of Gisors when it surrendered on 11 September 1419 (BNF, Fr. 26043/5419; Schnerb, *Bournonville*, pp. 321–4). Following the surrender of Gisors, the duke of Clarence besieged the fortress of Saint-Martin-le-Gaillard in which, according to Monstrelet (iii, pp. 344–5), were Rigault de Fontaines and Karados des Qesnes under the command of Philippe de Lis. Fontaines was knighted on the eve of the battle of Mons-en-Vimeu in 1421 (Monstrelet, iv, p. 59) and was still militarily active in the 1430s and 1440s. Huguet (*Aspects*, p. 156 n. 3) suggests that there might be a confusion between two Rigault or Regnault de Fontaines.

[188] Bouconvillers (Oise, arr. Beauvais, cant. Chaumont-en-Vexin). Jacques de Bouconvillers appears as a master of the household of Charles VI in 1417 (Rey, 'Un témoignage inédit',

at Pontoise the lord of l'Isle-Adam[189] and the lord of Melun[190]
at Meulan the lord of Aunoy[191]
at Mantes-la-Jolie *Jean d'Artye knight*[192]
at Vernon Jean de Courcelles knight[193] and the Bastard of la Baume of Savoy[194]
at La Roche-Guyon Olivier de Dampont[195]
at Monchaux-Soreng Robert de Pierrecourt[196]

---

p. 31). The lordship of Bouconvillers, confiscated from Jacques de Boquenvillers, rebel, was granted to Giles de Clamecy on 16 August 1421 (C 64/16 m. 27, DKR 42, p. 416). See also Lefèvre-Pontalis, 'Épisodes de l'invasion', pp. 261 n. 5 and 274.

[189] Val-d'Oise, ch. l. d'arr. Jean de Villiers, lord of l'Isle-Adam (1384–d. 1437), was entrusted by John the Fearless with the captaincy of the town of Pontoise in 1417.

[190] This may be Jean de Melun (c. 1396–1484), lord of Antoing, a devoted supporter of the last three Valois dukes of Burgundy. He participated in the military campaign of John the Fearless around Paris in the autumn of 1417. He was in the company of the duke just before the murder of Montereau in September 1419, and was present in the council of Philip the Good at Arras two months later which sealed a pact of alliance with the English king (Bonenfant, *Du meurtre*, p. 223, appendix no. 16). He was later heavily involved in the conflict between France and Burgundy, and rewarded for his service in 1432 with election as a knight of the Golden Fleece (Devaux, 'Jean de Melun, seigneur d'Antoing', pp. 64–7).

[191] Yvelines, arr. Mantes-la-Jolie, cant. Les Mureaux. Jean d'Aunoy, seigneur d'Aunoy, was 'écuyer d'écurie' in 1407 and *bailli* of Chaumont-en-Bassigny (1407–11 and 1413–18). He defended Paris in 1415 (*GR*, ii, p. 151; Demurger, 'Guerre civile', pp. 227–8).

[192] Yvelines, ch. l. d'arr. On 8 July 1416 Charles VI confirmed Jean de Tournebu, knight and chamberlain of the king, as captain of the town and fortress of Mantes (BNF, Clairambault 959/63; *GR*, iv, p. 78).

[193] Eure, arr. Les Andeleys, ch. l. cant. Jean de Courcelles, lord of Saint-Liebaut (d. 1435), was a councillor and chamberlain of Charles VI in 1411 and a staunch partisan of John the Fearless. After the duke's death, he fully embraced the dual monarchy. He was commissioned by Henry V to negotiate, on the English side, the surrender of the castle and town of Melun on 17 November 1420 (C 64/14 m. 14, DKR 42, p. 381) and later became master of the household of the duke of Bedford for whom he carried out several diplomatic missions (BNF, PO 383 Courcelles 6). He attended the coronation of Henry VI in Paris in 1431 and died childless in December 1435. See Mirot, 'Notes sur un manuscrit de Froissart', p. 312 n. 1; Mirot, 'Pierre de Fontenay', p. 311; *Cour amoureuse*, i, no. 144.

[194] Guillaume, Bastard of la Baume, lord of la Charme, is described as a captain of a company who, together with other captains from Savoy (Jean and Clavin du Clou), caused troubles in the Champagne region in August 1421 (*Choix de pièces inédites*, ii, p. 111). Waurin (iii, pp. 42–9, 56–9) devotes a long passage to him, explaining how he suddenly changed allegiance in 1423, rallying the Valois cause, and briefly occupying Cravant before he was captured by the English.

[195] Val-de'Oise, arr. Pontoise, cant. Vauréal. Olivier de Dampont, esquire, gave homage and fealty to Henry V on 24 February 1419 (C 64/10 m. 25, DKR 41, p. 755). 'Olivier Dampont' – possibly the same individual – who had been sergeant of the forest of Rouvray, died at Verneuil in 1424, leaving lands in the bailliage of Rouen (AN, Dom Lenoir 14, ff. 194–5, cited in Jones, 'Battle of Verneuil', p. 399).

[196] Seine-Maritime, arr. Dieppe, cant. Eu, rather than Monceaux in Oise, arr. Clermont, cant. Pont-Sainte-Maxence. According to Le Fèvre de Saint-Remy (*Chronique*, i, pp. 55–7), Robert de Pierrecourt, esquire, was at the siege of Saint-Rémy-du-Plain in 1412 where he was knighted by Waleran de Luxembourg, constable of France, before a battle took place against the relieving forces sent by the Orleanists.

at Eu the baron of La Heuze[197]
at Bouillancourt-en-Séry Gilles de Gamaches knight[198]
at Château-Gaillard the lord of Bacqueville[199] and the lord of Mauny[200]
at Ivry the lord of the place[201]

[197] Seine-Maritime, arr. Dieppe, ch. l. cant. This may be Jean de la Heuze, dit le *Baudrain* de la Heuze, although he is reported to have died at Harfleur, shortly after the surrender of the town in 1415 (AN, JJ 173/649). However, the same 'Johannes de la Heuse dicti le Baudreyn', or perhaps his son, was declared a rebel by Henry V and had his lands in Rouen and Caux confiscated and granted to Thomas Tunstall on 3 May 1419 (C 64/11 m. 38, DKR 41, p. 786). Robert de la Heuze, described by Demurger, 'Guerre civile', p. 265, as lord of La Heuze, was dead by 1414.

[198] Somme, arr. Abbeville, cant. Gamaches. Gilles de Gamaches was taken prisoner at the battle of Mons-en-Vimeu in 1421 (Monstrelet, i, p. 62). According to Berry (p. 109) he was captured by the duke of Burgundy himself before the town of Abbeville. He may have died at Verneuil in 1424 (Anselme, viii, p. 692).

[199] Eure, arr. et cant. Les Andelys. Guillaume IX Martel inherited the lordship of Bacqueville at the death of his father at Agincourt. He had been knighted by that time and had recently been made captain of Château-Gaillard. The stronghold continued to resist after the surrender of Rouen, which had brought about the surrender of all the other fortresses on the Seine including the castle of Bacqueville, which Guillame held in the name of his mother Marguerite. On 27 January 1419 Guillaume received a safe-conduct to come to Henry V in Rouen (C 64/10 m. 41, DKR 41, p. 722). The English king was possibly trying to obtain the surrender of Château-Gaillard using the lordship of Bacqueville as a leverage, but this failed. On 2 April Henry V granted the lordship of Bacqueville to Lord Roos (C 64/11 m. 79, DKR 41, p. 763). Château-Gaillard was blockaded from the end of March and was still resisting in December 1419. Deprived of access to fresh water, the castle was forced to surrender on 8 December. On the same day Guillaume and the other defenders received a safe-conduct to leave the place, but there is no mention in that of Mauny (C 64/11 m. 4, DKR 41, p. 808). Surviving musters and quittances show that Guillaume was actively serving Charles VII between 1420 and 1424. He may have died at Verneuil (Hellot, *Essai historique sur les Martel*, pp. 102–15).

[200] According to Monstrelet (iii, p. 338), Olivier de Mauny was the captain of the fortress of Château-Gaillard, who, together with his 120 men, gave long resistance to the earls of Huntingdon and Kent in 1419. If this Olivier de Mauny was the lord of Lignières and Lesnen who had been captured at Falaise and released in June 1418, as Henri de Moranvillé believes (*Songe véritable*, p. 188), this would mean that Mauny would have already broken his promise not to re-arm against the English only nine months after having given it to Henry V. But this contradicts M 9's later claim according to which Mauny broke his word at the battle of *le park l'evesque* which the chronicle situates in 1422 (f. 45v). The defender of Château-Gaillard may thus be a homonym, probably Olivier de Mauny (d. 1424), lord of Thiéville, knight, chamberlain of the king, who acted as lieutenant for the count of Aumale at Mont-Saint-Michel between 1420 and 1424 (Poli, p. cxxxvii). He might be the lord of Mauny who according to M 9 (f. 52v) was at Verneuil, where he died (Monstrelet, iv, p. 195).

[201] Settlements bearing the name Ivry lie on both sides of the River Eure. Ivry, which was given the suffix La Bataille after a battle of 1590, lies to the west of the River Eure and is the location of a castle (Eure, arr. Evreux, cant. Saint André de l'Eure). La Chaussée d'Ivry (Eure et Loir, arr. Dreux, cant. Anet), which is mentioned on f. 39v in the list of English captaincies, lies to the east of the river. Charles d'Ivry, baron of Ivry, knight, councillor and chamberlain of Charles VI, was also lord of Saint-Sauveur-le-Vicomte between 1394 and 1413. He was still officially captain of Saint-Sauveur but delegated the charge to Robert de Fréville (Delisle, *Histoire du château et des sires de Saint-Sauveur-le-Vicomte*, pp. 244–8). He was probably killed at Agincourt alongside his father, another Charles (*Cour amoureuse*, no. 116). On 23 June 1418, Sir John Blount was commissioned to

at Etrépagny Guillaume de Roncherolles[202]
at Courtonne-la-Meudrac *Jean de Famysson esquire*[203]
at La Rivière-Thibouville Guillaume de Thibouville knight[204]
at Chambois the lady of the place[205]
at Beaumesnil the lady of the place[206]
at Lisieux no captain, save for the bourgeois of the city[207]
at Pont-Audemer no captain[208]
at Fauguernon *Robert de Maillot*[209]
at Crèvecoeur-en-Auge [no name given][210]

---

treat with the baron of Ivry and the captains of the castles and towns of Ivry and Dreux (C 64/9 m. 20, DKR 41, p. 693). Pierre d'Orgessin, esquire, captain of the castle of Ivry, surrendered on 10 May 1419 (C 64/10 m. 2, DKR 41, p. 746).

[202]   Eure, arr. Les Andelys, cant. Gisors. Louis de Donmesnil, esquire, was captain of the castle of Etrépagny, surrendering the place to the duke of Exeter on 1 February 1419 (C 64/10 m. 3, DKR 41, p. 746). Guillaume V de Roncherolles may have died at Agincourt: his wife, Marguerite de Léon, dame de Hacqueville, was forced to leave the castle of Roncherolles and to take refuge in their estates at Gaillon. Three sons, including another Guillaume, allegedly died during the siege of Château-Gaillard (La Chesnaye, p. 292).

[203]   Calvados, arr. Lisieux, cant. Lisieux. Jean de Bienfaite was captain of the castle of Courtonne-la-Meurdrac when he negotiated its surrender to the English on 6 March 1418 (C 64/8 m. 3, Hardy, pp. 303–6).

[204]   Eure, arr. Bernay, cant. Beaumont-le-Roger, co. Nassandres. Guillaume de Thibouville, knight, was captain of the castle of La Rivière-Thibouville when he negotiated its surrender to the English on 11 March 1418 (C 64/8 m. 5, Hardy, pp. 292–4). The lordship of La Rivière-Thibouville and all the lands held by the late Louis de Thibouville were granted to Thomas, earl of Salisbury on 1 June 1418 (C 64/9 m. 13, DKR 41, p. 698).

[205]   This is presumably Chambois (Orne, arr. Argentan, cant. Argentan 2, co. Gouffern-en-Auge) where there is an eleventh-century keep. If Belleval (p. 167) is correct in designating Béatrix de Clermont-Nesle as the wife of Jean de Tilly, lord of Chambois, killed at Agincourt, this Béatrix might be the M 9 chronicle's lady of Chambois. Chambois had fallen into the hands of Henry V toward mid-October 1417. The castle and lordship, which were previously held by Jean de Tilly, knight, were granted to Henry Fitzhugh on 8 November 1417 (C 64/8 m. 7, Hardy, p. 280). On 11 October 1417, Jean de Tilly, knight, in the castle of Chambois, was provided by Henry V with safe-conducts for fifty people to leave the place (C 64/8 m. 23, Hardy, p. 177). We can assume that this Jean de Tilly was a relative or possibly the son of Béatrix.

[206]   Eure, arr. Bernay, ch. l. cant. Louise de Hangest appears as widow of Guillaume de Tournebu, knight, lord of Beaumesnil, in an inquiry into the guardianship of her children in June 1416 (AN, Dom Lenoir, 5, pp. 165–70, for which thanks to Adrien Dubois). She was, in all likelihood, the chronicle's lady of Beaumesnil. The castle and lordship of Beaumesnil, previously belonging to Guillaume de Tournebu, were granted to Robert, lord Willoughby on 24 May 1418 (C 64/9, m. 17, DKR 41, p. 695).

[207]   Calvados, ch. l. d'arr. Henry V had occupied Lisieux by 4 August 1417, which had been left undefended (Newhall, *English Conquest*, p. 57).

[208]   Eure, arr. Bernay, ch. l. cant. Pont-Audemer surrendered in the wake of the fall of Rouen (Monstrelet, iii, p. 309; Schnerb, 'Sauver', pp. 215–16) but the *vicomté* had been granted to the duke of Clarence in February 1418 (C 64/8 m. 11, Hardy, pp. 259–60).

[209]   Calvados, arr. Lisieux, cant. Pont-l'Evêque. There is a distant possibility that this was Robert de Mailly, an esquire from Picardy who died in 1419 or 1420.

[210]   Calvados, arr. Lisieux, cant. Mezidon-Canon.

at Chambois the lady of the place[211]
at Chailloué Jean le Beauvoisien[212]
at Conches-en-Ouche Guillaume Tournebeuf[213]
at Pont-l'Evêque Jean de Vieuxpont[214]
(36r) at Tilly Jean de Cantepie[215]
at Torigni-sur-Vire Thomas du Boys knight[216]
at Exmes Pierre le Beauvoisien knight[217]
at Exmes Jean de Tournebeuf knight[218]

---

[211] In addition to the Chambois in Orne noted earlier, there is another Chambois in Eure, arr. Bernay, cant. Verneuil-sur-Avre. A late twelfth-century castle lies close by at Avrilly. But it is more likely that the chronicle has simply repeated in error the earlier entry.

[212] Orne, arr. Alençon, cant. Sées. The chronicle attributes two captaincies to Jean le Beauvoisien, Chailloué and La Flèche. These are likely to have been shared between father and son. Jean le Beauvoisien, esquire, mustered in the retinue of Macé le Bailleul in Rouen on 24 September 1415 (BNF, Clairambault 9/73; Belleval, p. 302). On 28 April 1422, Henry V issued a pardon to 'Jean Bon Voisin' for having gone over to the enemy in order to pay the ransom of his father (C 64/17 m. 22, DKR 42, p. 441). Jean le Beauvoisien, esquire, is recorded as captain of La Flèche in three safe-conducts that he received between October 1433 and March 1434 (AN, KK 324 ff. 8v, 15r, 44r). Two other safe-conducts issued around the same time include a namesake who is qualified as 'le jeune', presumably his son (AN, KK 324 ff. 29v, 48r). Jean le Beauvoisien, esquire (possibly the elder), appeared among the witnesses of a truce sealed on 20 December 1438 with the earl of Dorset which was meant to bring peace in Maine and Anjou (Joubert, *Documents*, p. 35).

[213] Eure, arr. Evreux, ch. l. cant. A Guillaume Tournebeuf was *bailli* of Amiens in 1399 but it is uncertain whether this is the same person.

[214] Calvados, arr. Lisieux, ch. l. cant. Jean de Vieuxpont was son of Yves de Vieuxpont.

[215] Eure, arr. et cant. Les Andelys. The castle of Tilly, which belonged to Philippe de Harcourt (C 64/8 m. 12, Hardy, p. 253), had fallen into the hands of Henry V by 24 September 1417 (C 64/8 m. 25, Hardy, 153), but there is no mention of Cantepie. That said, evidence of at least one, and probably several, Jean de Cantepie has survived. A Jean de Cantepie mustered at Rouen as an esquire in the retinue of Guillaume Carbonnel on 24 September 1415 (BNF, Clairambault 25/74) and may have fought at Agincourt. A Jean de Cantepie, serving the dual monarchy, received wages for his service in arms around Paris in September 1429 (Viriville, *Histoire de Charles VII*, i, p. 121 n. 1). Another Cantepie acted against English rule in Normandy in 1434 (ibid., pp. 336–7).

[216] Manche, arr. Saint-Lô, cant. Condé-sur-Vire. Thomas du Boys, knight, seems to have remained in Normandy in the obedience of Henry V. On 8 March 1419 he and his wife, Marie Vierville, were granted livery of the lands of Catherine de la Luzerne, his mother (C 64/10 m. 24, DKR 41, p. 738). In the aftermath of Charles VII's reconquest, du Boys was engaged in a legal dispute to regain the ownership of the castle of Pirou (AN, K 68/47; Luce, ii, pp. 241–3 no. 293).

[217] Orne, arr. Argentan, cant. Argentan 2. Pierre le Beauvoisien was listed as an esquire in a muster made by the count of Aumale at Mont-Saint-Michel in 1420. A year later, he mustered together with fourteen esquires of his chamber under the captain of the Mont (BNF, Clairambault 57/171, 178; Poli, p. c, and preuves nos. 1010 and 1031).

[218] The Tabellionage of Rouen records Jean de Tournebeuf, knight, lord of Couronne, near Rouen, who sealed a contract with a Norman esquire, Robert Duval, and his wife for the purchase of their estates in return for a life annuity ('contrat en viager') (ADSM, 2E 1, registres du tabellionnage de Rouen; Péricard-Méa, 'Pèlerins par dévotion pure', p. 217). 'Jean Tournebeuse' appears in Glover's list of prisoners taken at Verneuil in 1424 (BL, Harley 782, f. 51r, printed in *L&P*, II, ii, pp. 394–9).

at Mortagne-au-Perche Jean de Montgoubert knight[219]
at Bellême the Bastard of Alençon[220]
at Verneuil-sur-Avre *Robert de Milant knight*[221]
at Longny-au-Perche Robert d'O knight, lord of Maillebois[222]
at La Motte d'Yversay Jean de Raveton knight[223]
at Tillières-sur-Avre Jean de Bellegarde, lord of Bellegarde[224]
at La Ferté-Vidame the *vidame* of Chartres[225]
at Châteauneuf-en-Thymerais the same *vidame*[226]
at Gacé Jean, lord of Cléry[227]

---

[219] Orne, ch. l. d'arr. Jean de Montgoubert appears in Glover's list of prisoners taken at Verneuil in 1424 (BL, Harley 782, f. 51r, printed in *L&P*, II, ii, pp. 394–9). A Jean de Montgoubert – possibly the same person – was in Pierre de Brézé's *Grande Ordonnance* company in the 1450s (Prosser, 'After the Reduction', p. 264).

[220] Orne, arr. Mortagne-au-Perche, cant. Ceton. The town of Bellême was captured in November 1417 when Henry V gave power to the earl of Warwick to deliver *bullettes* to all who wished to stay in its castellany (C 64/8 m. 19, Hardy, p. 202). Pierre, Bastard of Alençon was the brother of Duke Jean II of Alençon, according to Anselme (i, p. 272), and not his uncle, as the chronicle claims on f. 51v. The Bastard of Alençon took part in a military operation for the recapture of the fortresses of Beaumont and Fresnay in the early days of the English invasion together with Ambroise de Loré (Triger, *Le château et la ville*, p. 30).

[221] Eure, arr. Evreux, ch. l. cant. No information has been found on this captaincy.

[222] Orne, arr. Mortagne-au-Perche, cant. Tourouvre. Robert VII d'O, lord of O (d. 1451), whose father Robert VI died at Agincourt, was 'échanson' of Charles, duke of Bourbon to whom he paid homage for his lordships of Fresne, Baillet, Maillebois and Franconville on 18 January 1446 (La Chesnaye, xv, p. 91). The manor of O which had been held by his father was granted by Henry V to William FitzHarry on 21 November 1417 (C 64/8 m. 19, Hardy, p. 207).

[223] This was presumably the castle on the River Huisne in Perche, close to the village of Saint-Maurice-sur-Huisne, which was taken into English hands in January 1418 (C 64/8 m. 14, Hardy, pp. 235–6). Jean de Raveton (or Raneton), an esquire in the company of Guillaume Heudebert, mustered at Rouen on 3 October 1415 (BNF, Clairambault 59/196). Sixteen men including Jean de Raveton received a safe-conduct to leave the castle of O on 9 October 1417 (C 64/8 m. 23, Hardy, p. 178). Jean de Raveton, knight, received several safe-conducts in English territories in Maine in 1434 (AN, KK 324 ff. 48r, 53v, 56r, 69r).

[224] Eure, arr. Evreux, cant. Verneuil-sur-Avre. Jean de Bellegarde defended the interests of his wife Condorine de Mauléon (also called 'de Barbazan') against Renaud VI de Pons before the *Parlement* of Paris, in 1398 (Chavanon, 'Renaud VI de Pons', p. 212).

[225] Known at the time as La Ferté-Ernault. Eure-et-Loir, arr. Dreux, cant. Saint-Lubin-des-Joncheret. The *vidame* of Chartres was held by the Vendôme family in the fifteenth century. The person here is presumably Jean de Vendôme, knight, councillor and chamberlain of Charles VII. He had been taken prisoner by 1433 when he was ransomed by Walter Hungerford (C 76/115, m. 5, DKR 48, p. 294). He was important and close enough to Charles VII to receive 1000 *l.t.* towards the payment of his ransom, the king regretting that he could not help him more (BL, Add. Ch. 3744, 3805; Ambühl, *Prisoners*, pp. 168–9, 199).

[226] Eure-et-Loir, arr. Dreux, cant. Sain-Lubin-des-Joncherets.

[227] Orne, arr. Mortagne-au-Perche, cant. Vimoutiers. Jean IV de Mello, dit Hutin, knight, lord of Aumont, was also lord of Cléry. He rendered great service to Charles VI in his wars against the English and is alleged to have died at Agincourt. His heir, Jacques d'Aumont, inherited the lordship of Cléry (Anselme, iv, p. 873).

at Rugles Jacques de Neuville[228]
at Gaillon *Pierre du Couldray knight*[229]
at Le Goulet *Louis d'Abecourt*[230]
at Neaufles-Saint-Martin Jean de Saint-Cler knight, lord of the place[231]
at Baudemont the same Jean de Saint-Cler knight[232]
at Dangu Pierre de Saint-Cler[233]
at La Ferté-Frênel *the lord of Grippon*[234]
at Courville-sur-Eure *the lord of Vieuxpont*[235]
at L'Aigle [blank][236]

---

[228] Eure, arr. Bernay, cant. Breteuil. The captain of the fortress of Rugles at the time of its surrender on 18 October 1417 was Jean du Melle, esquire, lord of Champhaut (C 64/8 m. 3, Hardy, pp. 307–8). Jacques de Neuville, esquire, and Guillaume de la Perque, who had been commissioned by the lord of Ferrières and all those within the town and castle of Chambrais to negotiate their surrender, sealed a treaty on 9 March 1418 (C 64/8 m. 5, Hardy, pp. 294–6). Jacques de Neuville and his wife Catherine remained in English obedience, being confirmed on 6 June 1418 in the possessions they had held at the landing of Henry V in Normandy (C 64/9 m. 22, DKR 41, p. 691).

[229] Eure, arr. Les Andeleys, ch. l. cant. No information has been found on this captaincy.

[230] Eure, arr. Les Andelys, cant. Gaillon, co. Saint-Pierre-la-Garenne. Pierre de Jucourt and Charles de Longueval, knights, appear as captains of the castles of Le Grand Goulet and Le Petit Goulet in the treaty of surrender negotiated with Thomas, duke of Clarence, on 26 February 1419 (C 64/10 m. 4, DKR 41, p. 746; *Foedera*, ix, p. 699). Jean Recuchon and a lord of Abancourt (perhaps Louis d'Abecourt) had received a safe-conduct on 22 January 1419 to come to Henry V in the castle of Rouen (C 64/9 m. 1, DKR 41, p. 707). We can conjecture that these two men had been sent to Henry as a preliminary for surrender negotiations for the two castles.

[231] Eure, arr. Les Andelys, cant. Gisors. Pierre de Bourbon, lord of Préaux, was made captain of Neaufles on 13 October 1416 (*GR*, iii, p. 408), but it is 'noble homme' Jacques de Lille who appears as captain of the castle of Neaufles in the treaty for its surrender on 23 February 1419 (C 64/10 m. 4, DKR 41, p. 746). Jean, dit Bruneau, de Saint-Cler, lord of Saint-Cler, had a long career in the service of the duke of Burgundy and then of Charles VI, including the captaincy of Mantes (1390–1413) and the office of *garde de la prévôté* of Paris (1410–12). He is alleged, wrongly, to have died at Agincourt (*Songe véritable*, pp. 208–11).

[232] A castle in the commune of Bus-Saint-Rémy (Eure, arr. Les Andelys, cant. Vexin-sur-Epte).

[233] Eure, arr. Les Andelys, cant. Gisors. Pierre de Saint-Cler, knight, lord of Sérifontaine, a chamberlain of Charles VI (BNF, PO 2747, no. 27; *Songe véritable*, p. 211), was made captain of 'Neauphle-le-Château' on 26 February 1413 (BNF, Clairambault 782/92; *GR*, iv, p. 88). He died on 4 July 1416 (BNF, Clairambault 959/63; *GR*, iv, p. 88). According to Belleval (p. 253), Pierre was the 'lord of Saint Cler' who died at Agincourt.

[234] Orne, arr. Mortagne-au-Perche, cant. Rai. Might this be the same lord of Grippon who appears as captain of Louviers?

[235] Eure-et-Loir, arr. Chartres, cant. Illiers-Chambray. Might this be Jean de Vieuxpont, son of Yves de Vieuxpont (d. 1415) who appears as captain of Pont-l'Evêque?

[236] Orne, arr. Mortagne-au-Perche, cant. L'Aigle. No information has been found on this captaincy.

In the county of Maine
at Fresnay-sur-Sarthe *Jean de Combres knight*[237]
at Beaumont-sur-Sarthe Huet de Fontenay esquire[238]
at *Tonnoye Jean Canu knight*[239]
at Le Mans the lord of Fontaines[240] principal captain, the lord of Bellay[241] and Le Roncin,[242] sub-captains
at Saint-Aignan Guillaume de Maulny knight, lord of the place[243]
at La Guierche *Robert d'Asse* and the Spanish[244]

---

[237] Sarthe, arr. Mamers, cant. Sillé-le-Guillaume, formerly known as Fresnay-le-Vicomte. Ambroise de Loré was captain of Fresnay-le-Vicomte in 1418, according to Des Ursins (p. 547). It is not clear who Jean de Combres was. Isabelle II de Combres, dame de Bouloire et de Combres, inherited the lordship of Combres at the death of Jean III de Combres in 1405. Her second husband, Jean de Beaumont, acted as lord of Combres, paying rents to the abbaye du Pré in 1411. But this task was carried out by the dame de Combres between 1414 and 1425, which may suggest that Jean was dead by then. Isabelle died childless in 1425 (Vallée, 'Les seigneurs de Bouloire', pp. 241–54).

[238] Sarthe, arr. Mamers, cant. Sillé-le-Guillaume. Formerly known as Beaumont-le-Vicomte. Huet de Fontenay was among twelve knights and esquires who were handed over to the English as hostages for the payment of the ransom of the duke of Alençon in 1427, and who were released after payment (ADSM, 2E1, Registre du Tabellionage de Rouen, 1427–28, f. 113; Le Cacheux, *Rouen*, pp. 127–30, no. 56; see also Chartier, i, p. 57; *Pucelle*, pp. 249–50).

[239] Unidentified unless this should be read as Touvoie, a manor held by the bishop of Le Mans (Sarthe, arr. Mamers, cant. Savigné-l'Evêque). No information has been found on this captaincy.

[240] Sarthe, ch. l. d'arr. It is not easy to identify this lord of Fontaines. A Jean de Fontaines, lord of Fontaines, was active in the mid-1410s (Gonzales, pp. 228–31) According to the M 9 chronicle, several Fontaines, including the lord, died at Agincourt. According to des Ursins, a lord of Fontaines seized Beaumont-le-Vicomte with Ambroise de Loré in 1418 (pp. 547–8). For Cagny (p. 119) he was a captain in the Franco-Scottish contingent at Baugé in 1421. He may have been Jean, lord of Fontaine-Guérin, who was granted the lordship of Saint-Laurent-des-Mortiers on 26 February 1422 (Joubert, *Saint-Laurent des Mortiers*, pp. 346–7).

[241] Jean du Bellay, knight, was prisoner of the duke of Exeter in November 1418 (C 64/9, m. 8, DKR 41, p. 701). This is probably the same Jean du Bellay, an Angevin knight, who operated in Maine and Anjou in the early 1420s. He was among 2,000 French troops gathered by Guillaume de Narbonne in Anjou which defeated the English near Bernay in August 1422 (*Religieux*, vi, p. 476). Bellay and his acolyte Loré were captured during an attempt to seize the fortress of Fresnay-le-Vicomte four months later in November 1422 (Chartier, i, pp. 14, 30; *Pucelle*, p. 212). See note 766 for his possible capture at Cravant and putative death at Verneuil.

[242] Le Roncin (or Roussin), a French captain, fought at Baugé (AN, P 1334; Berry, p. 117 n. 3; Godefroy, *Histoire de Charles VI*, p. 732). He is described as captain of the castle of Châteaudun and 'gouverneur du pais' (possibly the comté of Dunois) toward the end of 1422 in a deposition made by Jean Baligaut in 1426 (*Pucelle*, p. 472; see also *Actes*, i, p. 56). His later activity as a *routier* in the 1440s is well documented (Tuetey, *Les Ecorcheurs*, i, pp. 56, 84, 162, 166; ii, pp. 402 and 435).

[243] Sarthe, arr. et cant. Mamers. Guillaume de Maulny must have inherited the lordship of Saint-Aignan from his father Hervé de Maulny sometime in the 1410s (Louis, 'Etudes féodales', pp. 334–6).

[244] Sarthe, arr. Le Mans, cant. Bonnétable. No information has been found on this captaincy.

at Assé-le-Riboul Guillaume de Saint-Denis[245]
at Sillé-le-Guillaume Pierre le Forestier and Olivier le Forestier, Bretons[246]
at Antoigny *Gawayn de Montigny*[247]
at Tucé Pierre Boterel knight[248]
at Loué Guyon du Coing esquire[249]
at Tennie Jean de Tournemine knight[250]
at Courmenant the same Jean de Tourmemine knight[251]
at Saint-Pierre-sur-Orthe *Jean Vachereau*[252]
(36v) at Saint-Thomas-de-Courceriers *Michel Taillebert*[253]

---

[245] Sarthe, arr. Mamers, cant. Sille-le-Guillaume. Guillaume de Saint-Denis, lord of Saint-Denis-sur-Sarthon, married Louise de Tyrel in the presence of the *bailli* of Alençon in 1423 (Allais, *Nobiliaire universel de France*, xvi, p. 515). Five years later, he was serving the English as a lieutenant of Sir William Glasdale at the siege of Orléans (Jarry, p. 713).

[246] Sarthe, arr. Mamers, ch. l. cant. Pierre and Olivier le Forestier, brothers, mustered at Sablé in April 1420 in the company of Robert Pouez (Morice, ii, p. 1006). The treaty of surrender of Sillé-le-Guillaume negotiated with the English on 1 October 1424 designated Olivier le Forestier as captain of the place (Planchenault, 'La conquête' (1925), pp. 25–72; see also Cosneau, p. 107). They may have shared this captaincy, as the chronicle claims. Pierre is unlikely to have attended the surrender, because, as a later legal suit reveals, he had been captured at Verneuil and taken to Alençon (AN, X1a 9201, f. 94v).

[247] Orne, arr. Alençon, cant. Magny-le-Desért. No information has been found on this captaincy.

[248] Sarthe, arr. Mamers, cant. Loué, co. Lavardin. Pierre Boterel, a Breton 'esquire banneret', was active around the time of the English conquest of Normandy. He mustered with Jean de Roussers at Paris in June 1416, and with Pierre de Rochefort, *maréchal de France*, at Bourges in June 1418. He was in the household of John V, duke of Britany in 1420 (Morice, ii, pp. 912, 961, 1067, 1069).

[249] Sarthe, arr. La Flèche, ch. l. cant. Guyon du Coing is described as captain of Sablé in 1428 when he and his men were defeated by English troops under the command of William Oldhall between Le Mans and Alençon according to Chartier (i, pp. 52–3) and *Pucelle* (p. 242). He shared the capture of Thomas, lord Scales with Jean Bouchet in June 1429 ('Extrait du Compte de Jehan Bouchet', ADS, E 300; Ledru, *Le château de Sourches*, pp. 352–3). As captain of Beaumont-le-Vicomte he was provided with six safe-conducts between 1433 and 1434 to travel across English-held territories (AN, KK 324, ff. 11v, 14v, 25r, 45v, 55v, 74r). Etienne du Plessis, dit Court Col, and Guiot du Coing, esquires, were deputies of Charles d'Anjou in an agreement sealed between them and representatives of the count of Dorset for bringing peace in Anjou and Maine, on 20 December 1438 (Joubert, *Documents*, pp. 31–8, no. 17).

[250] This could be Jean I de Tournemine (d. 1421), lord of la Hunaudaye, who is recorded as an executor of Guy de Laval's will in October 1415 (*Maison de Laval*, iii, p. 28) and who dealt with the marriage contract of Gilles de Rais and Beatrix de Rohan in November 1418 (Morice, ii, pp. 975–6). He was with Olivier de Blois immediately before the capture of Jean V (Morice, ii, p. 1001). The duke of Brittany granted his 'beloved cousin and loyal lord of la Hunaudaye' the manor of Montbran in July 1420 (*Lettres et mandements de Jean V*, III, no. 1411). Tournemine acted as a surety in the treaty for the release of Richemont in July 1420 (Morice, ii, pp. 1033–7). For a recent genealogical survey of the Tournemine, see Torchet, *Reformation des Fouages*, p. 406). We thank Professor Michael Jones for his help in identifying potentially three different Jean de Tournemines who appear in the M 9 chronicle.

[251] Sarthe, arr. Le Mans, cant. Sillé-le-Guillaume, co. Rouez.

[252] Mayenne, arr. Mayenne, cant. Évron. No information has been found on this captaincy.

[253] Mayenne, arr. Mayenne, cant. Évron. No information has been found on this captaincy.

at Sainte-Suzanne Ambroise de Loré knight[254]
at Sablé-sur-Sarthe *Guy de Laval knight*[255]
at Laval Guy Turpin knight[256]
at Mayenne *Jean* d'Avaugour knight[257]
at La Ferté-Bernard *Jean* d'Avaugour esquire[258]
at Clinchamps Jean Pesaz[259]

---

[254] Mayenne, arr. Laval, cant. Meslay-du-Maine. Ambroise de Loré (d. 1446), a knight from Maine and loyal supporter of Charles VII, fought relentlessly against the English in Maine and Normandy in the period covered by the chronicle, in which he is mentioned five times. Among his early feats of arms, he defeated Thomas Burgh in a chance encounter in 1417 (Des Ursins, p. 539) where he was described as a 'gentil escuyer' from the castle of 'Courseries' (Saint-Thomas-de-Courceriers?). He recaptured from the English Fresnay-le-Vicomte in 1418 and Beaumont-le-Vicomte in 1419 (he was knighted around that time). He was possibly captured twice between 1418 and 1419, but quickly found a way out of prison (Des Ursins, pp. 547–8, 559; Luce, i, p. 22 n. 2, 114 n. 6, 129 n. 1; Wylie, iii, p. 181; Triger, 'Une forteresse', p. 70). A letter of remission indicates that he was captain of Sainte-Suzanne in 1423 (Luce, i, p. 216, no. 68). See also *Journal d'un Bourgeois*, ed. Tuetey, p. 383 n. 1; Poli, p. cxxxiii; Charles, 'L'invasion', p. 18 n. 1; *Jeanne. Dictionnaire*, pp. 226–7.

[255] Sarthe, arr. La Flèche, ch. l. cant. Identification here is problematic. Guy XIII de Laval died at Rhodes in 1414. His son, the future Guy XIV of Laval, was only 10 in 1417. Guy de Laval – known as Guy de Gavre – became directly engaged with politics and military action around the time of Joan of Arc (*Maison de Laval*, iii, pp. 1–214). There is evidence of the existence of a Guy de Laval-Loué from a younger branch of the Lavals in 1419 (*Maison de Laval*, iii, p. 31). A last candidate is Guy de Laval, lord of Attechy, chamberlain of the duke of Orléans, but Gonzales (p. 340) could not find evidence of him after 1409.

[256] Mayenne, ch. l. d'arr. Guy Turpin served the king as knight banneret in 1416 (*Maison de Laval*, iii, pp. 29–30). At the beginning of the same year he clandestinely married his cousin, Anne de Laval (mother of the future Guy XIV). This led to a dispute before the *Parlement* of Paris in 1417 with his stepmother, Jeanne de Laval, who would eventually obtain the annulment of this union. The episode involved a short sojourn in prison for Turpin in the *conciergerie* of the Châtelet de Paris in June 1417. Guy de Turpin is therefore very unlikely to have been captain of Laval in 1417 (*Maison de Laval*, iii, pp. 17–20).

[257] Mayenne, ch. l. d'arr. The medieval suffix 'la juhez' is derived from the name of one of its earlier lords, Juhel. Jean des Vaux was made captain of Mayenne-la-Juhez by Yolande of Aragon in 1417 (AN, X2a 20, f. 64), replacing Guillaume d'Avaugour, not Jean. Des Vaux gathered under his command a great number of knights and esquires from Maine, amongst his friends and relatives, including Jean d'Avaugour, lord of Parc, his first cousin (AN, X2a 18). Taking advantage of the absence of Des Vaux in 1423, and betraying his cousin, Avaugour helped Jean de la Haie, baron of Coulonce, to seize control of Mayenne (AN, X2a 27; 246–7). Jean d'Avaugour stood as hostage for the payment of the ransom of Jean, duke of Alençon in 1427 (ADSM, 2E1, Registre du Tabellionage de Rouen, 1427–28, f. 113; Le Cacheux, *Rouen*, pp. 127–30, no. 56). See also Beauchesne, 'Jean des Vaux', pp. 235, 246–7.

[258] Sarthe, arr. Mamers, ch. l. cant. Evidence suggests that it was Louis d'Avaugour and not Jean who was captain of La Ferté-Bernard, commanding the town and castle in the name of Yolande of Aragon (ADS, E 271, no. 3; Charles, 'L'invasion anglaise', p. 188). Louis is given as captain by Chartier (i, p. 47).

[259] Given its place in the list within the section on Maine, this must be Clinchamps within Chemilli (Orne, arr. Mortagne, cant. Bellême) where there is a 'maison forte'. Jean Pesaz, esquire, was lord of Planches, which lies 30 km away from Clinchamps (*Archives départementales de la Sarthe, 4J 306: Sous-Série 4J. Chartier de Grandchamp. Répertoire numérique*, p. 45). In January

at Saint-Calais Jean Tibergeau[260]
at Pescheré Jean le Voyer, lord of the place[261]
at Bouloire *Astergon*[262]
at Montfort-le-Gesnois Michel de Ferrières[263]
at Château-l'Hermitage no captain[264]
at Bonnétable *Jean Courtvalain*[265]
at Ballon Hue de Chanay[266]
at La Faigne the lord of Périers[267]
at Le Grand-Lucé *Guillaume Papillon*[268]
at Château-du-Loir the lord of Maillé[269]
at La Suze-sur-Sarthe *Foulquet de Mauley*[270]
at Brûlon Jean de Mathefelon knight, lord of the place[271]

---

and May 1434 Pesaz and several men and women in his company received safe-conducts to cross English-obedient territories in Maine (AN, KK 324 ff. 31v, 65v).

[260] Sarthe, arr. Mamers, ch. l. cant. The Tibergeau family was from Saint-Calais. Jean Tibergeau, lord of la Mothe, was a vassal and a servant of Jean de Bueil, and possibly one of the authors of *Le Jouvencel*, according to Favre and Lecestre. The earliest evidence that Lecestre gathered about Tibergeau dates from 1427, when he, as captain of the men-at-arms of Beaufort and du Louroux, participated in the siege of La Lude (*Jouvencel*, i, p. x). Another Jean Tibergeau, his son or nephew, served as a man-at-arms in the company of de Bueil toward the end of 1428 (*Jouvencel*, i, pp. ccciv–cccv). Jean de Tibergeau was in Maine in 1434 (AN, KK 324 ff. 46r, 70v, 95r).

[261] Sarthe, arr. Mamers, cant. Montfort-le-Rotrou, co. Le Breil-sur-Mérize. Jean III le Voyer, lord of Pescheray, who succeeded his father Jean III who died at Agincourt, had the same fate at Verneuil nine years later (BNF, Fr. 22610, f. 191v). See Ledru, *Le château de Sourches*, pp. 77–81.

[262] Sarthe, arr. Mamers, cant. Saint-Calais. No information has been found on this captaincy.

[263] Sarthe, arr. Mamers, cant. Savigné-l'Evêque. Michel de Ferrières was an esquire of the count of Aumale in the garrison of Mont-Saint-Michel in 1421 and 1424 (Poli, p. cxx, *preuves* nos. 1039, 1063).

[264] Sarthe, arr. La Flèche, cant. Le Lude. No information has been found on this captaincy.

[265] Sarthe, arr. Mamers, ch. l. cant. No information has been found on this captaincy. This may be Jean Courtalain who paid 300 *l.t.* for his ransom to the English and Burgundians of the garrison of Chartres in 1421 (Merlet, *Registres et minutes*, p. 15).

[266] Sarthe, arr. Le Mans, cant. Bonnétable. This may be Hue de Chanay, knight bachelor, who mustered with nine esquires in his retinue at Le Mans on 19 July 1392 (Morice, ii, p. 611).

[267] Sarthe, arr. et cant. La Flèche, co. Pontvallain. This is probably Jean de Périers, knight, lord of Périers and la Gaulleraye, who gave an 'aveu' to the duke of Anjou for his lordship of la Gaulleraye on 24 November 1433 (AN, P 337/55–93; Espinay, *Fiefs du comté d'Anjou*, p. 46).

[268] Sarthe, arr. La Flèche, cant. Château-du-Loir. No information has been found on this captaincy.

[269] Sarthe, arr. La Flèche, ch. l. cant. This is most likely Hardouin VIII, lord of Maillé, a councillor of Charles VII, who defended Le Mans in 1418 together with Pierre de Rochefort. The two men were taken prisoner a few years later and shared their captivity in England (AN, X1a 9190, f. 303v; 9197, ff. 326v, 329; 9198, ff. 136, 152, 217). Maillé took part in the coronation of Charles VII in 1429, replacing an absent peer (Beaucourt, i, p. 62).

[270] Sarthe, arr. La Flèche, ch. l. cant. No information has been found on this captaincy.

[271] Sarthe, arr. La Flèche, cant. Loué. Jean de Mathefelon was the eldest son and heir of Jeanne le Cornu, dame de Sourches and Vassé (Ledru, *Le château de Sourches*, pp. 86–7, 359).

at Malicorne-sur-Sarthe the lord of the place[272]
at La Flèche Jean le Beauvoisien[273]
at Saint-Ouën-des-Toits Guillaume d'Orenge knight[274]
at Villaines-la-Juhel Pierre d'Anthenaise[275]
at Montaudin *the Bastard of la Fueillie*[276]
at La Tour-Emond Jean des Vaux knight[277]
at Meslay-du-Maine Guillaume Voyer knight[278]

On 11 November 1434 he received a safe-conduct authorising hunting outside the English obedience in Maine (AN, KK 324 f. 147v).

[272] Sarthe, arr. La Flèche, cant. La Suze-sur-Sarthe. The lord of Malicorne at this point was Antoine de Sourches, a knight from Maine, who died at the battle of Verneuil (Charles, 'L'invasion', p. 43).

[273] Sarthe, ch. l. d'arr. The two captaincies attributed to Jean le Beauvoisien – La Flèche and Chailloué – may in fact have been shared between father and son. Between October 1433 and March 1434 Jean le Beauvoisien, écuyer, is recorded as captain of La Flèche in three safe-conducts but two others include a namesake qualified as 'le jeune' (AN, KK 324 ff. 8v, 15r, 44r, 29v, 48r). It was possibly the elder who witnessed a truce in Maine and Anjou with Edmund Beaufort, earl of Dorset, on 20 December 1438 (Joubert, *Documents*, no. 17). A man of the same name mustered in the retinue of Macé le Bailleul in Rouen on 24 September 1415 (BNF, Clairambault 9/73). For the military activity of a Jean le Beauvoisien in the 1460s and 1470s see Contamine, *GES*, pp. 598–9; and Prosser, 'After the Reduction', p. 320.

[274] Mayenne, arr. Laval, cant. Loiron. A man of this name is found in the muster of Jean, lord of Landevy, at Mantes on 5 September 1386 (Lobineau, *Histoire de Bretagne*, ii, p. 660). Guillaume d'Orenge, knight, gave homage to the lord of Chemeré in 1415 (Beauchesne, 'Château du Coudray', p. 308). In 1417 Charles VI assigned Guillaume d'Orenge to defend the lands and castles of Anne de Laval (AN, X2a 17, cited in James, 'Anne de Laval (1385–1466)', p. 148).

[275] Mayenne, arr. Mayenne, ch. l. cant. The house of Anthenaise was based in the barony of Laval. Pierre d'Anthenaise, esquire, lord of Villeray, brother of Aymeric, was the youngest son of Jean d'Anthenaise and Jeanne Fresnel (Bonneserre de Saint-Denis, *Notice historique*, pp. 36, 42). According to Chartier (i, p. 158), he came to the defence of the castle of Pouancé during the siege of 1432. There is evidence of his presence in Maine in 1433 and 1434 (AN, KK 324 ff. 11v, 82r and v).

[276] Mayenne, arr. Mayenne, cant. Gorron. No information has been found on this captaincy.

[277] At Saint-Hilaire-du-Maine (Mayenne, arr. Mayenne, cant. Ernée). Jean des Vaux, seigneur des Horps (1365–?), hailed from an ancient family in southern Maine. In 1416 he was appointed a *chambellan* of Charles VI as reward for his services against the English. In the following year he became captain of Mayenne for Yolande of Aragon, widow of Louis, duke of Anjou, with a garrison of 200. He was wounded at Baugé (AN, X2a 18). His presence at the battle is noted on folio 42v of the chronicle. Whilst absent in another anti-English enterprise at Neuvillais near Sillé-le-Guillaume in 1422, Mayenne castle was seized by the baron of Coulonces, and the captaincy passed to Pierre le Porc, seigneur de Marolles en Larchamp. Des Vaux continued to fight against the English, being co-signatory of the surrender of Laval to Talbot on 15 March 1428. He was captured by the English (probably by Thomas Everingham) in May 1429, being taken to his former castle of Mayenne and ransomed for 2,000 *saluts* and 100 marcs of silver. He served Charles VII in the campaigns of that summer and was present at Patay. We also know that he purchased an English prisoner, Richard Hilton, from Raoul Girart (Beauchesne, 'Jean des Vaux', pp. 225–72).

[278] Mayenne, arr. Château-Gontier, ch. l. cant. Guillaume Voyer served in the company of his brother Jean at the siege of Pontorson in 1427 and shared in the profits of a prisoner (Jones, 'Comptes d'Auffroy Guinot', p. 97).

at Ramefort Jean de Saint-Aubin[279]
at La Chartre-sur-le-Loir Diego de Sales[280]
at Saint-Laurent-des-Mortiers Jacques de Scépeaux knight[281]
at Montmirail Huet des Prés *bailli* of Chartres[282]
at Nogent-le-Rotrou Florent d'Illiers knight[283]
at Mondoubleau Jean Descroix knight[284]

---

[279] Mayenne, arr. Château-Gontier, cant. Azé. See Joubert, *Le château de Ramefort de Gennes*. Jean de Saint-Aubin, écuyer, was captain of Ramefort in July 1434 (AN, KK 324 f. 85r). It is uncertain whether he is the Jean de Saint-Aubin who refused to acknowledge Henry V, thereby forfeiting his lands in the *bailliage* of Caux which were granted to William Bernard on 5 July 1419 (C 64/12 m. 41, DKR 42, p. 338), or the man of the same name who was later 'échanson' of Philip the Good (*Cour amoureuse*, ii, 735). It has been suggested that he was the son of Sir John St Aubyn (aft. 1376–1418) who was MP for Devon in 1414 (HOCa) but this is unlikely.

[280] Sarthe, arr. La Flèche, cant. Château-du-Loir. Diego de Sales was a Spaniard who served in the company of Jean de Torcy at Beaugency in September 1420 (BNF, Clairambault 100/119, 103/97). According to Monstrelet (iv, p. 195), a 'Dragon de Lasalle' died at Verneuil but we have evidence that he commanded a company of crossbowmen at Tours in May 1425 (BNF, Fr. 32510, f. 65v; Planchenault, 'La conquête' (1925), p. 10 n. 2).

[281] Mayenne, arr. Château-Gontier, cant. Azé. From a family based in Anjou, Jacques de Scépeaux, knight, was in Maine in 1434 (AN, KK 324 ff. 142r, 143v). He received safe-conducts in 1434 to travel outside the English obedience in Maine and Anjou (AN, KK 324 ff. 142r, 143v). His capture by Christopher Hanson is mentioned in the M 9 chronicle on f. 61r.

[282] Sarthe, arr. Mamers, cant. Saint-Calais. Uncle of two soldiers serving in the retinue of Perrinet de Gressart in 1435, Huet des Prés was taken prisoner by the garrison of Chartres in March of that year and later served in the garrison of Verneuil (Flamare, *Le Nivernais*, ii, p. 131; Bossuat, *Perrinet Gressart*, p. 235 n. 3).

[283] Eure-et-Loir, ch. l. d'arr. From Perche, in 1422 Florent d'Illiers (1400–75) married Jeanne de Coutes, an elder sister of the future page of Joan of Arc. He succeeded his father as captain of Châteaudun in 1424. He entered Orléans on 28 April 1429 at the head of 400 men-at-arms, including 230 men from his garrison, and went on to fight at Jargeau, Meung and Patay. He participated in the capture of Chartres on 13 April 1432 under Thibaut de Termes and was made chamberlain of the king shortly afterwards (*GR*, ii, pp. 125–6). He seized Meulan in 1435. We find him as captain of Nogent-le-Rotrou in 1437. In the 1440s he was in the service of Dunois as well as of the duke of Orléans. He was in charge of 800 men at the siege of Verneuil when Dunois left him in command on 8 August 1449 ('Le recouvrement de Normendie', in *Narratives of the Expulsion of the English from Normandy*, p. 260). He was *bailli* of Chartres between 1457 and 1461 (Gonzales, p. 294; *Jeanne. Dictionnaire*, pp. 768–9).

[284] Presumably Loir-et-Cher, arr. Vendôme, cant. La Perche. Jean d'Escroz or Descroix, knight, chamberlain of the duke of Orléans, received 100 *l.t.* from his master in 1416 to help him pay his ransom to the English (BL, Add. Ch. 3475–6). He was possibly captured at Agincourt with his master, or perhaps shortly afterwards since the duke gave him the captaincy of the castle of Château-Renault in November 1415, which he held until 1420 (Gonzales, pp. 200–1). On 22 August 1417, Jean Descroix, knight, was authorised to travel to England (C 64/8 m. 27, Hardy, p. 152). A Jean Descroix (perhaps the same person) was in Alençon after its surrender to Henry V, receiving a safe-conduct to leave the place on 23 November 1417 (C 64/8 m. 17, Hardy, p. 216). On 22 February 1418 we find a Jean Descroix in the town of Falaise, where he received another safe-conduct to go wherever he wished in France and then to return to England (C 64/8 m. 12, Hardy, p. 251). But it was surely a different Jean Descroix who was captain of Châtellerault in 1418 (Tours, AA 10). For Le Roulx, it was this last Jean Descroix who fought at Baugé and who became a councillor and

at *Saint-Rémy-du-Plain the lord of Vauhuet*[285]
at Torigni and Bazouges the lord of Escotais[286]
at Montsûrs Pierre d'Arquenay knight[287]
at Châteauneuf-sur-Sarthe *Jacques de Corches*[288]
at *Lisle-Ronde* Guillaume de Brévedent[289]
at Louplande *Louis de Valoges*[290]
(37r) at Ludon *Pierre Morel*[291]
at Le Lude *Henri de Moyen*[292]
at Guécélard *Jean Derien*[293]

---

chamberlain of Charles VII and governor of Vendôme in 1423 (BNF, Clairambault 37, p. 2812; Delaville le Roulx, *La domination bourguignonne à Tours*, p. 28 n. 1).

[285] This location is uncertain. Saint-Rémy-du-Plain (Ille-et-Villaine, arr. Fougères-Vitré, cant. Antrain) is too far distant. In the Norman rolls we find a surrender of the castle of Saint-Rémy-du-Plain on 23 October 1417 (C 64/8 m. 19, 21, Hardy, pp. 179, 189). Those noted as present within its castle, Michel Moyet, his son Gervais, and Guillaume de Remallart, received safe-conduct to depart (C 64/8 m. 19, 21, Hardy, pp. 179, 189). As Henry V was at Alençon at this point, the most likely fortification in the region was the castle 15 km to the south-west of Alençon at Saint-Rémy-du-Val (Sarthe, arr. et cant. Mamers). There is also a Saint-Rémy on the River Orne (Calvados, arr. Caen, cant. Thury-Harcourt), and it was presumably this parish where the inhabitants accepted English allegiance on 21 September 1417 (C 64/8 m. 25d, Hardy, p. 337).

[286] There are a number of possible locations here, but Bazouges (Sarthe, arr. et. cant. La Flèche) has a castle of the right date. Torigni is problematic since Torigni-sur-Vire (Manche, arr. Saint-Lô, cant. Condé-sur-Vire) is listed earlier and no other similar place name is known. Jean des Escotais, lord of Escotais (near Mayenne), was presented before the *Parlement* at Poitiers in 1423 as a noble knight who had always served the French king in his wars. The court had ordered the demolition of his castle of Escotais in 1422 because of the troubles caused to the neighbouring population. The order was enforced by Jean des Vaux. In retaliation, Escotais conspired with Jean de la Haye, baron de Coulonces, another enemy of des Vaux, to seize control of the town of Mayenne-la-Juhez in the absence of des Vaux in 1423. In 1425, when Mayenne was besieged by Salisbury, it was Pierre le Porc, knight, who acted as captain (AN, X2a 18, 27; X1a 9191; Beauchesne, 'Jean des Vaux', pp. 225–72).

[287] Mayenne, arr. Mayenne, cant. Evron et Meslay-du-Maine. Pierre d'Arquenay was chamberlain of the duke of Berry in 1398 (*Choix de pièces inédites*, i, p. 145). In 1424, he appears as lord of Varennes in a legal suit against Jean de Champagne before the *Parlement* of Paris (AN, X1a 4198, f. 40; Duchesne, 'Paroisse religieuse et féodale de la Poillée', p. 132). His continuing presence in Maine is revealed by a safe-conduct to him of 21 June 1434 to travel outside English obedience (AN, KK 324 f. 69v).

[288] Maine-et-Loire, arr. Segré, cant. Tiercé. No information has been found on this captaincy.

[289] Unidentified but probably the castle of Lisle, Mareil-en-Champagne (Sarthe, arr. La Flèche, cant. Brûlon). Guillaume de Brévedent, a Norman esquire from the Orne region, campaigned against the English in Normandy and Maine in the mid-1420s (Lefèvre-Pontalis, 'Épisodes de l'invasion anglaise', pp. 499–500).

[290] Sarthe, arr. La Flèche, cant. La Suze-sur-Sarthe. No information has been found on this captaincy.

[291] Eure-et-Loir, arr. Châteaudun, cant. Bonneval, co. Saumeray. No information has been found on this captaincy.

[292] Sarthe, arr. La Flèche, ch. l. cant. No information has been found on this captaincy.

[293] Sarthe, arr. La Flèche, cant. La Suze-sur-Sarthe. No information has been found on this captaincy.

at Baugé *Jean Cueurdommes knight*[294]
at Durtal Jean d'Averton knight[295]
at Belin the same d'Averton, lord of the place[296]
at Grez-en-Bouère Aymeric d'Anthenaise[297]
at Château-Gontier Hardouin de Mainbret knight[298]
at Craon Sylvestre de Scépeaux[299]
at Vitré the lord of Montjean[300]

---

[294] Maine-et-Loire, arr. Saumur, ch. l. cant. No information has been found on this captaincy.

[295] Maine-et-Loire, arr. Angers, cant. Tiercé. There may be confusion here over two generations. Payen I d'Averton, lord of Belin, inherited from his father Jean I d'Averton around 1406. He had a brother Jean d'Averton who appears as a vassal of the count of Laval in 1413 and of the duke of Alençon in 1437. Payen's death is unknown but he was still alive in 1429 when he commanded troops raised by the 'ladies of Laval' sent to Berry for the service of Charles VII. Payen's grandson, Jean II d'Averton, had already inherited from his father André IV by 1451. Jean II d'Averton owned a thirteenth-century manuscript ('Cy commence le tresor des ystoires compile') he acquired c. 1456 and which is now BL, ADD. MS. 19669 (Roquet, 'Recherches historiques sur Laigné-en-Belin', pp. 91–100).

[296] Belin is found in a suffix to a number of villages in close proximity south of Le Mans. This is probably Laigné-en-Belin (Sarthe, arr, Le Mans, cant. Éconnoy).

[297] Mayenne, arr. Château-Gonthier, cant. Meslay-du-Maine. Aymeric (1394–c. 1469) was the eldest son of Jean II, lord of Anthenaise and inherited the lordship in the early 1410s. Aymeric and his younger brother Pierre served Charles VII in the 1420s and 1430s. Aymeric (who on f. 53r is mistakenly referred to as 'Ambroys') was taken prisoner by Fastolf at Verneuil. His ransom was fixed at 2,800 *écus*. A later transaction between Aymeric and his nephew in 1445 reveals that Aymeric's brother, Pierre, loaned the money for the ransom. Aymeric was in command of the castle of Sillé-le-Guillaume in 1434 when besieged by the earl of Arundel. A surrender agreement with a conditional respite was agreed but the French failed to rescue the place and it surrendered by 12 March 1434 (AN, JJ 175/360). Aymeric d'Anthenaise together with a handful of men and women received two safe-conducts to travel safely outside the English obedience in Maine, in the course of that year (AN, KK 324 ff. 23r, 69v). See also Bonneserre de Saint-Denis, *Notice historique*, pp. 36–8; Triger, *Le château et la ville de Beaumont-le-Vicomte*, p. 55.

[298] Mayenne, ch. l. d'arr. A Hardouin de Mainbret stood as hostage for the payment of the ransom of Jean, duke of Alençon in 1427 (ADSM, 2E1, Registre du Tabellionage de Rouen, 1427–28, f. 113; Le Cacheux, *Rouen*, pp. 127–30, no. 56). He is called 'Hardouyn de Monbroez' by Chartier (i, p. 57) and 'Hardouin de Montlorées' in *Pucelle* (pp. 249–50).

[299] Mayenne, arr. et cant. Château-Gontier. Sylvestre (Sauvestre/Sevestre) de Scépaux appears as lord of l'Espronnière and la Touchardière. He received a safe-conduct to go outside the English obedience to hunt and fish in February 1434 (AN, KK 324 f. 35r).

[300] Ille-et-Villaine, arr. Fougères-Vitré, ch. l. cant. This is probably Guy de Laval, lord of Montjean, a cadet branch of the Laval (*Maison de Laval*, iii, p. 195). He participated in the battle of La Brossinières in September 1423, according to *Pucelle* (p. 216). He was sent to Orléans in the aftermath of the siege to join the royal army (Beauchesne, 'Jean des Vaux', p. 261) and was a member of a royal council at Crépy-en-Valois responding to the demands of the townspeople of Compiègne on the terms for their surrender in August 1429 (Champion, *Guillaume de Flavy*, p. 137, no. 15). Alternatively, it may be Jean II, lord Montjean, baron of Cholet and Sillé-le-Guillaume, who appears as councillor and chamberlain of the Dauphin Louis (the future Louis XI) in 1447 (Anselme, vii, pp. 175–6).

at La Guerche-de-Bretagne Jean de Champaine knight[301]
at Pouancé *Guillaume Boves*[302]
at Le Crotoy Jacques de Harcourt knight[303]
at Saint-Valéry-sur-Somme *Guillaume de Semembron knight*[304]
at Saint-Josse-sur-Mer *the said Guillaume, lord of the place*[305]
at Rue *Louis d'Ellecourt*[306]

(37v) Very soon after the landing had been made, the said victorious prince king began to make his conquest and took the castle of Bonneville-sur-Touques, which was surrendered to him. In it he installed and ordered as captain and keeper Sir John Kykley (Kyghley), knight.[307] From there he went on to lay siege before the town of Caen. After a certain length of time he made an assault on the town, as a result of which it was taken. After its capture he conquered, and had surrendered to him, many other towns and castles to which he ordered and appointed captains and keepers, to wit,

at Caen Sir Gilbert Umfraville, earl of Kyme, and Sir Gilbert Talbot[308]

---

[301]   Ille-et-Vilaine, arr. Fougères-Vitré, ch. l. cant. Le Galois d'Achy, captain of the town and castle of Alençon, together with more than sixty persons, including Jean de Champaine, knight, received a safe-conduct to depart on 24 October 1417 (C 64/8 m. 21, Hardy, pp. 187–8). Assuming this is the same person, Jean de Champagne, lord of Pescheseul, also fought at Baugé and Verneuil (Charles, 'L'invasion', pp. 83, 174–5).

[302]   Maine-et-Loire, arr. et cant. Segré. The identity of this Guillaume Boves is uncertain. A Guillaume des Boves, 'écuyer tranchant' of Philip the Bold and John the Fearless, died before 1427 (AN, J 771/10). Jean des Boves, whom Mirot presumed to be the son of Guillaume des Boves, received a grant from Henry VI on 26 April 1429 (AN, JJ 174/289; Mirot, 'Pierre de Fontenay', pp. 311, 325, 326–30). This Guillaume des Boves should not be confused with Guillaume de la Bove and his son (who was also called Jean), whose estates in Villeparisis were confiscated by Henry VI and granted to the Norman knight Roger de Bréauté on 24 September 1427 (AN, JJ 173/748; *Actes*, ii, pp. 356–7, no. 531).

[303]   Somme, arr. Abbeville, cant. Rue. Jacques de Harcourt, knight, baron of Montgomery, lord of Noyelles-sur-Mer and Wailly, was captured at Agincourt but released on parole soon after and received in Boulogne in November 1415 (*Registre des recettes et dépenses de la ville de Boulogne-sur-Mer 1415–1416*, p. 110). In 1418, he was made captain of the town and the castle of Le Crotoy (*La France gouvernée*, p. 202, no. 705; Bréard, 'Le Crotoy'). He commanded the castle for the duke of Burgundy but suddenly changed allegiance after the treaty of Troyes (Chastellain, i, pp. 88–9, 231–4). He fought the English in Ponthieu and Vimeu until 1423 when he was forced to surrender Le Crotoy (AN, JJ 172/477). He was killed in an attempt to seize the castle of Parthenay in 1428 (Belleval, p. 282).

[304]   Somme, arr. Abbeville, cant. Abbeville 2. No information has been found on this captaincy.

[305]   Pas de Calais, arr. Montreuil, cant. Etaples. No information has been found on this captaincy.

[306]   Somme, arr. Abbeville, ch. l. cant. No information has been found on this captaincy.

[307]   The treaty of surrender is dated 3 August 1417 (C 64/8 m. 6, Hardy, pp. 284–5). A John Kyghley esquire had crossed in the company of Lord Clifford in 1417 (E 101/51/2 m. 21) but no evidence has been found of his holding this captaincy. John Saint was captain of Touques by April 1421 (C 64/16 m. 41, DKR 42, p. 410).

[308]   The treaty of surrender of Caen castle was made on 9 September to be effected on the 19th (C 64/8 m. 6, Hardy, pp. 287–8). On 30 September Umfraville was appointed captain during royal pleasure (C 64/8 m. 26, Hardy, p. 159), holding office until the spring of 1421. On 1 October 1417 Gilbert Talbot was appointed as captain-general of the Marches of

at the same place as *bailli*, Sir John Popham[309]
at Torigni-sur-Vire the same Popham, lord of the place by virtue of a royal grant[310]
at Creully-sur-Seulles Sir Hartung van Clux, Knight of the Garter[311]
at Bayeux Lord Maltravers and Arundel[312]
at Argentan Lord Grey of Codnor[313]
at Chambois Lord Fitzhugh, lord of the place[314]
at Verneuil-sur-Avre Sir John Neville[315]
at Alençon my lord the duke of Gloucester and Sir Roland Lenthale as his lieutenant[316]
at Essay Sir William Hoddleston, *bailli* of Alençon[317]

Normandy during royal pleasure (C 64/8 m. 24, Hardy, p. 171), holding the office until 28 January 1418 (C 64/8 m. 11d, Hardy, p. 373). By 1 June 1418 we find Talbot in office as captain of the castle of Caen (C 64/9 m. 23d, DKR 41, p. 713), an office he seems to have held until his death on 19 October 1418 at the siege of Rouen.

[309] Sir John Popham* (c. 1395–1463), a Hampshire knight, was appointed *bailli* of Caen on 24 December 1417 (C 64/8 m. 15, Hardy, pp. 231–2) and held the office for the rest of Henry V's reign. He had served in the retinue of the duke of York in 1415 (E 101/45/2 m. 3), being knighted during the campaign or shortly afterwards. Indenting for forty men in February 1417 (E 101/70/1/574), he was part of an advance force which crossed to Harfleur before joining the main campaign in Normandy in the late summer. See also HOCb.

[310] Torigni was in English hands by 16 April 1418 (C 64/9 m. 40d, DKR 41, p. 708) and probably by February/March. The grant of the lordship was made to Popham on 5 May 1418 (C 64/9 m. 31, DKR 41, p. 686).

[311] Van Clux* (d. 1445) hailed from Silesia and proved a useful go-between for Henry V with the would-be emperor Sigismund, being rewarded with the Garter in May 1421. He served on the 1415 campaign (E 101/69/5/429; E 404/31/221; E 101/45/5 m. 4d; E 101/45/21 m. 6), and 1416 (*Foedera*, ix, p. 356) and 1417 (E 101/70/2/622) expeditions. He was granted the baronies of Creully and Courseulles as well as lands around Domfront on 22 May 1418 (C 64/9 m. 30, DKR 41, p. 688).

[312] There is no record of Lord Maltravers ever holding this office. Sir John Assheton (d. 1427) was appointed seneschal of Bayeux on 20 September 1417 (C 64/8 m. 2, Hardy, p. 320), a few days before the surrender which was agreed on 23 September (C 64/10 m. 10, DKR 41, p. 746). At some point before 3 April 1419 the captain was Sir John Grey of Ruthin* (1387–1439), but on that date Sir Richard Strother was appointed to replace him (C 64/11 m. 78, DKR 41, p. 763).

[313] Richard, lord Grey of Codnor was appointed captain on 13 October 1417 (C 64/8 m. 23, Hardy, p. 180) but died on 1 August 1418, probably in France. His eldest son, John, lord Grey (1396–1430) was captain by September 1419 (E 101/187/14 f. 19) and remained in post until his discharge on 9 October 1423 (BNF, NAF 1482/8; BL, Add. Ch. 91).

[314] Orne, arr. Argentan, cant. Argentan 2, co. Gouffern-en-Auge. The grant of Chambois to Fitzhugh was made on 8 November 1417, shortly after the surrender of the place (C 64/8 m. 7, Hardy, p. 280).

[315] Neville was appointed captain on 31 October 1417 (C 64/8 m. 21, Hardy, p. 193).

[316] Alençon was in Henry V's hands by 27 October 1417 but there is no formal record of the captaincy being held by the duke of Gloucester. Sir Roland Lenthale of Hampton Court (Herefs.) (1372–1450) was appointed *bailli* on 3 March 1418 (C 64/8 m. 8, Hardy, pp. 287–8) and was described in 1419–20 as 'gardien de la ville'. On 13 January 1420 the earl of Salisbury was appointed as captain to replace him (C 64/14 m. 14, DKR 42, p. 381).

[317] Sir William Hoddleston indented in 1417 for the service of twenty-four men (E 101/70/2/599) but is not known to have been captain of Essay. Sir John Tiptoft* (1378–1443)

at Falaise Lord Fitzhugh[318]
at Thury-Harcourt Sir Lewis Robessart[319]
at Condé-sur-Noireau Sir John Popham[320]
During Lent in the year 1417 (i.e. 1418) the said victorious prince and king who
was staying in Caen sent my lord the duke of Clarence, his brother, into the Auge
region and its neighbouring area in order to make conquests. The latter won and
conquered several towns, castles and fortresses in which, in the name of the said
victorious prince, he placed captains and keepers, to wit,
in the town and city of Lisieux, Sir John Kykley (Kyghley)[321]
at Fauguernon John St Albans[322]

---

took the surrender on 12 October 1417 and is described as captain in February 1418 (C 64/8
m. 23, 13, Hardy, pp. 180, 245) and in 1419–20 (E 101/187/14 f. 18). The earl of Salisbury is
found as captain in February 1420 (BNF, Fr. 25766/797). Hoddleston succeeded Sir Roland
Lenthale as *bailli* of Alençon on 13 November 1420 (C 64/14 m. 14, DKR 42, p. 381),
continuing in office until his death which had occurred by August 1422 (ADO, A 413).

[318] A treaty was agreed on 20 December 1417 for surrender of the town of Falaise on 2
January 1418 (C 64/8 m. 2, Hardy, pp. 312–13). No appointment is known following the
surrender of the castle on 16 February 1418 (C 64/8 m. 2, Hardy, pp. 308–12) but Fitzhugh
was certainly captain by 26 August 1418 (E 101/49/19).

[319] The earl of Warwick held the captaincy after its surrender in mid-December 1417 (C
64/8 m. 19d, Hardy, p. 370). On 14 February 1418 the castle and barony of Thury were
granted to Sir Lewis Robessart (c. 1390–1430) (C 64/8 m. 12, Hardy, p. 255). Lewis hailed
from Hainault but was already in the service of Henry V as prince from 1403, receiving letters
of denization on 8 March 1417. He served on the 1415 campaign in the royal household (E
101/69/3/366; E 101/45/5 m. 3d; E 101/407/10, m. 1). He crossed with the king on the 1417
expedition although no service record has as yet been found. He was knighted at the siege
of Caen (*First English Life*, p. 113) or in Caen on St Georges Day 1418 (Walsingham, *St Albans
Chronicle*, ii, p. 733). Marrying the widow of Hugh Stafford, lord Bourchier, after the latter's
death on 25 October 1420, he was summoned to parliament as Lord Bourchier from 1425.
He was made KG in May 1421. See also 'Louis Robessart – a Border-Crossing Knight',
www.englandsimmigrants.com; and Morgan, 'From Death to a View'.

[320] Popham's appointment at Condé is not evidenced. The grant of 1 July 1419 to Henry
Noon esquire notes that it had previously been held by Edward Holland, count of Mortain,
who died in early October 1418 (C 64/11 m. 30, DKR 41, p. 792). Noon, of Shelfhanger
and Tilney (Norfolk), who had served in Ireland with Fastolf in 1408 (CPR 1408–13, p. 41),
was a knight by June 1421 (CPR 1416–22, p. 369). He died during the siege of Meaux (TNA,
PROB 11/2B/407). The lordship of Condé-sur-Noireau was granted to Sir William Breton
on 18 December 1421 (C 64/16 m. 16, DKR 42, p. 420).

[321] Lisieux had a captain by 16 April 1418 (C 64/9 m. 40d, DKR 41, p. 708) but no name
is known until 13 August 1422 when a 'John Kirkeby' was appointed captain (C 64/17 m. 9,
DKR 42, p. 445). John de Kyghley crossed in the company of John, lord Clifford in 1417 (E
101/51/2 m. 26). A Sir John Kyghley (dead by 1436) had letters of protection in May 1420
in the retinue of the duke of Clarence (C 76/103 m. 7, DKR 44, p. 618) and was surely the
person appointed *bailli* of Rouen in January 1421 (C 64/14 m. 2 additional, DKR 42, p. 388),
serving to July 1422 (AN, Dom Lenoir 29, f. 65). He was captain of Louviers from 8 April
1421 and of Pont-de-l'Arche from 22 April 1421 (C 64/16 m. 41, DKR 42, p. 410; C 64/16
m. 40d, DKR 42, p. 425), holding both posts probably to the king's death.

[322] Fauguernon had a captain by April 1418 (C 64/9 m. 40d, DKR 41, p. 708) but his name
is not known. The identity of John St Albans is uncertain: there is a limited possibility that
he was the younger son of Sir John St Aubyn (d. October 1418) of Combe Raleigh (Devon)
who was MP for Devon in 1414 (HOCa).

at Courtonne-la-Meudrac John Aubin[323]
at Crèvecoeur-en-Auge *Sir Thomas Kirkby* lord of the place[324]
(38r) at Bernay William Howton[325]
at Auvilliers Robert [Ormesby cancelled] Horneby[326]
at Chambois Jacques de Neuville[327]
at Rugles Sir John Arthur[328]

---

[323]   Courtonne surrendered on 6 March 1418 (C 64/8 m. 3, Hardy, pp. 303–6). The identity of John Aubin is uncertain, although archers of this name are known. There is a limited possibility that he was the younger son of Sir John St Aubyn (d. October 1418) of Combe Raleigh (Devon) who was MP for Devon in 1414 (HOCa). There is no other evidence of Aubin holding the captaincy. In April 1421 the captain of Courtonne was John Sutton (C 64/16 m. 40d, DKR 42, p. 425) but on 15 July 1422 the latter was ordered to hand over the place to the papal administrator of the diocese of Lisieux since the castle had previously been held by the bishop of Lisieux (C 64/17 m. 12d, DKR 42, p. 451).

[324]   A man-at-arms of this name crossed in the retinue of Lord Clifford in 1417 (E 101/51/2 m. 21). It was perhaps the same man who served in the garrison of Caen in 1426 under Richard Woodville senior (BNF, Fr. 25767/188). A knight of this name is first seen in France from 1432 (BNF, Clairambault 207/111–20), and is still seen in service in 1437 when, described as of Surrey, he had letters of protection to cross to France with the earl of Warwick (C 76/119 m. 1, DKR 48, p. 319). A man of this name, although not a knight, was lieutenant of Lisieux in 1446–49 (AC Lisieux, CC 23 f. 10v, 25, p. 187), perhaps related to the John Kirkeby appointed captain of the same town on 13 August 1422 (C 64/17 m. 9, DKR 42, p. 445). No grant of Crèvecoeur is known but there are various grants of lands in Normandy to a Thomas Kirkeby esquire after 1423 (AN, JJ 172/293; *Actes*, ii, p. 319). On 11 October 1450 a Sir Thomas Kirkeby was granted duty-free export of wool and other goods from London to Calais for his long service to the king in France and Normandy and to help with his ransom since he was still a prisoner (CPR 1446–52, p. 404).

[325]   Eure, ch. l. d'arr. The first known captain is Richard Worcester on 3 April 1421 (C 64/16 m. 41, DKR 42, p. 410). A William Howton served in the retinue of Thomas, duke of Clarence, in 1415 (E 101/45/4 m. 3) and had letters of protection to cross with the duke in the 1417 expedition (C 76/100 m. 24, DKR 44, p. 590).

[326]   Seine-Maritime, arr. Dieppe, cant. Neufchâtel-en-Bray. Auvilliers had a captain by April 1418 (C 64/9 m. 40d, DKR 41, p. 708) but his name is not known. A number of Robert Hornebys and Ormesbys served in Normandy but all as archers.

[327]   Eure, arr. Bernay, cant. Verneuil-sur-Avre. The treaty of surrender is dated 9 March 1418 (C 64/8 m. 5, Hardy, pp. 294–6). One of the French signatories was Jacques de Neville, knight, described as deputy of the lord de Ferrières. The treaty left the latter in possession of the town and castle and all revenues in the duchy of Normandy which belonged to him and to his wife. It would appear, therefore, that de Neuville was left in command of the place under English allegiance.

[328]   Rugles surrendered on 18 October 1417 (C 64/8 m. 3, Hardy, p. 307). Sir William Porter (d. 1436) was appointed captain on 31 October (C 64/8 m. 21, Hardy, p. 192) and seems to have held the post until the death of Henry V (HOCa). John Arthur, of Clapton-in-Gordano (Somerset), may have crossed in the retinue of William, lord Botreaux in 1415 (E 101/45/18 m. 3) and served in Harfleur in 1418 (E 101/48/19). On 12 June 1418, still an esquire, he was granted the fief of Romilly (C 64/9 m. 22, DKR 41, p. 691). He was a knight by February 1420 when appointed *louvetier* in the *bailliages* of Alençon and Evreux (C 64/12 m. 33d, DKR 42, p. 357). He was captain of Conches from Michaelmas 1423 to 1425 (BNF, Fr. 4485, pp. 209–10; BNF, PO 108 Arthur 2) but no earlier captaincies are known. In 1432 he served in the army in the field under Robert, lord Willoughby at the siege of Saint-Célerin (BL, Add. Ch. 11759; BNF, Clairambault 207/111–20).

at Le Bec-Hellouin the Earl Marshal[329]
at Fresnay-sur-Sarthe Sir Robert Brent[330]
at Harcourt Richard Woodville esquire[331]
During this same Lent-tide the said victorious prince and king sent my lord of
Gloucester, his brother, into the Cotentin region in order to make conquests. The
latter won and conquered several towns, castles and fortresses in which, in the
name of the said victorious prince, he placed captains and keepers, to wit,
at Carentan Lord Botreaux[332]
at Pont-d'Ouve Davy Howell esquire[333]
at Saint-Lô Sir Reginald West[334]
at La Haye-du-Puits Sir John Assheton *bailli* of Cotentin[335]

---

[329] The treaty of surrender of the abbey and fortress is dated 4 May 1418 (C 64/9 m. 26,
DKR 41, p. 688). Ralph, lord Cromwell (1393–1456), one of the signatories, was captain by
at least April 1421 if not earlier (C 64/16 m. 40d, DKR 42, p. 425) but there is no evidence
of the Earl Marshal holding the post.

[330] Fresnay probably fell around 19 April 1420 (Triger, 'Une forteresse', p. 189). The
earliest known appointment to its captaincy is of Sir Robert Brent (d. 1421) of Cossington
(Somerset) on 11 January 1421 (C 64/14 m. 1, DKR 42, p. 387). As an esquire Brent had
served as a man-at-arms under the earl of Salisbury in 1417 (E 101/51/2 m. 9). He was a
knight by March 1419 (C 64/11 m. 78d, DKR 42, p. 314). On 13 January 1421 he was granted
lands in Maine including Sillé-le-Guillaume and Assé-le-Riboul (C 64/14 m. 4, DKR 42, p.
386) but he was killed at Baugé.

[331] The treaty of surrender to Clarence is dated 9 March 1418 (C 64/9 m. 29, DKR 41, p.
688). The *comté* of Harcourt was granted to Thomas, duke of Exeter on 1 July 1418 (C 64/10
m. 35, DKR 41, p. 728). On 18 April 1421 the captain was Henry Vernay (C 64/16 m. 40d,
DKR 42, p. 425). There is no other evidence of Woodville's holding the captaincy.

[332] Carentan surrendered on 16 March 1418 (C 64/8 m. 4, Hardy, pp. 300–3). Sir John
Assheton held the captaincy in 1419–20 (E 101/187/14 f. 18), and was still in post in May 1421
(C 64/16 m. 36d, DKR 42, p. 427). There is no evidence it was ever held by Lord Botreaux,
who does not appear to have been in Normandy at this time.

[333] Manche, arr. St.-Lô, cant. Carentan. Pont-d'Ouve surrendered on 17 March 1418
(C 64/10 m. 9, DKR 41, p. 746), the treaty being made by Sir John Robessart and Sir
William Beauchamp (d. 1421) of Powick and Alcester (Worcs.) on behalf of Gloucester.
William Rothlane was appointed captain on 21 May 1418 (C 64/9 m. 32, DKR 41, p. 686).
Davy Howell served as a man-at-arms in 1415 under Michael de la Pole, earl of Suffolk (E
101/46/2 m. 3), and in 1417 under the duke of Gloucester (E 101/51/2 m. 2), being found in
several garrisons thereafter, but there is no evidence he was ever captain of Pont-d'Ouve.

[334] Sir Reginald West (1395–1450), who became Lord de la Warre in 1427, led a company
of eighty in the 1417 expedition (E 101/51/2 m. 44). Saint-Lô surrendered on 12 March (C
64/8 m. 4, Hardy, pp. 298–300) and West was captain by 22 March (C 64/9 m. 37, DKR
41, p. 682). He was still in office in April 1421 (C 64/9 m. 37, DKR 41, p. 682) and probably
served to the death of Henry V.

[335] Assheton* (d. 1427), a Lancashire knight who had been a retainer of John of Gaunt and
a household knight of Joan of Navarre, was appointed *bailli* of Cotentin on 14 March 1418
(C 64/9 m. 36, DKR 41, p. 683), and features prominently in the military administration of
the conquest. He had led a retinue in the army of 1417 (C 76/99 m. 4, DKR 44, p. 588), but
its size is unknown (HOCa). The castle and barony of La Haye-du-Puits were granted to
John Cheyne esquire on 1 April 1418 (C 64/9 m. 33, DKR 41, p. 685). A man of this name,
probably the person described as a king's esquire in 1409 (CPR 1408–13, pp. 148), indented
for the service of sixteen men in 1415 (E 404/31/220; E 101/45/5 m. 2d) and is likely to be

at Valognes Thomas Burgh[336]
at Cherbourg Lord Grey of Codnor and after his death Sir Walter Hungerford[337]
at Coutances Lord Bergavenney[338]
at Saint-Sauveur-le-Vicomte Sir John Robessart[339]
at Avranches [cancelled: Thomas Burgh; added: *Philip Hall bailli* of Alençon][340]
at Pontorson Sir Robert Gargrave[341]
at Vire Lord Maltravers and Arundel[342]
at Saint-James (de-Beuvron) the same Lord Maltravers[343]
at Hambye the earl of Suffolk lord of the place[344]

---

the John Cheyne leading a sub-retinue under Lord Bergavenny in 1417 (E 101/51/2 m. 5), being active in Normandy thereafter and knighted during the siege of Rouen.

[336] Valognes had a captain from at least April 1418 (C 64/9 m. 40d, DKR 41, p. 708). Thomas Burgh (d. c. 1433), probably of Cowthorpe (Yorks. WR), was noted as captain in 1419–20 (E 101/187/14 f. 20). He had served in the retinue of the duke of Gloucester in 1415 (E 101/45/13 m. 2) and of the earl of March in 1417 (E 101/51/2 m. 7).

[337] The treaty of surrender for Cherbourg is dated 22 August 1418 (C 64/10 m. 8, DKR 41, p. 746). Sir Walter Hungerford* (1378–1449) of Farleigh Montfort (Somerset), who was made KG in 1421 and Lord Hungerford in 1436, was captain from at least 1 April 1419 (C 64/11 m. 71d, DKR 42, p. 316) but it is not known who was captain before this point. Hungerford had crossed with a retinue of eighty in 1415 (E 101/69/5/425; E 101/69/3/368; E 404/31/165; E 101/45/5 m. 5; E 101/45/20 m. 3) and 255 in 1417 (E 101/70/1/573, E 101/51/2 m. 19) (HOCa).

[338] Manche, ch. l. d'arr. Coutances surrendered on 16 March 1418 (C 64/8 m. 5, Hardy, pp. 296–8). Sir John Assheton, *bailli* of Cotentin, was captain in 1419–20 (E 101/187/14 f. 18) and was still in office in May 1421 (C 64/16 m. 36d, DKR 42, p. 427). There is no evidence the captaincy was held by Richard Beauchamp, lord Bergavenny.

[339] The treaty of surrender for Saint-Sauveur-le-Vicomte is dated 25 March 1418 (C 64/10 m. 6, DKR 41, p. 746). The name of the captain is not known but on 28 March 1419 the castle and lordship were granted in tail male to Sir John Robessart (C 64/11 m. 80, DKR 41, p. 763). Robessart (d. 1447), made KG in 1417, was the elder brother of Lewis and originally from Hainault, receiving letters of denization in 1423. Already a knight he had crossed with twenty-three men in 1415 (E 404/31/257; E 101/45/5 m. 3d; E 101/45/21 m. 19; E 101/44/30 m. 2) and with forty in 1417 (E 101/70/2/597; E 101/51/2 m. 41).

[340] The initial treaty of surrender is dated 14 September 1418 (C 64/10 m. 1, DKR 41, p. 746). The place was subsequently lost to the French but recovered on 14 July 1419. William de la Pole, earl of Suffolk, was appointed captain on 27 August 1419 (C 64/11 m. 25, DKR 41, p. 794). He was discharged of this post in October 1423 and Thomas Burgh appointed in his stead (BNF, Fr. 26046/142; Fr. 26046/184, printed in Luce, i, no. xxii), holding office until October 1429 (BNF, NAF 1482/65). There is no evidence that a Philip Hall ever held command at Avranches or that he was ever *bailli* of Alençon.

[341] By 12 March 1419 the captain was Lord Maltravers (C 64/10 m. 19d, DKR 41, p. 758). The identity of Robert Gargrave is uncertain. A man of this name, but not knighted, served as a man-at-arms on the 1417 expedition under Sir John Grey (E 101/51/2 m. 32).

[342] Vire surrendered on 21 February 1418 (C 64/8 m. 6, Hardy, pp. 289–92). John Smythes is noted as captain on 24 March 1418 (C 64/9 m. 37, DKR 41, p. 682). The account of the receiver-general of Normandy for April 1419–April 1420 gives the earl of March as captain (E 101/187/14 f. 17). There is no evidence Lord Maltravers ever held this post.

[343] No evidence has been found of this appointment.

[344] Hambye surrendered on 3 March 1418 (C 64/10 m. 10, DKR 41, p. 746). It was granted to the earl of Suffolk on 13 March (C 64/8 m. 2, Hardy, p. 319).

at *Bricqueville* (recte, Bricquebec) the earl of Suffolk, lord of the place[345]
(38v) During this same period this victorious prince sent my lord the earl of
Warwick to make conquests. The latter laid siege before the town and castle of
Domfront in Passais of Normandy. After a certain time they were surrendered and
delivered to him, and he installed a captain, Sir Hugh Stafford, Lord Bourchier,[346]
and he conquered many other places and fortresses into which he placed other
captains.

After the king and victorious prince had kept Lent and Easter and over-wintered
at Caen, in the following summer in the year 1418, at his command, my lord the
earl of March and the Lord Clifford were sent to him from the realm of England
with a large army.[347] The victorious prince laid siege before the town of Louviers,
where he was for the space of six weeks or thereabouts. It was surrendered and
delivered to him, and he made captain of it my lord the duke of Clarence, his
brother. The latter made Sir John Godard, knight, his lieutenant.[348] Around the
same time the victorious prince sent my lord the duke of Exeter to effect conquests.
The latter laid siege before the city and town of Evreux which was surrendered
and delivered to him after a certain time. He installed as captain Sir Gilbert Halsall
knight, who was made *bailli* of the place.[349] The victorious prince went to lay siege
before the town, bridge and castle of Pont-de-l'Arche, which, after a certain time,

---

[345] Whilst there is a Bricqueville-sur-Mer in the Cotentin, this is actually Bricquebec
(Manche, arr. Cherbourg, ch. l. cant.) since on 6 May 1419 William de la Pole, earl of
Suffolk, was granted the castle and lordship of Bricquebec (C 64/11 m. 55, DKR 41, p. 775).

[346] The treaty of surrender for Domfront, for which the earl of Warwick was the English
commissary, is dated 10 July 1418 (C 64/10 m. 8, DKR 41, p. 746). On 4 October the earl of
March was appointed lieutenant-general of the *bailliages* of Caen and Cotentin and of the
lordship of Domfront (C 64/9 m. 11, DKR 41, p. 741). By April 1419 Sir Hugh Stafford, lord
Bourchier, was captain of Domfront (C 64/11 m. 49, DKR 42, p. 318, though the calendar
gives the first name erroneously as Humphrey Stafford). Hugh died on 25 October 1420.

[347] This is a perplexing comment since the army which was indented in February 1418
did not involve these peers but rather the dukes of Exeter and Clarence, lord Fitzhugh, Sir
Gilbert Umfraville, Sir Richard Laken and Edward Holland, count of Mortain (E 403/634
m. 13). Lord Clifford and the earl of March were certainly at the siege of Louviers in May
1418 (C 64/9 m. 22d, DKR 41, p. 713).

[348] Troops were ordered on 9 June 1418 to be mustered at the siege (C 64/9 m. 23d, DKR
41, p. 713). On 5 July the king agreed to allow the inhabitants of Louviers to keep their
properties in return for a payment of 8,000 *écus* in two instalments at the end of August
and on 1 November (C 64/9 m. 21, DKR 41, p. 692). On 16 July the duke of Clarence was
empowered to receive the fealty of those of Louviers and Pont-de-l'Arche (C 64/9 m. 17,
DKR 41, p. 695). By 23 August Sir John Godard (1387–1420) was captain and *bailli* (C 64/9
m. 15d, DKR 41, p. 716). Godard, of Horton-in Ribblesdale (Yorks. WR), had interests in
the Morley inheritance since his mother was the widow of the fourth Lord Morley, who had
close service connections with Clarence, having served in his company in 1415 (E 101/45/4
m. 2, C 76/98 m. 13, DKR 44, p. 570).

[349] The surrender was made on 20 May 1418 (C 64/10 m. 8, DKR 41, p. 746). Sir John
Radcliffe (d. 1441) had already been appointed *bailli* on 2 May 1418 (C 64/9 m. 25d, DKR
41, p. 713). Sir Gilbert Halsall (c. 1390–1445) had replaced him in this role by 3 June 1419 (C
64/11 m. 42d, DKR 42, p. 320) and was appointed as both *bailli* and captain on 8 September
1419 (C 64/11 m. 25d, DKR 42, p. 325), holding the post until the death of Henry V. Halsall's
earlier service is not known but a man of this name, not knighted, is found in the garrison of
Harfleur in early 1416 (E 101/47/39). Halsall was the younger brother of Henry Halsall of

were surrendered and delivered to him, and of which (39r) he made captain my lord the duke of Clarence, his brother.[350]

In this year 1418 the said victorious prince, around the beginning of the month of August, laid siege before the city, town, castle and bridge of Rouen.[351] He was there for the space and time of around seven months until they were surrendered and delivered to him by composition. He appointed as captain my lord the duke of Exeter with my Lord Willoughby as his lieutenant, and Sir John Kykley (Kyghley) was made *bailli* of the place.[352] Soon after the said town of Rouen was surrendered, as has been said, the said king captured and had surrendered to him several other towns, castles and fortresses in which he appointed and commissioned captains, to wit,

at Caudebec Sir Lewis Robessart[353]

at Tancarville Sir John Grey, count of the place [added: by grant][354]

at Harfleur Sir John Grey[355]

Halsall, Lancs. (HOCb), Gilbert's Lancashire origins being noted by Worcester in *Itineraries*, pp. 3–4.

[350] Siege was being laid from late June 1418. On 16 July Clarence was empowered to receive the fealty of those of Louviers and Pont-de-l'Arche (C 64/9 m. 17, DKR 41, p. 695) and surrender was effected by the 20th (Newhall, *English Conquest*, p. 103). A reference dated 23 February 1421 notes Clarence as titular captain but he presumably held the post from the surrender. By the 1421 date, Sir Maurice Bruin was his lieutenant (C 64/15 m. 14d, DKR 42, p. 408), and was appointed captain in his own name on 3 April 1421 following Clarence's death at Baugé (C 64/16 m. 41, DKR 42, p. 410).

[351] Henry arrived before Rouen around 7 July (C 64/9 m. 16, DKR 41, p. 696). An initial treaty of surrender was agreed on 13 January 1419 (C 64/10 m. 5, DKR 41, p. 746).

[352] There is ample evidence in the Norman rolls and in the accounts of the receiver-general of the duchy that Exeter was captain from the time of the surrender of Rouen, remaining in post for the rest of Henry V's reign. Willoughby was described as lieutenant in April 1419 (C 64/11 m. 46d, DKR 42, p. 319), holding the post at least to the end of the year. The first English *bailli* of Rouen was Sir Walter Beauchamp* (1380–1430) of Bromham and Steeple Lavington (Wilts.), the younger brother of William. Walter had indented for seventeen men in 1417 (E 101/70/1/579) and was appointed *bailli* on 19 January 1419 (C 64/10 m. 38, DKR 41, p. 725) but returned to England with the king, now being also treasurer of the household, and hence treasurer of war. Sir John Kyghley was appointed *bailli* of Rouen on 14 January 1421 (C 64/14 m. 2 additional, DKR 42, p. 388) and was still in office on 7 July 1422 (AN, Dom Lenoir 29 f. 65).

[353] Caudebec had come to a treaty with the earl of Warwick on 7 September 1418 (C 64/10 m. 7, DKR 41, p. 746) but surrender was contingent on the outcome of the siege of Rouen. Robessart was given power, with Roger Fiennes, on 23 January 1419 to take the surrender and was appointed captain on the same date (C 64/9 m. 1, DKR 41, p. 708).

[354] Sir John Grey of Heton* (1384/91–1421) was granted the *comté* of Tancarville on 31 January 1419 (C 64/10 m. 41, DKR 41, p. 722). The younger brother of Sir Thomas Grey who had been executed for involvement in the Southampton plot, John had led a retinue of eighty men on the 1415 expedition (E 101/45/5 m. 2d) and 160 on the 1417 expedition (E 101/70/2/608; E 101/51/2 m. 32). He was made KG in 1419.

[355] Sir John Grey of Heton was appointed captain of Harfleur on 20 January 1420 at the point that the duke of Exeter gave up the post (C 64/12 m. 40, DKR 42, p. 339). He died at Baugé and was replaced as captain on 3 April 1421 by Sir Ralph Cromwell (C 64/16 m. 41, DKR 42, p. 410).

at Montivilliers Clement Overton escuier[356]
at Bellencombre Sir Thomas Rempston, lord of the place[357]
at Dieppe my lord William Bourchier, count of Eu by grant[358]
at Eu the same lord William, count of the place[359]
at Longueville-sur-Scie the Captal de Buch, count of the place[360]
at Arques Sir James Fiennes, *bailli* of Caux[361]

---

[356] Seine-Maritime, arr. Le Havre, cant. Le Havre 2. The treaty of surrender is dated 23 January 1419 (C 64/10 m. 9, DKR 41, p. 746). Sir Hugh Luttrell was captain by March 1420 (C 64/12 m. 6, DKR 42, p. 352), and probably from its surrender, since he was also in effective command at Harfleur. Clement Overton of New Romney, Kent (d. c. 1439) (HOCb), was appointed captain on 11 April 1420 (C 64/13 m. 15, DKR 42, p. 367) and remained in office until the place was lost to the French in 1436. He had been given lands in Bacqueville and elsewhere in the *bailliages* of Rouen and Caux in April 1419 (C 64/11 m. 56, DKR 41, p. 774) but it is not certain when he crossed to France. An archer of this name can be found in Camarthen under Thomas Beaufort, then earl of Dorset, in 1403 (E 101/43/21 m. 3). Clement was the brother of Thomas Overton who served as Fastolf's receiver-general but who then launched various complaints against his master (*English Suits*, XX, and pp. 300–1).
[357] Sir Thomas Rempston* (c. 1385–1458), of Rempstone and Bingham, Notts., was appointed captain of Bellencombre on 12 February 1419 (C 64/10 m. 32, DKR 41, p. 730) but there is no evidence he was ever granted the place (that William Worcester considered that he had been so rewarded is also mentioned in his later writings printed in *L&P*, II, ii, p. 622). By 24 January 1421 the captain was John Melton (C 64/15 m. 26d, DKR 42, p. 406). Rempston served on the 1415 campaign with thirty-one men (E 101/69/4/393; E 404/31/256; E 101/45/5 m. 1) and in 1417 with a company whose size is not known (C 76/100 m. 3, DKR 44, p. 602) (HOCa; and see also Payling, 'War and Peace', pp. 240–56).
[358] On 7 February 1419 Bourchier was given power to take the town into royal hands (C 64/10 m. 36, DKR 41, p. 727). The formal treaty of surrender made by the duke of Exeter is dated the next day (C 64/10 m. 1, DKR 41, p. 746), being ratified by the king on 9 March (C 64/10 m. 17, DKR 41, p. 742). Sir William Bourchier* (1374–1420) was appointed captain of Dieppe on 12 February 1419 (C 64/10 m. 32, DKR 41, p. 730). He had served with 120 men in 1415 (E 101/69/7/487; E 101/45/5 m. 5d; E 101/45/21 m. 18) and with 163 in 1417 (E 101/51/2 m. 23). He did not receive Dieppe by grant.
[359] The agreement to surrender is dated 15 February 1419 (C 64/10 m. 3, DKR 41, p. 746). On 12 February 1419 Sir Gilbert Umfraville was appointed captain in anticipation of the surrender (C 64/10 m. 4, DKR 41, p. 730). On 10 June 1419 Sir William Bourchier was granted the *comté* of Eu in tail male (C 64/11 m. 4, 33, DKR 41, pp. 789, 808) but he died at Troyes on 28 May 1420. On 18 October 1421 Robert Pygot was appointed captain of Eu and Monceaux (C 64/15 m. 26, DKR 42, p. 397).
[360] On 14 February 1419, shortly after its surrender, Sir Roger Fiennes (1384–1449) was appointed captain of Longueville (C 64/10 m. 32, DKR 41, p. 730) (HOCa). Gaston de Foix-Grailly (1390–1455), captal de Buch, vicomte of Benauges and Castillon, and lord of Puy-Paulin, was a supporter of Henry V from south-west France who served in Normandy and was made KG in 1438, although his elder brother John remained in French allegiance. As a reward, he was created count of Longueville on 11 June 1419 (C 64/11 m. 35, DKR 41, p. 789), the grant being reissued in tail male on 20 June (C 64/11 m. 35, DKR 41, p. 789).
[361] Sir Philip Leche (d. 1420) of Chatsworth (Derbys.) was appointed captain of Arques on 12 February 1419 (C 64/10 m. 32, DKR 41, p. 730). He had crossed with eleven in 1415 (E 101/69/7/482; E 404/31/166; E 101/45/5 m. 2d; E 101/45/22 m. 7) and 190 in 1417 (E 101/51/2 m. 17), but was killed at the siege of Melun in July 1420 (HOCa). Sir John Baskerville replaced him as captain of Arques on 29 July 1420 (C 64/14 m. 19, DKR 42, p. 379), holding the post to October 1422 (BNF, Fr. 25767/3). There is no evidence the place

at Aumale my lord of Warwick, who appointed a lieutenant at the place, Sir William Mountford[362]
at Neufchâtel Sir Philip Leche[363]
at Monceaux the same Sir Philip[364]
at Gournay Sir Gilbert Umfraville earl of Kyme[365]
at Bacqueville-en-Caux Lord Roos, lord of the place by grant[366]
at Château-Gaillard the same Lord Roos[367]
at Dangu Richard Woodville esquire[368]

---

was ever captained by James Fiennes* (1390–1450) of Hever and Knole (Kent), knighted in 1444 and created later Lord Saye and Sele in 1447 (HOCb). It was his elder brother Sir Roger Fiennes (d. 1449) who was *bailli* of Caux from 23 January 1419 (C 64/9 m. 1, DKR 41, p. 707). James Fiennes served in the 1415 (E 101/45/13 m. 4) and 1417 (E 101/51/2 m. 1) armies in the company of the duke of Gloucester. By February 1421 he was lieutenant at Caudebec to Sir Lewis Robessart (C 64/15 m. 26d, DKR 42, p. 406).

[362] On 19 May 1419 the earl of Warwick was granted the *comté* of Aumale (*Complete Peerage*, i, appendix J). At this stage it was probably not in English hands but it was by 8 January 1420 when the earl was given power to receive the homage of those within it (C 64/12 m. 44, DKR 42, p. 336). Sir William Mountford (d. 1452) of Coleshill (Warks.) was closely connected with Warwick, being steward of his household. He had served in the earl's retinue in 1415, presumably in Calais (C 76/98 m. 14, DKR 44, p. 569), and was in his company in 1417 but was not yet a knight (E 101/51/2 m. 1). He had that status in letters of protection to cross to France in July 1421 (C 76/104 m. 12, DKR 44, p. 628) (HOCa, b).

[363] The Earl Marshal was appointed captain of Neufchâtel on 12 February 1419 (C 64/10 m. 32, DKR 41, p. 730), but Sir Gilbert Umfraville replaced him as early as 21 February 1419 (C 64/10 m. 32, DKR 41, p. 731). Richard Walkstead was in post on 20 January 1421 (C 64/15 m. 26, DKR 42, p. 397). There is no evidence the captaincy of Neufchâtel was ever held by Sir Philip Leche.

[364] The place came into English hands in February 1419 (C 64/10 m. 3, DKR 41, p. 746) but there is no other evidence the command was ever held by Sir Philip Leche. On 18 January 1421 Robert Pygot was appointed captain of both Eu and Monceaux (C 64/15 m. 26, DKR 42, p. 397). On 10 May of the same year Sir Ralph Neville was appointed to the same posts (C 64/16 m. 41, DKR 42, p. 410), suggesting Pygot had been killed at Baugé.

[365] Gournay surrendered on 9 February 1419 (C 64/10 m. 36, DKR 41, p. 746). The Earl Marshal was appointed captain on 12 February (C 64/10 m. 32, DKR 41, p. 730) but on the following day the earl of Huntingdon was appointed to the same captaincy (C 64/10 m. 32, DKR 41, p. 730). On 23 December 1420 Sir John Grey of Ruthin was appointed captain (C 64/14 m. 10d, DKR 42, p. 384). There is no evidence it was ever captained by Umfraville.

[366] Seine-Maritime, arr. Dieppe, cant. Luneray. Roos was granted the castle and lordship of Bacqueville on 2 April 1419 (C 64/11 m. 79, DKR 41, p. 763). After his death at Baugé it was granted to Sir Thomas Beaumont (C 64/16 m. 28, DKR 42, p. 415).

[367] On 24 April 1419 the duke of Exeter was given power to take Château-Gaillard into royal hands (C 64/11 m. 12, DKR 41, p. 803). On 8 December 1419 Lord Roos was appointed captain (C 64/11 m. 4, DKR 41, p. 808). After his death at Baugé, Sir Alan Buxhill replaced him (C 64/16 m. 41, DKR 42, p. 410).

[368] The defenders of Dangu came in late January 1419 to surrender (C 64/10 m. 38, DKR 41, p. 726). The lordship was granted to Richard Woodville on 1 February (C 64/10 m. 12, DKR 41, p. 745) and on 4 February he was given power to take the castle into the king's hands (C 64/10 m. 36, DKR 41, p. 727). Woodville* (d. c. 1441) was closely associated with Henry V and active in the conquest of Normandy, although no specific records of his service in the 1415 and 1417 armies have been found (Pidgeon, *Brought up of Nought*, pp. 85–6).

at Saint-Clair-sur-Epte William Basset esquire, lord of the place[369]
at Neaufles-Saint-Martin the earl of Worcester[370]
at Gisors the same earl of Worcester[371]
at Bouconvillers John Burgh esquire *bailli* of Gisors[372]
at Mantes-la-Jolie the earl of March[373]
at Vernon Sir William Porter knight[374]
(39v) at La Roche-Guyon Guy le Bouteillier lord of the place[375]
at Meulan Sir Thomas Rempston and then Sir John Fastolf[376]

---

[369] Val-d'Oise, arr. Pontoise, cant. Vauréal. No such grant to a William Basset has so far been found.

[370] The treaty of surrender, made by Clarence, is dated 23 February 1419 (C 64/10 m. 4, DKR 41, p. 746). Richard Beauchamp, lord Bergavenny, was appointed captain of Neaufles on 2 February 1419 (C 64/10 m. 32, DKR 41, p. 730).

[371] Richard Beauchamp, lord Bergavenny, was appointed captain of Gisors on 1 October 1419 (C 64/11 m. 13, DKR 41, p. 802).

[372] Bouconvillers was captured on 31 August 1419 (Newhall, *English Conquest*, p. 141). On 14 April 1421 Adam Frost was appointed captain (C 64/16 m. 41, DKR 42, p. 410). Woodville was appointed *bailli* of Gisors on 16 November 1419 (C 64/11 m. 7, DKR 41, p. 806), John Burgh replacing him on 18 January 1421 (C 64/15 m. 26, DKR 42, p. 397), and holding office to at least May 1429 (BNF, PO 468 Burgh 4). Identification is uncertain but a John Burgh indented to serve with two other men-at-arms and nine archers in 1415 (E 404/31/236) and was probably in the royal household, appearing on a list of household men for the 1416 expedition (E 101/48/10/39). A man of this name served in the 1417 army in the company of Sir John Grey of Heton (E 101/51/2 m. 32) and was granted valuable lands in Normandy in April 1419 (C 64/11 m. 51, DKR 41, p. 778), holding a number of military commands to at least the mid-1430s.

[373] On 1 February 1419 Sir John Grey of Heton was appointed captain in anticipation of surrender (C 64/10 m. 40, DKR 41, p. 723) but, after the place submitted on 5 February, the earl of March was appointed to the captaincy (C 64/11 m. 28, DKR 41, p. 792).

[374] The treaty of surrender is dated 3 February 1419 (C 64/10 m. 5, DKR 41, p. 746). On 1 February 1419 Sir William Porter (d. 1436), of Wimpole (Cambs.), already described as captain of the town and castle of Vernon, was given power to receive all who wished to pay homage to the king (C 64/10 m. 40, DKR 41, p. 730). He remained in office to the death of Henry V but whilst in the company of the king in the early part of 1421, John Burgh was appointed as substitute (C 64/16 m. 38d, DKR 42, p. 426). Porter, originally from Rutland but with estates in Cambridgeshire and elsewhere through marriage, had been an esquire of Henry as prince of Wales and remained in his close service thereafter. He had crossed in 1415 with thirty-two men (E 101/45/5 m. 2d), being knighted during the campaign, and with 120 in 1417 (E 101/51/2 m. 31) (HOCa).

[375] Guy le Bouteillier, who had accepted English allegiance after defending Rouen castle for the French, participated in the English siege of the castle of La Roche-Guyon in early spring 1419 and was commissioned upon its surrender to take the castle into his hands on behalf of the king (C 64/11 m. 65, DKR 41, p. 771). Five months later, on 24 September, he was officially granted the lordship of La Roche-Guyon, 'lately held by the lord of La Roche Guyon' (C 64/11 m. 21, DKR 41, p. 797). Guy married, probably at the king's persuasion, Perrette Bureau de la Rivière, widow of Guy de La Roche Guyon (Mesqui et al., 'Guy le Bouteillier', pp. 135–6).

[376] Rempston was appointed captain of Meulan on 22 November 1419 (C 64/11 m. 6, DKR 41, p. 807), being replaced by Fastolf on 19 May 1421 (E 364/749; E 101/50/24 and 25).

at La Chaussée-d'Ivry my lord of Gloucester and later Arthur of Brittany, earl and lord of the place by grant[377]
at Damville Sir Christopher Curwen[378]
at Honfleur my lord the earl of Salisbury, and later my lord of Clarence, lord of the place by grant, who appointed as his lieutenant *Robert Inkbarrow* esquire[379]
at Conches-en-Ouche [added: Sir Richard Merbury][380]
at Breteuil [added: *Sir Ferry Mortimer, bailli* of Honfleur][381]

---

[377] The name given in the French text is 'Yvry la Chaucee', which suggests identification as La Chaussée-d'Ivry (Eure-et-Loir, arr. Dreux, cant. Anet). Yet the castle lies at Ivry-la-Bataille (Eure, arr. Evreux, cant. Saint-André-de-l'Eure). The surrender of Ivry, involving commissioners of the duke of Gloucester, is dated 10 May 1419 (C 64/10 m. 2, DKR 41, p. 746) but we do not know the name of any subsequent captain. The lordship of Ivry was granted to Richemont (1393–1458) on 10 January 1421 (C 64/14 m. 2 additional, DKR 42, p. 338). He had been captured fighting for the French at Agincourt but had accepted English allegiance in 1420, fighting for Henry V and VI until he changed his allegiance to Charles VII in 1425.

[378] Eure, arr. Bernay, cant. Verneuil-sur-Avre. Sir Christopher Curwen (d. 1450), of Workington (Cumb.), crossed in 1417 as a knight in the company of Sir John Neville (E 101/51/2 m. 22) (HOCa, b). He was granted on 30 January 1419 the fief of Cany (C 64/10 m. 16, DKR 41, p. 743), but is not proved to have any link with Damville. On 19 April 1419 the fief of Damville was granted to Peter Croft (C 64/11 m. 60, DKR 41, p. 774).

[379] The treaty of surrender of Honfleur made on behalf of Salisbury is dated 25 February 1419 (C 64/10 m. 4, DKR 41, p. 746) and involved a Walter Ynkebarow (which is probably a homophonic spelling of Interburgh). Walter Interburgh (dead by 1428), from Dorset, had been in the service of Bolingbroke and accompanied him to Prussia (*Expeditions to Prussia*, pp. lxii–lxxx, 246, 247, 251, 253, 255). By 1419 he was an annuitant of the duke of Clarence (*Household Accounts*, p. 642), having crossed in 1415 in the latter's company (E 101/45/4 m. 2). He may have crossed with Clarence in 1417 but the latter's muster does not survive. He is mentioned as captain of Honfleur in the account of the receiver-general of Normandy for April 1419–20 (E 101/187/14 f. 2v) and was probably captain from the surrender onwards since he received an order on 23 February 1419 concerning building works at Honfleur (C 64/10 m. 31d, DKR 41, p. 753). No Robert Inkbarrow is known.

[380] The place was garrisoned by late March 1419 (C 64/11 m. 78d, DKR 42, p. 314). The duke of Exeter appears as captain of Conches in the account of the receiver-general of Normandy for April 1419–20 (E 101/187/14 f. 16) and his appointment dated 26 March 1420 is found on the Norman rolls (C 64/13 m. 29, DKR 42, p. 362). He was replaced by Sir John Arthur at Michaelmas 1423 (BNF, Fr. 4491 f. 59). There is no evidence Richard Merbury was ever captain of Conches. No service of a man of this name is known before the army which accompanied Henry V back to France in 1421 where a Sir Richard Merbury appears in the retinue of Richard Beauchamp, earl of Worcester (E 101/50/1 m. 1). Both the knight and an esquire called by the same name are found in various Normandy garrisons thenceforward, and receive land grants, but their relationship to the Merbury families of Cheshire and Herefordshire remains uncertain.

[381] A *vicomte* of Breteuil was appointed by the English as early as June 1418 (C 64/9 m. 23d, DKR 41, p. 713): this relates to the administrative unit in Eure, arr. Bernay, ch. l. cant. A sergeant of the town and castle of Breteuil was appointed on 10 February 1419 (C 64/10 m. 32d, DKR 41, p. 752) but the location in Eure is not known to have had a castle. The reference to Ferry Mortimer may therefore relate to Breteuil in Oise, arr. Clermont, cant. Saint-Jussé-en-Chaussée, although no one of this name has been identified nor any *bailli* of Honfleur.

At the beginning of the following year, 1419, there began, through ambassadors, negotiations on a final peace between the two realms of France and England. During this time the town of Pontoise was taken and captured by assault. My lord the duke of Clarence was appointed captain. He made Ralph, lord Cromwell his lieutenant.[382]

(40r) In the year 1420 the treaty of final peace between the two kings and kingdoms of France and England, which was mentioned above, was agreed, concluded and confirmed. By its terms, the said victorious prince and king married, in the town of Troyes in Champagne, my lady Catherine, daughter of the king of France, Charles, sixth of that name, and became heir and regent of France by adoption.[383] Soon after this treaty and marriage had been effected and completed with the Queen of France, Isabel, acting on behalf of the king, the duke of Burgundy and several other lords, the said victorious prince and king with all his army laid siege to the town and city of Sens in Burgundy.[384] He was there for the space of a fortnight or thereabouts, and took with him the said King Charles. The town was surrendered and delivered to the two kings and the lord of Jonvelle[385] was put in as captain and keeper. The two kings then departed from there, and the victorious prince went to lay siege before the town and castle of Montereau-Fault-Yonne,[386] the place where John, duke of Burgundy had been killed. After he had besieged it for ten weeks or thereabouts, the town and castle were surrendered and delivered to him. The body of Duke John was found there but it had not been buried fittingly. For this reason, Duke Philip of Burgundy, his son, had the body buried afresh in

---

[382] On 2 February 1419 Sir Gilbert Umfraville had been appointed captain of Pontoise in anticipation of its capture (C 64/10 m. 32, DKR 41, p. 730). On 1 August, the day after Pontoise was taken by assault, the earl of Huntingdon appointed to the captaincy (C 64/11 m. 30, DKR 41, p. 791) but the duke of Clarence was made captain instead on 17 August (C 64/11 m. 30, DKR 41, p. 792). Ralph Cromwell's lieutenancy to Clarence at Pontoise is confirmed by AN, Dom Lenoir 14, f. 23. Cromwell (c. 1393–1456) had been in the household of Clarence and served with him on the 1412 campaign as well as in 1415 (E 101/45/4 m. 2). His service under Clarence continued throughout the conquest, where we find him at the siege of Caen in 1417 (C 64/8 m. 20, Hardy, p. 195), and in March 1418 lieutenant of Clarence as constable of the army (C 64/8 m. 10, Hardy, pp. 265–6). The Norman rolls show his presence at a number of surrenders. He was also involved in diplomatic negotiations with the French towards the treaty of Troyes. In April 1421 he was appointed captain of Harfleur (C 64/16 m. 41, DKR 42, p. 410). But his service in France after the death of Henry V was sporadic as he held several important positions in the minority government, including that of Treasurer. William Worcester mentions in his *Itineraries* (p. 359) that Henry Inglose was 'taken prisoner in the Vale of Ververie near Senlis in an action with Lord de Cromwell'.

[383] Aube, ch. l. d'arr. The treaty was sealed at the cathedral of Troyes on 21 May 1420. Henry married Catherine* (1401–37) at the church of Saint Jean in Troyes on 2 June.

[384] Yonne, ch. l. d'arr. The siege began on 5 June and the town surrendered on 11 June, with the treaty negotiated by Sir John Cornwall (Wylie, iii, p. 208).

[385] This may be Jean de la Trémoille, lord of Jonvelle. The captain of Sens in 1424 was Pierre le Verrat (AN, X1a 4795, f. 5r).

[386] Seine-et-Marne, arr. Provins, ch. l. cant. The army arrived at Montereau on 16 June. The town was taken after an assault on 24 June but the castle surrendered on 1 July (Wylie, iii, pp. 209–10), the siege lasting nowhere near the ten weeks claimed in the M 9 chronicle.

an honourable manner.[387] Once these things had been carried out and completed, the said victorious prince made the earl of Warwick captain and keeper of the said town and castle.[388] The same prince and king departed and laid siege before the town and castle of Melun where he was for the space of around seven months.[389] With him at that siege were King Charles of France, his father-in-law, and the king of Scotland,[390] and many other princes and lords, to wit,

my lord the duke of Clarence[391]   }

my lord the duke of Bedford[392]   } all brothers of the victorious prince and king

my lord the duke of Gloucester[393]   }

my lord the duke of Burgundy[394]

my lord the duke of Bar[395]

---

[387] Duke John ('The Fearless', 1371–1419), murdered by the Dauphin's associates on 10 September 1419, had initially been buried in the parish church of Montereau. His recovered body was taken for reburial at the Charterhouse of Champol outside Dijon.

[388] No other evidence has been found of Warwick's captaincy. By October 1423 Sir William Bucton was captain of Montereau (BNF, Fr. 21495/12), and by October 1426 the captain was Thomas Guerard, who continued his service from October 1427 (BNF, Fr. 4484 ff. 142–5v). Its French captain had been Guillaume de Chaumont, knight, lord of Guitry (C 64/14 m. 26, DKR 42, p. 375).

[389] Seine-et-Marne, ch. l. d'arr. The siege began on 13 July. In negotiations led by Sir Walter Hungerford, Jean de Roubaix and Jean de Courcelles, the place agreed on 17 November to surrender (Wylie, iii, pp. 210–11), suggesting the siege actually lasted four rather than seven months. Worcester, in his *Itineraries* (p. 359), claimed that the siege lasted thirty-one weeks and three days.

[390] James I, king of Scotland (1394–1437), had been captured by the English in 1406, shortly before his accession to the throne whilst fleeing to France for fear of his uncle, Robert, duke of Albany. Held as a prisoner in England, he had been brought to France by Henry V in the summer of 1420 in the hope that his presence would dissuade the Scots who were fighting for the Dauphin.

[391] On 3 November 1420 Clarence's troops at the siege were ordered to be mustered (C 64/14 m. 15d, DKR 42, p. 391).

[392] John, duke of Bedford* (1389–1435) had brought about 2,800 troops from England in the late spring (E 101/49/36; E 404/36/271), many of whom were deployed at this and other sieges (Wylie, iii, p. 211). On 6 August and 3 November 1420 the duke's troops were ordered to be mustered at the siege (C 64/14 m. 19d, DKR 42, p. 390; C 64/14 m. 15d, DKR 42, p. 391).

[393] The duke of Gloucester was keeper of England and therefore not in France at this time.

[394] Duke Philip (1396–1467) was commissioned on 12 July 1420 to maintain the siege on the side of the town towards Brie, i.e. the eastern side (C 64/14 m. 5d, DKR 42, p. 375, printed in *Foedera*, x, p. 4).

[395] Cardinal Louis de Bar (1370/5–1430), bishop of Châlons (1423–30) and bishop-administrator of Verdun, inherited the duchy of Bar from his elder brother Edward who died at Agincourt. In August 1419 he adopted as his successor his grand-nephew, René of Anjou (1409–80). René, a minor, was placed under the tutelage of Charles II, duke of Lorraine, who became his father-in-law in October 1420 and presented himself until 1424 as 'mainbour' and governor of the duchy of Bar. M 9's duke of Bar who is present at Melun may refer to Cardinal Louis or Charles II, but there is no other evidence of the presence of either. Cardinal Louis was a Burgundian supporter, but Charles II's loyalty was not evident until he swore to observe the treaty of Troyes in May 1422 (Schnerb, *Bulgnéville*, pp. 11–14; *Jeanne. Dictionnaire*, pp. 543–4, 953–4).

(40v) the prince of Orange[396]
the earl of March[397]
the earl of Huntingdon[398]
the earl of Stafford[399]
the earl of Somerset[400]
the Earl Marshal[401]
the earl of Warwick[402]
the earl of Worcester[403]
the earl of Suffolk[404]
Arthur of Brittany, count of Ivry[405]
Charles Beaumont knight, alferez of Navarre[406]

---

[396] The principal interests of Louis II of Chalon-Arlay (c. 1388–1463) lay in the Dauphinée but he offered military support to Henry V and the duke of Burgundy. However, he withdrew during the siege (Wylie, iii, p. 213).

[397] On 3 November 1420 March's troops at the siege were ordered to be mustered (C 64/14 m. 15d, DKR 42, p. 392).

[398] On 3 November 1420 Huntingdon's troops at the siege were ordered to be mustered (C 64/14 m. 15d, DKR 42, p. 392).

[399] Humphrey, earl of Stafford* (1402–60), created duke of Buckingham in 1444. He was with the king in France in 1420 for the sealing of the treaty of Troyes but then returned to England with the king. He indented for forty men in the army which crossed with Henry V to France in the summer of 1421 (E 101/70/6/724; E 101/50/1).

[400] John Beaufort* (1404–44), elevated to duke of Somerset in 1443, succeeded to the earldom at the death of his elder brother Henry on 25 November 1418. His presence at the siege of Melun is also noted by Walsingham (*St Albans Chronicle*, ii, p. 755). It does not seem that in 1420 he held a command but he was with the king in France. He was captured at Baugé in the following spring.

[401] On 3 November 1420 the Earl Marshal's troops at the siege were ordered to be mustered (C 64/14 m. 15d, DKR 42, p. 391).

[402] On 3 November 1420 Warwick's troops at the siege were ordered to be mustered (C 64/14 m. 15d, DKR 42, p. 392).

[403] There is no reference to the service of the earl at the siege but he was with the king at the siege of Sens in June (C 64/14 m. 29d, DKR 42, p. 388) and in Paris in December 1420 (C 64/14 m. 12d, DKR 42, p. 393).

[404] On 3 November 1420 Suffolk's troops at the siege were ordered to be mustered (C 64/14 m. 15d, DKR 42, p. 392).

[405] Richemont was escorted to Henry V, then besieging Melun, on 28 October 1420 (*PPC*, ii, pp. 277–9; Cosneau, p. 58). He was granted on 10 January 1421, after the siege ended, the lands of Ivry, Aumale Garentières and Berenguierville (C 64/14 m. 2 additional, DKR 42, p. 388) in a possible attempt to cement an Anglo-Breton alliance. Thenceforward he was called, as in the chronicle, 'count of Ivry', a title highlighting his vassalage to the English.

[406] Charles de Beaumont (1361–1432), grandson of Philip III, king of Navarre, and count of Evreux, was one of the English king's important supporters in south-west France, holding lands in Labord and Noailhan near Bordeaux. In 1379 he had been appointed 'alferez' (standard bearer) of Navarre by his uncle Charles 'the Bad' of Navarre. He served on the 1415 campaign with twelve men and was probably at Agincourt (E 101/45/5 m. 5d; E 101/45/21 m. 15). He was active in the conquest of Normandy, being present at the siege of Rouen (C 64/ C 64/ 9 m. 8d, DKR 41, p. 718) and in the subsequent campaign along the Seine valley (C 64/11 m. 31d, DKR 42, p. 323).

the count of Perche[407]
the count of Mortain[408]
the earl of Ormond[409]
Le conte d'Essemont
the count of Eu[410]
the count of Tancarville[411]
the count of Longueville, Captal de Buch[412]
the count of Saint-Pol[413]
the count of Braine[414]

---

[407] Thomas Montague, earl of Salisbury, had been granted the *comté* of Perche by Henry V on 26 April 1419 (C 64/11 m. 52, DKR 41, p. 777). On 3 November 1420 Salisbury was commissioned to muster troops at the siege of Melun under Clarence, Bedford and the earl of March (C 64/14 m. 15d, DKR 42, p. 391). It is strange, however, that the chronicle should use here his French rather than his English title. An alternative identification is Thomas Beaufort (1405–31), the third son of John, earl of Somerset (d. 1410) and Margaret Holland, who had married as her second husband the duke of Clarence. Thomas (d. 1431) was created count of Perche after the earl of Salisbury's death but there is no evidence of his presence in France at this point.

[408] Edward Holland, count of Mortain, was dead by 18 October 1418 (C 64/9 m. 10, DKR 41, p 700). Edmund Beaufort (1406–55) was created count of Mortain in 1427. He had letters of attorney in March of 1427 to cross to France (C 76/109 m. 11, DKR 48, p. 247) and was at the siege of Montargis in the summer of that year (BNF, Fr. 4484 f. 69v). He had been captured at Baugé alongside his elder brother John and had been released only recently.

[409] James Butler, earl of Ormond (1392–1452), inherited his earldom in 1405. He had letters of attorney to cross to France in April 1418 (C 76/101 m. 10, DKR 44, p. 604) and is believed to have served at the siege of Rouen. On 10 February 1420 he was appointed lieutenant in Ireland and is unlikely to have been in France at this point.

[410] Sir William Bourchier, who had been granted the *comté* of Eu in June 1419, died at Troyes on 28 May 1420 and cannot therefore have been present at the siege of Melun. There is no evidence that his son and heir Henry (1404–83) was in France at this point.

[411] Sir John Grey of Heton had been granted the *comté* of Tancarville on 31 January 1419 (C 64/10 m. 41, DKR 41, p. 711). That he was at the siege is suggested by a grant made to him there on 1 November 1420 of a house in Harfleur (C 64/14 m. 4, DKR 42, p. 381).

[412] According to Monstrelet (iii, p. 333) Gaston de Foix had been 'principal conducteur des Anglois' in the surprise capture of the town of Pontoise in August 1419. It is possible, though not otherwise evidenced, that he was at the siege of Melun. He played a prominent role in the negotiations between his elder brother John I de Foix and Henry V in the early 1420s (Vale, *English Gascony*, pp. 87–90).

[413] Philippe of Burgundy (1404–30), count of Saint-Pol and Ligny (1415–30) and duke of Brabant (1427–30), younger son of Duke Anthony, was brought up at the Burgundian ducal court following the death of his father at Agincourt. Despite his young age, John the Fearless entrusted him with the safeguard of Paris in January 1419. The count was heavily involved in the negotiations which led to the treaty of Troyes and attended the marriage of Henry V and Catherine on 2 June. If present at the siege of Melun, he may have left early since he was in Brabant by the end of September trying to settle a dispute between the Estates of Brabant and his elder brother Duke John IV (Dynter, *Chronique des ducs de Brabant*, I, p. 76; Uyttebrouck, *Le gouvernement du duché de Brabant*, i, pp. 506–12; ii, p. 729).

[414] Jean VI, count of Roucy and Braine, died at Agincourt. His daughter, Jeanne de Roucy, married Robert de Sarrebrück (c. 1400–c. 1462) in 1417 who thus became count. But Robert's presence at Melun for the English is implausible since he was a Dauphinist supporter operating in eastern France (Toureille, *Robert de Sarrebrück*, pp. 38–9, 67–74). The

the count of Ligny[415]
the count of Vaudemont[416]
the count of Joigny[417]
Lord Roos[418]
Lord Maltravers[419]
Lord Grey of Codnor[420]
Lord Bourchier[421]
Lord Audeley[422]
Lord Willoughby[423]
Lord Clinton[424]
Lord Clifford[425]
Lord Ferrers of Groby[426]

---

chronicle's mention of the same count of Braine at the siege of Meaux suggests that the authors mistook Braine for Brienne. This would mean that Pierre de Luxembourg appears twice in this list, both as count of Brienne ('Braine') and lord of Enghien ('Anguyan').

[415] Philippe de Saint-Pol was also count of Ligny. This is a case of the chronicle mentioning twice the same person within the same list under a different patronym.

[416] Antoine de Lorraine (d. 1458) inherited the county of Vaudémont (1415) from his father Ferry de Lorraine who died at Agincourt. He also inherited a claim, which never materialised, to the duchy of Lorraine which would eventually lead to the battle of Bulgnéville in 1431. In 1419 he was among the captains of the Burgundian party serving in Perthois and Bassigny, and he continued to serve the duke in the early 1420s. In reward for his services, Henry VI granted him the lands of Démuin and Mézières-en-Santerre which were confiscated from Charles d'Esneval in 1425 (AN, JJ 173/231) and in 1427 the lordships of Vaux and Vauchelle-en-Ponthieu (AN, JJ 174/37; Schnerb, *Bulgnéville*, pp. 17–21). His presence at the siege of Melun in 1420 is not noted elsewhere.

[417] Guy de la Trémoille (d. 1438), comte de Joigny, had suffered the ravaging of his lands by the Dauphinists late in 1420 but before the siege of Melun had ended, according to Monstrelet (iv, p. 33). He was granted by Charles VI in January 1421 the lordships of La Loupière, Brion, Brecy, and Vieuchamp in compensation and reward for his services (Anselme, iv, p. 180).

[418] On 3 November 1420 John, lord Roos's troops at the siege were ordered to be mustered (C 64/14 m. 15d, DKR 42, p. 392).

[419] On 3 November 1420 Lord Maltravers's troops at the siege were ordered to be mustered (C 64/14 m. 15d, DKR 42, p. 392). He died on 21 April 1421.

[420] John Grey (1396–1431), who became lord of Codnor at his father Richard's death in 1418, was serving in Normandy by April 1419 (C 64/11 m. 48d, DKR 42, p. 318), and was commissioned on 11 November 1420 at the siege of Melun to investigate complaints against the earl of Salisbury (C 64/14 m. 14d, DKR 42, p. 392).

[421] Hugh Stafford, lord Bourchier, died on 25 October 1420.

[422] James Tuchet, fifth lord Audley (c. 1398–1459), led a retinue of troops brought to France by the duke of Bedford in the spring of 1420 (E 101/49/36 m. 5). He remained in France after the expiry of his six-month indenture (C 76/103 m. 4, DKR 44, p. 620) but returned to England with the king in February 1421.

[423] On 3 November 1420 Lord Willoughby was commissioned to carry out various musters at the siege of Melun (C 64/14 m. 15d, DKR 42, p. 392).

[424] There is no evidence that William, lord Clinton served in France after 1416.

[425] On 3 November 1420 Clifford's troops at the siege were ordered to be mustered (C 64/14 m. 15d, DKR 42, p. 392).

[426] No service in France by William, lord Ferrers of Groby is known.

Lord Ferrers of Chartley[427]
Lord Fitzwalter[428]
Lord Talbot[429]
Lord Furnival[430]
Lord Fitzhugh[431]
(41r) Sir John Cornwall, Lord Fanhope[432]
Lord Scrope of Bolton[433]
Lord Scrope[434]
Lord Harington[435]
Sir William Phelip, Lord Bardolf[436]

---

[427]   On 3 November 1420 Lord Ferrers's troops at the siege of Melun were ordered to be mustered (C 64/14 m. 15d, DKR 42, p. 392).

[428]   On 3 November 1420 the troops at the siege of Melun of Sir Walter Fitzwalter*, seventh baron Fitzwalter of Woodham Walter and Dunmow, Essex (c. 1400–31), were ordered to be mustered (C 64/14 m. 15d, DKR 42, p. 392). Whilst serving at the siege in late July, Walter had been appointed master of Henry's 'herthounds' (C 64/14 m. 18, DKR 42, p. 378).

[429]   Gilbert, lord Talbot died at the siege of Rouen on 19 October 1418. It is possible that the Lord Talbot mentioned here is John, lord Talbot (at that date Lord Furnival) but on 3 November 1420 the troops at the siege of Sir William Talbot, John's younger brother, were ordered to be mustered (C 64/14 m. 15d, DKR 42, p. 392).

[430]   On 3 November 1420 troops at the siege of Melun under John, lord Furnival (c. 1387–1453) were ordered to be mustered (C 64/14 m. 15d, DKR 42, p. 392). This was the first known service in France of the man who became John, lord Talbot* (1387–1453) at the death of his niece (the daughter of Gilbert, lord Talbot) in December 1421, and earl of Shrewsbury in 1442. He had a very extensive career in France until his death at Castillon in 1453 (Pollard, *John Talbot*).

[431]   On 3 November 1420 Fitzhugh was commissioned to muster at the siege of Melun troops in the royal household (C 64/14 m. 15d, DKR 42, p. 391).

[432]   On 3 November 1420 Cornwall's troops at the siege of Melun were ordered to be mustered (C 64/14 m. 15d, DKR 42, p. 392).

[433]   Richard, lord Scrope of Bolton died at the siege of Melun on 29 August (C 64/14 m. 17, DKR 42, p. 380).

[434]   Presumably this is Sir John Scrope of Masham who is known to have been serving in Normandy in 1419, and who crossed to France in the army which accompanied the king in the summer of 1421 (E 101/70/5/695; E 101/50/1 m. 4d, C 76/104 m. 16, DKR 44, p. 625). So far no other evidence has been found of his presence at the siege of Melun.

[435]   William, lord Harington* (1390–1458) of Aldingham (Lancs.) had succeeded his brother John who died on 11 February 1418 in France. In 1415 he probably served in the retinue of the duke of Gloucester (E 101/45/13 m. 2). Now a knight, he served in his brother's company in the 1417 expedition (E 101/51/2 m. 14). It is difficult to distinguish his service in Normandy from that of his namesake Sir William Harrington of Hornby (d. 1440), who had become a KG. But we can see that William, lord Harington mustered at Mantes in July 1419 (C 64/11 m. 31d, DKR 42, p. 323) and therefore is likely to have been with the king in the campaign which followed. He does not appear to have served in France after the death of Henry V.

[436]   On 3 November 1420 Phelip's troops at the siege of Melun were ordered to be mustered (C 64/14 m. 15d, DKR 42, p. 391). Sir William Phelip of Dennington, Suffolk (1380–1441), had close connections with the king, being treasurer of the household 1421–22. He indented for the sevice of forty men in 1415 (E 101/45/5 m. 3; E 101/45/22 m. 39; E 101/44/30 no. 4, m. 5; E 101/45/1; E 101/46/16; E 358/6 m. 5) and led a company of eighty-six in 1417 (E 101/51/2 m. 29). Active in Normandy, he was made KG in 1418/19, perhaps linked to

Lord Scales[437]
Lord Carew[438]
the lord of Duras[439]
the lord of La Lande[440]
the lord of Montferrand[441]
Lord Lovel[442]
the lord of Boutras and of Bourg[443]
the lord of Chastellux[444]   }

---

service at the siege of Rouen. He was known as Lord Bardolf from c. 1437, reflecting his marriage to the heiress Joan Bardolf (HOCa).

[437] Thomas, lord Scales (1399–1460), then an esquire, served in the 1417 army in the retinue of the earl of Warwick (E 101/51/2 m. 12) but there is no information on his subsequent career in France until he crossed in the army which accompanied the king in the summer of 1421. He inherited the barony of Scales at the death of his brother Robert on 1 July 1419 and paid homage for his lands in February 1421.

[438] No other references have been found to the presence of Thomas, lord Carew at the siege of Melun. He was serving at sea in May 1420 (E 101/48/9 no. 1, m. 4).

[439] Galhart III de Durfort (d. c. 1443), lord of Duras and Blanquefort, was a Gascon lord loyal to the English crown, son of Galhart II who had been seneschal of Aquitaine from 1399 to 1415. In August 1423 he was made *prévôt* of the city of Bayonne (C 61/119, item 29), and became seneschal of the Landes in July 1434 (C 61/125, item 97). He was married to the sister of John IV de Lalande. See also *Documents sur la Maison de Durfort*, ii.

[440] Johan IV de Lalande (or La Lande), lord of La Brède and La Lande (d. 1433), was a Gascon lord. In 1426 he married Johana de Foix, daughter of Gaston de Foix (Meaudre de Lapouyade, 'La maison de Bordeaux et les premiers captaux de Buch', pp. 143–4; C 61/135 item 3).

[441] Bertrand (or Bérard) III de Montferrand (1380–1446), of Montferrand near Bordeaux, came from a noble Gascon family with a long tradition of loyalty to the English. He probably came to England with Joan of Navarre and had a long military career, both in Normandy, where he held various captaincies in the 1430s and 1440s (Curry, 'Military Organisation', ii, pp. cx, cxxvi, cxxxv), and in Gascony, where he also became lord of Gassac (Vale, *English Gascony*, pp. 98, 174–5). By 1423 he was chamberlain to the duke of Bedford whom he served in various diplomatic and administrative capacities, but by the early 1440s he was suffering financial difficulties through loss of lands and offices (*Bedford Inventories*, ed. Stratford, pp. 414–17). See also Communay, *Essai généalogique sur les Montferrand*, pp. xxi–xxiii.

[442] On 3 November 1420 the troops at the siege of William, seventh baron Lovel (1397–1455) were ordered to be mustered (C 64/14 m. 15d, DKR 42, p. 392). Although this is his first mention in the M 9 chronicle he had served on the 1415, 1416 and 1417 campaigns and had been present in Normandy in the autumn of 1419 if not earlier.

[443] Assuming the identification is correct – the addition of 'de Bourg' is perplexing – William, lord Botreaux (1389–1462) took out letters of protection on 3 April 1420 for service in France (C 76/103 m. 8, DKR 44, p. 617), but no other evidence has been found of his service at the siege of Melun.

[444] Claude de Beauvoir (d. 1453), lord of Chastellux, was a vassal and a loyal servant of the dukes of Burgundy. He fought at Agincourt and played a prominent role in the capture of Paris in 1418, in the aftermath of which he was appointed marshal of France. Charles VI made him his lieutenant and general-captain of Normandy that same year: he enjoyed some military successes in Upper Normandy, and suffered a stinging defeat before the walls of Louviers in August 1418 (Schnerb, '"A l'encontre des Anglois"', pp. 203–4). In 1419 the king made him his lieutenant and captain-general of Saint-Denis with 600 men-at-arms and 600 archers to protect it from the English. He participated in Burgundian embassies

the lord of L'Isle-Adam[445] } marshals of France
the lord of Vergy[446]
the lord of Châtillon[447]
the lord of Crouy[448]
the lord of Saint-George[449]

---

dispatched to Henry V (C 64/11 m. 37, DKR 41, p. 787; Bonenfant, *Du meurtre*, p. 31), and attended the English king's marriage on 2 June 1420 (Monstrelet, iii, pp. 389–90). His participation at the siege of Melun is not otherwise evidenced. He was officially discharged as marshal on 22 January 1421 but continued to serve the duke of Burgundy and the English king (Chastellux, *Histoire généalogique de la Maison de Chastellux*, pp. 79–97).

[445] Jean de Villliers, lord of L'Isle-Adam, had been appointed marshal of France by John the Fearless in 1418 after the capture of Paris. Monstrelet (iv, p. 9) also mentions his presence at the siege of Melun where Henry V expressed his dislike for him. In 1421 he was accused of conspiracy, deprived of his office and thrown into jail. He was eventually released in 1422 after the death of Henry V and fully exonerated in 1423.

[446] Despite the original spelling of Vergier, this is surely Antoine de Vergy (d. 1439), lord of Fouvent, Champlitte, count of Dammartin, whom Monstrelet also designates as 'seigneur de Vergy'. He became a chamberlain of John the Fearless in 1408 and was wounded at Montereau as he tried to defend the duke. There is no other evidence of his presence at the siege of Melun. He served the double monarchy in eastern France in the late 1420s and early 1430s (Caron, 'Antoine de Vergy', pp. 11–13).

[447] Guillaume, lord of Châtillon and La Ferté-en-Ponthieu, was given the government of Reims and its surrounding lands, together with the office of *Grand Queux de France*, in 1418. He captured Château-Thierry from the Orleanists at some point in the following year (AN, JJ 172/363). He embraced the double monarchy. On 24 September 1420 he was given full power and authority to subdue all towns and fortresses in Brie and Champagne by Henry V 'en nostre ost devant nostre ville de Melun' (AN, JJ 172/184), confirming his presence. According to Monstrelet (iv, p. 136), Châtillon and the Bastard of Thian captured La Ferté-Milon in 1423, the year in which he might also have been knighted by Salisbury, perhaps at Cravant (Anselme, viii, p. 839). He contributed to the negotiations at Arras in 1435 and served Charles VII afterwards.

[448] Antoine de Croÿ, lord of Crouy, and count of Porcien (c. 1402–c. 1475), a Burgundian supporter, was with Philip the Good at the siege of Crépy-en-Laonnois in February 1420 and accompanied his master to Troyes, attending the marriage of Henry V and Catherine of France (Monstrelet, iv, pp. 374–5, 389–90). His presence at the siege of Melun is likely but not otherwise evidenced. We find him militarily active in the early 1420s, taking oaths of the inhabitants of Saint-Riquier which was handed over to the duke after the battle of Mons-en-Vimeu in August 1421; in the army for the relief of the siege of Cosne-sur-Loire in the summer of 1422; negotiating the surrender of Dommart (Ponthieu) in 1423 (Monstrelet, iv, pp. 73, 107, 143); and in 1424 supporting the duke in Brabant and Hainault against the duke of Gloucester (Monstrelet, iv, pp. 212, 226). He was councillor and chamberlain of Philip the Good by 1426 (Win, 'Antoine de Croÿ', pp. 33–8).

[449] The career in arms of Guillaume de Vienne (d. 1434), lord of Saint-Georges and Sainte-Croix, began in 1379. He remained loyal to the dukes of Burgundy throughout, defending Artois in 1415, participating in the entry to Paris in 1418, and being present at the murder of Montereau. He was taken prisoner by the Armagnacs but cannot have been in captivity for long as he escorted the body of his master to Champmol after its recovery in July 1420. In May 1422 he was made captain-general of Burgundy, serving also on the ducal council in later years. His last action appears to have been at the siege and surrender of Grancey in August 1434 (ACO, B 11880; Caron, 'Guillaume de Vienne', pp. 3–4; Schnerb, *Jean Sans Peur*, p. 694).

the lord of Pesmes[450]
the lord of Enghien[451]
the lord of La Trémoïlle[452]
the lord of Jonvelle[453]
Hue de Lannoy knight[454]

---

[450] His presence at Melun is not evidenced elsewhere but is not improbable.

[451] Pierre de Luxembourg, count of Conversano and Brienne, and lord of Enghien (1390–1433), was a supporter of the Anglo-Burgundian regime. He took part in the siege of Melun, being captured on his way back home in the county of Brienne by Perron de Luppé and others who took him to Meaux (Monstrelet, iii, p. 413). During the siege of that place, his brother, Jean de Luxembourg, managed to secure his release through the mediation of Henry V (Monstrelet, iv, p. 80). The treaty of surrender anticipated that Pierre de Luxembourg was quit from any obligation toward Perron de Luppé (AN, J 646, no. 21(2)). He was subsequently commissioned by Henry V to negotiate and receive the surrender of various places in northern France (AN, JJ 172/61, 96, 128). On 5 June 1422 he was granted estates confiscated from the lord of Argilliers (AN, JJ 172/129). In the 1420s, he played a prominent role in the ducal council of Brabant. Like his elder brother Jean de Luxembourg, he was elected as knight of the Golden Fleece in the first round of elections in 1430 (Win, 'Pierre de Luxembourg', pp. 22–4).

[452] Georges de la Trémoïlle (d. 1445), lord of Sully and La Trémoïlle, is better known for his intrigues at the court of Charles VII in the late 1420s and his hostility toward Philip the Good. Yet this had not always been the case. The house of La Trémoïlle had developed ties with Burgundy in the second half of the fourteenth century. Georges and his brother Jean, lord of Jonvelle, began their career in Burgundy and Jean remained loyal to the dukes although Georges' allegiance wavered in the early 1420s. Evidence shows that some garrisons under his command in July 1424 ravaged the Auvergne, shouting 'Vive Bourgogne!' (AN, X1a 18, cited in Beaucourt, ii, pp. 145–6). His presence at the siege of Melun is not evidenced elsewhere and seems unlikely (Vissiére, 'Georges de La Trémoïlle' pp. 15–30; Contamine, *Charles VII*, pp. 133–5).

[453] Jean de la Trémoïlle, lord of Jonvelle, younger brother of Georges, held the hereditary office of first chamberlain of the duke of Burgundy after his elder brother defected (Schnerb, *Jean Sans Peur*, pp. 333–4). He was also great master of the household of John the Fearless, an office he kept under Philip the Good. He was in the Burgundian army which seized Paris in 1418 and participated in negotiations with the Orleanists in 1419. He was present at the murder of Montereau and fought at the battle of Mons-en-Vimeu in August 1421. His presence at Melun is not evidenced elsewhere but he attended the marriage of Henry V and Catherine of France (Monstrelet, iv, p. 389). On 24 July 1427 Henry VI gave 'his loved and loyal councillor, great master of the household and first chamberlain of the duke of Burgundy' the lands confiscated from his brother Georges (AN, JJ 173/716; *Les La Trémoïlle*, i, pp. 168–70, no. 14; Caron, 'Jean de la Trémoïlle, seigneur de Jonvelle', pp. 24–5).

[454] Hue de Lannoy (1384–1456), lord of Santes, Beaumont and Ijsselmonde, was a trusted and loyal servant of the dukes of Burgundy and a staunch supporter of the dual monarchy. He survived Agincourt in 1415 and was in the Burgundian contingent which took Pontoise in 1417. He was councillor and chamberlain of Charles VI in 1418–19 and part of the French delegation which negotiated the treaty of Troyes in 1420. His presence at the siege of Melun is not otherwise evidenced but is likely. He was named master of the crossbowmen of France towards the end of 1421 and is found campaigning in northern France afterwards in the company of Jean de Luxembourg (Monstrelet, iv, pp. 80, 83, 89), levying troops in Flanders for the relief of the siege of Cosne-sur-Loire in the summer of 1422 (Monstrelet, iv, p. 107). He took part in the battle of Montépilloy in 1429 (Monstrelet, iv, p. 345). Pro-

Jean de Courcelles knight,[455] 'garde du corps' of King Charles
the lord of Varambon[456]
the lord of Jalons
Guy de Bar knight[457]
Sir John Fastolf[458]
Sir Philip Leche[459]
Sir [added: John] Rodenal[460]
Sir John Heron[461]

English, he was against the reconciliation with Charles VII in 1435 (Brand, 'Hue (Hugues) de Lannoy', pp. 14–17).

[455] Jean de Courcelles was commissioned on 17 November 1420 by Henry V, together with Walter Hungerford and Jean de Roubaix, to negotiate the surrender of the castle and town of Melun (C 64/14 m. 14, DKR 42, p. 381).

[456] Francois de la Palud, lord of Varambon (d. 1456), a subject of the duke of Savoy, served the dukes of Burgundy from 1418, acting then as an ambassador with Benedict XIII. There is no other evidence of his presence at the siege of Melun. In February 1421, he served the duke at the siege of Villeneuve-sur-Yonne (*Livre des Trahisons*, p. 161). In 1423 he was in Cravant when besieged by the French and was present at the battle on 30 July, although this is not noted in the M 9 chronicle. In 1425 he was sent to relieve the siege of Haarlem. In the following year he took part in a crusading expedition in Cyprus where he may have been taken prisoner. We find him four years later serving the prince of Orange in the Dauphiné, participating in the battle of Anthon (11 June) in which he was wounded, captured and ransomed. On 12 June 1431, he committed to serve in the army of Antoine, comte de Vaudémont, with 200 men-at-arms (ACO, B 1647, f. 129v; Schnerb, *Bulgnéville*, pp. 136–7), and was present at the battle of Bulgnéville (Paviot, 'François de La Palud', pp. 257–92).

[457] Guy, dit le Veau, de Bar, lord of Presle, was a Burgundian captain, councillor and chamberlain of John the Fearless and Philip the Good. He was responsible, together with Claude de Chastellux and L'Isle-Adam, for the successful seizure of Paris in 1418, and held the office of *prévôt* from late May 1418 to 3 February 1419 (*GR*, iv, p. 312), as well as being lieutenant-general in Normandy between 20 August and 10 October 1418 (*GR*, iv, p. 245). His presence at the siege of Melun is wholly possible but not otherwise evidenced. He later served the double monarchy, being rewarded in September 1423 with estates in the Nivernais worth 1,500 *l.t.* per year confiscated from Dauphinists (AN, JJ 172/364). In this grant his defence of the town of Cravant under French siege was noted, 'jusques a ce que lesdis ennemis ont esté combatuz et deconfiz moiennant l'aide de nostre seigneur devant icelle ville, en laquelle besongne icellui Guy de Bar, nostre chevalier, c'est (sic) vaillamment emploié et exposé sa personne'. The chronicle, however, makes no mention of his participation in the battle of Cravant. He was *bailli* of Sens and Auxerre from 11 May 1424 to at least 5 October 1427, probably losing office when the town of Sens surrendered to Charles VII in December 1428 (*GR*, v, p. 444; Demurger, 'Guerre civile', pp. 231–2).

[458] No other evidence of the presence of Fastolf at the siege of Melun has been found. He was appointed captain of the Bastille Saint-Antoine in Paris on 24 January 1421 (Nichols, 'Appointment of Sir John Fastolf'; E 101/50/5).

[459] According to Monstrelet and Waurin, Leche was killed in the taking of a barbican but won praise from the duke of Burgundy (Wylie, iii, p. 211). He was dead by 2 August 1420 (C 64/14 m. 18, DKR 42, p. 379).

[460] On the assumption this should be identified as the treasurer of the royal household, Sir John Rothenale, he was dead by 2 August 1420 (C 64/14 m. 18, DKR 42, p. 379) but would have previously been in the company of the king.

[461] Sir John Heron (d. 1420) of Thornton, Northumberland, who was already militarily active in the late 1370s, had died at the siege of Melun by 24 September 1420 since on that

Sir Maurice Bruin[462]
Sir William, lord Bonville[463]
Sir Peter Tempest
Sir Robert Tempest[464]
(41v) and several others. When the kings and lords had held siege there for about seven months, the town and castle of Melun were surrendered and delivered to the kings. The enemy who were inside had no more food to sustain their lives. Barbazan,[465] the chief captain, was taken prisoner. Afterwards, the victorious prince appointed and established my lord the earl of Huntingdon as captain and

------

date the duke of Clarence was granted the wardship of his son, a minor (CPR 1422–29, p. 451; see also CFR 1413–22, p. 33; and *Calendar of Inquisitions Post Mortem*, xxi, p. 121). He had taken out letters of protection in the retinue of the duke in 1415 and 1417 (C 76/98 m. 12, C 76/100 m. 7, DKR 44, pp. 575, 591), making his will for the expedition (LR 14/1), and appears in the duke's 1415 muster with a company of thirty-five men (E 101/45/4 m. 1). The Norman rolls reveal Heron's involvement in surrenders made to Clarence in 1417–18. Thanks to Dr Michael Warner for references to his will and death.

[462] Sir Maurice Bruin (1385–1466) had lands in Hampshire, Essex, Dorset and Kent but resided primarily in Essex. Although he is known to have served under the duke of Clarence as an esquire in 1415 (E 101/45/4 m. 2) and as a knight in 1417 (C 76/100 m. 6, DKR 44, p. 600), and to have been in Normandy in the summer of 1419 (C 64/11 m. 29d, DKR 42, p. 324), his presence at the siege of Melun is not otherwise evidenced. He was captain of Gaillon in January 1421 (BL, Add. Ch. 1066), and lieutenant of Pont-de-l'Arche from at least February 1421 (C 64/15 m. 14d, DKR 42, p. 408), being appointed captain there on 3 April (C 64/16 m. 41, DKR 42, p. 410).

[463] This was presumably William Bonville* (1392/3–1461) of Chewton, Somerset, who was elevated as Lord Bonville in 1445. He served under the duke of Clarence as a man-at-arms in 1415 (E 101/45/4 m. 2) and a knight in 1417 (C 61/117 m. 6), taking out letters of attorney to continue his service in France under the duke in January 1418 (C 76/100 m. 4, DKR 44, p. 601) and subsequently acting as one of his executors. He served again in France in the early years of Henry VI, and again in Gascony in the 1440s.

[464] Robert Tempest led a retinue in troops taken by the duke of Bedford to France in the spring of 1420 (E 101/49/36 m. 2), some of which were detailed to the siege. But he was not a knight and his identity remains uncertain.

[465] Arnaud-Guilhem, lord of Barbazan (c. 1360–d. 1431), was a Gascon captain from Bigorre, chamberlain of Louis, duke of Orléans, and a fervent supporter of the Orleanist cause throughout the civil war. He was captain of Melun when it was besieged by Henry V in 1420. At its surrender he was taken prisoner, together with 600 men-at-arms in the garrison. Charles VII granted 6,000 *l.t.* to him in 1426 to help pay his enormous ransom of 32,000 *saluts d'or* (BNF, PO 187 Barbazan 35, 36), but he had to wait another four years to regain his freedom. The problem was not simply financial. He was suspected of taking part in the murder of John the Fearless. In the parliament of 1429 the lords asked Bedford and his council in France to establish the truth of this, and more importantly whether his release might be prejudicial to the 'great peace'. They hoped to secure an exchange for Lord Talbot, who had been captured at Patay, instead of surrendering him to Philip the Good. Barbazan was eventually released from his prison in Château-Gaillard through the intervention of La Hire who seized the fortress by surprise in February 1430 (Monstrelet, iv, pp. 350–1). Later that year, in July 1430, Barbazan received 2,000 *francs* from Charles VII to help him '[se] remettre sus de notre prison des Anglois et pour servir en ses guerres ainsi que paravant faisions' (BNF, PO 187 Barbazan 39, 40). He died at the battle of Bulgnéville on 2 July 1431 (Demurger, 'Guerre civile', p. 232; Gaussin, 'Les conseillers', p. 107; Schnerb, *Bulgnéville*, pp. 47–52; Gonzalez, pp. 26–9; Schnerb, *Jean Sans Peur*, pp. 706–9).

keeper of the said town and castle.[466] The three kings, as well as the princes and lords mentioned above, went to the city of Paris and there the noble and victorious prince was proclaimed as heir and Regent of the realm of France. Charles of Valois, son of King Charles, who called himself the Dauphin of Vienne, was proclaimed incapable of succeeding to the throne of France and deprived of that succession.[467] Once these matters and other ordinances had been made and established for the government of the realm of France, the victorious prince sought licence from King Charles, his father-in-law, and of the queen to go into England, and to take with him the queen, his wife, to have her crowned. He appointed the duke of Exeter as captain of Paris and my lord the Earl Marshal as captain of Pontoise.[468] For the keeping of France and Normandy he appointed and commissioned my lord the duke of Clarence, his brother, as his lieutenant-general, and my lord the earl of Salisbury as his particular lieutenant in Normandy beyond the River Seine.[469] He went off to England taking with him Queen Catherine his wife, who was crowned at Westminster near to London as Queen of England, and he made provision for her estate and assigned her dower.[470]

(42r) In the year 1420 during Lent (i.e. 1421) the said victorious prince was in the realm of England. Because truces and abstinences of war for Anjou and Maine entered into between the said victorious prince on the one hand and the duke of Anjou on the other, had been broken, my lord of Clarence, his brother and lieutenant-general of France and Normandy, assembled all the garrisons of Normandy in the town of Bernay. Departing from there, he entered into the territory of Maine and passed beyond the River Huisne at Pont-de-Gennes.[471] He moved on from there to Le Grand-Lucé where he crossed the River Loir and entered into the region of Anjou, riding before the city of Angers[472] where he made several knights, to wit,
Sir William Roos[473]

---

[466] This appointment is not found in any official source. Monstrelet (iv, p. 282) gives the appointment by Charles VI and Henry V of Pierre de Veroult as captain after the surrender (who may be Pierre de Verruyes mentioned at note 737). By January 1423 Edward Heron esquire was captain of Melun (CPR 1422–29, p. 22). Gilbert Umfraville is also noted as captain in some chronicles.

[467] Henry and Charles VI entered Paris on Advent Sunday (1 December 1420). The *lit de justice* through which the Dauphin was declared incapable of succession was held on 23 December.

[468] On 10 January 1421 Exeter was given power to govern the English in Paris and elsewhere during the absence of Thomas, duke of Clarence (C 64/15 m. 22d, DKR 42, p. 407) who had held the captaincy of Paris in the previous year (*GR*, iv, p. 292). The Earl Marshal was captain of Pontoise by at least the end of January 1421 (E 101/50/19 no. 1).

[469] Salisbury was appointed lieutenant in Normandy on 13 November 1420 (C 64/14 m. 14, DKR 42, p. 381) but had held a similar position from April 1419 (C 64/11 m. 65, DKR 41, p. 772). On 18 January 1421 Clarence was appointed commander of all troops in Normandy (C 64/15 m. 17d, DKR 42, p. 408).

[470] Henry and Catherine landed in England on 1 February 1421. Catherine was crowned in Westminster Abbey on 23 February.

[471] Now within Montfort-le-Gesnois (Sarthe, arr. Mamers, cant. Savigné-l'Evêque).

[472] Maine-et-Loire, ch. l. d'arr.

[473] A William Roos was probably a younger brother of John, lord Roos (b. 1397) but there is some uncertainty on identification. A man-at-arms of this name is found in the retinue of

Sir Henry Godard[474]
Sir Rowland Ryde[475]
and several others

Once this was done he returned to Beaufort-en-Vallée,[476] taking prisoners and booty. He lodged at Beaufort until Easter Eve (22 March) at the beginning of the year 1421. After a certain time he heard news that the enemy, to wit,
the duke of Alençon[477] who called himself lieutenant-general of the king
the count of La Marche, French[478]
the count of Comminges[479]
the count of Astarac[480]
the count of Aumale[481]
the count of Peyteure[482]
the vicomte of Rohan[483]

William Cromwell within the overall company of the duke of Clarence in 1415 (E 101/45/4), and in the retinue of Sir Hugh Luttrell for the 1417 campaign (E 101/51/2 m. 11).

[474]   The younger brother of Sir John Godard, and therefore born after 1387, Henry served in the retinue of Clarence in the 1415 expedition (E 101/45/4 m. 2) and of Thomas Carew in 1417 (E 101/48/14 m. 9) and was noted for his actions at the siege of Falaise (C 64/8 m. 12, Hardy, p. 255). Still an esquire, he crossed to France again in the army led by the duke of Bedford in the spring of 1420 (E 101/49/36 m. 6).

[475]   A Roland de Rede served as a man-at-arms in the retinue of Sir William Elmeden in the 1417 army (E 101/51/2 m. 24). Subsequent service under Richard Woodville in Normandy between 1421 and 1424 is also in evidence, followed by service in the garrison of Caen, but no knight of this name has so far been discovered.

[476]   Maine-et-Loire, arr. Angers, ch. l. cant.

[477]   The presence of Jean II, duke of Alençon (1409–76) at Baugé is unlikely as he was barely 12 years old at the time.

[478]   Jacques II de Bourbon, count of la Marche (d. 1438), seems to have been in Italy at this point through his marriage to Queen Joanna II of Naples (Huart, 'Jacques de Bourbon', p. 286).

[479]   The allegiance of Matthieu de Foix, count of Comminges (c. 1389–1453), brother of Jean, count of Foix and Gaston de Foix, captal de Buch, waivered between the Burgundian and the Dauphinist sides. At this point he was operating in the south and his presence at Baugé is unlikely (Pailhes, 'Mathieu de Foix, comte de Comminges', pp. 93–4).

[480]   Jean II, count of Astarac (d. 1458), was probably serving the Dauphin Charles at that time but his presence in northern France is unlikely.

[481]   Jean de Harcourt (1396–1424), count of Aumale, took possession of the captaincy of Mont-Saint-Michel for the Dauphin in May 1420, following the defection of Robert Jolivet (Luce, i, pp. 22–3, 98–9, no. 6). He was given full authority by the Dauphin on 23 June 1420 to wage war against the English (ADM, H 15351; Poli, p. 84, no. 988). He mustered at Sablé (45 km from Baugé) on 1 October 1420 with five knights bachelor, fifteen esquires and eleven mounted archers (BNF, Clairambault, 57/171, 178; Poli, p. 86, no. 1010). At Tours (80 km from Baugé) on 1 April 1421, he sent an order to his lieutenant, Olivier de Mauny, lord of Thiéville (Luce, i, pp. 107–8, no. 10). In light of this evidence, Aumale's presence at Baugé, which, curiously, is not mentioned in other chronicles, seems very likely.

[482]   The Dauphin was count of Poitiers at this point, having succeeded his elder brother John, but he was not at the battle.

[483]   Alain VIII, viscount of Rohan, and count of Porhoët (d. 1429), as well as his son and heir, the future Alain VIII, were supporters of Jean V de Montfort, duke of Brittany, who did not break with the English until after Baugé, when the duke sealed an alliance with the

the vicomte of Thouars[484]
the vicomte of Châtellerault[485]
the vicomte of Amboise[486]
the lord of L'Aigle[487]
the Bastard of Alençon[488]
the Bastard of La Marche[489]
the Bastard of Vendôme[490]
(42v) the lord of Champagne[491]
Baudouin de Champagne knight, lord of Tucé[492]

Dauphin at Sablé on 8 May 1421. The Rohans' participation at Baugé on the French side is thus very unlikely (Cosneau, pp. 60–1; Halgouet, *La Vicomté de Rohan*, pp. 78–85).

[484] Pierre II, lord of Amboise (d. 1422) and viscount of Thouars from 1399, who was in the entourage of the Dauphin in 1417 and 1418, seems to have died childless in 1422 and not in 1426, as is claimed in some studies (*RDP*, vii, p. 42 n. 1). His participation at Baugé is not otherwise attested.

[485] Louis d'Harcourt (1384–1422), viscount of Châtellerault, was made archbishop of Rouen on 16 January 1409, an office he held until the Norman capital fell into the hands of Henry V in January 1419. He took refuge in Poitou, where he stayed until his death in November 1422, being buried in the church of Châtellerault, the *vicomté* reverting to his elder brother (*RDP*, vii, pp. 436n, viii, p. 302n). The participation of this cleric at Baugé is unlikely and not otherwise attested.

[486] There was no vicomte of Amboise at that time. Pierre de Harcourt was lord of Amboise and viscount of Thouars. This is seemingly a case of the same individual appearing twice in the list.

[487] Jean de Blois (d. 1454), lord of L'Aigle, and count of Penthièvre from 1433, was forced to flee from Brittany after the unsuccessful coup orchestrated by his mother Marguerite de Clisson against Duke Jean in 1420. He took refuge in the Limousin where he served Charles as Dauphin and king. He was reconciled with the duke of Brittany in the late 1420s thanks to the mediation of Richemont (Anselme, vi, pp. 104–5; Beaucourt, i, p. 116; Cosneau, pp. 53–9).

[488] The presence of the Bastard of Alençon at Baugé is also noted in Cagny (p. 157) and the *Religieux* (vi, p. 455).

[489] Jean, Bastard de la Marche, a natural son of Jean I de Bourbon, comte de la Marche, is described as captain and governor of La Marche in a legal suit brought before the *Parlement* of Paris in 1425. He appears as a knight in a payment made to him in 1436 (Thomas, *Le comté de la Marche et le Parlement de Poitiers*, pp. 114, 119; Thomas, *Les états provinciaux*, i, p. 265 n. 1).

[490] This Bastard of Vendôme is unidentified. There is evidence of a Jean, Bastard of Vendôme as captain of francs-archers operating in the second half of the fifteenth century (Contamine, *GES*, pp. 359–60). The man intended is unlikely to be Guillaume, Bastard of Wandonne, who was militarily active in the first half of the fifteenth century, and who was a captain in the company and household of Jean de Luxembourg (Schnerb, *Bournonville*, p. 211 n. 13; *Jeanne. Dictionnaire*, pp. 1045–6).

[491] Jean de Champagne, seigneur de Pescheseul, brought 1,000 combatants from Angers to the battle of Baugé according to the 'Chronique de Parcé'. Two years later, he fought at Verneuil, as 'grand maréchal d'Anjou', together with his nine sons, commanding a company of 600 lances. He was severely wounded but survived, yet seven of his sons perished, according to the same chronicle (Charles, 'L'invasion', pp. 82–3). We have been unable to consult the printed edition of *La Chronique de Parcé*.

[492] The participation at Baugé of Baudouin de Champagne, lord of Tucé, also seems to be evidenced in the *Journal de Jean du Bellay*, according to Planchenault ('La conquête' (1925), p. 14 n. 1), but we have not managed to identify this source.

Antoine de Champagne knight[493]
the lord of Fontaines[494]
the lord of Bellay[495]
the lord of Averton and Belin
Caignart captain
the lord of Rambures[496]
Tanguy du Chastel knight[497]
Jean de Tournemine knight[498]
the lord of Assé-le-Riboul[499]

---

[493]   Antoine de Champagne is identified on f. 50v as a brother of Baudouin de Champagne.

[494]   The presence at Baugé of the lord of Fontaines, possibly Jean, lord of Fontaines-Guérin, is widely attested in chronicles.

[495]   His presence at Baugé is also mentioned in Cagny (p. 119).

[496]   André, lord of Rambures, son of David de Rambures who died at Agincourt, fought alongside Jacques de Harcourt in Ponthieu and Vimeu in the early 1420s (Monstrelet, iv, p. 42). Henry V confiscated his lordships in Normandy in March 1419 (C 64/10 m. 3, DKR 41, p. 744). His lordship of Rambures-en-Vimeu was confiscated by Henry VI in August 1423 (AN, JJ 172/286). Although his presence at Baugé is not noted elsewhere, it is not unlikely. Monstrelet (iv, p. 370) has him as captain of Aumale in 1429 when the town surrendered to the earl of Stafford. Taken prisoner, Rambures was sent to England where he spent six to seven years in captivity. He was released on parole in September 1436, leaving hostages behind for the payment of his ransom, which seems to have been completed by March 1439 (C 76/117 m. 3; C 76/118 m. 4 and 18; C 76/119 m. 12; C 76/121 m. 18, DKR 48, pp. 305, 308, 309, 313, 315, 325).

[497]   Tanguy II du Chastel (1370–1449), a Breton knight, chamberlain of the duke of Orléans in 1407 and in the service of the duke of Anjou in 1410, became marshal of the Dauphin Louis in 1412. A fervent supporter of the Orleanists, he was provost of Paris in 1413 and 1414, and governor and captain of La Rochelle as well as seneschal of Saintonge between 1414 and 1416. He fled Paris with the Dauphin Charles when the Burgundians took control of the city in 1418. He was involved in the murder of John the Fearless on the bridge of Montereau. It cannot be ascertained whether he was present at Baugé since he was carrying out a mission in the Midi in February 1421. He was appointed 'mareschal des guerres de Monseigneur le Regent (i.e. the Dauphin Charles)' in 1422, and participated in several military operations. He came to the relief of Meulan when it was besieged by the English in February 1422, but failed. Five months later, in June 1422, La Charité-sur-Loire surrendered to him. He accompanied Charles VII into Auvergne at the end of 1424. His influence at court diminished in favour of Richemont (Mirot, 'Vie politique de Tanguy du Chastel', pp. 101–4; Demurger, 'Guerre civile', pp. 243–4; Gonzales, pp. 185–9; Schnerb, *Jean Sans Peur*, pp. 703–6; Cassard, 'Tanguy du Chastel', pp. 83–104).

[498]   This may be Jean II de Tournemine, lord of la Hunaudaye (d. 1427), who was the principal heir of Jean I (d. 1421) and Isabeau de Beaumanoir. Both father and son were supporters of the duke of Brittany. It is therefore unlikely that either fought at Baugé, since the duke had not officially broken with the English until 8 May 1421 when he sealed an alliance with the Dauphin at Sablé. Subsequently, Jean II raised troops against the English: his company of twenty-six esquires and ninety-seven archers mustered at Château-Gontier in August 1421, and in September he held 493 men under Richard Bretagne (Morice, ii, pp, 1086, 1090). According to Gruel (p. 57) he was killed at Saint-James-Beuvron in 1427. Our thanks to Professor Michael Jones for information on Jean I and II.

[499]   Dreux Riboul, knight, succeeded as lord of Assé and Lavardin following the death of his elder brother Jean at or around the time of Agincourt. He died heirless by 1436 when the lordship of Assé was the object of a legal dispute (Roquet, 'Mansigné', p. 186).

the lord of Bueil[500]
the lord of Gaules[501]
the lord of Graville[502]
the lord Albret[503]   }
the lord of La Fayette[504] } marshals of France
the baron of Coulonces[505]

---

[500] According to Guillaume Tringant (*Jouvencel*, ii, p. 271), Jean V, lord of Bueil (1406–67), began his illustrious career as page of Guillaume II, viscount of Narbonne, who died at Verneuil. His presence at Baugé is not otherwise known: Verneuil may have been his first battle (ibid., i, p. x).

[501] Pierre le Mornay, dit Gauluet, lord of Gaules (c.1360–1423), knight banneret, a chamberlain of the duke of Orléans and Charles VI, had had a long military career by 1421. He supported the Orleanists during the civil war. He fought at Agincourt and his disappearance from the records for the next two years may suggest that he had been taken prisoner. He is described as marshal of the duke of Orléans and the count of Vertus in a letter of 14 April 1419, in which Tanguy du Chastel, who called Gauluet his 'brother', delegated to him the charge to muster the army raised in the name of the Dauphin against the lord of Partenay. His presence at Baugé is not unlikely but is nowhere else mentioned. On 7 July 1422 Gauluet received 500 *l.t.* from the Dauphin for his good services in the war. He died in May 1423 at La Ferté-Hubert (Guessard, 'Gauluet ou le sire de Gaules', pp. 466–7).

[502] This may be Guy de Malet, lord of Graville, or else his son and heir, Jean de Malet. Their presence at Baugé is feasible.

[503] Charles II d'Albret (c. 1402–71) was an ally of Henry V at the time of Baugé, appointing two proctors to perform an oath of loyalty to Henry V as duke of Guyenne on 25 September 1420 (E 310/1095; Vale, *English Gascony*, p. 82). On 9 February 1421, about a month and a half before the battle of Baugé, he renewed an earlier agreement with Jean de Foix confirming the league of Aire of 1418 (Archives Départementales des Basses Pyrénées, E 342, no. 60, cited in Vale, *English Gascony*, p. 83). Charles II d'Albret was never marshal of France. There may be confusion here with his father Charles I d'Albret who had been constable of France.

[504] Gilbert III Motier (c. 1380– c. 1463), lord of La Fayette, was a trusted servant of the duke of Bourbon who made him his lieutenant in Guyenne in July 1415, which explains why he was not at Agincourt where the duke was captured. Together with the lords of Préaux and Gaules, he was entrusted with the defence of Rouen in June 1417, and subsequently that of Caen with Jean de Montenay before Henry V's arrival: he may have been present during the siege of Caen. He was in an embassy dispatched by Charles VI to Normandy in late September (C 64/8 m. 26, Hardy, pp. 155–6), and was later in the town of Falaise (C 64/8 m. 20, Hardy, p. 197), whose surrender he negotiated in December, gaining a safe-conduct to leave in January 1418 (C 64/8 m. 2, 16, Hardy, pp. 312–15, 227). He was appointed captain of Lyon in February 1418 and governor of the Dauphiné in 1420. He became marshal of France by the end of September 1420 and his presence at Baugé is widely attested in chronicles (Bouillé, *Un conseiller de Charles VII*, chs 4–9).

[505] Jean de la Haye, baron of Coulonces (d. 1427), held one of the most significant fiefs in Lower Normandy. On 1 March 1418 it was confiscated by Henry V and granted to Louis Bourgeois, a Norman who played a major role in the administration of the duchy for the English (C 64/8 m. 9, Hardy, p. 268). He was deeply engaged in the war against the English in the 1420s, as this chronicle and other sources show. His presence at Baugé is not noted elsewhere but, according to the *Religieux* (vi, p. 474), he and Ambroise de Loré led the vanguard of a French army under the joint command of the count of Aumale and the viscount of Narbonne which marched on Bernay and defeated in the field the English garrison in August 1422.

the lord of Auzebosc[506]
the lord of de Vieuxpont[507]
Alain Giron, captain[508]
Guillaume Remon dit Marjolaine, captain[509]
Le Roncin, captain[510]
Oudin Chenart, captain[511]
Florent d'Illiers knight[512]
Jean d'Avaugour knight[513]

---

[506] Louis d'Estouteville (d. 1464), lord of Auzebosc and of Estouteville (from 1437), was the elder son of Jean II, lord of Estouteville who had been taken prisoner at Harfleur in 1415. He had married Jeanne Paynel, lady of Bricquebec and Hambye, by 10 April 1419, when her lordship of Moyon was confiscated by Henry V (C 64/11 m. 53, DKR 41, p. 776). He served in the garrison of Mont-Saint-Michel from 1420 and became captain on 2 September 1425, holding the office until his death. His presence at Baugé is nowhere else attested (Poli, p. cxix, nos. 684, 777, 983; Luce, *La France pendant la guerre de Cent ans*, pp. 217–79).

[507] Laurent de Vieuxpont (b. 1407), baron of Neubourg, was placed under the tutelage of Jean de Coutes, dit Minguet, at the death of his father at Agincourt. He was only 14 at the time of Baugé. In 1432 Dunois entrusted him with the guard of the castle of Courville (Durand, 'Chronologie des premiers seigneurs de Courville', pp. 258–60).

[508] Alain Giron (d. 1438) was a Breton captain known to be active in the 1420s and 1430s. In 1425–26, commanding troops with Theodore de Valperga, he was paid over 5000 *l.t.* by the estates of La Marche to spare lands from pillage and ransom (Thomas, *Les états provinciaux*, ii, pp. 37–8, no. 14). He was sent to the relief of Montargis in 1427 (Gruel, p. 195), and was captain of Senlis, probably in 1429 (Flammermont, *Histoire de Senlis*, pp. 107–8, nos. 17–18). He was killed fighting in Lorraine under Richemont in 1438 (Cosneau, p. 286).

[509] Guillaume Remon, dit Marjolaine, was a Dauphinist captain in northern France in the first half of the 1420s. He held La Ferté-Milon with his acolyte, Jean du Pont, before it fell into the hands of the English in May 1422 (AN, JJ 172/373).

[510] The presence of Le Roncin (or Roussin) at Baugé is attested in an extract from a register of the *chambre des comptes* of Anjou (AN, P 1334; Berry, p. 117 n. 3; Godefroy, *Histoire de Charles VI*, pp. 732, 472; see also *Actes*, i, p. 56).

[511] Notarial records for the county of Dunois record a transaction made between Pierre de Vaucouleurs and Oudin Chenart, husband of Jeanne d'Auvilliers, for the succession of Guillaume de Morsans (Merlet, *Registres et minutes*, p. 15). Oudin Chynart appears in Glover's list of prisoners taken at Verneuil (BL, Harley 782, f. 51 r, printed in *L&P*, II, ii, pp. 394–9).

[512] Florent d'Illiers was militarily active at the time, but his presence at Baugé is not noted elsewhere.

[513] M 9 distinguishes two Jean d'Avaugours here and in the list of garrisons in Maine: Sir Jean d'Avaugour, captain of La Mayenne, and Jean d'Avaugour, esquire, captain of La Ferté-Bernard. See above note 256 for possible confusion between Sir Jean d'Avaugour, Louis and Guillaume d'Avaugour. The latter fled from Paris with Tanguy du Chastel and the Dauphin when the Burgundians entered the capital in 1418 (AN, Xia 9200, f. 293; Cosneau, p. 85 n. 3), and was in the close entourage of the Dauphin in the early 1420s, lending a substantial sum to him in December 1420 which was paid back to him in September 1421 (Morice, ii, p. 1089). The Dauphin had given his 'amé et feal conseiller et chambellan', Guillaume d'Avaugour, the guard and captaincy of the castle du Bris in Dauphiné, as we learn in a letter dated 15 April 1421 which stated the difficulty that he encountered in taking possession of the stronghold (Archives de Grenoble, B3223 bis, f. 180; published in Beaucourt, i, p. 456). He was present at the meeting of Richemont and Charles VII at Angers, in October 1424, where he appears as *bailli* of Touraine (Cosneau, p. 85). His presence at Baugé is plausible.

Jean des Vaux knight[514]
Jehan d'Avaugour, captain of La Ferté-Bernard
Jean Descroix knight[515]
Roberton Descroix[516]
Girart de Lawe, captain
Jean de Montgoubert knight
the lord of Goussall, Spanish
Diego de Sales, Spanish
André Lombart, traitor[517]
the lord of Grippon
Poton, lord of Xaintrailles[518]
Jean de Raveton knight

---

[514] Sir Jean de Vaux claimed to have fought and been wounded at Baugé (AN, X2a 18, pleas of 31 August 1423, cited in Beauchesne, 'Jean des Vaux', p. 239).

[515] The presence of a Jean Descroix, knight, at Baugé is attested in Berry (p. 100), *Religieux* (vi, p. 454) and in a register of the *chambre des comptes* of Anjou, cited in Godefroy, *Histoire de Charles VI* (p. 732).

[516] Both Chartier (i, p. 58) and 'Geste des nobles' (p. 132) mention Roberton Descroix among the French captains who recaptured Le Mans in May 1428, although the M 9 chronicle does not note them on that occasion. Roberton, described on this occasion as an esquire, escorted supplies and Joan of Arc to Orléans between 29 April and 4 May 1429 (Raguier's accounts in *Journal du siège*, pp. 195–8).

[517] André Lombart (Andrew Lombard) appears as the traitor who deceived the duke of Clarence in several English accounts of Baugé (Milner, 'Baugé', pp. 498–500; BL, Lansdowne MS 204, f. 214v). Hall (p. 106) calls him Andrew Forgusa. John Streeche (Taylor, 'Chronicle of John Strecche', pp. 45–6, 50–1) claims that he had at one time served with the duke of Clarence, mentioning that the duke had disciplined him for looting Pontoise at its capture in 1419 which had led to him joining the French. No existing links with Clarence have been discovered in military or household records.

[518] Poton de Xaintrailles (c.1400–61), lord of Xaintrailles (Lot-et-Garonne), was a Gascon nobleman of middling status and a vassal of the count of Armagnac. Xaintrailles and La Hire were frequently associated in the chronicles of the time. Xaintrailles' service to the Dauphin, and future king Charles VII, began in 1418 and culminated with the reconquest of Normandy and Aquitaine in the 1450s, but his participation at Baugé is not noted elsewhere. He was captured at the battle of Mons-en-Vimeu in August 1421 (Monstrelet, iv, p. 62). Toward the end of the year the duke of Burgundy purchased him from one of his men for 1,200 *écus d'or* (ADN, B 1925, f. 123r). We do not know the terms for his release, but it is interesting to note that the two men, Xaintrailles and Duke Philip, remained on good terms. According to Monstrelet (iv, p. 181), Jean de Luxembourg ambushed Xaintrailles and other French near Guise in 1424, but released him in April or May that year upon the promise never to return north of the Loire unless accompanied by Charles VII. Yet Xantrailles fought at Verneuil, at the siege of Orléans, and at Patay where he captured Talbot and ceded him to Charles VII in return for 12,500 *réaulx* (Chartier de Thouars, AN, 1 AP 175/27), going on to participate in the coronation expedition of Charles VII. It was around that time that the king made him 'grand écuyer de France'. Xaintrailles was captured at least once more in the 1430s and may have recovered his freedom through an exchange with Talbot in 1433. In 1437, the king ordered 4,200 *l.t.* as part of 6,000 *réaulx* to be granted to Xaintrailles, described as his 'premier escuier de corps', in order to compensate for the losses incurred in being kept prisoner in England and to help him pay his great ransom (BL, Add. Ch. 3804). (See also the notice of Xavier Hélary on Xaintrailles in *Jeanne. Dictionnaire*, pp. 1049–50.)

Jean de Beauvau knight[519]
(43r) the lord of Précigné[520]
Pierre Chapperon knight[521]
Pierre de Beauvau knight[522]
Guy de Fromentières knight[523]
Jean de Champagné knight, lord of la Montagne[524]
the lord of Montbourcher[525]

---

[519]   Jean III de Beauvau, father of Pierre and Bertrand de Beauvau, lord of Précigné, died in 1391.

[520]   Bertrand de Beauvau (d. 1474), lord of Précigné, hailed from a noble family of Anjou, being the younger brother of Pierre de Beauvau. He appears as 'premier écuyer' of Louis II of Anjou in the act of 1416 which granted him Précigné as reward for his past services in Sicily. The grant was confirmed in 1425 by Yolande of Aragon for his services in defending Maine and Anjou against the English (AN, P 1344, no. 603). Evidence of his activity in the 1420s is relatively scarce. In November 1422, Pierre de Beauvau was made captain of the town of Angers, while Bertrand became captain of the castle, an office he held to his death. He had joined the service of the crown as 'écuyer d'écurie' by 1429. At the death of his elder brother in 1435, Bertrand replaced him as councillor of Charles VII and became influential at the royal court, participating regularly in the royal council to 1459 and carrying out diplomatic missions from the mid-1440s (Gaussin, 'Les conseillers', p. 107; Bidet, 'La noblesse', pp. 471–99; Matz, 'Les orientations religieuses').

[521]   Pierre Chapperon, a knight from Auvergne, had been captain of Le Mans in 1418 (*Les La Trémoïlle*, i, p. 258), presumably just before Baudouin de Champagne, lord of Tucé.

[522]   Pierre de Beauvau (d. 1435), lord of Beauvau, Champigny-sur-Veude and La Roche-sur-Yon, was son and heir of Jean III de Beauvau (d. 1391) and elder brother of Bertrand de Beauvau, as well as a chamberlain of Louis II of Anjou in 1414, for whose will he was executor. He was captain of Bayeux until his resignation in 1416, and participated in the failed attempt to recapture Harfleur. He served the Dauphin in 1418, participating in the meeting of Montereau where he was meant to take the oath of John the Fearless. His presence at Baugé is not noted elsewhere. He became captain of the town of Angers in November 1422. He accompanied Louis III of Anjou in Italy, in whose name he governed Calabria between 1424 and 1427. His was named governor of Provence in 1429 and attended the coronation of Charles VII in July before returning to Italy (Gaussin, 'Les conseillers', p. 107; Bidet, 'La noblesse', pp. 471–99; Matz, 'Les orientations religieuses').

[523]   Guy de Fromentières was from Maine and took part in military operations in Maine and Anjou in 1426. According to Tringant, he was present at the siege of the fortress of Le Lude (*Jouvencel*, ii, p. 374). He was at the siege of Gallerande in May 1426, with eleven men-at-arms and four archers in his company (BNF, Fr. 20684, p. 548, published in Planchenault, 'La conquête' (1933), pp. 149–51). He was a brother-in-arms of Philip Gough and associated with him in a 'butin' at the time of Patay in June 1429 (AN, Xia 9193, f. 157r). A Guyon de Fromentières, possibly the same man, was active in Maine in 1434 (AN, KK 324 f. 73v) and in April 1439 was captain of Château-du-Loir (*Jouvencel*, i, p. xvi n. 2).

[524]   Jean I de Champagné, knight, lord of la Montagne, Louvigné and Rochecaude, was a chamberlain of Pierre II, duke of Brittany. He received wages as a ducal officer in 1442 and participated in the ducal celebration of the epiphany of 1447 (La Chesnaye, 15 or suppl. 3 (1786), pp. 177–8).

[525]   This may be Bertrand de Montbourcher who is found in the retinue of Bertrand de Montauban, marshal of Brittany, in 1419 (Morice, ii, pp. 1105–7), and in the Ligue against Penthièvre in 1420 (ibid., ii, p. 1060). In March 1425 he was assigned to the defence of the 'Renais' together with the lord of Châteaugiron, the vicomte of la Bellière and Jean de Saint-Gilles, lord of Beton (ibid., ii, p. 1166; *Lettres et mandements de Jean V*, iii, pp. 150–2, no.

the lord of Châteaugiron[526]
Jean de Mathefelon knight
Guy Turpin knight
Guillaume de Mauny knight[527]
Guillaume de la Mote knight[528]
and the Scottish
the earl of Buchan[529]
the earl of Wigtown[530]
Sir William Stewart[531]
Sir William Douglas[532]

1622). In 1427 he appears as captain of Saint-Aubin-du-Cormier (ibid., v, p. 78, no. 2677) and in March 1440, Duke Jean granted letters of privilege to him, being then described as his chamberlain (ibid., iv, p. 239, no. 2410).

[526] Patri III, lord of Châteaugiron, was a supporter of the Montfort dukes of Brittany, being present at the ducal council on 7 September 1420 (*Lettres et mandements de Jean V*, iii, pp. 7–8, no. 1404), being pardoned by the duke on 30 December 1422 in a long-running case concerning the abduction of a minor (ibid., iii, p. 98, no. 1544), and being given a horse by the duke in 1426 (ibid., iii, p. 198, no. 1725). He died at the siege of Pontorson in 1427 (Gruel, p. 57).

[527] This Guillaume de Mauny (or Maulny) is likely to be the lord of Saint-Aignan, captain of that place in 1417. He, like Guy de Fromentières, took part in military operations in Maine and Anjou in 1426 (Cosneau, p. 123). He was at the siege of Gallerande in May 1426 with fifteen men-at-arms and twenty-two archers in his company (BNF, Fr. 20684, p. 548, in Planchenault, 'La conquête' (1933), pp. 149–51). His presence in Maine in 1433 and 1434 is also evidenced (AN, KK 324 ff. 15r, 22r, 37r, 72r).

[528] A Breton, Guillaume de la Mote, chamberlain of the duke of Brittany, stepped down as captain of Saint-Malo in September 1415 (*Lettres et mandements de Jean V*, ii, p. 113, no. 1569bis). He was apparently still alive in 1433 when, chamberlain to Duke Jean V, he was commissioned by the duke to enquire about pillages at sea committed against the English (ibid., iv, p. 54, no. 2084). It is possible, however, this is not the man listed here. According to Gruel (p. 44), Guillaume de la Mote died at the siege of Saint-James-Beuvron in 1426 together with his father Alain de la Mote. The widow of a Guillaume de la Mote appears in Maine in April 1434 (AN, KK 324 f. 55v).

[529] John Stewart, second earl of Buchan* (c. 1381–1424), was the younger son of Robert Stewart, the duke of Albany, who acted as regent for King James I during the latter's captivity. He was commander of the Scots at Baugé (Scottish chroniclers have him fighting in single combat against the duke of Clarence) and was created constable of France in early April 1421 as a reward (AN, KK 50 f. 2v). He was subsequently active in Perche and responsible for the French capture of Avranches in 1422. He participated in the 1424 Scottish army alongside his father-in-law, the earl of Douglas, and was killed at Verneuil.

[530] Archibald Douglas (1390–1439), the future fifth earl of Douglas, known by his courtesy title earl of Wigtown, had served in the Scottish troops sent in 1419 to support the Dauphin. As a reward for his service at Baugé the Dauphin created him comte de Longueville, a title given by Henry V in June 1419 to the captal de Buch. He returned to Scotland in early 1423 and succeeded to the earldom of Douglas at the death of his father at the battle of Verneuil. Thenceforward he seems to have used 'duke of Tourraine' as his principal title, that honour having been given to his father by Charles VII in April 1424.

[531] William Stewart of Castlemilk (d. 1429) was the son of Sir Alexander Stewart of Darnley (d. 1404) by his second wife, and an active participant in Scottish support for the Dauphin. He was killed alongside his half-brother John at Rouvray (the battle of the Herrings) in 1429.

[532] There were two William Douglases in France between 1419 and 1421. One was William Douglas of Lugton who was a cousin of the lord of Dalkeith and who died in 1421 (Fraser,

Sir John Turnbull[533]
Sir Robert Lyle[534]
Sir William Cunningham[535]
Sir Alexander Meldrum[536]
Sir Alexander Home[537]
Sir John Balglavy[538]
Sir William Lyle[539]
Sir John Haliburton[540]
Sir John Crawford[541]

Douglas Book, iii, pp. 57–8). The second was an illegitimate son of James Douglas, second earl of Douglas (d. 1388), being granted the barony of Drunlanrig by his father. This William Douglas was therefore a cousin of Archibald Douglas, the fourth earl, who granted him the barony of Hawick. He fought in support of the Dauphin from 1419 but was defeated by an English force at Fresnay in early 1420 (Brown, *Black Douglases*, p. 218). He is also thought to have died in 1421 but this is uncertain.

[533]   The Turnbulls were a border family with a seat at Minto castle in Roxburghshire but several branches by 1400. A John Turnbull of Langton was constable of Newark Castle for the fifth earl of Douglas in 1439 (Fraser, *Douglas Book*, iii, no. 406) and may be the man listed here. Another John considered in 1390 that he was suffering from leprosy and so made a grant of his lands to Sir William Stewart of Dalswintoun; it is possible that he later served in France and was killed at Cravant, his lands being inherited, as well as the dispute with Stewart, by his son Walter (*New Statistical Account of Scotland: Roxburgh, Peebles, and Selkirk*, p. 363).

[534]   Sir Robert Lyle of Duchal in Renfrewshire was back in Scotland by late 1423. He subsequently received a safe-conduct to escort James I back to Scotland from England, acting as a hostage for the Scottish king in 1424–25 (our thanks to Professor Michael Brown for this information).

[535]   This was not the Sir William Cunningham who was head of the family and lord of Kilmaurs (East Ayrshire) since he died in 1415, his heir being Robert Cunningham (d. c. 1450). There has been debate over whether he had a younger brother called William but the outcome is inconclusive (*Scots Peerage*, iv, p. 231). More likely the William Cunningham listed here is Robert's cousin, son of Archibald Cunningham, who is mentioned in a charter of entail from 1415 (*Calendar of Laing Charters*, no. 94).

[536]   This is most likely Alexander Meldrum of that ilk, who acquired Fyvie and other lands through marriage to the daughter of Henry Preston of Formartine (Temple, *Thanage of Fermartyn*, p. 22). He was dead by 1445 when the wardship of his heir and lands was granted to Alexander Forbes (NRS, GD 248/397/1). We are grateful to Professor Michael Brown for this reference.

[537]   Sir Alexander Home (1368–1424) of Berwickshire had close links with Alexander, fourth earl of Douglas. Although the M 9 chronicle lists him amongst the dead at Cravant he probably met his end at Verneuil in the following year.

[538]   A man of this name was a prisoner of Richard Neville, earl of Salisbury, in 1438 (*Rot. Scot.*, ii, p. 302) but has otherwise eluded identification.

[539]   A William Lyle, uncle of Robert, was still alive in 1452 (*RMS*, i, no. 871; *Registrum Monasterii de Passelet*, pp. 250–3).

[540]   This may have been a son of Walter of Dirleton, the first lord Haliburton, who was a cousin of the earl of Wigtown, but is more likely a junior kinsman of the main line, the John Haliburton who was dead by 1424 (*RMS*, ii, no. 8).

[541]   This is a common name but may be John, the son of Roger Crawford of Daleglis (Ayrshire), an area from which many troops in this campaign hailed.

Sir William Kennedy[542]
Sir John Grey[543]
the lord of Concressault[544]
and many others, both French and Scottish, had assembled in great power in a town with a castle, called Baugé,[545] intending an encounter with my lord of Clarence. The latter spoke with André Lombart, who was a traitor twice over, and enquired what power the enemy had and what number they were. Lombart replied that the enemy were only in small number and were not strong enough to acquit themselves even against half of the power of my lord of Clarence, and that he would therefore have a very fine and honourable victory. My lord of Clarence, thinking (43v) that the traitor was telling him the truth, gave orders for the deployment of the archers of his company, to wit, Sir [blank], Sir [blank] knights of Portugal, captains of Fresnay-sur-Sarthe,[546] and with them, the bastard of Clarence,[547] and told them to await him in the said location of Beaufort until his return, telling them also that he wished that the other nobles and himself should have the honour of the destruction (of the French). But it turned out quite the opposite, for which reason there was much sadness and sense of loss. My lord of Clarence and the nobles of his company, passing through narrow pathways, encountered the enemy already in battle formation, thanks to the warning of the aforementioned traitor Lombart who had sold the duke. They had set up significant ambushes by their men to prevent the duke and his company escaping without being killed or taken prisoner. The enemy immediately overran the duke on all sides. The duke and his nobles defended themselves as valiantly as they could, but finally my lord of

---

[542] A Hugh Kennedy was recorded by Walter Bower as present at Baugé and a Fergus Kennedy is also believed to have been active in France in 1420 (Fraser, *Memoirs of the Maxwells of Pollok*, i, no. 28).

[543] A Scottish John Grey known to have been active in France was the cleric who was archdeacon of Galloway who was proctor of the English nation at the university of Paris (Watt, *Biographical Dictionary of Scottish Graduates*, pp. 233–6). In December 1421 he witnessed an act made by the earl of Wigtown and is also involved in an act concerning the will of Robert Maxwell in 1420 (Fraser, *Memoirs of the Maxwells of Pollok*, i, no. 28).

[544] John Stewart of Darnley* (c. 1380–1429) was the eldest son of Sir Alexander Stewart of Darnley (d. 1404) by his first wife. His service in France began in 1419 as constable of the army of Scotland. He was rewarded by the Dauphin in 1421 with a grant of the lordship of Concressault (Cher, arr. Bourges, cant. Sancerre) (Ditcham, 'Employment of Foreign Mercenary Troops', p. 23).

[545] Maine-et-Loire, arr. Saumur, ch. l. cant.

[546] The first known appointment to the captaincy of Fresnay is of Sir Robert Brent in January 1421. No Portuguese captains are known. The place had first been besieged by Salisbury in April–May 1420 and a French army of relief defeated, according to Walsingham (*St Albans Chronicle*, ii, p. 745).

[547] John, Bastard of Clarence, was an illegitimate son of the duke. That he had been responsible for recovering his father's body and bringing it back to Canterbury for burial is confirmed by a royal grant made to him in July 1428 (CPR 1422–29, pp. 489–90). He continued to serve in France after his father's death. In early 1430 he was co-commander with Sir John Kyghley, Thomas Burgh and Henry Fenwyk of troops sent to France which recovered Torcy in August (Ratcliffe, 'Military Expenditure', pp. 40–1). This was perhaps in response to his petition (SC 8/96/4753) complaining of poverty and asking to serve the king in France or elsewhere, or to make other provision for his maintenance. On 3 July 1431 he was appointed captain of Dublin castle (CPR 1429–36, p. 122).

Clarence was pitiously killed and several other lords were taken prisoner or killed, some of whose names follow, to wit,

the earl of Somerset[548]   }
the earl of Huntingdon[549]   }
the count of Perche[550]   }
Lord Fitzwalter[551]   }
Sir John Grey, count of Tancarville[552]   }
Sir John Barker[553]   }
Sir Ralph Neville[554]   }
Sir Henry Inglose[555]   }

---

[548] John Beaufort, earl of Somerset, was in the hands of the Scot Laurence Vernon after the battle but was sold to Charles VII in 1423. He was not released until 1438 (Ambühl, *Prisoners*, pp. 68–9).

[549] The earl of Huntingdon, in the hands of John Stewart, earl of Darnley, after the battle, was released in 1425 after a complex prisoner exchange involving the count of Vendôme, taken at Agincourt, and Raoul de Gaucourt and Jean d'Estouteville, prisoners from the siege of Harfleur (Ambühl, *Prisoners*, p. 67).

[550] This title was not at this point held by Thomas Beaufort (d. 1431), the third son of John, earl of Somerset (d. 1410), since he was only granted it after the death of the earl of Salisbury, but that must be who is meant here. Thomas was in the hands of John Stewart after the battle. By 1427 he was part of an abortive proposed exchange of prisoners and was subsequently in the hands of Tanguy du Chastel. The precise date of his release is uncertain but he was serving in France by the summer of 1430 (Ambühl, *Prisoners*, pp. 67–8).

[551] Fitzwalter had been appointed captain of Vire in January 1421 (C 64/14 m. 1, DKR 42, p. 388). He was held prisoner for four years but received two grants of lands during his captivity, in September 1421 the fief of La Roche Tesson (BL, Add. Ch. 1422, AN, Dom Lenoir 25/61), and in 1424 the fief of La Haye-du-Puits (ADSM, Rouen Echiquier 1424 f. 104v), as well as livery of his lands in England in 1423. From June 1425 we find him in action in the conquest of Maine (BL, Add. Ch. 95).

[552] Grey (of Heton) was killed at Baugé.

[553] A John Barker had crossed as a man-at-arms in 1417 under the earl of Warwick (E 101/51/2 m. 12). A man-at-arms of this name is found at the siege of Pontorson in March and April 1427 under Thomas Burgh (BNF, Fr. 25767, no. 211; BL, Add. Ch. 11573). A John Barker of Dore, 'gentliman', took the oath of 1434 (CPR 1429–36, p. 411) to keep the peace. But no knight of this name has been found.

[554] Ralph (d. 1458) was a younger son of Ralph, first earl of Westmorland (d. 1425). He was certainly serving in France in March 1418 when, still an esquire, he received a land grant (C 64/9 m. 40, DKR 41, p. 679). If captured at Baugé, he was soon released since we find him, now described as knight, appointed captain of Monceaux (Oise, arr. Clermont, cant. Pont-Sainte-Maxence) on 10 May 1421 (C 64/16 m. 41, DKR 42, p. 410).

[555] Henry Inglose (c. 1380–1451), of Dilham and Loddon, Norfolk, was related through his maternal grandmother to Sir John Fastolf. In later years, a room was kept for him at Caister where he was a councillor and intended feoffee of Sir John. He had participated in the 1412 campaign under Clarence, as had Fastolf. He was almost certainly at Agincourt and in 1417 was in Clarence's company (C 76/100 m. 5, DKR 44, p. 601), being one of the first to enter Caen. He was involved in the taking of various surrenders in January 1418 (C 64/8 m. 20d, Hardy, pp. 358–9), though it is unlikely he was appointed captain of Beaumont as has been claimed. He was a knight by May 1418 (C 76/101 m. 9, DKR 44, p. 605). Worcester noted in his *Itineraries* (pp. 361, 359) those with whom Inglose lodged at the siege of Rouen, and also credited him with being the first man into Caen with the duke of Clarence at its capture. Inglose was captured at Baugé but had regained his freedom by November 1422 when he

Sir William Bowes[556]   }
Sir William Longton[557]   } prisoners
Thomas Burgh esquire[558]   }
Sir William [cancelled: Heron] Wolf[559]   }
Sir Edmund Heron[560]   }

---

planned to return to France for service with the earl of Suffolk in Lower Normandy (C 76/106 m. 20, DKR 48, p. 221). He also worked to secure the release of his companion William Bowet (CCR 1422–31, p. 54; Morton, 'Henry Inglose', in HOCb, where it is also suggested Fastolf helped him pay a ransom in 1416, which suggests he may have served with Fastolf in the garrison of Harfleur at that date).

[556] There is a problem of identification here between a Sir William Bowes and a Sir William Bowet, both of whom served in Clarence's company in 1415 (E 101/45/4 m. 1, 2). The name given in the original text is 'Bowys'. Sir William Bowes of Durham (1389–c. 1460) or of Streatlam (1391–1448) was a retainer of Clarence from 1414 and can be seen from the Norman rolls to be active in Normandy in 1418–19. Other chronicles mention his capture at Baugé and we can trace him in royal service from 1422 although there is confusion between the various generations of the Bowes family. Sir William Bowet (1373–1422), who was also taken prisoner at Baugé, was of Cumbrian stock but married as his second wife Ann (or Amy) Paston, the widow of Sir John Calthorp (d. 1415) of Norfolk, thereby bringing him into the Fastolf circle. Ann wrote to William Paston in 1418 before her husband departed for the siege of Rouen requesting funds to assist in his preparations, a letter considered to be the first of the great Paston collection (Richmond, 'How the First "Paston Letter" came to be written in Suffolk'). Sir William Bowet's retinue was ordered on 24 October 1420 to be mustered at Corbeil along with that of the duke of Clarence (C 64/14 m. 18d, DKR 42, p. 391). Sir Henry Inglose was engaged in the negotiations for his release, but Bowet died before this was achieved. Inglose had married Bowet's widow by 1427. Worcester claimed in his *Itineraries* (p. 361) that the two men were amongst a group sharing lodgings at the siege of Rouen (Richmond, *Paston Family: First Phase*, pp. 207, 214–23).

[557] A William Longeton was in the royal household during the 1415 campaign (E 101/407/10 m. 2) but so far no knight of this name has been identified.

[558] Burgh's capture led to some of his soldiers trying to remove him from his captaincy of Valognes by persuading the earl of Salisbury to appoint John Botiller in his stead, which the earl did on 3 April (C 64/16 m. 41, DKR 42, p. 410). On 14 April John Assheton was ordered to arrest the men who were wishing to deliver the place to Botiller by force (C 64/16 m. 37d, DKR 42, p. 426). Burgh seems to have been released quickly since he was in post again at Valognes on 15 May (C 64/16 m. 36d, DKR 42, p. 427). Intriguingly, Burgh also faced a complaint in the Paris *Parlement* in 1430 from an archer in his garrison of Avranches that he had unfairly taken one of his prisoners (Ambühl, *Prisoners*, p. 114).

[559] William Worcester claims in his *Itineraries* (p. 359) that 'Sir William Wolf of Suffolk, from Wales, was once a groom, knight with the duke of Clarence', adding on p. 361 that Wolf was knighted by Clarence at Paris in a 'roode in the time of Henry VI on St Lawrence's Eve (9 August)'. Since that post-dates Baugé where the duke was killed, it is perhaps the eve of that battle which is meant or else 1419 when Clarence was in the Paris area. Wolf served as a man-at-arms in the retinue of Thomas, earl of Arundel in 1415 (E 101/47/1) and captured Marshal Boucicaut at Agincourt (E 358/6 m. 2). He was a knight by 1422 when he crossed with expeditionary troops (E 403/655 m. 1), and served on commissions in Suffolk in the mid-1420s (CPR 1422–29, p. 570). In the coronation expedition of 1430 he crossed with a retinue of twelve men (E 101/70/4/659; E 404/46/278).

[560] Heron (d. 1426), probably the younger brother of Sir John Heron of Thornton, Northumberland, served in 1415 and in 1417 in the retinue of Sir John Grey of Heton (BL,

Sir Richard Benet[561]   }
Sir William Crafford[562]   }
Sir William Roos[563]   }
(44r) Sir William Roos (sic)   }
Richard Waller esquire[564]   }
Sir Guillotin de Lansac[565]   } prisoners
Sir Richard Strother[566]   }

Harley 782, f. 79v; E 101/51/2 m. 32). If captured at Baugé then he had been released by early January 1423 when he was captain of Melun (CPR 1422–29, p. 22).

[561] No knight of this name has been discovered. All men with this name serving in France did so as archers. A Richard Benet had letters of protection in May 1428 to cross to Ireland in the service of the then lieutenant John Sutton (CPR 1422–29, p. 471). William Worcester speaks of a Benet in connection with Castle Combe, one of Fastolf's estates (*Itineraries*, p. 265).

[562] Crafford (d. 1463) was lieutenant of Sir John Kyghley as *bailli* of Rouen and as captain of Pont-de-l'Arche in October 1421 (C 64/16 m. 25d, DKR 42, p. 432) although not yet a knight. He seems to have been knighted by July 1424 and was serving in Normandy in the 1430s and 1440s. On 16 May 1442 he was made a poor knight of Windsor, the grant noting his service in Normandy and France from the initial siege of Harfleur, his suffering from wounds in hand, foot and head, and being taken prisoner (CPR 1441–46, p. 170).

[563] There is some confusion here since Sir William is later noted as killed at the battle. The William Roos killed is considered to be the brother of John, lord Roos (as Walsingham, *St Albans Chronicle*, ii, p. 763, also notes). There was another William Roos in Normandy although not a knight. If captured, he cannot have been in captivity long since in February 1422 he was appointed captain of Bricqueville-sur-Mer (Manche, arr. Avranches, cant. Bréhal), a castle which had been granted to the earl of Huntingdon who was in captivity following the battle of Baugé (C 64/16 m. 7, DKR 42, p. 423). It may be the same William Roos who served in the garrison of Pontoise in the late 1430s and early 1440s (BNF, Clairambault 202/6, 7, 10, 11, 13–15).

[564] Richard Waller* (c. 1395–c. 1462) of Groombridge, Kent, served in the 1415 army as a man-at-arms in the company of Sir William Bowes (E 101/45/4 m. 1). He seems to have been in the garrison of Louviers by August 1418 (C 64/9 m. 15d, DKR 41, p. 716). Nothing further is known of him until he took out letters of attorney in June 1424 to cross to France (C 76/106 m. 3, DKR 48, p. 231). His capture at Baugé is not evidenced elsewhere but the gap in his service is suggestive. His service in France stretched into the 1440s and he was one of Fastolf's feoffees in 1452 (Smith, 'Aspects of the Career of Sir John Fastolf', p. 116).

[565] The Gascon Guilhem-Amaniu Andron was lord of Lansac (Gironde, arr. Blaye, cant. L'Estuaire) and was called Guillotin de Lansac in financial records of Lancastrian Normandy. He was captain of Louviers from January 1423 (BNF, Fr. 25767/9) to at least December 1429 (BNF, Fr. 4488 p. 272). His company, under his brother Mondot, served in the early stages of the Loire campaign of 1428 (BNF, Fr. 4488 f. 111v). We also find him in reinforcements in Rouen in June 1436 (BL, Add. Ch. 189). On 12 May 1437 he was appointed seneschal of the Agenais 'because of his long service in the wars in the kingdom of France and the duchy of Aquitaine as well as the great and excessive sums he owes because he has often been prisoner of the king's enemies' (C 61/127, entry 60).

[566] Strother, a Northumberland knight, crossed in the retinue of the duke of Clarence in 1417 (C 76/99 m. 4, DKR 44, p. 588). He had a land grant in February 1418 (C 64/8 m. 11, Hardy, p. 258) and was captain of Bayeux from April 1419 (C 64/11 m. 78, DKR 41, p. 763) to at least January 1420 (BNF, PO 2730 Strother 3). If captured at Baugé, he was not a prisoner for long since in October 1422 we find him serving under the earl of Suffolk at Coutances and Saint-Lô (BNF, Fr. 25766/809).

Sir Gilbert Umfraville[567]
Sir Robert Vere, brother of the earl of Oxford[568]
Sir William Roos[569]
Sir Henry Godard
Sir Robert Brent   } dead
Sir John Knyvet[570]
Sir Robert Bitvelaine[571]
Sir James Ryde
Sir John Pudsey[572]
Sir Thomas Marney[573]

and many others. Immediately after the two knights of Portugal and the Bastard of Clarence had heard the news that my lord of Clarence and his company had been falsely betrayed, they departed in great haste with all the archers hoping to arrive in time to help the said lord and to give battle with the enemy. But the latter, hearing news of the approach of the archers, did not dare wait for battle and hastily retreated, going off with their prisoners. They did not have time to carry off with them the body of my lord of Clarence, therefore it suited them to leave it

---

[567] After an extensive career in France, Umfraville was killed at Baugé intestate and childless.

[568] Robert de Vere (d. 1461) was the younger brother of John de Vere (1408–62), the twelfth earl of Oxford who had inherited as a minor at his father's death on 15 February 1417. Assuming this is the correct identification (rather than a family member of the previous generation), he was too young to be in military service in 1421 and did not die at Baugé, instead being knighted alongside his brother in 1426. From the 1439 expedition onwards (E 101/53/22 m. 3) he was serving in Gascony, where he was seneschal in 1441 and 1445. He served in the 1443 expedition to France under John Beaufort, duke of Somerset (E 101/54/5, m. 1), and in the last years of the duchy (HOCb).

[569] Dugdale claimed that Sir William, younger brother of John, lord Roos, died at the battle alongside his brother (Atkinson, *Cartularium abbathiae de Rievalle*, pp. 361–2).

[570] Sir John Knyvet (1395–1415) of Southwick (Northamptonshire), Hamerton (Hampshire) and Mendlesham (Suffolk) was knight of the shire for Northamptonshire in the parliament of December 1421, and therefore did not die at Baugé (HOCa). He served on the 1417 expedition in the company of Sir John Blount (E 101/51/2 m. 6). Worcester claimed in his *Itineraries* (p. 361) that he lodged at the siege of Rouen with Henry Inglose and others.

[571] From an ancient family with interests in Northamptonshire, Bedfordshire and Norfolk, Robert crossed to France in the retinue of Clarence in 1415 (E 101/45/4 m. 2). His subsequent service is unknown. William Worcester claims in his *Itineraries* (p. 361) that he was knighted by Clarence at Paris in a 'roode in the time of Henry VI on St Lawrence's Eve (9 August)' but since that post-dates Baugé where both men were killed, it is perhaps the eve of that battle which is meant or 1419 when Clarence is known to have been in the Paris area.

[572] Sir John Pudsey of the West Riding of Yorkshire, and a supporter of the Percies in 1403, led a retinue under Clarence in the 1415 army (E 101/45/4 m. 2) but does not appear to have served in 1417–18 since we find him appointed to various commissions in the West Riding (CPR 1416–22, pp. 144, 196). There is debate as to whether he died at the battle of Baugé or not.

[573] Thomas Marney (before 1381–1421) of Layer Marney, Essex, served in Clarence's retinue in 1415 (E 101/45/4 m. 2) and was a knight by November 1416 (CCR 1413–19, p. 375). He took out letters of attorney in July 1419, and of protection in December 1419, for service in Normandy under Clarence (C 64/11 m. 32, 2, DKR 41, pp. 790, 808) but the details of his actual activities are not known. He died at the battle of Baugé.

behind. When the knights (of Portugal) and the Bastard saw that the enemy had made off and retreated in this manner, they took up, with tears, sighs and lamentation, the bodies of my lord of Clarence and those of the other lords who had been killed with him, and carried them away with them. The rest they buried as best they could. Then they returned to the county of Maine and passed before the city of Le Mans,[574] killing the people and devastating the country through which they crossed. They came to the town of Alençon where they took their leave and returned each of them to the garrison to which they belonged.

(44v) In the year 1421 in the month of May, the most noble and victorious prince crossed the sea with a notable army and landed at Calais.[575] He came into Normandy and laid siege before the town and castle of Dreux, at which siege he made and appointed the king of Scotland captain-in-chief and governor.[576] After this siege, which lasted for the space of six weeks or thereabouts, the town and castle were surrendered and delivered to the victorious prince, and he appointed my lord the earl of Worcester as captain and keeper.

Soon after the taking of the town and castle of Dreux the most noble and victorious prince heard news that the enemy had assembled in great power in the region of Orléans.[577] He rode off and went with all his host towards and right up to the city of Orléans. The enemy did not dare to wait for him but had already departed and passed over the River Loire. As a result, the victorious prince returned without doing anything more and passed before Beaugency.[578] From there he went straight on to lay siege to the town and market of Meaux in Brie.[579] This siege lasted for the space of around nine months. In his company at this siege were the lords whose names follow:

my lord the duke of Exeter[580]

the earl of March[581]

the earl of Warwick[582]

---

[574] Sarthe, ch. l. d'arr.

[575] Henry landed at Calais on 11 June 1421, an army of over 4,000 being raised for service in France (Wylie, iii, pp. 318–19).

[576] Dreux was invested by 18 July and surrendered on 20 August (Wylie, iii, pp. 326–7). By 3 September 1421 the captain of Dreux was Sir Gilbert Halsall (C 64/16 m. 23d, DKR 42, p. 432). No appointment of the earl of Worcester is known but he was present at the siege, at which on 1 August 1421 the king granted him the lands of Sir Gilbert Umfraville who had been killed at Baugé (C 64/16 m. 30, DKR 42, p. 414).

[577] Loiret, ch. l. d'arr. Henry moved into the area in hope of bringing the Dauphin to battle (Wylie, iii, p. 328).

[578] Loiret, arr. Orléans, ch. l. cant.

[579] Seine-et-Marne, ch. l. d'arr. The siege began in mid-October 1421.

[580] The chronicle omits the presence of the duke of Exeter at the siege of Melun where he was commissioned by the king on 18 November 1420 to take the surrender of the town and castle in the name of the king of France (C 64/14 m. 14, DKR 42, p. 381). For his presence at the siege of Meaux, see Wylie, iii, p. 338.

[581] The earl of March led a retinue of 120 in the army which returned with the king in the summer of 1421 (E 101/70/5/704; E 101/50/1 m. 1) and which went on to serve at the siege of Meaux. He had been created KG in May 1421.

[582] The earl of Warwick led a retinue of 200 men in the army which returned with the king in the summer of 1421 (CPR 1416–22, p. 388) and which went on to serve at the siege of Meaux.

the earl of Stafford[583]
the earl of Worcester[584]
Arthur of Brittany, count of Ivry[585]
the count of Brienne[586]
Lord Clifford[587]
Lord Furnival[588]
Lord Lovel[589]
Lord Audeley[590]
the lord of Seyntmer who died there
the lord of Aucourt who died there
(45r) *the lord de la Swych*[591]
Lord Morley[592]
Sir John Cornwall, Lord Fanhope, and his son who died during the siege[593]

---

[583] The earl of Stafford led a retinue of forty in the army which returned with the king in the summer of 1421 (E 101/70/6/724; E 101/50/1 m. 1) and which went on to serve at the siege of Meaux.

[584] The earl of Worcester led a retinue in the army which returned with the king in the summer of 1421 (E 101/50/1 m. 1–2) and which went on to serve at the siege of Meaux, but was killed by a cannonball during the siege on 18 March 1422.

[585] Richemont came to the siege of Meaux with a Breton contingent (Cosneau, p. 64).

[586] This is presumably Pierre de Luxembourg, count of Conversano and Brienne, lord of Enghien. He was a prisoner of the French in Meaux, but released during the siege through the intervention of his brother, Jean de Luxembourg, and Henry V (Monstrelet, iv, p. 80), who specified that he should join the siege upon his release. He was commissioned by the king, alongside Exeter, Warwick and Hungerford, to receive the oath of around a hundred men in the market of Meaux to abide by the terms of the treaty of surrender (AN, J 646, no. 21(1)).

[587] John, lord Clifford led a retinue in the army which accompanied the king to France in the summer of 1421 (E 101/50/1 m. 1) and which went on to serve at the siege of Meaux. He had been made KG in May 1421. He was killed at the siege on 13 March 1422.

[588] John, lord Furnival (better known as John, lord Talbot*) led a retinue in the army which accompanied the king to France in the summer of 1421 (E 101/70/5/706; E 101/50/1 m. 1) and which went on to serve at the siege of Meaux. He inherited the barony of Talbot in December 1421.

[589] William, lord Lovel led a retinue in the army which returned with the king in the summer of 1421 (E 101/50/1 m. 1) and which went on to serve at the siege of Meaux.

[590] James Tuchet, lord Audeley led a retinue in the army which returned with the king in the summer of 1421 (E 101/50/1 m. 1) and which went on to serve at the siege of Meaux.

[591] This bears some resemblance to 'Zouche' but William, lord Zouche of Haringworth was only 19 at this point and is not known to have been in France.

[592] Thomas, fifth baron Morley (1393–1435) led a retinue of forty in the army which returned with the king in the summer of 1421 (E 101/70/6/710; E 101/50/1 m. 1) and which went on to serve at the siege of Meaux. This appears to be his first service in France although Worcester noted him as a lodging mate of Sir Henry Inglose and others at the siege of Rouen (*Itineraries*, p. 361).

[593] Sir John Cornwall (who was not created Lord Fanhope until 1432) led a retinue of 120 in the army which returned with the king in the summer of 1421 (E 101/70/5/708; E 101/50/1 m. 3) and which went on to serve at the siege of Meaux (Wylie, iii, p. 339). His son, another Sir John (b. 1403), served as a man-at-arms in his retinue but was killed by a cannonball at the siege in December 1421. Allegedly, his father witnessed this and was so distressed he vowed never to fight against Christians again.

Lord Ferrers of Chartley
Lord Botreaux
Lord Clinton[594]
Lord Harington[595]
Lord Willoughby[596]
Lord Fitzhugh, chamberlain of the king[597]
Jean Germeyn marshal
Sir John Fastolf[598]
Sir Lewis Robessart[599]
Sir William Gascoigne, who died there[600]
Sir John Radcliffe[601]

---

[594] There is no evidence that William, lord Clinton was in France at this point.

[595] Explicit evidence of the presence of William, lord Harington at the siege of Meaux has not been found.

[596] There is doubt about his presence at the siege of Meaux because he seems to have been in England in 1421–22 but he crossed to France in June 1422 with 120 men (CPR 1416–22, p. 445).

[597] Given his office of chamberlain, it is highly likely that Lord Fitzhugh was with the king at the siege. At the siege camp on 16 January 1422 Henry made him a land grant (C 64/16 m. 36d, DKR 42, p. 427).

[598] Fastolf's whereabouts are not certain at this stage, but on 18 July 1421 an order was issued to muster his troops and also those he held in the Bastille St Antoine in Paris (C 64/16 m. 36d, DKR 42, p. 427).

[599] Whilst Robessart's presence at the siege is not evidenced, his closeness to the king, who had appointed him his standard bearer four days after the sealing of the treaty of Troyes (C 64/14 m. 26, DKR 42, p. 375), makes it likely that he was. We find an order issued on 12 November 1421 for the muster of his troops at the siege (C 64/16 m. 23d, DKR 42, p. 433).

[600] Sir William Gascoigne (d. 1422) of Gawthorpe (Yorks. WR) was the son of the eponymous chief justice of the Common Bench (1400–13). He served as a man-at-arms in the retinue of the earl of Northumberland in 1417 (E 101/51/2 m. 37) and is known to have been a knight by October 1419 when he held a Genoese prisoner (C 76/102 m. 8, DKR 44, p. 612) and in May 1420 when his troops were ordered to be mustered at Pontoise (C 64/13 m. 9d, DKR 42, p. 373). (Walsingham (*St Albans Chronicle*, ii, p. 751) mentions him in connection with the king's march to Troyes around this time.) He went back to England, presumably with the king, but returned in the army which accompanied Henry in the summer of 1421 with a retinue of forty (E 101/50/1 m. 3). He was killed at the siege of Meaux on 22 March 1422 (HOCa, HOCb).

[601] Sir John Radcliffe* (d. 1441) hailed from Lancashire but became lord of the manor of Attleborough (Norfolk) through his marriage to Cecily Mortimer, who was Fastolf's half-sister (and the widow of Sir John Harling). He served with twenty-three men in the 1415 campaign, all of whom were put into garrison at Harfleur (E 101/69/6/464; E 101/45/5 m. 6; E 358/6 m. 8). He may have been present at Agincourt himself, but was serving in Harfleur in the spring of 1416 (E 101/45/11 m. 3). He served with eighty men on the 1417 campaign (E 101/70/2/600; E 101/51/2 m. 40) and was appointed *bailli* of Evreux on 2 May 1418 even before the place surrendered (C 64/9 m. 25d, DKR 41, p. 713), holding the office until the appointment of Gilbert Halsall on 12 March 1419 (C 64/10 m. 14, DKR 41, p. 744). His career then shifted to Gascony after his appointment as constable of Bordeaux on 16 May 1419, but he served in the parliament of December 1420 and seems to have been in northern France in the spring of 1421, receiving a commission on 5 May to inspect all fortifications and garrisons (C 64/16 m. 35d, DKR 41, p. 428), though there is also some evidence he was back in Gascony. His presence at the siege of Meaux is not otherwise evidenced (Reeves, 'Sir John Radcliffe'; HOCa, HOCb).

Sir Robert Harling[602]
Sir William Phelip
Sir William Porter[603]
Sir Thomas Rempston[604]
Sir William Gascoigne [sic], who died at the siege from an arrow,
and many others. After the siege had been maintained there against the said town and market for the space of around nine months, to wit, around the month of August in the year 1422, the town and market of Meaux were surrendered and delivered to the victorious prince,[605] and all the gentlemen and other men of war who were inside surrendered themselves to the will of the said victorious prince. Before the siege had been laid, the Bastard of Vaurus[606] had had a very large number of poor labourers arrested and cruelly killed, taking them prisoner whilst they were carrying out (45v) their work. They had then been hanged from a very high tree called 'Ourme' [Elm]. When the victorious prince came to lay siege their bodies were shown to him by my lord the duke of Exeter. He had great pity for them and had them taken down and reburied. He swore that if he could catch the Bastard he would be inclined to give him a similar death to that which he had given to the poor labourers, and from the same tree. This came to pass, since as soon as the Bastard of Vaurus came and surrendered himself to the will of that victorious prince, the latter immediately had him led to the tree, where he was hanged and where he died. Peron de Lupé[607] and all the other defenders were made prisoners.

---

[602] Sir Robert Harling (d. 1435) of East Harling (Norfolk) led a retinue of fourteen in the army which accompanied the king back to France in the summer of 1421 (E 101/50/1 m. 3). He was a nephew of Fastolf (the son of Sir John Harling and Cicely, Fastolf's sister) and his service seems to have begun in the garrison of Harfleur in 1416 (E 101/47/39). In the 1417 expedition he crossed in the company of Sir John Blount (E 101/51/2 m. 6).

[603] Sir William indented to provide eighty men for the army which accompanied the king back to France in the summer of 1421 but did not muster in person, suggesting he was already in France (E 101/70/5/694; E 101/50/1 m. 4).

[604] Rempston led a retinue of forty men in the army which returned with the king in the summer of 1421 (CPR 1416–22, p. 388) and which went on to serve at the siege of Meaux.

[605] Seine-et-Marne, arr. Meaux, ch. l. cant. The final surrender of the market was on 10 May 1422 (*Foedera*, x, p. 212). The siege therefore lasted for about seven months, not nine.

[606] On 30 November 1417, the Dauphin Charles gave to his 'bien amé le bastart de Warus, escuier', 250 *l.t.* for good services rendered in time of war (Chartier, iii, p. 249 n. 2; Bove, 'Deconstructing', p. 531). Between 26 August and 30 November 1419, with nineteen 'écuyers' of his household, he joined the company of Arnaud de Barbazan, then captain of Melun (BNF, PO 2946 Vauruz, 65445; published in Bove, 'Deconstructing', p. 519). English administrative records (Devon, *Issues of the Exchequer*, p. 355) and the *Religieux* (vi, p. 451) designate Guichard Chissé as captain of Meaux at the surrender, while English and Burgundian chroniclers attribute the role to the Bastard of Vaurus (Ambühl, 'Henry V and the Administration of Justice', p. 81). The circumstances of his execution, hanged at the tree where he hanged his victims, are widely reported in chronicle accounts, but these accounts also provide more (gruesome) details. There is a general consensus that his head was cut off and stuck on a lance, possibly his own banner, which was firmly attached to the top of the tree, while his body was suspended from a branch (Fénin, pp. 354–5; *Journal d'un Bourgeois*, ed. Beaune, p. 184; Monstrelet, iv, p. 96; *Religieux*, vi, p. 451; Des Ursins, p. 566).

[607] Pierre de Lupé, dit Pierron, a knight from Auvergne, may have been taken prisoner at Agincourt (Belleval, p. 386). He was a Dauphinist supporter who served in northern France in the late 1410s and the early 1420s. He had captured Pierre de Luxembourg, count

Some of them were sent to England and others were taken to various towns and castles and put into different prisons.[608]

During the siege of Meaux Olivier de Mauny,[609]who had been captain of the castle of Falaise and who had by the composition and surrender of that castle made an oath that he would never make war against that victorious prince, assembled – thereby infringing his oath and acting against his faith and promise – a great power of men of war both French and Bretons, to wit,

the lord of Montbourcher[610]
the lord of Coynon
the lord of Châteaugiron
the lord of Tinténiac[611]
the lord of la Houssaye[612]

and several others. He entered the Cotentin region where he carried out many evil actions.[613] He would have done more but as soon as he heard the news of the enterprise my lord the earl of Suffolk, who was governor of Lower Normandy,[614] assembled

Lord Scales[615]

Sir John Assheton *bailli* of Cotentin[616]

---

of Conversano and Brienne, towards the end of 1420 and had brought him to Meaux (Monstrelet, iii, p. 413). In December 1420 he was captain of the fortress of Montaigu (C 64/14 m. 12, DKR 42, p. 382), but evidence shows that he was defending Meaux during the siege and that he was present there with his prisoner. The treaty of surrender of Meaux on 2 May 1422 anticipated that Lupé would have his life spared once he surrendered the fortresses which were in his hands and that he released Luxembourg from any obligation (AN, J 646, no. 21(2)). Montaigu, Soupir and Braine negotiated their surrender on 28 May 1422; the main provision was for Lupé, given as captain of Montaigu, to have his life spared (AN, J 1039/2). There is evidence of his captivity in England for the years 1422 and 1423 but not later (E 404/309, 330). According to Monstrelet (iv, p. 196) he died at Verneuil.

[608] In June 1422, 151 prisoners from Meaux were taken to England (Wylie, iii, p. 351).

[609] The identity of Olivier de Mauny has already been discussed. Chartier (i, pp. 48–9) and *Pucelle* (p. 233) also designate Mauny as leading Franco-Breton troops at the battle of *le park l'evesque*. On 1 May 1422 Henry V rewarded Robert Passage with a life grant for having captured and handed Mauny over to the crown (CPR 1416–22, p. 437).

[610] This may be Bertrand de Montbourcher.

[611] Jeanne de Laval, widow of Bertrand du Gueslin, was lady of Tinténiac at this time, dying in 1433 (Broussillon, *La Maison de Laval*, ii, p. 401).

[612] This may be Eustache de la Houssaye who was a supporter of the duke of Brittany in 1420 (Morice, ii, p. 1060). He committed to observe the terms of the treaty of Amiens in 1423 and in September 1427 took the oath to uphold the peace of Troyes (Morice, ii, pp. 1127, 1201). He appears as a chamberlain of Duke Jean V in the records around that time (Morice, ii, p. 1223).

[613] The strategically important town of Avranches fell to the French in December 1421.

[614] Suffolk had been made KG in May 1421.

[615] Scales led a retinue in the army which accompanied the king to France in the summer of 1421 (E 101/70/5/699; E 101/50/1 m. 3; C 76/104 m. 18, DKR 44, p. 622), which went on to serve at the siege of Meaux.

[616] Assheton held this office until at least February 1422 (BL, Add. Ch. 11319) and probably to Henry V's death.

John Banaster esquire[617]
Rys ap Madoc esquire[618]
and several other men of war of the garrisons of the area, and rode against the enemy. He came to meet them near a castle called *le park l'evesque*.[619] There they assembled, one side against the other (46r), and on both sides performed many fine deeds of arms. At the end the French and the Bretons, who could no longer endure the actions of the English, ran off in flight and defeat. There died on the French side *the lord of Coynon*, the lord of Châteaugiron and several others, and the lord of la Houssaye and Olivier de Mauny knight were taken prisoner along with several others. As soon as the news of the capture of Olivier was taken to that victorious prince, the latter ordered him to be brought before him. He said to him words of this kind: 'Old man, you had made an oath and promise to us that you would never make war against us and our subjects. You are a long-established knight and ought to have kept your promise. Because you have never before done anything like this in terms of falsehood and breaking your word, we do not crave your death but give you life and a trip to England to learn to speak English.' Afterwards he was taken to England where he later died.[620]

In that same year in the month of August, soon after the town and market of Meaux had been surrendered and conquered, that victorious prince came to the city of Paris.[621] Immediately there were surrendered and delivered to him all the places and fortresses which the French held and occupied in the Ile-de-France, in the Laonnais, and in Brie and Champagne. All of the enemy took themselves off to beyond the Loire having promised and sworn (not to resist).

Soon afterwards, to wit, around the feast of the Assumption of Our Lady (15 August), news was brought to that victorious prince that the enemy in great power

---

[617] A man-at-arms of this name served in the retinue of the duke of Gloucester in 1415 but was invalided home (E 101/44/30 no. 1, m. 4; E 101/45/13 m. 4; E 101/50/26). It may be the same person found subsequently in the garrison of Harfleur (E 101/47/39), in Fastolf's retinue at the siege of Pontorson in 1427 (BNF, Fr. 25767/216, 25768/225), as Fastolf's lieutenant at Alençon in the same year (BNF, Fr. 25768/329), under Sir Robert Harling at Meulan in 1431 (AN, K 63/10/35) and under John Handford and then Richard Guethin at Mantes in 1432 (BNF, Fr. 26279/198; BNF, Fr. 25770/702).

[618] A Rees ap Madoc Lloyd was an archer recruited in South Wales for the 1415 campaign (E 101/46/20 no. 3, m. 1) but it is uncertain whether this is the same person as Rys ap Madoc who served as a man-at-arms in the retinue of the earl of Salisbury in the 1417 army (E 101/51/2 m. 9). The latter also served as a man-at-arms ordered to the defence of Le Mans in June 1436 under Fastolf (BNF, Fr. 25772/1046).

[619] Unidentified but presumably a holding of the bishop of Avranches. Possibly 'Les Pas', north-east of Pontorson. This incident seems to have occurred in December 1421 (Wylie, iii, p. 343). Chartier (i, p. 48) mentions the attack of Mauny and others against the English 'before le Parc-l'Evesque, before Avranches' and the capture of Mauny. Both he and *Pucelle* (p. 233) date this 'battle' of *le park l'evesque* to 1425.

[620] For payments in July 1422 concerning the bringing of Olivier to England, see Devon, *Issues of the Exchequer*, p. 375. He seems to have died in captivity. Hall (1809), p. 109, claims that he was buried in the White Friars in London.

[621] Henry moved from Meaux around 26 May to meet his wife at Vincennes, making a formal entry to Paris on 30 May 1422 (Wylie, iii, p. 406).

had laid siege before the town of Cosne in Burgundy.[622] In order to rescue the town, the victorious prince assembled and created a very large army and departed from the town of Paris. He went as far as the town of Corbeil[623] seven leagues from Paris where he started to become ill. For that reason, he appointed my lord (46v) the duke of Burgundy as his lieutenant-general for the campaign.[624] He also appointed as his lieutenant for the English his brother my lord the duke of Bedford.[625] The two dukes carried out the expedition and went directly to Cosne. As soon as the enemy heard the news of the coming of the lords for the rescue of the town, they did not dare wait longer and so raised their siege. They took themselves off to such an extent that when the lords arrived they could not find any enemy. So the town was rescued. The victorious prince returned from the town of Corbeil to a castle near to the town of Paris called the Bois de Vincennes.[626] Here his illness became worse and worse. After the last rites towards God Our Creator had been performed and completed, he gave up his soul in full devotion. Alas, what pity, what sadness, what lamentation, what loss, what damage was this. It was the last day of August in the year of grace 1422. Afterwards his body was taken to England and buried in the abbey of Westminster near the city of London alongside his predecessors as kings.[627] Weep, all you princes, lords, nobles, bourgeois, people, and all good, true and loyal subjects, the death and loss of so very noble and victorious a prince, your protector and defender.

Soon after the decease of that victorious prince, because his son and heir was still a minor under age, to wit, about nine months old, in order to provide for the guard, government, safe keeping and defence of the kingdom of France, it was ordered, appointed and established, by the consent of all the lords and nobles, both spiritual and temporal, and by the commons of the land, that my lord the duke of Bedford, eldest brother of the late victorious prince, be Regent of the realm of France.[628] Soon after he accepted the appointment, which was around 1 January in the year 1422 (i.e. 1423), he heard (47r) news that the town and bridge of Meulan on the river (Seine) had been taken by surprise attack by the lord of Graville and other enemies. Therefore, he armed himself and assembled, to wit, [added: Richard Woodville esquire, Robert Harling of Norfolk knight, at that point lieutenant of the place][629]

---

[622]   Now Cosne-Cours-sur-Loire (Nièvre, ch. l. d'arr). Cosne had agreed to surrender to the Dauphin on 12 August. The duke of Burgundy had agreed to a *journée*, asking Henry V to send troops to assist, but the Dauphinist troops withdrew (Wylie, iii, pp. 409–10).

[623]   Now Corbeil-Essones in the southern suburbs of Paris (Essone, arr. Evry, cant. Corbeil-Essones). The king moved from Paris to the castle of Vincennes on 7 July 1422, but then moved to Corbeil, only to be brought back, seriously ill, to Vincennes by mid-August (Wylie, iii, p. 415).

[624]   To date, no official appointment has come to light but joint action is evidenced in the chronicles (Wylie, iii, p. 410). For further discussion, see Lobanov, 'Anglo-Burgundian Military Cooperation', p. 63.

[625]   Bedford crossed to France in early May 1422 (Wylie, iii, p. 401).

[626]   Val-de-Marne, arr. Nogent-sur-Marne, ch. l. cant.

[627]   Henry's funeral took place in Westminster Abbey on 7 November 1422.

[628]   The formal proclamation of Bedford as Regent was made in Paris on 19 November 1422 (Fauquembergue, ii, pp. 72–5).

[629]   Fastolf was still captain on 6 November 1422 (BNF, Fr. 25766/810) but Harling mustered as captain of Poissy and Meulan on 1 November (BNF, Fr. 25766/816) and continued as captain of Meulan after the recovery of the place until Michaelmas 1425 (BNF, Fr. 4491 f. 72).

my lord the earl of Salisbury
my lord the earl of Suffolk
Lord Scales
the young Lord Poynings[630]
Sir John Fastolf, master of the household of the Regent and seneschal of Normandy[631]
and several others, and laid siege before the town and bridge of Meulan. The siege lasted around two months.[632] Finally, the lord of Graville surrendered and delivered the town and castle to my lord the Regent, and made an oath to be the true and loyal subject of, and obedient to, the king our sovereign lord and my lord the Regent. But soon afterwards, going against his oath, he returned to being an enemy. My lord the Regent made [blank] captain of the town and bridge.

In the year beginning at Easter in the year of grace 1423, my lord of Bedford began negotiations to treat for marriage between himself and Lady Anne,[633] sister of Philip, duke of Burgundy. During this period of time, Arthur of Brittany, count of Richemont and count of Montfort (who had taken the oath to the most victorious prince King Henry the Fifth, of whom mention has been made previously, and who had been given the county of Ivry), left secretly, acting against his faith and oath, and went to Flanders. From there he went across country to give himself up to the enemy of the king and of my lord the Regent.[634] As a result, when the men to whom he had committed the keeping of the castle of Ivry heard news of his surrender, they held the castle against the king and my lord the Regent. To strengthen their position, they installed alongside themselves within the castle Girault de la Pallière[635] and a large number of the enemy who rode through the area, which

---

[630] Robert, lord Poynings (1382–1446) could hardly be described as young in 1423. This may therefore be his son, Sir Richard Poynings of Slaugham (Sussex) and Okeford Fitzpayn (Dorset) who was active in France, being killed near Orléans on 10 June 1429. Richard had crossed in the expeditionary army which accompanied the king to France in June 1421 (E 101/50/1 m. 1) and seems to have been knighted in 1423 (HOCb).

[631] Fastolf is not known to have held this title but on 17 January 1424 he was appointed 'gouverneur et superveeur de toutes les villes, chasteaulx et forteresses' in Normandy and in the parts of Maine which were appatised (BNF, Fr. 26047/200), having powers similar to those held by Richard Woodville as seneschal of Normandy under Henry V. Woodville had been reappointed to that role on 11 March 1423 (BNF, Fr. 26046/47).

[632] The town had been taken by the Dauphinists in early January and the treaty of surrender was agreed on 1 March 1423. According to Monstrelet, who included the text of the treaty, Bedford's English commissioners for the surrender were the earl of Salisbury, Sir John Fastolf, Richard Woodville, and Nicholas Burdet (Monstrelet, iv, p. 138).

[633] Anne (1404–32) was the daughter of Duke John the Fearless.

[634] The chronicle is misleading here since Richemont did not defect to the French until June 1424 (Cosneau, p. 79).

[635] Girault de la Pallière, a Gascon gentleman supporting Charles VII in northern France, seized the fortress of Ivry by surprise in 1423 (AN, JJ 172/442, printed in *Actes*, i, pp. 76 7; see also JJ 173/87; and *Journal d'un Bourgeois*, ed. Tuetey, p. 191 n. 2). He acted as captain when the fortress was besieged by the English and negotiated its surrender in the summer of 1424 (Monstrelet, iv, p. 190; *Journal d'un Bourgeois*, ed. Tuetey, p. 194 n. 1). The castle of Rochefort (Yvelines) seized by the English in 1426 was recaptured by La Pallière in 1427, only to fall again into the hands of Salisbury in 1428 (*Journal d'un Bourgeois*, ed. Tuetey, p. 205 n. 1; see also *Pucelle*, p. 256). Giraut de la Pallière was in the army gathered by Richemont

lay in royal obedience, robbing and pillaging the poor subjects and committing (47v) as much evil as they could. Despite this, the Regent continued with his objective. The marriage was agreed and effected, and they were together at Troyes in Champagne.[636] At this betrothal there were in the company of the Regent, to wit,

my lord the earl of Salisbury
my lord the earl of Suffolk
Lord Scales
Lord Ferrers and Chambrois[637]
[Sir John Fastolf, deleted]

and several others. Once the marriage was consummated, the prince left Troyes in order to go to Paris. On his journey he took and captured several castles and fortresses: Traînel,[638] Bray-sur-Seine[639] and several others. Afterwards he went to Paris, where he was well received, with honour and great joy. The enemy occupying two fortresses were committing excessive damage and harm to the citizens of Paris and to the poor people of the neighbourhood. As a result, the Parisians petitioned the Regent that it might please him to provide so that the enemy would be driven out of these places, which were Passy[640] and Orsay.[641] At their request and petition, in order to capture the two castles, the Regent ordered and appointed Sir John Fastolf, the master of his household, with a significant army. Sir John immediately laid siege before the castle of Passy which surrendered to him within a short space of time. The captain of the place, called Guillaume dit Marjolaine esquire,[642] became

---

which raised the siege of Montargis in 1427 (BNF, Fr. 26084, f. 550; cited in Cosneau, p. 145). He was already in Orléans in September 1428 with fifteen men-at-arms, and stayed there throughout the English siege (Hémon Raguier's accounts in *Journal du siège*, pp. 159, 168, 171, 174, 178, 184, 190, 194). He then took part in the siege of Jargeau, the battle of Patay, and Charles VII's coronation expedition (ibid., p. 205; see also Cosneau, p. 171).

[636] Anne was married by proxy to the duke of Bedford at Montbard on 17 April 1423 and in person at the church of Saint John in Troyes on 13 May 1423. The marriage cemented the treaty made at Amiens on 13 April between Bedford, Philip, duke of Burgundy and Arthur de Richemont on behalf of his brother Jean V, duke of Brittany (1389–1442). Arthur married Anne's elder sister Margaret at Dijon on 10 October 1423.

[637] In the Norman rolls there is a protection to the lord of Ferrieres de Chambois on 5 April 1419 (C 64/11 m. 78, DKR 41, p. 673), so, on the face of it, this is a Frenchman. In the late fifteenth century, however, the family of Ferrers of Groby had a Chambois pursuivant.

[638] Aube, arr. et cant. Nogent-sur-Seine.

[639] Seine-et-Marne, arr. et cant. Provins.

[640] Identification is problematic. The sense of the passage implies a location close to Paris, so that Passy-sur-Seine (Seine-et-Marne, arr. Provins, cant. Provins) suggests itself. Yet no fortifications are known there, whereas there is a thirteenth-century castle at Passy-en-Valois, Aisne, arr. Soissons, cant. Villers-Cotterêts.

[641] Identification is problematic. Orsay is in Essone, arr. et cant. Palaiseau, but no fortifications are known. Waurin also names the location as Orsay, which he notes as lying between Paris and Montlhéry. According to Waurin, Orsay was besieged by the earl of Salisbury, with the siege lasting three weeks (Waurin, iii, p. 34). Monstrelet (iv, p. 155) gives the same location but no commander on behalf of Bedford is named and the siege is given as six weeks in duration. An alternative is Oulchy-le-Château (Aisne, arr. Soissons, cant. Villiers-Cotterêts), close to Passy-en-Valois, which has a thirteenth-century castle.

[642] A royal grant to Fastolf issued in January 1433 confirms that Guillaume Remon was taken prisoner by Fastolf at Passy-en-Valois in 1423 (AN, JJ 175/203). Yet Fastolf's hopes for a high ransom – Remon, according to Fastolf, had undertaken to pay an astonishing 22,000

Fastolf's prisoner by virtue of the surrender. Afterwards Fastolf lay siege (48r) to the castle of Orsay but the enemy who were within the place immediately came to a composition and surrendered the place. Fastolf appointed captains and keepers in these castles and then returned to Paris to my lord the Regent.

In the year 1423 [added: around the month of July] the count de Ventadour,[643] the count de Comminges,[644] Sir William Stewart constable of Scotland[645] and several others to the number of 20,000 men of war of the enemy party laid siege to the town and castle of Cravant[646] in the county of Auxerre in Burgundian territory. Straightaway my lord the Regent and my lord the duke of Burgundy assembled a great power. The names of the leading lords, knights and esquires present in it follow, to wit,

my lord the earl of Salisbury lieutenant-general of my lord the Regent[647]
Lord Willoughby[648]
the young Lord Poynings
Lord Moleyns[649]

écus d'or – were thwarted by Bedford who ordered Remon to be released and relieved of any obligation to pay a ransom as part of a transaction to obtain the surrender of Compiègne in 1424. Fastolf's claims for compensation were eventually met ten years later. The case is discussed in detail in Armstrong, 'Sir John Fastolf', pp. 123–33.

[643] Jacques, count of Ventadour (d. 1424), was taken prisoner at Agincourt (AN, X1a 9190, f. 125v). He was a chamberlain of the Dauphin, fighting on his behalf in the Charolais and the Mâconnais, in May 1420 (BNF, Clairambault 111/8677). His presence and capture at Cravant are widely reported in chronicles (Berry, p. 112; Monstrelet, iv, pp. 158–9; *Pucelle*, p. 191), as also his death at Verneuil. See also *RDP*, vii, pp. 363–74, no. 1003, and 363 n. 2. An act sealed between Perrinet Gressart and Jeanne de Château de Montaigne indicates that the count, who had been captured by a man of Perrinet Gressart, had been released by April 1424 (Flamare, *Le Nivernais*, i, p. 215, p.j. no. 8; Bossaut, *Perrinet Gressart*, p. 18 n. 2).

[644] Matthieu de Foix, count of Comminges, and his elder brother John I, had continued negotiations with the English after the death of Henry V. In April 1423, John I was yet again asked to take the oath of his younger brother (*L&P*, I, pp. 1–6; Vale, *English Gascony*, p. 94).

[645] Sir William is here confused with his half-brother John Stewart of Darnley who was constable of the army of Scotland.

[646] Yonne, arr. Auxerre, cant. Joux-la-Ville. The Franco-Scottish army laid siege to the Burgundian-held town in late June. The Anglo-Burgundian army set out from Auxerre on 30 July and the battle took place on the next day. The chronicle omits mention of the earl of Suffolk who was most certainly present.

[647] Salisbury is described in documents of the spring of 1423 as 'lieutenant general en Normandie et partout le pais conquis es parties du Maine' (BNF, Fr. 26046/56) but his area of activity had moved to Champagne and Brie by June.

[648] Willoughby crossed from Dover in late May 1423, having indented on 26 March to serve with 160 men (E 101/71/2/2).

[649] This is unlikely to be Sir William Moleyns (1378–1425) of Stoke Poges (Bucks.) who is not known to have served in the wars (HOCa). His son, another William, born in 1405, was certainly serving in France from 1426, mustering as a man at arms under the earl of Salisbury at the siege of La Ferté-Bernard on 4 March (BL, Add. Ch. 94) and taking out letters of attorney to cross to France in June 1427 (C 76/109 m. 7, DKR 48, p. 250). In the summer of 1428 he led a retinue of eighty men within the 1,200 men ordered to join in France with Salisbury's expeditionary army and which ended up at the siege of Orléans. On 23 December 1428 he and William Glasdale (described as 'freres' – brothers-in-arms – as joint captains) indented with 46 men-at-arms and 138 archers to continue in service (BNF, PO

Sir Thomas Rempston[650]
Sir William Oldhall[651]
Sir John Pashley[652]
Sir Thomas Fleming[653]
Sir Edmund Heron[654]
Sir John Grey[655]

47117 Moulins 11; Jarry, pp. 92–5). Moleyns mustered his men at the bastide on the bridge on the same day (BNF, Fr. 25768/328). He was killed at Joan of Arc's attack on 8 May 1429, where Glasdale also died (C 139/45/38 mm. 1–2). Neither William senior or junior was a baron but the daughter of the latter married Sir Robert Hungerford, son of Walter, lord Hungerford, and was created Lord Moleyns in 1445.

[650] Rempston had letters of protection to cross to France in July 1423 (C 76/106 m. 13, DKR 48, p. 226), probably crossing as one of the thirteen knights in the expeditionary troops under the duke of Exeter. He was captain of Argentan from Michaelmas 1423 (BNF, Fr. 4485, pp. 273–4), a post he held to April 1430 (BL, Add. Ch. 11508; BNF, PO 79 Apowell 2).

[651] William Oldhall (1395–1460) of East Dereham (Norfolk) and Hunsdon (Herts.) indented with Thomas Beaufort, earl of Dorset (duke of Exeter), for the service of himself and three archers in the 1415 army (E 101/69/7/503). It is uncertain whether Oldhall was at Agincourt but he was certainly serving in the garrison of Harfleur in 1416 (E 101/47/39). He does not appear in subsequent musters of the Harfleur garrison and is probably the 'William Holdhall' who crossed in the retinue of Sir John Blount in the 1417 army (E 101/51/2 m. 6). William Worcester in his *Itineraries* (pp. 355, 361) claims that he was a member of Exeter's household, and that he shared lodgings at the siege of Rouen with Henry Inglose and others. The duke of Exeter brought troops to France in the early summer of 1423: it is probable Oldhall was one of the 182 men-at-arms for which he indented (E 404/39/163; E 403/658 and 661; C 76/106 m. 14, DKR 48, p. 225), although we also find letters of protection in July 1423 for service in the retinue of the earl of Suffolk (C 76/106 m. 12, DKR 48, p. 225). He may have been knighted at Cravant although Worcester (*Itineraries*, p. 335) claims that he was dubbed at Verneuil. He had a long career in France, serving there until at least the mid-1440s (HOCb).

[652] John Pashley (1398–1453) of Smeeth (Kent) and Pashley (Sussex) had letters of protection in July 1422 to cross to France, though not yet a knight (C 76/105 m. 1, DKR 44, p. 638). It is possible that he had served in 1417 in the company of William Swinburne (d. 1422), who had married his widowed mother (HOCa). John's service between 1423 and 1425 remains obscure. He was a man-at-arms in the garrison of the Tower of London in 1425–26 (E 101/51/21 mm. 2, 3) and married the daughter of Richard Woodville senior, its commander. In 1426 he indented for a company of ninety in an expeditionary army for France under the general command of the earl of Warwick (E 404/42/309; E 403/675; C 76/108 m. 2, DKR 48, p. 243), having been dubbed a knight along with the young king and his brother-in-law Richard Woodville junior at Whitsun 1426.

[653] A Thomas Fleming crossed as a man-at-arms under the earl of Arundel in 1415 (E 101/47/1 m. 2). In 1417 we find a Thomas Fleming senior and junior under the earl of Salisbury (E 101/51/2 m. 9). A man of this name is found in various garrisons and companies through to the late 1440s, most notably as lieutenant to Ogard at Caen between 1438 and 1448 (BNF, Fr. 26065/3768, 25778/1822) but he was not a knight until 1441.

[654] Heron was most likely knighted at Cravant since he was certainly of this status by October 1423 (*Calendar ... of Papal Letters, 1417–31*, p. 306).

[655] Sir John Grey of Ruthin* (1387–1439), eldest son of Reginald, lord Grey of Ruthin (1362–1440), led a retinue of sixty in 1415 (E 404/31/159; E 101/45/5/ m. 4d; E 101/45/22 m. 38; E 101/45/18; E 101/45/1; E 101/47/17; E 358/6 m. 6), and indented for a retinue of

Sir Reginald Grey[656]
Sir John Arthur
Sir Henry Biset[657]
Sir William Peyto[658]
Sir Richard Lowick[659]
Sir John Crafford
Sir Gilbert Halsall[660]

---

120 in 1417 (E 101/70/2/590). His service, including captaincy of Bayeux before April 1419, and of Gournay 1420–22, can be traced in the Norman rolls. He was made KG in 1436.

[656] Sir Reginald Grey (1401–85) was a half-brother of Sir John Grey of Ruthin. He crossed in the army which accompanied the king in the summer of 1421 (E 101/50/1 m. 2; in a company raised by his father). He succeeded Sir John as captain of Gournay in September 1423, holding the post to Michaelmas 1424 (BNF, NAF 1482/14; BNF, Fr. 4491 f. 76).

[657] No service by Henry Biset before 1426 has been discovered and his origins are obscure. A Henry Biset released claims to the property he had inherited from his father in Cudham and Downe in Kent in 1379 but that would make him quite old by the mid-1420s (C 146/3574; thanks to Dr Kleineke for this reference). It is even possible that he was French. A Biset family is known in Normandy in 1421 (C 64/16 m. 38, DKR 42, p. 412), and French origins might explain why French chroniclers show an unusual interest in him. In March 1426, already a knight although the date of his dubbing is not known, he served under the earl of Salisbury at the siege of La Ferté-Bernard (BL, Add. Ch. 94) and at the second siege of Mont Aimé (BNF, Fr. 32510 f. 369r). He served at the siege of Montargis (BNF, Fr. 4484 f. 59–60v), during which, according to the chronicle of Jean Raoulet, he fought a successful diversionary battle with 400 men against the French (Chartier, iii, p. 192). His presence at the siege of Montargis is also noted in Monstrelet (iv, p. 272) and Waurin (iii, p. 216). He was in service under Salisbury at Nogent in April 1428 (BNF, Fr, 4484 f. 43v), and on the Loire campaign, mustering in December 1428 he mustered in the retinue of Sir John de la Pole at Meung-sur-Loire (BL, Add. Ch. 1102). He appears in lists prepared in the sixteenth century, probably from the chronicle, by Robert Glover of presences at the battles of Cravant and Verneuil (BL, Harley 782 f. 51; *L&P*, II, ii, pp. 385, 394).

[658] There is no evidence beyond the chronicle and other lists made by William Worcester that Sir William Peyto (c. 1394–1464) of Chesterton (Warks.) was in France at this time. Later in 1423 he became a retainer of the earl of Warwick. The first firm evidence of his service is the expeditionary army of 1432 where he crossed with 180 men (E 404/48/320; E 403/703). He served on a number of later expeditions (1439, 1443 and 1449) and also held various offices in France, including the lieutenancy of Rouen under Talbot's captaincy in the early 1440s (HOCa).

[659] Richard Lowick, probably from Northumberland, crossed to Normandy in 1417 under Sir John Neville (E 101/51/2 m. 22) and was granted lands in the duchy in April 1419 (C 64/11 m. 45, DKR 41, p. 782). On 15 April 1421 he was given command of Mantes (C 64/16 m. 38d, DKR 42, p. 426), a post he held until the winter of 1422 when replaced by Sir Alan Buxhill (BNF, PO 483 Buxhill 2). We find him at the siege of Mont-Aimé in 1426–27 (BNF, Fr. 32510 f. 369v), defending Chartres in February 1428 (BNF, Fr. 4484 f. 139), at Montigny in April 1428 by which time he was a knight (BNF, Fr. 4484 f. 43), and on the Loire campaign of 1428, culminating at the siege of Orléans (Jarry, pp. 133–4). He continued in service into the 1430s, with the last reference to his service in December 1436 when he was lieutenant of Verneuil for William Neville, lord Fauconberg (ADE II F/4069). On 18 July 1438 he was made a poor knight of St George's Chapel at Windsor castle (CPR 1436–41, p. 176).

[660] Halsall had added the captaincy of Dreux to his captaincy of Evreux from September 1421 (C 64/16 m. 23d, DKR 42, p. 432), holding both posts until 1 October 1422 (BNF, PO 1487 Harpelay 2). He then returned to England but took out letters of protection and of

Sir Lancelot de Lisle[661]
William Glasdale[662]
(48v) Matthew Gough,[663] Digon Amore[664]
Rys ap Madoc
Jenkin Banaster[665]
and many others.
And of the Burgundians
the lord of Saint-George, lieutenant-general for the duke of Burgundy[666]

---

attorney in mid-May 1423 (C 76/106 m. 16, DKR 48, p. 224), no doubt to participate in the expeditionary army which crossed that summer (Ratcliffe, 'Military Expenditure', pp. 6–8). He was reappointed captain of Dreux on 2 November 1423 (BNF, Fr. 4485 pp. 205–7), holding the post until the summer of 1424 (BNF, Fr. 26265/123). At some point – perhaps at Cravant or Verneuil – he was made a knight banneret, a status he certainly had by 1425 (BNF, Fr. 32510 f. 368).

[661] Lancelot de Lisle (d. 1429), of Hampshire, crossed in 1417 as a man-at-arms in the retinue of the earl of Salisbury (E 101/51/2 m. 9). That he had a close link to the earl is seen by his acting as his commissary in the surrender of Honfleur in 1419 (C 64/10 m. 4, DKR 41, p. 746) and by the bequest of 20 marks in the earl's will (*Register of Henry Chichele*, ii, p. 393). Since he was a knight by July 1424 he may have been dubbed at Cravant.

[662] Glasdale (d. 1429) crossed as an archer under the earl of Salisbury in 1417 (E 101/51/2 m. 10) and by November 1420 was master of the earl's household (BNF, PO 1338 Glasdale 3; *English Suits*, pp. 294–5). In August 1421 he was granted lands near Orbec (C 64/16 m. 31, DKR 42, p. 414). Worcester (*Itineraries*, pp. 3–5) speaks of him as hailing from 'Blackmoor beyond York', now called Glaisdale (Yorks. NR).

[663] Gough (Goch)* (c. 1390–1450) was from Maelor but came to settle at Hewelsfield near St Briavels (Gloucs.) and became a famous warrior applauded in Welsh poetry (www.biography.wales; Probert, 'Matthew Gough', pp. 34–44). Although there are claims he was at Agincourt this cannot be substantiated in the surviving records. If he can be identified with Morgan Gough then he may have crossed as a man-at-arms under Lord Bergavenny in 1417 (E 101/51/2 m. 5). William Worcester (*Itineraries*, p. 351) claims that his father was bailiff of the Talbot manor of Hanmer and his mother the nurse of the future John, lord Talbot. He does not appear in the records of English military administration until March 1427 when he was at the siege of Pontorson in the retinue of Fastolf (BNF, Fr. 25767/216). Claims of his presence at Cravant and Verneuil derived from his presence in lists made by Robert Glover in the late sixteenth century (BL, Harley 782, ff. 51r–52r), which, as discussed in Chapter 5, appear to come from the M 9 chronicle.

[664] The nationality of Amore is uncertain. He may have been the Richard More who crossed to France in the summer of 1421 as a man-at-arms under Richard Beauchamp, earl of Worcester (E 101/50/1 m. 2), who subsequently led his troops to eastern Champagne, but Amore's description as 'seigneur de Blandery', modern-day Blanderie, close to Mons and Tournai, suggests he was a Hainaulter. (We are grateful to Professor Valérie Toureille for this identification.) He was captain of Montigny-le-Roi for the English in 1424–25 and served at the siege of Arzillières in the spring of 1426 (BNF, Fr. 35210 f. 367; Lobanov, 'Anglo-Burgundian Military Cooperation', pp. 133–6).

[665] No Jenkin Banaster has been found but as the first name is a common diminutive of John this may be the same person as noted earlier or else his son. If the latter, it is possible that the service record noted earlier may relate to two generations.

[666] His son, also called Guillaume de Vienne, was present at Cravant where, according to Monstrelet (iv, pp. 158–9), he was dubbed knight, but there is no evidence of the presence of the lord of Saint-Georges himself.

the count of Joigny[667]
the count of Brainé[668]
the lord of Chastellux marshal of Burgundy[669]
the lord of Vergy[670]
the Bastard of Vergy[671]
the lord of Châtillon[672]
the lord of Crouy[673]
the lord of Lisle-Adam[674]
the lord of Pesmes[675]
the Bastard of Thian[676]
Perrinet Gressart[677]
François l'Arragonais[678]

---

[667] The presence of Guy de la Trémoïlle, count of Joigny, is also in Monstrelet (iv, p. 158).
[668] Probably the count of Brienne is meant but his presence is not attested elsewhere and is unlikely.
[669] The presence of Claude de Beauvoir, lord of Chastellux, is also attested in Berry (p. 112). He was made marshal of France in 1418.
[670] This is probably Antoine de Vergy whose presence at Cravant is also mentioned by Monstrelet (iv, p. 158).
[671] A Jean, Bastard of Vergy, was active in Lorraine during the wars of succession. See Toureille, *Robert de Sarrebrück*, pp. 196 n. 384, and 169.
[672] According to Monstrelet (iv, p. 136), the lord of Châtillon and the Bastard of Thian captured La Ferté-Milon in 1423. Anselme (viii, p. 839) claims that Thomas Montague, earl of Salisbury, knighted Châtillon in 1423. This may have been at Cravant.
[673] There is no other evidence of Antoine de Croÿ's presence at Cravant.
[674] Jean de Villiers, lord of Lisle-Adam, being cleared of charges put forward before Henry V's death, was already back in action towards the beginning of 1423 when he recaptured the town of La Ferté-Milon which had briefly fallen into the hands of Dauphinists (AN, JJ 172/363; Monstrelet, iv, p. 136). His presence at Cravant is not evidenced elsewhere. His participation in the siege of the Pont-de-Meulan is mentioned by Monstrelet (iv, pp. 136–7). Between 1425 and 1428, he served Philip the Good in Hainaut and Holland. He was back to the French capital in 1429 which he defended against the French, and was made once again captain of Paris. In January 1430, he was rewarded for his loyal service to the dukes of Burgundy since 1417 with his election as a member of the Order of the Golden Fleece (Schnerb, 'Jean de Villiers, seigneur de L'Isle-Adam', pp. 32–3; Schnerb, 'Jean de Villiers, seigneur de L'Isle-Adam, vu par les chroniqueurs bourguignons', pp. 105–21).
[675] There is no other evidence of the presence of Guillaume de Grandson, lord of Pesmes, at Cravant.
[676] There is no other evidence of the presence of the Bastard of Thian at Cravant.
[677] Perrinet Gressart (d. 1438) was a 'chef de bande' or captain of *routiers*, operating mainly in the Nivernais between 1419 and 1435, holding the strategic stronghold of La Charité-sur-Loire between December 1423 and 1435. He was present at Cravant; he is likely to be the 'Perrinet', who, according to Monstrelet (iv, p. 162), chased the French combatants who fled the battlefield. An act dated April 1424 shows that it was one of Gressart's men who captured the count of Ventadour at the battle of Cravant (Bossuat, *Perrinet Gressart*, p. 18).
[678] François de Surienne, dit l'Aragonais (c. 1398–1462), was a close companion of Perrinet Gressart whose niece, Estinette de Gréseville, he married in 1426. He was a *routier* in the pay of the English and was elected as knight of the Garter in 1447. In 1449 he seized the town of Fougères which gave Charles VII a pretext to resume the war. In the early 1420s he was in the service of the duke of Burgundy defending the Charolais, together with Gressart in

Jean de Gingins[679]
David du Clou[680]
Henri Chauffour[681]
and many others totalling, English and Burgundians together, around 15,000 soldiers. They came before the said town of Cravant in order to relieve it and to give battle to the enemy. The River Yonne, which passes in front of Cravant, lay between the enemy who were laying siege and the English and Burgundians who had come to relieve the town. As a result, the latter could not easily assemble to give battle because the enemy were guarding very strongly the river bank and the passage of the river. Despite this situation, the English and Burgundians, jointly and with equal courage, threw themselves into the river both on foot and on horse. Crossing over it in force, they joined battle with the enemy. (49r) There was a very strong and hard fight in that location. Finally, the enemy could not endure any longer the great blows of the English and Burgundians and ran off in defeat. In the rout and during the battle were killed and taken prisoner of the enemy around 800 soldiers. Here follow the names of the principal lords and other nobles who were killed and captured:

the count of Ventadour	}
the count of Astarac[682]	}
the count of Comminges[683]	} dead
the count of Tonnerre[684]	}

1421. He fought a duel at Chalon against a partisan of the Dauphin called Jean du Mayne in July 1423 (Aubrée, *Mémoires*, ii, p. 218), and was taken prisoner afterwards. The duke of Burgundy gave him 200 *livres* to help him pay his ransom on 21 August 1424 (ACO, B 11886). He may have been at Cravant and been taken prisoner there (Bossuat, *Perrinet Gressart*, esp. pp. 44–5).

[679] Jean de Gingins, lord of Divonne, was an esquire from Savoy who served the dukes of Burgundy. Like the du Clou brothers, he took an active part in the civil wars of the 1410s. He was present at the siege of Montereau in July 1420 and received 100 *francs* from Duke Philip for his past service to himself and his father (ADN, B 1920, f. 104v; Schnerb, 'Bourgogne et Savoie', esp. pp. 22–3). We can assume he was present at the sieges of Melun (1420) and Meaux (1422). Of note, Waurin (iii, p. 62) records the presence of two other Savoyards at Cravant, Amé de Viry and Guigue de Sallenove, the latter being a frequent companion of arms of Jean de Gingins (on Sallenove see Schnerb, 'Bourgogne et Savoie', pp. 21–2). Thanks to Professor Schnerb for drawing our attention to these Savoyards. After the peace of Arras, Jean de Gingins settled in Savoie (Amiet, 'Le Livre d'Heures de Jean de Gingins', pp. 95–7).

[680] The brothers Jean, Amé and Clavin du Clou were mercenaries from Savoy in the service of the dukes of Burgundy. There is no evidence of a David du Clou (Schnerb, 'Bourgogne et Savoie', pp. 20–2).

[681] Henri de Chauffour, according to Chastellain (i, pp. 122–3), had been fatally wounded in 1420.

[682] Jean II, count of Astarac's (d. 1458) allegiance was still wavering at that time. His presence at Cravant is highly unlikely.

[683] The count of Comminges is no more likely than Astarac to have fought at Cravant.

[684] Hugues de Chalon (d. 1424), count of Tonnerre, succeeded his elder brother Louis II who died childless by the end of 1422. Since Louis had supported the Dauphin, the *comté* of Tonnerre had been confiscated by John the Fearless on behalf of the king and given to the future Duke Philip the Good, who returned it to the family in the early 1420s. Hugues was also a Dauphinist. He served on Charles VII's embassy to the duke of Savoy in late 1422 (BNF, Fr. 32511 f. 34). His participation and capture at the battle of Cravant

Coquart de Cambron knight[685]   }
      The Scots
the lord of Saint Johnson[686]   }
John Balglavy   }
Sir John Turnbull   }
Sir John Haliburton   }
Sir Robert Lyle   }
Sir William Cunningham   }
William Douglas esquire[687]   } dead
Sir Alexander Home   }
Sir William Lyle   }
Sir John Rotherford   }
Sir William Crawford[688]   }
the lord of Concressault[689]   }
Sir George Lyle   }

Sir Alexander Meldrum   } prisoners
Sir Louis de Serigny   }

After this battle and glorious victory had been won – for which the lords gave thanks and praise to God and to His glorious mother – the English and Burgundian lords departed together. The Burgundians went off to their own country and my lord of Salisbury and the other English lords returned to Paris to my lord the Regent who received them with great joy and honour. At that battle no man of name from their party died, and only a few others, who do not need to be mentioned here.

(49v) In this time, soon after the town of Cravant had been recovered as has been said, my lord the Regent appointed and ordered my lord the earl of Salisbury as lieutenant-general on behalf of the king and of himself for the land of France, Brie and Champagne.[690] Sir John Fastolf was appointed lieutenant for the king and for my lord the Regent in Normandy in the bailliages of Rouen, Evreux, Alen-

---

are not impossible although there is no other evidence of it and he must like Ventadour have secured release since we know that he was killed at Verneuil (Monstrelet, iv, pp. 195–7; Cagny, pp. 132–5; *Pucelle*, pp. 197–8; Caron, 'Vie et mort d'une grande dame', pp. 147–90; Schnerb, *L'état*, pp. 198–9).

[685] Coquart de Cambron was still alive at the time of Verneuil.

[686] In 1489 the head of the Hospitallers Order in Scotland was given the title 'Lord Saint John' and made a parliamentary peer but no other man of this title is known in Scotland nor is it obvious that this is a French title granted to one of the Scottish military leaders in the service of Charles VII.

[687] A William Crawford was in the service of Archibald, fourth earl of Douglas, at this point (Fraser, *Douglas Book*, iiii, no. 356).

[688] The Sir William Crawford serving in 1421 had a son William but he inherited his father's barony of Drumlanrig and is not known to have died in 1423.

[689] Having been granted this lordship by the Dauphin in 1421, John Stewart of Darnley was rewarded by Charles as king in 1422 with the lordship of Aubigny-sur-Nère (Cher, arr. Vierzon, ch. l. cant.). He was supported by the king in paying his ransom after his capture at the battle of Cravant but was not released in time to participate in the battle of Verneuil (Ambühl, *Prisoners*, pp. 70, 198).

[690] Salisbury had been appointed to this command in early June 1423 (Warner, 'Montague Earls of Salisbury', p. 165).

çon and the lands beyond the River Seine, and also to the governorship of Anjou and Maine.[691] William Glasdale was appointed *bailli* and captain of Mâcon.[692] Sir Thomas Gargrave[693] and Sir Thomas Fleming were appointed captains of Montigny.[694] Sir Edmund Heron and Digon Amore were appointed captains of Vertus[695] in Champagne, and Matthew Gough was made captain of [blank].

Once this had been done, my lord of Salisbury laid siege to the tower and castle of Fontaine-sous-Montaiguillon[696] in Brie whose captains were the Bretons

---

[691] On 17 January 1424 Fastolf was appointed 'gouverneur et superveeur de toutes les villes, chasteaulx et forteresses' in Normandy and in those parts of Maine which were appatised (BNF, Fr. 26047/200) but he seems to have held authority at least in the duchy of Alençon earlier. In September 1424 we find him described as lieutenant of the king in Alençon and below the River Seine (BNF, Fr. 4485 p. 319) and in January 1425 'gouverneur d'alençon et lieutenant du comte du Maine' (BNF, Fr. PO 566 du Busc 14). His appointment by the duke of Bedford as governor of Anjou and Maine of 11 March 1425 exists in a later copy in College of Arms, Arundel 26, ff. 59–63.

[692] Sâone-et-Loire, ch. l. d'arr. On 2 November 1423 Glasdale mustered his men before the *bailli* of Mâcon Philibert de Saint-Léger (BNF, Fr. 25767/45), suggesting he was not himself *bailli*. At the end of the next month we find him described in the municipal records of Mâcon as 'capitaine general sur le fait de la guerre au bailliage de mascon' (AM Mâcon, BB 13 f. 98r; Lobanov, 'Anglo-Burgundian Military Cooperation', p. 108).

[693] Thomas Gargrave crossed in the retinue of the duke of Clarence in 1415 (E 101/45/4 m. 3) but we can only speculate that he did the same in 1417 since the muster for the duke's company does not survive. We find him active in Normandy from at least the summer of 1421 (C 64/16 m. 36d, DKR 42, p. 427). He was lieutenant of Château-Gaillard by April 1422 (C 64/17 m. 25d, DKR 42, p. 447), probably being in command of the place after the death at the siege of Meaux of Lord Clifford. He was knighted between 1424 and 1426. The earl of Salisbury was appointed on 7 October 1426 captain of Montigny-le-Roi as well as of Nogent (Haute-Marne, arr. Chaumont, ch. l. cant.) as part of his commission to make war in Champagne (BNF, Fr. 32510 f. 369). Gargrave took command at Montigny from April 1427 first as the *procureur* for Salisbury, then from June as lieutenant, until Sir Lancelot de Lisle was appointed captain in January 1428 (BNF, Fr. 4484 ff. 43v, 149r–52v, 153r). Gargrave was knighted between September 1424 and March 1426 and is known also to have served under the earl of Salisbury at the sieges of La Ferté-Bernard (BL, Add. Ch. 94) and Mont-Aimé (second siege) in Champagne (BNF, Fr. 32510 f. 369v).

[694] Montigny-le-Roi, now known as Val-de-Meuse (Haute-Marne, arr. Langres, cant. Bourbonne-les-Bains).

[695] Marne, arr. Épernay, ch. l. cant. Heron was retained with 800 men for the safekeeping of Beauce and Gâtinais on 16 March 1425 (BNF, Fr. 32510 f. 368) and also served at the siege of Mont-Aimé which ended in January 1426 (ibid., f. 367r). Vertus fell to the Dauphinists in September 1426. Heron and Amor tried to hold out but were both killed, Heron on 26 September (ibid., f. 369). The place was subsequently retaken by the earl of Salisbury.

[696] Seine-et-Marne, arr. Provins, cant. Villiers-Saint-Georges, co. Louan-Villegruis-Fontaine. The siege lasted from the summer of 1423 well into 1424 (Lobanov, 'Anglo-Burgundian Military Cooperation', p. 98).

Pregent de Coëtivy[697] and Guillaume Bourgeois.[698] After the siege had lasted for about six months, the tower and castle were surrendered and delivered into the hands of the earl of Salisbury. Prégent de Coëtivy and Guillaume Bourgeois took an oath that they would never make war against the king and my lord the Regent in the area north of the River Loire. Based on this condition they departed. During the siege it so happened that the Bastard of Baume[699] and a man called *Caignart*, captains of Courcillon (Corcelles),[700] carried out a raid into the Mâconnais. By chance, Matthew Gough esquire and others of his company were in the field on their own venture and came across the Bastard of Baume and Caignart. Meeting each other, they engaged in a very bitter fight. This was a fine little action, and pretty hard going. At the end, the Bastard took flight. Seeing this, Matthew left all his company, and followed the Bastard alone right to Courcillon. When the Bastard realised that he could not seek safety inside that place, he abandoned his horse and went into the ditches in the hope of finding safety. Matthew Gough, however, got down from his horse and followed the Bastard. Despite the men inside Courcillon throwing stones and other things (50r) in a desire to save their captain, Matthew took the Bastard prisoner, leading him away with him. He then presented him to my lord the earl of Salisbury who was then at the siege of Fontaine-sous-Montaiguillon. In recognition of the bravery which Matthew Gough had shown, the earl gave him a fine courser with the full right of thirds[701]

---

[697] Prégent de Coëtivy (c. 1399–d. 1450), lord of Coëtivy, knight, councillor and chamberlain of the king, was a devoted supporter of Charles VII and a nephew of Tanguy du Chastel. His later career – he became admiral of France in 1439 – is well known but evidence for the earlier part of his career is thin (Anselme, vii, pp. 842–3). The *Religieux* (vi, pp. 460–2) describes him as a lieutenant-general for war of the Dauphin in Champagne in 1421 when he, along with Tugdal de Kermoysan, was besieged in the fortress of Montaiguillon; both were taken prisoner when the place was surrendered. The *Religieux* and M 9 are describing the same incident but dating it differently. Other chronicles and a legal suit suggest that M 9's dating is correct (AN X1a 4795, f. 5r; *English Suits*, pp. 148–9).

[698] Tugdual de Kermoysan (d. 1450), dit 'le Bourgeois' (called here Guillaume Bourgois), was a Breton, a Montfortist and an active supporter of Charles VII. He held Montivilliers with nine esquires under his command in 1416 (Morice, ii, p. 928). In 1420 he was given the responsibility by the duchess of Brittany to raise troops in France for the siege of Champtoceaux where Duke Jean V was held prisoner (Lobineau, *Histoire de Bretagne*, ii, p. 545). He was captain of Montaiguillon when it was besieged by Salisbury in 1423, and was taken prisoner with Prégent de Coëtivy when the place surrendered (see the previous note). He disappears from the sources until 1429 when he fought at Patay. He operated in the Ile-de-France between 1435 and 1439 under the command of the constable and took an active part in the reconquest of Normandy in the 1440s (Trévédy, *Les compagnons bretons de Jeanne d'Arc*, pp. 19–27).

[699] Guillaume, Bastard of la Baume, lord of La Charme, harassed the English besieging Montaiguillon but was captured as he was retreating to Châteaurenard (AN, X1a 4795, f. 5r). He was released on parole by Salisbury on the promise to obtain the surrender of the Châteaurenard, Charny and other fortresses, and to pay a large ransom, but considered himself quit from any obligation when his hostages, who were kept in captivity in Sens, managed to escape. See also *English Suits*, p. 148.

[700] Corcelles-en-Beaujolais, south of Mâcon (Rhône, arr. Villefranche-sur-Saône, cant. Belleville).

[701] An allusion to the contemporary sharing of war profits between king, captain and soldier on a thirds and thirds-of-thirds basis (Hay, 'Division of the Spoils of War').

which would have been his for the prisoner, as well as all the Bastard's inheritance. That was how Matthew's reputation for honour and bravery first started.

You have heard earlier how my lord of Bedford, the Regent, had negotiated a marriage between himself and Lady Anne of Burgundy, and how he went to the city of Troyes in order to finalise and confirm this marriage. During the time of his journey, Sir John de la Pole,[702] brother of the earl of Suffolk and the latter's lieutenant in the Basses Marches of Normandy and in the captaincy of Avranches,[703] assembled all of the garrisons of the Basses Marches to the number of around 2,000 soldiers and rode into Anjou towards the city of Angers,[704] and thence to the abbey of La Roë,[705] and to a nunnery where he stayed for three days. Then he returned to an unfortified town near the castle of La Gravelle,[706] all the time taking prisoners, animals and every other kind of booty he could find. Whilst there, the enemy arrived, to wit,

the count of Aumale[707]

the vicomte of Narbonne[708]

the lord of Laval[709]

---

[702] John de la Pole (post-1396–1429) may have begun his career in the garrison of Harfleur in 1416–17 (E 101/47/39; E 101/48/17). He crossed, now as a knight, with the army which accompanied the king in the summer of 1421 (E 101/50/1 m. 3; E 101/50/28 m. 10) and served in his brother's garrisons of Saint-Lô and Coutances from October 1422 (BNF, Fr. 25766/809; Fr 25767/1). On 30 July 1423 he was given power by Bedford to receive Mont-Saint-Michel into Henry VI's obedience (BNF, Fr. 26046/94, printed in Luce, i, no. xx). He was killed near Orléans on 10 June 1429 (*'Gregory's chronicle'*, p. 164).

[703] The earl of Suffolk was 'gardien du pays' of Coutances and Avranches, as well as of the castle and town of Saint-Lô and the town of Coutances from 10 October 1422 (BNF, Fr. 4485 p. 324), but was discharged from the captaincy of Avranches with effect from 10 December 1423 because he was occupied elsewhere (BNF, Fr. 26046/184).

[704] Maine-et-Loire, arr. Angers, ch. l. cant.

[705] An Augustinian house founded by Robert d'Abrissel in 1098, which lies in a village of the same name in the south-west of Mayenne, 33 km from Laval (Mayenne, arr. Château-Gontier, cant. Saint-Aignan-sur-Roë). The church and claustral buildings still survive.

[706] Mayenne, arr. Laval, cant. Loiron.

[707] The count of Aumale's command of the French troops which defeated John de la Pole at the battle of La Gravelle is widely reported (Berry, p. 113; Chartier, i, pp. 35–8; Monstrelet, iv, p. 146; 'Geste des nobles', p. 193; *Pucelle*, p. 215; Cagny, pp. 129–31).

[708] Guillaume de Lara, vicomte de Narbonne (d. 1424), an Orleanist and staunch supporter of Charles VII, was heavily involved in the war against the English (Anselme, vii, pp. 765–6). He commanded a ship in the attempt to recover Harfleur in 1416 and was in Paris in 1417 when the French capital was besieged by the Burgundians. He was captured in May 1418 but soon released. As a close councillor of the Dauphin, he signed the peace of Ponceau in July 1419 and was deemed responsible for the murder of Montereau at which he was present. He fought at Baugé in 1421 and was in command at the siege of Cosne in 1422, according to Berry (pp. 100 and 105). The 'Geste des nobles' (p. 193) is the only other chronicle to mention his participation at La Gravelle.

[709] It can reasonably be assumed that the person meant was Guy XIV de Laval (d. 1486), the elder brother of the lord of Lohéac. He served on Charles VII's coronation campaign: a letter describing his first encounter with Joan of Arc has survived. The lordship of Laval was elevated to a *comté* by Charles VII at his coronation (*Maison de Laval*, iii, pp. 212–44; *Jeanne. Dictionnaire*, p. 799). Chartier (i, p. 35) mentions Guy de Laval at La Gravelle, but *Pucelle* (p. 216) specifies that this is Guy de Laval, lord of Montjean.

the lord of Lohéac[710]
the lord of Champagne[711]
Jean d'Avaugour knight
Jean des Vaux knight[712]
the lord of Parc[713]
Guy de Champchevrier knight[714]
(50v) Ambroise de Loré knight[715]
Pierre le Porc knight[716]
Guillaume de Pontbriant knight[717]
Pierre d'Arquenay knight
the lord of Escotais
Baudouin de Champagne knight, lord of Tucé[718]
Antoine de Champagne knight, his brother
Hardouin de Mynedere knight[719]
Pierre Hérisson knight[720]

---

[710] André de Laval (1406–85), lord of Lohéac, admiral of France (1437–39) and marshal of France from 1439, was prominent in Charles VII's reconquest of Normandy and Aquitaine. According to *Pucelle* (pp. 215–16) the count of Aumale asked Anne, lady of Laval, to send her elder son to fight the English at La Brossinière (or La Gravelle), but curiously, this elder son is identified by the chronicler as André de Laval, lord of Lohéac. His presence at La Gravelle, where he seems to have been dubbed a knight, is also noted in Cagny (pp. 129–31) and Chartier (i, pp. 35–8). See also *Jeanne. Dictionnaire*, p. 799.

[711] Possibly Jean de Champagne, seigneur de Pescheseul.

[712] De Vaux's presence is possible but not evidenced elsewhere.

[713] The Breton house du Parc seems to be a cadet branch of the Avaugour. This may be Jean du Parc, knight, lord of la Motte-du-Parc, who served Duke Jean V in 1419 and 1420 (Allais, *Nobiliaire universel*, pp. 260–312, esp. p. 281).

[714] Possibly Guy de Champchevrier, lord of Soudé, an Angevin knight who appears in a letter from Henry VI to Charles VII, dated 3 February 1444 (o.s.) (Baudier, *An History of the Memorable and Extraordinary Calamities of Margaret of Anjou*, pp. 5–9). This letter which Baudier claimed had been provided to him by the auditor of the *chambre des comptes* in Paris has raised suspicion (Cron, 'The Champchevrier Portrait', pp. 321–7). Significantly, Guy de Champchevrier appears in the letter as a prisoner of war of Sir John Fastolf; he had broken his word and escaped his prison. Henry VI asked Charles VII to have him escorted back to England.

[715] The participation of Ambroise de Loré in the battle of La Gravelle is also noted in Chartier (i, p. 35) and *Pucelle* (i, p. 215).

[716] According to Alphonse Angot, there were two Pierre le Porcs (d. 1451) militarily active. The participant at La Gravelle, also noted in Monstrelet (iv, p. 146), was a Breton lord (his homonym was from Maine). He accompanied the duke of Brittany on his expedition to France in May 1418 and was governor of Fougères from 1427 to 1439. An aid of 2,000 *saluts d'or* was levied on the inhabitants of the *bailliage* of Caen and Cotentin to pay for the handing over to justice of Pierre le Porc 'chevalier, rebelle et adversaire du roi' in 1433 (Luce, ii, p. 16 no. 137; see also BNF, Fr. 25771/867; and *Dictionnaire historique, topographique et biographique de la Mayenne*, ii (angot.lamayenne.fr/).

[717] No man of this name has been discovered. There is possible confusion with Jean de Pontbriant.

[718] His presence at La Gravelle is not unlikely but there is no other evidence of it.

[719] This may be Hardouin de Mainbret.

[720] After the execution of her first husband, Jean de Montaigu, in 1412, Jacqueline de la Grange married Pierre Hérisson, knight, captain of Sablé in Maine (Breul, *Théatre des*

Louis de Trémagon knight[721]
Guy Turpin knight[722]
Jean de Loré knight[723]
Jean de Champigny knight
Robert de Chauvigny knight
the lord of la Feillée[724]
Guy d'Orenge knight[725]
Jean de la Rochière knight[726]
the lord of Juigné[727]
the lord of Juvigny
the lord of Bellay[728]
the lord of Fontaines[729]
the lord of Malicorne[730]
the lord of la Suze[731]

Antiquitez de Paris, p. 955). He was captured at the battle of Verneuil.

[721]   According to Chartier (i, p. 35) and *Pucelle* (p. 216) Louis de Trémagon and Amboise de Loré fought on horseback at the battle of La Gravelle.

[722]   Guy Turpin seems to have taken refuge in Flanders following the annulment of his union with Anne de Laval in 1417 (*Maison de Laval*, iii, pp. 17–20), which makes it unlikely that he was present at La Gravelle.

[723]   On 12 July 1434 Jean de Loré, knight, obtained a safe-conduct to go to Brittany (AN, KK 324 f. 79r).

[724]   Sylvestre, lord of la Feillée, was a councillor of Jean V, duke of Brittany, present at his council on multiple occasions between 1421 and 1433 (*Lettres et mandements de Jean V*, iii, p. 88, no. 1527, p. 98, no. 1546, p. 119, no. 1527, pp. 232–3, no. 1815; iv, p. 52, no. 2079). He supported the Montfort against the Penthièvre in 1420 (Morice, ii, p. 1060). In October 1424, he accompanied Richemont to his meeting with Charles VII at Angers (Morice, i, p. 1148). He was at the siege of Pouancé in 1432 (Jones, 'Comptes d'Auffroy Guinot', p. 84). His presence at La Gravelle is not unlikely but there is no other evidence of it.

[725]   Guy (or Gui) d'Orenge, lord of La Feuillée en Alexain (near Laval), appears as a vassal of the countess of Laval in 1413 (Bétencourt, *Noms féodaux*, p. 32). He married Alienor of Villeprouvée, in 1420 (Beauchesne, *Le château de la Roche-Talbot*, p. 284). He was active in Maine in 1434 (AN, KK 324 f. 74v).

[726]   A Breton lord, Jean de la Rochière appears in a list of recipients of New Year's gifts from Duke Jean V on 1 January 1434 (Jones, 'Comptes d'Auffroy Guinot', p. 96).

[727]   This may be Jean II le Clerc, esquire, lord of Juigné, who, according to La Chesnaye (xiii, pp. 296–7), defeated the English at Saint-Denis-d'Anjou in 1440.

[728]   His presence at La Gravelle is not unlikely but there is no other evidence of it.

[729]   This is presumably Jean, lord of Fontaines-Guérin, the same 'lord of Fontaines' who is described in the chronicle as chief captain of Le Mans in 1417, and who had the lord of Bellay and le Roncin as captains *particuliers*. The presence of the lord of Fontaines at the battle of La Gravelle is also noted in Monstrelet (iv, p. 146).

[730]   Antoine de Sourches (d. 1424), lord of Malicorne, a knight of Maine, died at Verneuil (Charles, 'L'invasion', p. 43; Viriville, *Histoire de Charles VII*, i, p. 418).

[731]   Jean de Craon (c. 1362–1432), lord of La Suze in Maine, was a close ally of the duke of Brittany and tutor of the infamous Gilles de Rais. He gave assistance to Duke Jean V when abducted and imprisoned by the Penthièvre, and was duly rewarded over the summer of 1420 with rights and lands confiscated from the plotters (Broussillon, *La Maison de Craon*, ii, pp. 106–7, nos. 914–17). He was among the negotiators for the release of Richemont in July

the lord of Champagne[732]
Louis le Gros knight[733]
Hue le Gros knight, his brother[734]
Guy de Laval knight[735]
the lord of Assé-le-Riboul
the lord of Averton and Belin
the lord of la Saugière
Jean le Voyer knight[736]
Jean le Bervier knight[737]
Pierre de Verruyes knight[738]
Jean de Beaurepaire knight[739]
Jean le Beauvoisien
Jean d'Avaugour
and several others to around 6,000 soldiers. Finding the English in disarray (51r),
they came down suddenly upon them, thereby bringing defeat and forcing them
to flee.[740] At this defeat were taken prisoner and killed lords, knights and esquires,
some of whose names follow, to wit,

Sir John de la Pole   }
John Basset[741]   } prisoners

1420 (ibid., p. 117, no. 918). Queen Yolande of Aragon made him lieutenant-general for war in the provinces of Anjou and Maine (Joubert, 'Le testament du Jean de Craon', p. 341).

[732] Named earlier in the same list.

[733] Louis le Gros, esquire, was the elder son and heir of Hue le Gros, knight, lord of Brestel, and Marie de Tucé (BNF, PO Tussé, no. 17265, cited in Leblanc, 'La Laire', pp. 22–4). He served in three different companies over that year: under the command of Jean de Bueil in February, Guillaume de Tucé in September and Louis de Clermont in November (Morice, ii, pp. 245, 256, 262).

[734] Hue le Gros (or le Groux), lord of Brestel, knight, was active in Maine in May 1434 (AN, KK 324 f. 58r).

[735] The participation of Guy de Laval, lord of Montjean, in the battle of La Brossinières is also reported in *Pucelle* (p. 216). He was apparently sent to the king in Orléans in the aftermath of the siege to join his army (Beauchesne, 'Jean des Vaux', p. 261).

[736] This Jean le Voyer may be the lord of Pescheray who is described as captain of Pescheray in 1417, but we might ask why he is not called lord of Pescheray here. The lord of Pescheray died at Verneuil (Ledru, *Le château de Sourches*, p. 81). A 'Jean de Vayer' is active in Maine in October 1433 and June 1434; on the earlier occasion he received permission to go to Pescheray, La Ferté, Sablé, Angers and La Guierche (AN, KK 324 ff. 10v and 71r).

[737] Unidentified unless Jean le Verrier, hostage for the duke of Alençon.

[738] This may be a member of the Verruyes family from Poitou. An act of the *Parlement* of Paris of 13 July 1377 mentions a Pierre de Verruyes (AN, X1C 35; *RDP*, v, p. 92 n. 2).

[739] A Jean de Beaurepaire, esquire, mustered at Rouen on 24 September 1415 in the retinue of Jean de Hareng, an esquire of the duke of Alençon (BNF, Clairambault 58/31). On 9 October 1417, Jean de Beaurepaire, together with six others residing in Sees, was given a safe-conduct to leave the place (C 64/8 m. 23, Hardy, p. 178). According to Chartier (i, p. 120), Jean de Beaurepaire died in an encounter with the English besieging the castle of Saint-Célerin (Maine) in April 1429. Whether these were one and the same person remains uncertain.

[740] This defeat is dated from chronicle evidence to 26 September 1423 (Beaucourt, ii, p. 14).

[741] Within the early years of the regency, a John Basset is found as a man-at-arms in the garrison of Pontoise in 1422 (E 101/50/19) and Rouen in 1426 (BL, Add. Ch. 1424), but there

John Offord, lieutenant of Falaise[742] }
Jean Affourd, marshal of Argentan }
[added: John Clifton knight][743]
and several others to the number of about 1,000 Englishmen.

In the winter following in the same year, 1423, Yvon du Puis,[744] *Girart de Lawe*[745] and Gauthier de Brusac,[746] esquires of the enemy party, assembled with their men and crossed over the River Loire. They rode the most covertly and secretly that they could, so much so that they came almost right up to the town of Compiègne[747] without any information about them being known at that place or in the surrounding area, and in such a way that one Friday morning when it was extremely foggy they took the town by surprise assault.[748] As soon as my lord the Regent heard

---

are also archers of this name in March 1423 under Andrew Ogard as captain of Vire (BL, Egerton Ch. 149) and March 1424 in the retinue of Richard Woodville as seneschal (BNF, NAF 20522/14).

[742] A Thomas Offord was lieutenant of Falaise from at least 12 March 1423 (BNF, Fr. 25767/33) and was still in post at Michaelmas 1424 (BNF, Fr. 4491 ff. 46r–46v). A John Affourd is found at Argentan in the early 1430s (for instance, BNF, Fr. 25769/533), being lieutenant to the earl of Salisbury's bastard son in 1431–32 (BL, Add. Ch. 182; BNF, Fr. 25770/728).

[743] Sir John Clifton (d. 1447) of Buckenham (Norfolk) had crossed as an esquire under Michael de la Pole senior, earl of Suffolk, in 1415 (E 101/46/24 m. 3) and as a knight under William de la Pole, earl of Suffolk, in 1417 (E 101/51/2 m. 13), implying that he was dubbed during the Agincourt campaign. In the army which accompanied the king again to France in the summer of 1421 he led a retinue of thirty-seven men (E 101/50/1 m. 3). On 28 September 1421 he was appointed captain of Vire (C 64/16 m. 22, DKR 42, p. 417), holding the post until March 1423 when replaced by Andrew Ogard (BL, Egerton Ch. 149), perhaps as a result of his capture. Worcester (*Itineraries*, p. 361) claims that he was lodged with William Bowet, Henry Inglose and various others at the siege of Rouen.

[744] Yvon du Puy (or Puis) was a captain retained by Charles VII's ordonnance of 1439, with Chartres as his garrison base (Escouchy, *Chronique*, iii, p. 9). He was by then a seasoned warrior, though not necessarily the most successful according to Monstrelet who describes his capture at Mons-en-Vimeu in 1421 (iv, p. 63), and at Verneuil in 1424 (iv, p. 196). He is also portrayed as twice defeated in the 1430s in encounters against Burgundians in Picardy in 1431 (v, p. 30) – he was then captain of Braine (AN, X1a, 78, f. 271r) – and Reims in 1435 (Monstrelet, v, p. 132). His capture of Compiègne in 1423, which he then held for a short while, contrasts with this string of failures. Monstrelet (iv, p. 174), Fénin (p. 219) and *Trahisons* (p. 176) also record Yvon du Puis's leading role in the surprise capture of Compiègne which was 'eschellée par faulte de guet'. See also Contamine, *GES*, pp. 269–71.

[745] An 'Angerot de Laux' is found in Monstrelet (iv, p. 174) and 'Ogelot du Lan (or Lau)' in Fénin (p. 219) but has not been identified.

[746] Gauthier Brusac (d. 1445) and his brother Mondot were in the service of Charles VII. 'Brusac' (though it is not clear which brother) received a horse from the king, and his men were paid 160 *écus* in 1428 (*Les La Trémoïlle*, i, pp. 141–2). Gauthier was in the French army gathered to raise the siege of Saint-Célerin in 1432 and participated in the capture of Dieppe in 1433 (Chartier, i, pp. 132, 140). He is described as 'écuyer d'écurie' and captain of Crépy-en-Valois on 9 June 1436 (BNF, PO 542 542, Brusac 2; *GR*, v, p. 424). He was sénéchal of Limousin between 1437 and 1439 (*RDP*, viii, p. 221 n. 1), and made his name at the same time as a 'chef de routiers' (*Cronique Martiniane*, p. 27 n. 1). Monstrelet (iv, p. 174) and Fénin (p. 219) also record his leading role in the surprise capture of Compiègne.

[747] Oise, ch. l. d'arr.

[748] The capture of Compiègne has been dated to 10 January 1424, which was a Tuesday (Beaucourt, ii, p. 14).

news of its capture he assembled an army in order to recover it, and laid siege to the town.[749] On one side of the river were the earl of Suffolk, the count of Ligny and several others, and on the other side, the lord of L'Isle-Adam, the *prévôt* of Paris,[750] Sir Thomas Gargrave, lieutenant at Rouen for the earl of Warwick who was its captain,[751] and several others. The enemy were strong within the town and had plenty of food, which threatened to make the siege last a long time. There was also fear that the enemy within might receive assistance from their own side. As a consequence, my lord the Regent had someone called Guillaume Remon (51v) dit Marjolaine esquire brought to him because he was the master and captain of the enemy who were in the town of Compiègne.[752] Remon had been taken prisoner at Passy by Sir John Fastolf. My lord the Regent had Remon put onto a cart and tied up there, with a rope around his neck so that he was ready to be hanged. Marjolaine was led in that state before the town and in full view of the enemy, with a declaration that if they did not surrender the town into the obedience of the king and the Regent, he would be hanged by the neck and thereby strangled to death. Because of the loyalty that they had to their captain who was in such danger of death and because of the love they had towards him, in addition to their belief that no aid would be coming, the enemy came to a composition and surrendered the town, on condition that Marjolaine might be delivered and they would leave freely with all their goods, horses, and equipment.

After the town of Compiègne had been recovered and conquered, as has been described, the Regent received frequent complaints of the horrible and limitless evil deeds and damage committed on a daily basis by the enemy occupying the castle of Ivry. He therefore assembled a new army and sent it to lay siege to Ivry, to wit,

the earl of Salisbury
the earl of Suffolk
Lord Willoughby[753]
Lord Scales
Lord Poynings[754]

---

[749] Compiègne had fallen to the Dauphin's supporters on 7 January 1424. The siege began in late February and the town surrendered on 13 April (BNF, Fr. 4485 p. 129).

[750] Simon Morhier (c. 1390–1450), a pro-Burgundian knight from the Chartrain, was appointed to this post by the duke of Bedford on 1 December 1422, holding it until the 1430s (Thompson, *Paris*, p. 68) and subsequently serving the English in Normandy as treasurer of the duchy. He had previously been master of the household of Queen Isabeau.

[751] The earl of Warwick was captain of Rouen from at least Michaelmas 1422 (BNF, Fr. 26044/5761), with Gargrave as lieutenant from at least 15 October 1422 (ADSM, 100J 33/3).

[752] Armstrong, 'Sir John Fastolf and the Law of Arms', from AN, JJ 175/66–7.

[753] Willoughby, Scales and Walter Hungerford were commissioned by Bedford to besiege Ivry as early as 17 September 1423 (BNF, PO 3050 Willeby 2). The earl of Suffolk, assisted by John Harpelay, *bailli* and captain of Evreux, and Sir Gilbert Halsall, captain of Dreux, was paid from 22 June 1424 for the siege of Ivry (BNF, Fr. 4485 pp. 292–4). The involvement of Salisbury is uncertain at this point.

[754] Robert, lord Poynings indented for the service of eighty men on 2 February 1424 for a thirty-day campaign to relieve Le Crotoy (E 404/40/155), and on 8 February for the six-month service of 240 men within an expeditionary army for France of 1,641 (E 101/71/2/11), many of whose troops joined with Bedford for the actions of the summer. Shipping records show Lord Poynings crossed from Sandwich to Calais in early June (E 403/666, under 8 June).

and many others with a notable army. They laid siege before the castle of Ivry, and maintained it for about six weeks.[755] During this time the enemy put together a large army in order to bring aid to the place. In this army were the princes and lords whose names follow, to wit,

the duke of Alençon chief and lieutenant-general[756]

the Bastard of Alençon, his uncle[757]

(52r) the count of Aumale[758]

the count of Ventadour[759]

the count of la Tonnerre[760]

the count of Maulévrier[761]

the count of Forez[762]

---

[755] The earl of Suffolk was paid from 22 June 1424 for the siege (BNF, Fr. 4485 pp. 292–4), but some garrison detachments had mustered there in mid-May, including troops from Pont-de-l'Arche (BNF, Fr. 25767/75).

[756] John II, duke of Alençon, was only 15 when he was captured at Verneuil and taken to Le Crotoy (BNF, Fr. 4485, ff. 433r and v). He led the operations at Verneuil, was taken prisoner (by Fastolf, it would seem, for which Bedford offered the latter 5,000 marks) and remained for three years in captivity, regaining his freedom in September 1427 in return for payment of a ransom of 200,000 *écus*, part of which was paid upon his release, and leaving twelve hostages behind as guarantee for the payment of the remainder (Le Cacheux, *Rouen*, pp. 127–30, no. 56; *Pucelle*, pp. 249–50; Cagny, pp. 136–7). According to *Pucelle* (p. 300), the ransom was paid and the hostages released by June 1429. Fastolf claimed that he never received from the duke of Bedford the full 5,000 marks due to him (*PL Gairdner*, iii, pp. 58–9; Smith, 'Aspects of the Career of Sir John Fastolf', p. 4).

[757] Pierre, Bastard of Alençon was the brother of Duke Jean II of Alençon, according to Anselme (i, p. 272), and not his uncle. His participation in the siege of Ivry and his capture at Verneuil are also mentioned in Monstrelet (iv, pp. 172, 196) and Chartier (i, p. 43). Pierre was wounded at Verneuil and left among the dead, similar to his brother, until they were both taken prisoner (Anselme, i, p. 272). The Bastard of Alençon also appears in Glover's list of prisoners taken at Verneuil in 1424 (BL, Harley 782, f. 51r, printed in *L&P*, II, ii, pp. 394–9). His name is also mentioned in a contract for the sale of the barony of Fougères to the duke of Brittany on 31 December 1428 (Anselme, i, p. 272).

[758] The participation and death of Jean de Harcourt, count of Aumale, at Verneuil are widely reported in chronicle accounts.

[759] The participation and death of Jacques, count of Ventadour, at Verneuil are widely reported in chronicle accounts.

[760] The death of Hugues de Chalon, count of Tonnerre, at the battle of Verneuil is widely reported in chronicle accounts, but not in M 9 (Monstrelet, iv, p. 195; Cagny, p. 135; *Pucelle*, p. 198).

[761] This reference is puzzling. Pierre II de Brézé (d. 1465), lord of la Varenne, who, at some point, became count of Maulévrier (to the north of Rouen), was apparently still under the tutelage of his mother in February 1435 (AN, X1a, 9190, f. 75; *RDP*, viii, p. 178 n. 2). His father, Pierre I de Brézé, lord of la Varenne, chamberlain of Charles VII, is likely to have been alive in 1423, but he did not bear the title of count of Maulévrier (Anselme, viii, p. 270). For Pierre II, who became grand sénéchal of Normandy, see Pierre Bernus, 'Essai sur la vie de Pierre de Brézé (vers 1410–1465)', pp. 7–17; Prosser, 'After the Reduction'; Contamine, 'A l'abordage'.

[762] Jean I, duke of Bourbon (1384–1434), was also count of Forez by inheritance from his mother but was still in captivity in England in 1424 following his capture at Agincourt.

the vicomte of Narbonne[763]
the lord of Graville
the lord of Gaules[764]
the lord of Malicorne[765]
the lord of Mauny[766]
the lord of Bellay[767]
the lord of Fontaines[768]
the lord of Montfort Lailleur
Louis de Harcourt knight, lord of Bonnétable[769]
the lord of Tucé[770]
the lord of Champaigney
the lord of Montjean and of Sillé-le-Guillaume[771]
the lord of la Suze[772]

---

[763] The participation and death of Guillaume Lara, vicomte of Narbonne, at Verneuil are widely reported. According to Monstrelet (iv, pp. 195–6), his body once found was quartered and hanged at the gallows because of Narbonne's involvement in the murder of John the Fearless.

[764] Pierre le Mornay, dit Gauluet, lord of Gaules, could not have participated at the battle of Verneuil as he died in May 1423.

[765] Antoine de Sourches, seigneur de Malicorne, a knight of Maine, died at Verneuil (Charles, 'L'invasion', p. 43; Viriville, *Histoire de Charles VII*, i, p. 418).

[766] This may be Guillaume Crespin, lord of Mauny and Bec-Crespin, who supported Charles VII in his wars against the English. His presence and death at Verneuil are not unlikely: Monstrelet (iv, p. 195) reports the death of a lord of Mauny at Verneuil. Jacqueline d'Auvrichier, Crespin's wife, was described as his widow in 1425 when she received a grant of 300 *l.* from the king (Anselme, vi, p. 635). Poli (p. cxxxvii) suggests that this lord of Mauny was Olivier de Mauny, lord of Thiéville.

[767] This may be Jean de Bellay whose participation and capture at Cravant are noted in Monstrelet (iv, p. 157), Berry (p. 112), and Tringant (*Jouvencel*, ii, p. 268) but not in the M 9 chronicle. He would have needed an early release from imprisonment, as the count of Ventadour, to be present in the French army heading to Verneuil. The du Bellay who died at Verneuil may be a sibling called Pierre du Bellay (Tringant, *Jouvencel*, ii, p. 268 n. 4). The 'sire du Bellay' also appears in Glover's list of prisoners taken at Verneuil in 1424 (BL, Harley 782, f. 51r, printed in *L&P*, II, ii, pp. 394–9).

[768] There is no other evidence of the participation of Jean, lord of Fontaine-Guérin in the battle of Verneuil, let alone of his death. He died in 1428 (Joubert, *Saint-Laurent des Mortiers*, pp. 346–7).

[769] Gérard de Harcourt, knight, baron of Bonnétable, died at either Agincourt or Verneuil (Anselme, v, pp. 139–40; Bouzy, 'Les morts d'Azincourt', p. 243). His son, Jean de Harcourt, knight, baron of Bonnétable, gave homage to Charles VII in 1449 for his barony of Beaufou and in 1450 for his barony of Tilly and lordship of Fontaine-le-Henry (Anselme, v, pp. 139–40).

[770] There is no other evidence of the presence of Bauduin de Champagne, lord of Tucé, at Verneuil.

[771] Jean II, lord Montjean, baron of Cholet and Sillé-le-Guillaume, appears as councillor and chamberlain of the Dauphin Louis (the future Louis XI) in 1447. He was the son of Jean I and Anne de Sillé, who married after the death of her first husband Jean de Craon, lord of la Suze, who appears next in the list (Anselme, vii, pp. 175–6).

[772] There is no other evidence of the presence of Jean de Craon, lord of la Suze, at Verneuil.

the lord of Amboise[773]
the lord of Beaumesnil[774]
the lord of Auzebosc[775]
the lord of Moyon[776]
the baron of Coulonces[777]
the baron of Biards[778]
Jean de Tollevast knight[779]
Jean de Villiers knight[780]
Nicole Paynel knight
Jacques Paynel knight, his brother

---

[773]   The lordship of Amboise was under the direct suzerainty of Charles VII at that time. The chronicle is probably referring to Louis d'Amboise (d. 1469), vicomte of Thouars, who succeeded his uncle in 1422, and who is better known for his intrigues at the court of Charles VII in 1429–30 (Peyronnet, 'Les complots de Louis d'Amboise', pp. 115–35). There is no other evidence of his participation in the battle of Verneuil, let alone of his death there.

[774]   Jean II de Tournebu, lord of Marbeuf and Beaumesnil, was the elder son of Guillaume de Tournebu who died at Agincourt. He stood as hostage for the payment of the ransom of the duke of Alençon in 1427–29 (Le Cacheux, *Rouen*, pp. 127–30, no. 56). This may imply that he fought at Verneuil. Anselme (vi, p. 740) and Fierville ('Histoire généalogique de la maison et de la baronnie de Tournebu', at pp. 326–7) confuse father and son.

[775]   There is no other evidence of the presence of Louis d'Estouteville, lord of Auzebosc, at Verneuil.

[776]   The lordship of Moyon was in the possession of Jeanne Paynel after the death of Nicole Paynel, her father, in 1414. In 1419, as we have seen, Jeanne married Louis d'Estouteville, lord of Auzebosc. It is likely, therefore, that the chronicle is referring twice to the same man. This doubling of names in direct succession occurs elsewhere in the chronicle, as in the case of the lord of Amboise and the vicomte of Thouars.

[777]   It is relevant to note that the chronicle overlooks the participation of Jean de la Haye, baron de Coulonces, at the earlier battle of La Gravelle, despite his presence being noted by Monstrelet (iv, p. 146), lengthily commented on by Chartier (i, pp. 35–7) and *Pucelle* (pp. 215–17) because of existing tensions between Aumale and Coulonces, and celebrated by Berry (p. 113) who gave him full credit for the victory: 'le baron de Coulonches s'i porta si vaillanment et fut a cheval par derriere sus les Englois; ce qui fut cause de gangner la bataille'. According to the same source (p. 117), Coulonces, who was present at the battle of Verneuil, commanded the right wing of mounted troops. The *Chroniques de Normandie* (pp. 72–3), which also make no mention of Coulonces at La Gravelle, report divisions between Coulonces and the duke of Alençon 'pour avoir l'onneur' at the battle of Verneuil, which resulted in Coulonces stepping aside during the battle and leaving the field when it turned out badly for the French.

[778]   There is no other evidence of the presence of Guillaume le Soterel, baron des Biards, at Verneuil.

[779]   The brothers Tollevast must have lost their father during the English invasion of Normandy or else not long before. Jean de Tollevast, esquire, the elder, together with at least two of his brothers, was absent from the duchy on 21 March 1419 when Henry V granted to Robin de Tollevast, esquire, another brother, who had remained in the duchy under English rule, his portion of the inheritance from their late father (C 64/11 m. 71, DKR 41, p. 768). There is later evidence of a Jean de Tollevast, knight, in Maine in November 1433 (AN, KK 324 f. 19r).

[780]   Jean de Villiers, esquire, appears as a vassal of the countess of Laval in 1413 (Bétencourt, *Noms féodaux*, p. 32). Provided it is the same person, Jean de Villiers later stood hostage for the payment of the ransom of the duke of Alençon in 1427–29 (Le Cacheux, *Rouen*, pp. 127–30, no. 56).

Jean d'Onnebaut knight
Henri de Tilly knight[781]
Louis de Braquemont knight[782]
Jean de Tournebeuf knight[783]
Gauvain de la Haye knight[784]
Jean Pigache knight[785]
Rigault de Fontaines knight
Robert de Dreux knight[786]
(52v) *Olivier de Milanc knight, lord of Saint-Célerin*[787]
Coquart de Cambron knight[788]
Pierre le Beauvoisien knight
Pierre de Bereville knight
Jean de Bourgneuf knight
Grognet de Vassé knight[789]
the lord of Escotais
Pierre d'Arquenay knight

---

[781] This may be Henri de Tilly who with his wife Jeanne Bouterie sold the *vicomté* of Maisnières to the abbey of Corbie in 1424 ('Archives de l'abbaye de Corbie, Trésor généalogique de D. Villevielle, vol. 54', as cited in Belleval, *Mémoire sur les comtes de Ponthieu*, p. 14).

[782] Louis de Braquemont's presence at Verneuil is noted in Monstrelet (iv, p. 196), who, unlike the M 9 chronicle, included him among the dead.

[783] There is no other evidence of the presence and capture of Jean de Tournebeuf, lord of Couronne, at Verneuil.

[784] Gauvain de la Haye, esquire, appears among fifty-one esquires in the company of Loivier de Mauny, knight banneret, at Sours, near Chartres, on 4 July 1421 (Morice, ii, p. 1086).

[785] Jean Pigache, esquire, mustered at Rouen on 23 September 1415 (BNF, Clairambault 69/54). The lordship of Bouceel in the *vicomté* of Avranches was confiscated from Jean and André Pigache, rebels, and granted to William Glasdale in 1420 (*Extrait du registre des dons*, p. 151). On 12 August 1422, Henry V handed back to Olivier de Mehubert and Robine, his wife, the fief of Bouceel which had been unlawfully detained for forty years by Jean Pigache, Pierre Pigache, Guillaume and Nicolas de Verdun, described as rebels (C 64/17 m. 8, DKR 42, p. 445). Jean Pigache, esquire, joined the garrison of Mont-Saint-Michel where he mustered in the company of Nicole Paynel on 1 May 1421 (Luce, i, p. 112, and n. 4).

[786] Robert de Dreux (d. 1478), lord of Beaussart, vidame and baron of Esneval, lost his father Gauvain de Dreux at Agincourt. Robert de Dreux was still a minor at the death of his mother in 1421 (C 64/16 m. 14, DKR 42, p. 421). See also Anselme, i, p. 212. For his later life and career, see Prosser, 'Affinity'.

[787] Unidentified. A Louis de Meullent, lord of Saint-Célerin, is described as a knight banneret in 1387 (Anselme, ii, p. 407). Olivier is presumably a member of the same family.

[788] Coquart de Cambron, knight, is one of nine named 'familliers et obbeissans de hault noble et puissant prince' the duke of Alençon who guaranteed to the twelve hostages for the duke of Alençon to do their utmost for the fulfilment of the ransom agreement (Le Cacheux, *Rouen*, pp. 127–30, no. 56).

[789] Jean II, alias Grognet de Vassé, lord of Sourches, was still a minor at the death of his father in the second half of 1423 (Ledru, *Le château de Sourches*, pp. 325–6). He spent part of his youth at the court of Jean II, duke of Alençon. In April 1434, he had safe-conducts to go to Laval, Château-Gontier, Sainte-Suzanne and Le Mans (AN, KK 324 f. 174). See also Ledru, *Le château de Sourches*, pp. 82–96.

Robert de Feschal knight[790]
Olivier de Feschal knight[791]
Guy d'Orenge knight
Guillaume d'Orenge knight
Ambroise de Loré knight
Guy de Champchevrier knight
Antoine de Champagne knight[792]
Samson de Sens knight[793]
Robert d'Aungne knight
the lord of la Rochebouet[794]
Guillaume de Mauny knight
the lord of Pont-Bellengier[795]
Guillaume de la Mote knight
Jean de Thévalle knight[796]
Ambroise de Gaigné knight[797]
Guillaume de Verdell knight

---

[790] On 9 July 1434, Guillaume de Boiffroult, a prisoner in Domfront, and Robert de Feschal paid six *saluts* to the English for a three-month safe-conduct to travel into enemy territory with three men and three women in their company (AN, KK 324 f. 75v).

[791] Olivier de Feschal (d. c. 1465), knight, was a loyal supporter of Charles VII. He served him as Dauphin at the siege of Bourges with 160 men-at-arms on 4 February 1418 (Morice, ii, p. 987). He mustered with a larger retinue of 300 men-at-arms and 100 archers at Melun on 12 July 1419 (Morice, ii, p. 989). He was present at Orléans when the siege was lifted in May 1429 and became governor of Laval in 1430, succeeding Lancelot Frézeau. As captain of Laval he received several safe-conducts in Maine to cross English-obedient territories in 1434 (AN, KK 324 ff. 61r, 142r, 144v). He was appointed as a commissioner for the truce in Anjou and Maine negotiated between deputies of Jean, duke of Alençon and Charles d'Anjou, on the one side, and Edmund Beaufort, earl of Dorset, on the other, on 20 December 1438 (Joubert, *Documents*, pp. 31–8, no. 17). See also Angot, *Dictionnaire historique, topographique et biographique de la Mayenne*, ii: art. Feschal (Olivier de).

[792] Presented on f. 50r as a brother of Baudouin de Champagne, lord of Tucé.

[793] Samson de Sens (or Cens) (d. 1475), knight, was provided with a safe-conduct to go outside the English obedience in Maine for hunting in January 1434 (AN, KK 324 f. 163r). He appears as a knight and lord of la Rochebouet (Maine) when negotiating rents and properties in Parigné with the bishop of Le Mans in an act dated 22 March 1453 (Le Paige, *Dictionnaire topographique*, ii, p. 452). He died in 1475 and was buried in the church of the abbey of Chalocé (collecta.fr/image.php?id=13644).

[794] Samson de Sens seems to have been the lord of la Rochebouet. This appears to be yet another case of M 9 mentioning twice the same individual under two different names (using patronym and toponym).

[795] This may be Guillaume du Pont-Bellengier (Pont-Bellenger in Calvados) whom we find in Maine provided with three safe-conducts issued between October and December 1434 (KK 324 ff. 144v, 147r, 150r).

[796] Jean de Thévalle, lord of Thévalle, knight, obtained two safe-conducts from the English to circulate in Maine in July and October 1434 (AN, KK 324 ff. 81v and 142v). See also Angot, *Dictionnaire historique, topographique et biographique de la Mayenne*, iii: art. Thévalle.

[797] Ambroise de Gaigné, knight, obtained a safe-conduct for a duration of eight days to go outside the English obedience for hunting in Maine in October 1434 (AN, KK 324 f. 145r). He appears as lord des Vallées and Saint-Denis in 'déclarations censuelles' made to him in 1450 and 1453 (*Archives du Cogner*, p. 255).

Hue le Gros knight
Guillaume de Montahier knight
Jean des Vaux knight
Jean Odart knight[798]
Jean de la Rochière knight
Pierre de Beauvau knight[799]
Jean Quatrebarbes
Jean le Verrier knight[800]
Robert de Boiscornu knight
Jacques de Mathefelon knight[801]
Pierre le Voyer knight, lord of Bellay[802]
Hardouyn de Myndiere knight[803]
the lord of Averton[804]
the lord of Assé-le-Riboul
(53r) the lord of Pescheray[805]
Jean de Villeprouvée knight[806]
Jacques de Scépeaux knight[807]
Galois d'Achy
Jean de Beaurepaire knight
Guillaume Bellengier knight[808]

[798] Jean Odart, knight, lord of Chandoiseau and la Varenne, councillor and chamberlain of Charles VII, served under the constable Albret in the wars in Gascony against the English in 1405. In June 1423, a man of this name, who was still alive in 1461, made a donation to the abbey of Bourgueil for the remembrance of his late wife, Isabeau Mangé, and daughter, Isabelle (Busserolle, *Archives des familles nobles de la Touraine, de l'Anjou, du Maine et du Poitou*, i, pp. 240–1). A Sir Jean Oudart, knight, received a safe-conduct to go outside the English obedience in Maine in April 1434 (AN, KK 324 f. 51r). He had a long life, if indeed this was one and the same person.

[799] Pierre de Beauvau seems to be in Calabria in 1424.

[800] This may be Jean le Verrier, knight, who stood as hostage for the payment of the ransom of the duke of Alençon in 1427–29 (Le Cacheux, *Rouen*, pp. 127–30, no. 56).

[801] Jacques de Mathefelon, lord of Lancheneil, died at Verneuil, according to Angot, *Dictionnaire historique, topographique et biographique de la Mayenne*, ii: art. Mathefelon.

[802] Pierre le Voyer obtained two safe-conducts to go outside the English obedience in Maine between October and December 1434 (AN, KK 324 ff. 142v, 152v).

[803] This may be Hardouin de Mimbret, who stood as hostage for the duke of Alençon.

[804] This may be either Payen I d'Averton, lord of Belin, or Jean d'Averton, yet both of them were alive after Verneuil and there is no other evidence of their presence at Verneuil.

[805] Jean IV le Vayer, lord of Pescheray, died at Verneuil on 17 August 1424, leaving as heir his brother Patry (BNF, Fr. 22610 f. 191; Ledru, *Le château de Sourches*, p. 81).

[806] Jean de Villeprouvée, esquire, lord of Villeprouvée, made his will on 4 August 1424 (BNF, Duchesne, 56, f. 59 sq) and died at the battle of Verneuil (Achon, 'Les seigneurs de Courceriers', pp. 22–5).

[807] Jacques de Scépeaux, knight, obtained several safe-conducts to circulate in English-obedient Maine in 1434 (AN, KK 324 ff. 142r, 143v, 148v).

[808] On 2 August 1434, Guillaume Bellengier paid one *salut* for a three-month *congé* from Maine (AN, KK 324 f. 89r). A Guillaume Bellenger appears as a liegeman of Baudouin de Tucé in 1453 (ADS, E 114 (online), cited in Robveille and Froger, 'La communauté d'habitants de Pont-de-Gennes', p. 396).

Robert de Freulay knight
Guillaume de Chauvigné knight[809]
Pierre le Porc knight
Robert de Montchauvel knight
the lord de la Marvaille knight
Lancelot Goyon knight, baron of Brittany[810]   }
Jean de Chauvigné lord of la Montaigne[811]   }
Jean de Tournemine knight[812]   }
Jean de Pontbriand knight[813]   }
Jean Giffart knight[814]   }
Jean Girart knight[815]   }

---

[809] Guillaume de Chauvigné appears in a letter addressed by the nobility of the barony of Craon to their lord, Georges de la Trémoille, on 14 May 1428, by which they committed to pay him 1,200 *écus* if he could secure a truce or abstinence of war with the English which would protect them from plundering and depredations (Joubert, *Histoire de la baronnie de Craon*, pp. 338–40).

[810] Probably Lancelot Goyon, lord of Lude and la Roche-Goyon, who mustered as an esquire banneret in the company of Pierre de Rochefort, marshal of France, at Bourges in June 1418 (Morice, ii, p. 961). He commanded 100 men-at-arms at Gien-sur-Loire to serve the Dauphin in March 1419 (Lobineau, *Histoire de Bretagne*, ii, p. 912; Morice, ii, p. 965). He was chamberlain of Duke Jean V in 1421 (Morice, ii, p. 1084) and was in the company of the duke on his journey to Amiens. See also Anselme, v, p. 380.

[811] Unless there is confusion with Jean de Champagné, knight, lord of la Montagne, who was listed as at Baugé, this is surely Jean de Chauvigné, esquire, lord of Chauvigné-en-Craonnais, who acted as lieutenant of Pierre de Beauvau during the latter's captaincy of Mayenne (1446–53) (Beauchesne, *Pierre de Beauvau*, pp. 120, 128; Bellier, 'Les seigneurs du Boisfroust', pp. 23–47).

[812] This could be either Jean II de Tournemine, lord of la Hunaudaye (d. 1427), who was listed at Baugé, or Jean de Tournemine, lord of Barrach (d. 1440), who joined the royal forces with sixteen esquires in March 1419 (Morice, ii, p. 984). He was newly retained by Duke Jean V in 1420, and acted as captain of Ile de Ré for the constable in June 1432 (Jones, 'Comptes d'Auffroy Guinot', p. 65). See also Torchet, *Reformation des Fouages de 1426*, p. 408.

[813] Jean de Pontbriand, lord of Pontbriant (inheriting from his father in 1437), described as a rebel in May 1418, had his estates within the *comté* of Avranches confiscated by Henry V and redistributed to Thomas Whiteney (C 64/11 m. 62, DKR 41, p. 773). He defended Mont-Saint-Michel in 1427, being captured during a sally, perhaps the battle of la Gueintre in April 1427. He was taken prisoner a second time by the English of Tombelaine in 1435 (Poli, p. cxlvii and preuves nos. 1038, 1124 and 1216; Lainé, *Archives généalogiques*, i, pp. 2–4).

[814] Jean Giffart, knight, lord of Plessis-Giffart and Fail, fought under the banner of Richemont at Agincourt where he was also captured (Gruel, p. 18). Jean V, duke of Brittany, made him his chamberlain in May 1421 (*Lettres et mandements de Jean V*, iii, p. 68, no. 1492; Morice, ii, p. 1084). In October 1424, a few months after Verneuil, Duke Jean gave his chamberlain a protection against all legal suits whilst absent in France with Richemont (*Lettres et mandements de Jean V*, iii, p. 133, no. 1595).

[815] Jean Girart, esquire, mustered at La Charité-sur-Loire in the company of the Bastard of Ivry in June 1422 (Morice, ii, p. 1124). He was apparently with Richemont when the latter seized Pontorson for Charles VII in February 1426 (BNF, Fr. 20684 f. 48v), and defended Montargis in 1427 (BNF, Fr. 35210 f. 58v). We find him in Orléans in 1429 and subsequently in the coronation expedition (ibid., f. 60v). He was captain of Chablis in 1432 when he was captured by Perrinet Gressart (ACO, B 11917). He was paid 200 *francs* for his service to

Henri de Puscalec knight[816]   } Bretons
Pierres Boterel knight   }
Jean Testenowe knight   }
the Bastard of Beaumanoir[817]   }
Olivier le Forestier   }
Pierre le Forestier[818]   }
the lord of Grippon[819]
Aymeric d'Anthenaise[820]
Pierre d'Anthenaise
Foulquet Pezas[821]
Guyon du Coing
Jannequin Kend[822]

Charles VII in Maine and Anjou in 1435 (*Les La Trémoïlle*, i, p. 208). See also Planchenault, 'La conquête' (1925), p. 16 and n. 4, 5; Bossuat, *Perrinet Gressart*, p. 170 n. 4.

[816] In 1418, Henri de Puscalec accompanied Jean V, duke of Brittany, in his voyage to France (Morice, ii, p. 967). He was also serving Dauphin Charles at that time as one of his 'écuyers d'écurie'. He lent much money to the Dauphin for the transport of the Scottich army to France and was granted, as a guarantee for repayment, the lordship of Taillebourg and Chastelaillon in 1421 (Morice, ii, p. 1089), and acted as negotiator with the Scottish in 1422. He was governor of La Rochelle in 1420 but was relieved of this office in 1426 (Delayant, 'Le procès des frères Plusquellec', pp. 217–51; Beaucourt, i, pp. 351, 406).

[817] Geoffroy, Bastard of Beaumanoir, Breton, is known to have been active in the 1430s. He received a safe-conduct to go to the (Valois-obedient) place of Beaumont on 16 February 1434 (AN, KK 324 f. 38r). He was paid for his service against the English in Maine and Anjou as captain of Château-du-Loir for Charles VII in 1435 (*Les La Trémoïlle*, i, p. 207). He fought in Brie in the company of Xaintrailles and Gaucourt in 1437 (Monstrelet, iii, p. 346). Two years later, he was retained by Charles VII's ordonnance of 1439 and placed in La Gravelle, together with Jean Girart and the Bastard of Sorbier (Beaucourt, iii, p. 411). Finally, in 1453, we find him serving the count of Clermont in Gascony (Monstrelet, v, p. 293; Beaucourt, v, pp. 268–9).

[818] Pierre le Forestier, Olivier's brother, was captured at the battle of Verneuil, taken to Alençon and put to ransom (AN, X1a 9201, f. 94v).

[819] Raoul Tesson, lord of Grippon (1422), was on the English side at that time.

[820] Aymeric d'Anthenaise participated in the battle of Verneuil and was taken prisoner by Fastolf. The sum for his ransom which was fixed at 2,800 *vieux écus d'or* was loaned by his brother Pierre (Bonneserre de Saint-Denis, *Notice historique*, p. 37).

[821] Foulquet Pezas (from Maine) and a 'Jannequin' or 'Rennequin' were captains of the castle of Montmirail (arr. Mamers) for the duke of Burgundy when the place surrendered to the army of the Dauphin in June 1421 (*Religieux*, vi, pp. 461–2; Des Ursins, p. 569). The two men are said to have changed allegiances on that occasion (see also Charles, 'L'invasion', p. 31). On 19 July 1433 he received a safe-conduct from the English for himself and three men in his company to go to various places in Maine including La Guierche and Montmirail (AN, KK 324 f. 83r).

[822] Jannequin (Jehanequin, Jehennekin, Jennekin or Jannekyn) Kend esquire operated in Maine. The proximity between the names in this list suggests that he was Foulquet Pezas's joint captain of Montmirail designated merely as 'Jannequin' or 'Rennequin' in chronicles. Kend appears as captain of La Guierche in November 1433 (AN, KK 324 ff. 14v, 16r), and may have received a visit from Pezas earlier that year. Jannequin was the recipient of no fewer than seven safe-conducts between November 1433 and April 1434 to circulate in Maine outside the

Huet de Fontenay[823]
Michel Tailleuer
Hue de Chanay
Charles de Villiers[824]
La Manne
Fouquet de Coulonges[825]
Guillaume de Landereposte[826]
(53v) and many other knights, esquires and other soldiers up to a total of about 40,000 men. As soon as news came to my lord the Regent, he assembled all he reasonably could, both English and Normans,[827] and went off to the siege in order to reinforce it. When the enemy heard the news that the Regent was present at the siege in person, they did not dare go there but took themselves off to Verneuil-sur-Avre in Perche. This town surrendered to them immediately. When the enemy inside the castle of Ivry saw that help to them had failed and that they had nothing more to eat, they came to a composition, surrendering the castle to the king and my lord the Regent and leaving the place.[828] My lord the Regent placed keepers into the castle. With all his host, in which were, to wit,[829]
my lord the earl of Salisbury
Lord Willoughby

English obedience (AN, KK 324 ff. 16r, 29v, 32vo, 34r, 46v, 52r). He was paid 300 *écus* for his service to Charles VII in Maine and Anjou in 1435 (*Les La Trémoïlle*, i, p. 208).

[823] Huet de Fontenay stood as hostage for the payment of the ransom of the duke of Alençon in September 1427 and 1429 (Le Cacheux, *Rouen*, pp. 127–30, no. 56). According to *Pucelle* (p. 300), the ransom was paid and the hostages released by June 1429.

[824] Charles de Villiers received a safe-conduct to go outside the English obedience in Maine in October 1434 (AN, KK 324 f. 143r).

[825] Fouquet de Coulonges was a man-at-arms in the garrison of La Mayenne under the captaincy of Jean des Vaux (1417–23). The heirs of des Vaux and Coulonges were engaged in a legal suit before the *Parlement* of Paris over the ransom of an English prisoner, John Clifton, captured by Foulquet and worth 4,000 *l.t.* At stake was the payment of a tenth of this ransom which, according to the usages of war, should devolve to the captain (AN, X1a 84, arrêt du 8 mars 1454; Beauchesne, 'Jean des Vaux', p. 238). We know that Clifton was captured at the battle of Formigny in 1450, and was bound to pay 800 marks for his ransom (C 81/1546/78; Jones, 'Ransom Brokerage', p. 223), but des Vaux probably died around 1430 (Beauchesne, 'Jean des Vaux', p. 272).

[826] Landreposte, or Lande-Poutre, was based in La Mayenne and was active in Maine in 1434 (AN, KK 324 f. 148r). We also find a Gervaise Landreposte in the same area. See also Ledru, *Le château de Sourches*, p. 99.

[827] A *semonce des nobles* was issued in Normandy on 8 May, with troops finally being ordered to assemble at Vernon by 3 July for service under Bedford against the enemy attempting to raise the siege of Ivry (BNF, Fr. 26047/257; BNF, NAF 7626/232; AN, K 62/12; Luce, i, no. xxvi; *L&P*, II, i, pp. 24–8).

[828] The place agreed to surrender on 15 August 1424 if not relieved, and ten hostages were handed to the earl of Suffolk as guarantee (BNF, Fr. 4485 p. 436). Ivry was surrendered to the earl of Suffolk on that day (BNF, Fr. 4491 f. 40).

[829] Pay to Bedford's army for the *journée* is detailed in BNF, Fr. 4485 pp. 296–306. Of those in the chronicle's list, Salisbury, Reginald Grey, Fastolf, Salvain, Halsall, Blount, Harling, Harpelay, Merbury, Burgh, Montgomery, Butler, Guethin, Robessart, Burdet and Minors are noted in the account, but there are others paid who are not mentioned here, such as the earl of Suffolk, Andrew Ogard and Richard Woodville senior.

Lord Scales
Lord Poynings who was ill
Sir John Grey
Sir Reginald Grey of Ruthin brothers
Sir John Fastolf
[added: Sir John [cancelled: salvyan] Salvain *bailli* of Rouen][830]
Sir Lancelot de Lisle[831]
Sir John Pashley
Sir Gilbert Halsall
Sir John Grey of Northumberland[832]
Sir Thomas Blount[833]
Sir Robert Harling
Sir William Oldhall[834]
Sir John Harpelay[835]
Sir Alan Buxhill[836]

---

[830] Salvain (from Yorks. ER) crossed in the army from England brought by the duke of Bedford in 1420 (E 101/49/36 m. 1), and had a long career in military service in France. He was *bailli* of Rouen from at least Michaelmas 1423 (BNF, Fr. 4485 pp. 220–1), retaining this office to at least 1448, and knight by at least the winter of 1424, probably being dubbed at Verneuil.

[831] On 1 July 1424 Lisle had been in command of the earl of Salisbury's retinue as governor of Champagne and Brie (BL, Add. Ch. 11520).

[832] If this is meant to be Sir John Grey of Heton it is an error since the latter was killed at Baugé, leaving a son who was a minor.

[833] Thomas Blount (c. 1383–1456) of Barton Blount (Derbys.) crossed in the troops led by the duke of Bedford in the spring of 1420 (E 101/49/36 m. 6) but was back in England to serve in parliament at the end of the year. He crossed again in the summer of 1423 (C 76/106 m. 15, DKR 48, p. 224), and soon became captain of Saint-Lô, holding office to 1425 (BNF, Fr. 4485 pp. 190–2). He had been knighted by the time of the battle of Verneuil (HOCa).

[834] Oldhall had crossed in the expeditionary army of the summer of 1424 with 180 men (E 404/40/188).

[835] Harpelay, who hailed from Dorset, served as a man-at-arms in the garrison of Harfleur in 1416 (E 101/47/39), in the army which the duke of Bedford brought to France in 1420 (E 101/50/28 mm. 2d and 4d) and in that which accompanied the king back to France in 1421 (E 101/50/28 mm. 6 and 7), and in the garrison of Rouen in 1422 (E 101/50/22). He became captain and *bailli* of Evreux in October 1422, holding office to 1425 (BNF, PO 1487 Harpelay 2; BL, Add. Ch. 1419). He was probably knighted at Verneuil since he was certainly a knight by February 1425 when serving in the conquest of Maine (AN, K 62/11/19).

[836] Buxhill (1382–after 1436) was the posthumous son of Sir Alan Buxhill (d. 1381), who had been prominent in the fourteenth-century French wars, and his second wife, Maud Francis. His mother subsequently married John Montague, third earl of Salisbury (d. 1400). Hence Alan was the elder half-brother of Thomas Montague, earl of Salisbury (d. 1428). His military career was underway by 1414 when, already a knight, he was serving in the Calais march (C 76/96 m. 13, DKR 44, p. 550). Any service on the 1415 expedition has not been identified, but he served in the 1416 rescue of Harfleur in the retinue of the earl of Salisbury (C 76/99 m. 25, DKR 44, p. 580). In 1417 he was in the retinue of the Earl Marshal (E 101/51/2 m. 27; C 76/100 m. 23, DKR 44, p. 590), and was active in the conquest of Normandy, being granted the lordship of Clinchamp in April 1419 (C 64/11 m. 68, DKR 41, p. 770), a title he certainly used (*English Suits*, VIII). He was appointed captain

Sir John Arthur
Sir Richard Merbury
Sir Thomas Gargrave
Thomas Burgh [added: an esquire valiant in arms][837]
William Glasdale[838]
Matthew Gough [added: captured as a prisoner in the pursuit, taken to a town in Perche but then surrendered with the town]
John Banaster
(54r) Rys ap Madoc
Richard Waller
John Burgh
Sir Philip Branche[839]
Sir John Montgomery[840]

---

of Château-Gaillard in April 1421 (C 64/16 m. 41, DKR 42, p. 410) and was captain of Fresnay-le-Vicomte by June 1422 (C 64/17 m. 19, DKR 42, p. 442) but was replaced by Fastolf in September. We find him briefly as captain of Mantes in December 1422 (BNF, PO 483 Buxhill 2) but he probably returned briefly to England since he took out letters of attorney in November 1423 in the retinue of Bedford (C 76/106 m. 10, DKR 48, p. 227).

[837] Burgh was indeed active and mobile, and appears many times in the records. In addition to his captaincy of Avranches (1423–29), he also served as captain of Pontorson in October 1423 (*Actes*, i, p. 400), Ardevon in September 1424, linked to the siege newly laid to Mont-Saint-Michel (BNF, Fr. 25767/95), Tombelaine, an island close to the Mont, from at least 1427 to 1429 (BNF, Fr. 25768/250, 415), and as lieutenant of Domfront in October 1428 (BNF, Fr. 26051/970). He participated in the siege of Pontorson in 1427 (BNF, Fr. 25767/211; BL, Add. Ch. 11573), and was marshal of the host at the siege of Château-Gaillard in 1430 (BNF, Fr. 26053/1350). He was then expected to join the Burgundians for the siege of Compiègne in 1430 but other forces were sent as he was still busy before Château-Gaillard (ADN, B 302/15576). (We are grateful to Dr Lobanov for this reference.) We find him in 1430 as captain of Fresnay (BL, Add. Ch. 11748) and of Exmes from 1431 to his death on 12 February 1433 (BNF, Clairambault 144/104; Motey, 'La ville d'Exmes', p. 121).

[838] At the time of the battle of Verneuil Glasdale was probably *bailli* of Alençon.

[839] Branche (d. 1427), of Fleet (Lincs.), was a knight by 1401 and had married Fastolf's half-sister Margaret. In November 1408 he had letters of protection for service in Ireland in the retinue of Prince Thomas (CPR 1408–13, p. 41), as did Fastolf. Branche served in Clarence's company in 1415 (E 101/45/4 m. 2) and probably also in 1417. His activity in Normandy can be seen in the Norman rolls. According to William Worcester (*Itineraries*, p. 361) he shared lodgings at the siege of Rouen with William Bowet, Henry Inglose and others. In the years leading up to the battle of Verneuil we see him as captain and *bailli* of Mantes and captain of Saint-Germain-en-Laye (BNF, PO 492 Branche 2 and 3), but he suffered a defeat near Mortagne when leading a force against French incursions in December 1422 (*Actes*, ii, pp. 361–2; *Religieux*, vi, pp. 476–9; Chartier, i, pp. 16–18).

[840] Sir John Montgomery (d. 1449) of Faulkbourne (Essex) had Welsh origins and early connections with Henry V's household as prince. He served on the 1415 campaign with three archers (E 404/31/331; E 101/45/5 m. 3d; E 101/47/30; E 358/6 m. 10d), the whole retinue being detailed into Harfleur garrison where he continued to serve in the first quarter of 1416 (E 101/47/39). He crossed in 1417 in the retinue of Sir John Cornwall (E 101/51/2 m. 35) and was active in the conquest, being a knight by June 1418 (C 64/9 m. 22d, DKR 41, p. 713). According to Walsingham (*St Albans Chronicle*, ii, p. 733), he was knighted at Caen on St George's Day 1418. He was appointed captain of Maulévrier (Seine-Maritime, arr. Rouen, cant. Notre-Dame-de-Gravenchon) in September 1419 (C 64/11 m. 12, DKR 41, p. 803) and of Domfront on 20 October 1420 (C 64/14 m. 15, DKR 42, p. 391), holding the

Sir William Crafford
Sir John Kyghley
Sir Ralph Butler[841]
Sir William Torbok[842]
Richard Guethin[843]
Sir Henry Biset
Sir Roland Standish[844]
Sir John Robessart[845]
Sir Nicholas Burdet[846]

---

latter post until at least late August 1428 (BNF, Fr. 25768/251). He was briefly captain of Argentan between October and November 1423 (BNF, Fr. 4485, pp 273–4). By 1420 he had become the brother-in-law of Sir Ralph Butler by marriage to the latter's sister. See HOCb; and Bogner, '"Military" Knighthood', pp. 104–26.

[841] Butler (d. 1473) of Sudeley (Gloucs.) was appointed captain of Arques and *bailli* of Caux on 1 October 1422 (BNF, NAF 1482/16), posts he held to the early 1430s. He was also *bailli* of Rouen during the king's visit in 1431 (BNF, PO Le Boutellier 110; BNF, Fr. 26054/1650; BL, Add. Ch. 3695). In 1423 he was also captain of Saint-Valéry-en-Caux (BNF, Fr. 26046/67), and was first chamberlain and councillor of Bedford from at least November 1423 (BNF, Fr 25767/44). He was probably knighted at the battle of Verneuil. Appointed Chief Butler in 1435, he had a long career in royal service, being elevated to the barony of Sudeley in 1441.

[842] William de Torbok, from Knowsley (Lancs.), served as a man-at-arms in the retinue of William Ashton in the army taken by Bedford to France in 1420 (E 101/49/36 m. 8). He had letters of protection and attorney to cross in the 1424 expedition under Christopher Preston (C 76/106 mm. 4 and 5, DKR 48, p. 230). He was probably knighted at Verneuil, and crossed again to France in the coronation expedition in the retinue of the duke of Norfolk (C 76/112 m. 9, DKR 48, p. 276).

[843] Richard Guethin of Builth was captain of the garrison of Exmes from the spring of 1424 to at least the summer of 1425 (AN, K 62/11/22; AN, K 62/18/9), also serving as captain of Essay from Michaelmas 1423 to 1424 (BNF, Fr. 4485 pp. 264–5), whose detachment he led to Ivry and the battle of Verneuil. No further service is known until 1432 when, now a knight, Guethin was captain and *bailli* of Mantes (BNF, Fr. 26055/1813), remaining in post until 1438 (BNF, Fr. 25774/1262), after which he was captain of Conches and *bailli* of Evreux until the end of the same year (BNF, Fr. 25775/1379). He disappears from the record thereafter, which suggests he had died. Guto'r Glyn composed two poems for him (www.gutorglyn.net).

[844] From Dukesbury (Lancs), Roland (1399–1435) was a man-at-arms in Harfleur in the early months of 1416 (E 101/47/39). He led a retinue of eighty men in the 1424 expeditionary army (E 404/40/171) and participated in the siege of Guise (BNF, Fr. 4485 p. 408) and possibly at Verneuil. But he then seems to have returned to England since he crossed with other members of his family in the expeditionary army of the summer of 1425 (E 404/41/194; E 403/669). We find him later at the siege of Orléans by which time he was a knight (Jarry, p. 112). He continued in service in the early 1430s, being appointed captain of Louviers after its recovery in 1431 but charged to effect its demolition (BNF, Fr. 25770/62). From July 1434 to his death he was captain and *bailli* of Evreux (ADE II F 4069; BNF, Clairambault 139/77).

[845] John Robessart went to England with Henry V in 1421 but returned with the army which accompanied the king back to France (E 101/70/5/702). In the early stages of Bedford's regency he was captain of Caudebec (BL, Add. Ch. 3566; BNF, Clairambault 191/128).

[846] Nicholas Burdet (d. 1441), from Warwickshire, served as a man-at-arms under Humphrey, duke of Gloucester, in 1415 (E 101/45/13 m. 4) but is not known to have served in the conquest of Normandy. He crossed in 1420 with troops under the duke of Bedford

Thomas Lound[847]
William Minors[848]
George Rigmaiden[849]
William Kyrkeby[850]
Thomas Everingham[851]

(E 101/49/36 m. 2). He was captain of Neufchâtel from 1 October 1422 to April 1424 (BL, Add. Ch. 25838; BNF, Fr. 4485 pp. 241–8), but also served at Bedford's siege of Meulan and was appointed Grand Butler of Normandy by the duke in April 1423 (AN, K 62/10). By the time of the battle of Verneuil, where he seems to have been knighted, he had been appointed captain of Carentan and *bailli* of Cotentin (BNF, Fr. 4485 pp. 189–90) in which capacity he was charged on 26 August 1424 with laying siege to Mont-Saint-Michel (BNF, Fr. 26047/309; Luce i, no. xxxiv). He was captured by the French in May 1425 but must have been released quickly as he was back in service by the following year.

[847] The assumption must be that Lound (often given as Lounde) was at the battle in the contingent of 240 from Fresnay and Alençon under Fastolf (BNF, Fr. 4485 p. 296). He mustered under Fastolf at Alençon on 5 September 1424 for the conquest of Maine (BNF, Fr. 25767/93). In 1426 he launched a case in the *Parlement* of Paris against Sir Alan Buxhill (*English Suits*, VIII, and pp. 297–8). In this he claimed to be of knightly stock and to have served in various campaigns on the southern frontier. His service had probably begun at Harfleur; a Thomas Launde mustered there in early 1416 (E 101/47/39). Lound certainly crossed in 1417 as a man-at-arms under Henry, lord Fitzhugh (E 101/51/2 m. 3).

[848] William Minors was a yeoman of the crown in 1413 (CPR 1422–29, p. 54) and served as an archer in the king's household on the 1415 expedition (E 101/45/18 m. 8). He served the king in the conquest of Normandy since on 28 April 1419 he was given lands near Caen (C 64/10 m. 29, DKR 41, p. 732). On 29 November 1422 he was appointed captain of Harfleur (BNF, Fr. 4485 pp. 213–15), a post he held until the loss of the town in 1435. He continued in military service in Normandy thereafter, until at least the mid-1440s. For the Ivry/Verneuil action he led a detachment of sixteen from Harfleur (BNF, Fr. 4485 pp. 203–5).

[849] George Rigmaiden was from Westmorland but developed interests in Woodacre and Garstang (Lancs.). It is not certain when his military service began but he was serving in a force in Normandy under Robert, lord Willoughby in the early 1420s (E 101/46/33 m. 1). His service in 1424 is uncertain but in the 1430s he was in the garrison of Alençon and was its lieutenant in 1433–34 (BNF, PO 2487 Rigmaiden 2). In July 1433 he was described in Breton ducal accounts as captain of Mayenne-la-Juhez (though it seems he was actually lieutenant there to Fastolf (AN, KK 324 f. 215r) and retained as a ducal chamberlain in Brittany (Lobineau, *Histoire de Bretagne*, ii, p. 1033). According to William Worcester (*Itineraries*, p. 353) Rigmaiden was one of a number of men, headed by Fastolf, who participated in the 'rescous' of Caen in 1434 (*Itineraries*, p. 353).

[850] There are a number of men with this name. One served as an archer in the garrison of Harfleur from 1416 to 1418 (E 101/47/39; E 101/48/17; E 101/48/19) and as a man-at-arms in 1421 (ADSM, 100J/30/32). A man of this name mustered at Alençon as a man-at-arms in Fastolf's company on 5 September 1424 for the conquest of Maine (BNF, Fr. 25767/93).

[851] Firm identification here is difficult. According to the Agincourt roll, a Thomas Everingham was present on the 1415 expedition in the company of Sir John Everingham, who is commonly believed to have died at the battle (BL, Harley 782, f. 83). In 1417 a Thomas Everingham crossed in the retinue of Henry, lord Fitzhugh (E 101/51/2 m. 3). A man of the same name took out letters of protection to cross in June 1422 (C 76/105 m. 2, DKR 44, p. 637). A Thomas Everingham served in the garrison of Alençon (now captained by the duke of Bedford with Fastolf as his lieutenant) between at least 1434 (including service in a garrison detachment at the *journée* of Sillé-le-Guillaume) and 1437, being Fastolf's lieutenant at the later date (BNF, Fr. 25771/826; BNF, Fr. 25771/843; BNF,

and others, both English and Norman to a total of about 10,000 soldiers. As soon as the Regent had definite news that the enemy had taken the town of Verneuil-sur-Avre, he departed and rode straight towards the enemy. He sent notification to the duke of Alençon, to the duke of Douglas and the earl of Buchan, constable of Scotland, that if they wanted to await him there, he would come to see them. Their response was that he could come as boldly as he wished; they would await him and be ready to receive him. So on the vigil of the feast of the Assumption of Our Lady in the month of August (14 August),[852] my lord the Regent arrived before the town of Verneuil where he found the enemy ready and in battle formation.[853] In that location, before he gave battle against the enemy, he created as a knight banneret Sir John Fastolf who had previously been only knight bachelor. Once this had been done, the two sides came together in hostile fashion for an exceptionally cruel and terrible battle. But at the end, as it pleased God our Creator and the Glorious Virgin, victory inclined towards, and then remained with, the English. The enemy were defeated in this battle (54v) and there were taken prisoner or killed princes, lords and other knights and esquires, both French and Scots, whose names follow, to wit,

the duke of Alençon	}
the Bastard of Alençon	}
Louis de Trémagon knight[854]	} prisoners
Pierre Hérisson knight[855]	}
Jean Tournebœuf, knight, lord of Courronne	}

the count of Aumale	}
the count of Ventadour	}
the vicomte of Narbonne	}
the lord de la Forest	}
the lord of Graville[856]	}
the lord of Gaules[857]	}
the lord of Fontaines	}

Fr. 25774/1279), and continuing at Alençon under Edmund Beaufort. One candidate is Thomas Everingham of Stainborough near Sheffield but he was closely associated from 1427 with John, lord Talbot and died with him at Castillon in 1453 (Pollard, *John Talbot*, pp. 76–7). Another possibility is Thomas Everingham (d. c. 1461) of Newhall in Thurlaston (Leics.) who was MP for Leicestershire in 1449 and 1453. If the latter, then his service in France ended in time for him to establish himself in Beverley by 1440 (HOCb).

[852] The Feast of the Assumption is 15 August. The battle is commonly deemed to have occurred on 17 August 1424. The English recovered Verneuil on the following day (Beaucourt, ii, pp. 15–16).

[853] The *journée* had been fixed for 14 August (Beaucourt, ii, p. 15).

[854] There is no other evidence of the presence and capture of Louis de Trémagon at Verneuil.

[855] The capture of Pierre Hérisson, knight, is also noted in Monstrelet (iv, p. 196). He received 2,000 *livres* from Charles VII to help him pay his ransom (Lainé, *Archives généalogiques*, vi, p. 53).

[856] The death of the lord of Graville is also noted in Chartier (i, p. 43) and Monstrelet (iv, p. 195). He appears in the latter source as 'le seigneur de Graville ancien' by way of differentiating Guy de Malet from his son Jean.

[857] He was already dead in 1423.

the lord of Amboise   } dead
the viconte de Thouars[858]   }
the lord of Bellay[859]   }
the lord d'Averton   }
the lord of Assé-le-Riboul[860]   }
Le Roncin[861]   }
Oudin Chenart   }
Yvon du Puis[862]   }
Pierre de Champagne knight[863]   }
Pierre Boterel knight, Breton   }
Robert de Dreux knight   }
Jean de Montgoubert knight   }
the *bailli* of Touraine[864]   }
Pierre Chapperon knight   }
the lord of Malicorne   }
the lord of Bourg Nouvel   }
Jean de Tournebu knight lord of Beaumesnil }
[cancelled: Jean de Tournebeuf knight]   }
Louis de Harcourt knight, lord of Bonnétable }

---

[858] This is another example of the chronicle mentioning twice the same person under a different name. Given we have two examples in succession, there is reason to suspect that the authors were deliberately inflating the list.

[859] Monstrelet (iv, p. 195) mentions the death on the battlefield of Verneuil of 'le seigneur de Belloy'. According to Tringant (*Jouvencel*, ii, p. 268), Jean du Bellay died at Verneuil, but there may be a confusion with a brother of du Bellay called Pierre (ibid., n. 4).

[860] Dreux Riboul, knight, lord of Assé and Lavardin, was apparently still alive in 1436.

[861] Le Roncin was among the leaders of the cavalry on the left wing according to Berry (pp. 117–18: 'se frappa ledit Roncin dedans leur Bataille le premier et la fut tué'). See also Monstrelet, iv, pp. 193, 195. His death is uncertain: there is ample evidence of a 'le roussin' operating as an écorcheur in the 1440s.

[862] Yvon du Puis did not die at Verneuil but his participation in this battle is noted elsewhere. Monstrelet (iv, p. 196) claims that he was made prisoner.

[863] Pierre de Champagne (d. 1485) followed Louis III, duke of Anjou, in his conquest of Naples, and was handsomely rewarded for his service with the titles of viceroy of Naples, great marshal, count of Aquila, prince of Montorio, and the castellany of Villaines-la-Juhel. Upon his return to France in 1426, Pierre de Champagne was present at all battles until the eventual expulsion of the English. He gave homage to René of Anjou, king of Sicily and Jerusalem, for his lands and lordship of Pescheseul and Champagne on 21 September 1439, being described as 'cousin, councillor and chamberlain', and still holding the office of 'maréchal de nos royaumes'. He also served in arms against the English in the 1440s and participated in the battle of Formigny in 1450. He became a knight of Anjou's order of the Croissant in 1449 (Allais, *Nobiliaire universel de France*, pp. 380–1; Perrier, 'Les Chevaliers du Croissant', p. 38; Angot, *Dictionnaire historique, topographique et biographique de la Mayenne*, i: art. Champagne (de)).

[864] Guillaume d'Avaugour was *bailli* of Touraine 1417–25 and 1440–46. He abandoned his functions as *bailli* in 1425 because of his suspected involvement in the murder of John the Fearless, but Charles VII, of whom he was a trusted servant, assigned him a pension on the income from the 'grenier à sel' of Tarascon (Beaucourt, ii, p. 102 n. 6). There is no other evidence of his presence at Verneuil, let alone of his death.

Michel de Ferrières[865]   }
Jean Pigache knight   }
Jean Quatrebarbes knight[866] }
(55r) and the Scots
the duke of Touraine, earl of Douglas[867]   }
James Douglas his son[868]   }
the earl of Buchan constable of France   }
the earl of Wigtown[869]   } dead
Sir Alexander Meldrum   }
Sir Henry Balglavy   }
Sir John Sterlyng   }
Sir William Hamilton[870]   }
Sir James Grey   }
Sir Robert Kennedy   }

and many others both French and Scots to the number of about 9,000 men, according to Mountjoye, King of Arms for the enemy party. On the English side no man of name worthy of mention died.

At the same juncture, John de Luxembourg, count de Ligny,[871] with a certain number of Englishmen in his company, to wit,
Sir Thomas Rempston[872]

---

[865] Ferrières appears in Glover's list of prisoners taken at Verneuil (BL, Harley 782, f. 51r; *L&P*, II, ii, pp. 394–5).

[866] This is probably Jean Quatrebarbes, lord of la Rongère (d. 1459), chamberlain of Charles VII (La Chesnaye, xi, p. 607). A Jean Quatrebarbes, esquire, mustered in the company of Raoul de Montbourcher on 24 September 1415 in Rouen (Morice, ii, p. 910). Probably the same Jean Quatrebarbes, now a knight, had two safe-conducts to circulate between Maine and Brittany in February and June 1434 (AN, KK 324 ff. 40v, 64v).

[867] Archibald Douglas, fourth earl* (1372–1424), had not participated in earlier Scottish military assistance to the Dauphin, having even promised in 1421 to serve Henry V with 400 men (*Foedera*, x, pp. 123–4). But the Dauphin persuaded him to serve in the army which landed at La Rochelle in March 1424, creating him duke of Touraine on 19 April (AN, J 680/79). He was killed at Verneuil and buried in the cathedral of Tours.

[868] The second son of Archibald, fourth earl of Douglas was part of the army which landed at La Rochelle in March 1424. He was killed alongside his father at the battle of Verneuil.

[869] The earl of Wigtown, eldest son of the fourth earl of Douglas, was not present in the Scottish army sent to France in 1424 and became fifth earl of Douglas at his father's death at Verneuil.

[870] This may be the stepbrother of John Stewart of Darnley. A William Hamilton was the son of Janet Keith of Gelston who married Alexander Stewart of Darnley as her second husband. William had two brothers, Andrew and John Hamilton of Cadzow, and held Bathgate by grant from his mother in 1407 (*RMS*, i, no. 890, 911; Ditcham, 'Employment of Foreign Mercenary Troops', p. 57).

[871] Jean III de Luxembourg (c. 1390–1441), count of Guise and Ligny, lord of Beaurevoir, was a close ally of the house of Burgundy and a fervent supporter of the dual monarchy. He was heavily involved in military campaigns against the partisans of Charles VII in Picardy, and in 1424 conquered the county of Guise belonging to René of Anjou. He inherited the county of Ligny after the death of Philippe de Saint-Pol in 1430 (B. Schnerb, 'Jean III de Luxembourg', pp. 29–31).

[872] Rempston was commissioned by Bedford for six months from 6 April 1424 with a company of 100 men-at-arms and 300 archers from the garrisons of Normandy to lay siege to Guise (BNF, Fr. 4485 pp. 280–2).

Nicolas Warberton[873]
William Lynoz
and several others, English as well as Burgundians and Picards, had laid, and were
holding, siege before the town and castle of Guise-en-Thièrache.[874] This was surrendered to him by composition along with the castle of Hirson[875] and several
other castles and fortresses in the vicinity of the town of Guise.

After the battle and glorious victory won by my lord the Regent, as has been
said, the enemy who had retreated into, and who were still in, the town of Verneuil
made a composition (55v) that by surrendering and delivering the town and castle of Verneuil they could leave freely with their goods, horses and equipment.
And so they did. My lord the Regent appointed as captain and keeper *Sir Philip
Hall*.[876] Then the Regent departed, returning towards the city of Rouen with great
honour, joy and victory. From there he went on to Paris. In that place soon afterwards, he commissioned and appointed Lord Scales, Sir John Fastolf, and Sir John
Montgomery with around 2,000 men in their company to go off to make conquest
in the territories of Anjou and Maine.[877] In the month of September in the year 1425
[1424 cancelled][878] they entered into the land and county of Maine and laid siege to
the castle of Beaumont-sur-Sarthe whose captain was Huet de Fontenay esquire.[879]
Within a fortnight he surrendered the castle by an agreement whereby some of
those inside remained and became prisoners and others left freely. From there the

---

[873] Warberton and Lynoz are not mentioned in any of the records of the siege, but a
Nicholas Weberton is found as a man-at-arms in the garrison of Gisors under Richard
Merbury in August 1428 (BNF, Fr. 25767/90), and William Lynoz was active in various
companies detailed to service in the Vexin against brigands and for the protection of roads
over the winter of 1428–29 (e.g. AN, K 63/1/7; BNF, Fr. 25766/319; BL, Add. Ch. 11620–1),
but also at the siege of Orléans under Jenkin Orell in January 1429 (BNF, Fr. 25766/398).

[874] Aisne, arr. Vervins, ch. l. cant. The siege was laid between 6 April and 18 September
1424 (Beaucourt, ii, p. 15). The treaty of surrender, made by Jean de Luxembourg and
Thomas Rempston with the defenders, is given in full in Monstrelet, iv, pp. 199–205.

[875] Aisne, arr. Vervins, ch. l. cant.

[876] There is no record of a Sir Philip Hall holding this command or indeed of any knight
of this name. The only Philip Hall appearing in musters is an archer in Bernay in 1446
(BNF, Fr. 25777/1712). Lord Scales was captain of Verneuil from 1422 to at least 1425 (BNF,
Fr. 4485 f. 425) and Fastolf by May 1427 (BL, Add. Ch. 7944).

[877] This commission of 25 August 1424 and the resulting payments to Fastolf, Montgomery,
Scales and others in their company (such as Ogard) are detailed in the account of Pierre
Surreau, receiver-general of Normandy (BNF, Fr. 4485 pp. 319–20). Fastolf is described
there as councillor and master of the household of the Regent, lieutenant of the king in
the pays d'Alençon and beyond the Seine, and led a force of 240 men. Montgomery, with
seventy-two men, was captain of Domfront. Scales had a company of 120 men. In addition
to the 400 under their command, small companies were also drawn from a number of
garrisons in Lower Normandy. The appointment exists in a sixteenth-century copy (BL,
Arundel MS 26, f. 4, printed in Planchenault, 'La conquête' (1925), pp. 24–5) and in an
earlier copy in College of Arms, Arundel 26, f. 56v).

[878] The campaign began in September 1424. Fastolf mustered his 800 men at Alençon on
6 September (BNF, Fr. 25767/93).

[879] The English took the place around 21 September 1424 but it was later recovered,
probably in the spring of 1425. The earl of Salisbury retook it after a second siege in mid-
July 1425 (Planchenault, 'La conquête' (1925), pp. 6, 13; Triger, *Le château et la ville de Beaumont-
le-Vicomte*, p. 33).

English went to lay siege before the castle of Tennie [inserted over deletion of 'Thouvioye'][880] at a league near the city of Le Mans whose captain was Jean de Tournemine[881] knight, Breton. The latter surrendered the castle after eight days, with the defenders being allowed to depart, a baton in their hands.[882]

From there they went before the castle of Sillé-le-Guillaume whose captains were Pierre le Forestier[883] and Olivier de Forestier,[884] Bretons. Within six days they surrendered the castle by an agreement which allowed them to leave freely but by which they were to pay a large sum of money for which the captains stood as pledges and hostages. The English then went before the castles of Saint-Pierre-sur-Orthe and Saint-Thomas-de-Courceriers whose captains were *Michel Tailleuer* and Guillaume Vachereau.[885] The latter made a composition to surrender the places or else to fight within a month next following. For that purpose they handed over hostages. During this time the English lords captured other places, to wit, Rouessé-Vassé[886] and Courmenant, and several others which were abandoned to them by the captains and men inside who fled and did not dare await the arrival of the English lords. Before the end of the month (56r) the lords returned before the castles of Saint-Pierre-sur-Orthe and Saint-Thomas-de-Courceriers in order to receive them into the obedience of the king and of my lord the Regent, or else to give battle. Despite the fact that the enemy did not appear, the captains, going against their oath and promises, did not wish to deliver the fortresses and abandon their hostages, who saw what was happening, immediately beheaded the hostages before the fortresses and then returned to their own places. Soon after these things had been done, which was around the feast of Candlemas (2 February 1425), the lords mentioned earlier, accompanied by 1,500 troops, carried out a raid towards the River Loir and took by assault the outer defences of the castle and fortress of La Chartre-sur-le-Loir.[887] The keep held out although it surrendered a few days later and Richard Guethin esquire was made captain. During this time the English

---

[880]   Touvoie was a manor held by the bishop of Le Mans (Sarthe, arr. Mamers, cant. Savigné-l'Evêque). The siege of Tennie (Sarthe, arr. Mamers, cant. Loué) by Fastolf is mentioned in Chartier (i, pp. 43–4, as 'Tennye').

[881]   This could be either Jean II de Tournemine, lord of la Hunaudaye, or Jean de Tournemine, lord of Barrach.

[882]   Planchenault ('La conquête' (1925), p. 6) suggests on geographical grounds that the taking of Tennie must have followed that of Sillé.

[883]   Pierre le Forestier was likely still to be in prison in Alençon, following his capture at Verneuil. However, his presence in Sillé-le-Guillaume, or even his shared captaincy of that place with his brother Olivier before his capture, appear credible.

[884]   Olivier le Forestier stood as captain of the tower and fortress of Sillé-le-Guillaume in the treaty of surrender between himself, Scales (described as marshal), Fastolf, and Montgomery dated 1 October 1424. A sixteenth-century copy is in British Library Arundel MS 26, f. 4r (printed by Planchenault, 'La conquête' (1925), pp. 25–7), with an earlier copy in College of Arms, Arundel 26, f 55

[885]   Guillaume Vachereau served during Charles VII's recovery of Normandy in 1449–50, according to La Roque, *Histoire généalogique de la Maison de Harcourt*, iv, p. 1720.

[886]   Given as two separate places in the French text but now one location known by this name (Sarthe, arr. Mamers, cant. Sillé-le-Guillaume).

[887]   The place had been captured by 1 May 1425 when English troops under Sir William Bucton mustered there (BL, Add. Ch. 11536).

lords fortified Montfort-le-Gesnois,[888] to which Thomas Lound esquire was made captain.[889] After this they returned to their places and garrisons with their booty and prisoners.

In the following year, 1425, my lord the Regent appointed the earl of Salisbury lieutenant-general in the name of the king and of himself, and sent a notable army to the region of Anjou and Maine to carry out a conquest there.[890] The names of the lords in this company are as follows, to wit,

Lord Scales

Sir John Fastolf, grand master of the household of my lord the Regent and governor of Anjou and Maine[891]

Sir John Grey, son of the lord Grey of Ruthin[892]

Sir Reginald Grey, his son[893]

Sir Alan Buxhill[894]

Sir Thomas Blount

Sir William Oldhall[895]

Sir Lancelot de Lisle[896]

(56v) Sir Andrew Ogard[897]

---

[888] Sarthe, arr. Mamers, cant. Savigné-l'Evêque, previously known as Montfort-le-Rotrou. It was captured by the English by early December 1424 but then lost and recovered by Salisbury in his campaign of 1425 (Planchenault, 'La conquête' (1925), pp. 6, 13).

[889] Thomas Lound had also been appointed by Sir Alan Buxhill, lord of Clinchamp in Maine, to defend the castle of Clinchamp, but had been dismissed for his oppression of the local population (*English Suits*, VIII).

[890] Salisbury's campaign into Maine, where we find the title 'capitaine general ordonne par le roi pour la guerre de son royaume de France' (AN, K 62/18/7), began in mid-July since a quittance dated 20 August 1425 concerns a payment for the second month (BNF, Fr. 4491 f. 28v).

[891] Fastolf was certainly at the siege of Le Mans in late June 1425 (BNF, Fr. 26048/432).

[892] Sir John Grey of Ruthin led a retinue of 160 in the expeditionary army sent from England in May 1425, his half-brother Sir Reginald leading a retinue of eighty men (E 404/41/191, 179; E 403/669; Ratcliffe, 'Military Expenditure', p. 17).

[893] Sir Reginald was in fact the half-brother of Sir John Grey.

[894] Sir Alan is known to have mustered in the company of the earl of Salisbury at the siege of La Ferté-Bernard in March 1426 (BL, Add. Ch. 94). He subsequently served at the second siege of Mont-Aimé (BNF, Fr. 32510 f. 369r. BNF, Fr. 4484 ff. 37r–37v).

[895] Oldhall had been appointed captain of Essay in September 1424 (BNF, Fr. 4491 f. 82), a post he held to 1438 (BNF, Fr. 26065/3620), often combining the position with that of *bailli* of Alençon.

[896] Lisle indented for 120 men in the expeditionary force sent from England in the summer of 1425 (E 404/41/185; E 403/669) and was marshal of Salisbury's army for the conquest of Maine (BL, Add. Ch. 17,629; Planchenault, 'La conquête' (1925), pièce justificative IV).

[897] Sir Andrew Ogard (d. 1454) was a Dane who made his career in the French wars and obtained letters of denization in England in 1433. He was in the household of the duke of Bedford from at least 1423, becoming second chamberlain and councillor by November 1430, and, like Fastolf, was one of the duke's executors. His career in France continued well into the 1440s, and gave him rewards as well as good connections. This included a marriage to the daughter of Sir John Clifton whose estates in Norfolk he was able to acquire, making him a relatively close neighbour of Fastolf (*Bedford Inventories*, ed. Stratford, pp. 417–21). His death in 1454, and the dimensions of the house he had built in Stanstead Abbots (Essex), were noted by William Worcester in his *Itineraries* (p. 47). His first military command was

Sir John Montgomery
[added: Thomas Popham knight][898]
Lord Ferrers and Chambrois
William Glasdale[899]
Matthew Gough
Richard Wytherton[900]
Thomas Gower[901]
Robert Stafford[902]

---

as captain of Touques from October 1422 (BNF, Fr. 25766/815), a command he held until late in 1430 (BNF, Fr. 26274/109) and again from 1434 to 1438 (ADC, F 1547 (2); BNF, Fr. 25774/1336). At the battle of Verneuil, at which he was knighted, he led a contingent from the garrison of Vire of which he was also captain, a command he continued to hold to 1430 (BNF, Fr. 4485 pp. 139–40; BNF, Fr. 25769/507), and again from 1431 to 1437 (BNF, Fr. 26053/1480, BNF, NAF 8602/5). He participated in the initial campaign into Maine in the autumn of 1424 (BNF, Fr. 4485 pp. 81, 121, 321). It is puzzling, given his link to Fastolf in Bedford's service, that the chronicle mentions him for the first time only in 1425, and in particular that there is no mention of his presence at the battle of Verneuil (HOCb).

[898] An error for Sir John Popham, who had indented with 120 men in the expeditionary army which crossed in May 1425 (E 403/669; E 404/41/187). Popham was amongst those charged with command of the force as it crossed (CPR 1422–29, p. 299, Ratcliffe, 'Military Expenditure', p. 19).

[899] Glasdale was *bailli* of Alençon from late 1425 or July 1426 (ADO, A 1402), and captain of Fresnay from at least early 1426 (BNF, Fr. 26049/574) – he had probably replaced Fastolf at Michaelmas 1425 – holding both offices until his death. He continued to participate in the conquest of Maine, mustering for this purpose in April 1426 (BNF, Fr. 25767/143).

[900] It is possible this is the Richard Warberton who mustered several times in Lord Willoughby's retinues: at Rouen in November 1425 for the conquest of Maine (AN, K 62/18/19); in April 1426 at the siege of La Ferté-Bernard (ADSM, 100J/30/31); in May 1426 for the conquest of Maine (AN, K 62/25/4); and in a detachment of the garrison of Rouen at the siege of Bonneval in July 1426 (BNF, Fr. 25767/156). A Richard Wedirton indented for the service of forty men in the expeditionary army which accompanied the duke of Bedford back to France in March 1427 (E 403/677; E 404/43/175) and is found at the siege of Montargis in late August (BNF, Fr. 4484 f. 72v).

[901] Thomas Gower served as a man-at-arms in the retinue of John, lord Roos, on the campaign of 1415 (E 101/50/26; E 101/44/30/1 m. 14) and in the retinue of Richard Beauchamp, lord Abergavenny, in 1417 (E 101/51/2 m. 5). He mustered at Alençon in September 1424 in Fastolf's company for the campaign in Maine (BNF, Fr. 25767/93). In December 1428 he was lieutenant of Falaise to Talbot (AN, K 63/1/10). He held many important military offices thereafter: *bailli* and captain of Evreux in 1430 (BNF, Fr. 25769/509); lieutenant at Alençon in February 1431, being replaced by Fastolf in November (AN, K 63/10/75, 63/13/32). From 1439 he was involved in the command of Cherbourg (BNF, Fr. 26066/3897) and was still there at the loss of 1450.

[902] Exactly when Robert Stafford began his service in France is not known. In a suit against Lord Talbot in the Paris *Parlement* (*English Suits*, XIX, pp. 305–6) he claimed that he had served first the duke of Clarence and later the earl of Salisbury. On 18 May 1419 he had been granted lands in the *bailliage* of Caux and Rouen (C 64/11 m. 39, DKR 41, p. 786). In 1424 he acted as a musterer of Oldhall's troops at Essay (BNF, Fr. 25767/110) and in 1426 of troops under Glasdale at Fresnay-le-Vicomte (AN, K 62/25/2; BNF, NAF 8605/105). By his testimony in the *Parlement* case Stafford had been made captain of La Ferté-Bernard by Salisbury but was accused of negligence in letting the place be captured by the French in February 1427. As a result, his lands in Normandy had been

Thomas Burgh
Thomas Everingham
William Kyrkeby[903]
and several others to the number of about 10,000 men of war. He entered the area of Maine in the month of June and laid siege to the city of Le Mans[904] whose principal captain was Baudouin de Champagne,[905] knight, seigneur de Tucé, with Guillaume de la Mote, knight, and Huet de Fontenay as sub-captains. After the siege had lasted for about six weeks and those inside saw that they would not be relieved, they entered into negotiations for an agreement whereby they would surrender and deliver into the obedience of the king and of my lord the Regent, the city and all the townspeople, churchmen, soldiers and others who wished to stay there freely and with all their goods and their inheritances undiminished. Those who did not wish to stay would be allowed to leave with all their goods, horses, and equipment. Of that city Sir John Fastolf, governor of the area, was, and remained, captain.[906] In coming to lay siege before the city of Le Mans the earl of Salisbury passed before the castle of La Guierche two leagues from Le Mans and lodged there for about a fortnight until the enemy who were inside the city surrendered the place to him. After Le Mans had been surrendered and captured as described, various castles and fortresses were surrendered and placed into the obedience

---

transferred to John, lord Talbot. Stafford began a suit of recovery against Talbot in the *Parlement* in June 1430, claiming that he had always behaved well but others had let him down. But it was counter-claimed that he had not maintained the right number of men in La Ferté and had been absent at Le Mans (which was true) when the enemy attacked. Stafford retorted that Salisbury had not given him enough men even though he had held thirty more than his indenture required, that the enemy had been let in by the people of the town, including Salisbury's *procureur*, and that no resistance could be offered as the cannoneer had gone off with the cannon and the keeper of the artillery had gone off with the crossbows. After an inquiry, judgment was made in Stafford's favour in February 1433 and his lands were restored to him. He also seems to have enjoyed good relations with Talbot since, from the summer of 1435 onwards to the end of the occupation, he was a member of his personal retinue (BNF, Fr. 25772/944 (1435); BNF, NAF 8606/102 (1448)), along with stints in Talbot's garrisons of Caudebec where he was master porter, and in Rouen, where he was sometime *quaternier* of La Porte Cauchoise, as well as service at various sieges and field actions. He also seems to have had control of Talbot's seal (Pollard, *John Talbot*, pp. 87–9, 96).

[903] Various archers of this name are seen in the 1415 musters but it is possible that he was the William Kirkeby serving in Harfleur from the spring of 1416, initially as an archer and from at least 1421 as a man-at-arms (E 101/47/39; E 101/48/17; E 101/48/19; ADSM, 100J/30/32). He may also be the man-at-arms who mustered at Meung under Sir Thomas Rempston in September 1428 (BNF, Fr. 25768/303). Later service by a man of this name can be seen in musters but it is impossible to know if they relate to the same person.

[904] Part of a treaty of surrender for Le Mans dated 2 August 1425 is found in a London Chronicle (BL, Cotton Julius B 1, ff. 71–2, printed in Planchenault, 'La conquête' (1925), pp. 27–9) but it does not mention names other than that of Salisbury. The exact start date of the siege is a matter of debate (Planchenault, 'La conquête' (1925), p. 13) but there are references to Salisbury's presence in late June and July (BNF, Fr. 4491 f. 33v).

[905] He had been captain of Le Mans from at least 1424.

[906] Planchenault, 'La conquête' (1925) (p. 18) considered that the earl of Suffolk was actually captain with Fastolf as lieutenant.

of the king and my lord the Regent. Captains were appointed to them, some of whose names follow, to wit,

(57r) Saint-Calais, where Richard Guethin esquire was made captain

Château-l'Hermitage *et la saigne*,[907] where Matthew Gough esquire was made captain

Guécélard, where John Banaster esquire was made captain[908]

Malicorne-sur-Sarthe, where William Glasdale esquire was made captain

L'Isle-sur-Brûlon, where Sir Lancelot de Lisle knight was made captain

Louplande, where Henry Branche was made captain[909]

Montsûrs, where Sir William Oldhall knight was made captain[910]

La Suze-sur-Sarthe, where *John Suffolk* esquire was made captain,

and many others were demolished and dismantled.

In this same year around the month of September, my lord the earl of Salisbury and the other lords named above who were in his company laid siege before the town and castle of Sainte-Suzanne whose captain was Amboise de Loré, knight.[911] Within a fortnight the latter came to an agreement and surrendered the town and castle to the earl, on the condition that they (i.e. the defenders) would make an oath not to make war or take up arms against the English for a year. By this means they departed with their goods, save for the cannoneers who were kept back and delivered to my lord the earl to do with them what he wished. He had them all hanged with a cannonball tied to their leg. The earl made Sir John Popham captain and keeper of Sainte-Suzanne.[912] The earl then left straightaway and laid siege before the castle of Mayenne whose captain was the lord of Escotais.[913] The siege lasted for around six weeks until they made an agreement that they would surrender the castle and depart with their lives, goods, horses and equipment.[914] Sir John Montgomery was appointed and made captain and keeper of the castle.[915]

---

[907] The meaning of *la saigne* is not clear but the place may be Mansigné, a few kilometres to the south-west of Château-l'Hermitage.

[908] Banaster was lieutenant to Fastolf at Alençon in the summer of 1427 (BNF, Fr. 25768/239).

[909] Henry Branche was a man-at-arms in Fastolf's company for the campaign in Maine which mustered at Alençon on 5 September 1424 (BNF, Fr. 25767/93). He was Fastolf's nephew, being the son of his half-sister and Sir Philip Branche, who was in the same muster. Henry is mentioned, and his relationship with Fastolf noted, by Chartier (i, p. 56) in connection with an action near Sainte-Suzanne during the siege of Montargis, but this incident is not found in the M 9 chronicle.

[910] John Popham was sent to inspect the garrison of Montsûrs on 29 November 1425 (BNF, Fr. 7626 f. 401, cited in Planchenault, 'La conquête' (1925), p. 21).

[911] The siege began in late August and continued until at least the last week of September (BNF, Fr. 4491 f. 29; Planchenault, 'La conquête' (1925), p. 19). Chartier (i, p. 45) and *Pucelle* (p. 228) also name Ambroise de Loré as captain of the town and fortress of Sainte-Suzanne in August–September 1425. A letter of remission indicates that Loré was already captain of that place in 1423 (Luce, i, p. 216, no. 68).

[912] Popham was certainly captain by 29 November 1425 (BNF, NAF 7676/461).

[913] Chartier (i, p. 46) and *Pucelle* (pp. 226–7) name the captain as Pierre le Porc.

[914] Surrender was probably on 31 October 1425 (Planchenault, 'La conquête' (1925), p. 21).

[915] Montgomery had returned to England with Bedford in December 1425 and served as MP for Hertfordshire in the parliament which met at Leicester from 18 February to 1 June, but had letters of protection on 8 July 1426 to return to France (C 76/108 m. 6, DKR 48, p.

When winter was nearly over, to wit, around the feast of the Purification of Our Lady (2 February 1426), the earl of Salisbury laid siege to the town and castle of La Ferté-Bernard,[916] whose captain was *Jean* d'Avaugour dit Chieure.[917] The siege lasted until just after Easter. During the time of the siege (57v), a financial deal was plotted and executed by a Gascon of the English allegiance with Charles de Villiers, Pierre le Beuf, Pierre d'Anthenaise,[918] Aymeric d'Anthenaise,[919] and Guillaume de Landrerepost,[920] all of whom adhered to the enemy side. The deal was that the Gascon would admit these men into the castle of Alençon in return for the enemy giving him money. This deal was carried out as planned. The Gascon informed the earl of Salisbury, who ordered Robert, lord Willoughby and Sir John Fastolf to go to meet these men of the enemy party. On the day which had been assigned by the Gascon and the men of the enemy to make delivery of the castle, such men, with others in their company to the total of 2,000 soldiers, came in the morning close to Alençon thinking that they would indeed, and without difficulty, enter it. But it all turned out otherwise, since Lord Willoughby and Sir John Fastolf, who had left the siege of La Ferté accompanied by 2,000 English, came to meet and surround the enemy close to Alençon. At that spot all of the aforesaid men of the enemy party were killed or taken prisoner save for Pierre d'Anthenaise who took to flight and escaped. After this action had happened, Lord Willoughby and Sir John Fastolf returned to the siege before La Ferté to the earl of Salisbury who received them with great joy because of the defeat they had inflicted.

Very soon after Easter it happened that the enemy who were in La Ferté-Bernard, seeing that no help or aid was coming to them, that their victuals were greatly dwindling, and that it was in vain that they might keep the town and castle against the English who each day and night launched fierce assaults and skirmishes in various ways, negotiated and came to an agreement with the earl. They surrendered and delivered to him the castle and town whereby they might leave

---

242). By 1433/34 Fastolf was captain of Mayenne-la-Juhez with George Rigmaiden as his lieutenant (AN, KK 324).

[916] For payments for English soldiers at the siege of La Ferté-Bernard in January and February 1426 see BNF, Fr. 4491 f. 26v. The siege was still in train on 1 March 1426 when Salisbury wrote a letter from it (Cosneau, p.j. xxxiv), and his troops mustered there on 4 March 1426 (BL, Add. Ch. 94).

[917] Louis d'Avaugour, esquire, commanded the town and castle of La Ferté-Bernard in the name of Yolande of Aragon (ADS, E 271, no. 3; Charles, 'L'invasion anglaise', p. 188). The garrison surrendered in February 1426 after a three- or four-month-long siege. Ignoring the clauses of the treaty, Salisbury kept Avaugour prisoner, but he escaped (Chartier, i, p. 46). La Ferté-Bernard was recaptured by the French in January 1427 (Joubert, *Documents*, p. 21, no. 10).

[918] Pierre le Beuf was a man-at-arms in the garrison of Touques under Jean Carbonnel, lord of Sourdeval, in the 1450s (Prosser, 'After the Reduction', p. 267; Raguier's accounts in *Journal du siège*, p. 194).

[919] Aymeric d'Anthenaise was taken prisoner at Verneuil and put to ransom by Fastolf but may have regained his freedom by February 1426. He definitely survived this ambush as we find him acting as captain of Sillé-le-Guillaume when the place surrendered again to the English in 1434 (AN, JJ 175/360).

[920] Guillaume de Landreposte was still alive in 1434.

with their goods, horses and equipment. The earl of Salisbury was made lord of the place by a grant which was made to him by my lord the Regent.[921]

Around the same time during this siege, to wit (58r) in the period of Lent (13 February–31 March 1426), Sir Thomas Rempston,[922] Sir Philip Branche,[923] Sir Nicholas Burdet[924] and other English in their company, to the number of around 500 men, took and fortified the town of Saint-James (de-Beuvron) on the marches of Brittany. As soon as Arthur of Brittany, count of Richemont, heard news of this fortification, he ordered the barons of Brittany and others of the enemy party to assemble with the people of the Brittany region.[925] They numbered, all groups together, about 60,000 to 80,000 people. They came to lay siege before the town of Saint-James, inflicting on the English many hard and cruel assaults. But the English who were inside defended themselves valiantly like lions, so much so that, after a particularly tough assault carried out by the Bretons on the town which troubled the English much, the latter sallied out of the town and attacked the Bretons in their positions. The Bretons were so scared that, shamefully and in cowardly manner, they fled and lifted the siege, leaving their possessions, foodstuffs and weapons. In this defeat 4,000 or more of these Bretons were killed or taken prisoner.

In the year 1426 in the month of May my lord the Regent duke of Bedford appointed and ordered the earl of Warwick as lieutenant-general of the king and of himself, discharging the earl of Salisbury.[926] Warwick had recently arrived from England accompanied by 6,000 soldiers.[927] He entered Maine and laid siege before the town of Château-du-Loir. Within eight days it was surrendered to him by [blank] who was captain, and Matthew Gough esquire was installed as captain and keeper.

Afterwards he went before the castle of Mayet.[928] Within two days it was surrendered and delivered to him and he appointed as captain John Winter esquire[929]

---

[921] Robert Stafford was appointed captain by Salisbury. The place was recaptured by the French in early 1427 (Joubert, *Documents*, p. 21, no. 10; *English Suits*, XIX) but was back in English hands by late January 1428 (BL, Add. Ch. 3617).

[922] Rempston is singled out for mention in Monstrelet (iv, p. 285) along with the earl of Suffolk.

[923] Branche was dead by October 1427 and probably was killed during Richemont's siege of Saint-James (CFR 1422–30, p. 187).

[924] Burdet was back in England by February 1427 (CPR 1422–29, p. 404).

[925] On 1 March 1426 Salisbury wrote from the siege of La Ferté-Bernard to prompt a call out of Norman and English troops given this French threat to Saint-James (Cosneau, p.j. xxxiv).

[926] During Bedford's absence in England he had appointed three 'lieutenants general sur le fait de la guerre', Warwick in the regions of France, Vermandois, Champagne, Brie and Gastinois, Salisbury in Normandy, Anjou, Maine, Chartrain and Beausse, and Suffolk in the Basses Marches of Normandy (C 31/8/136/16), but in August 1426 Warwick became 'lieutenant du roy en France et Normandie ou fait de sa guerre' (BNF, Fr. 26049/614). None the less Salisbury is seen by October as 'capitaine general ordonne sur le fait de la guerre en Champagne et Brie' (BNF, Fr. 32510 f. 368v).

[927] The earl of Warwick seems to have remained in France but entered into indentures in England in late July 1426 for an expeditionary company of 400 men which crossed to Calais at the end of August to join him. Another three companies totalling 400 men crossed to Cherbourg around the same time for actions in Lower Normandy (E 404/42/308–11; E 403/675).

[928] Sarthe, arr. La Flèche, cant. Le Lude.

[929] Archers of this name are found in the retinues of the duke of Clarence and the earl of Huntingdon in 1415 (E 101/45/4 m. 9, 45/7 m. 1), and under the latter in 1417 (E 101/51/2

who was lord (58v) of the place by a grant made to him by my lord the Regent. Then Warwick went before the castle of Le Lude which was surrendered to him, and he appointed as captain William Glasdale. Because the earl had heard news that the enemy were assembling in the region of Beauce, he made his course towards that area hoping to locate and meet the enemy. But he did not find them and returned without doing anything else. At his return he laid siege to the castle of Montdoubleau whose captain was Roberton Descroix, esquire.[930] After three weeks Roberton surrendered the place on the terms that the enemy should leave with their goods, horses and armour. The earl made and appointed captain and keeper Lord Willoughby. Once this had been done, the earl returned towards the duke of Bedford, the Regent, who was then in the town [blank].

In this same year around the feast of the Purification of Our Lady (2 February 1427) the lord of Rostrenen,[931] marshal of Brittany, assembled a great company of Bretons and went to fortify the town of Pontorson. Whilst this fortification was being undertaken, the lord of Rostrenen, accompanied by 1,000 soldiers or more, made a raid into Normandy to the southern limits of the Cotentin right up to the town and city of Avranches. But the English of the garrison of that place made a sortie against the Bretons and defeated them, putting them to flight. The lord of Rostrenen was taken prisoner and a large part of his men were killed or captured. As soon as news came to the duke of Bedford of the fortification of Pontorson he immediately called for siege to be laid before the town by the earl of Warwick, his lieutenant-general, with Lord Scales, Sir John Fastolf,[932] Sir John Popham, Sir Thomas Rempston, Sir Nicholas Burdet, Matthew Gough[933] and several others in the earl's company, forming a notable army of about 7,000 soldiers.[934] Because there was a necessity for victuals during the siege, Lord Scales,[935] with Sir John Harpelay knight, *bailli* of

m. 26). On 12 July 1421 John Winter esquire (d. 1445) entered into a 'brotherhood-in-arms' agreement with Nicholas Molyneux at Harfleur (Oxford, Magdalen College, Southwark 213, in McFarlane, 'A Business Partnership in War and Administration'). In November 1428 he was a man-at-arms within Talbot's personal retinue at the siege of Orléans (BNF, Fr. 25768/318). It was as a soldier under Talbot that he had been involved in the rescue of Le Mans in May of the same year and in the suit in the Paris *Parlement* which this triggered (*English Suits*, XVII, and p. 309). By 1433 he was controller of the revenues of the duke of Bedford in Maine and Anjou (AN, KK 324 f. 1). No grant of Mayet to Winter has been found.

[930] Loir-et-Cher, arr. Vendôme, ch. l. cant. The siege took place over September (Beaucourt, ii, p. 24). Sir John Popham mustered at the siege on 24 September 1426 (BL, Add. Ch. 11566).

[931] Pierre VIII (d. 1440), lord of Rostrenen, was chamberlain of Jean V, duke of Brittany, in August 1421, and became a trusted lieutenant of Richemont, assisting him in the war against the English. According to Gruel (pp. 51–3), whose account is fairly close to that of the M 9 chronicle, Richemont, having fortified the town of Pontorson, left the place in the hands of Rostrenen as his captain in 1426 or 1427, but the latter was subsequently captured during a raid near Avranches (at Pontaubault). See also Trévédy, *Compagnons bretons*, pp. 6–19.

[932] In March Fastolf had 200 men at the siege of Pontorson (BNF, Fr. 26049//691, printed in Luce, i, no. lxxxvii).

[933] Gough mustered as a man-at-arms in the retinue of Fastolf at the siege of Pontorson (BNF, Fr. 25767/216; BNF, Fr. 25768/225).

[934] Warwick was commissioned in January 1427 to lay siege to Pontorson with an army of 2,400 (AN, K 62/32, printed in Luce, i, lxxxv; Beaucourt, ii, p. 25).

[935] The action of Scales as commander of a supply convoy is also noted in Monstrelet, iv, p. 288.

Cotentin,[936] Sir William Breton knight, *bailli* of Caen,[937] (59r) Sir Raoul Tesson, Sir John Carbonnel and many others to the number of 3,000 soldiers, English as well as Normans, departed from the siege and went to seek victuals as well as equipment and armaments. As they returned to the siege via the tidal causeways of Mont-Saint-Michel,[938] they met a large force of the enemy, to wit,

the baron of Coulonces[939]

the lord of Auzebosc captain of Mont-Saint-Michel[940]

the lord of Montbourcher[941]

the lord of Châteaugiron[942]

the lord of Tinténiac[943]

the lord of Montauban[944]

the lord of Châteaubriant[945]

---

[936] Harpelay was *bailli* of Cotentin from at least 25 January 1426 (BNF, Fr. 25767/133).

[937] Breton had become *bailli* of Caen late in 1422 (BNF, Fr. 26046/1), holding office to 25 April 1430 (BNF, Fr. 22468/126). Men of this name had served as men-at-arms in 1415 under Lord Camoys (E 101/47/13 m. 1) as well as the earl of Arundel (E 101/47/1 m. 2). In 1417 Breton crossed as a knight under Sir Gilbert Umfraville (E 101/51/2 m. 33), suggesting he had been dubbed during the 1415 campaign. The Norman rolls show his prominence in the conquest, especially in the defence of Caen, where he was granted a number of houses and where he served as captain in 1421–22. He also held the captaincy of Bayeux from 29 September 1422 (BNF, NAF 1482/5) to at least 29 September 1427 (BNF, Fr. 26049/634). Breton was used as an agent by Fastolf to transfer money for him to England (Smith, 'Aspects of the Career of Sir John Fastolf', p. 4).

[938] Reference here is to what are called the 'Chemins des grèves', pathways across the bay along which visitors are led by experts who know the safe passages and tides.

[939] The attempt of Jean de la Haye, baron of Coulonces, to relieve Pontorson, his confrontation with the English at *La Gueintre* and death are also reported in the *Chronique du Mont-Saint-Michel* (Luce, i, pp. 28–9). We find a similar account in Chartier (i, p. 60) and *Pucelle* (p. 263) which wrongly situate the events in 1429.

[940] Louis d'Estouteville, lord of Auzebosc, was indeed captain of Mont-Saint-Michel in 1427.

[941] This is probably Bertrand de Montbourcher.

[942] Gruel (p. 57) reports the death of Patri III, sire de Châteaugiron, at the siege of Pontorson in 1427.

[943] At this point there was a lady of Tinténiac rather than a lord.

[944] Guillaume de Montauban (d. 1432), lord of Montauban, had already had a long political and military career in the service of dukes Jean IV and Jean V of Brittany by this time (he is believed to have been born long before 1370). For a while in the 1410s, he was also at the royal court, acting as chancellor of Queen Isabeau and chamberlain of the Dauphin Louis. Acting on behalf of the duchess of Brittany, Montauban was sent on an embassy to Henry V for the release of Richemont in June 1420 (Morice, ii, pp. 1021–2) and was still in France in September that year (*Lettres et mandements de Jean V*, iii, p. 29, no. 1437). He escorted Richemont to Angers for his meeting with Charles VII in October 1424 (Cosneau, pp. 84–5, 500–1, p.j. xviii). He was on the council of Jean V in February 1425 (*Lettres et mandements de Jean V*, iii, pp. 144–5, no. 1612). According to Gruel (p. 51) he was in Richemont's army which came to build up the defence of Pontorson in 1427. See also Merion-Jones et al., 'Le château de Montauban-de-Bretagne', pp. 704–5.

[945] Robert de Dinan (d. 1429) succeeded his father as lord of Montafilant and Châteaubriant in 1419. He was in the close entourage of Duke Jean V who addressed him in October 1420 as his 'dearest and most beloved cousin' (*Lettres et mandements de Jean V*, iii, p. 35, no. 1447). He sat regularly in the duke's council between 1420 and 1423 (ibid., iii, pp. 6–103). He escorted Richemont to Angers for his meeting with Charles VII in October 1424 (Cosneau, pp.

and many others to the number of 6,000 troops. There Lord Scales and the English dismounted and fought valiantly against the enemy. There was a fierce battle on both sides but at the finish, the enemy could no longer endure the great blows of the English, and took to flight in defeat. The baron of Coulonces was killed, and more than 1,000 Frenchmen were killed or taken prisoner.

After this fine and noteworthy act of destruction, Lord Scales and others of his company took themselves off with their victuals, weapons and prisoners in great joy and honour, to the siege (of Pontorson) where they were received very warmly by the earl of Warwick. During the siege Christopher Hanson and other soldiers of the garrison of Sainte-Suzanne to the number of [blank] soldiers carried out an enterprise in the region of Anjou, going right up to a castle called Ramefort. They took this castle by surprise attack and assault. When this capture came to the knowledge of the enemy, who had assembled 20,000 persons or more to give aid to the town of Pontorson, they broke off their campaign and went to lay siege to the castle of Ramefort. (59v) They were there for ten whole days until the English inside the place, seeing the great number in the enemy forces before them when they themselves were so few and also realising that their food supplies were failing, were compelled to come to a composition with the enemy and to surrender the castle to them, on terms that they might leave with their own lives intact but lose all their possessions, horses and armour. Once this had happened, the enemy left and did not come to Pontorson to provide assistance. Soon afterwards the lord of Rais,[946] so-called lieutenant of the king in the regions of Anjou and Maine, with the lord of Montjean,[947] the lord of Beaumanoir,[948] the lord of Tucé, *bailli* of Tours, and several others to the number of 3,000 soldiers entered Maine and laid siege to the castle of Malicorne-sur-Sarthe

---

500–1, p.j. xviii). According to Gruel (pp. 51, 53) he was in Richemont's army which came to build up the defence of Pontorson in 1427, and replaced the lord of Rostrenen as captain of Pontorson after the latter's capture by the English near Avranches. He was supported by his brother, Bertrand de Dinan, lord of Huguestières, marshal of Brittany.

[946] The first deed of arms of Gilles de Laval (1405–40), lord of Rais, was involvement in the rescue operation aimed at releasing Duke Jean V from his prison at Champtoceaux (*Maison de Laval*, iii, p. 43 no. 1162). He later fought with Richemont against the English. His involvement in the campaign in Maine in 1427 and the capture of the fortresses of Malicorne and Ramefort are noted in Chartier (i, pp. 51, 53) and *Pucelle* (pp. 242–3). He changed patron afterwards, swearing 'inviolable loyalty' to Georges de la Trémoille in April 1429 (*Les La Trémoïlle*, i, p. 183). He was made marshal of France by Charles VII on the day of the coronation, 17 July 1429 (AN, X1a 8604, f. 106v; Cosneau, p. 174 n. 4). His career ended in dramatic fashion, being tried and executed for the murder of children and 'invocations of demons' (*Jeanne. Dictionnaire*, pp. 947–8).

[947] This may be Guy de Laval, lord of Montjean, or Jean II, lord of Montjean.

[948] This is either Jacques de Dinan, lord of Beaumanoir and Montafilant (d. 1444), or Jean de Beaumanoir, seigneur d'Assé et de Lavardin, who married Marie Riboul. The lord of Beaumanoir escorted Richemont to his meeting with Charles VII at Angers in October 1424 (Cosneau, pp. 500–1, p.j. xviii). He appears as governor of the town and castle of Sablé-sur-Sarthe when he mustered in Angers with seventy-two men-at-arms in August 1425 en route to the frontiers of Maine to confront the English following their capture of Le Mans (Anselme, viii, p. 577). The lord of Beaumanoir's presence at the siege and capture of the fortresses of Ramefort, Lude and Malicorne in 1427 are reported by *Pucelle* (pp. 252–3) and Chartier (i, pp. 52–3, 57). Jacques de Dinan was made 'grand bouteiller of France' in April 1428 (Beaucourt, i, p. 568). He also fought at Patay (AN, X1a 9201, ff. 145r and v; 9193, ff. 157r sq; 9194, f. 144r; AN, X2a, ff. 197v, 305rv; *PPC*, iv, pp. 149–50; Little, *Parlement of Poitiers*, pp. 173–4) and was present at the coronation of Charles VII (Monstrelet, iv, p. 339).

whose lieutenant and keeper was Oliver Kathersby esquire.[949] They conquered the castle and took prisoner Oliver and all the others inside. From there they went off to the castle of Le Lude where William Blackburne[950] was lieutenant and keeper under William Glasdale esquire. They attacked the castle and took it by assault. All those inside were killed or taken prisoner. Afterwards they made a raid into the countryside and then returned because they realised that the earl of Warwick would not raise the siege which he had laid, and was continuing to maintain, before the town of Pontorson. Also they had heard news that the English were assembling to fight them and the enemy did not dare wait. Those inside the town of Pontorson realised that they would not have any help, knowing also that their victuals were starting to fail and that the English were every day launching attacks on them. They negotiated and came to an agreement with the earl of Warwick whereby they would surrender and deliver the town of Pontorson into the hands of the earl of Warwick in return for being allowed to go freely with their goods, their horses and equipment.[951]

After this the earl appointed Lord Roos[952] and Lord Talbot[953] as keepers and captains of the town[954] and then returned to the Regent. Subsequently by an agreement made that there should be a state of truce and an abstinence (60r) of

---

[949] Fastolf was at the siege of Pontorson in March and early April but left after 10 April 1427 with 100 troops to go to the rescue of Malicorne (BNF, NAF 1482/47; BNF, Fr. 26050/749). Oliver, whose name is given in a number of different forms, hailed from Battersby (Yorks. NR). If he was the Oliver Bathirsby who served in Normandy in 1418 under Sir William Huddlestone within the company of the Yorkshire lord, Henry, lord Fitzhugh (E 101/49/19), he had a very long career. From 1434 to 1438 he served in the garrison of Fresnay, captained by Fastolf, and in garrison detachments serving in the field (BNF, Fr. 25771/815; BNF, Fr. 25767/195; BNF Fr. 25772/1043; AN, K 64/10/8bis; AN, K 64/8/2; BNF, Fr. 25774/1309 and 1310). After Fastolf left France we find him serving under Sir Richard Woodville at Alençon in 1442 (BNF, Fr. 25776/1602) and Lord Scales at Domfront in 1443–46, in the last year as his lieutenant (BNF, Fr. 25777/1651 and 1714; BL, Add. Ch. 1231). According to a list made by William Worcester he was still in that office at the French reconquest (*L&P*, II, ii, p. 633). Chartier (i, p. 30) mentions him as marshal of Fresnay in connection with an incident apparently in 1422.

[950] Surviving muster records show a man-at-arms of this name in the personal retinue of Lord Talbot from 1436 (BNF, Fr. 25774/1214), but archers of this name are found in the retinue of the duke of Glocuester in the 1417 expedition (E 101/51/2 m. 1) and of John, lord Clifford in the army which accompanied the king back to France in the summer of 1421 (E 101/50/1 m. 1), as well as in the garrison of Coutances under Sir John de la Pole in March 1423 (BNF, Fr. 25767/1) and Sir John Harpelay in 1426 (AN, K 64/1/34).

[951] A *journée* was fixed for 1 May but the French did not appear and the English occupied Pontorson on 8 May (Beaucourt, i, p. 26).

[952] Thomas, lord Roos (1406–30) inherited the barony at the death of his brother John at Baugé in 1421, and married a daughter of Richard Beauchamp, earl of Warwick. He might seem too young to be the Thomas Rous serving as a man-at-arms in the army which crossed with the king in 1421 but his service at this date is not impossible (E 101/50/1 m. 4). His presence in France in 1426 is not otherwise evidenced, nor his presence at the battle of Verneuil. He was knighted alongside the young king at Whitsun 1426. He indented for the service of 160 men for the expeditionary army which crossed in March 1427 at the duke of Bedford's return to France (E 403/677 mm. 11, 17; E 404/43/170), having seisin of his lands in that same year. He died at a skirmish in France on 18 August 1430 during the 'coronation expedition' for which he also indented for 160 men (E 404/46/210).

[953] Talbot indented for a company of 320 in the expeditionary army which crossed in March 1427 at the duke of Bedford's return to France (E 403/677 mm. 11, 17).

[954] According to Monstrelet (iv, p. 288) it was Scales whom Warwick appointed captain at Pontorson. He was certainly in post by 6 January 1428 (AN, K 63/1/12). In the summer of

war between the Regent and the duke of Brittany, the two towns and fortresses of Pontorson and Saint-James-de-Beuvron were dismantled. Soon afterwards, the lord of Rais and others of the enemy who had entered into the county of Maine, as you have heard earlier, took themselves off. Christopher Hanson, Philip Goth,[955] Martin Godefroy,[956] the wall-scaler, and several others of the garrison of Sainte-Suzanne to the number of twenty to thirty English, went off on a venture. One morning, Jacques de Scépeaux,[957] who was captain and keeper of the castle of Saint-Laurent-des-Mortiers, came out of the castle with several French and went to the church of the same place, which was outside the castle gate, so that they could hear mass. During the time they were saying mass, the English named earlier entered by crafty means through the castle gate and took the castle. Jacques de Scépeaux became the prisoner of Christopher Hanson. Following this, they guarded the castle, and Sir William Oldhall knight was appointed as its captain and keeper.

In this same year around the month of [blank] Sir John Fastolf, the English knight, governor of Anjou and Maine, assembled the men of the garrisons of the area and other men of his retinue and laid siege before the castle and fortress of Saint-Ouën-des-Toits close to the town of Laval whose captain, for the French, was Guillaume d'Orenge, knight. At the end of eight days he surrendered the castle to Fastolf by composition whereby he and all those who were inside had their lives guaranteed, save for one man who was guilty of defamation and who had said several hurtful words for which he was executed. The captain was taken prisoner.

From there Fastolf left and went to lay siege before the castle of La Gravelle. At the end of eight days those who were inside came to an agreement to surrender the fortress on a particular day if they were not rescued and if the enemy did not find themselves in the majority before the place on that same day. In order to hold to this agreement and to fulfil it, the enemy (6ov) delivered and handed over pledges and hostages, namely Guillaume de Cordouen[958] and *Jean de la Maisière*, esquires. When these had been taken and received by Fastolf, he left the place and went to my lord the Regent in Paris and informed him of the agreement and composition.

---

the following year his soldiers demolished the place without his licence (BNF, Fr. 4488 pp. 238–40).

[955] Goth had mustered at Alençon on 5 September 1424 in Fastolf's company for the invasion of Maine (BNF, Fr. 25767/93).

[956] The surname 'Godefroy' is found in both England and France at this point but the first name Martin suggests a French origin for this person. A Martin Gieffroy served as an archer under Robert, lord Willoughby on field service in Lower Normandy in January 1432 (BNF, Clairambault 207/102) and as an archer in September 1433 at the siege of Bonsmoulins (AN, K 63/24/11).

[957] The Scépeaux were a large family implanted in Maine and Anjou (Angot, *Dictionnaire historique, topographique et biographique de la Mayenne*, iii, Scépeaux (de)). There is evidence of the presence of Jacques de Scépeaux, knight, in Maine and Anjou in October and November 1434 (AN, KK 324 ff. 142r, 143v 148v).

[958] Guillaume de Cordouen gave homage to the lord of Sillé in 1455 (ADS, E 21; Termeau, 'La Forêt de Sillè-le-Guillaume', p. 19). Guillaume de Cordouen, described as lord of Mimbré and Chaigné, gave homage to the lord of Corbon in 1457 (ADS, E 293). In 1461, Guillaume de Cordouan, esquire, seigneur de Mimbré, gave homage to Marie de Sillé for his fief of Cherré (ADS, 4J 64; *Archives départementales de la Sarthe, Sous-série 4J; Chartier de Grandchamp*, p. 11).

As a result, the Regent raised an army in order to go on the assigned day to fight or to take surrender of the place. In his company were
the count of Mortain[959]
Lord Roos
Lord Talbot
Sir John Fastolf
Sir John Montgomery
Sir John Popham
Sir William Oldhall
Sir Thomas Blount[960]
Sir Nicolas Burdet
[added: *Sir Philip Hall*
Sir Jehan de Aubemond
Sir John Radcliffe][961]
and many others to the number of about 20,000 men of war. The Regent rode to the abbey of [blank] in the hope of fighting the enemy who had, it was said, assembled in great strength. Despite this, the enemy did not appear on the assigned day. As a result, my lord the Regent sent Fastolf to receive the surrender of the fortress as had been agreed and promised. The enemy who were inside were very well provided with victuals and had therefore gone against their agreements and promises and had abandoned their pledges and hostages. The latter were beheaded in full view of those in the place. Once this was done my lord the Regent went home with all his host without doing anything further. (61r) After the departure of the Regent, that is, around the feast of St Michel (29 September) in the year 1426,[962] Sir John Fastolf was discharged from the government of the areas of Anjou and Maine and in his place Lord Talbot was appointed.[963] Around Lent[964] the latter carried out a secret enterprise through which the town of Laval was taken and won by surprise attack using ladders for the assault. But the lord of Lohéac and many nobles and bourgeois in the town retreated into the castle and held themselves there for about four days. During this period, they negotiated and came to an agreement with Lord Talbot that the lord of Lohéac[965] and all the other noble men of war, bour-

---

[959]   This must be Edmund Beaufort (c. 1406–55), although he did not receive this title until 22 April 1427. He had indented for 160 men in the expeditionary army which crossed in March 1427 at the time of the duke of Bedford's return to France (E 403/677; E 404/43/158) and was present at the siege of Montargis in August–September 1427 (BNF, Fr. 4484 f. 69v).

[960]   On 17 September 1426 Blount took out letters of protection to serve in France (C 76/109 m. 18, DKR 48, p. 243).

[961]   Radcliffe was appointed seneschal of Aquitaine on 3 March 1423, crossing to Bordeaux in June, but was in England from the summer of 1425 to May 1429 when, shortly after his election as KG, he agreed to lead 800 reinforcements to France (*PPC*, iii, pp. 326–7; E 404/45/140).

[962]   The chronology is confused here since Bedford crossed to England in December 1425 and did not return to France until March 1427.

[963]   The exact date of Talbot's appointment is not known but he was 'gouverneur du pays de Maine' by 17 April 1428 (BNF, Fr. 26050/870).

[964]   The chronology here is problematic. The Lent indicated here must be 1428 since Laval was taken by Talbot on 13 March 1428 (Beaucourt, ii, p. 30).

[965]   On 19 June 1428, Jeanne and Anne de Laval, along with Guy XIV, committed to reimburse all those who had contributed to pay the remainder of the ransom of André de

geois and others who had retreated into the castle should leave it freely by paying 20,000 *écus* for everything. The castle was thereby handed over and Lord Talbot appointed and ordered as its keeper and captain there and in the town Sir Gilbert Halsall knight.[966] He remained captain and keeper up to the time that siege was laid before the city of Orléans at which he was killed. After that, Matthew Gough esquire was appointed keeper and captain holding the office to the time of the *journée* before Senlis,[967] which will be mentioned later.

Around the time Matthew Gough was going to the assigned day for action (i.e. the *journée* at La Gravelle), thanks to the treason of a renegade miller who kept a mill next to the walls of Laval, the enemy were able to ride into the town and to win it, putting it under their obedience.

In the year 1427[968] around the feast of Pentecost (1 June) the enemy carried out a large-scale and secret enterprise. They gathered to the number of 6,000 men of war, including the lords whose names follow:

the lord of Albret[969]	} marshals of France
the lord of La Fayette[970]	}
(61v) the lord of Montjean[971]
the lord of Bueil[972]
the lord of Orval[973]
the lord of Tucé[974]

Laval, lord of Lohéac, to Lord Talbot as in the treaty of surrender of the castle of Laval. The outstanding sum amounted to 8,000 *écus d'or*. Contributors included Jean de Craon, lord of la Suze, Gilles de Laval, lord of Rais, Baudouin de Champagne, lord of Tucé, Jean, lord of Bueil and Bertrand de Beauvau (*La Maison de Laval*, iii, pp. 73–4, no. 1208).

966 Halsall had taken out letters of protection in February 1427 (C 76/109 m. 13, DKR 48, p. 247) and can be assumed to be the knight banneret in Talbot's company in the expeditionary army of that year (Ratcliffe, 'Military Expenditure', pp. 22–4). We find him in Talbot's personal retinue at the siege of Orléans in January 1429 (BL, Add. Ch. 11612).

967 Oise, ch. l. d'arr. The *journée* refered to here is the aborted battle between armies under the dukes of Bedford and Alençon at Montépilloy on 15 August 1429. This mention indicates that the context of the chronicle had been planned beyond the end point of the existing manuscript.

968 This is an error for 1428. The French took Le Mans on 25 May 1428.

969 The involvement of Charles II d'Albret, marshal of France, in the recapture of Le Mans is nowhere else evidenced.

970 The involvement of Gilbert III Motier, lord of La Fayette, in the failed attempt to recapture Le Mans is nowhere else evidenced. He had been marshal since 1420.

971 This may be Guy de Laval, lord of Montjean, or Jean II, lord of Montjean.

972 On 28 May 1428, Jean, lord of Bueil, knight, gave a quittance to the king for 120 *l.t.* for participation in the operation 'pour le recouvrement de la dicte ville du Mans' (BNF, Clairambault, 23/1669; Ledru, 'Tentative des français', pp. 7–8).

973 Guillaume d'Albret (d. 1429), lord of Orval, was the younger brother of Charles II d'Albret. His leading role in this attempt to recapture Le Mans is reported in various chronicles. Louis de Cars, knight, chamberlain of the king, gave quittance for 1,000 *écus d'or* on behalf of Guillaume d'Albret for his expenses in the recovery of the city (BNF, Clairambault, 43/3201; Ledru, 'Tentative des français', p. 8).

974 Baudouin de Tucé, knight, lord of Tucé and *bailli* de Touraine, gave a quittance on 23 May 1428 for participation in the recovery of Le Mans (BNF, Clairambault, 28/2055; Ledru, 'Tentative des français', p. 8).

the lord of Beaumanoir[975]
La Hire[976]
Regnault Guillaume, his brother[977]
and many others. Thanks to the help and treason of some churchmen and bourgeois of the city of Le Mans, the enemy entered and gained the city by a [blank].

The English who were within the city retreated into the castle which had newly been built and whose lieutenant and keeper was Thomas Gower. They defended themselves there very powerfully and valiantly against the enemy. For the whole day of the following [blank] the enemy carried out strong and notable assaults, so much so that more than half the English were wounded or killed by the arrows of the French. There was a danger that the place would be taken had it not been that news of the capture of the city came to Lord Talbot. He hastily assembled the soldiers of the garrison of which he was captain[978] and others of the vicinity. To wit, Lord Scales
Sir Thomas Blount[979]
Sir Thomas Rempston[980]
Sir William Oldhall
Matthew Gough

---

[975] The involvement of the lord of Beaumanoir (either Jacques de Dinan or Jean de Beaumanoir) in this operation is also reported in *Pucelle* (p. 251).

[976] Etienne de Vignolles, dit la Hire (c. 1390–1443), from the Landes in Gascony, was a well-known captain in the service of Charles VII whose extensive military activities during the 1420s and the 1430s caused much ink to flow. His participation in the attempted recapture of Le Mans in May 1427 is reported in Chartier (i, p. 58) and *Pucelle* (p. 251). Raoulet (in Chartier, iii, p. 194) and Tringant (*Jouvencel*, ii, p. 275) add the presence of La Hire's 'inseparable' companion, Jean, dit Poton, de Xaintrailles. See also Lediou, *Esquisses militaires*; and Bloch, 'Etienne de Vignolles'.

[977] La Hire had four brothers who served in arms, largely in support of their brother: Amadoc, Arnaud or Renaud-Guillaume, Pierre-Renaud (dit le bourg) and Jean Benoît (Bloch, 'Etienne de Vignolles', p. 106). Arnaud or Regnault-Guillaume, whom M 9 describes as taking part in the attempted capture of Le Mans, may also be the 'frere d'Hiere' reported as participating in the capture of La Ferté-Bernard in a report to Bedford in January 1427 (Joubert, *Documents*, pp. 21–2, no. 10). An entry of the *Livre des Miracles* (pp. 55–7, no. 104) suggests that Regnault-Guillaume was in garrison in Vendôme in 1426 and/or 1427. There is evidence of Arnault-Guillaume's presence in Maine and Anjou in 1433–34 (AN, KK 324 ff. 38v, 45r, 67v, 82r).

[978] It is unclear which garrison is meant as Talbot did not hold any captaincies at this point other than Pontorson, to which he had been appointed after its surrender in early May 1427. According to Cosneau (p. 137), his captaincy at Pontorson was jointly with the earl of Warwick but the chronicle names Lord Roos as co-captain (f. 59v). It is possible that Talbot's regional command in Maine and Anjou, which he held by mid-April, gave him control of certain garrisons.

[979] Blount's whereabouts in the summer of 1427 are uncertain. On 16 October 1427 his company mustered at Essay for the conquest of Maine and Anjou but he himself is not included in the muster list (BNF, Fr. 25768/260). His service was notable enough to lead in January 1428 to a grant of lands in the area of Crépy-en-Valois, Meaux and Soissons (AN, JJ 173/719).

[980] The recovery of Le Mans by the English on 28 May 1428 led to a suit in the *Parlement* of Paris, which began in August 1428, by Sir John Popham, Sir William Oldhall, Sir Thomas Rempston and William Glasdale against John, lord Talbot, John Winter, John Felawe and Richard Gildon over prisoners (*English Suits*, XVII).

William Glasdale[981]
Oliver Kathersby of Battersby
Osbern Mundeford[982]
Nicolas Molyneux[983]
Thomas Lound[984]

and many others to the number of 700 soldiers. They left Alençon by night and rode to a castle two leagues away from the city of Le Mans, called La Guierche. There Lord Talbot sent an order to Matthew Gough (62r) that he should ride on ahead alone and spy out the state of the enemy. Talbot would follow straight afterwards and they would meet on the road so that Gough could tell him what he had found out. In fulfilment of the command which had been given to him, Gough rode on ahead in a very guileful manner without being spotted or recognised by the enemy. Early in the morning just after daybreak he entered the castle of Le Mans and spoke to Thomas Gower who told him the deployment of the enemy who were within the town. Afterwards Gough ate some bread and had a drink, then left. He met Lord Talbot and Lord Scales about a mile away from [blank]. He told them all he had seen.

Straightaway the lords and their company dismounted and entered the castle.

By such means they entered the city of Le Mans around 5 o'clock in the morning,[985] and began to cry in a loud voice 'Our Lady, Saint George, Lord Talbot'. The French who were still asleep in their beds were completely terror-stricken and got up as quickly as they could. They began to flee, some of them naked

---

[981]   Glasdale was at this point *bailli* of Alençon, holding the post from at least July 1426 to his death on 8 May 1429 (BNF, Fr. 26049/668, 669).

[982]   Mundeford (d. 1460), of Hockwold (Norfolk), appears in musters as a man-at-arms, and sometime marshal, in Fastolf's garrison of Fresnay-le-Vicomte from 1432 (BNF, Fr. 25770/734) to 1438 (BNF, Fr. 25774/1297), continuing in service there after Fastolf's retirement from France (BNF, Fr. 25775/1386). His service before 1432 is likely but elusive. (It was his father who had crossed as a man-at-arms in 1415 under Sir John Colville, one of the duke of Clarence's captains (E 101/45/4 m. 1)). He was *bailli* and captain of Le Mans by 1445 and in that capacity refused to fulfil the royal order to surrender the place to the French. In September 1448 he was appointed treasurer-general of the duchy of Normandy as well as captain of Fresnay and Pont-l'Evêque. When Charles VII invaded, he was captured at Pont-Audemer on 12 August 1449. He was released thanks to the mediation of Andrew Trollope, his brother-in-law and also his lieutenant at Fresnay, as part of the surrender agreement for Fresnay. He continued in military service as marshal of Calais in the early 1450s and was killed at Sandwich by the Yorkists whilst trying to raise reinforcements for Lancastrian-held Guînes.

[983]   Nicholas Molyneux entered into a 'brotherhood-in-arms' agreement with John Winter in July 1421 (Oxford, Magdalen College, Southwark 213, in McFarlane, 'A Business Partnership in War and Administration'). In 1422 we find him as a foot man-at-arms in the garrison of Rouen (E 101/49/31). From at least 1427 he was Fastolf's representative in the collection of garrison wages, and by 1433 he was the knight's receiver-general in France as well as the accounting official for the duke of Bedford's income in Maine and Anjou (AN, KK 324). Between 1445 and 1447 he was receiver of Richard, duke of York's lands in France (McFarlane, 'A Business Partnership in War and Administration', pp. 157–8, 161–3).

[984]   Lound may have been associated with Fastolf's garrison of Alençon in this action, but in March he had served at the siege of Pontorson under Thomas Burgh, being involved in late April in an action with Burgh along the Breton frontier (BNF, Fr. 25767/2; BL, Add. Ch. 11573).

[985]   The rescue of Le Mans occurred on 28 May 1428.

save for their nightshirts, and climbed over the walls. Others took themselves off through the gates and saved their lives as best they could, abandoning their clothes, horses, helmets, armour, equipment and weapons. In that recovery and victorious rout around three to four hundred French were killed or taken prisoner.

Soon afterwards, to wit, around the feast of the Nativity of St John the Baptist (24 June 1427), the Regent lay siege to the town of Montargis[986] from both sides of the river which passed through there and which was called [blank]. He gave command to the earl of Suffolk and to Sir John (62v) de la Pole, his brother, with around 600 soldiers.[987] In addition, the Regent ordered the earl of Warwick who was his lieutenant-general to be at Larchamp[988] with a certain number of men so that he could reinforce the siege if necessary and, if the French came, to give help to those who were inside.

The siege lasted for about two months.[989] The French, to wit,
the lord of Boussac, marshal of France[990]
La Hire[991]
Poton de Xaintrailles[992]
and many others to the number of 3,000 soldiers rode out as secretly as they could towards the siege. They found the English in the section under Sir John de la Pole to be in disarray because of the failure to keep good watch and because of the

---

[986] Loiret, ch. l. d'arr. The town lies on the River Loing. English troops may have first appeared before Montargis on 1 July (BNF, Fr. 26050/807).

[987] On 21 May 1427 Suffolk was appointed captain-general and lieutenant for war in the Vendomois, Chartrain, Beauce and Gastinois with a total force of 2,000 men, of which 1,200 were from the expeditionary army which had been sent from England and the remainder raised in France. It was in this capacity that he lay siege to Montargis, mustering there on 17 August and 1 September, as did his brother Sir John de la Pole (BNF, Fr. 4484 f. 45v).

[988] Mayenne, arr. Mayenne, cant. Ernée. Warwick, 'captain-general and lieutenant for war for the whole of France', was commissioned on 21 July 1427 for three months to lay siege to Montargis and other places held by the enemy in Beauce and Gastinois (BNF, Fr. 4484 f. 65v).

[989] The siege was laid from July to September 1427. Soldiers from England arrived in late August under Edmund Beaufort and others to boost the troops raised in France (BNF, Fr. 4484 ff. 68–71; Toureille, *Montargis*, pp. 24–5).

[990] Jean de Brosse (1375–1433), lord of Boussac, a councillor and chamberlain of the king, was made 'maréchal de France' sometime in 1426 or 1427. He was involved in court intrigue, orchestrating the murder of Jean du Vernet, dit le Camus de Beaulieu, in June 1427. In May 1428, he participated in the capture of Bourges by the count of Clermont who had rebelled against Charles VII, but the two men were soon pardoned and reconciled with the king. Boussac then became a loyal and devoted subject. His taking part in the relieving of the siege of Montargis is nowhere else evidenced, but is feasible since the lord of Boussac was still an ally of Richemont and may have gone with him to Jargeau over the summer of 1427 (*Jeanne. Dictionnaire*, p. 582). On the other hand, there may be confusion with Gauthier de Brusac whose presence at the siege of Montargis is mentioned in Monstrelet (iv, p. 273) and the *Cronique Martiniane* (p. 7).

[991] La Hire's presence and prominent role in this rescue operation are widely reported in chronicle accounts (Toureille, *Montargis*, pp. 46–50).

[992] The presence of Poton de Xaintrailles at Montargis is evidenced in three chronicle accounts, namely Raoulet (in Chartier, iii, p. 193), Cagny (p. 136) and Gruel (p. 58), but not in Monstrelet, Berry, Chartier or *Pucelle*.

negligence and indolence of Sir John.[993] They launched an attack on them and put them to flight, killing and taking prisoners to the number of about 2,000 English. Sir John himself crossed the river on a horse towards the other section of the siege where his brother, the earl of Suffolk, was. By such means was he saved.

As soon as the earl of Warwick heard the news of the French attack, he left his location of Larchamp and hastily went off to join the siege. With a big effort he rallied the English and offered to give battle to the French. The latter had already retreated into the town of Montargis but refused to give battle. Seeing that was the case and that they could do no more for the time being to raise and break the siege, the English lords lifted and broke the siege, departed, and withdrew, leaving behind and losing all the ordnance that they had taken to the siege.[994] They took themselves back to my lord the Regent.

(63r) In the year of grace 1428 around the feast of Pentecost (23 May) the earl of Salisbury as lieutenant of the king of England and France crossed over the sea with a noteworthy army of 7,000 men or thereabouts, landing at Calais.[995] From there he passed through the region of Picardy, making his way towards the city of Paris in which my lord the Regent was at this point.[996] After they had spoken together the earl left Paris with his army and went to lay siege before the town and castle of Janville in Beauce.[997] After a fortnight he launched an assault of the town by force and dint of which he took and conquered it. But the French retreated inside the castle and defended themselves as much as they could. After another fortnight the French who were in the castle surrendered and handed over both themselves and the castle to the will of the earl. The latter, for various reasons, put some of them to death and the others he held as prisoners.

Immediately afterwards, the earl went to lay siege before the town of Beaugency.[998] This siege lasted for about a fortnight, during which period those in the town negotiated and came to an agreement with the earl that they would surrender the

---

[993] Monstrelet (iv, p. 273) notes an attack on the camp of John de la Pole, making no comment on his lack of defence but mentioning that he saved himself in a little boat ('se sauva en un petit bateau'). Gruel (p. 58) suggests that it was the area defended by Sir Henry Biset which was poorly defended, and where the French found the English asleep because they had kept watch all night.

[994] The English withdrew on 5 September, after suffering casualties in a French attack, and the place was delivered to Dunois (ADL, 2 J 2435; Beaucourt, ii, p. 28; Toureille, *Montargis*, pp. 55–6).

[995] Salisbury's indenture for an expeditionary army of 2,400 men is dated 24 March 1428 (E 101/71/2/28). He crossed with 2,694 men in mid-July, the larger size being explained by his taking advantage of an indenture clause which allowed more archers to be recruited in place of men-at-arms. He was appointed on 29 July 1428 as 'lieutenant general sur le fait de la guerre du roi et du regent partout le royaume de France' and a force of 1,600 was detailed in France to join with him for the campaign (BNF, Fr. 4484 ff. 106–7).

[996] The earl met Bedford in Paris around 6–9 August 1428 when a payment of 3,000 *l.t.* was agreed from 1 July for six months for his command of the campaign (BNF, Fr. 4484 ff. 107–8v).

[997] Eure-et-Loir, arr. Chartres, cant. Voves. The earl's troops mustered at Janville on 20 August (BNF, Fr. 4484 f. 110). Sir Richard Grey was appointed captain of Janville at its capture (Jarry, p. 82) but died at the siege of Orléans on 3 May 1429.

[998] The earl's troops mustered there on 26 September 1428 (BNF, Fr. 4484 f. 110v) with surrender on the previous day (Beaucourt, ii, p. 32).

place, on condition that all those living in the obedience of the English should preserve their lives and all their goods and possessions. From there the earl went before Meung-sur-Loire[999] but those inside surrendered immediately through a similar agreement to those at Beaugency. In the same way those in the town of Jargeau surrendered.[1000] Once the earl had put captains and keepers into these towns and places, that is, in the month of September 1428, he laid siege to the city of Orléans but on one side of it only.[1001] In this city the main captains and governors were the Bastard of Orléans (Dunois)[1002] and the bishop of the place.[1003] They had a large number of men of war under them, both French and Scottish. After the place had been besieged for the space of around [blank] those inside made a sally by the bridge and skirmished with the English. The latter (63v) received them well and they all fought bravely against each other. But finally the French could no long bear the actions and charges of the English and began to lose confidence and to turn to flight towards the bridge in order to save their skins. However, the English pursued them so hotly that they entered into the bulwark of the bridge. This bulwark, along with the tower which was at the end of the bridge, was won by the English and many of the French inside were killed or taken prisoner. Once this had been done the earl appointed and ordered as captain of the tower and bulwark William Glasdale esquire.[1004]

Quite soon, and within a short time after the taking and capture of the tower – in which there was a room, amongst other chambers, which had a window barred with iron bars through which you could see all along the bridge and into the city – several lords and other Englishmen frequently went to this window to observe and

---

[999] Loiret, arr. Orléans, ch. l. cant. Salisbury appeared before the walls on 5 September (Beaucourt, ii, p. 32).

[1000] Loiret, arr, Orléans, cant. Châteauneuf-sur-Loire.

[1001] Salisbury's siege from the south began on 12 October (Beaucourt, ii, p. 32).

[1002] Jean, Bastard of Orléans (c. 1402–68), count of Dunois (1439) and Longueville (1443), was the illegitimate half brother of Charles, duke of Orléans, and Jean d'Angoulême, who were both held captive in England at that time, so that the defence of the house of Orléans in his brothers' prolonged absence was his responsibility. The M 9 chronicle omits the prominent role that he played in lifting the siege of Montargis in 1427 for which he was generously rewarded by Charles VII, who called him his 'amé et féal cousin, conseilliez et chambellan' (BNF, Fr. 20382/19; BNF Fr. 20379 f. 134, cited by Bord, 'Jean, Bâtard d'Orléans', pp. 100–1). Along with several other captains he came to reinforce the defence of Orléans on 25 October 1428, according to the *Journal du siège* (pp. 10–13). The accounts of Hémon Raguier record a payment of 155 *l.t.* made to him for a company of twelve men-at-arms and seven archers who had entered the city on 30 October 1428 (Raguier's accounts in *Journal du siège*, pp. 164–6, no. 5). He then took command of the city (AN, U 821, ff. 199–210v, cited in Bord, 'Jean, Bâtard d'Orléans', p. 104). See also *Jeanne. Dictionnaire*, pp. 674–6.

[1003] John of Kirkmichael, alias Jean de Saint-Michel, a Scot of noble birth, doctor in civil and canon law, may have been a chaplain of Archibald, earl of Douglas, duke of Touraine, who died at Verneuil. He was bishop of Orléans between 1426 and 1435, and a councillor of Charles VII in the same period. He was in Orléans when the siege began, and left the place after the battle of Rouvray only to return after the siege had been lifted. He was present at the coronation of Charles VII (*Jeanne. Dictionnaire*, pp. 783–4).

[1004] By late December Glasdale held command at this location alongside William Molins, with a garrison of 144 men (BNF, Fr. 25768/328; Jarry, pp. 95–6). He died at the storming of Les Tourelles by Joan of Arc, an event commonly dated to 8 May 1429.

look out into the city. Those inside the city were annoyed by this. As a result, they had one of the master cannoneers aim a cannon straight against the window to shoot when necessary. One day around dinner time,[1005] the earl of Salisbury, Sir Thomas Gargrave,[1006] Glasdale and others came into the tower and entered the chamber. The earl went straight to the window and began to look out towards the city. Immediately the son of the master cannoneer noticed that there were people at the window. So he took the fuse and did just what his father, when going off for his dinner, had shown and instructed him. He fired the cannon and let fly a ball directly against the window, which broke the iron bars. The earl was hit on the head by one of the bars, or else by the shattering of the ball, to such an extent that it took out one of his eyes and smashed up a quarter of his head right through to his brain. Sir Thomas Gargrave was also hit by another exploding shot to such a degree that he died two days later.[1007] The earl (64r) was taken to Meung-sur-Loire where he lay ill for about eight days. During this time he made disposition for his soul as a good Christian should, received the sacrament of the Holy Church and the true body of Our Lord. Then he gave up his soul to God the Father and to Jesus Christ his son.[1008]

The very sad news came to the Regent of the death of this most noble, victorious and valiant lord. It was not surprising that he had great sadness and displeasure in his heart because of this. He appointed and ordered as lieutenant-general on behalf of the king and himself the earl of Suffolk, who was at the siege, making him chief captain of the siege and of all the army, and giving him the command, government and direction of it.[1009] In order to reinvigorate and reinforce the siege he sent, to wit,

Lord Talbot[1010]

Lord Scales[1011]

[1005] The date of Salisbury's accident was most likely 27 October 1428.

[1006] Gargrave was certainly present with the earl of Salisbury on the campaign to the Loire, and at the sieges of Janville, Beaugency and Orléans (BNF, Fr. 4488 ff. 110r–110v), having previously commanded a contingent of the earl's troops detailed to the siege of Montargis (ff. 55–8).

[1007] Gargrave did not die. Financial records show that he was still at the siege in December 1428–January 1429 (Jarry, pp. 127–8). According to Monstrelet (iv, p. 459) and Berry (pp. 150, 433), he participated, as captain of Nogent-le-Roy, in the battle of Bulgnéville on 2 July 1431. By October 1432 he was also captain of Montigny-le-Roy (ACO, B 1649, f. 122v), a post he presumably held until the breach with Burgundy in 1435. Assuming this is the same person, he was in the garrison of Pontoise in 1439 (AN, K 67/1/40; BNF, Clairambault 202/6, 7, 10, 11) and then of Mantes, of which he was lieutenant by September 1442 (BNF, Fr. 25766/1538; BNF, NAF 8637/51).

[1008] The earl died on 3 November 1428, his body being brought back to England for burial at Bisham (Berks.)

[1009] Suffolk provided a company of 160 of the 1,200 troops raised in France to join with Salisbury's expeditionary army (ADE, IIF 4069; BNF, Clairambault 188/84). On 22 December he entered into an indenture with Bedford for the service of 400 men at the siege, also being paid 333*l.* 6*s* 8*d.t.* per month as commander from 27 October (Jarry, pp. 107–10).

[1010] Talbot entered into an indenture with Bedford on 23 December 1428 for 232 men for the siege (Jarry, pp. 110–11).

[1011] Scales was appointed on 15 December to the command of the army at the siege, alongside Suffolk and Talbot (BNF, Fr. 26051/997, printed in Jarry, pp. 233–4). On 23

Sir John Fastolf[1012]
Sir Thomas Rempston[1013]
Sir Ralph Neville[1014]
Sir Gilbert Halsall[1015]
Sir Lancelot de Lisle[1016]
Sir Henry Biset[1017]
[added: *Sir Henry Mortimer*]
and several others in a notable army. They continued the siege and, in addition, had constructed and established several bastides in front of the gates of that city in order to place restrictions on those inside. Around the time of the following Lent (9 February–27 March 1429), because victuals and equipment were starting to fail at the siege, it was decided and ordered that Sir John Fastolf and Sir Thomas Rempston with their men should go to the Regent in Paris in order to seek out and bring back with them to the siege victuals and equipment. (64v) When they had arrived in Paris, they had loaded onto carriages, carts and horses, by the order of the Regent, a large quantity of foodstuffs, including grains, flour, oats, and also military equipment. In order that they could conduct and escort these to the siege more securely, Sir Simon Morhier knight, *prévôt* of Paris, was ordered, with the crossbowmen of the *cinquantaine* of Paris[1018] in his company as well as some of the men of the household of the Regent, to go with Fastolf and Rempston to escort the victuals to the siege. They left together with about 1,500 soldiers, and went with all the stuff to Janville in Beauce. They left Janville on a morning when there was

---

December he entered into an indenture with Bedford for 200 men to serve at the siege (Jarry, pp. 112–14).

[1012] On 22 November Fastolf entered into an indenture with Bedford for service at the siege with eighty men, a new indenture for 200 men being issued on 12 January (Jarry, pp. 97–100).

[1013] Rempston's presence on the Loire campaign is evidenced by musters from August 1428 to April 1429 (BNF, Fr. 25768/291; BNF, Fr. 25768/299; BL, Add. Ch. 11614; BNF, Fr. 25768/352; BL, Add. Ch. 11629). On 8 December 1428 Thomas Afford entered into an indenture on Rempston's behalf for ninety men, with a new indenture issued to Rempston for sixty men on 12 January 1429 (Jarry, pp. 101–4). Rempston was captured at the battle of Patay.

[1014] Ralph had served in Coutances and Saint-Lô under the earl of Suffolk in October 1422 (BNF, Fr. 25766/809) and was captain of Coutances himself in 1425–26 (BNF, Fr. 25767/139). By summer 1424 he had become a household knight of the duke of Bedford's household and commanded, together with Sir John Handford, part of Bedford's personal retinue sent to the siege of Gaillon in May 1424 (BNF, Fr. 4485 p. 283). On 15 December 1428 he entered into an indenture with Bedford for the service of forty men at the siege of Orléans (Jarry, pp. 42–3).

[1015] Halsall mustered in Lord Talbot's personal retinue at the siege on 29 January 1429 (BL, Add. Ch. 11612).

[1016] Lisle served with a retinue of 140 men within the 1,200-strong army assigned to join with Salisbury's expeditionary army on its arrival in France (BNF, Clairambault 173/44; BL, Add. Ch. 7947). He was marshal of Salisbury's army at the siege of Orléans (Jarry, pp. 87–90). On 30 January 1429, when returning from negotiations with the Dauphinists before Orléans, he was killed by a cannonball (*Journal du siège*, p. 4).

[1017] Biset was killed at the French assault on Jargeau in June 1429 (Boucher de Molandon, *L'armée anglaise*, p. 130).

[1018] The *cinquantaine* was a crossbow company organised by the citizens of Paris.

a very heavy frost and it was very cold, making their way towards the siege. When they had gone as far as the vicinity of a village called Rouvray-Sainte-Croix,[1019] in open country, they spotted quite a long way off the enemy French coming against them. The French were about nine or ten thousand strong, with both French and Scots. The names of some of them follow, to wit,

Sir Charles de Bourbon, eldest son of the duke of Bourbon[1020]
Sir William Stewart constable of Scotland[1021]
the count of Perdriac[1022]
the Bastard of Orléans[1023]
Jean de Vendôme, knight, vidame of Chartres[1024]
the lord of Thouars[1025]

[1019] Loiret, arr. Orléans, cant. Meung-sur-Loire. This location for the 'Battle of the Herrings' is preferred to Rouvray-Saint-Denis (Eure-et-Loir, arr. Chartres, cant. Voves), following Cooper, *Real Falstaff*, pp. 53–5.

[1020] Charles (1404–56), count of Clermont and then duke of Bourbon, was the elder son of Duke Jean and Marie de Berry and inherited the titles and estates from his father in 1434 when the latter eventually died in captivity in England. Charles had been captured by the Armagnacs on the bridge of Montereau in 1419, and from then had fought on the Dauphinist side. He was captain-general of Languedoc and Guyenne for Charles VII between 1420 and 1424. He entered the party of Arthur de Richemont, constable of France, in 1425, and received the duchy of Auvergne, but fell into disgrace along with Richemont in 1427. Charles VII soon recalled him, however, because of his supposed capacity as a military leader, to intercept a supply convoy to the English army besieging Orléans in 1429. His commanding role and presence at Rouvray are widely reported in chronicle accounts and narrative sources. He subsequently participated in the coronation campaign of Charles VII who made him lieutenant of the 'pays en deçà de la Seine', but he soon retired to his estates (*Jeanne. Dictionnaire*, pp. 571–2).

[1021] Sir William Stewart was not constable. That office was held by his half-brother Sir John Stewart of Darnley, lord of Concressault.

[1022] Bernard d'Armagnac (1396–1462), count of Pardiac, was the second son of Bernard d'Armagnac, count of Armagnac, the constable of France killed in Paris in 1418. Bernard junior was lieutenant-general for Charles VII in the *bailliage* of Macon and the *sénéchaussée* of Lyon in 1422, but was replaced by the maréchal of Séverac by the end of the year. He sealed an alliance with Clermont and Richemont in 1427, ordered the killing of Séverac that year, and plotted against Charles VII in 1428. Pardiac and Clermont assembled the Estates of Auvergne which voted a subvention of 30,000 *livres* for relieving the siege of Orléans in October 1428. His participation in the battle of Rouvray and the siege of Orléans is nowhere else noted. Pardiac was not allowed to join the coronation expedition. He would only return to grace in 1436, but thereafter became a loyal and dedicated subject of Charles VII (*Jeanne. Dictionnaire*, pp. 96, 160 and 901–2).

[1023] According to the *Journal du siège* (p. 36), the Bastard of Orléans left the city of Orléans with 200 men to join the count of Clermont and the constable of Scotland in Blois on 10 February. His presence at the battle of Rouvray is widely reported in the *Journal du siège* (pp. 41–2) and other narrative accounts such as Monstrelet (iv, p. 311), *Pucelle* (p. 267) and Tringant (*Jouvencel*, ii, p. 276)

[1024] According to the *Journal du siège* (p. 100), Jean de Vendôme, vidame de Chartres, joined the royal army in Orléans after the capture of Jargeau in June 1429. There is no other evidence that he was present at the battle of Rouvray.

[1025] This must be Louis d'Amboise, viscount of Thouars, whose presence in the French army at Rouvray is also noted in Monstrelet (iv, p. 311), *Pucelle* (p. 267), Cagny (p. 138), and the *Journal du siège* (p. 37).

the lord of Lohéac[1026]
the bishop of Orléans[1027]
the lord of L'Aigle[1028]
the lord of Beauvau[1029]
the lord of Tucé[1030]
the lord of Maillé[1031]
the lord of Orval[1032]
the Bastard of La Trémoille[1033]
Jean de la Roche[1034]
La Hire and his brothers[1035]
Poton de Xantrailles[1036]
(65r) Ferrebourg captain[1037]

[1026] According to the *Journal du siège* (p. 100), André de Laval, lord of Lohéac, joined the royal army in Orléans after the capture of Jargeau in June 1429. There is no other evidence that he was present at the battle of Rouvray.

[1027] John of Kirkmichael is believed to have left Orléans after the battle of Rouvray. There is no evidence that he took part.

[1028] There is no other evidence that Jean de Blois, lord of L'Aigle, was present at Rouvray.

[1029] There is no other evidence that Pierre de Beauvau, lord of Beauvau, was present at Rouvray.

[1030] There is no other evidence that Baudouin de Champagne, lord of Tucé, was present at Rouvray. According to Tringant (*Jouvencel*, ii, p. 273) Tucé played an important role at the battle of Montépilloy in August 1429.

[1031] There is no other evidence that Hardouin VIII, lord of Maillé, was present at Rouvray, but he later took part in Charles VII's coronation expedition (Beaucourt, i, p. 62).

[1032] The accounts of Hémon Raguier indicate that Guillaume d'Albret, lord of Orval, came to the defence of the city of Orléans in September 1428 (Raguier's accounts in *Journal du siège*, p. 161). His participation at the battle of Rouvray where he died is widely reported in narrative sources.

[1033] A Bastard of La Trémoille, possibly Jacques, was paid 100 *francs* for serving Charles VII in arms in Maine and Anjou in c. 1435 (*Les La Trémoille*, I, pp. 207 and 289).

[1034] Jean de la Roche, lord of Barbezieux and Vertueil, a French captain and a *routier*, caused much trouble in Poitou, Saintonge, Limousin and Angoumois in the second half of the 1420s to the subjects of Charles VII, but obtained an extensive letter of abolition from the latter for himself and his men in April 1431 (AN, X2a 20, f. 32vo, printed in *RDP*, viii, pp. 8–20, no. 1026). By such means Charles VII was able to re-align and gain the support of a turbulent captain, to whom he granted the office of seneschal of Poitou in November 1431 (AN, X1a 8604, f. 111; *RDP*, viii, pp. 33–5, no. 1031). There is no evidence that he was at Rouvray, but a famous letter of Guy and André de Laval to their mother Jeanne mentioned that Jean de la Roche had joined Charles VII's coronation army in June 1429 (*Procès de condamnation*, v, pp. 105–11). His later activities as an *écorcheur* are well documented in chronicles. See also Clément-Simon, 'Un capitaine de routiers sous Charles VII, Jean de la Roche', pp. 41–65.

[1035] La Hire's presence at Rouvray is widely reported in chronicles (Bloch, 'Etienne de Vignolles', pp. 59–60).

[1036] Poton de Xaintrailles' presence at Rouvray is reported in several chronicles (Monstrelet, iv, p. 311; *Jouvencel*, ii, p. 276; *Journal du siège*, pp. 37–8).

[1037] This is probably a Breton captain called Ferbourg, Ferrebourg, Forbourg or Fourbourg, who captured the town and castle of Bonmoulins in August 1429, of which he was then made captain by the duke of Alençon until the place surrendered to the earl of Arundel in

the Bourg de Bar[1038]
Pierre Jaillet[1039]
Blanchefort[1040]
Henri de Villeblanche[1041]
the Bastard of Vendome
Pevot captain
Estevenot de Tallauresse[1042]
Jean Foucaut knight[1043]

1432. That same year we find him harrying ('courir') in Normandy with Ambroise de Loré (Chartier, i, pp. 110, 151 and 160; *Pucelle*, p. 334).

[1038] Le Bourg de Bar, possibly a bastard of Guy de Bar, was captured on 9 February by the English and the Burgundians on his way from Orléans to Blois, where the count of Clermont was, and handed over to Talbot. He seems to have regained his freedom on 7 May when the English raised the siege and left him behind (*Pucelle*, pp. 297–8; *Journal du siège*, pp. 36 and 90).

[1039] This is probably Pierre Jaillet or Jaillot (d. 1448), esquire, whom we find raiding in Normandy in 1432 with Ambroise de Loré and Ferbourg (Chartier, i, p. 151). Jaillet, together with the lord of Rambouillet, captured by assault ('prins d'eschielles') the Pont de Meulan in September 1435, and made himself its captain (AN, JJ 177/131, cited in *Journal d'un Bourgeois*, ed. Tuetey, p. 308 n. 2), an office he held until his death in 1448 (*GR*, iv, pp. 84–5).

[1040] This is probably Jean de Blanchefort (d. 1450), a French esquire from Berry. He acted as lieutenant of the maréchal of Saint-Sever in Orléans in March 1429, when he received the wages for sixty-two men-at-arms and forty-two archers under his command (Raguier's accounts in *Journal du siège*, p. 184). He became captain of the fortress of Breteuil around 1430, holding it until 1434 when a treaty sealed between Richemont and the count of Etampes anticipated that the place would be destroyed. He served Charles VII in arms in Normandy in the 1430s, and continued to wage war on Burgundian soil after the treaty of Arras, causing much trouble in Hainaut. Blanchefort was in the service of Charles VII by at least the siege of Pontoise in 1441. A royal ordonnance of 1443 or 1444 included him in a list of royal captains, commanding 100 lances (AN, 1 AP, 177). He died at the siege of Saint-Sauveur-le-Vicomte in 1450. Blanchefort caused much ink to flow in Monstrelet's chronicle, but not before 1430. M 9's reference appears unique in this respect. See also *Cronique Martiniane*, pp. 36–7; Escouchy, *Chronique*, pp. 290–1; Contamine, *GES*, p. 596.

[1041] Henri de Villeblanche was in the company of the constable Richemont at the entry to Paris in April 1436, holding the royal banner. He was later grand master of the household during the reign of Pierre II, duke of Brittany, between 1450 and 1457. He was arrested for his presumed involvement in the murder of Gilles de Rais in October 1457, but released six months later for lack of evidence (Cosneau, pp. 247, 265, 445).

[1042] This may be Estevenot de Tallauresse (d. 1477), a Gascon, who was present at the sieges of Meaux in 1439 and Pontoise in 1441, and who served in the army of the Dauphin in 1444. He was a lieutenant of the lord of Orval in 1445 and a captain of the 'grande ordonnance' in 1448. He kept his functions under Louis XI until his death in 1477 (Contamine, *GES*, pp. 411–12).

[1043] Jean Foucaut (d. 1465), knight, from the Limousin, lord of Saint-Germain-Beaupré, participated in the defence of Orléans and the subsequent campaign in the Loire Valley (Raguier's accounts in *Journal du siège*, p. 192). His presence at Rouvray is not evidenced elswhere but is not unlikely. He participated in the battle of Montépilloy in mid-August 1429 and defended Lagny against Bedford in 1430. It must around that time that he was taken prisoner by the English. The English knight John Cressy handed over his captive Jean Foucaut to the crown for 2,000 *saluts d'or* in April 1432 (BNF, PO 929 Cressy 2). Foucaut remained captain of Lagny until at least September 1440 (*GR*, iv, p. 120). He was in the household of the duke of Orléans in the late 1440s and the 1450s and was apparently made

Guillaume de Lyons knight[1044]
Robert de Savoye knight
Gautier Brusac[1045]
Pierre de Brusac knight[1046]
Pierre de Beauvau knight[1047]
Ambroise de loré knight[1048]
the lord of Bourg Guarrat[1049]
the lord of Bueil[1050]
Pierre de Champagne[1051]
Pierre de Verruyes knight
Kennedy, a Scotsman[1052]
the bourc de Mascaras[1053]

'podestat d'Asti' (Champion, *Vie de Charles d'Orléans*, pp. 268–72, 387, 402). See also Ambuhl, *Prisoners of War*, pp. 194–5; *Jeanne. Dictionnaire*, pp. 717–8.

[1044] Guillaume de Lyons, son of Pierre de Lyons, received the *sergenterie* of Montfort in the *vicomté* of Pont-Authou as a fief from Charles VI in June 1408 (Vauchez, 'En réserve de la royauté', p. 401).

[1045] Gautier Brusac, esquire, participated in the defence of Orléans, the subsequent campaign in the Loire Valley and the coronation campaign (Raguier's accounts in *Journal du siège*, pp. 191–2, 204). His presence at Rouvray is not evidenced elsewhere but is likely.

[1046] Pierre de Brusac, a son of the knight Mondot de Brusac and a nephew of Gautier de Brusac, participated in the siege of Meaux in 1439, and appears in the records as an 'écuyer d'écurie' of Charles VII in 1444. His activities as 'capitaine d'écorcheurs' in that period are well recorded (Tuetey, *Les Écorcheurs*, i, pp. 68, 162, 292; Beaucourt, iii, pp. 17n, 133n, 388; Contamine, *GES*, pp. 268–9).

[1047] Pierre de Beauvau also appears as lord of Beauvau in this list, another example of a double entry.

[1048] Ambroise de Loré, knight, participated in the defence of Orléans, the subsequent campaign in the Loire Valley and the coronation campaign in 1429 (Raguier's accounts in *Journal du siège*, pp. 192, 204). His presence at Rouvray is not evidenced elsewhere, but it is not unlikely.

[1049] A 'Bourg Guarrat' received a horse from Charles VII worth 100 *écus* in October 1428 (*Les La Trémoïlle*, i, p. 138). The same individual described as 'Bourg Garzat' in the account of Hémon Raguier received compensation of 135 *l.t.* for the loss of his horse killed before the bastides of Orléans in December 1428 or January 1429 (Raguier's accounts in *Journal du siège*, p. 179). 'Bourg' in this instance seems to refer to bastard origins.

[1050] Jean V de Bueil came to the defence of Orléans in October 1428. He was subsequently in the escort of a second supply convoy to Orléans in April and May 1429 and later accompanied the king in his coronation campaign (Raguier's accounts in *Journal du siège*, pp. 164–6, 197, 199). Tringant (*Jouvencel*, ii, pp. 276–7), who includes the battle of Rouvray in his narrative, does not mention the presence of Jean de Bueil, nor is his presence at Rouvray evidenced elsewhere.

[1051] There is no other evidence of the presence of Pierre de Champagne at Rouvray.

[1052] Possibly Hugh Kennedy of Ardstynchar, who had served under John Stewart, earl of Buchan. He was present at the battles of Baugé and Verneuil and continued in the service of the French king in the early 1430s.

[1053] Raymond, bourc (or bourg) de Mascaras (in Gers), seigneur de Las, is described as a retainer of George de la Trémoïlle in a letter of Perrinet Gressart to the duke of Burgundy in June 1426 (ACO, B 11916; Bossuat, *Perrinet Gressart*, p. 134 n. 4). He appears in royal accounts as the recipient of a horse in October 1428 (*Les La Trémoïlle*, i, p. 138). There is no evidence

the bourg de Comylliam
Teodoro de Valperga knight lombard[1054]
Giles de Saint-Simon knight[1055]
the lord of Chabannes[1056]
Roberton Descroix[1057]
Prégent de Coëtivy[1058]
Guillaume Bourgeois[1059]

---

elsewhere of his presence at Rouvray. The accounts of Hémon Raguier signal his presence at the coronation campaign in June 1429 (*Journal du siège*, p. 201), along with his companions in arms, Thibaut de Thermes, Arnaud Guillaume de Bourguignan, and Bertand de Toujouse. In 1430, these men defended the town of Marigny against Guillaume, lord of Châteauvillain, whom they took prisoner. The original ransom contract drawn up in January 1431 mentions the four men plus Jacques d'Espailly, also called Fort-Espice, Mascaras's brother-in-arms, as joint masters of Châteauvillain (BNF, Coll. Bourgogne, 99, f. 263; Bossuat, *Perrinet Gressart*, p. 137 n. 2). See also Bossuat, 'Les prisonniers de guerre', pp. 10–11.

[1054] Teodoro de Valperga (d. 1459), knight, from a noble family of Piemont, was a diligent supporter of Charles VII throughout a thirty-year career in France, mainly military, and as a royal officer in Auvergne, Macon and Dauphiné. According to Berry (p. 114), he had arrived in France from Lombardy in 1423, participating in the capture of Jean de Toulongeon, marshal of Burgundy. Berry (p. 117) also has him at Verneuil in 1424. A letter of remission granted to Jean de Novare in April 1447 dates back his arrival in France some twenty years earlier, as well as that of his captain Valperga who is there described as councillor and chamberlain of Charles VII and *bailli* of Lyon (Tuetey, *Les Ecorcheurs*, ii, pp. 476–8, no. 108). The account of Hémon Raguier brings evidence of Valperga's sporadic presence in Orléans between December 1428 and May 1429 (Raguier's account in *Journal du siège*, pp. 178, 186, 189). According to Monstrelet (iv, p. 311), Valperga fought at Rouvray. After the siege he took part in a campaign in the Loire Valley (*Journal du siège*, p. 201). See also Tuetey, *Les Ecorcheurs*, ii, p. 477; Gaussin, 'Les conseillers', p. 126; *Jeanne. Dictionnaire*, pp. 1027–8.

[1055] Gilles de Rouvroy, dit de Saint-Simon, knight, lord of Rasse, had a military career of over forty years in the service of Charles VII and then Louis XI. He became a lieutenant of Richemont and followed him in his military expeditions and in his disgrace between 1427 and 1434. Saint-Simon was present at the rescue of Montargis in 1427 (Monstrelet, iv, p. 272), and fought at Patay with Richemont where, according to Monstrelet (iv, p. 332), he was knighted. It is unlikely that he was present at Orléans or on the coronation expedition. See also Anselme, iv, pp. 406–7; Lefèvre-Pontalis, 'Épisodes de l'invasion anglaise' (1895), pp. 452–3.

[1056] Jacques de Chabannes (d. 1453), lord of Charlus and la Palice (1431), was only at the start of a long and eventful military career in 1429, which reached its climax in the 1450s. He was appointed grand master of the household of Charles VII in 1451 and fought in the victory at Castillon in 1453. He came to the defence of Orléans in October 1428 (Raguier's accounts in *Journal du siège*, p. 165), being at the head of a substantial company of 120 men-at-arms and 120 archers. His presence at the battle of Rouvray is also noted in Monstrelet (iv, p. 311) and the *Journal du siège* (p. 35). See also *Cronique Martiniane*, pp. xix–xx; and *Jeanne. Dictionnaire*, p. 604.

[1057] Roberton Descroix appears in the escort of a second supply convoy to Orléans in April or May 1429, and later participated in the campaign in the Loire Valley and the coronation campaign (*Journal du siège*, pp. 197 and 204).

[1058] There is no other evidence of the presence of Prégent de Coëtivy at Rouvray.

[1059] Although the first name is given as Guillaume, the surname le Bourgeois and his place in the list immediately after Prégent de Coëtivy identifies this man as Tugdual de Kermoysan. He was present at the siege of Jargeau and in the coronation campaign in June 1429 according to Raguier's accounts in *Journal du siège* (pp. 95 and 108).

(65v) and many others. Fastolf drew up and placed all the English and others of his company into battle order. In front of each archer he had planted a sharpened stake in order to break the force of the cavalry when the enemy charged. To the rear he had placed and tethered together all the horses and carts which the English had brought with them. There they waited the arrival of the enemy. The latter arrived and assaulted the English within the enclosure which they had made. The English defended themselves very vigorously and valiantly, so much so that the French were defeated. They retreated, shamefully losing the field and fleeing. In this noble victory and defeat were killed

Sir William Stewart constable of Scotland and his brother[1060]

the lord of Orval

the lord of Châteaubrun[1061]

Jean de Lesgo knight[1062]

and many other French and Scots to the number of around twenty-five.

After this noble and glorious victory Sir John Fastolf and all those of his company, of which not a single man deserving of mention was killed or wounded, left with their victuals and equipment. They took themselves off to the siege where they were notably received with great joy and honour by the earl of Suffolk and other lords. Following this victorious rout, the siege was maintained and continued until just after Easter (27 March) which began the year of grace 1429, with continual great and marvellous skirmishes, assaults and other acts of war by one side against the other. The siege continued up to the month of May, at which point the enemy were in very great strength, with lords and other knights, esquires and nobles, some of whose names follow, to wit,

the duke of Alençon[1063]

[1060] The constable was Sir John Stewart of Darnley, who was indeed killed at Rouvray and subsequently buried in the cathedral of Orléans. The chronicle mentions him earlier as lord of Concressault. After his release from captivity following the battle of Cravant, he had served Charles VII loyally, winning victories against the English near Mont-Saint-Michel (which led to Charles granting him the *comté* of Evreux, then in English hands) and raising the English siege of Montargis in 1427. He had returned to Scotland in 1428 to recruit more troops to aid the Valois king. His half-brother Sir William Stewart was also killed at Rouvray.

[1061] This may be Jean de Naillac (d. 1429), lord of Châteaubrun, whose death at Rouvray is reported in Monstrelet (iv, p. 313) and *Pucelle* (p. 269). Jean de Naillac was seneschal of Limousin from 1423 until at least 1428 (Thomas, *Les états provinciaux*, i, pp. 344–5), when he also became 'grand panétier' of France. See also Anselme, viii, p. 665.

[1062] Jean de Lesgo, knight, was taken prisoner by Claude de Chastellux in 1421 and kept in captivity for his alleged involvement in the murder of John the Fearless (BNF, Coll. Bourgogne, 29, ff. 180, 187). He was eventually released through an exchange with three prisoners in 1423 (Bossuat, *Perrinet Gressart*, p. 48 n. 1). He was captain of Bonny and Beaulieu in 1423 (AN, JJ 179, f. 89v) and chamberlain of the king in 1425. In March 1428 he received orders from Charles VII to reinforce the garrisons in the fortresses of the Loire (Bossuat, *Perrinet Gressart*, p. 95). The account of Hémon Raguier records the presence of Jean de Lesgo in the garrison of Orléans from September 1428 to January 1429 (Raguier's accounts in *Journal du siège*, pp. 158, 168, 169, 172 and 178). His presence and death at Rouvray are noted in Monstrelet (iv, p. 313) and *Pucelle* (p. 269).

[1063] According to the testimony he gave at the retrial of Joan of Arc in March 1456, the duke was not present in Orléans in the final phase of the siege, but joined the royal army at the beginning of June 1429 when it was about to engage in the siege of Jargeau (*Procès en nullité*, i, pp. 380–8).

the Bastard of Orléans[1064]
the Maid[1065]
La Hire[1066]
the lord of Rais[1067]
the lord of Loré[1068]
Robert Baudricourt knight, captain of Vaucouleurs[1069]]

[added: Let it be remembered in the year of our Lord God 1450 on the last day of July Cherbourg, the last town in Normandy was delivered to Thomas Gonell in the time of King Henry VI]

[added: Normandy contains six days' journeying in length and four in breadth, and there are within it a hundred towns and strong castles, seven cities and five bishoprics as well as the archbishopric of Rouen. At the time of the last conquest Charles VII reigned in France.]

[added: In the year of the Lord 1440 Charles duke of Orléans was delivered out of prison in England, having been a prisoner for twenty-five years. He paid for his ransom 400,000 crowns.]

[1064] In his deposition at the retrial of Joan of Arc in 1456, the Bastard of Orléans (Dunois), describing himself as lieutenant-general of Charles VII 'sur le fait de la guerre' and having the guard of Orléans ('ayant la garde'), gave ample details on Joan of Arc's arrival at Orléans on 29 April and the events which led to the raising of the siege on 8 May (*Procès en nullité*, i, pp. 316–26).

[1065] Joan of Arc (1412–31) reached Orléans with a supply convoy coming from Blois on 29 April 1429. She was accompanied by Gilles de Laval, lord of Rais, Jean de Brosse, lord of Boussac, Louis de Graville, lord of Culant, La Hire and Ambroise de Loré. See the deposition of Dunois in *Procès en nullité*, i, pp. 316–26.

[1066] Etienne de Vignolles, dit la Hire, arrived in Orléans on 25 October 1428, and appeared in every single episode of the siege including the battle of Rouvray and the ultimate lifting of the siege, as the *Journal du siège*, the extracts of the account of Hémon Raguier and the accounts of the city of Orléans show.

[1067] Gilles de Laval, lord of Rais, first arrived in Orléans with Joan of Arc and the supply convoy on 29 April 1429 (*Journal du siège*, p. 74). See also the deposition of Dunois in *Procès en nullité*, i, pp. 316–26.

[1068] On 9 February, Ambroise de Loré first arrived in Orléans with Joan of Arc and the supply convoy on 29 April 1429 (*Journal du siège*, p. 74). See also the deposition of Dunois in *Procès en nullité*, i, pp. 316–26.

[1069] Robert de Baudricout (d. 1454), lord of Blaise, had been captain of Vaucouleurs for Charles VII for probably more than ten years by February 1429, when, yielding to the insistence of Joan of Arc, he agreed to take her to Charles II, duke of Lorraine, and subsequently organised an escort to lead her to Charles VII in Chinon, whilst he remained in Vaucouleurs. The chronicle's suggestion that Baudricourt accompanied Joan of Arc to Orléans is incorrect. See *Jeanne. Dictionnaire*, pp. 551–2.

Appendix:
Additional material by William Worcester bound into College of Arms MS M 9

Measurements: width 19 cm, length 26.5 cm
Paper, with watermark of bull's head and star
In the hand of William Worcester

A le sege de Leysnye [inserted above: sur Marn] qui estoit [inserted above: envy-ron] le viij jour de juing [deleted: A°] lan notre seigneur m¹ iiij^c xxxij que estoit mise de par Johan regent le royaume de Ffraunce duc de Bedford[2]
Johan counte de Arundelle
Robert seigneur de Wyllughby
Le seigneur de Lysleadam marchall de Fraunce
Sire Andreu Ogard chambylyn dudit Regent
Sir Johan Salvayn le bayllyff de Roon
Sire John Montgomery bayllyff de Caux
Sire Rauff Nevylle
Syr Rauff Standyssh
Sir John Hanfford
Sir Richard Guethyn de Walys
Sir Richard Haryngton le bayllyff de Evreux
Sir William Fulthorp
Sir Thomas Gryffyn de Hibernia
Sir de Aumont Fraunceys
Sir Richard Standysh
Philip de Vauderey [deleted: norman]
Le Galloys denney FFerrerys
Sire John Cauvan
Thomas Gerard capitaine Motreaw de Lancasshyre
[deleted: reddit] [inserted above: postea] traditone [deleted: postea] reddidit Montreaw Faut yon adversariis domini regis circa mensem octobre' anno christi 1435 post rescussum sancti dionisii

Annotations

At the top right-hand corner is the page number 'cxx' written in the same style as the page numbers of the chronicle.

---

[1]   Seine-et-Marne, arr. Torcy, cant. Lagny-sur-Marne.
[2]   A three-letter illegible word is followed by a decorative squiggle probably of a later date.

Above the text we find in a later hand: Jesus maria Amen dico vobis amen, and directly underneath it, preceded by an ornamental squiggle, Thome Chorum Anglororum.

Below the text, in a different later hand: Thomas Hudson marchant taillour of London

HALF PAGE FOLLOWING FOLIO 120. NOTES ON ACTIONS IN 1434–35.

Measurements: width 17.6 cm, length 13.2 cm
Paper, watermark of bull's head and star
In hand of William Worcester, with many deletions and amendments. The hand is sometimes difficult to read. Uncertain readings are in italics.

1434 Mowtreaw faut [deleted: yin] yon[3] perditum fuit post reddicionem de Meaulx per tradicionem et per obsidionem

Pount Melank perditum fuit tempore Ricardi Merbery militis capitanei [deleted: tempore quo circa] mense octobris proxime post obitum ducis de Bedford tempore obsidionis Seynt Denys per tradicionem

Boys Vincent [underlined] perditum fuit [deleted: die] in quadragesima proxime post obitum ducis Bedford

Pounteys [deleted: fuit] dominus Wyllughby capitaneus et Johannes Ryppley locumtenens eius sunt per treyson perditum per insurrectionem gentium ville et per dominum Lysleadam mareschallum *fideliter tradita* regi Henrici vj die jovis in crastino Ash Wenday proxime post mortem ducis de Bedfordie et postea le Shroseeven proxime sequen' infra annum predictum duobus diebus fuit [inserted above the line: dicta villa adquisita] adquisitum per dominum Talbot dominum Fauconberge *quod* Ricardus dux Eboracis prius applicuit in Francie per scalyng et Petro Durant [deleted: fut] de Vasconia fuit principalis scalator

Die veneris in septianam pasche idest [deleted: per] idest per v dies proxime festum pasche fuit Parys perditum per treyson

1435 Seynt Denys [deleted: perditum fuit] fuit reskewed circa festum sancti Michaelis [inserted above the line: post mensem dux Bedfordie obiit] per comitem Arundell Johannem dominum Talbot et le Bastard Seynt Poule et fratrem suuum, Long Gregory de Wallia Sire John Kyrelle Hugonem Standysh milites et Mathe' Gough fuit captus in transitu suo apres les rescus Seynt Denys (*illegible word follows*) [deleted: pount vyr] Baudwynye per unam leucam ultra Pount Melant et per *tria miliara* citra Pounteys usque Roon per le garrison de Beauvays et Thomas Kyryelle miles evadit de captione prisonarii et Johannes Fastolf miles iacebat dicta nocte in villa de Gysors. Saluo.

Per stabilitatem et cautela gentium Ffrancorum adversariorum [inserted above line: Willelmus Buketon miles de hospicio ducis Bedfordie perdidit] per scalas intraverat et ceperit [paper damaged] … domino Reges fideliter custodunt quam prisonarium … qui perdidit … per treyson

---

[3] Montereau-Fault-Yonne, Meulan, Vincennes, Pontoise, Paris, Saint-Denis, Beauvais and Gisors are the places mentioned.

Bibliography

UNPUBLISHED PRIMARY SOURCES

Alençon, Archives Départementales de l'Orne, série A
Caen, Archives Départementales du Calvados, série F
Caen, Musée des Beaux Arts, Collection Mancel
Chartres, Archives Départementales du Loiret, série 2J
Dijon, Archives Départementales du Côte d'Or, série B
Evreux, Archives Départementales de l'Eure, sous série IIF
Evreux, Archives Municipales série AA, BB, CC
Le Mans, Archives Départementales de la Sarthe, série E, 4J
Lille, Archives du Nord, série B
Lisieux, Archives Communales de Lisieux, série B, CC
Mâcon, Archives Municipales, série BB
Mantes, Archives Municipales, série B, CC
Paris, Archives Nationales de France, série J, JJ, K, KK, P, U, X1a, X1c, X2a, 1 AP,
    Dom Lenoir Mi. 104
Paris, Bibliothèque Nationale de France, manuscrits français, nouvelles acquisi-
    tions françaises, pièces originales, Collection Clairambault, Collection de
    Bourgogne
Rouen, Archives Départementales de la Seine Maritime, série 100 J, 2E Tabel-
    lionage, G, Echiquier
Rouen, Bibliothèque municipale, Collection Martainville, Leber, MS Y
Saint-Lô, Archives Départementales du Manche, série A, H
Gloucester Record Office, Microfilm 12 (from Berkeley Castle D1/21/01/002/
    00/00)
London, British Library, Additional Charters, Additional Manuscripts, Cotton
    MS, Egerton Charters, Harley MS, Lansdowne MS, Royal MS, Sloane MS
London, College of Arms, Arundel MS, MSS L and M
London, Lambeth Palace Library, MS 506
London, The National Archives, C 47 Chancery Miscellanea, C 54 Close rolls, C
    61 Gascon rolls, C 64 Norman rolls, C 65 Parliament rolls, C 66 Patent rolls, C
    76 French or Treaty rolls, C 71 Scotch rolls, C 77 Welsh Rolls, C 81 Warrants,
    C 138 and 139 Inquisitions Post Mortem, E 28 Council and Privy Seal, E 101
    Exchequer Accounts Various, E 358 Miscellaneous Accounts, E 364 Foreign
    Accounts, E 403 Issue Rolls, E 404 Warrants for Issue, LR 14 Office of the
    Auditors of Land Revenue: Ancient Deeds, PROB, SC 8 Ancient Petitions
Norfolk Record Office, Norwich Public Library Manuscript Collection MS 7197
Oxford, Magdalen College, Fastolf Papers; Hickling Papers; Southwark

PUBLISHED PRIMARY SOURCES

Actes de la chancellerie d'Henri VI concernant la Normandie sous la domination anglaise (1422–1435), ed. P. Le Cacheux, Société de l'Histoire de Normandie, 2 vols (Rouen, 1907–08)

Archives départementales de la Sarthe, 4J 306: Sous-Série 4J. Chartier de Grandchamp. Répertoire numérique, ed. H. Boullier de Branche (Mende, 1991)

Archives du Cogner, ed. J. Chappée, and L. J. Denis, 3 vols (Paris and Le Mans, 1903–07)

The Bedford Inventories. The Worldly Goods of John, duke of Bedford, Regent of France (1389–1435), ed. J. Stratford (London, 1993)

Bethencourt, Jean de, *The Canarian or Book of the Conquest and Conversion of the Canarians in the year 1402*, ed. P. Bontier and J. le Verrier, translated by R. H. Major (London, 1872)

The Book of Chivalry of Geoffroi de Charny, ed. R. W. Kaeuper and E. Kennedy (Philadelphia, 1996)

Bouvier, Giles le, dit Berry Herald, *Les chroniques du roi Charles VII*, ed. H. Couteault, L. Celier and M.-H. Jullien de Pommerol, Société de l'Histoire de France (Paris, 1979)

Bovet, Honorat, *The Tree of Battles*, translated by G. W. Coopland (Liverpool, 1949)

Bueil, Jean de, *Le Jouvencel*, translated by C. Taylor and J. H. M. Taylor (Woodbridge, 2020)

Cagny, Perceval de, *Chronique*, ed. H. Moranvillé (Paris, 1902)

Calendar of Entries in the Papal Registers Relating to Great Britain and Ireland: Papal Letters, 14 vols, ed. W. H. Bliss and J. A. Twemlow (London, 1893–1960)

Calendar of Fine Rolls: Henry VI, 1452–1461 (London, 1939)

'Calendar of French Rolls' in *Annual Report of the Deputy Keeper of the Public Records*, 44 (London, 1883), pp. 543–638; 48 (London, 1887), pp. 217–450

Calendar of Inquisitions Post Mortem, vol. 21, 6–10 Henry V (1418–1422), ed. J. L. Kirby and J. H. Stevenson (London, 2002)

Calendar of the Laing Charters AD 854–1837, ed. J. Anderson (Edinburgh, 1896)

'Calendar of Norman Rolls' in *Annual Report of the Deputy Keeper of the Public Records*, 41 (London, 1880), pp. 671–810; 42 (London, 1881), pp. 313–452

Calendar of Patent Rolls, Henry V and Henry VI (London, 1891–1916)

Calendar of State Papers: Milan, 1385–1618, ed. A. B. Hinds (London, 1912)

Cartulaire des sires de Rays (1160–1449), ed. R. Blanchard, 2 vols (Poitiers, 1898–99)

Cartularium abbathiae de Rievalle, ed. J. Atkinson, Surtees Society (1889)

Catalogue analytique des archives de M. le Baron de Joursanvault, contenant une précieuse collection de manuscrits, chartes et documents originaux au nombre de plus de quatre-vingt mille concernant l'histoire générale de France, 2 vols (Paris, 1838)

Champollion-Figéac, J.-J. (ed.), *Lettres des rois, reines et autres personnages des cours de France et d'Angleterre depuis Louis VII jusqu'à Henri IV*, 2 vols (Paris, 1839–47)

Chartier, Jean, *Chronique de Charles VII, roi de France*, ed. A. Vallet de Viriville, 3 vols (Paris, 1858)

Chastelain, George, *Œuvres*, ed. J. Kervyn de Lettenhove, 4 vols (Brussels, 1863–66)

Choix de chroniques et mémoires, ed. J. Buchon (Paris, 1838)

Choix de pièces inédites relatives au règne de Charles VI, ed. L.-C. Douët-D'Arcq, 2 vols (Paris, 1863–64)

Chronica maiora of Thomas Walsingham (1376–1422), ed. D. Preest and J. G. Clark (Woodbridge, 2005)

A Chronicle of England during the Reigns of the Tudors from AD 1485 to 1559, ed. W. H. Douglas, Camden, new series, 11 (London, 1875)

'Chronicle of John Strecche for the Reign of Henry V (1414–1422)', ed. F. Taylor, *Bulletin of the John Rylands Library* 16 (1932), pp. 137–87

Chronique du Mont-Saint-Michel (1294–1376), ed. S. Luce, 2 vols (Paris, 1879–83)

La Chronique de Parcé, ed. H. de Berranger (Le Mans, 1953)

Chronique du Religieux de Saint-Denis contenant le règne de Charles VI de 1380 à 1422, ed. L. Bellaguet, 6 vols (Paris, 1829–52, reprinted 1994)

Comptes généraux de l'état bourguignon entre 1416 et 1420, ed. M. Mollat, 3 vols (Paris, 1965–69)

Cousinot, Guillaume, *Chronique dite de la Pucelle*, ed. A. Vallet de Viriville (Paris, 1859)

Cronique Martiniane, ed. P. Champion (Paris, 1907)

The Dicts and Sayings of the Philosophers: The Translations Made by Stephen Scrope, William Worcester, and an Anonymous Translator, ed. C. F. Bühler, Early English Text Society, o.s. 211 (London, 1941)

Documents sur la Maison de Durfort (XIe–XVe siècle), ed. N. de Peña, vol. II (Bordeaux, 1977)

Dynter, Edmond de, *Chronique des ducs de Brabant*, 3 vols (Brussels, 1854–60)

English Suits before the Parlement of Paris, 1420–1436, ed. C. T. Allmand and C. A. J. Armstrong, Camden Fourth Series, 26 (London, 1982)

Escouchy, Mathieu de, *Chronique*, ed. G. du Fresne de Beaucourt, 3 vols (Paris, 1863–64)

Expeditions to Prussia and the Holy Land made by Henry of Derby, ed. L. ToulminSmith, Camden Second Series, 52 (1894)

Extrait du registre des dons, confiscations, maintenues et autres actes faits dans le duché de Normandie pendant les années 1418, 1419 et 1420, ed. C. Vautier (Paris, 1828)

Fabyan, R., *New Chronicles of England and France*, ed. H. Ellis (London, 1811)

Fénin, Pierre de, *Mémoires*, ed. M. L. E. Dupont (Paris, 1837)

The First English Life of Henry V, ed. C. L. Kingsford (Oxford, 1911)

Foxe, J., *The First Volume of the Ecclesiasticall History, contayning the Actes and Monuments of thinges passed in euery kynges time* (London, 1576)

'Fragment d'une version française des chroniques de Saint-Denis', in *Chronique de Charles VII de Jean Chartier*, ed. A. Vallet de Viriville, 3 vols (Paris, 1858)

La France gouvernée par Jean Sans Peur: les dépenses du receveur général du royaume, ed. B. A. Poquet de Haut-Jussé (Paris, 1959)

Gesta Henrici Quinti. The Deeds of Henry V, ed. F. Taylor and J. Roskell (Oxford, 1975)

'Geste des nobles françois', in Guillaume Cousinot, *Chronique dite de la Pucelle*, ed. A. Vallet de Viriville (Paris, 1859), pp. 105–204

Godefroy, D., *Histoire de Charles VI, roy de France … par Jean Juvenal des Ursins, archevesque de Rheims* (Paris, 1653)

Grafton, R., *A Chronicle at Large* (London, 1569)

Grafton's Chronicle or History of England, ed. H. Ellis, 2 vols (London, 1809)

'Gregory's chronicle', in *The Historical Collections of a Citizen of London in the Fifteenth Century*, ed. J. Gairdner, Camden, old series, 17 (1876)

Gruel, Guillaume, *Chronique d'Arthur de Richemont, connétable de France, duc de Bretagne (1393–1458)*, ed. A. le Vavasseur (Paris, 1890)

Hall's Chronicle, ed. H. Ellis (London, 1809)

Ham, R. E. (ed.), 'The Autobiography of Sir James Croft', *Bulletin of the Institute of Historical Research* 50 (1977), pp. 48–57

Hardyng, John, *Chronicle*, ed. H. Ellis (London, 1812)

Hellot, A., *Les chroniques de Normandie 1223–1453* (Rouen, 1881)

Household Accounts from Medieval England, ed. C. M. Woolgar, 2 vols (London, 1992–93)

Index Britanniae scriptorum quos ex variis bibliothecis non parvo labore collegit Ioannes Baleus, cum aliis, ed. R. L. Poole and M. Bateson, Anecdota Oxoniensa, Medieval and Modern Series 9 (Oxford, 1902), revised by C. Brett and J. Corley (Oxford, 1990)

Issues of the Exchequer, ed. F. Devon (London, 1837)

Jarry, L., *Compte de l'armée anglaise au siège d'Orléans, 1428–1429* (Orléans, 1892)

Jones, M. (ed.), 'Les Comptes d'Auffroy Guinot, trésorier et receveur général de Bretagne, 1430–1436: édition et commentaire', *Journal des Savants* (2010), pp. 17–109, 265–306

Journal d'un Bourgeois de Paris, 1405–1449, ed. C. Beaune (Paris, 1990)

Journal d'un Bourgeois de Paris, 1405–1449, ed. A. Tuetey (Paris, 1881)

Journal de Clément de Fauquembergue, 1417–1435, ed. A. Tuetey, 3 vols (Paris, 1903–15)

Journal du siège d'Orléans (1428–1429) augmenté de plusieurs documents, notamment des comptes de ville (1429–1431), ed. P. Charpentier and C. Cuissard (Orléans, 1896)

Juvénal des Ursins, Jean, *Histoire de Charles VI*, ed. J. A. C. Buchon (Paris, 1836)

La Roque, G.-A. de, *Histoire généalogique de la maison de Harcourt*, 4 vols (Paris, 1662)

Le Fèvre de Saint-Rémy, Jean, *Chronique*, ed. F. Morand, 2 vols (Paris, 1876–81)

Le Jouvencel, ed. C. Favre and L. Lecestre, 2 vols (Paris, 1887–89)

Le Livre des miracles de Sainte-Catherine-de-Fierbois (1375–1470), ed. Y. Chauvin (Poitiers, 1976)

'Le livre des trahisons de France', in *Chroniques relatives à l'histoire de la Belgique sous la domination des ducs de Bourgogne, II: Textes français*, ed. J. Kervyn de Lettenhove (Brussels, 1873), pp. 1–258

Le Songe véritable, ed. H. Moranvillé (Paris, 1891)

Legge, M.-D. (ed.), *Letters and Petitions from All Souls MS 182*, Anglo-Norman Text Society, 3 (1941)

Legnano, Giovanni da, *Tractatus de Bello, de represaliis et de duello*, ed. and trans. T. Erskine Holland (Washington, 1917)

Leland, J., 'Ad Georgium Ferrarium', *Principium, ac Illustrium Aliquot et Eruditorum in Anglia Virorum, encomia, trophaea, genethliaca et epithalamia* (London, 1589)

Les La Trémoïlle pendant cinq siècles, ed. L.-C. de La Trémoïlle, 5 vols (Nantes, 1890–06)

Letters and Papers Illustrative of the Wars of the English in France During the Reign of Henry the Sixth, King of England, ed. J. Stevenson, 2 vols in three parts (London, 1861–64)

Lettres et mandements de Jean V, duc de Bretagne, de 1402 à 1442, ed. R. Blanchard, 5 vols (Nantes, 1889–95)

Lobineau, G.-A. (ed.), *Histoire de Bretagne, composée sur les titres et les auteurs originaux*, 2 vols (Paris, 1707)

Lucas, S. C. (ed.), *A Mirror for Magistrates: A Modernized and Annotated Edition* (Cambridge, 2019)

Mandements et actes divers de Charles V, 1364–1380, recueillis dans les collections de la Bibliothèque Nationale, ed. L. Delisle (Paris, 1874)

Merlet, L., *Registres et minutes des notaires du comté de Dunois (1369 à 1676). Inventaire Sommaire* (Chartres, 1886)

Monstrelet, Enguerran de, *Chronique*, ed. L. Douët d'Arcq, 6 vols (Paris, 1857–62)

Musée des Archives Départementales. Recueil de fac-simile héliographiques de documents tirés des Archives des préfectures, mairies et hospices (Paris, 1878)

Narratives of the Expulsion of the English from Normandy, ed. J. Stevenson (London, 1863)

Nichols, J. G., 'An Original Appointment of Sir John Fastolfe to be Keeper of the Bastille of St. Anthony at Paris', *Archaeologia* 44 (1873), pp. 113–22

Ordonnances des rois de France de la troisième race, 23 vols (Paris, 1823–49)

Paris pendant la domination anglaise (1420–1436), ed. A Longnon (Paris, 1878)

A Parisian Journal, 1405–1449, ed. J. Shirley (Oxford, 1968)

The Parliament Rolls of Medieval England, 1275–1504, ed. C. Given-Wilson, P. Brand, S. Phillips, W. M. Ormrod, G. Martin, A. Curry and R. Horrox, 16 vols (Woodbridge and London, 2005)

The Paston Letters AD 1422–1509, ed. J. Gairdner, 6 vols (London, 1872)

Paston Letters and Papers of the Fifteenth Century, 2 parts, ed. N. Davis (Oxford, 2005)

Paston Letters and Papers of the Fifteenth Century, Part 3, ed. R. Beadle and C. Richmond (Oxford, 2005)

Pitts, J., *De Illustribus Angliae Scriptoribus* (Paris, 1619)

Pizan, Christine de, *The Book of Deeds of Arms and Chivalry*, ed. C. C. Willard, trans. Sumner Willard (Pennsylvania, 1999)

Proceedings and Ordinances of the Privy Council of England, ed. N. H. Nicolas, 7 vols (London, 1834–37)

Procès de condamnation et de réhabilitation de Jeanne d'Arc, ed. J. Quicherat, 5 vols (Paris, 1841–49)

Procès en nullité de la condamnation de Jeanne d'Arc, ed. P. Duparc, 5 vols (Paris 1977–89)

Recueil des documents concernant le Poitou contenus dans les registres de la chancellerie de France, ed. P. Guérin, vol. VII: 1403–30; vol. VIII: 1430–47; vol. X: 1456–64 (Poitiers, 1888–1906)

The Register of Henry Chichele Archbishop of Canterbury, 1414–1443, ed. E. F. Jacob, 4 vols (Oxford, 1937–47)

Register of the Great Seal of Scotland (Registrum Magni Sigilli Regum Scotorum), ed. J. M. Thompson et al., 10 vols (Edinburgh, 1882–1914)

Registre de Délibérations du Conseil de Ville de Reims (1422–1436), ed. S. Guilbert (Reims, 1990–91)

Registre des recettes et dépenses de la ville de Boulogne-sur-Mer 1415–1416, ed. E. Dupont (Boulogne, 1883)

Registrum Monasterii de Passelet, ed. C. Innes (Glasgow, 1832)

Remarks and Collections of Thomas Hearne, ed. H. E. Salter, Oxford History Society, 65 (Oxford, 1914)

'Rôles normands et français et autres pièces tirées des archives de Londres par Bréquigny en 1764, 1765 et 1766', *Mémoires de la Société des Antiquaires de Normandie*, 3e série, 23 (1865)

Rotuli Normanniae, ed. T. D. Hardy (London, 1835)

Rotuli Scotiae in turre Londensi et in domo capitulari Westmonasteriensi asservati, ed. J. Caley, 2 vols (London, 1814)

Rouen au temps de Jeanne d'Arc et pendant l'occupation anglaise, 1419–1449, ed. P. Le Cacheux (Rouen, 1931)

Seymour, Edward, duke of Somerset, *Edward, Duke of Somerset: To all of the Realme of Scotlande*, printed by Richard Grafton (London, 1547)

Shakespeare, William, *The First Part of King Henry IV*, ed. H. Wiel and J. Weil, New Cambridge Shakespeare (Cambridge, 1997)

Shakespeare, William, *The First Part of King Henry VI*, ed. M. Hattaway, New Cambridge Shakespeare (Cambridge, 1990)

Stow, J., *Annales* (London, 1592)

Tanner, Thomas, *Bibliotheca Britannico-Hibernica* (London, 1748)

Taylor, F., 'The Chronicle of John Streeche for the Reign of Henry V', *Bulletin of the John Rylands Library* 16 (1932), pp. 137–87

Testamenta Vetusta, ed. N. H. Nicolas (London, 1826)

Thomas, A. (ed.), *Le comté de la Marche et le Parlement de Poitiers: 1418–1436; recueil de documents inédits tirés des Archives nationales précédé d'une étude sur la géographie historique de la Marche aux 14e et 15e siècle* (Paris, 1910)

The Thomas L. Gravell Watermark Archive, compiled and maintained by D. W. Mosser and E. W. Sullivan II (www.gravell.org)

Timbal P.-C. et al., *La guerre de Cent Ans vue à travers les registres du Parlement, 1337–1369* (Paris, 1961)

Titi Livii Foro-Juliensis Vita Henrici Quinti, ed. T. Hearne (Oxford, 1716)

Troubles Connected with the Prayer Book of 1549, ed. N. Pocock, Camden, new series, XXXVII (London, 1884)

Tudor Royal Proclamations, vol. 1, ed. P. L. Hughes and J. F. Larkin (London and New Haven, 1964)

Vita et Gesta Henrici Quinti, ed. T. Hearne (Oxford, 1727)

Walsingham, Thomas, *St Albans Chronicle, vol. II 1394–1422*, ed. J. Taylor, W. Childs and L. Watkiss (Oxford, 2011)

Warner, J. C. (ed.), *John Bale's Catalogue of Tudor Authors. An Annotated Translation of Records from the Scriptorum illustrium maioris Brytanniae… catalogus (1557–1559)* (Tempe, 2010)

Waurin, Jean de, *Recueil des croniques et anchiennes istories de la Grant Bretaigne a present nommé Engleterre, 1399–1422*, ed. W. Hardy, 5 vols (London, 1868)

Worcester, William, *The Boke of Noblesse*, ed. J. G. Nichols (London, 1860)

Worcestre, William, *Itineraries*, ed. J. Harvey (Oxford, 1969)

SECONDARY SOURCES

Achon, C. de, 'Les seigneurs de Courceriers (1422–1552) (Suite)', *Bulletin de la commission historique et archéologique de la Mayenne* 10 (1895), pp. 19–63, 133–49

Allais, N.-V., *Nobiliaire universel de France*, 22 vols (Paris, 1877)

Allmand, C. T., *Lancastrian Normandy 1415–1450. The History of a Medieval Occupation* (Oxford, 1983)

Allmand, C. T., 'France-Angleterre à la fin de la Guerre de Cent Ans: Le "Boke of Noblesse" de William Worcester', in *La France anglaise au Moyen Age, Actes du 111ème Congrès national des sociétés savantes, Poitiers 1986* (Paris, 1988), pp. 104–11

Allmand, C. T. and Keen, M. H., 'History and the Literature of War: The Boke of Noblesse of William Worcester', in *War, Government and Power in Late Medieval France*, ed. C. Allmand (Liverpool, 2000), pp. 92–105

Allmand, C. T., *The De Re Militari of Vegetius: The Reception, Transmission and Legacy of a Roman Text in the Middle Ages* (Cambridge, 2014)

Ambühl, R., *Prisoners of War in the Hundred Years War. Ransom Culture in the Late Middle Ages* (Cambridge, 2013)

Ambühl, R., 'Hostages and the Laws of War: The Surrender of the Castle and Palace of Rouen (1449–68)', in *Medieval Hostageship, c. 700–c. 1500*, cd. M. Bennett and K. Weikert (Abingdon, 2017), pp. 188–205

Ambühl, R., 'Joan of Arc as *prisonnière de guerre*', *EHR* 132 (2017), pp. 1045–76

Ambühl, R., 'Henry V and the Administration of Justice: The Surrender of Meaux, 1422', *Journal of Medieval History* 43 (2017), pp. 74–88, reprinted in *Agincourt in Context: War on Land and Sea*, ed. R. Ambühl and C. Lambert (London, 2018), pp. 74–88

Ambühl, R. and Dodd, G., 'The Politics of Surrender: Treason, Trials and Recrimination in the 1370s', in *Ruling Fourteenth Century England: Essays in Honour of Christopher Given-Wilson*, ed. R. Ambühl, J. Bothwell and L. Tompkins (Woodbridge, 2019), pp. 227–63

Amiet, R., 'Le Livre d'Heures de Jean de Gingins', *Zeitschrift für schweizerische Kirchengeschichte* 77 (1983), pp. 95–147

Angot, A., *Dictionnaire historique, topographique et biographique de la Mayenne de l'abbé Alphonse Ango*, 4 vols (Mayenne, 1900–10)

Anselme de Sainte Marie, Père, *Histoire généalogique et chronologique de la maison royale de France*, 9 vols (3rd edn, Paris, 1726–33)

Appendix to the Second Report of the Royal Commission on Historical Manuscripts (London, 1871)

Armstrong, C. A. J., 'Sir John Fastolf and the Law of Arms', in *War, Literature and Politics in the Late Middle Ages*, cd. C. T. Allmand (Liverpool, 1976), pp. 46–56

Armstrong, C. A. J., 'La double monarchie France-Angleterre et la maison de Bourgogne (1420–1435): le déclin d'une alliance', *Annales de Bourgogne* 37 (1965), pp. 81–112, reprinted in C. A. J. Armstrong, *England, France and Burgundy in the Fifteenth Century. Collected Studies* (London, 1983), pp. 343–74

Aston, M., *Lollards and Reformers* (London, 1984)

Aubert de la Chesnaye-Desbois, F.-A., *Dictionnaire de la noblesse, contenant les généalogies, l'histoire et la chronologie des familles nobles de la France*, 19 vols (Paris, 1863–76)

Aubrée, G., *Mémoires pour servir à l'histoire de France et de Bourgogne*, 2 vols (Paris, 1729)

Baker, J. H., *The Men of Court 1440 to 1550. A Prosopography of the Inns of Court and Chancery and the Courts of Law*, 2 vols, Selden Society Supplementary Series 18 (London, 2012)

Bale, J., *Illustrium majoris Britanniae scriptorium* (Wesel and Ipswich, 1548)

Bale, J., *Scriptorum illustrium majoris Britanniae Catalogus* (Basel, 1557–59)

Balon, J., *La Maison de Namur sur la scène de la grande histoire, 1196–1429* (Namur, s.d.)

Barber, M. J., 'The Books and Patronage of Learning of a Fifteenth-Century Prince', *The Book Collector* 12 (1963), pp. 308–18

Barbey, F., *Louis de Chalon, Prince d'Orange, seigneur d'Orbe, Echallens, Grandson, 1390–1463* (Lausanne, 1926)

Barker, J., 'The Foe Within: Treason in Lancastrian Normandy', in *Soldiers, Nobles and Gentlemen: Essays in Honour of Maurice Keen*, ed. Peter R. Coss and C. Tyerman (Woodbridge, 2009), pp. 305–20

Barron, C., *London in the Later Middle Ages. Government and People 1200–1500* (Oxford, 2004)

Baudier, M., *An History of the Memorable and Extraordinary Calamities of Margaret of Anjou, Queen of England* (London, 1737)

Beadle, R., 'Sir John Fastolf's French Books', in *Medieval Texts in Context*, ed. G. D. Caie and D. Renevy (London, 2008), pp. 96–112

Beauchesne, A. de, *Le château de la Roche-Talbot et ses seigneurs* (Mamers, 1893)

Beauchesne, A. de, 'Château du Coudray et les chatellenies de Chemeré et de Saint-Denis-du-Maine: La Châtellenie de Chemeré (suite et fin)', *Extrait du Bulletin de la Commission d'Histoire et Archéologie de la Mayenne*, 19 (1902) (Mayenne, 1903)

Beauchesne, A. de, 'Jean des Vaux, capitaine de Mayenne pendant la guerre de Cent Ans', *Revue Historique et Archéologique du Maine* 73 (1913), pp. 225–72

Beauchesne, A. de, *Pierre de Beauvau, seigneur de la Bessière, capitaine de Mayenne pendant les dernières années de la guerre de Cent Ans* (Le Mans, 1924)

Beaucousin, L. A., *Histoire de la principauté d'Yvetot, ses rois et ses seigneurs* (Rouen, 1884)

Beaune, C., *The Birth of an Ideology. Myths and Symbols of Nation in Late-Medieval France*, translated by S. Ross Huston and F. L. Cheyette (Berkeley and Oxford, 1991)

Beaurepaire, C. de Robillard de, 'Notes et documents concernant l'état des campagnes de la Haute Normandie dans les Derniers Temps du Moyen Age', *Recueil des Travaux de la Société Libre d'Agriculture, Sciences, Arts et Belles-Lettres de l'Eure*, 3e série, 8 (1862–63), pp. 347–784

Beauvais de Saint-Paul, P. D., *Essai historique et statistique sur le canton et la ville de Mondoubleau* (Le Mans, 1837)

Belleval, R. de, *Azincourt* (Paris, 1865)

Belleval, R. de, *Mémoire sur les comtes de Ponthieu de la deuxième race et sur les familles qui sont issus d'eux* (Paris, 1868)

Bellier, L., 'Les seigneurs du Boisfroust, 1370–1550: construction et projection d'une lignée aristocratique', *La Mayenne, Archéologie et Histoire* 20 (1997), pp. 23–47

Bémont, C., 'Bréquigny, Louis Georges Oudard Feudrix de', *Encyclopaedia Britannica* (1911 edn)

Bernus, P., 'Essai sur la vie de Pierre de Brézé (vers 1410–1465)', Position des Thèses de l'Ecole des Chartes, 1906, pp. 7–17

Bétencourt, Dom, *Noms féodaux ou noms de ceux qui ont tenu fief en France dans les provinces d'Anjou, Aunis, Auvergne* (Paris, 1867)

Bidet, L., 'La noblesse et les princes d'Anjou: la famille de Beauvau', in *La noblesse dans les territoires angevins à la fin du Moyen Age, Actes du colloque international organisé par l'Université d'Angers, Angers-Saumur, 3–6 juin 1998*, ed. N. Coulet and J.-M. Matz, Collection de l'Ecole française de Rome, 275 (Rome, 2000), pp. 471–99

Black, W. H., *Catalogue of the Arundel Manuscripts in the College of Arms* (London, 1829)

Bloch, J., 'Etienne de Vignolles, dit "la Hire" (c. 1385–1443), seigneur féodal, capitaine charismatique, homme d'état', unpublished mémoire de Maîtrise (Université de Louvain-la-Neuve, 2015)

Boffa, S., 'Antoine de Bourgogne et le contingent brabançon à la bataille d'Azincourt', *Revue belge de philologie et d'histoire*, 72 (1994), pp. 255–84

Boffey, J., *Manuscript and Print in London c. 1475–1530* (London, 2012)

Bogner, G., '"Military" Knighthood in the Lancastrian Era: The Case of Sir John Montgomery', *Journal of Medieval Military History* 7 (2009), pp. 104–26

Bonenfant, P., *Philippe le Bon, sa politique, son action* (Brussels, 1944)

Bonenfant, P., *Du meurtre de Montereau au traité de Troyes* (Brussels, 1958)

Bonneserre de Saint-Denis, L. S., *Notice historique et généalogique sur la maison d'Anthenaise, 980–1878* (Angers, 1878)

Bord, P., 'Jean, Bâtard d'Orléans (1402–1468): étude d'un bâtard princier dans le royaume de France au XVe siècle', unpublished PhD thesis (Université de Lille, 2019)

Bossuat, A., *Perrinet Gressart et François Surienne, agents de l'Angleterre* (Paris, 1936)

Bossuat, A., 'Les prisonniers de guerre au XVe siècle: la rançon de Guillaume de Châteauvillain', *Annales de Bourgogne* 23 (1951), pp. 7–35

Boucher de Molandon, R. and Beaucorps, A. de, *L'armée anglaise vaincue par Jeanne d'Arc sous les murs d'Orléans* (Paris, 1892)

Bouillé, A. de, *Un conseiller de Charles VII, le maréchal de La Fayette (1380–1463)* (Lyon, 1955)

Bouzy, O., 'Les morts d'Azincourt: leurs liens de familles, d'offices et de parti', in *Hommes, cultures et sociétés à la fin du moyen âge: liber discipulorum en l'honneur de Philippe Contamine*, ed. P. Gilli and J. Paviot (Paris, 2012), pp. 221–55

Bove, B., 'Deconstructing the Chronicles: Rumours and Extreme Violence during the Siege of Meaux (1421–1422)', *French History* 24 (2010), pp. 501–23

Bozzolo, C. and Loyau, H., *La cour amoureuse dite de Charles VI; étude et édition critique des sources manuscrites: armoiries et notices biographiques*, 3 vols (Paris, 1982–92)

Brand, H., 'Hue (Hugues) de Lannoy, seigneur de Santes, de Beaumont et d'Ijsselmonde', in *Les Chevaliers de l'Order de la Toison d'or au XVe siècle. Notices bio-bibliographiques*, ed. R. de Smedt (Frankfurt, 2000), pp. 14–17

Bréard, C., 'Le Crotoy et les armements maritimes des XIVe et XVe siècles', *Mémoires de la société des antiquaires de Picardie*, série 4, 4 (1903), pp. 1–214

Breul, J. de, *Théatre des Antiquitez de Paris* (Paris, 1639)

Briquet, C., *Filigranes. Dictionnaire historique des marques du papier*, 4 vols (Geneva, 1907)

Broadway, J., 'Lennard, Sampson (d. 1633)', *ODNB*, article 16446 [accessed 16 November 2020]

Broussilon, B. de, *La maison de Craon (1050–1480), étude historique, accompagnée du cartulaire de Craon*, 2 vols (Paris, 1893)

Broussillon, B. de, *La Maison de Laval, 1020–1605: étude historique, accompagnée du cartulaire de Laval et de Vitré*, 5 vols (Paris, 1895–1903)

Brown, M., *The Black Douglases. War and Lordship in Late Medieval Scotland, 1300–1455* (Edinburgh, 1998)

Bühler, C. F., 'Sir John Fastolf's Manuscripts of the Epitre d'Othéa and Stephen Scrope's Translation of This Text', *Scriptorium* 1–3 (1949), pp. 123–8

Buridant, C., *Grammaire nouvelle de l'ancien français* (Paris, 2000)

Bush, M., *The Government Policy of Protector Somerset* (London, 1975)

Busserolle, J. X. Carré de, *Archives des familles nobles de la Touraine, de l'Anjou, du Maine et du Poitou*, 2 vols (Tours, 1889–90)

Campbell, L. and Steer, F., *A Catalogue of Manuscripts in the College of Arms Collections*, vol. 1 (London, 1988)

Carolus-Barré, L., 'Compiègne et la Guerre, 1414–1430', in *La 'France Anglaise' au Moyen Age, Actes du 111ème Congrès national des sociétés savantes, Poitiers 1986* (Paris, 1988), pp. 383–92

Caron, M.-T., 'Vie et mort d'une grande dame: Jeanne de Chalon, comtesse de Tonnerre (vers 1388–vers 1450)', *Francia* 8 (1980), pp. 147–90

Caron, M.-T., 'Guillaume de Vienne, seigneur de Saint-Georges et de Sainte-Croix', in *Les Chevaliers de l'Order de la Toison d'or au XVe siècle. Notices bio-bibliographiques*, ed. R. de Smedt (Frankfurt, 2000), pp. 3–4

Caron, M.-T., 'Antoine de Vergy, seigneur de Fouvent, de Champlitte, comte de Dammartin', in *Les Chevaliers de l'Ordre de la Toison d'or au XVe siècle. Notices bio-bibliographiques*, ed. R. de Smedt (Frankfurt, 2000), pp. 11–13

Caron, M.-T., 'Jean VI de Vergy, seigneur de Saint-Dizier, Vignory, La Fauche, Pont-sur-Saone', in *Les Chevaliers de l'Ordre de la Toison d'or au XVe siècle. Notices bio-bibliographiques*, ed. R. de Smedt (Frankfurt, 2000), pp. 70–1

Caron, M.-T., 'Jean de la Trémoïlle, seigneur de Jonvelle', in *Les Chevaliers de l'Ordre de la Toison d'or au XVe siècle. Notices bio-bibliographiques*, ed. R. de Smedt (Frankfurt, 2000), pp. 24–5

Caron, M.-T., 'Philippe, seigneur de Ternant', in *Les Chevaliers de l'Ordre de la Toison d'or au XVe siècle. Notices bio-bibliographiques*, ed. R. de Smedt (Frankfurt, 2000), pp. 59–60

Cassard, J.-C., 'Tanguy du Chastel, l'homme de Montereau', in *Le Trémazan des du Chastel: du château fort à la ruine* (Brest, 2004), pp. 83–104

Catalogue of Additions to the Manuscripts 1756–1782: Additional Manuscripts 4101–5017 (London, 1977)

Catalogue of the Arundel Manuscripts in the College of Arms, ed. W. H. Black (London, 1829)

Caumont, A., 'Relation de la visite des forteresses du bailliage de Caen en 1371', *Mémoires de la Société des Antiquaires de Normandie* 11 (1840), pp. 185–204

Chambers, J., 'Dialect Acquisition', *Language* 68 (1992), pp. 673–705

Champion, P., *Guillaume de Flavy, capitaine de Compiègne* (Paris, 1906)

Champion, P., *Vie de Charles d'Orléans* (Paris, 1911)

Chapman, A., 'The Posthumous Knighting of Dafydd Gam', *Journal of Medieval History* 43 (2017), pp. 89–105

Charles, R., 'L'invasion anglaise dans le Maine de 1417 à 1428' (publié par Louis Froger), *Revue historique et archéologique du Maine* 25 (1889), pp. 62–103

Chastellux, H.-P.-C. de, *Histoire généalogique de la Maison de Chastellux* (Paris, 1869)

Chavanon, J., 'Renaud VI de Pons, vicomte de Turenne et de Carlat, seigneur de Ribérac, etc Lieutenant du roi en Poitou, Saintonge et Angoumois Conservateur des trêves de Guyenne (vers 1348–1427)', *Extrait des Archives historiques de la Saintonge et de l'Aunis* 21 (1902) (Paris, 1903)

Clegg, C. S., 'Holinshed [Hollingshead], Raphael (c. 1525–1580?)', *ODNB*, article 13505 [accessed 30 November 2020]

Clément-Simon, G., 'Un capitaine de routiers sous Charles VII, Jean de la Roche', *Revue des questions historiques* 58 (1895), pp. 41–65

Collins, H., *The Order of the Garter 1348–1461. Chivalry and Politics in Late Medieval England* (Oxford, 2000)

Collins, H., 'Sir John Fastolf, John Lord Talbot and the Dispute over Patay: Ambition and Chivalry in the Fifteenth Century', in *War and Society in Early Modern Britain*, ed. D. Dunn (Liverpool, 2000), pp. 114–40

Communay, A., *Essai généalogique sur les Montferrand de Guyenne* (Bordeaux, 1889)

The Complete Peerage, revised edition of original edition by G. E. Cokayne, ed. V. Gibbs, 14 vols (London, 1910–98)

Contades, G. de, *Rasnes, histoire d'un château normand* (Paris, 1884)

Contamine, P., *Guerre, état et société à la fin du Moyen Age: études sur les armées des rois de France, 1337–1494* (Paris, 1972)

Contamine, P., 'Un serviteur de Louis XI dans sa lutte contre Charles le Téméraire: Georges de la Trémoille, sire de Craon (vers 1437–1481)', *Annuaire Bulletin de la Société d'Histoire de France* 97 (1976/77), pp. 63–80

Contamine, P., *War in the Middle Ages*, translated by M. C. E. Jones (London, 1984)

Contamine, P., 'À l'abordage! Pierre de Brézé, Grand sénéchal de Normandie, et la guerre de course (1452–1458)', in *La Normandie et l'Angleterre au Moyen Âge*, ed. P. Bouet and V. Gazeau (Caen, 2003), pp. 307–58

Contamine, P., *Charles VII. Une vie, une politique* (Paris, 2017)

Contamine, P., Bouzy, O. and Hélary, X., *Jeanne d'Arc. Histoire et dictionnaire* (Paris, 2012)

Cooper, S., *The Real Falstaff: Sir John Fastolf and the Hundred Years War* (Barnsley, 2010)

Cosneau, E., *Le Connétable de Richemont (Artur de Bretagne), 1393–1458* (Paris, 1886)

Courroux, P., *Charles d'Albret: le connétable d'Azincourt* (Bordeaux, 2019)

Cron, B. M., 'The "Champchevrier Portrait": A Cautionary Tale', *The Ricardian* 12 (2001), pp. 321–7

Curry, A., *The Hundred Years War* (Basingstoke, 1983)

Curry, A., 'Military Organisation in Lancastrian Normandy 1422–1450', 2 vols, unpublished PhD thesis (CNAA/Teesside Polytechnic, 1985)

Curry, A., 'Towns at War: Relations between the Towns of Normandy and Their English Rulers, 1417–1450', in *Towns and Townspeople in the Fifteenth Century*, ed. J. Thomson (Gloucester, 1988), pp. 148–72

Curry, A., 'The Nationality of Men-at-Arms Serving in English Armies in Normandy and the 'pays de conquête', 1415–1450: A Preliminary Study', *Reading Medieval Studies* 18 (1992), pp. 135–63

Curry, A., 'English Armies in the Fifteenth Century', in *Arms, Armies and Fortifications in the Hundred Years War*, ed. A. Curry and M. Hughes (Woodbridge, 1994), pp. 39–68

Curry, A., 'The Organisation of Field Armies in Lancastrian Normandy', in *Armies, Chivalry and Warfare in Medieval Britain and France*, ed. M. Strickland (Stamford, 1998), pp. 207–33

Curry, A., *The Battle of Agincourt. Sources and Interpretations* (Woodbridge, 2000)

Curry, A., *Agincourt. A New History* (Stroud, 2005)

Curry, A., 'After Agincourt, What Next? Henry V and the Campaign of 1416', *The Fifteenth Century* 7 (2007), pp. 23–51

Curry, A., 'The Battle Speeches of Henry V', *Reading Medieval Studies* 34 (2008), pp. 77–97

Curry, A., 'The Military Ordinances of Henry V: Texts and Contexts', in *War, Government and Aristocracy in the British Isles c. 1150–1500: Essays in Honour of Michael Prestwich*, ed. C. Given-Wilson, A. Kettle and L. Scales (Woodbridge, 2008), pp. 214–49

Curry, A., 'John, Duke of Bedford's Arrangements for the Defence of Normandy in October 1434: College of Arms MS Arundel 48, folios 274r–276v', *Annales de Normandie* 62 (2012), pp. 235–51

Curry, A., 'Henry V's Harfleur: A Study in Military Administration, 1415–1422', in *The Hundred Years War (Part III). Further Considerations*, ed. L. J. A. Villalon and D. J. Kagay (Leiden and Boston, 2013), pp. 259–84

Curry, A., 'Representing War and Conquest, 1415–1429: The Evidence of College of Arms Manuscript M9', in *Representing War and Violence 1250–1600*, ed. J. Bellis and L. Slater (Woodbridge, 2016), pp. 139–58

Curry, A., 'Foreign Soldiers in English Pay. Identity and Unity in the Armies of the English Crown, 1415–1450', in *Routiers et mercenaires pendant la guerre de Cent Ans. Hommage à Jonathan Sumption*, ed. G. Pépin, F. Boutoulle and F. Lainé (Bordeaux, 2016), pp. 303–16

Curry, A., 'The Garrison Establishment in Lancastrian Normandy in 1436 According to Surviving Lists in Bibliothèque Nationale de France manuscrit français 25773', in *Military Communities in Late Medieval England. Essays in Honour of Andrew Ayton*, ed. G. P. Baker, C. L. Lambert and D. Simpkin (Woodbridge, 2018), pp. 237–69

Curry, A., 'The Norman Rolls of Henry V', in *People, Power and Identity in the Late Middle Ages. Essays in Memory of Mark Ormrod*, ed. G. Dodd, H. Lacy and A. Musson (Abingdon and New York, 2021), pp. 265–82

Curry, A., 'Une chronique écrite par des soldats: College of Arms MS M 9 et la guerre de Cent Ans en Normandie au quinzième siècle', in *Maîtriser le temps et façonner l'histoire. Les historiens normands aux époques médiévale et moderne*, ed. F. Paquet (Caen, forthcoming)

Curry, A., 'Basset, Peter (fl. 1415–1437)', *ODNB*, article 1642 [accessed 22 April 2021]

Cuzacq, P., 'Un célèbre capitaine landais, Etienne de Vignolles dit La Hire; Rion-des-Landes, au moyen-age', *Bulletin de la Société des Sciences, Lettres et Arts de Bayonne* (1901), pp. 93–112, 119–26

Day, J. F. R., 'Cooke, Robert (d. 1593)', *ODNB*, article 6148 [accessed 19 November 2020]

Dees, A., *Atlas des formes et des constructions des chartes françaises du 13e siècle* (Tübingen, 1980)

Delaville le Roulx, J., *La domination bourguignonne à Tours et le siège de cette ville (1417–1418)* (Paris, 1877)

Delayant, I., 'Le procès des frères Plusquellec', *Archives historiques du Poitou* 2 (1873), pp. 217–51

Delisle, L.-V., *Histoire du château et des sires de Saint-Sauveur-le-Vicomte: suivie de pièces justificatives* (Valognes, 1867)

Demurger, A., 'Guerre civile et changements du personnel administratif dans le royaume de France de 1400 à 1418: l'exemple des baillis et sénéchaux', *Francia* 6 (1978), pp. 151–298

Denis, L.-J., 'Confrérie des prêtres du doyenne de Beaumont, érigée en l'église paroissiale de Vivoin, sous le patronage de la sainte Vierge', *Revue du Maine* 40 (1886), pp. 113–46, 273–320

Devaux, J., 'Jean de Melun, seigneur d'Antoing, d'Epinoy, de Sottengheim, de Beaumetz, de Mets-en-Couture, de Saulty, et de Wingles, connétable de Flandre, vicomte de Gand, prévôt de Douai et châtelain de Bapaume', in *Les Chevaliers de l'Order de la Toison d'or au XVe siècle. Notices bio-bibliographiques*, ed. R. de Smedt (Frankfurt, 2000), pp. 64–7

Devereux, E. J., 'Empty Tuns and Unfruitful Grafts: Richard Grafton's Historical Publications', *The Sixteenth Century Journal* 21 (1990), pp. 33–56

Ditcham, B., 'The Employment of Foreign Mercenary Troops in the French Royal Armies, 1415–70', unpublished PhD thesis (University of Edinburgh, 1978)

Driver, M. W., '"Me fault faire": French Makers of Manuscripts for English Patrons', in *Language and Culture in Medieval Britain. The French of England c. 1100–c. 1500*, ed. J. Wogan Browne et al. (Woodbridge, 2009), pp. 420–43

Dubosc, F., 'Manuscrit inédit tiré des archives de la maison de Matignon', *Journal des Savants de Normandie* (1844), pp. 33–51

Duchesne, L., 'Paroisse religieuse et féodale de la Poillée', *Revue du Maine* 45 (1899), pp. 48–62

Dupont-Ferrier, G., *Gallia Regia, ou état des officiers royaux des bailliages et des sénéchaus-sées, de 1328 à 1515*, 7 vols (Paris, 1942–46)

Durand, R., 'Chronologie des premiers seigneurs de Courville: Courville et Vieuxpont, notice généalogique', *Mémoires de la Société Archéologique d'Eure-et-Loir* 12 (1895–1900), pp. 243–93

Elder, J. A., 'A Study of the Beauforts and Their Estates 1399–1540', unpublished PhD thesis (Bryn Mawr College, 1964)

Elton, G., *Reform and Reformation: England 1509–1558* (Cambridge, MA, 1977)

Erler, M. C., 'The Guildhall Library, Robert Bale and the Writing of London History', *Historical Research* 89 (2016)

Espinay, D. de, *Fiefs du comté d'Anjou aux XIVe et XVe siècles* (Angers, 1900)

Favreau, R., 'Pierre de Brézé (vers 1410–1465)', *Société des Lettres, Sciences et Arts du Saumurois* 117 (1968), pp. 25–38

Fenster, T. and C. Collette (eds), *French in Medieval England: Networks, Exchanges, Collaborations. Essays in Honour of Jocelyn Wogan-Browne* (Woodbridge, 2017)

Ferguson, M. G., 'Grafton, Richard (1506/7–1573)', *ODNB*, article 11186 [accessed 22 June 2020]

Fiasson, D., 'Un chien couché au pied du roi d'Angleterre? Robert Jolivet, abbé du Mont Saint-Michel (1411–1444)', *Annales de Normandie* 64 (2014), pp. 47–72

Fierville, C., 'Histoire généalogique de la maison et de la baronnie de Tournebu, d'après les archives inédites de cette famille', *Mémoires de la Société des Antiquaires de Normandie* 26 (1867), pp. 170–367

Flamare, H. de, *Le Nivernais pendant la Guerre de Cent Ans*, 2 vols (Nevers and Paris, 1913)

Flammermont, J., *Histoire de Senlis pendant la seconde partie de la guerre de Cent Ans (1405–1441)*, in *Mémoires de la Société de l'Histoire de Paris* 5 (1869)

Flourac, L., *Jean Ier, comte de Foix, vicomte souverain de Béarn, lieutenant du roi en Languedoc. Etude historique sur le Sud-Ouest de la France pendant le premier tiers du XVe siècle* (Paris, 1884)

Fraser, W., *Memoirs of the Maxwells of Pollok*, 2 vols (Edinburgh, 1863)

Fraser, W., *The Douglas Book*, 4 vols (Edinburgh, 1885)

Fresne de Beaucourt, G. du, *Histoire de Charles VII*, 6 vols (Paris, 1881–91)

Froger, L., 'La paroisse de Pirmil pendant l'invasion anglaise, 1423–1435', *Revue historique et archéologique du Maine* 41 (1897), pp. 281–95

Frondeville, H. de, 'La Vicomté d'Orbec pendant l'occupation anglaise (1417–1449)', *Etudes Lexoviennes* 4 (1936), pp. 1–115

Gaussin, P.-R., 'Les conseillers de Charles VII (1418–1461)', *Francia* 10 (1982), pp. 67–130

Géographie du département de la Seine-Inférieure. Ouvrage posthume de M. l'abbé J. Brunel, continué et publié par l'abbé A. Tougard, Arrondissement d'Yvetot (Rouen, 1876)

George, D., 'A Lost Annotated Text and an Unrecognized Folio Corrector', Shakespeare Association of America Seminar, 45th annual meeting, Georgia, 5–8 April 2017

Germain, L., 'Recherches sur les actes de Robert de Baudricourt depuis 1432 jusqu'à 1454', *Bulletin mensuel de la société d'archéologie lorraine et du musée historique lorrain* 2 (1902), pp. 218–30

Gerville, C. Duhérissier de, 'Recherches sur les anciens châteaux du département de la Manche (arrondissements d'Avranches et de Mortain)', *Mémoire de la Société des Antiquaires de Normandie* 4 (1828), pp. 58–196

Given-Wilson, C., *Chronicles. The Writing of History in Medieval England* (London and New York, 2004)

Gonzales, E., *Un prince en son hôtel: les serviteurs des ducs d'Orléans au XVe siècle* (Paris, 2004)

Gransden, A., *Historical Writing in England c. 1307 to the Early Sixteenth Century* (London, 1982)

Grübl, K., 'La standardisation du français au Moyen Âge: point de vue scriptologique', *Revue de Linguistique Romane* 77 (2013), pp. 343–83

Guessard, F., 'Gauluet ou le sire de Gaules (1380–1423)', *BEC* 9 (1847–48), pp. 441–73

Halgouet, H. du, *La Vicomté de Rohan et ses seigneurs* (Saint-Brieuc, 1921)

Harriss, G. L., 'Fastolf, Sir John (1380–1459)', *ODNB*, article 9199 [accessed 22 April 2021]

Hay, D., 'The Division of the Spoils of War in Fourteenth Century England', *Transactions of the Royal Historical Society* 4 (1954), pp. 91–109

Hébert, P., 'Les pèlerinages dans les statuts des confréries normandes jusqu'à la fin du XVIe siècle', *Revue de l'Avranchin et du pays de Granville* 80 (2003), pp. 211–32

Hébert, P., 'Nouveau regard sur la confrérie Saint-Jacques et Saint-Christophe de Bernay', *Connaissance de l'Eure* 136 (2005), pp. 28–31

Hellot, A., *Essai historique sur les Martel de Basqueville et sur Basqueville-en-Caux (1000–1789), d'après des documents inédits* (Rouen, 1879)

Herman, P. C., 'Hall, Edward (1497–1547)', *ODNB*, article 11954 [accessed 22 June 2020]

Holder, N., *The Friaries of Medieval London from Foundation to Dissolution* (Woodbridge, 2017)

Huart, A., 'Jacques de Bourbon, roi de Sicile, frère mineur, cordelier à Besançon, 1370–1438', *Études franciscaines* 22 (1909), pp. 266–86, 354–74

Hughes, J., 'Stephen Scrope and the Circle of Sir John Fastolf: Moral and Intellectual Outlooks', *Medieval Knighthood IV. Papers from the Fifth Strawberry Hill Conference*, ed. C. Harper-Bill and R. Harvey (Woodbridge, 1993), pp. 109–46

Hughes, J., 'Scrope, Stephen (1397–1472)', *ODNB*, article 66283 [accessed 12 May 2021]

Huguet, A., *Aspects de la guerre de cent ans en Picardie maritime, 1400–1450*, 2 vols (Amiens, 1943–44)

Huillard-Bréholles, J., 'La rançon du duc de Bourbon Jean Ier, 1415–1436', *Mémoires présentés à l'Académie des Inscriptions et Belles-Lettres* 8 (1874), pp. 37–91

Ingham, R., 'Later Anglo-Norman as a Contact Variety of French', in *The Anglo-Norman Language and its Contexts,* ed. R. Ingham (Woodbridge, 2010), pp. 8–25

Ingham, R., 'L'anglo-normand et la variation syntaxique en français médiéval', in *Actes du XXVème colloque international de linguistique et de philologie romane,* ed. M. Iliescu, H. Siller-Runggaldier and P. Danler, vol. 6 (Berlin, 2011), pp. 163–74

Ingham, R., *The Transmission of Anglo-Norman: Language History and Language Acquisition,* Language Faculty and Beyond, Research Monograph Series no. 9 (Amsterdam and New York, 2012)

Ingham, R., 'The Maintenance of French in Later Medieval England', *Neuphilologische Mitteilungen* 115 (2015), pp. 623–45

James, E., 'Anne de Laval (1385–1466): une héritière au pouvoir', unpublished Master's thesis (Université d'Angers, 2013)

James, M. R., *A Descriptive Catalogue of the Manuscripts in the Library of Lambeth Palace: The Medieval Manuscripts* (Cambridge, 1932)

Jefferson, L., 'MS Arundel 48 and the Earliest Statutes of the Order of the Garter', *EHR* 109 (1994), pp. 356–85

Johnson, P., *Duke Richard of York 1411–60* (Oxford, 1988)

Jones, M. K., 'Ransom Brokerage in the Fifteenth Century', in *Guerre et société en France, en Angleterre et en Bourgogne, XIVe–XVe siècles*, ed. P. Contamine, C. Giry-Deloison and M. Keen (Villeneuve-d'Asq, 1991), pp. 221–35

Jones, M. K., '"Gardez mon corps, sauvez ma terre" – Immunity from War and the Lands of a Captive Knight: The Siege of Orléans (1428–29) Revisited', in *Charles d'Orléans in England (1415–1440)*, ed. Mary-Jo Arn (Cambridge, 2000), pp. 9–26

Jones, M. K., 'The Battle of Verneuil (17 August 1424): Towards a History of Courage', *War in History* 9 (2002), pp. 375–411

Jordan, W., *The Chronicle and Political Papers of Edward VI* (London, 1966)

Jordan, W., *Edward VI: The Young King* (Cambridge, MA, 1968)

Joubert, A., 'Les invasions anglaises en Anjou en XIVe et XVe siècles', *Extrait de la Revue d'Anjou* (1872)

Joubert, A., 'Les negotiations relatives à l'évacuation du Maine par les Anglais (1444–1448) et deux attaques anglais contre la Lude en 1371', *Extrait de la Revue historique et archéologique du Maine* 8 (1880) (Mamers, 1881)

Joubert, A., 'Ramefort des Gennes et ses seigneurs au XVe siècles d'après les archives inédits du chateau de la Sionnière', *Extrait de la Revue historique et archéologique du Maine* 8 (1880) (Mamers, 1881)

Joubert, A., 'Le marriage d'Henry VI et Margaret d'Anjou d'après les documents publiés en Angleterre', *Extrait de la Revue historique et archéologique du Maine* 13 (1883)

Joubert, A., *Le château seigneuriale de Saint-Laurent des Mortiers d'après les documents inédits (1356–1789)* (Mamers, 1884)

Joubert, A., *Les monnaies frappés au Mans en nom d'Henry VI (1425–1432)* (Mamers, 1886)

Joubert, A., *Le chateau de Ramefort de Gennes et ses seigneurs aux XIVe et XVe siècles d'après des documents inédits* (Mamers, 1888)

Joubert, A., *Histoire de la baronnie de Craon de 1382 à 1626 d'après les archives inédites du chartier de Thouars (Fonds Craon)* (Angers/Paris, 1888)

Joubert, A., *Une tentative des anglais contre Château-Gontier en 1421 d'après des documents inédits* (Mamers, 1888)

Joubert, A., 'Documents inédits pour servir à l'histoire du Maine au XVᵉ siècle', *Revue historique et archéologique du Maine* 5 (1879), pp. 110–23, reissued as *Documents inédits pour servir à l'histoire du Maine de 1424 à 1452 d'après les archives du British Museum, et du Lambeth Palace de Londres* (Mamers, 1889)

Joubert, A., 'Le testament du Jean de Craon, seigneur de la Suze et de Chantocé (avant 1432)', *Revue historique et archéologique du Maine* 27 (1890), pp. 340–6

Jouet, R., 'Un vicomte de Falaise attentif aux intérets du roi (vers 1370–1380): autour de la baronnie d'Annebecq', *Annales de Normandie* 26 (1976), pp. 81–7

Kaeuper, R., *Medieval Chivalry* (Cambridge, 2016)

Keen, A., 'A Short Account of the Recently Discovered Copy of Edward Hall's Chronicle', *Bulletin of the John Rylands Library* 24 (1940), pp. 255–62

Keen, A. and Lubbock, R., *The Annotator. The Pursuit of an Elizabethan Reader of Halle's Chronicle* (New York, 1954)

Keen, M. H., 'Brotherhood in Arms', *History* 47 (1962), pp. 1–17

Keen, M. H., *The Laws of War in the Later Middle Ages* (London, 1965)

Kelly, H. A., *Divine Providence in the England of Shakespeare's Histories* (Cambridge, MA, 1970)

Kibbee, D., *For to Speke Frenche Trewely: The French Language in England, 1000–1600* (Amsterdam, 1991)

King, A., 'War and Peace: A Knight's Tale. The Ethics of War in Sir Thomas Gray's Scalacronica', in *War, Government and Aristocracy in the British Isles, c. 1150–1500: Essays in Honour of Michael Prestwich*, ed. C. Given-Wilson, A. Kettle and L. Scales (Woodbridge, 2010), pp. 148–62

King, J. N., 'Bale, John (1495–1563)', *ODNB*, article 1175 [accessed 8 April 2020]

Kingsford, C., *English Historical Literature in the Fifteenth Century* (Oxford, 1913)

Kipling, G., *The Triumph of Honour. Burgundian Origins of the Elizabethan Renaissance* (The Hague, 1977)

Kosto, A., *Hostages in the Middle Ages* (Oxford, 2012)

Kristol, A., 'L'enseignement du français en Angleterre (XIIIe–XVe siècles): Les sources manuscrites', *Romania* 111 (1990), pp. 289–330

La Morandière, G. de, *Histoire de la Maison d'Estouteville en Normandie* (Paris, 1903)

Labov, W., *Principles of Linguistic Change: Social Factors* (Oxford, 2001)

Labutte, A., *Histoire du royaume et des rois d'Yvetot* (Paris, 1871)

Lainé, P. L., *Archives généalogiques et historiques de la noblesse de France ou Receuil de preuves, mémoires et notices généalogiques*, 11 vols (Paris, 1828–50)

Le Paige, M., *Dictionnaire topographique, historique, généalogique et bibliographique de la Province et du Diocèse du Maine*, 2 vols (Paris, 1777)

Leblanc, E., 'La Laire', *Bulletin de la Commission historique et archéologique de la Mayenne* 3 (1891), pp. 13–42

Ledieu, A., *Esquisses militaires de la guerre de Cent Ans – La Hire et Xaintrailles* (Lille and Paris, 1887)

Ledru, A., *Le château de Sourches au Maine et ses seigneurs* (Paris and Le Mans, 1887)

Ledru, A., *Anne de Laval et Guy Turpin* (Laval, 1888)

Ledru, A., 'Tentative des français sur Le Mans en 1428', *Province du Maine* 3 (1895), pp. 1–9

Lefèvre-Pontalis, G., 'Compte-rendu du cartulaire de la seigneurie de Fontenay-le-Marmion, provenant des archives de Matignon', par Gustave Saige, Monaco, 1895, *BEC* 59 (1888), pp. 165–8

Lefèvre-Pontalis, G., 'Épisodes de l'invasion anglaise: la guerre de partisans dans la Haute-Normandie (1424–1429)', *BEC* 54 (1893), pp. 475–521; 55 (1894), pp. 259–305; 56 (1895), pp. 433–508; 97 (1936), pp. 102–30; 54 (1893), p. 519

Lefèvre-Pontalis, G., *Le siège de Meulan 1423* (Versailles, 1903)

Leguai, A., 'Le problème des rançons au XVe siècle: la captivité de Jean Ier, duc de Bourbon', *Cahiers d'Histoire* 6 (1961), pp. 41–58

Leguai, A., *Les ducs de Bourbon pendant la crise monarchique du XVe siècle. Contribution à l'étude des apanages* (Paris, 1962)

Lenoir, J.-L., *Preuves généalogiques et historiques de la maison d'Harcourt* (Paris, 1907)

Leroux, Roger, *Histoire de la ville de Soissons*, 2 vols (Soissons, 1839)

Lester, G. A., 'The Books of a Fifteenth-Century English Gentleman, Sir John Paston', *Neuphilologische Mitteilungen* 88 (1987), pp. 200–17

Lewis, P., *Later Medieval France. The Polity* (London, 1968)

Little, G., *The Parlement of Poitiers: War, Government and Politics in France, 1418–1436* (London, 1981)

Lobanov, A., 'Anglo-Burgundian Military Cooperation 1420–1435', unpublished PhD thesis (University of Southampton, 2015)

Lodge, R. A., *A Sociolinguistic History of Parisian French* (Cambridge, 2004)

Lodge, R. A., 'The Sources of Standardisation in French – Written or Spoken?', in *The Anglo-Norman Language and Its Contexts*, ed. R. Ingham (Woodbridge, 2010), pp. 26–43

London, H. S., 'Walter Bellengier, Ireland King of Arms, 1467–87', *Notes and Queries* 203 (1958), pp. 232–6

London, H. S., *The Life of William Bruges, the First Garter King of Arms* (London, 1970)

Longford, W., 'Some Notes on the Family of Osbaldeston', *Transactions of the Historic Society of Lancashire and Cheshire* 87 (1935), pp. 59–85

Louis, V. A., 'Études féodales. Le fief de Chères et ses seigneurs', *Revue du Maine* 1 (1876), pp. 321–84

Luce, S., 'La Maine sous la domination anglaise en 1433 et 1434', *Revue des questions historiques* (Paris, 1878), pp. 226–41

Luce, S., *La France pendant la guerre de Cent Ans. Épisodes historiques et vie privée aux XIVe et XVe siècles*, 2e série (Paris, 1893)

Lucas, S. C., *'A Mirror for Magistrates' and the Politics of the English Reformation* (Amherst, 2009)

Lucas, S. C., 'Hall's Chronicle and the Mirror for Magistrates: History and the Tragic Pattern', in *The Oxford Handbook of Tudor Literature, 1485–1603*, ed. M. Pincombe and C. Shrank (Oxford, 2009), pp. 356–71

Lucas, S. C., 'Holinshed and Hall', in *The Oxford Handbook of Holinshed's Chronicles*, ed. F. Heale, I. W. Archer and P. Kewes (Oxford, 2012), pp. 204–16

Lucas, S. C., '"The Consent of the Body of the Whole Realm": Edward Hall's Parliamentary History', in *Writing the History of Parliament in Tudor and Stuart England*, ed. P. Cavill and A. Gajda (Manchester, 2018), pp. 60–76

Lusignan, S., *La langue des rois au Moyen Âge. Le français en France et en Angleterre* (Paris, 2004)

Lusignan, S., *Essai d'histoire sociolinguistique: le français picard au Moyen Âge* (Paris, 2012)

Marchello-Nizia, C., *La langue française aux XIVe et XVe siècles* (Paris, 1997)

Martin, G., *Histoire et généalogie de la Maison d'Harcourt* (Lyon, 1994)

Massey, R. A., 'Lancastrian Rouen: Military Service and Property Holding, 1419–49', in *England and Normandy in the Middle Ages*, ed. D. Bates and A. Curry (London, 1994), pp. 269–86

Masson d'Autume, M. de, *Cherbourg pendant la guerre de Cent Ans, de 1354 à 1450* (Cherbourg, 1948)

Mattéoni, O., *Servir le prince: les officiers des ducs de Bourbon à la fin du Moyen Âge (1356–1523)* (Paris, 1998)

Matz, J. M., 'Les orientations religieuses d'un officier angevin: Bertrand de Beauvau († 1474)', in *Les officiers et la chose publique dans les territoires angevins (xiiie–xve siècle): vers une culture politique? Gli ufficiali e la cosa pubblica nei territori angioini (XIII–XV secolo): verso una cultura politica?* (Rome, 2020) (online)

McFarlane, K. B., 'The Investment of Sir John Fastolf's Profits of War', *Transactions of the Royal Historical Society* 7 (1957), pp. 91–116, reprinted in K. B. McFarlane, *England in the Fifteenth Century. Collected Essays*, ed. G. L. Harriss (London, 1981), pp. 175–98

McFarlane, K. B., 'William of Worcester. A Preliminary Survey', in *Studies Presented to Sir Hilary Jenkinson*, ed. J. C. Davies (Oxford, 1957), pp. 196–221, reprinted in K. B. McFarlane, *England in the Fifteenth Century. Collected Essays*, ed. G. L. Harriss (London, 1981), pp. 199–224

McFarlane, K. B., 'A Business Partnership in War and Administration, 1421–1445', *Past and Present* 22 (1962), pp. 3–15, reprinted in K. B. McFarlane, *England in the Fifteenth Century. Collected Essays*, ed. G. L. Harriss (London, 1981), pp. 151–74

McLaren, M-R., 'Fabyan, Robert (d. 1513)', *ODNB*, article 9054 [accessed 27 November 2020]

Mead, V., 'Walter Belyngham, Esperance Pursuivant', *Coat of Arms*, third series, 12 (2016), p. 103

Meaudre de Lapouyade, M., 'La maison de Bordeaux et les premiers captaux de Buch, étude historique et généalogique', *Extrait des Actes de l'Académie Nationale des Sciences, Belles-Lettres et Arts de Bordeaux* xi, 1937–38 (1939)

Menage, G., *Histoire de Sablé* (Paris, 1683)

Merion-Jones, G., Jones, M., Meuret, J. and Amiot, C., 'Le château de Montauban-de-Bretagne: paysage, histoire, monument', *Mémoires de la Société d'Histoire et d'Archéologie de Bretagne* 94 (2016), pp. 673–736

Merrilees, B., 'La simplification du système vocalique de l'anglo-normand', *Revue de Linguistique Romane* 46 (1982), pp. 319–26

Merriman, M., *The Rough Wooings: Mary Queen of Scots, 1542–1551* (East Linton, 2000)

Mesqui, J., Le Roy, C. and Le Roy, J., 'Guy le Bouteillier, le château de Roche-Guyon, et le Maître de Fastolf vers 1425', *Bulletin Monumental* 166 (2008), pp. 135–50

Millar, G., *Tudor Mercenaries and Auxiliaries 1485–1547* (Charlottesville, VA, 1980)

Millet, H., 'Qui a écrit "Le Livre des fais du bon messire Jehan le Maingre dit Bouciquaut"?', in *L'Église du Grand Schisme 1378–1417*, ed. H. Millet (Paris, 2009), pp. 136–47

Milner, J., 'The English Enterprise in France, 1412–13', in *Trade, Devotion and Governance. Papers in Later Medieval History*, ed. D. J. Clayton, R. G. Davies and P. McNiven (Stroud, 1994), pp. 80–101

Milner, J., 'The Battle of Baugé, March 1421: Impact and Memory', *History* 91 (2006), pp. 484–507

Milner, J., 'The English Commitment to the 1412 Expedition to France', *The Fifteenth Century* 11 (2012), pp. 9–24

Mirot, A., 'Vie politique de Tanguy du Chastel', *Positions de thèse de l'Ecole de Chartes* (1926), pp. 101–4

Mirot, L., 'Notes sur un manuscrit de Froissart et sur Pierre de Fontenay, seigneur de Rancé, son premier possesseur', *BEC* 83 (1922), pp. 297–330

Mirot, L., 'Pierre de Fontenay, seigneur de Rancé', *BEC* 83 (1922), pp. 297–330

Moréri, L., *Le Grand Dictionnaire historique, ou le mélange curieuse de l'histoire sacrée et profane*, 10 vols (Paris, 1759)

Morgan, D., 'From Death to a View; Louis Robessart, Johan Huizinga and the Political Significance of Chivalry', in *Chivalry in the Renaissance*, ed. S. Anglo (Woodbridge, 1990), pp. 93–106

Morice, P., *Mémoires pour servir de preuves à l'histoire civile et ecclésiastique de Bretagne*, 3 vols (Paris, 1742–46)

Morton, C., 'Henry Inglose: A Hard Man to Please', *The Fifteenth Century* 10 (2011), pp. 39–52

Motey, H., 'La ville, le château et le pays d'Exmes pendant l'occupation anglaise de 1417 à 1422', *Bulletin de la Société Historique et Archéologique de l'Orne* 8 (1889), pp. 101–48

Murphy, N., 'Henry VIII's French Crown: His Royal Entry into Tournai Revisited', *Historical Research* 85 (2012), pp. 617–31

Murphy, N., *The Tudor Occupation of Boulogne. Conquest, Colonisation and Imperial Monarchy 1544–1550* (Cambridge, 2019)

Nall, C., *Reading and War in Fifteenth-Century England: From Lydgate to Malory* (Woodbridge, 2012)

Nall, C. and Wakelin, D., 'Le déclin du multilingualisme dans The Boke of Noblesse de William Worcester et dans son codicille', *Médiévales* 68 (2015), pp. 73–91

New Statistical Account of Scotland: Roxburgh, Peebles, and Selkirk (Edinburgh, 1845)

Newhall, R. A., *The English Conquest of Normandy, 1416–1424: A Study in Fifteenth-Century Warfare* (New Haven and London, 1924)

Nicolas, N. H., *History of the Battle of Agincourt* (1st edition London, 1827; 2nd edition 1831; 3rd edition 1833)

Nichols, J. G., 'Peter Basset. A Lost Historian of the Reign of Henry V', *Notes and Queries*, second series, 9 (1860), pp. 421–2

Nycz, J., 'Changing Words or Changing Rules? Second Dialect Acquisition and Phonological Representation', *Journal of Pragmatics* 52 (2013), pp. 49–62

Orme, N., 'Worcester [Botoner], William', *ODNB*, article 29967 [accessed 22 April 2021]

Ornato, M., *Répertoire prosopographique de personnages apparentés à la couronne de France aux XIVe et XVe siècles* (Paris, 2001)

Pailhes, C., 'Mathieu de Foix, comte de Comminges', *Les Chevaliers de l'Order de la Toison d'or au XVe siècle. Notices bio-bibliographiques*, ed. R. de Smedt (Frankfurt, 2000), pp. 93–4

Paravicini, W., *Die Preussenreisen Des Europäischen Adels*, 2 vols (Sigmaringen, 1989–95)

Paviot, J., 'François de La Palud, seigneur de Varambon, un encombrant seigneur du XVe siècle', in *Hommes, cultures et sociétés à la fin du moyen âge: liber discipulorum en l'honneur de Philippe Contamine*, ed. P. Gilli and J. Paviot (Paris, 2012), pp. 257–92

Pavlenko, A., 'L2 Influence on L1 in Late Bilingualism', *Issues in Applied Linguistics* 11 (2013), pp. 175–205

Payling, S., 'War and Peace: Military and Administrative Service amongst the English Gentry in the Reign of Henry VI', in *Soldiers, Nobles and Gentlemen: Essays in Honour of Maurice Keen*, ed. P. Coss and C. Tyerman (Woodbridge, 2009), pp. 240–58

Perchet, E., *Recherches sur Pesmes. Première partie* (Gray, 1896)

Péricard-Méa, D., 'Pèlerins par dévotion pure', in *Compostelle et cultes de saint Jacques au Moyen Âge*, ed. D. Péricard-Méa (Paris, 2000), pp. 199–220

Perrier, E., 'Les Chevaliers du Croissant', *Annuaire du Conseil héraldique de France* 19 (1906), pp. 99–164

Peyronnet, G., 'Les complots de Louis d'Amboise contre Charles VII (1428–1431): un aspect des rivalités entre lignages féodaux en France au temps de Jeanne d'Arc', *BEC* 142 (1984), pp. 115–35

Pidgeon, L., *Brought up of Nought. A History of the Woodvile Family* (London, 2019)

Piolin, L.-P., *Histoire de l'église du Mans*, 10 vols (Le Mans, 1858)

Plaisse, A., *La baronnie du Neubourg. Essai d'histoire agraire, économique et sociale* (Paris, 1961)

Planchenault, R., 'De l'utilité pour l'histoire de France de quelques chroniques anglaises de la première moitié du XVème siècle', *BEC* 85 (1924), pp. 118–28

Planchenault, R., 'La conquête du Maine par les Anglais: la campagne de 1424–1425', *Revue historique et archéologique du Maine*, série 2, 5 (1925), pp. 3–32

Planchenault, R., 'La conquête du Maine par les Anglais: les campagnes de Richemont (1425–1427)', *Revue historique et archéologique du Maine*, série 2, 13 (1933), pp. 125–85

Planchenault, R., 'La conquête du Maine par les Anglais: la lutte des partisans (1427–1429)', *Revue historique et archéologique du Maine*, série 2, 18 (1938), pp. 47–60

Poli, O. de, *Les défenseurs du Mont-Saint-Michel (1417–1450)* (Paris, 1895)

Pollard, A. F., *England under Protector Somerset* (London, 1900)

Pollard, A. F., 'Edward Hall's Will and Chronicle', *Bulletin of the Institute of Historical Research* 9 (1931), pp. 171–7

Pollard, A. J., *John Talbot and the War in France 1427–1453* (London, 1983)

Pollard, G., 'The Bibliographical History of Hall's Chronicle', *Bulletin of the Institute of Historical Research* 10 (1932), pp. 12–17

Pope, M., *From Latin to Modern French with Especial Consideration of Anglo-Norman Phonology and Morphology* (Manchester, 1934)

Prestwich, M., *Armies and Warfare in the Middle Ages: The English Experience* (London and New Haven, 1999)

Price, G., 'Anglo-Norman', in *Language in the British Isles*, ed. P. Trudgill (London, 1934)

Probert, Y., 'Matthew Gough, 1390–1450', *Transactions of the Honourable Society of Cymmrodorion* (1961), pp. 34–44

Prosser, G. L. L., 'After the Reduction. Restructuring Norman Political Society and the Bien Public 1450–65', unpublished PhD thesis (University College London, 1996)

Prosser, G., 'Affinity as a Social World: Marriage Brokerage, Maintenance and Lateral Networks. A Magnate Affinity in 15th Century Normandy: The Followers of Pierre de Brézé, comte de Maulevrier (1450–1465)', in *Liens personnels, réseaux, solidarités en France et dans les îles Brittaniques (xie–xxe siècle). Personal Links, Networks and Solidarities in France and the British Isles (11th–20th Century)*, ed. D. Bates (Paris, 2006), pp. 29–58

Puisieux, L. F., *Siège et prise de Rouen par les Anglais (1418–1419) principalement d'après un poème anglais contemporain* (Caen, 1867)

Ramsay, N., 'London. Clarenceux King of Arms and the Office of Arms', in *Corpus of British Medieval Library Catalogues 14: Hospitals, Towns and the Professions*, ed. N. Ramsay and J. M. W. Willoughby (London, 2009)

Ramsay, N., 'Richard III and the Office of Arms', in *The Yorkist Age. Proceedings of the 2011 Harlaxton Symposium*, ed. H. Kleineke and C. Sterre (Donington, 2013), pp. 142–63

Ramsay, N., 'Glover, Robert (1543/44–1588), herald', *ODNB*, article 10833 [accessed 18 November 2020]

Ramsay, N. and Willoughby, J. M. W., 'London Guildhall', in *Corpus of British Medieval Library Catalogues 14: Hospitals, Towns and the Professions*, ed. N. Ramsay and J. M. W. Willoughby (London, 2009)

Ratcliffe, H., 'The Military Expenditure of the English Crown 1422–1435', unpublished MLitt thesis (University of Oxford, 1980)

Raven, J., *The Business of Books: Booksellers and the English Book Trade 1450–1850* (London, 2007)

Reeves, A. C., *Lancastrian Englishmen* (Washington, 1981)

Reeves, A. C., 'Sir John Radcliffe, K. G. (d. 1441): Miles Famossissimus', *Journal of Medieval Military History* 11 (2013), pp. 183–214

Rey, M., 'Un témoignage inédit sur l'Hôtel du Roi: Le Journal de la dépense du premier semestre 1417', *Annales Littéraires de l'Université de Besançon* (1955), pp. 3–32

Reynolds, C., 'English Patrons and French Artists in Fifteenth-Century Normandy', in *England and Normandy in the Middle Ages*, ed. D. Bates and A. Curry (London, 1994), pp. 299–313

Richardson, G., *Renaissance Monarchy: The Reigns of Henry VIII, Francis I, and Charles V* (London and New York, 2002)

Richmond, C., *The Paston Family in the Fifteenth Century. The First Phase* (Cambridge, 1990)

Richmond, C., *The Paston Family in the Fifteenth Century. Fastolf's Will* (Cambridge, 1996)

Richmond, C., *The Paston Family in the Fifteenth Century: Endings* (Cambridge, 2002)

Richmond, C., 'How the First "Paston Letter" Came to Be Written in Suffolk', *Proceedings of the Suffolk Institute of Archaeology and History* 41 (2005–08), pp. 461–6

Richmond, C., 'Sir John Fastolf, the Duke of Suffolk and the Pastons', *The Fifteenth Century* 8 (2008), pp. 73–103

Ringe, D. and Eska, J. F., *Historical Linguistics: Toward a Twenty-First Century Reintegration* (Cambridge, 2013)

Robinson, C., *Register of Scholars Admitted into the Merchant Taylors' School from 1562 to 1874*, I (London, 1882)

Robveille, A. and Froger, L., 'La communauté d'habitants de Pont-de-Gennes', *La Province du Maine* 16 (1908), pp. 309–25, 341–57, 385–98

Roger, J.-M., 'Guy Le Bouteillier', in *La guerre et la paix, frontières et violences au Moyen Âge, Actes du 101e Congrès national des sociétés savantes, Lille 1976* (Paris, 1978), pp. 271–331

Roger, J.-M., 'Simon Morhier en Normandie', *Bulletin philologique et historique (jusqu'à 1610) du comité des travaux historiques et scientifiques* (Paris, 1981), pp. 101–64

Roquet, H., 'Mansigné', *Revue historique et archéologique du Maine* 85 (1929), pp. 17–37, 131–45, 171–202

Roquet, M., 'Recherches historiques sur Laigné-en-Belin', *Bulletin de la Société d'Agriculture, Sciences et Arts de la Sarthe* 32 (1889–90), pp. 51–144

Rothwell, W., 'English and French in England after 1362', *English Studies* 82 (2001), pp. 539–59

Rowe, B. J. H., 'A Contemporary Account of the Hundred Years' War from 1415 to 1429,' *EHR* 41 (1926), pp. 504–13

Rowe, B. J. H., 'John, Duke of Bedford as Regent of France 1422–35: His Policy and Administration in the North', unpublished BLitt thesis (University of Oxford, 1927)

Rowe, B. J. H., 'Discipline in the Norman Garrisons under Bedford, 1422–35', *EHR* 46 (1931), pp. 551–78

Rowe, B. J. H., 'The Estates of Normandy under the Duke of Bedford, 1422–35', *EHR* 46 (1931), pp. 194–208

Rowe, B. J. H., 'John, Duke of Bedford and the Norman 'Brigands', *EHR* 47 (1932), pp. 583–600

Rowe, B. J. H., 'Henry VI's Claim to France in Picture and Poem', *The Library*, 4th series, 13 (1933), pp. 77–88

Rowe, B. J. H., 'The *Grand Conseil* under the Duke of Bedford', in *Oxford Essays in Medieval History Presented to Herbert E. Salter* (Oxford, 1934), pp. 207–34

Sauvage, H., *Les capitaines et gouverneurs du château de Saint-Lô pendant la guerre de Cent Ans, de 1337 à 1453* (Paris, 1902)

Scarisbrick, J. J., *Henry VIII* (Berkeley, 1968)

Schmid, M. S. and Köpke, B., 'The Relevance of First Language Attrition to Theories of Bilingual Development', *Linguistic Approaches to Bilingualism* 7 (2017), pp. 637–67

Schnerb, B., 'Aspects de l'organisation militaire dans les principautés bourguignonnes', unpublished PhD thesis (Université de Paris IV, Paris-Sorbonne, 1988)

Schnerb, B., 'Bourgogne et Savoie au début du XVe siècle: evolution d'une alliance militaire', *Publication du Centre Européen d'Études Bourguignonnes* 32 (1992), pp. 13–29

Schnerb, B., *Bulgnéville (1431): l'état bourguignon prend pied en Lorraine* (Paris, 1993)

Schnerb, B., *Enguerrand de Bournonville et les siens: un lignage noble du Boulonnais aux XIVe et XVe siècles* (Paris, 1997)

Schnerb, B., 'Jean III de Luxembourg, comte de Guise et de Ligny, seigneur de Beaurevoir', in *Les Chevaliers de l'Order de la Toison d'or au XVe siècle. Notices bio-bibliographiques*, ed. R. de Smedt (Frankfurt, 2000), pp. 29–31

Schnerb, B., 'Jean de Villiers, seigneur de L'Isle-Adam', in *Les Chevaliers de l'Order de la Toison d'or au XVe siècle. Notices bio-bibliographiques*, ed. R. de Smedt (Frankfurt, 2000), pp. 32–3

Schnerb, B., 'Jean de Villiers, seigneur de L'Isle-Adam, vu par les chroniqueurs bourguignons', *Publication du Centre Européen d'Études Bourguignonnes* 41 (2001), pp. 105–21

Schnerb, B., *Jean Sans Peur: un prince meurtrier* (Paris, 2007)

Schnerb, B., 'Morelet de Béthencourt. Service, carrière et délinquance en milieu de cour', *Revue du Nord* 380 (2009), pp. 449–72

Schnerb, B., '"Sauver les meubles". A propos de quelques traités de capitulation de forteresses du début du XVe siècle', in *Frieden schaffen und sich verteidigen im Spätmittelalter*, ed. G. Naegle (Munich, 2012), pp. 215–66

Schnerb, B., *L'état bourguignon* (Paris, 2014)

Schnerb, B., '"A l'encontre des Anglois". Les défenseurs de la Normandie entre 1417 et 1419', in *La guerre en Normandie (xi–xv siècle)*, ed. A. Curry and V. Gazeau (Caen, 2018), pp. 195–216

Scofield, C. L., *The Life and Reign of Edward IV*, 2 vols (London, 1923)

The Scots Peerage, ed. J. B. Paul, 9 vols (Edinburgh, 1904–14)

Sharp, R., 'Tanner, Thomas (1674–1735)', *ODNB*, article 26963 [accessed 8 April 2020]

Short, I., *Manual of Anglo-Norman*, Anglo-Norman Text Society Occasional Publications, 7 (London, 2007)

Siddons, H. P., *Heraldic Badges in England and Wales*, 4 vols (London, 2009)

Sleigh-Johnson, N. V., 'The Merchant Taylors Company of London 1580–1645', unpublished PhD thesis (University College London, 1989)

Smedt, R. de (ed.), *Les Chevaliers de l'Ordre de la Toison d'or au XVe siècle. Notices bio-bibliographiques* (Frankfurt, 2000)

Smith, A., 'Aspects of the Career of Sir John Fastolf (1380–1459)', unpublished DPhil thesis (University of Oxford, 1982)

Smith, R. M., 'The Date and Authorship of Hall's Chronicle', *Journal of English and Germanic Philology* 17 (1918), pp. 252–66

Spencer, D., 'The Provision of Artillery for the 1428 Expedition to France', *Journal of Medieval Military History* 13 (2015), pp. 179–92

Spencer, D., 'The Development of Gunpowder Weapons in Late Medieval England', unpublished PhD thesis (University of Southampton, 2016)

Spencer, D., *Royal and Urban Gunpowder Weapons in Late Medieval England* (Woodbridge, 2019)

Sutton, A. and Visser-Fuchs, L., 'Richard III's Books: XII. William Worcester's Boke of Noblesse and His Collection of Documents on the War in Normandy', *The Ricardian* 9 (1991), pp. 154–65

Sutton, A. and Visser-Fuchs, L., *Richard III's Books. Ideals and Reality in the Life of a Medieval Prince* (Stroud, 1997)

Tanner, T., *Bibliotheca Brittanico-Hiberniae* (London, 1748)

Taylor, C., *Chivalry and the Ideals of Knighthood in France during the Hundred Years War* (Cambridge, 2013)

Taylor, C., 'John Talbot, John Fastolf and the Death of Chivalry', in *People, Power and Identity in the Late Middle Ages*, ed. G. Dodd, H. Lacy and A. Musson (London, 2021), pp. 324–40

Temple, W., *The Thanage of Fermartyn*, New Spalding Club, 51 (1894)

Termeau, M., 'La Forêt de Sillé-le-Guillaume, Notes d'Histoire', *Revue du Maine* 100/101 (1944), pp. 18–43

Thomas, A., *Les états provinciaux de la France centrale sous Charles VII*, 2 vols (Paris, 1879)

Thompson, G. L., *Paris and Its People under English Rule. The Anglo-Burgundian Regime 1420–1436* (Oxford, 1991)

Thorpe, D. E., 'Documents and Books: A Case Study of Luket Nantron and Geoffrey Spirleng as Fifteenth-Century Administrators and Textwriters', *Journal of the Early Book Society* 14 (2011), pp. 195–215

Thorpe, D. E., 'Writing and Reading in the Circle of Sir John Fastolf (d. 1459)', unpublished PhD thesis (University of York, 2012)

Torchet, H., *Reformation des Fouages de 1426. Diocèse ou évêché de Saint-Brieuc* (Paris, 2016)

Toureille, V., *Robert de Sarrebrück ou l'honneur d'un écorcheur (v. 1400–v. 1462)* (Rennes, 2014)

Toureille, V., *Montargis et la guerre de Cent Ans. La rescousse de Montargis (1427)* (Brest, 2017)

Trévédy, J., *Les compagnons bretons de Jeanne d'Arc* (Saint-Brieuc/Rennes, 1896)

Triger, R., 'Une forteresse du Maine pendant l'occupation anglaise: Fresnay-le-Vicomte de 1417 à 1450', *Revue historique et archéologique du Maine* 19 (1886), pp. 27–105, 185–239

Triger, R., *Le château et la ville de Beaumont-le-Vicomte pendant l'invasion anglaise (1417–1450)* (Mamers and Le Mans, 1901)

Triger, R., 'Sainte-Suzanne aux XIe et XVe siècles', *Revue historique et archéologique du Maine* 61 (1907), pp. 45–77, 121–68

Trotter, D., 'Not as Eccentric as It Looks: Anglo-French and French French', *Forum for Modern Language Studies* 39 (2003), pp. 427–38

Trotter, D., '"Une et indivisible": Variation and Ideology in the Historiography and History of French', *Revue roumaine de linguistique* 51 (2006), pp. 359–76

Tuetey, A., *Les Ecorcheurs sous Charles VII. Episodes de l'histoire militaire de la France au XVe siècle d'après des documents inédits*, 2 vols (Montbéliard, 1874)

Uyttebrouck, A., *Le gouvernement du duché de Brabant au bas moyen âge (1355–1430)*, 2 vols (Brussels, 1975)

Vale, M. G. A., *English Gascony 1399–1453. A Study of War, Government and Politics during the Later Stages of the Hundred Years War* (Oxford, 1970)

Vale, M. G. A., 'Sir John Fastolf's "Report" of 1435: A New Interpretation Reconsidered', *Nottingham Medieval Studies* 17 (1973), pp. 78–84

Vallée, E., 'Les seigneurs de Bouloire (1329–1466)', *Province du Maine* 10 (1902), pp. 241–54

Vallet de Viriville, A., *Histoire de Charles VII, roi de France, et de son époque, 1403–1461*, 3 vols (Paris, 1863–65)

Vallez, A., 'Jean II duc d'Alençon, pair de France, comte du Perche, vicomte de Beaumont, seigneur de Fougères', in *Les Chevaliers de l'Order de la Toison d'or au XVe siècle. Notices bio-bibliographiques*, ed. R. de Smedt (Frankfurt, 2000), pp. 90–3

Vauchez, A., 'En réserve de la royauté: la vicomté de Pont-Authou', *Annales de Normandie* 23 (1990), pp. 393–40

Vissiére, L., 'Georges de La Trémoille et la naissance du parti angevin', in *René d'Anjou (1409–1480). Pouvoirs et gouvernement*, ed. L. Bourquin, J.-M. Matz and N.-Y. Tonnerre (Paris, 2011), pp. 15–30

Wagner, A., *Heralds and Heraldry in the Middle Ages* (London, 1939)

Wagner, A., *The Records and Collections of the College of Arms* (London, 1952)

Wakelin, D., 'William Worcester Writes a History of His Reading', *New Medieval Literatures* 7 (2005), pp. 53–71

Wakelin, D., *Humanism, Reading and English Literature, 1430–1530* (Oxford, 2007)

Walker, A. T., 'The Westminster Tournament Challenge (Harley 83 H 1) and Thomas Wriothesley's Workshop', *British Library Journal* (2011), pp. 1–13

Warner, M., 'The Montagu Earls of Salisbury c. 1300–1428: A Study in Warfare, Politics and Political Culture', unpublished PhD thesis (University College London, 1991)

Watt, D., *A Biographical Dictionary of Scottish Graduates to AD 1410* (Oxford, 1977)

Whetham, D., *Just Wars and Moral Victories: Surprise, Deception and the Normative Framework of European War in the Later Middle Ages* (Leiden, 2009)

Wijsmann, H., 'History in Transition. Enguerrand de Monstrelet's Chronique in Manuscript and Print (c. 1450–c. 1600)', in *The Book Triumphant. Print in Transition in the Sixteenth and Seventeenth Centuries*, ed. M. Walsby and G. Kemp (Leiden and Boston, 2011), pp. 199–252

Willetts, P., *Catalogue of Manuscripts in the Society of Antiquaries* (Woodbridge, 2000)

Win, P. de, 'Antoine de Croÿ, seigneur de Crouy, comte de Porcien', in *Les Chevaliers de l'Order de la Toison d'or au XVe siècle. Notices bio-bibliographiques*, ed. R. de Smedt (Frankfurt, 2000), pp. 33–8

Win, P. de, 'Pierre de Luxemborg, comte de Saint-Pol, de Conversano et de Brienne, seigneur d'Enghien', in *Les Chevaliers de l'Order de la Toison d'or au XVe siècle. Notices bio-bibliographiques*, ed. R. de Smedt (Frankfurt, 2000), pp. 22–4

Wogan-Browne, J. C., Kowaleski, M., Mooney, L., Putter, A. and Trotter, D. (eds), *Language and Culture in Medieval Britain: The French of England, c. 1100–c. 1500* (Woodbridge, 2009)

Wylie, J. H., 'Notes on the Agincourt Roll', *Transactions of the Royal Historical Society*, third series, 5 (1911), pp. 105–40

Wylie, J. H. and Waugh, W. T., *The Reign of Henry the Fifth*, 3 vols (Cambridge, 1914–29)

Yorke, R., 'Barker, Sir Christopher (d. 1550)', *ODNB*, article 1389 [accessed 17 November 2020]

Yorke, R., 'Wriothesley [formerly Writhe], Sir Thomas (d. 1534)', *ODNB*, article 30075 [accessed 17 November 2020]

Zeeveld, W. G., 'The Influence of Hall on Shakespeare's English Historical Plays', *English Literary History* 3 (1936), pp. 317–53

WEBSITES

anglo-norman.net
biography.wales
englandsimmigrants.com (individual studies)
english.nsms.ox.ac.uk/holinshed
historyofparliamentonline.org
gasconrolls.org
gravell.org
gutorglyn.net
himanis.huma-num.fr
ihd.cnrs.fr
medievalsoldier.org